GREAT
OUTDOORS
U.S.A.

Fall is a beautiful time of year to camp on Matanuska Glacier in Alaska (page 26).

GREAT
OUTDOORS
U.S.A.

1,000 ADVENTURES
ACROSS ALL 50 STATES

NATIONAL GEOGRAPHIC

WASHINGTON, D.C.

Cool off in a stunning
limestone grotto near
Austin, Texas (page 607).

CONTENTS

Lake and alpine views, along with switchbacks and rollers, await on the Van Sickle Trail in South Lake Tahoe, Nevada.

Introduction

The beauty of the United States resides in the scope of its diversity. From the deserts of Arizona to the rocky coastline of Maine, from the sandy shores of Florida to the peaks of Colorado, the country offers a dazzling range of natural landscapes—and is ripe for exploring.

In *Great Outdoors U.S.A.*, National Geographic helps you explore all of the country's rich environments in unique ways, from sandboarding to kitesurfing, sailing to snowboarding, rock climbing to spelunking, experiencing outdoor art festivals to picking berries. Featuring 1,000 adventures in total, this comprehensive guide offers 20 activities in every state.

Got a spare weekend—or a few hours? Tackle a hike that's just a short drive—or walk—from your own backyard. Or, even better, use this book as your bucket list to crisscross the country on one epic road trip.

In these inspiring pages, you'll find state-by-state adventures big (bungee jumping over the Kentucky River, page 240) and small (walking the botanical gardens of historic Sandwich, Massachusetts, page 293). And there's something for *everyone*, including trips for adrenaline junkies (raft the Class V rapids of the Upper Youghiogheny River in Maryland, page 287); bird-watchers (look to the skies along Ohio's Little Miami State and National Scenic River, page 490); and those who want accessible options (see the playgrounds and trails at Burns Park in Arkansas, page 59, and wheelchair-friendly routes in Kentucky's Abraham Lincoln Birthplace National Historical Park, page 237), high-soaring activities (ride a hot-air balloon in Albuquerque, New Mexico, page 437), and more.

Take it from us: You'll be hard-pressed to stay inside after perusing the wealth of information in this enticing book. So grab your gear, get out there, and start exploring!

—Allyson Johnson
Senior Editor, National Geographic Books

ADVENTURE ICONS

 ATV & Off-roading
 Biking
 Bird-watching
 Boating
 Camping
 Climbing & Spelunking
 Cold-weather Activities

 Fishing
 Forests
 Gardens
 Hiking
 Horseback Riding
 Kayaking & Canoeing
 Parks

 Road Trips
 Sand-boarding
 Sightseeing
 Skiing & Snow-boarding
 Skydiving
 Snorkeling & Diving
 Stargazing

 Surfing
 Swimming & Tubing
 Wine & Food
 Wildlife-spotting
  Yoga
 Zip-lining

Don't miss the sunset views
in Cheaha State Park.

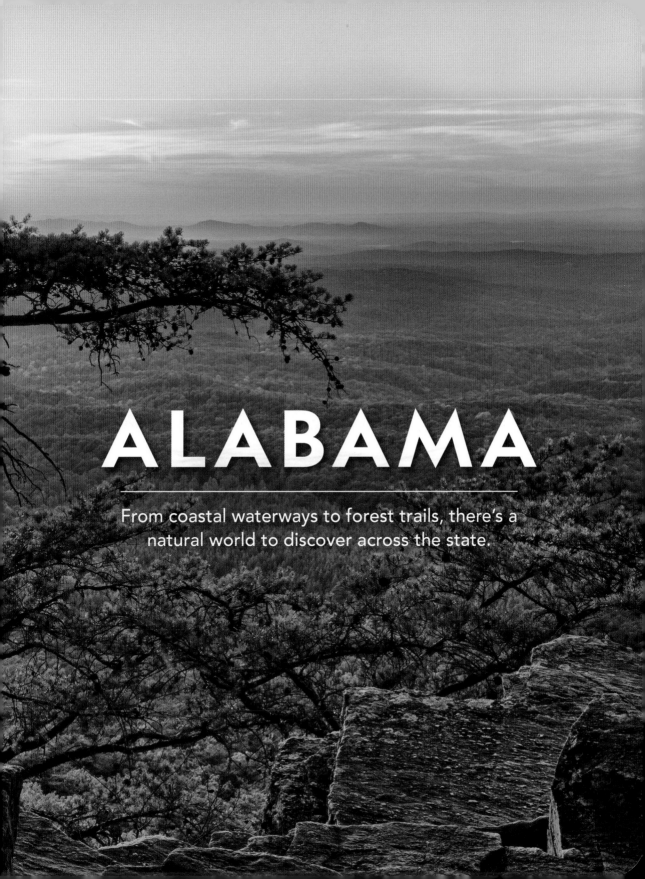

ALABAMA

From coastal waterways to forest trails, there's a
natural world to discover across the state.

TENNESSEE

Neversink
Pit

Dismals
Canyon

Cherokee
Rock Village

Sipsey
Fork

Coosa
River

Pinhoti Trail,
Sweetwater Lake

Red Mountain
Park

Coosa

GEORGIA

Majestic
Caverns

A L A B A M A

MISSISSIPPI

Chewacla
State Park

Alabama
Nature Center

Lagoon
Park

Tuskegee
National Forest

Selma to Montgomery
National Historic Trail

Blount
Cultural Park

Chattahoochee
River

Walter F. George Reservoir
(Lake Eufaula)

Chattahoochee

Sepulga

Sepulga
River

Perdido
River Trail

FLORIDA

Dauphin
Island

Back Bay
Blueway

Gulf of Mexico

LOUISIANA

Show off your skills—and get your thrills—rappelling into the 162-foot-deep (49 m) open-air pit.

Sink Into Neversink Pit

Few outdoor experiences are more primordial than staring into the gaping maw of a gigantic hole in the earth. When it comes to holes, Alabama's Neversink Pit is in a class of its own. Tucked away in the mountain town of Fackler, this 40-foot-wide (12 m) abyss (actually a sinkhole) boasts a stomach-plunging depth of almost 16 stories. Rain-fed cascades spill down its moist walls, on which you can find unusual species of ferns, vines, and moss. Winter visitors will also encounter ice sheets along the pit's walls.

Extensively photographed but ecologically fragile, Neversink Pit is owned and managed by the Southeastern Cave Conservancy (SCC), which allows hikers and climbers to visit the cave through a permitting system. (You can secure a permit by visiting the SCC's website.) A steep woodland hike of just over half a mile (0.8 km) leads to the mouth of Neversink Pit. From here, the only way to reach the cavernous 100-foot-wide (30 m) floor of the pit is to rappel down.

The vertical drop from the lip of Neversink Pit to the bottom is 162 feet (49 m). At the top, the SCC has established two permanent rig sites for rappellers, each of which offers two bolts. (Climbers are asked to not use nearby trees for rigs, as this stress can have a destructive effect on the trees.) Rappellers should be experienced, with caving knowledge and the proper safety equipment. They should also be familiar with a single-rope technique.

As you begin your descent into the darkness of Neversink, keep an ear open for the telltale squeak of the resident bats that roost by the thousands in the pit's nooks and crannies.

Even if you don't have the skills to descend, a hike to Neversink and looking over its ledge is worth the effort.

Fackler, AL | **Season:** Year-round

A Walk in the Park

Choose your own adventure on the trails at Red Mountain Park.

The long ridgeline of Red Mountain that looms over Birmingham is a window into industrial history. During the 19th and 20th centuries, miners bored through the mountain searching for iron ore, coal, and limestone. After the last mine closed in 1962, Red Mountain was left largely untouched for 50 years and its vegetation resurged, inspiring an idea. Why not transform a 4.5-mile (7.2 km) section of the mountain into a recreational park with trails to the old mining infrastructure?

Today, Red Mountain Park is one of the largest urban parks in the United States—more than 70 percent larger than New York's Central Park. The park boasts 17 miles (27 km) of walking, hiking, and mountain biking paths that weave through the mountainside woods and offers free off-road electric wheelchairs and accessible routes. Also, Remy's Dog Park has been recognized as one of the "10 Great Southern Dog Parks" by *Southern Living*.

Birmingham, AL   Season: Year-round

The Big Bass Capital of the World

Of the 13 lakes that make up the Alabama Bass Trail, Lake Eufaula is *the* fishing destination. Built by the Army Corps of Engineers, this 45,181-acre (18,284 ha) reservoir on the Alabama-Georgia border is part of the Chattahoochee River. The largemouth and spotted bass are so prominent here that the nearby town of Eufaula decided to brand itself the "Big Bass Capital of the World."

The shoreline offers an impressive array of brush where bass shelter and spawn in the springtime, before moving onward to numerous tributaries that spill into the lake.

As you enter Eufaula, you'll find fishing gear retailers, bait shops, and a 12-foot-tall (3.7 m) jumping bass statue. Boat rentals and fishing charters are available from Chewalla Creek Marina, or use one of several public access points along the lakes.

Eufaula, AL | Season: Spring and fall

Cast your line and try your luck at Lake Eufaula.

Just Around the River Bend

The abundant waterways of southern Alabama's River Heritage come in all denominations, and often, they contain surprises. The Sepulga River flows roughly 60 miles (97 km) through pine, dogwoods, and limestone walls that resemble a shallow gorge. But the waters of this snug river get deeper and choppier than one might expect, and one of the most interesting ways to experience this is by paddling the Sepulga River Canoe Trail.

Starting at Travis Bridge (near Brewton) and extending 29 miles (47 km) south to Cottonhouse Landing in Conecuh National Forest, the canoe trail features Class I rapids, swimmable beaches, caves, and impressive cascades such as Pigeon Creek Falls, which is located near the trail's midpoint at Bull Slough Bridge.

The riverbed around here is also known to contain fossilized shark teeth: relics of the Eocene era, when ocean covered most of Alabama. Bring goggles or a snorkeling mask and scoop up these ghostly denticles yourself.

Conecuh County, AL | **Season:** Year-round

> "DISMALS CANYON'S MOST UNUSUAL TREASURE—ITS NAMESAKE—EMERGES AFTER SUNDOWN."

Nighttime Spectacular

Alabama is one of the most biologically diverse states in the United States, and this badge of honor is on full display in the twisted sandstone passageways of Dismals Canyon. More than 300 million years ago, this area was a festering swamp, a patch of land literally raised by geologic activity during the Paleozoic era. Gallons of draining water cut the canyon walls now festooned with verdant moss and ferns.

Now a national natural landmark, Dismals Canyon features a 1.5-mile (2.4 km) hiking trail on which you'll follow Dismals Creek to boulder piles, roaring cascades, natural bridges, and a sunken forest that contains preserved bluff shelters and grottoes once used by Paleo-Americans and, later, the Cherokee and Chickasaw peoples. You'll explore these features amid more than 350 species of flora, including towering Canadian hemlocks. But Dismals Canyon's most unusual treasure—its namesake—emerges after sundown.

As darkness falls, the canyon walls come alive with "dismalites": carnivorous fly larvae that emit a ghostly blue glow. Biologically related to glowworms found in Australia and New Zealand, these tiny bioluminescent insects require a humid climate, hanging surfaces on which they can build their webs, and an endless buffet of insects to trap and ingest. Dismals Canyon provides the perfect environment. Against the canyon walls at night, the dismalites resemble stars against a pitch-black sky.

To observe the dismalites in all their luminary beauty, your best bet is a guided night tour of the canyon. Starting at the Country Store that welcomes visitors to Dismals Canyon, guided trips last 45 minutes and reservations are recommended.

Phil Campbell, AL | Season: Spring and fall

Hike through moss-covered Dismals Canyon for an otherworldly adventure.

An Island (Bird) Sanctuary

Many visitors to Dauphin Island—from French explorers expanding their grasp of Louisiana territory to American families dreaming of summer homes on the Gulf of Mexico—have put down roots on the beaches of this 14-mile (22.5 km) barrier island. But North American birds long preceded the island's human migration. Each winter, hundreds of avian species swoop through Dauphin Island's saw palmetto woodlands and salt marshes.

Thanks to the efforts of the Audubon Society and the Dauphin Island Bird Sanctuaries, you can witness these winged island residents in their element. Many birders head straight for the Audubon Bird Sanctuary on the island's east end, where a three-mile (4.8 km) trail system allows visitors to explore 137 acres (55 ha) of coastal woods, wetlands, and dunes. But the Dauphin Island Bird Sanctuaries' 11 protected places allow you to explore lesser known birding environments across the island, such as tupelo tree swamps or elevated "mound" forests.

Dauphin Island, AL | Season: Spring

A blue heron rests at Dauphin Island.

Dam Good Rapids

Approximately 85 million years ago, an asteroid the size of a sports arena slammed into Alabama at 43,000 miles an hour (69,200 km/h), killing the local dinosaurs and leaving behind a four-mile-wide (6.4 km) crater. The Coosa River rumbles along the western edge of that crater, and you can glimpse its dramatic rock formations from the seat of your kayak.

For paddlers, the asteroid yielded more than abstract geographic sculptures. The unsettled layers of rock over which the Coosa flows produce an impressive array of rapids. Wetumpka, the town through which the most paddled segment of the Coosa passes, gets its name from the Creek word for "rumbling waters." Local outfitters offer white-water kayak rentals and transportation to the bottom of the Walter Bouldin Dam, where you'll put in and paddle south through oak and hickory forest into a buffet of shoals.

Just how placid or choppy the Coosa might be during your visit depends on the amount of water released by the dam that day. These variable flows are publicly scheduled in advance. For a gentle and meditative river voyage with more involved paddling, go on a day when the water output is 2,000 cubic feet (57 m³) a second. The higher outputs, ranging from 4,000 to 10,000 cubic feet (113 to 283 m³) a second will bring more rapids to life. Moccasin Gap is the most formidable obstacle, where kayakers can choose between a Class II and Class III bypass.

Wetumpka, AL | Season: Late spring to early fall

Through-State Hiking

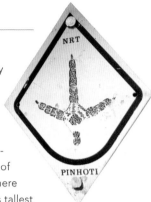

When forester and conservationist Benton MacKaye mapped out his vision for the Appalachian Trail (AT) in 1925, he foresaw a trail that wandered from the mountains of northern Alabama to the wilderness of northern Maine. Instead, the trail began from Springer Mountain in Georgia.

But the "missing link" of MacKaye's original idea lingered in the minds of Alabama and Georgia hikers, and in 1972, construction began on the Pinhoti Trail. A 339-mile (546 km) passage of stone and soil, the Pinhoti Trail ambles northeast from Flagg Mountain (Alabama's southernmost peak of 1,000-plus feet/305-plus m) through Talladega National Forest to Georgia's Cohutta Wilderness. From there, the Benton MacKaye Trail continues to Springer, fulfilling MacKaye's vision.

If you've wondered what it might have been like to hike the AT in its infancy, before it was "broken in" by hiker hordes, consider section hiking the Pinhoti Trail.

Flagg Mountain to Talladega National Forest, AL Season: Fall to spring

Beyond regional hiking groups, the trail is relatively unknown. A few trail highlights are longleaf pine forests where the average tree is 200 years old, waterfalls, rocky scrambles, and panoramic views of the Cheaha Wilderness (where the trail ascends Alabama's tallest mountain).

First-time section hikers often begin at Pine Glen Campground with a gentle six-mile (10 km) out-and-back hike along Shoal Creek to Sweetwater Lake, one of the trail's most beautiful tent sites. Birders should head for the Trammel Trailhead, which offers access to red-cockaded woodpecker nesting sites along a two-mile (3.2 km) stretch of the trail. To avoid scorching temperatures, plan your hike for the window between October and March.

A Woodsy Retreat

Bigger isn't always better when it comes to woodlands, and Tuskegee National Forest—the smallest national forest in the United States—proves the point by packing a surprising heft of history and ecology into its 11,000 acres (4,450 ha). In 1959, President Eisenhower declared the woods a protected space—giving it time to recover from decades of logging activity that began in the early 20th century.

As you wander through magnolias and dogwood trees on the park's 7.7-mile (12.4 km) Bartram Trail, you'll encounter native flora like trillium and cranefly orchids. You'll also hear planes taking off from Moton Field, next door to the forest. This airstrip is where America's first Black military aviators—the Tuskegee Airmen—were trained during World War II. The Army airfield closed in 1946; the space is used as a municipal airport today.

Walk through majestic groves on the Bartram Trail.

Tuskegee, AL Season: Spring to fall

Civil rights marchers faced violent attacks from police on the Edmund Pettus Bridge in 1965.

> "THE WORLD WATCHED AS CIVIL RIGHTS ACTIVISTS WALKED 54 MILES (87 KM) FROM SELMA TO MONTGOMERY."

Stepping Into History

Of all the marches undertaken in U.S. history, the 1965 voting rights march is among the most important. The world watched as civil rights activists walked 54 miles (87 km) from Selma to Montgomery, Alabama, registering Black voters and suffering violence and blockades from the police and white supremacists. The march was one of many efforts that led to the Voting Rights Act of 1965. Decades later, in 1993, Congressman John Lewis (one of the marchers) suggested the route be preserved.

Three years later, the Selma to Montgomery National Historic Trail was green-lit and "blazed" with informative signs commemorating important events along the march route. The trail's vast midsection follows U.S. Route 80 and is best taken as a drive or on bicycle. The bookending trail segments in Selma and Montgomery are easily walkable.

Starting from Selma's Brown Chapel A.M.E. Church, a haven for march organizers, you'll proceed through the city to the Edmund Pettus Bridge in Selma, where the infamous "Bloody Sunday" attack on marchers took place. En route to Montgomery, the Lowndes Interpretive Center offers illuminating exhibits that show what it was like for marchers to walk and camp on the busy road for days (the center is built on the site of a former tent city for marchers).

The final leg of the trail crosses the grassy quads at City of St. Jude, where Harry Belafonte organized a concert for the marchers. The route concludes at the Alabama State Capitol in downtown Montgomery. Here, on white marble steps, Dr. Martin Luther King, Jr., delivered his "How Long? Not Long" speech to the crowd.

Montgomery to Selma, AL | **Season:** Year-round

A cascade falls into
Little River Canyon
National Preserve.

1. WHITE-WATER RAFTING ON THE CHATTAHOOCHEE RIVER

Rumbling between Phenix City, Alabama, and Columbus, Georgia, the Chattahoochee offers one of the most powerful urban white-water runs in the South. Class II and Class IV rapids explode against the prows of kayaks.

2. EXPLORE LAGOON PARK TRAILS

Montgomery is a city surrounded by twisting rivers and immense junglelike woods. But it wasn't until the late 2010s when 176 acres (72 ha) of these hardwood forests were opened to hikers, cyclists, and birders with the construction of the Lagoon Park Trails system, which spans five miles (8 km) of pine flats, woodlands, and creeks.

3. SEE WILDLIFE AT ALABAMA NATURE CENTER AT LANARK

Explore 350 acres (142 ha) of rustling oak and pine woodlands, cypress swamps, streams, and meadows. Labyrinthine trails and boardwalks offer opportunities to spot eastern box turtles and red-bellied woodpeckers.

4. FIND CULTURE AT BLOUNT CULTURAL PARK

Home to the Montgomery Museum of Fine Arts, this oasis southeast of downtown boasts Old English–style stone bridges along a 3.5-mile (5.6 km) trail network that ambles past duck ponds, sculptures, fountains, and picnic greens.

5. SPELUNK MAJESTIC CAVERNS

Alabama's superlative "Big Cave"—one of the state's few publicly accessible caves—lures would-be spelunkers into the depths of the Appalachians. The cathedral-like main chamber of Majestic Caverns is more than 10 stories tall and 100 yards (90 m) long. Innumerable onyx-marble stalagmites and stalactites decorate this great hall of stone.

6. MOUNTAIN BIKE CHEWACLA STATE PARK

Central Alabama mountain biking clubs played an authorial role in shaping more than 30 miles (48 km) of bike trails that swerve and plunge through the woodlands of Chewacla. Keep an eye peeled for red foxes, curious rock formations, and thunderous waterfalls along this challenging trail system.

7. LAUNCH AT THE COASTAL ALABAMA BACK BAY BLUEWAY

Alabama's Gulf Coast contains protected waterways that lead to cypress swamps, freshwater lakes, and secluded sandy beaches. The Back Bay Blueway opens these serene channels to adventurous kayakers and paddleboarders with 21 launch sites and four water-based trails that span from Gulf Shores to Fort Morgan.

8. SUBMERGE YOURSELF IN THE PERDIDO RIVER TRAIL

Epic hiking might not seem like an intuitive activity for coastal Alabama but the 18-mile (29 km) river trail bucks convention, taking you along a former stagecoach route through white cedar swamps and longleaf pine forests permeated by salty sea breeze from the Gulf of Mexico. The trail visits sandbars that double as swimming holes.

9. CLIMB AT CHEROKEE ROCK VILLAGE

Picture a lonely town made of sandstone boulders and rock formations, and you'll have a glimpse of this mountaintop outcropping with stunning views of Weiss Lake. But it's the top-rope climbing along Sand Rock, the park's premier pinnacle of stone, that draws adventurers from near and far.

10. RAINBOW TROUT FISH AT SIPSEY FORK

Located beneath a dam at Smith Lake, the Sipsey Fork is often described as Alabama's only year-round rainbow trout fishery, thanks to monthly fish stocking by the state. The clear, cool water helps the trout flourish and you're free to cast here without a permit (limit five trout).

Camellia

All aboard! The Alaska Railroad winds through the beautiful south side of Denali National Park (page 27).

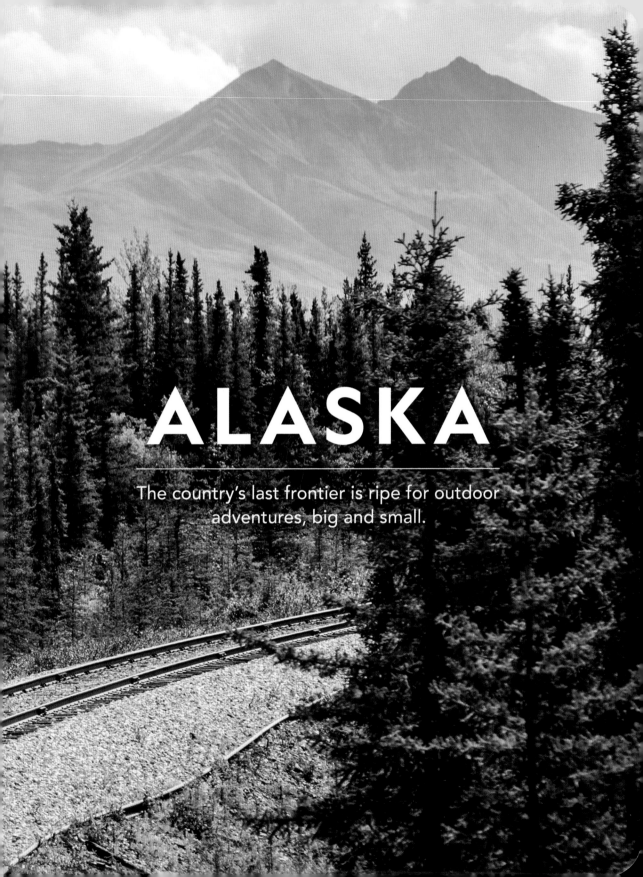

ALASKA

The country's last frontier is ripe for outdoor
adventures, big and small.

A R C T I C

*Chukchi
Sea*

RUSSIA

RUSSIA
U.S.

*Bering
Sea*

A L A

"TO THE LOVER OF
WILDERNESS, ALASKA
IS ONE OF THE MOST
WONDERFUL COUNTRIES
IN THE WORLD."
—JOHN MUIR

*Lake Clark National
Park & Preserve*

*Wood-Tikchik
State Park*

*Katmai National
Park & Preserve*

*Alaska
Marine
Highway*

P A C I F I C

OCEAN

Beaufort Sea

NUNAVUT

Arctic National
Wildlife Refuge

NORTHWEST
TERRITORIES

CANADA
U.S.

YUKON

C A N A D A

Black Diamond
Golf Course

Denali
Park Road

Alaska
Highway

Alaska
Railroad

Wrangell-St. Elias
National Park & Preserve

Tony
Knowles
Coastal
Trail

Matanuska
Glacier

Paul Claus bush
plane flightseeing

Alyeska
Resort

Chugach
Mountains

SKA

Alsek &
Tatshenshini Rivers

BRITISH
COLUMBIA

Seward
dogsledding

Icy Bay

Kenai Fjords
National Park

Glacier Bay National
Park & Preserve

Gulf of Alaska

Inside
Passage

U.S.
CANADA

OCEAN

Sleep Tight (On a Glacier)

A 27-mile (43 km) tongue of ice flowing down from the Chugach Mountains, Matanuska Glacier is noteworthy for several reasons. Most important, it's still growing rather than retreating like so many other glaciers. It's also the largest glacier nearly accessible by car in the United States. And it offers the rare opportunity to camp on its surface overnight.

On the opposite side of Matanuska River from the glacier's main facade, MICA Guides maintains a tented summer camp atop the glacier. After reaching the camp via helicopter, campers check into a roomy safari-style tent with queen bed, camp chairs, and down comforter. The one-night adventure includes dinner and breakfast prepared and served by the camp staff.

Besides hiking across the glacier surface with a MICA guide, campers have the option of guided ice climbing and rappelling into a deep glacial crevasse. And there's plenty of time to just chill (pun intended) in Matanuska sunshine.

Matanuska Glacier, AK | **Season:** Late May to early September

Make camp overlooking the Matanuska Glacier and Chugach Mountains.

Extreme Flightseeing

Bush pilots have been taking to the skies above the Last Frontier since the 1920s. In a state that remains largely roadless, they transport passengers and supplies to remote settlements and whisk thousands of tourists on scenic flights each year.

Among the pantheon of legendary bush plane pilots is Paul Claus, who owns and operates Ultima Thule Lodge in the backcountry of Wrangell–St. Elias National Park. The only way to reach the lodge is his air taxi from McCarthy. And flying with Claus is the ultimate thrill.

Among his three aircraft is a canary yellow Piper Super Cub stripped of everything not absolutely necessary for safe flight to make the plane as light as possible.

A typical day in the air with Claus might include a slow-motion corkscrew landing on top of a glacier, alighting on a grassy ledge on the side of a 1,000-foot (305 m) cliff for a closer look at Dall sheep or mountain goats, or gliding onto a gravel beach beside an alpine lake where grizzly bears are feasting on wild berries. Claus and his aircraft can also expedite fly-in fishing, hiking, kayaking, climbing, or other adventures.

See the sights from new heights on a bush plane tour.

Wrangell–St. Elias National Park, AK | **Season:** Year-round

A Road Trip Like No Other

No other route is quite like it anywhere in Alaska. Stretching 92.5 miles (148 km) into the heart of the national park, Denali Park Road offers an ever changing panorama of glaciers, rivers, wildlife, and the snowy Alaska Range.

Hikers and bikers can traverse the entire length of the road on their own. Six roadside campgrounds take reservations or have backcountry permits for those who wish to overnight in the bush. The easternmost stretch between the visitors center and Savage River (Mile 15) is open to all private vehicles, but driving beyond that point requires a day permit acquired through an annual lottery or reservations at Teklanika River Campground (Mile 29).

Another way to explore Denali Park Road is hopping aboard the old school buses that ply the route daily. In addition to a trip down memory lane for those who once rode the vintage buses to school, it's far and away the easiest way to cruise the route.

Denali National Park, AK | **Season:** Summer to early fall

Green transit buses offer hop-on, hop-off service along the road; brown buses like the Tundra Wilderness Tour feature driver-guides with an encyclopedic knowledge of Denali and often a great sense of humor. Both green and brown buses stop at viewpoints, exhibits, restrooms, and for wandering wildlife along the way.

Those staying at the wilderness lodges in Kantishna at the road's western end (Mile 92) reach their digs via private or park shuttle. Or if money is no object, fly in by air taxi and land at a remote gravel airstrip. Before scheduling your trip along Denali Park Road, check the national park's website as weather conditions and natural events like rockslides may impact your route.

Grizzly Paparazzi

Alaska's most iconic wildlife image is a grizzly fishing for salmon. The shot is most often snapped along the Brooks River in Katmai National Park and Preserve, where brown bears gather between July and September to bulk up before winter hibernation.

Katmai's Pacific shore also hosts one of the largest concentrations of bears on the planet. On Hallo Bay, Moraine Creek, and Swikshak Lagoon, bruins venture onto the mudflats or into shallow water to feast on salmon and clams. The Cook Inlet coast of nearby Lake Clark National Park and Preserve is also great for bear sightings, especially on the salt marshes and mudflats near Chinitna Bay and sedge-filled meadows along Silver Salmon Creek.

Bear aficionados can overnight at Brooks Camp or book a fly-in tour with outfitters in Anchorage.

A pair of grizzlies play in the meadows near Lake Clark.

Katmai National Park and Preserve, AK | **Season:** July to September

Icy Bay is surrounded by the Tyndall Glacier (center) and Mount Saint Elias.

> "THE NEAREST HUMANS ARE
> MOST LIKELY 70 MILES
> (110 KM) AWAY IN EVERY
> DIRECTION."

Kayak Camping and Sightseeing in Icy Bay

Imagine Yosemite on the coast, an iceberg-filled fjord rather than a mountain valley, its aquamarine waters fed by huge glaciers and dozens of unnamed waterfalls, some of them tumbling down 1,000-foot (305 m) granite cliffs: That's what Icy Bay is all about.

Located along a remote stretch of the Gulf of Alaska at the confluence of the panhandle with the rest of the state, the pristine bay lies in one of the more remote corners of Wrangell–St. Elias National Park and Preserve. A century ago, the bay didn't exist. But the retreat of Guyot, Tyndall, and Yahtse Glaciers created a void that gradually filled.

Reaching Icy Bay is part of the adventure. It starts with a domestic flight to Yakutat, followed by a bush plane flight over massive Malaspina Glacier (the world's largest piedmont glacier) to a gravel beach at Kageet Point near the bay's mouth. Setting off in kayaks, expect several hours of steady paddling—with the possibility of sighting whales, dolphins, and other sea creatures along the way—to reach primitive camping spots above the high tide line on Tsaa Fjord or Taan Fjord.

Having established a base camp, kayakers can easily explore the 30-mile-long (48 km) bay on day paddles through a maze of icebergs and the mist zone beneath thunderous waterfalls. Shore landings provide opportunities to probe ice caves or the outer edge of glaciers, or snap photos of the bay with a backdrop of the world's highest coastal mountain range. All the while knowing that the nearest humans are most likely 70 miles (110 km) away in every direction.

Wrangell–St. Elias National Park, AK | **Season:** Spring and summer

Fly-Fish With a View

Sprawling across a wilderness as big as Delaware, Wood-Tikchik is the nation's largest state park and one of Alaska's best spots for fly-fishing. Located on the western side of the state near Bristol Bay and the Bering Sea, the park safeguards a dozen glacial lakes and several large rivers framed by the snowy Wood River Range.

Whether you're angling for trout, char, grayling, pike, or the park's five different types of salmon, fishing the waters of Wood-Tikchik is the stuff of angler legend. Many of the estimated 50 million fish that gather in Bristol Bay each year make their way up the park's rivers to spawn.

Most anglers overnight at one of the five fly-in fishing lodges inside the park. Open from June to early October, they provide everything you need for days of fishing. Outfitters in Anchorage and nearby Dillingham also offer fly-in day trips and multiday float trips.

Wood-Tikchik, AK | **Season:** June to October

> "WHETHER YOU'RE ANGLING FOR TROUT, CHAR, GRAYLING, PIKE, OR THE PARK'S FIVE DIFFERENT TYPES OF SALMON, FISHING THE WATERS OF WOOD-TIKCHIK IS THE STUFF OF ANGLER LEGEND."

There's rarely a more beautiful setting to cast your luck on a fly-fishing trip.

Big jumps await on the ledges of Alyeska Resort's downhill slopes.

Searching for Fresh Powder

Girdwood started life in the late 1890s as a supply camp for gold miners and stop along the historic Iditarod Trail. By the 1990s it was producing precious metals of a much different kind—Olympic medals captured by alpine skiers Tommy Moe and Hilary Lindh, and snowboarder Rosey Fletcher. All three of them based at the town's Alyeska snow sports resort.

With a winter season that stretches from early December to May, Alyeska has grown from a single rustic downhill run mostly frequented by locals into a major international skiing and snowboarding center with world-class facilities. Located about an hour's drive from Anchorage along the Seward Highway, the mountain now boasts more than 70 total runs—a third of them black diamond—served by eight lifts including a fully enclosed, heated tram. In addition to fixed runs, Alyeska offers helicopter skiing and snowboarding, and

six remote snowcat-accessed runs in the Chugach Range.

There's always plenty of fresh powder. The region's subarctic climate dumps an average of more than 200 inches (500 cm) of snow each year at the base of the mountain and an incredible average of around 650 inches (1,650 cm) each year at the top of the runs. That makes Alyeska the nation's snowiest resort.

Taking time off from the slopes, visitors can rent bikes to navigate three fat-tire trails that meander through the scenic Girdwood Valley or try their luck at ice fishing on a frozen-over alpine lake. Alyeska also offers three miles (4.8 km) of groomed Nordic trails and plenty of scope for snowshoeing in the valley's forests and meadows.

Girdwood, AK **Season:** December to May

You'll have to paddle past icebergs on Alsek Lake.

Float of a Lifetime

Considered one of the world's great river trips, a float down Alsek River and the tributary Tatshenshini takes rafters through a pristine wilderness draped in glaciers and boreal forest, and framed by the peaks of the world's highest coastal mountain range.

The journey covers 140 river miles (225 km) of the Yukon Territory, the northwest corner of British Columbia, and the Alaska Panhandle. The put-in is a remote place called Dalton Post, just off the Haines Highway in Canada, the takeout at Dry Bay in Glacier Bay National Park and Preserve. Though most of the river is rated Class II or lower, there are some Class III and occasional Class IV rapids to spike your heart rate.

Veteran rafters run the Alsek-Tatshenshini on their own, but most folks opt for a guided trip with outfitters like MT Sobek, OARS, or Nahanni River Adventures. Trips normally take 10 days to two weeks.

Yukon (Canada) and AK | **Season:** July to October

Arctic Safari

Tucked up in Alaska's northeast corner beside the Arctic Ocean and Yukon border, Arctic National Wildlife Refuge (ANWR) is home to an immense array of animals from polar bears, muskoxen, and tundra wolves to more than 200 bird species and a Porcupine caribou herd that numbers nearly 200,000.

Nearly as big as the state of Maine, the refuge also shelters diverse terrain and vegetation, from 9,000-foot (2,750 m) mountains far enough south to support spruce, birch, and aspen groves to an extensive coastal plain covered in classic Arctic tundra. Wild rivers, alpine lakes, glaciers, and coastal wetlands are also part of ANWR's geographical equation.

Away from the reserve's controversial coastal oil and gas drilling zone, the wildlife is largely undisturbed by mankind. A few small Alaska Native villages account for

Willow ptarmigan

the entire population. But more telling is the fact that parts of ANWR are more remote—farther from roads, towns, and other human-made features—than anywhere else in the nation.

However, that extreme remoteness also makes it difficult to explore. Though you could bushwhack your way across the tundra from the nearest road outside the refuge or pilot a boat along the often ice-choked Arctic coast, the only practical means is flying in.

Expeditions Alaska offers several ANWR safari options including a packrafting trip along 140 miles (225 km) of the Canning River to the Arctic Ocean in midsummer and a polar bear photo tour in October that includes boat excursions to view the huge white beasts on ice floes.

Arctic National Wildlife Refuge, AK | **Season:** Spring to fall

Drive the Alaska Highway for scenic views of snow-covered mountains and conifer woods.

Cruise the Alaska Highway

Constructed during World War II as a strategic inland route to supply military bases in Alaska, this celebrated thoroughfare is on the bucket list of every die-hard road warrior.

Most of the route is outside of its namesake state, a 1,500-mile (2,400 km) drive between Dawson Creek and Fairbanks through the wilds of British Columbia, the Yukon Territory, and east-central Alaska. The highway wasn't fully paved until 1992, which makes for a much smoother ride than the original gravel roadbed.

Among the highway's natural highs are Stone Mountain Provincial Park in British Columbia (BC), Kluane National Park in the Yukon, and the Tanana River corridor in Alaska.

There's also history, especially in and around Whitehorse, hub of the Klondike gold rush.

Most everyone who drives the Alaska Highway these days travels with an inch-thick copy of *The Milepost*, a comprehensive guidebook to the entire route and other highways in BC, the Yukon, and Alaska.

Dawson Creek to east-central AK | **Season:** Year-round

Put your crampons on to backpack across the Root Glacier in Wrangell–St. Elias National Park.

1. CYCLE THE ANCHORAGE COAST

Rent a standard, tandem, or electric bike from Pablo's in downtown Anchorage to cruise the 22-mile (35 km) Tony Knowles Coastal Trail along Cook Inlet. Keep an eye out for moose and beluga whales, and the bird-watching is sublime; you can also learn about the infamous 1964 Good Friday earthquake at Earthquake Park.

2. CHOPPER OVER CHUGACH

Hop aboard a helicopter at Knik River Lodge northeast of Anchorage for a scenic flight into the Chugach Range punctuated by a walk across the top of Knik Glacier. AK Helicopter Tours can also arrange dogsledding, ice or rock climbing, heli-skiing and snowshoeing, fat-tire biking and hiking deep in the Chugach wilderness.

3. SAIL THE INSIDE PASSAGE

Explore Sitka, Glacier Bay, Baranof Island, and elsewhere in Southeast Alaska under canvas aboard the S/V *Arcturus*. Multiday journeys aboard the 54-foot (16 m), two-masted ketch include all meals, accommodation for up to six passengers, and activities like visiting hot springs, hiking, and kayaking. Another plus: The boat is fully heated.

4. GOLF THE TUNDRA

Beware of moose on the fairways, putt across concrete-like greens frozen year-round by permafrost, and watch out for a wily golf ball–stealing fox at Black Diamond Golf Course. Located off the Parks Highway between Denali and Fairbanks, the nine-hole course is open from late May to September.

5. UNLEASH YOUR POOCH POWER

You don't have to race the legendary Iditarod to get a taste of dogsledding in the Alaska wilderness. Kennels based in Girdwood, Willow, Juneau, and Seward offer sledding adventures that last anywhere from one hour to a couple days. Visit the National Park Service kennels at Denali to learn more about the intrepid huskies.

6. KAYAK GLACIER BAY

Explore the national park—far away from cruise ships—on a kayak journey into a wilderness that John Muir called "a solitude of ice and snow and newborn rocks." Whether on a guided or independent trip, paddlers should be prepared for breaching whales and grizzly bears, extreme tides, and gnarly pressure waves.

7. TAKE A RAILROAD ADVENTURE

Connecting Anchorage with Seward, Denali, and Fairbanks, the Alaska Railroad offers passenger cars with outdoor viewing decks and a winter Nordic ski train, as well as adventure activities at whistle stops along the route, ranging from a jet boat excursion on the Talkeetna River to a Denali zip line and nine holes at the country's northernmost golf course.

8. FLIT AROUND BY FERRY

Explore the Alaska Marine Highway at your own pace aboard ferries that call on 30 ports along the Inside Passage, Gulf of Alaska, Cook Inlet, Kodiak Island, and the Aleutians. Ideal for independent or backpacking travelers, the boats visit remote destinations like Dutch Harbor, Cold Bay, and Petersburg. Mainline ferries feature overnight cabins and restaurants.

9. KAYAK CAMP THE KENAI

Sure, you can see the Kenai Fjords on a day sail from Seward. But the only way to really know the remote national park is kayak camping along the rocky shores of Resurrection Bay, Aialik Bay, or super-remote Harris Bay. Both guided and independent paddlers hop a water taxi to/from drop-off points inside the park.

10. HIKE FROM BASE CAMP IN WRANGELL–ST. ELIAS

Only a small fraction of America's largest national park is accessible by road. But bush planes can transport hikers deep into the wilderness, landing on grass, gravel, and even glaciers. St. Elias Alpine Guides offers fly-in base camps in Skolai Pass, Nizina Glacier, Bremner ghost town, and other spots in the vast reserve.

Cottonwood trees line the trails at Tsegi Overlook at Canyon de Chelly National Monument (page 49).

ARIZONA

The Copper State offers year-round sun, red rocks, grand canyons, and exhilarating sky-high thrills.

UTAH

COLORADO

NEVADA

Vermilion Cliffs
National Monument

Arizona
Strip

Colorado

Antelope
Canyon

Canyon de Chelly
National Monument

Colorado
River

Grand Canyon
National Park

Grand Canyon
South Rim

Kingman

Arizona
Snowbowl

Petrified Forest
National Park

Red Rock
State Park

Slide Rock
State Park

Granite Dells and
Prescott National Forest

NEW MEXICO

Lake
Havasu

Colorado

A R I Z O N A

CALIFORNIA

Superstition
Mountains

Sonoran
Desert

Sierra
Estrella

Saguaro
National Park

Organ Pipe Cactus
National Monument

U.S.
MEXICO

Sierra
Vista

Gulf of
California

S O N O R A

Flagstaff Peak in the Wasatch Mountains offers epic sunrise views.

Flagstaff Winter Wonderland

Arizona snow sports may seem like an oxymoron. But those who've spent the cold-weather season in the Flagstaff area know that white winters are more common than not. Elevations reaching 12,000 feet (3,660 m) complement cold fronts blowing in from the north to produce a nifty sprinkling of fresh powder.

Situated a 30-minute drive from Flagstaff on the western flank of the San Francisco Peaks, the Arizona Snowbowl is the state's premier downhill skiing and snowboarding spot. Average snowfall is 260 inches (660 cm), and eight lifts serve the resort's 55 pistes. There's a ski and ride school, ski and snowboard rental, and ski biking for those who want to glide across the snow on something different.

Flagstaff, AZ | Season: Winter

Nearby Arizona Nordic Village offers the state's best cross-country skiing and snowshoeing on a network of 27 trails in Coconino National Forest. The trails vary between groomed and fresh snow; quite a few are also dog- and fat bike–friendly. Nordic Village also offers rentals and lessons, as well as accommodation in cabins and yurts.

The Forest Service maintains a network of snowmobile trails around Flagstaff, and it's possible to hike the Arizona Trail in winter as it snakes through the region. Lake Mary Road leads south from Flagstaff to the family-friendly Mormon Lake Ski Touring Center and its 21 miles (34 km) of groomed cross-country routes. Farther south, Sunrise Park Resort on the White Mountain Apache Reservation offers skiing and snowboarding, snow tubing, and horse-drawn sleigh rides.

Splash into summer in Oak Creek's natural pools.

Sedona Swimming Holes

Though flowing for fewer than 50 miles (80 km) on either side of Sedona and with much of the waterway shallow enough to walk or wade across, fabled Oak Creek boasts some of Arizona's most beloved swimming holes, places where families have been going for generations to beat the state's notorious summer heat.

Just off Highway 89A north of Sedona, Slide Rock State Park takes its name from a natural slide that channels the creek (and hundreds of kids each day) down a slippery red-rock ledge. Framed by the majestic walls of Oak Creek Canyon, Slide Rock has been named among America's top 10 swimming holes.

Over on the west side of Sedona, Red Rock Crossing offers another family-friendly summer oasis that includes shallow pools and tiny waterfalls, riverside picnic areas, and a mysterious collection of rock cairns that supposedly marks one of Sedona's celebrated vortex spots.

Sedona, AZ | **Season:** Late spring to early fall

Alone on the Strip

Larger than six states, the vast Arizona Strip remains the state's most remote and least inhabited corner. Cut off from the rest of the state by the Grand Canyon and Colorado River, the landscape blends sagebrush and chaparral with piñon-juniper-ponderosa pine forest and the desert scrub of deeply indented canyonlands.

With few paved roads, the best way to explore much of the region is by foot, four-wheel drive, or often both, as many of the trailheads are at the end of rough roads.

Pipe Spring National Monument offers insight into the Arizona Strip's oddball history before you veer off onto roads to Grand Canyon–Parashant National Monument. As the Park Service warns, "Be equipped to leave pavement, cell service, and the 21st century behind" when you venture into the remote reserve in pursuit of solitude, wilderness, and vertiginous views of the Grand Canyon from Whitmore Canyon, Kelly Point, and Twin Point overlooks.

Mohave County, AZ | **Season:** Year-round

Spot old wagons and relics at Pipe Spring National Monument.

Ride (or hike) the Wave—a one-of-a-kind sandstone formation.

Catch a (Rock) Wave

A massive stone barricade along the Arizona-Utah border, the Vermilion Cliffs were little known to outsiders until 2000, when the area became a national monument via presidential decree. Since then, its multicolored mesas, buttes, slot canyons, and 3,000-foot (910 m) palisades have attracted a growing number of visitors seeking the ulti-mate in Arizona desert solitude or a glimpse of seldom seen wildlife like the California condor.

Although the park's namesake cliffs are viewable from Highway 89A between Page and Jacob Lake, most of the monument is accessible only by four-wheel drive or foot. Long day hikes or multiday backpacking are the best ways to experience a wide variety of terrain. Hikers need a permit for visiting mind-blowing spots like Paria Canyon, Coyote Buttes, and the Wave, the latter a much photographed swirl of red, orange, and golden sandstone.

Marble Canyon, AZ | **Season:** Year-round

> "ONE OF THE GREAT SAGAS OF AMERICAN EXPLORATION IS THE FIRST KNOWN FLOAT TRIP DOWN THE COLORADO."

Rafting the Big One

Whether you accomplish the feat by raft, kayak, or wooden dory, making the roller-coaster run down the Colorado River in northern Arizona is an incredible adventure. Beyond the fact that it boasts numerous Class IV and Class V rapids—as well as a few monster Class X rapids that only the most experienced river rats should attempt—the Colorado runs through some of the globe's biggest and most impressive canyons.

One of the great sagas of American exploration is the first known float trip down the Colorado, an 1869 expedition led by one-armed Civil War veteran John Wesley Powell. They navigated the wild river in heavy wooden boats, forerunners of today's lightweight dories. And it was definitely scary. "The spectacle is appalling," wrote expedition member George Bradley.

That adrenaline rush is part of the thrill of running the Colorado in modern times. Because most of the river in northern Arizona falls within Grand Canyon National Park and Lake Mead National Recreation Area, navigation on the Colorado is strictly regulated to enhance safety, prevent overuse, and protect the area's natural and cultural assets.

Private individuals can undertake their own white-water expedition with a noncommercial river permit from the Park Service. However, most people opt for a guided commercial trip through experienced outfitters with a park concession.

Those who aren't ready for gnarly rapids can book one-day float trips on smooth water between Glen Canyon Dam and Lees Ferry. Multiday trips through the Grand Canyon last anywhere from three days to three weeks with takeout at Phantom Ranch, Whitmore Wash, Diamond Creek, or Lake Mead.

Grand Canyon National Park, AZ | **Season:** April to October

Take on the roaring rapids of the Colorado River while paddling through the Grand Canyon.

Pipe Dream

🚲 Sprawling across a huge chunk of desert along the Arizona-Mexico frontier, Organ Pipe Cactus National Monument is ready-made for remote cycling. Bikes are verboten on hiking trails but are welcome on all park roads, many of them unpaved and off the beaten track.

Kris Eggle Visitor Center is the jumping-off point for several long, scenic rides. Heading east, Ajo Mountain Drive offers a 21-mile (34 km) loop to Arch Canyon and the Bull Pasture. Meandering off to the west, Puerto Blanco Drive makes a 41-mile (66 km) loop that includes Dripping Spring, Golden Bell Mine, and La Abra Plain.

It's hard to miss the park's namesake organ pipe cactus or the tall saguaro as you're pedaling around. But bikers should keep an eye out for 27 other cactus species found in the park, including barrel, cholla, prickly pear, hedgehog, pincushion, devil's club, and Sonoran queen of the night.

Organ Pipe Cactus National Monument, AZ | **Season:** Year-round

It's worth the early wake-up to catch the sunrise at Organ Pipe.

Saddle Up for Saguaros

🏇 It's an image straight out of a Western movie—a string of riders and their horses moving through a forest of towering cacti in the Arizona desert. The best place to re-create that scene is in and around Saguaro National Park.

The park is split into two units: the Tucson Mountain District to the west of Tucson and the Rincon Mountain District on the east side of town. Both boast equestrian-friendly trails, horse trailer parking, and nearby stables offering guided rides.

Rincon Mountain is larger and slightly wilder, a rugged expanse of desert covered in thousands of saguaros. The lush Cactus Garden area near the visitors center offers flat and fairly easy rides, while trails into the highlands require more time and skill to reach lofty viewpoints and remote canyons.

Guided saddle trips are offered by a dozen stables in the area, including Tanque Verde Ranch. Founded in 1868, the ranch offers breakfast and sunset rides, one-hour walk and lope rides, and a half-day ride that ventures deep into the Rincon Mountains. Trailheads at Sendero Esperanza, El Camino del Cerro, and Cam-Boh offer access to horseback rides inside the Tucson Mountain District along cactus-studded routes like the Golden Gate Multiuse Trail, Coyote Pass Loop, and Sendero Esperanza Trail.

More equestrian trails crisscross neighboring Tucson Mountain County Park, home to the Old Tucson Studios, where hundreds of Western movies have been filmed since 1939.

Tucson, AZ | **Season:** Year-round

Hiking the Big Ditch

Along with the Appalachian and Pacific Crest Trails, hoofing it into the Grand Canyon is one of the great adventures of American hiking. Even a brief descent from the South Rim provides an entirely different take on the world's most famous canyon. At the other end of the trekking spectrum, hard-core hikers can take more than a month to walk the gorge from end to end.

There are two classic canyon hikes. The most popular is a two-day loop via the Bright Angel and South Kaibab Trails with an overnight at Phantom Ranch (camping and cabins) or Indian Garden (camping only). Total distance: 19.2 miles (31 km). The other is the Rim to Rim hike, normally undertaken as a three-day hike with nights at Phantom Ranch and Cottonwood Campground. Total distance: 23 miles (37 km) via the South/North Kaibab route or 24 miles (39 km) via the Bright Angel/North Kaibab.

Grand Canyon National Park, AZ | **Season:** Year-round

No matter what time of year you visit Grand Canyon National Park, you are bound to run into other people on those routes. Despite the heat, the Bright Angel Trail gets

Cactus wren

mighty crowded during late spring, summer, and early fall. But the canyon boasts plenty of other routes that are much less traveled.

Among the alternate ways to descend into the canyon from the South Rim are the Tanner, New Hance, Grandview, and Hermit Trails. Each of these routes intersects with the epic Tonto Trail, which runs 95 miles (153 km) across the canyon bottom between Red Canyon and Garnet Canyon.

Free-Fall Over Eloy

A free fall from 15,000 feet (4,570 m) lasts around 60 seconds. But it feels like an eternity as you plunge toward the Sonoran Desert, Phoenix, and the Superstition Mountains on one side, Tucson and the Santa Catalina Range on the other, and the town of Eloy straight below.

That's the thrill of jumping with Skydive Arizona. Based in Eloy, it's the world's largest drop zone. Tandem jumps offer an introduction to the sport. Ratcheting up the thrill, Skydive Arizona also offers wingsuit instruction.

The Sonoran Desert's clear, dry skies enable around 340 days of skydiving each year. In addition to 15 aircraft—the world's largest fleet of skydiving planes—Skydive Arizona's drop zone features a vertical wind tunnel for "body flight," indoor skydiving, as well as campsites and RV hookups for overnight stays.

Take to the skies above the desert.

Eloy, AZ | **Season:** Year-round

Lake Havasu is a water lover's paradise.

> "WITH MORE THAN 400 MILES (640 KM) OF SHORELINE, IT'S A PLAYGROUND OF TITANIC PROPORTIONS."

Water Play on Lake Havasu

Wet and wild is the unofficial motto of an Arizona water body that has evolved from a World War II military rest camp into one of the world's premier water sports destinations. With more than 400 miles (640 km) of shoreline and around 60 miles (97 km) of navigable water-ways—and more than 300 days of sunshine each year—it's a playground of titanic proportions.

Powerboats and personal watercraft, wakeboarding and waterskiing, canoeing, kayaking, paddleboarding, and even scuba diving—Havasu has it all. As well as a full-service marina, watercraft rental outlets, boat-in bars and restaurants, and 119 boat-in campgrounds.

Created in the 1930s by the construction of Parker Dam, Lake Havasu stretches around 26 miles (42 km) from stem to stern. Almost nothing lined its desert shores until 1968, when chain saw and outboard motor mogul Robert McCulloch purchased London Bridge and moved the historic British span lock, stock, and stone to Lake Havasu City.

Lake Havasu's central and southern sections are the realm of powerboaters, especially those seeking a campground or secluded cove. Boaters can snap selfies at Red Rock or Balance Rock, play a round of five holes on the executive golf course at Black Meadow Landing, or grab lunch beside Parker Dam.

With no wake zones and powerboat restrictions, Havasu National Wildlife Refuge at the lake's northern end lures canoers and kayakers. In addition to more than 300 bird species, desert bighorn sheep, and wild burros, paddlers can visit the shoreline petroglyphs and venture through the deep Topock Gorge.

Lake Havasu City, AZ | **Season:** Year-round

Explore the wonders of
Lower Antelope Canyon's
sandstone formations.

1. HUNT FOR SUPERSTITIOUS TREASURE

You likely won't find the fabled Lost Dutchman Mine or the Apache portal to the underworld, but the Superstition Mountains just east of Phoenix offer plenty of flora and fauna treasure. More than 40 hiking and horse trails fan out across a federal wilderness area established in 1939.

2. BIKE THE GRAND CANYON

Cyclists can cruise the Village Greenway, Rim Trail, or Hermit Road, some of the more energetic ways to explore the South Rim. Bright Angel Bicycles near the Mather Point visitors center rents cruisers and road bikes, plus tagalongs and trailers for kids. They also offer three-hour guided bike tours.

3. TREK TO TRIASSIC TREES

Most visitors never stray far from viewpoints along Highway 180 in the Petrified Forest. But the northern Arizona national park features half a dozen awesome backcountry routes, including an 8.5-mile (13.7 km) out-and-back to the Red Basin Clam Beds and a 7-mile (11 km) Wilderness Loop through 210-million-year-old petrified trees.

4. EXPLORE CANYON DE CHELLY

Jointly managed by the Navajo Nation and the National Park Service, this imposing red-rock canyon is both a scenic wonder and showcase of ancestral Puebloan cliff dwellings. Visitors can explore the national monument on guided walks or rides with Navajo outfitters like Ancient Canyon Tours and Justin's Horseback Tours.

5. GLIDE OVER THE SIERRA ESTRELLA

Get ready for loops, rolls, thermaling, and maybe even flying upside down during a glider ride over the Sonoran Desert and Sierra Estrella Mountains south of Phoenix. Based at the Estrella Sailport, Arizona Soaring offers aerobatic or scenic flights with veteran pilots as well as courses for those who want to pilot their own glider.

6. FLOCK FOR FEATHERS

The nation's "greatest little birding festival," Southwest Wings takes flight each spring in and around Sierra Vista. The event includes day trips with professional guides to primo birding spots like Coronado National Memorial, Fort Huachuca, Madera Canyon, and the Santa Cruz Valley in search of more than 500 avian species recorded in Arizona.

7. AMBLE THROUGH ANTELOPE CANYON

The Navajo people called it Tsé Bighánílíní—"The Place Where Water Runs Through Rocks"—an apt description for a slot canyon that seems sculpted by an artist rather than a random act of nature. The only way to visit the Navajo tribal park is on a guided hike with a certified tribal outfitter.

8. ROAD TRIP TO A GHOST TOWN

The desert of western Arizona is riddled with ghost towns, abandoned or backwater burgs that once thrived on gold or silver mining. Starting from Phoenix or Kingman, a looping road trip takes in seven Wild West relics, including Agua Caliente, Castle Dome, Swansea, Oatman, Chloride, Hackberry, and Vulture City.

9. DRIFT OVER SEDONA

Clear skies, steady updrafts, and incredible red-rock scenery give Sedona almost ideal conditions for hot-air ballooning. Taking flight from a site near Red Rock State Park, Northern Light Balloon Expeditions takes passengers high above fabled Oak Creek and past stately sandstone landmarks like Cathedral Rock and the distant Mogollon Rim.

10. PADDLE PRESCOTT'S BACKCOUNTRY

Arrayed on either side of Prescott in Arizona's central highlands, three lakes expedite excellent paddling against a backdrop of the rocky Granite Dells and piñon pines of Prescott National Forest. From late spring through early fall, Prescott Outdoors rents canoes, kayaks, and stand-up paddleboards at all three water bodies.

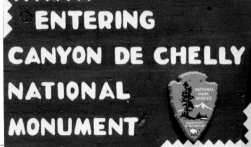

ENTERING CANYON DE CHELLY NATIONAL MONUMENT

Known for their lakes, the Ozark Mountains (page 63) also offer verdant mountainsides with miles of hiking trails.

ARKANSAS

From scenic waterways to renowned mountain bike trails,
find surprises throughout the Natural State.

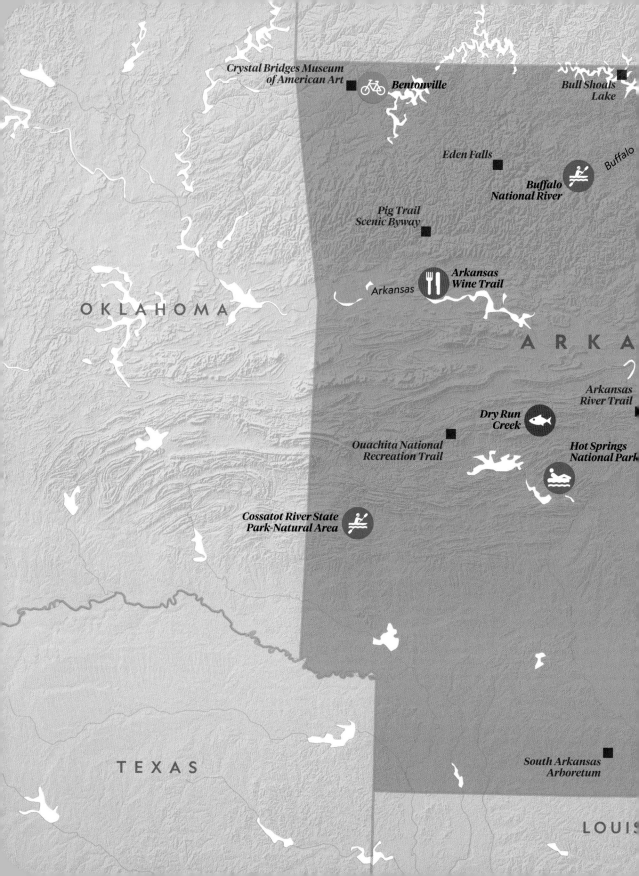

Crystal Bridges Museum
of American Art

Bentonville

Bull Shoals
Lake

Eden Falls

Buffalo
National River

Buffalo

Pig Trail
Scenic Byway

Arkansas
Wine Trail

Arkansas

OKLAHOMA

ARKA

Arkansas
River Trail

Dry Run
Creek

Ouachita National
Recreation Trail

Hot Springs
National Park

Cossatot River State
Park-Natural Area

TEXAS

South Arkansas
Arboretum

LOUIS

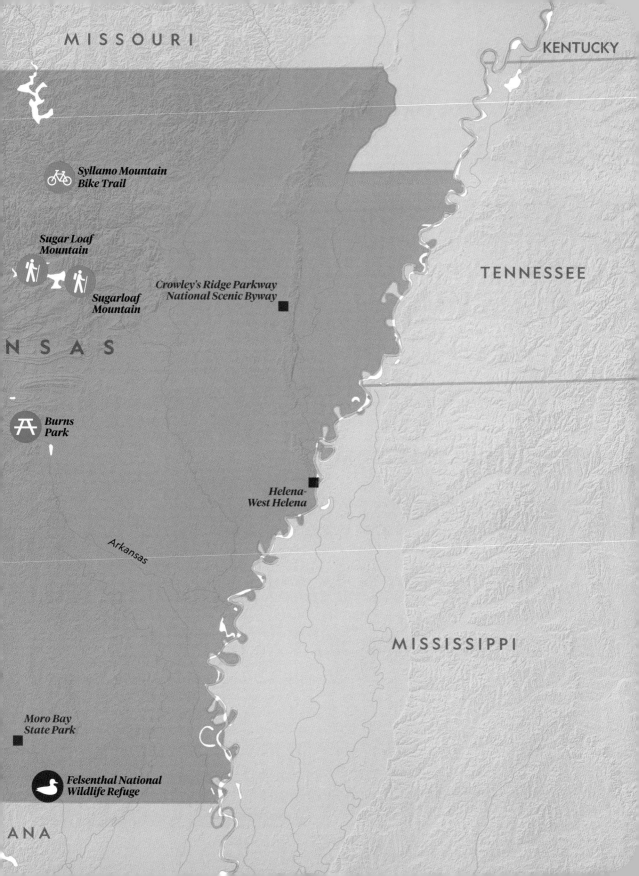

MISSOURI

KENTUCKY

Syllamo Mountain
Bike Trail

Sugar Loaf
Mountain

TENNESSEE

Sugarloaf
Mountain

Crowley's Ridge Parkway
National Scenic Byway

N S A S

Burns
Park

Helena-
West Helena

Arkansas

MISSISSIPPI

Moro Bay
State Park

Felsenthal National
Wildlife Refuge

ANA

Two Summits, One Day

Little known fact: In northern Arkansas, two 600-foot-plus (180 m) peaks with the same name lie 18 miles (29 km) apart as the crow flies. Sugarloaf Mountain sits on the mainland near the town of Heber Springs. Meanwhile, Sugar Loaf Mountain rises from the middle of Greers Ferry Lake. But the two peaks are so eerily similar that legend has it early explorers who paddled through the region on the Little Arkansas River often mistook one for the other.

See the two peaks for yourself by hiking both summits in one day. Hike the 0.66-mile (1.1 km) round-trip trail east of Heber Springs to the summit of Sugarloaf, then sprint down, drive 25 miles (40 km) northwest to Peters Sugar Loaf Marina, where you can rent a canoe, and paddle out to the island. Hike 0.8 mile (1.3 km) to the summit, have a picnic, then paddle back to the mainland to overnight at none other than Sugar Loaf Campground near the marina.

Heber Springs and Greers Ferry Lake, AR | Season: Year-round

Sugarloaf Mountain overlooks the Little Red River.

Soak at Hot Springs National Park

This haven of therapeutic bathing dates back thousands of years, starting with the Cherokee, Caddo, Quapaw, and other Native Americans who came to this region in the heart of the Ouachita Mountains to mine novaculite, a rock used to make tools and weapons.

In the process they discovered the mineral spas. Legend has it that tribes used these soothing waters as a place to set aside their differences and soak in peace.

In 1804, President Thomas Jefferson sent the Dunbar-Hunter expedition to explore the recently acquired lands within the Louisiana Purchase. The group "discovered" the hot springs, and the area became a frontier resort town. In 1913 a fire destroyed many of the original wooden structures, which were gradually replaced with resplendent, fire-resistant buildings with marble walls and stained glass windows.

All nine of the elegant historic bathhouses that make up "Bathhouse Row" are still standing. Only two, however, the Buckstaff and Quapaw, are still used as spas. Guests can soak in their mineral-rich waters or bathe in a human-made "cave" surrounding the water naturally flowing from the outdoor springs.

Soak in the hot mineral waters of Hot Springs National Park.

Hot Springs, AR | Season: Year-round

Wheels Up in Bentonville

Bentonville, a modest midwestern city of 50,000 nestled in the hills of northwest Arkansas, has exploded into the self-proclaimed "mountain biking capital of the world" over the past decade. Its ascendance is largely thanks to the descendants of Walmart founder Sam Walton, whose corporate empire is headquartered here. Walton's grandsons Tom and Steuart, both avid cyclists, had an epiphany that the ancient limestone surrounding the city could be the ultimate base for a mountain biker's playground, so they hired a crew to carve a network of purpose-built trails through its bluffs and valleys.

The trails keep expanding. Combined, Benton and neighboring Washington Counties contain a running total of 322-plus miles (518 km) of single-track. "Slaughter Pen," an easy to expert 23-plus-mile (37 km) trail system, is easily accessible from downtown. Five minutes away is Coler Mountain Bike Preserve, a playground with natural and human-made features like gap jumps, tabletops, and bridges for riders who want to practice skills and get sendy.

The mountain biking utopia extends beyond trails. Starting from Crystal Bridges Museum of American Art, cyclists can ride through the world-renowned sculptures of the outdoor OZ Art NWA museum and end up at a live concert at The Momentary outdoor venue. Sign on to hone skills through camps like Bike School Bentonville. Take half- or full-day rides with seasoned guides from Shift Outdoors, or multiday bikepacking adventures with 37 North Expeditions. Or sleep in a bed at the Bike Inn, a renovated motel with amenities like bike tools and showers outside and places to hang your two wheels inside.

Bentonville, AR | Season: Year-round

The Mississippi Flyway

A watery, 76,000-acre (30,760 ha) oasis in south-central Arkansas, Felsenthal National Wildlife Refuge is an intricate system of rivers, swamps, lakes, creeks, and sloughs dominated by the Ouachita and Saline Rivers. It contains the largest green tree reservoir in the world, a bottomland hardwood forest that is lightly flooded in the fall and winter, making it an ideal habitat for white ibis, great egrets, anhingas, and the endangered red-cockaded woodpecker.

Because of its location along the Mississippi Flyway, the refuge is also a mecca for migrating shorebirds, neotropical songbirds, birds of prey, and waterfowl. In the best years, more than 300,000 waterfowl flock to the reserve.

The best way to see the birds is to get on the water. The refuge has three self-guided water trails ranging in length from 1 mile (1.6 km) to 3.7 miles (6 km).

A female red-winged blackbird perches on a sweet gum tree.

Huttig, AR | Season: Year-round

> "BUFFALO HAS THE DISTINC-
> TION OF BEING NAMED THE
> FIRST EVER 'NATIONAL RIVER.'"

A River Runs Through It

Originating in the Boston Mountains of the Ozark Plateau, 135 miles (217 km) of the 153-mile-long (246 km) undammed Buffalo has the important distinction of being named the first ever "national river" (established in 1972). This portion managed by the National Park Service meanders through three designated wildernesses, is lined by dramatic limestone and sandstone bluffs, and is the habitat for 12 species of game fish. The best way to experience it is by placidly floating on an inner tube, fly-fishing from a canoe, or paddling in technical white water.

Dependent largely on rainfall, river levels fluctuate greatly throughout the year. Segmented into three main paddling sections, the upper district is narrow with fast water, especially in the spring. Not surprisingly, it contains the most technical white water for expert kayakers, especially the six-mile (10 km), Class II to III-plus stretch between Boxley and Ponca. Farther downstream in this section is a 4-mile (6.4 km) stretch rife with smallmouth bass.

The middle Tyler Bend district, from Carver to South Maumee, is ideal for lazy paddling on hot summer days, with ample sandbars for picnicking and deep pools for swimming. The 12-mile (19 km) reach between Gilbert and South Maumee is an especially uncrowded option. Be forewarned that it's a long day's paddle, especially when the river is low.

The river's easternmost section from North Maumee to the White River is often accessible year-round and offers peaceful paddling with vistas to interesting bluffs and shoals, as well as great fishing between Buffalo Point and Rush. For those with limited time, the one- to two-hour paddle between Dillards Ferry and Buffalo Point offers a glimpse at the appropriately named Skull Rock.

Northern AR | **Season:** Year-round

The Buffalo National River is particularly breathtaking when autumn hues take over its banks.

An Angler's Delight

"If you give a man a fish, you feed him for a day. If you teach a man to fish, you feed him for a lifetime." So goes the popular proverb, which seems specially coined for Dry Run Creek, a custom-designed park that consists of a trout stream lined by ramps, walkways, and fishing platforms built to provide easy access for kids and those with mobility impairments.

The three-quarter-mile-long (1.2 km) creek starts at the Norfork National Fish Hatchery, a cold-water hatchery that raises an estimated 1.5 million trout a year, and ends at the confluence with the Norfork River. From the banks or wading, licensed anglers using artificial, barbless hooks are welcome to fish its nutrient-rich water, stocked with rainbow, brown, and cutthroat trout. Be prepared to catch a lunker and know how to release it quickly and painlessly.

> "A CUSTOM-DESIGNED PARK THAT CONSISTS OF A TROUT STREAM LINED BY RAMPS, WALKWAYS, AND FISHING PLATFORMS BUILT TO PROVIDE EASY ACCESS FOR KIDS AND THOSE WITH MOBILITY IMPAIRMENTS."

Mountain Home, AR | **Season:** Year-round

Choose your lure for a fly-fishing trip on Dry Run Creek.

Walk or bike across the old covered bridge, just one of many fun sites in Burns Park.

Play at Burns Park

This sprawling green space in North Little Rock, across the Arkansas River from the state capital, is one of the largest city parks in the country and a peaceful oasis for all. Covering 1,700 acres (690 ha), it offers something for everyone: accessible playgrounds, an 18-hole golf course, two 18-hole disc golf courses, 21 outdoor tennis courts, horseback riding, hiking and mountain bike trails, outdoor pavilions for picnicking, and access to the Arkansas River, among other amenities.

The park's namesake, William Milton Burns, was an indefatigable pillar of the community who served as physician, two-term mayor, school board member, and park visionary. In 1948 Burns started the push to buy 870 acres (352 ha) of government land next to Camp Joseph Robinson Army Base. With the help of other volunteers, he built a lake, a fishing area for kids, and a covered bridge that still stands.

Since Burns's day, the park has more than doubled in size and straddles both sides of Interstate 40. In 2019, the Arkansas River severely flooded the southern half of the park, but it has rebounded nicely. Right off the interstate, it's an ideal oasis for travelers to stretch their legs on the Arkansas River Trail, a portion of which runs through the park, or eat lunch under the oaks. History buffs will appreciate the park's pre–Civil War cabin constructed in 1849 and other historic relics. If there's too much to see and do in one day, bunk down on-site at the Burns RV Park and Campground.

North Little Rock, AR | **Season:** Year-round

Boardwalk bike trails run through Ozark National Forest.

An Epic Trail Ride

Unlike the celebrated urban trails of Bentonville, this 50-mile (80 km) network of mostly single-track trails for those with the skills and endurance lies off the grid in the heart of the Ozark–St. Francis National Forests. With terrain from easy flow to exposed technical single-track, the Syllamo Mountain Bike Trail has earned its coveted status as an International Mountain Biking Association "Epic" ride, a designation reserved for technically and physically challenging routes that offer a true backcountry riding experience.

A good launching point is from the Blanchard Springs Campground on the southwest side of the trail network. A spur trail just past Campsite 13 connects to the 12.3-mile-long (19.8 km) Jack's Branch Loop, which in turn connects to the 11.8-mile (19 km) Scrappy Mountain Loop, and so on. Download the GPS file from Trailforks and be sure to carry what you need: extra tubes, food, water, and first aid.

Mountain View, AR : **Season:** Year-round

Follow the Arkansas Wine Trail

The mountainous Arkansas River Valley in the northwest corner of the state has an ideal climate for growing grapes, a tradition that dates back two centuries. It began in the late 1800s, when a German immigrant named Jacob Post settled on 80 acres (32 ha) near the town of Altus and realized that the moderate climate and sandy soil were almost identical to the fine winemaking regions of Germany. Post opened a winery, which is still run today by his great-great-grandson Paul.

Post Winery, which grows a multitude of grape varietals, including its signature muscadine, is one of more than 20 located along the loosely defined "Arkansas Wine Trail" that stretches almost 200 miles (320 km) from Eureka Springs to Hot Springs. The centerpiece is the cluster of wineries around Altus, from Wiederkehr Village north of town that has been family owned and operated since 1880, to Cowie Wine Cellars on the south side of the Arkansas River, home to the only wine museum in the United States devoted to the history of winemaking in Arkansas.

Like a mini–Napa Valley, all the wineries around Altus are distinct. Wander through the stunning vineyards of Chateau Aux Arc, the world's largest planter of Cynthiana grapes; visit the 35-year-old table-grape vines of Dahlem Vineyard; explore the historic century-old cellar at Mount Bethel Winery; and sip the expertly blended wines of Dionysus Wine and Brew. Save room for the granddaddy of them all, Post Winery, which now has more than 30 wines to its name.

Northwest AR : **Season:** Year-round

Kayak racers ply the rapids of the Cossatot River.

Paddle the Skull Crusher

The French meaning of Cossatot, the name of this 26-mile-long (42 km) National Wild and Scenic River in the Ouachita Mountains of southwest Arkansas, is "skull crusher." It's an apt name, especially for two particularly challenging sections: The first is Cossatot Falls, a series of six Class II to V rapids with strong hydraulics that can suck kayakers under and spit them out. The second is Devil's Hollow Falls, a six-foot (1.8 m) diagonal ledge across the river with craggy, uplifted rocks below that make it extremely hazardous.

If these challenges sound less than exhilarating, enjoy the waterway from solid ground. Twelve miles (19 km) of the river are lined by Cossatot River State Park-Natural Area. It has four trails that span almost 20 miles (32 km), along which hikers can search for the 28 rare plant species in the park, including the heart-shaped leaves of the twistflower and the spectacular pink bursts of the compact blazing star.

Mena, AR | **Season:** Mid-fall through late spring

Take in outdoor strolls and local artistry at the Crystal Bridges Museum of American Art.

1. SNAP A SELFIE AT EDEN FALLS

One mile (1.6 km) down the Lost Valley Trail along the Buffalo National River, hikers will encounter a multitiered waterfall that plunges 53 feet (16 m) to the base of a box canyon. It's the perfect spot to strike a pose before continuing up a spur trail that ends at a dark cave through which a 25-foot-long (7.6 m) waterfall cascades.

2. DRIVE CROWLEY'S RIDGE PARKWAY NATIONAL SCENIC BYWAY

This 198-mile-long (319 km) route through northeast Arkansas sits atop the Upper Arkansas Delta, a 200-foot-high (60 m) ridge that parallels the Mississippi River. The beautiful route passes seven state parks and winds through the hardwoods of the Ozark–St. Francis National Forests. Time your trip to coincide with the annual King Biscuit Blues Festival in Helena.

3. SMELL THE AZALEAS AT THE SOUTH ARKANSAS ARBORETUM

With two miles (3.2 km) of paved trails meandering through this lush 12-acre (5 ha) park in El Dorado, you'll find never ending vantage points to see and smell the fragrant rainbow of azaleas that bloom from March to May. Come autumn, the black gum, yellow poplar, and beech trees flame red, orange, and yellow.

4. FERRY ACROSS BULL SHOALS LAKE

State Highway 125 dead-ends at Bull Shoals Lake, a snaky 80-mile-long (130 km) reservoir in the Ozark Mountains of northern Arkansas. In 20-minute intervals, the state's last remaining free and public ferry will transport you and your car to the opposite shore of this big lake that's wildly popular for boaters, anglers, and swimmers.

5. HIKE THE OUACHITA NATIONAL RECREATION TRAIL

The Arkansas portion of this epic hiking trail starts in Talimena State Park and ends 222 miles (357 km) later in Pinnacle Mountain State Park, 15 miles (24 km) east of Little Rock. Climbing from 600 to 2,600 feet (183 to 793 m), the trail traverses the pine and oak forests of the Ouachita Mountains.

6. DRIVE THE PIG TRAIL SCENIC BYWAY

This 19-mile (31 km) scenic byway through the rugged Boston Mountains region of northwest Arkansas' Ozarks starts in the town of Brashears and follows Arkansas Route 23 south to its intersection with I-40. The road winds through a tunnel of foliage any time of year, but it is especially beautiful during spring wildflower season.

7. CYCLE THE ARKANSAS RIVER TRAIL

What originated as a 16-mile (26 km) paved loop trail along both banks of the Arkansas River has been expanded to an 88-mile (142 km) "Grand Loop" that extends all the way to Pinnacle Mountain State Park.

8. RENT A CABIN AT MORO BAY STATE PARK

At the convergence of Raymond Lake, Moro Bay, and the Ouachita River sits 117-acre (47 ha) Moro Bay State Park, an oasis for anglers. The park's most unique features are its five fully equipped modern cabins that sit on stilts in a canopy of trees overlooking the bay. Kayak and fishing boat rentals are nearby.

9. VISIT A CIVIL WAR–ERA VILLAGE

In 1863 Helena was the site of a battle instigated by Confederate forces trying to run out the Union Army, which was using the town as a haven for runaway slaves. Two decades later, Mark Twain forever memorialized Helena as "one of the prettiest situations on the [Mississippi] river."

10. VISIT CRYSTAL BRIDGES MUSEUM OF AMERICAN ART

This one-of-a-kind museum sits on 120 acres (49 ha) in Bentonville and houses masterworks from the colonial era to the present. Take it all in, then catch your breath on five miles (8 km) of multipurpose trails meandering through the Ozark–St. Francis National Forests. Don't miss the stone grotto covered in quartz crystals.

Red apple blossoms

Joshua Tree National Park
(page 77) is an outdoor
enthusiast's playground.

CALIFORNIA

Coastal oases, desert dunes, lush forests, and mountain retreats make California an outdoor mecca.

OREGON

IDAHO

UTAH

Shasta
Lake

NEVADA

Fort
Bragg

North Fork
American River

Lake
Tahoe

Napa
Valley

Mono and
June Lakes

West Marin

Presidio of
San Francisco

Half Dome,
Yosemite National
Park

Big Basin Redwoods
State Park

CALIFORNIA

Santa Cruz

Death Valley
National Park

Garrapata
State Park

PACIFIC OCEAN

Mount
Whitney

Guadalupe-Nipomo
Dunes Wildlife Refuge

Joshua Tree
National Park

ARIZONA

Huntington Beach
(Surf City, U.S.A.)

Temecula
Valley

Trans-Catalina
Trail

San Diego-La Jolla
Underwater Park
Ecological Reserve

U.S.
MEXICO

BAJA
CALIFORNIA

SONORA

Vineyards spread out across Napa Valley, but you'll find plenty more to do here than just sip.

Napa Valley Sans Wine

To say this world-famous region is all about wine is not wrong. But the 30-mile-long (48 km) valley, just an hour from San Francisco, is also graced with good weather, state parks, and an outdoor lifestyle as ripe as the fruit feeding its more than 375 tasting rooms.

Northern Californians love a good hike, and Bothe-Napa Valley State Park doesn't disappoint with its miles of hiking trails that meander through stands of coastal redwood trees. Early risers will appreciate a bird's-eye view aboard a hot-air balloon just after dawn, a popular way to appreciate Napa Valley's lush rolling hills, especially in the fall. Family-friendly Lake Berryessa, Napa County's largest lake, is an oasis on hot summer days, when temperatures hover in the 90s, and boating, swimming, wakeboarding, and paddling offer some beat-the-heat relief.

The 12.5-mile (20 km) Napa Valley Vine Trail connects South Napa to the town of Yountville, and is ideal for leisurely bike rides, with some Napa Valley companies offering guided tours. Summer not only means sipping outdoors; it also means an agenda chockablock with outdoor concerts, from cozy gatherings in the park to big-name-heavy gatherings such as BottleRock.

Along Highway 29, Napa Valley's main thoroughfare, the 35-foot (11 m) "Bunny Foo Foo" sculpture at Hall Winery is hard to miss and is just one of 35 contemporary pieces freckled around the pretty grounds. For a mellow day on the water, rent a kayak or paddleboard from the docks in downtown Napa, and see why the Napa River is one of the area's best kept paddling secrets.

Napa Valley, CA   Season: Year-round

Roam the sand dunes in search of wildlife.

Discover Hollywood History in the Dunes

For 18 miles (29 km) along California's Central Coast, these shifting sand dunes are home to roughly 200 species of birds and more than 100 species of rare plants and animals. If it weren't for the mighty Pacific crashing nearby, the Sahara might swirl to mind. Perhaps that's why Hollywood filmmaker Cecil B. DeMille chose the location for his 1923 epic, *The Ten Commandments*. When finished filming, he ordered the set and its accoutrements buried in sand where they remained hidden for 60 years.

Some props have turned up over the years and are on display at the Guadalupe-Nipomo Dunes visitors center. Maps are available, and information about local flora and fauna, points of interests, and the importance of conservation can be learned on private, naturalist-led walks through the sandy slice of the Central Coast.

Guadalupe, CA | **Season:** Year-round

Hang Ten in Surf City

Huntington Beach earns its nickname—Surf City—for good reason, and in no short part because of its 10 miles (16 km) of sandy beaches, gnarly curls, and more than 50 surf contests held here each year, including the U.S. Open of Surfing.

Local surfers of all levels paddle out between the pier to the "cliffs" to catch a variety of waves, while visitors and newbies can find plenty of schools to help perfect their own hang-ten style in a few short hours. The city perpetuates the hang-ten lifestyle by way of an International Surfing Museum, the Surfers' Hall of Fame, and the Surfing Walk of Fame, all within walking distance of the shoreline.

Huntington Beach officially adopted the Surf City U.S.A. nickname in January 2008, and embraced the title full on, as evidenced by myriad bars, restaurants, and shops whose names reflect and honor the quintessentially Californian pastime.

Huntington Beach, CA | **Season:** Year-round

The "Nude Dude Naked Surfer" stands outside Huntington Beach.

Paddle the crystal clear waters of Emerald Bay State Park.

Do It All in the Lake of the Sky

One of California's most beloved destinations, Lake Tahoe, from a Washoe word interpreted to mean "Lake of the Sky," sits 6,200 feet (1,890 m) above sea level, surrounded by Sierra Nevada peaks. Not only is Lake Tahoe known for its 300-plus days of annual sunshine, but the region has also earned a reputation as a year-round outdoor playground. Whether downhill or cross-country skiing in Olympic Valley, cannonballing from a lakeside dock, strolling along the Truckee River, or mountain biking on the 165-mile (266 km) Tahoe Rim Trail, there's something for every effort level. Sipping a Tahoe-crafted beer on a pine-shaded deck or dipping into the icy water along 70 miles (110 km) of pristine shoreline in hot summers are rites of passage. Stand-up paddleboarding and kayaking don't get better than in the blue-green and appropriately named Emerald Bay, which harbors Lake Tahoe's only island, and where divers can peruse the Maritime Heritage Trail, an underwater world of sunken artifacts.

Lake Tahoe, CA | Season: Year-round

Stand among the giants in
Sequoia National Park.

> "COAST REDWOODS STRETCH FROM THE OREGON BORDER TO BIG SUR, AND FROM THE EASTERN SIERRA TO THE SEA."

Hug a Giant

Few things inspire awe like California's massive redwood and sequoia trees, and experiencing their majesty is pretty easy in Northern California, where coast redwoods stretch from the Oregon border to Big Sur, and from the Eastern Sierra to the sea.

Soaring to the top of the list is Sequoia National Park, home to the largest tree in the world (by trunk volume), including a behemoth named General Sherman and the second largest tree in the world, General Grant.

At Big Basin Redwoods State Park, California's oldest state park, ramble along 80 miles (130 km) of trails to waterfalls and ocean views. Situated about 100 miles (160 km) southwest of Sacramento, Calaveras Big Trees State Park harbors two groves of giant sequoias, as well as the "Discovery Tree," a massive redwood stump that fell around 1850.

Near the Oregon border, the densely forested Jedediah Smith Redwoods State Park is just a few miles inland from the ocean and contains 7 percent of all the old-growth redwoods left in the world, and a handful of trails cover only a fraction of its expanse.

When it comes to iconic drives, Avenue of the Giants rolls for 31 miles (50 km) through one of the most beautiful redwood groves in the state. Meanwhile, in Southern California, Carbon Canyon Regional Park features a 10-acre (4 ha) grove of young coastal redwoods planted in 1975.

The newbies might be smaller and younger than their Northern California brethren, but a walk along the 2.5-mile (4 km) Carbon Canyon Nature Trail gives a sneak peek to the next generation of California giants.

Northern CA | **Season:** Year-round

Sea Life in San Diego

For underwater adventure without a trip out to sea, the 6,000-acre (2,430 ha) La Jolla Underwater Park and Ecological Reserve within San Diego's city limits can't be beat. A Disneyland for snorkelers, divers, kayakers, swimmers, and underwater photographers, the park is split into two sections: the Ecological Reserve and Marine Life Refuge.

Slip in at sandy La Jolla Cove and explore kelp beds with strands growing up to 100 feet (30 m), rocky reefs, and two submarine canyons. Two artificial reefs also attract and enhance marine life, which is plentiful. Bright orange garibaldi (California's state fish) are easy to spot, as are pregnant leopard sharks that hang out in the warm shallow water of the sand flats between June and December. Often frolicking in the water are seals and sea lions, along with other sea creatures that call this magical marine paradise home. Or make your way to Turtle Town, aptly named for its population of green sea turtles.

San Diego, CA | **Season:** Year-round

Sea lions swim in the waters of La Jolla Cove.

Play in the Presidio

There are city parks and then there's the Presidio. Hemmed into the northwest corner of San Francisco, between the San Francisco Bay and the Pacific Ocean, the 1,500-acre (600 ha) former military base is easily one of the most enjoyable places to spend a day, and home to 330 native plant species, 323 bird species, 30 butterfly species, three watersheds, a tidal marsh, and a freshwater lake.

An army post from 1776, well before California was a state, until 1994, the Presidio served soldiers from Spain, Mexico, and the United States. These days, the historic landmark and national park have been reborn, offering city dwellers and visitors a chance to blend the great outdoors and California history.

With 25 miles (40 km) of hiking and biking trails, a serene military cemetery, and more than 400 historic

California poppy

buildings that house museums, inns, a bowling alley, and a visitors center, you might need more than one day to experience the Presidio. Public art lovers will find North America's largest collection of British artist Andy Goldsworthy's work on public view, including "Wood Line," a walkable 1,200-foot (370 m) installation of recycled eucalyptus trunks that begs for an Instagram post. San Francisco's Golden Gate Bridge is part of the park too, as is Baker Beach, a must for sunset watching, and Crissy Field, a former landing strip now popular for walking, jogging, dog walking, and picnicking along a sandy beach, both with stunning bridge views.

Golfers can take a swing at the Presidio Golf Course, one of the oldest public courses on the West Coast.

San Francisco, CA | **Season:** Year-round

Live It Up in Death Valley

Its foreboding moniker (named by a lost group of gold-seeking pioneers in 1849) makes Death Valley seem like an empty wasteland, a misconception fueled by the fact that it is the hottest and driest place on Earth. With summer temps reaching 120°F (50°C) or more, Death Valley is unquestionably a vast land of emptiness and extremes, counting within its borders the lowest place on Earth—the Badwater Basin Salt Flats at 282 feet (86 m) below sea level—and Telescope Peak, rising more than 11,000 feet (3,350 m). But it's also full of curiosities, outdoor endeavors, and natural wonders that make it one of the most unique places in the state.

Once a mining hot spot, no pun intended, and a film location for *Star Wars, Robinson Crusoe on Mars,* and *The Twilight Zone,* Death Valley is now a place where more than a million annual visitors come to make memories, pursue unique adventures, and snap photos.

Death Valley, CA | **Season:** Spring, fall, and winter

Zabriskie Point and Dantes View, overlooking the salt flats, at sunrise and sunset are just a couple of ideal picture spots.

Hiking trails of varying degrees of difficulty crisscross the valley floor and rocky canyons. Other Death Valley surprises include the Mesquite Flat Sand Dunes (bring your own sand sled), the 600-foot-deep (180 m) Ubehebe volcanic crater, and the saw-toothed and sharp salt mounds known as Devils Golf Course.

Scenic drives abound, some to more remote locations that may require a four-wheel drive to access, such as Death Valley's Racetrack Playa, a dry lake bed across which rocks unexplainably move, leaving their mysterious tracks in the dehydrated earth.

A Fork in the River

Just a short distance from Sacramento and San Francisco in Gold Country, the American River is the most popular white-water rafting destination in California. Originating near Lake Tahoe, the river's three main forks—the South, Middle, and North—flow down through the Sierra foothills, serving up heart-pounding fun. However, it's the 88-mile-long (142 km) North Fork that's a utopia for hard-core rafters in search of Class IV and V thrills.

Unlike the other two branches, the North Fork is not dam controlled and slaloms its way through steep narrow canyons whose walls reach up to 4,000 feet (1,220 m) high. Technical skills, and maybe a little bravery, are required to navigate the wild white water of the North Fork. For landlubbers who want to experience panoramic views of the North Fork's white-water action without getting wet, the easy Lake Clementine Trail is just right.

The North Fork boasts challenging—and fun—rapids.

Sacramento, CA | **Season:** Year-round

> ## "THESE ANCIENT MINERAL SPIRES LOOK AS IF THEY'VE HAILED FROM ANOTHER PLANET."

Mono County's Great Lakes

The lakes of California's Mono County impress nature lovers looking for unusual geology, high-altitude adventure, and camera-pleasing scenes.

Mono Lake is one the oldest lakes in the Western Hemisphere (more than a million years old). It has long been a muse for artists and photographers, but the water's high salinity and alkalinity have created an ecosystem that supports brine shrimp and alkali flies, which attract millions of migratory birds each year.

But it's the unusual tufa formations that draw visitors to Mono Lake. These ancient mineral spires, formed by freshwater springs bubbling into alkaline water, look as if they've hailed from another planet.

Fifteen miles (24 km) south, California State Route 158 circles away from Highway 395. Called the June Lake Loop, the scenic road is known for its fall foliage and lakes. June Lake, just one mile (1.6 km) long and a half mile (0.8 km) wide, is more than just a pretty place to snap an Instagram selfie. Paddlers, swimmers, sunbathers, and hikers stake claim to the beach and trails during summer.

Nearby Gull Lake is popular with trout fisherman and campers, while walkers can enjoy an easy, two-mile (3.2 km) trail around the lake. More serious hikers should lace up at Silver Lake, where they'll find access to the Ansel Adams Wilderness and Yosemite National Park, as well as connections to the Pacific Crest and John Muir Trail systems.

There are more than a hundred lakes throughout the area, including gorgeous Twin Lakes, with its 300-foot (90 m) waterfall, and Convict Lake, whose name comes with a storied past.

Mono County, CA | **Season:** Year-round

Tufa formations jut out from Mono Lake.

Each June, Lake Skinner hosts a wine and balloon festival.

1. HIKE THE TRANS-CATALINA TRAIL

A mere 22 miles (35 km) off Southern California's famed beaches, Santa Catalina Island boasts a rugged interior that invites two-footed adventurers to hoof the 38.5-mile (62 km) trail. The steep ups and downs in hot temps during summer can be punishing, but beachside campgrounds, unrivaled island views, and unusual wildlife, including resident bison and endemic gray foxes, are the payoff.

2. STRETCH YOUR LEGS IN GARRAPATA STATE PARK

California's iconic Highway 1 between charming Carmel-by-the-Sea and glorious Big Sur is de rigueur, and this park is perfectly placed for a pit stop to hike into the Santa Lucia Mountains or stroll along the coastal trails. Wildflowers bloom bright each spring, and sea lions and sea otters are often spotted, as are gray whales during their annual migration.

3. CAMP NEAR GIANT BOULDERS IN JOSHUA TREE NATIONAL PARK

With 124 campsites for RVs, trailers, and tents, Jumbo Rocks Campground—as the name suggests—is surrounded by supersize granite boulders, and it is one of the few campsites that takes reservations. Its central location makes exploring the park's desert wilderness a breeze. At night, the star-illuminated sky is equally bewitching.

4. BOAT TO A 250-MILLION-YEAR-OLD CAVERN

On the north end of Shasta Lake, a collection of subterranean caves hides glistening stalagmites, stalactites, and colorful limestone formations that prove aging can be graceful. The caverns are only accessible with a guide and via a boat ride across sparkling Shasta Lake and require maneuvering about 600 stairs.

5. ASCEND AN ICON IN YOSEMITE NATIONAL PARK

The stunning wilderness of Yosemite is world famous, but perhaps nothing is more recognizable than Half Dome, the park's most iconic rock that rises more than 8,800 feet (2,680 m) above sea level. Permits and advanced planning are essential.

6. TAKE THE BEST DAY TRIP EVER TO WEST MARIN

Remarkably close to San Francisco yet delightfully unplugged and rural, West Marin is where untouched beaches, lush forests, and sleepy California towns combine into one idyllic destination, where sampling local oysters and cheese, and exploring Point Reyes National Seashore's vast expanse of protected coastline is an easy day trip.

7. RETURN TO YESTERYEAR AT THE SANTA CRUZ BEACH BOARDWALK

Founded in 1907, California's oldest surviving amusement park is awash with nostalgic delight. Two historic landmarks, the Giant Dipper wooden roller coaster and the Looff Carousel, along with 35 other rides, thrill all ages. The boardwalk has made cameos in several major films, and screens family-friendly movies on the sand during summer.

8. FLOAT ABOVE TEMECULA VALLEY

The serenity of a hot-air balloon ride is unparalleled, especially when below are the rolling hills and award-winning vineyards of the Temecula Valley, Southern California's largest viticultural area, and one of the state's best kept oenophile secrets. The two joys combine each June at an annual wine and balloon festival.

9. CHECK OFF MOUNT WHITNEY

If visiting the highest mountain in the contiguous United States is on your list (hello 14,505 feet/ 4,421 m!), check the box in the town of Lone Pine on the Mount Whitney Trail, a strenuous 22-mile (35 km) round-trip hike with an elevation gain of more than 6,000 feet (1,830 m). For mere mortals, a condensed 2.5-mile (4 km) version along the Lone Pine Lake Trail does the trick too.

10. BIKE THE RAILS IN FORT BRAGG

Pedal along the tracks of California's world-famous Skunk Train into a sometimes silent though bird-filled forest of towering redwoods, Douglas firs, and carpets of ferns. The two-seater, four-wheel bikes have an electric assist and were built especially for this unique rail-trail adventure.

Dream Lake reflects the surrounding peaks at sunrise in Rocky Mountain National Park (page 84).

COLORADO

Boasting 300 annual days of sunshine, it's no wonder
Colorado tops outdoor adventurer bucket lists.

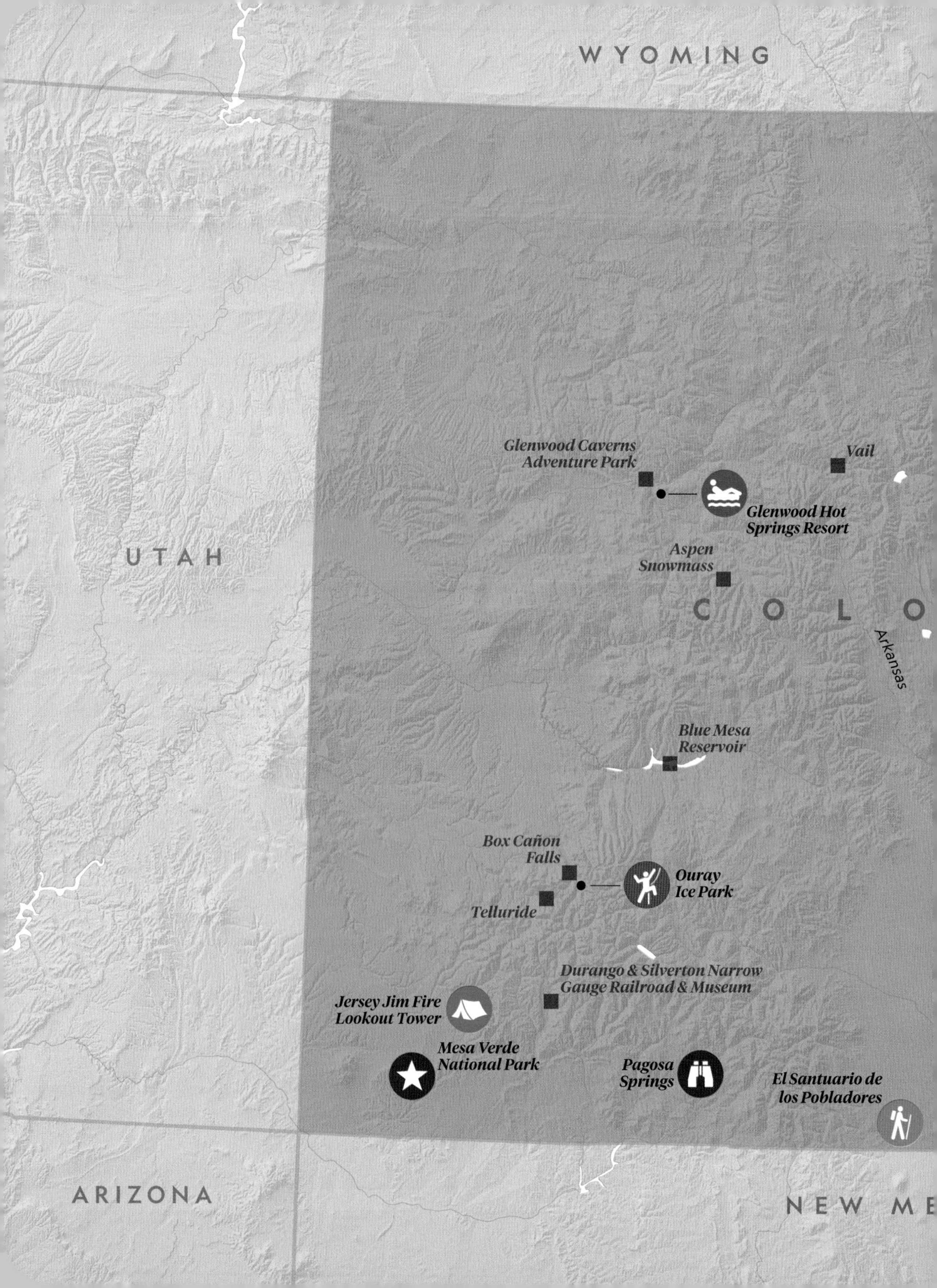

WYOMING

UTAH

Glenwood Caverns
Adventure Park

Vail

Glenwood Hot
Springs Resort

Aspen
Snowmass

C O L O

Arkansas

Blue Mesa
Reservoir

Box Cañon
Falls

Ouray
Ice Park

Telluride

Durango & Silverton Narrow
Gauge Railroad & Museum

Jersey Jim Fire
Lookout Tower

Mesa Verde
National Park

Pagosa
Springs

El Santuario de
los Pobladores

ARIZONA

NEW ME

NEBRASKA

Estes Park

Rocky Mountain
National Park

Boulder
Creek

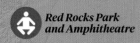
Red Rocks Park
and Amphitheatre

R A D O

Manitou
Incline

Paint Mines
Interpretive Park

KANSAS

Arkansas
River

Arkansas

Great Sand Dunes
National Park & Preserve

KICO

OKLAHOMA

Climbing on Thick Ice

The small former mining town of Ouray is known as the Switzerland of America, as well as Colorado's ice-climbing capital. It's home to Ouray Ice Park, a human-made ice-climbing park on the natural Uncompahgre Gorge. It boasts more than 200 ice and mixed climbs and 17,000 vertical feet (5,180 m) of terrain.

Open mid-December to March, the park welcomes nearly 10,000 climbers who rappel down (most climbs are accessed from the top) and then defy gravity by scaling up a near-vertical wall of ice. Named after the animated cartoon, South Park has 32 routes and is popular with beginners.

The water used to form the ice is overflow from Weehawken Spring. Crampons (ice-climbing boots with metal spikes) and helmets are required. The park is free to use, but it does not rent gear or provide guides or lessons. Several stores in Ouray rent supplies, and outfitters provide various ice-climbing services.

Ouray, CO   Season: Mid-December to March

Climbers can challenge themselves on the frozen Pick o' the Vic.

Stargaze and Discover Ancient Dwellings

Certified as the world's 100th International Dark Sky Park in 2021, Mesa Verde's high elevation, arid climate, and clear skies make the 52,485-acre (21,240 ha) national park an ideal stargazing destination. Time your visit during a new moon, when the sky is darkest, and park at a pullout such as the Geologic, Mancos, or Montezuma Valley Overlooks. Look up and prepare to be mesmerized by the same breathtaking Milky Way the ancestral Puebloan people, the park's original inhabitants, witnessed nearly 1,400 years ago.

In the morning, discover how the ancestral Puebloans lived with a visit to the national park. Though the ancestral Puebloans deserted the area by around A.D. 1300, the cliff dwellings, pottery, and tools remained. The largest and most famous cliff dwelling, the Cliff Palace, includes more than 150 individual rooms and 20 kivas used for religious rituals.

Cliff Palace is closed, but you can still go on ranger-led tours to explore the Long House, the park's second largest cliff dwelling. The tour includes a 2.25-mile (3.6 km) hike and a climb up two 15-foot (4.5 m) ladders.

With clears skies, you can sometimes spot the Pleiades, Venus, and Jupiter.

Mesa Verde, CO   Season: Year-round

Rock the Yoga Mat

Awaken your chakras with a meditative 7 a.m. yoga session at the Red Rocks Park and Amphitheatre, about 17 miles (27 km) southwest of Denver. A national historic landmark, Red Rocks is renowned for its geologically formed open-air amphitheater that has hosted a variety of concerts, from orchestral to hip-hop, since 1906. However, on Saturdays and Sundays in summer, certified instructors from local studio The River Yoga lead a couple thousand yoga enthusiasts in an hour-long Vinyasa flow session.

Participants show up as early as 6 a.m. to secure a spot among the amphitheater benches, surrounded by 300-foot (90 m) sandstone monoliths called Ship Rock and Creation Rock. The crowd stretches to warrior and downward dog poses in unison, while taking in panoramic views of downtown Denver. After the yoga session, stop by the visitors center to learn about the park's musical history (the Beatles and Jimi Hendrix played here), or

head over to the 1931 Pueblo Revival–style Trading Post, featuring the Colorado Music Hall of Fame, which pays homage to some of the state's famous musicians, including John Denver, Dianne Reeves, Philip Bailey, and Judy Collins.

Across from the trading post, you'll find the Trading Post Trail, which takes hikers on a 1.4-mile (2.3 km) loop to see the Fountain and Lyons formations, blooming wildflowers, and pine trees. The multiuse Red Rocks Trail, which continues to Jefferson County's Matthews/Winters Park, is a six-mile (10 km) loop that permits biking. The trails are accessible year-round from an hour before sunrise to an hour after sunset.

In addition to live performances, Red Rocks Park also screens movies in the amphitheater during the summer.

Morrison, CO | Season: Year-round

The historic Our Lady of Guadalupe Parish church

Inside a Labyrinth

Next to the site of the 1858 Our Lady of Guadalupe in Conejos, near the border of Colorado and New Mexico, visitors can walk through a prayer labyrinth called El Santuario de los Pobladores.

At six feet (1.8 m) tall and 135 feet (40 m) in diameter, this outdoor labyrinth is one of the largest adobe buildings constructed in the 21st century. The structure honors the heritage of the San Luis Valley, where early settlers built their homes with mud bricks. Four processional experiences lead pilgrims to the center of the labyrinth, where they'll find a chapel with two view platforms.

Representing the Mysteries of the Rosary, the circular labyrinth also took design inspiration from Hopi sand paintings, India's mandalas, and ancient Tibetan tapestries. Though spiritual in nature, the quiet meditative walk can signify a person's journey toward self-discovery.

Conejos County, CO | Season: Year-round

> "ROCKY MOUNTAIN IS ONE OF THE HIGHEST PARKS IN THE UNITED STATES."

Hike the Rockies Alongside Llamas

Explore majestic Rocky Mountain National Park, 70 miles (110 km) north of Denver, with a worthy hiking partner: a llama. Several adventure outfitters, including Wildland Trekking, Kirks Mountain Adventures, and Spruce Ridge Llamas, offer guided day trips and overnight excursions with a herd of hardworking llamas that double as porters.

Adept at climbing rocky terrains, these trained llamas help transport supplies—tents, cooking equipment, sleeping bags—from trails to campsites. Though friendly, llamas don't like to be ridden, but they might just be willing to pose for a toothy selfie.

Before President Woodrow Wilson established the national park in 1915, the region was hunting and foraging grounds for Ute and Arapaho tribes, and home for gold miners and homesteaders. The park has more than 350 miles (560 km) of hiking trails that lead to cascading waterfalls, crystal clear alpine lakes, jutting granite mountains, and spruce fir forests.

With elevation that reaches 14,259 feet (4,346 m), Rocky Mountain is one of the highest parks in the United States. Llama-guided hikes range from a trek to the peak summit of the 13,425-foot (4,092 m) Mummy Mountain to a backcountry journey along the Finch Lake Trail to a lake that bears the same name.

With various ecological zones, you might encounter a wide range of animals, including moose, bighorn sheep, mule deer, eagles, or owls. During spring and summer, hundreds of species of wildflowers blanket the landscape. And when fall arrives, the towering quaking aspens turn into brilliant shades of yellow, red, and orange. When night falls, bright stars cover the skies.

Rocky Mountain National Park, CO | **Season:** Late spring to fall

Llamas carry gear on a hike through the Weminuche Wilderness in Rocky Mountain National Park.

Spend the Night on the Lookout

Park history buffs can spend one to two nights at the Jersey Jim Fire Lookout Tower, a former U.S. Forest Service fire lookout residence from the 1940s to the 1970s. Renovated in 1991, the 55-foot-tall (17 m) tower retains its original lookout equipment: two twin beds, propane heater, lamp, and refrigerator. A pulley on the deck brings up your supplies and water, which is available from a hand pump at the nearby Transfer Campground.

The humble structure has windows on all sides, with views of San Juan National Forest, as well as sunrise and sunset. Evenings, stargaze from the deck or read about past fire lookout experiences in a historic logbook kept in the living quarters.

Reservations are available from late May to mid-October, but time your visit with leaf-peeping season so you can catch a glimpse of fiery orange and golden aspens.

> "THE HUMBLE STRUCTURE HAS WINDOWS ON ALL SIDES, WITH VIEWS OF SAN JUAN NATIONAL FOREST, AS WELL AS SUNRISE AND SUNSET."

Dolores, CO | **Season:** May to October

Wake up to one-of-a-kind views after a night in the Jersey Jim Fire Lookout Tower.

Pagosa Springs Resort sits on the banks of the San Juan River. The mineral-rich waters of the Mother Spring are a draw.

The Historic Hot Spring Loop

In Colorado, there are nearly 100 developed and undeveloped hot springs, heated natural mineral water that's said to boost blood circulation, relieve pain, treat skin irritations, and reduce stress. For the ultimate wellness road trip, embark on the 720-mile (1,160 km) Colorado Historic Hot Springs Loop from Denver to Pagosa Springs to Steamboat Springs, which highlights 17 thermal hot springs destinations.

Take a therapeutic soak in the world's largest mineral hot springs pool at Glenwood Hot Springs Resort, located around 160 miles (260 km) west of Denver. Funneled from the Yampah Spring, the thermal spring water is a heated 104°F (40°C) in the Therapy Pool and a warm 90°F to 93°F (32–34°C) in the large main pool. "Yampah" means "big medicine" in the Ute language, and its repu-

tation for healing has drawn visitors from all over the world since 1888.

In Pagosa Springs Resort, the Mother Spring—the world's deepest geothermal hot spring—feeds 25 pools, including the Marco Polo with views of the San Juan River, and Serendipity, which has a cascading waterfall. Built in 1867, the historic bathhouse at the Mount Princeton Hot Springs Resort in Nathrop is open daily to the public. The soaking pool's water temperature reaches up to 105°F (40.5°C).

Next to the bathhouse, the resort's Creekside Hot Springs are divided into individual pools with temperatures ranging from 70°F to 120°F (21–49°C). Local favorite Strawberry Park Hot Springs in Steamboat Springs has a series of natural hot springs, surrounded by a lush alpine forest. Overnight guests can stay in a train caboose, covered wagon, or rustic cabin.

Denver to Steamboat Springs, CO   Season: Year-round

Find light rapids on a tube ride down Boulder Creek.

Float Down Boulder Creek

Snowmelt from the Rocky Mountains flows to the cottonwood-shaded Boulder Creek, setting it up as the perfect environment for tubing. Contrary to a relaxing lazy river, the float trip down Boulder Creek is more like white-water tubing with chutes and rapids.

Before you go, check the Mile High Flood District website to make sure the water level is between 40 and 200 cubic feet (1.1 to 5.7 m³) a second. The higher the water level, the faster you'll travel on your tube. Most people start tubing from Eben G. Fine Park downstream to 55th Street, but if you prefer a shorter, gentler float, you should hop off at the Boulder Public Library a mile (1.6 km) east.

Bring your own tube or rent from a nearby store, and be sure to wear a life jacket, water shoes, a helmet, and a wet suit (the water can be chilly). Tubing season is from May to August.

Boulder, CO | **Season:** Summer

High Above the Rocky Mountain High

Soar across the clear Colorado skies in a hot-air balloon. A number of outfitters throughout Colorado offer balloon rides over landscapes ranging from lakes, streams, and fields to the neatly stacked suburban homes and snowcapped Rocky Mountains.

On brisk, clear mornings with calm winds, the outfitter's crewmember will check you in and conduct a safety briefing. After you climb into the wicker or rattan basket, the crewmember will light the burners and the balloon will gently rise to a few thousand feet aboveground.

Flights are typically an hour long, and most rides culminate with a champagne or cider toast. In summer during balloon festivals, the Colorado skies are painted with a whimsical kaleidoscope of colorful balloons. Some festivals, including the Labor Day Lift Off in Colorado Springs and Colorfest in Pagosa Springs, illuminate the night sky with evening balloon launches.

At the Labor Day Lift Off, a 40-plus-year tradition, more than 70 hot-air balloons take to the sky. On Saturday and Sunday, the resting balloons inflate and ignite their burners at sunset, casting a glow across the festival grounds. Similarly, Colorfest, held since 1986, fills the sky, along with a wine, beer, and food festival on the ground.

Colorado Springs, CO | **Season:** Spring to fall

The Manitou Incline gains more than 2,000 feet (610 m) in less than a mile (1.6 km).

Climb the Manitou Incline

Ascend 2,000 feet (610 m) in less than a mile (1.6 km) at the Manitou Incline in Colorado Springs. The trailhead starts at 6,600 feet (2,010 m) above sea level, so make sure you're accustomed to high altitude.

Made up of 2,744 railroad ties, this intimidating trail has an average grade of 41 percent, with some portions as steep as 68 percent. The incline was originally built for cable cars used to transport pipeline materials to Pikes Peak. After the pipelines were completed, the funiculars were turned into a tourist attraction but closed due to rockslide damages in 1990.

Reopened to the public in 2013, the stairway trail is a near-vertical hike to the summit. There are benches and two bailout points along the way where hikers can cut short the journey and return to the trailhead via the Northern Incline Return Trail. Those who have the endurance to push forward will be rewarded with great views of Pikes Peak and Manitou Springs. The downhill journey is about four miles (6.4 km) on the switchbacked century-old Barr Trail, zigzagging through Douglas firs, ponderosa pines, and scrub oaks.

Colorado Springs, CO | **Season:** Year-round

Great Sand Dunes National Park boasts North America's tallest dunes, some rising up to 750 feet (230 m).

1. RIDE THE ALPINE COASTER IN ESTES PARK

Get a rush of adrenaline when you ride down the alpine Mustang Mountain Coaster at Sombrero Ranch. With more than 2,000 feet (610 m) of twisty turns along the hills at the base of Mount Olympus, the mountain coaster can travel up to 30 miles an hour (48 km/h). The ride is open year-round.

2. EXPLORE PAINT MINES INTERPRETIVE PARK

The park's 3.4-mile (5.5 km) Paint Mines Trail leads through prairies and otherworldly badlands toward a ravine of 55-million-year-old hoodoos and sandstone-capped spires in pastel hues of yellow, orange, pink, and magenta. The best time to see the Paint Mines is a couple hours after sunrise or before sunset.

3. FIND YOURSELF IN THE LOST FOREST AT ASPEN SNOWMASS

Walk across sky bridges tucked among towering aspens, zip-line at high speed, and rappel down to the next zip-line platform. Other amenities include a gondola, a climbing wall, hiking trails, disc golf course, Trout Hook Fishing Pond, and an alpine coaster. Lost Forest is open June to October.

4. WHITE-WATER RAFT THE ARKANSAS RIVER

Raft though world-famous Class III rapids at Browns Canyon National Monument near Buena Vista. The thrilling run navigates past dramatic granite cliffs that transform colors when the sun hits at different times of the day. Notable exhilarating rapids include House Rock, Zoom Flume, and Seidel's Suckhole.

5. SAND-SURF AT GREAT SAND DUNES NATIONAL PARK

Sandboard or sled down the tallest dunes in North America at Great Sand Dunes National Park. Hike 0.7 mile (1.1 km) from the parking lot to the small- and medium-size slopes or head another half mile (0.8 km) for high ridges. Sandboards and sleds are available for rent at nearby Oasis market.

6. HELI-SKI IN TELLURIDE

A helicopter takes cross-country skiers to the backcountry and experienced downhill skiers and snowboarders to the top of the San Juan Mountains for a day of secluded adventure. Founded in 1982, Helitrax is a full-service operation that includes a guide, snowboard or powder skis and poles, lunch and snacks, and avalanche transceivers. Guests can be dropped off at more than 100 locations, depending on skill levels and terrain preference.

7. SALMON FISH AT BLACK CANYON OF THE GUNNISON

The largest body of water in Colorado, the Blue Mesa Reservoir in Curecanti National Recreation Area is home to kokanee salmon, the landlocked version of sockeye salmon. The fish can be caught by trolling with lead-core line and a quality hook (tip: white shoepeg corn makes a great bait).

8. FLIT TO THE FAIRY CAVES

In 1897, the Fairy Caves became the first cave system in the world to have illuminated electric lights. Today, the caves are the main attractions at Glenwood Caverns Adventure Park, America's only mountaintop theme park. In addition to a 40-minute guided tour, Glenwood Caverns also offers a two-hour spelunking trip through narrow corridors and deep into rarely visited chambers.

9. BIKE THE COLORADO TRAIL FROM SILVERTON TO DURANGO

Mountain bike 535 miles (860 km) through alpine terrain on one of the world's best long-distance mountain bike trails. Elevation for most of the ride is around 10,000 feet (3,050 m), with peaks of 13,000 feet (3,960 m). Cyclists pass through several national forests, mountain ranges, and wilderness areas.

10. HIKE AT BOX CAÑON FALLS

Walk down to the base of the 285-foot-tall (87 m) falls that gushes through the glacial-carved quartzite canyon. Birders should keep their eye out for black swifts that nest there in June. You can also climb 200 feet (60 m) for an aerial view of the waterfall and the peaks of Amphitheater Cirque from the half-mile (0.8 km) High Bridge Trail.

Sheffield Island Lighthouse is one of the "castles of the sound" and a favorite summer destination.

CONNECTICUT

New England charm abounds from the mountain peaks
to the coastal, rocky shores.

MASSA

NEW YORK

CONNE

Long Isl

**Mohawk Mountain
Ski Area**

Macedonia
Brook Loop

Farmington

**Farmington
River**

Farmington Canal
Heritage Trail

The Glebe House Museum &
Gertrude Jekyll Garden

Housatonic

**Marsh Botanical
Garden**

Housatonic
River

Weir Farm National
Historical Park

**The Adventure Park at
The Discovery Museum**

*Norwalk
Islands*

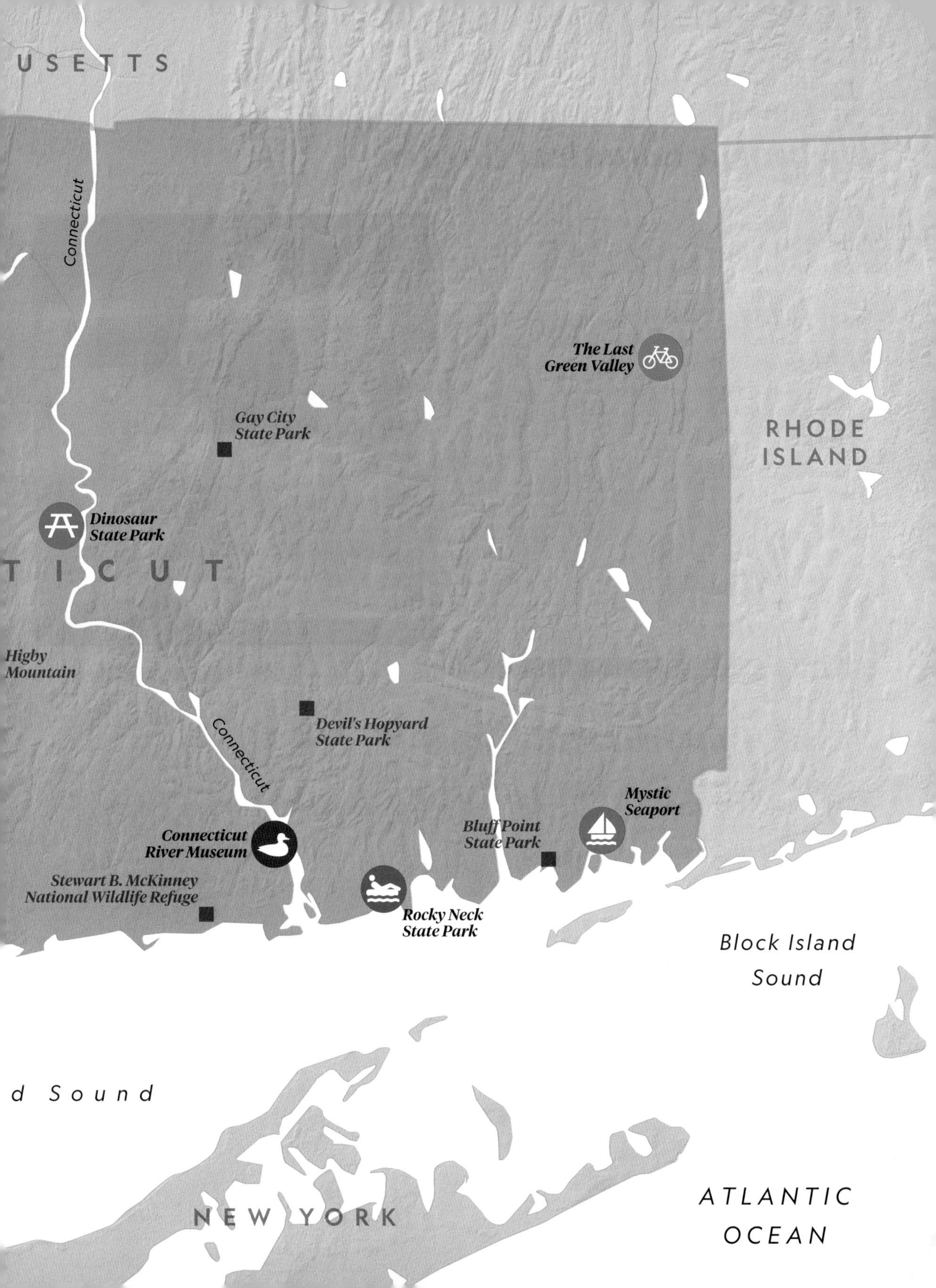

USETTS

RHODE
ISLAND

Connecticut

The Last
Green Valley 🚲

Gay City
State Park ■

🏕 Dinosaur
State Park

TICUT

Higby
Mountain

Connecticut

Devil's Hopyard
State Park ■

Mystic
Seaport ⛵

Bluff Point
State Park ■

Connecticut
River Museum 🦆

Stewart B. McKinney
National Wildlife Refuge ■

Rocky Neck
State Park 🛶

Block Island
Sound

d Sound

NEW YORK

ATLANTIC
OCEAN

Ivy League Botanical Garden

In a compact state like Connecticut, you're never too far from a gurgling wetland or a crop of wildflowers. Yale's Marsh Botanical Garden affirms this, less than two miles (3.2 km) away from downtown New Haven. At the foot of "Science Hill," a hub of biological lab spaces on Yale's campus, more than 1,200 species of flowers, shrubs, and trees take root on eight acres (3 ha) of gardens and greenhouses.

The oldest tree here, a giant white oak thought to be 307 years old, was once described by the garden's assistant director Kunso Kim as "a witness to Yale." Indeed, walking among the flora here can feel like a communion with ancient ancestors. From the hillside bog garden where native Connecticut plants bloom beside a natural spring during the spring and summer, to the climate-controlled greenhouses that nurture rainforest and desert specimens like *Pereskia* cacti, the natural world feels improbably localized at Yale.

New Haven, CT | Season: Year-round

The Ivy League university gets top marks for its botanical garden.

Fossil Hunt in a State Park

The ancient floodplains of the Connecticut River Valley hide many secrets. In 1966, a bulldozer operator made a startling discovery while breaking ground for highway infrastructure near Rocky Hill. Preserved in a sandstone slab were the footprints of a bipedal dinosaur, which paleontologists believe to have been *Dilophosaurus* (the venom-spitting carnivore that took out Newman in *Jurassic Park*).

Further excavation revealed more than 2,000 fossilized tracks of a dinosaur known as *Eubrontes*. The state decided to preserve these specimens by establishing Dinosaur State Park, where the famous tracks are now spotlit within a large geodesic dome. The "trackway" continues outside, some of it exposed and other sections still buried. During summer, you can take home a piece of history by mining for fossils and minerals in the park's on-site sluice or by creating a plaster cast of a dinosaur footprint.

Gentle trails around the park's lush 80 acres (32 ha) of woods and swamps are flanked with more than 250 species of plants and trees—many of which were growing here when dinosaurs roamed the valley.

Learn about the prehistoric era at exhibits in the park.

Rocky Hill, CT | Season: Summer

Choose Your Own Adventure at Rocky Neck

Connecticut is a smorgasbord of leafy, sun-splashed state parks where you can swim, hike, and spot wildlife without forking over hefty entrance fees. People avail themselves of these parks year-round, and nowhere is this on more prominent display during summer than along the sandy beaches of Rocky Neck State Park. Nutmeg State residents and visitors alike flock here to paddle, picnic, scuba dive, and cast their lines for blackfish and flounder. But just as enticing as the shoreline is the ecology of the park.

Rocky Neck's 710 acres (287 ha) include salt marshes, tidal waterways, and an unusual coastal thicket of young oak trees and shrubs (think of this as the transitional zone between a meadow and a forest). Bride Brook, sloshing through the park, is one of the busiest "runs" for herring as they travel up from the Long Island Sound to spawn in freshwater ponds. Baker's Cave, a dank chamber in a jumble of boulders, is rumored to have been named for a man who hid here and avoided service during the Revolutionary War. Thanks to a well-blazed trail system, you could spend an entire day exploring these features. Or two days, if you feel like booking one of the park's 160 campsites, which are open May through September. Ospreys (in the summer) and cranes, herons, and mute swans (in the fall) make their way to these waters and their cattails and rose mallows.

The "crown jewel" reputation of Rocky Neck is exemplified by the Ellie Mitchell Pavilion, which curves along the park's western shoreline. The wooden pillars of this beautiful masonry walkway were all harvested from trees in Connecticut's state parks and forests.

East Lyme, CT | **Season:** Year-round

Eagle Scout

From December through March, the illustrious birds of prey travel here from as far north as Canada to take shelter in the trees along the river's southern stretch and hunt for fish in the mostly unfrozen waters. Because the tree limbs are mostly bare, winter in Connecticut is one of the most opportune times to observe bald eagles in their element.

But how? The Haddam branch of the Audubon Society and the Connecticut River Museum of Essex both offer wintertime eagle-spotting cruises in boats with open decks and heated cabins. Reservations are a must, as birders scoop up slots fast. As you prowl along the river, your guide will offer a historical primer on the river's ecology, pointing out the surprising array of plants and animals that share the riverbanks with eagles.

Essex, CT | **Season:** December to March

A bald eagle guards her nest.

Catch—or take part in—a ski race at Mohawk Mountain.

> "ITS EIGHT CHAIRLIFTS OFFER PRIMO ACCESS TO 26 SIDEWIND- ING AND PLUNGING TRAILS."

The Home of Snowmaking

Winter is relative in New England, and Walter Schoenknecht learned this the hard way. In 1947, the Connecticut-born skier and his wife, Peg, leased land in Mohawk State Forest and built a network of ski trails and towrope lifts. The only thing missing was snow. A winter drought left the initially popular ski area barren and unusable. But instead of shutting down, Schoenknecht decided to fix the problem by providing his own snow.

A series of experiments, such as hauling truckloads of ice to Mohawk Mountain Ski Area and chipping them into "snow," yielded a breakthrough. Schoenknecht and his partners were able to create snow by using an air and water compressor (a staple of tobacco farming). The trails were now reliably blanketed with packed powder when the clouds couldn't deliver, but Schoenknecht's invention had ripple effects far beyond Connecticut. It was a game changer for ski resorts, and it is why Mohawk Mountain is called "the home of snowmaking."

With 650 feet (200 m) of vertical drop, Mohawk might look modest, but its eight chairlifts offer primo access to 26 sidewinding and plunging trails, many of which can be skied after dark thanks to night lighting. Toward the summit, several of these trails connect with snowshoe and cross-country ski paths that will take you deeper into Mohawk State Forest.

You can use these trails year-round and discover the mountain's nearby oddities, like a black spruce bog with some of the most abundant peat moss in Connecticut. Or hilltop towers the American Telephone and Telegraph Company (now AT&T) once used to broadcast radio signals. But when the days get darker and the temperature drops, *there will be snow.*

Cornwall, CT | **Season:** Winter

Fish the Norwalk Islands

Located roughly one mile (1.6 km) off the Connecticut coast, the Norwalk Islands are a hodgepodge of rocks, sand, clay, oyster beds, and coastal vegetation like beach roses. With more than 25 islands to explore, these terminal moraines are a curiosity for kayakers, swimmers, and tent campers alike.

But it's the bluefish, trout, fluke, and dogfish that travel through the waters around the glacial islands that lure anglers from across New England. Striped bass are especially coveted. In midsummer, they can often be caught near Greens Ledge Light, while late fall visitors tend to have better luck off the easternmost beaches of Cockenoe Island, the largest of the islands.

You'll need a boat or kayak to traverse shallow waters if you want to get close enough to poke around the island beaches and boulder jumbles. But whether you're planning on casting in deeper water or closer to shore, local outfitters offer boat rentals and charters.

> "IT'S THE BLUEFISH, TROUT, FLUKE, AND DOGFISH THAT TRAVEL THROUGH THE WATERS AROUND THE GLACIAL ISLANDS THAT LURE ANGLERS FROM ACROSS NEW ENGLAND."

Norwalk, CT | **Season:** Spring to fall

Set sail in the waters surrounding Norwalk Islands and cast a line for bass and bluefish when the winds are calm.

Adventure Park's rope courses are fun for all ages.

Adventure and Discovery Await

It's easy to think of Fairfield County as one sprawling New York suburb. But to do so is to miss the forest for the trees—especially when you can climb and soar through those trees on one of the most expansive zip-line and rope courses in New England.

Hidden within five acres (2 ha) of deciduous woodlands behind Bridgeport's science center—the Discovery Museum—Adventure Park applies the ski resort model to its 13 treetop trails, rating them by level of difficulty and exposure. Double-black trails are the most rigorous and scary, while purple and yellow are ideal for beginners. Unlike zip-line courses where you link up with a group of visitors, Adventure Park lets you choose between a guided "hike" or a solo traverse.

Before setting off on the course, you'll receive a thorough walk-through from staff on how to use your harness and clip yourself to the safety cables that connect more than 180 elevated platforms amid the trees. A low-stakes practice course gives you the chance to hone your moves and steel your nerves for the adventure ahead. From there, your trail of choice will take you across a dizzying array of wire-and-wood obstacles like suspension bridges, ladders, floating steps, and the occasional tube slide.

The various rope courses and aerial trails are thrilling but efficient enough that you can try several in the span of one visit. If you find yourself out of your element midcourse, the park also offers outdoor ax-throwing lanes where you can enjoy a different kind of calculated risk-taking.

Bridgeport, CT | **Season:** Spring to fall

Oak leaves and acorns

Paddle rapids like Satan's Kingdom on the Farmington River.

Tube Like Twain

The Connecticut River Valley is where Mark Twain wrote *The Adventures of Huckleberry Finn,* and his lavish Hartford home is now a preservation site. But 19 miles (31 km) west of here is a more exciting way to pay homage to the author. Thanks to a local rafting outfitter, you can emulate Huck Finn's journey down the Mississippi by tubing the lively waters of the Farmington River.

Operating from Memorial Day weekend through mid-September, Farmington River Tubing sets you up with life jackets and inner tubes before sending you on a 2.5-mile (4 km) journey down the river. You'll float past chirping woodlands and bounce through three sets of rapids. One of these rapid runs will take you through Satan's Kingdom gorge (named for the rigors of building railroads in this rocky area). Lifeguards are posted at rapids to assist tubers if needed. When you complete the journey, a bus will transport you back to your vehicle.

New Hartford, CT **Season:** Summer

Cruise Through the Mystic

In the 19th century, the economy of Mystic was powered by whale oil—the standard fuel for lamps then. From the docks of the Mystic Seaport, listen to the fluttering of sails as wooden tall ships ventured beyond Long Island Sound to hunt the coveted sperm whale. These voyages could last for months or years, and some tall ships never made it back to unload their bounty of blubber.

Since the whaling boom, the Mystic Seaport has been repurposed for more recreational uses. But a deep reverence for the sea endures, and you can explore the maritime heritage of the harbor in several ways. Hop aboard the *Argia*, a two-masted topsail schooner, for a briny ride past lighthouses, estuaries, and rocky islands. Or venture farther inland up the Mystic River on the 110-year-old *Sabino* steamboat.

On the river, you'll find the Mystic Seaport Museum, home to the last surviving vessel of an American whaling fleet that once boasted 2,700 ships. The *Charles W. Morgan* took its inaugural ride across the harbor in 1841, before embarking on 37 whaling voyages spanning from the Arctic to the tropics. At 106 feet (32 m) long, with three main masts and the capacity to hoist more than 7,000 square feet (650 m²) of sail, the *Charles W. Morgan* is a stunning relic of a lost era. With admission to the museum, you can walk the ship's decks and observe the preserved try-pots that sailors would use for reducing blubber to oil, before exploring the claustrophobic crew quarters below.

Stonington, CT **Season:** Spring to early fall

Stop at the Huntington Homestead, a national historic landmark and the birthplace of statesman Samuel Huntington.

Bike the Last Green Valley

Stretching from Hartford into south-central Massachusetts is a 1,100-square-mile (2,850 km²) passage of verdant forests, flowering fields, and lively streams that ripple past 35 rural towns. This is the Last Green Valley National Heritage Corridor, half the size of Grand Canyon National Park, with only 300,000 residents spread across nearly 707,000 acres (286,115 ha) of undeveloped woods and historic farmlands.

It's one of the most pristine patches of the Nutmeg State, and the most exhilarating way to experience it is from behind the handlebars of a bike. Route 169, a scenic byway, climbs and winds through the valley, serving as an artery for cyclists looking to branch off onto quieter paths such as Prudence's Trail, which visits the villages of Scotland and Moosup over 55 wooded miles (89 km). The 41-mile (66 km) Roseland Trail, which departs from a Gothic Revival mansion where presidents summered, is another favorite for atmospheric biking.

Danielson, CT | **Season:** Spring to fall

Old Drake Hill Flower Bridge
is one of three surviving
Parker truss bridges.

1. BIKE THE FARMINGTON CANAL HERITAGE TRAIL

Steamships and trains once chugged along the Farmington Canal. But in recent decades, conservationists and trail builders leveraged 56 miles (90 km) of the waterway for a more environmentally friendly purpose by creating the Heritage Trail. It runs north from New Haven to Suffield past farms, forests, and mountains like Sleeping Giant.

2. EXPLORE STEWART B. MCKINNEY NATIONAL WILDLIFE REFUGE

Connecticut's rocky coastline is speckled with islands that serve as R&R venues for birds like the endangered roseate tern. The refuge, which includes 70 miles (110 km) of coastal habitats, was the first federal conservation site in the state. Explore its trails by foot, or kayak to the islands.

3. CROSS-COUNTRY SKI AT GAY CITY STATE PARK

If you've ever wanted to ski past the icy ruins of a ghost town, set the controls for Gay City. Its 11 miles (18 km) of ungroomed trails wind through the park past crumbling relics of the titular "city," a once thriving mill town that was ruined by a fire in 1879.

4. SUMMIT HIGBY MOUNTAIN VIA THE MATTABESETT BLUE TRAIL

The horseshoe-shaped trail is a 61-mile (98 km) grand tour of Connecticut's state parks and land trusts that leads to the sunny summit of Higby Mountain. This long, exposed ridge features tall traprock cliffs overlooking Middletown, and the 9-mile (14 km) out-and-back hike up the Mattabesett Blue Trail includes lots of rock scrambling.

5. LOOP THROUGH BLUFF POINT STATE PARK

One of the last stretches of undeveloped coastline in Connecticut, the peninsular Bluff Point extends into Long Island Sound and includes 806 acres (326 ha) of tidal wetlands, ragged cliffs, and forested sand dunes. Thanks to the paved 3.6-mile-long (5.8 km) Bluff Point Trail that loops through the park, you can also savor the scenery from a bike.

6. FACE YOUR DEMONS AT DEVIL'S HOPYARD STATE PARK

Chapman Falls, a crashing 60-foot (18 m) cascade, is the first thing you'll find upon entering Devil's Hopyard. But as its name suggests, the park is something of a shrine to Puritan superstition. A rooty 2.2-mile (3.5 km) trail through shadowy hemlock woods leads to Devil's Oven, a rock formation with an ominous cave.

7. MAKE MEMORIES AT WEIR FARM NATIONAL HISTORICAL PARK

The former residence of impressionist painter J. Alden Weir is a preserved dreamscape of rolling hills, flowering fields, and old stone walls that inspired Weir. The park offers free drawing and painting supplies at the visitors center, so you can return home with a memory that you can hang on a wall.

8. CLIMB THE MACEDONIA BROOK LOOP

Postcard-worthy views of New York's Catskills are the reward of this 6.8-mile (11 km) loop trail. The steep, rocky climb to the top of Cobble Mountain (the highpoint of the ridge) makes this trail a challenge for hikers visiting Litchfield County—it's an ascent on par with New England's toughest trails.

9. WHITE-WATER RAFT ON THE HOUSATONIC RIVER

Appalachian Trail hikers love the placid ripple of the Housatonic as they enter the Berkshires. But downstream, the river sloshes with rapids that can make for an ideal beginner's white-water adventure. Clarke Outdoors, a West Cornwall outfitter, leads guided rafting trips on the iconic river as it rumbles past meadows and bridges.

10. STROLL THROUGH BLOOMS AT GERTRUDE JEKYLL GARDEN

The horticulturist Gertrude Jekyll designed hundreds of beloved gardens across the U.K. during the 20th century. But her stateside footprint is contained to a little-known nook in the Litchfield Hills. At the Glebe House Museum—a historic Georgian colonial home—Jekyll's only U.S. garden blooms with life and is open to visitors year-round.

Walk along the Christina River for views of downtown Wilmington.

DELAWARE

From sandy stretches to rocky ledges to bird-watching trails, Delaware abounds with activities and beautiful natural scenery.

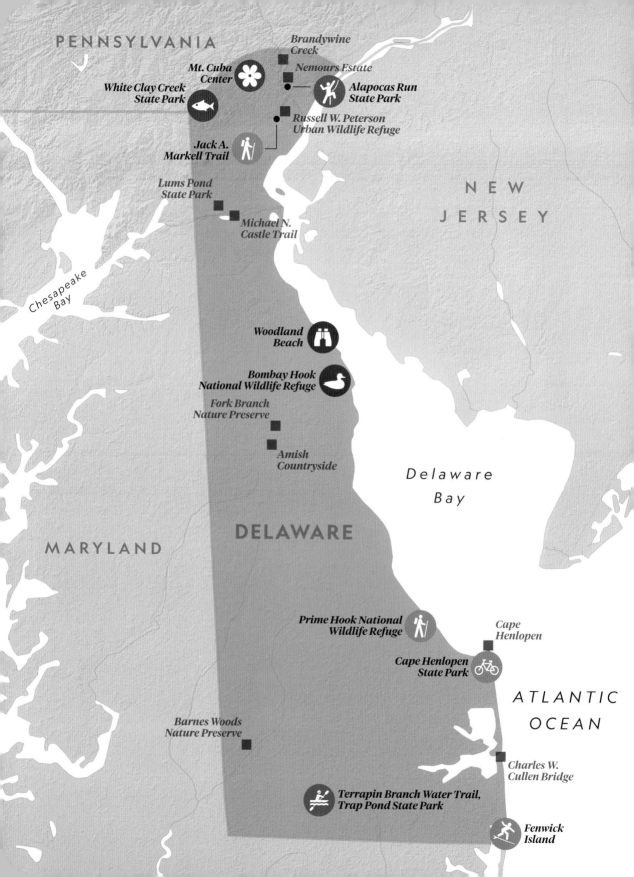

Alapocas Run State Park's rock wall is nestled in the trees.

Rock Climb in the City

When you're constructing a city like Wilmington, you need stone. Lots of it. To ensure a steady supply, the builders behind the state's northern metropolis blasted quarries along a section of the Brandywine Creek. This once ravaged landscape has since regrown, and today it's known as Alapocas Run State Park.

Named for one the Brandywine's tributaries, the park still contains the walls of the old quarries. The sheets of metamorphic blue gneiss rock can take on a mixed hue of blue and earthier tones in certain lighting conditions. But gawking at these cliffs is just half the fun. Climbers venture here to test their skills on the park's 78-foot-tall (24 m) climbing wall—the only natural rock-climbing wall in Delaware.

Wilmington, DE | Season: Year-round

Located off the park's Northern Greenway multiuse trail (which runs all the way to Brandywine Park in Wilmington), the blue gneiss wall is affixed with top-rope anchoring systems. You can try scaling the wall by affixing a rope to one of these anchors, having your partner belay you from below and using the mossy cracks of the wall to hoist yourself up. Or you can rappel to the base of the wall from the top, observing the rock formations and sometimes, seasonal cascades that trickle down the cliff.

Other than the requisite climbing gear, all you need is a free climbing permit from the Delaware State Parks website and you're ready to scale. And if you're still getting the hang of harness prep or choosing the best crags, the park offers climbing courses during the summer.

White Clay Creek is home to bluegill and crappie.

Cast Away

The shallow waters of White Clay Creek flow through sunny deciduous woods, practically inviting you to wade in. And that's exactly what anglers have been doing since the state of Delaware protected the waterway by founding White Clay Creek State Park in 1968. Several times each year, the creek is stocked with rainbow and brown trout, making it possible to go fishing here well into the fall, when the park woodlands take on heavenly gold and auburn hues.

April through June and October through November are the most popular times to reel in trout from the creek. (You'll need to purchase a trout stamp from the park before casting amid those windows.) But the titular creek is the tip of the iceberg when it comes to robust fish populations within the park. Those who explore Cattail and Millstone Ponds will find bluegill, crappie, and largemouth bass, which the park allows you to catch and release.

Newark, DE | **Season:** Spring and fall

See the Horseshoe Crab Migration

The horseshoe crab is actually a member of the spider family, and along the eastern seaboard, you'll find their molted shells on beaches. Delaware Bay boasts the largest concentration of these aquatic arachnids during spawning season. Each spring—in May and June—horseshoe crabs emerge from their wintry sleep on submerged continental shelves. They storm the beaches of Delaware like it's D-Day, laying their eggs in the sand and ensuring generational continuity.

The horseshoe crab spawn is one of the most unique natural events that you can witness in Delaware. At venues like Woodland Beach and Bowers Beach (both located in Kent County), it's not uncommon to see horseshoe crabs clustered in droves, like a crowd at a music festival. For the best "show," hit the beaches when high tide, sunset, and a new or full moon happen to coincide. Usually, seven nights in spring fit these criteria.

Woodland and Bowers Beach, DE | **Season:** Spring

Thousands of horseshoe crabs migrate to Woodland Beach every spring.

Sitting on the branches of a tree in Bombay Hook is a group of great egrets, one of many bird species you'll spot here.

Bird-Watching in Bombay Hook

If you've ever wondered how the federal government spends the money made from hunting permit sales, Bombay Hook National Wildlife Refuge is a best-case scenario. All 16,000 acres (6,475 ha) of this coastal waterfowl sanctuary were purchased from private landowners with the proceeds from federal duck stamps, and pintail ducks are just one of more than 350 bird species observed here.

Gentle hiking trails and scenic drives wander throughout the refuge, offering prime access to the tidal salt marshes where many of the visiting birds take shelter. (The trails feature 30-foot-tall [9 m] observation towers.) Migratory birds from North and South America like the yellow warbler tend to converge here during fall and spring, while shorebirds such as the sandpiper and red knot arrive en masse in May. But don't overlook the resident red foxes, river otters, and muskrats, which can be seen literally chewing the scenery year-round.

Smyrna, DE | **Season:** Spring and fall

Paddle your way through
swampy woodlands.

"SPOT GREAT BLUE HERONS, OWLS, TURTLES, SNAKES, AND THE OCCASIONAL BALD EAGLE WITH STARTLING INTIMACY."

The Terrapin Branch Water Trail

The bald cypress tree, a staple of the American South, is sparsely encountered elsewhere. But the northernmost pocket of naturally occurring bald cypresses in the United States is hidden in Trap Pond State Park, one of Delaware's first state parks. Here, 100-foot-tall (30 m) trees and their hanging mosses are partially submerged in the waters of a former industrial logging pond.

Taking in these bald cypresses from the shoreline is entrancing, but the ultimate way to pay homage to these arbors is by kayaking or canoeing the Terrapin Branch Water Trail. Marked by signs posted in the swamp water and spanning two miles (3.2 km), this unique water trail will take you into the depths of the swamp, where you can spot great blue herons, owls, turtles, snakes, and the occasional bald eagle with startling intimacy. In the early morning hours, crepuscular beams of sunlight flare through the swamp's mists, creating a visual spectacle known as "god rays."

The bald cypress swamp is located along the northern shore of Trap Pond, and to reach the trailhead, you'll need to paddle there first. Most visitors choose to begin their hike at the Baldcypress Nature Center, off the park's main access road. A dock is located steps away, and kayak and canoe rentals are available there. As you paddle across Trap Pond toward the swamp, a few lone bald cypress trees in the middle of the pond offer a taste of what's ahead. As you approach the swamp, look for a yellow sign for the Terrapin Branch Water Trail. The trail is an out-and-back route, so it's best to turn around when your energy starts to fade.

Laurel, DE | **Season:** Spring to fall

Hike or Bike Through Wetlands

The sandy "point" of Cape Henlopen is where the Delaware seashore meets the Atlantic Ocean. Its dunes and pine forests have hosted visitors ranging from the Algonquin peoples who came here to fish in the surf to soldiers who manned the coastal defense artillery at Fort Miles during World War II. Today, more than six miles (10 km) of the cape are preserved as one of Delaware's state parks (which also happens to be the eastern terminus of the American Discovery Trail from Delaware to California).

Nab one of the free on-site bikes or lace up your hiking shoes for a 3.2-mile (5 km) jaunt on the Gordons Pond Trail, which features elevated boardwalk through wetlands. Considering camping? Nestled within the piney dunes are tent sites and primitive cabins that connect to the Walking Dunes Trail (2.6 miles/4 km). And for a stunning vista of the cape, climb the observation tower at the Fort Miles Historic area and savor the sea breeze at the top.

Lewes, DE | **Season:** Spring to fall

The Delaware shore beckons visitors to the Atlantic.

A Beachy Refuge for Wildlife

About 10,144 acres (4,105 ha) of saltwater and freshwater marshes, wooded swamps, and grasslands make an ideal pit stop for millions of migratory birds on their way south each winter. The U.S. Fish and Wildlife Service established Prime Hook National Wildlife Refuge in 1963 to ensure that this pocket of Delaware Bay's west shoreline would offer reliable haven for more than 308 species of birds, which coexist here with reptiles such as hognose snakes, mammals like the red fox, and plenty of snackable insects.

Named for the purple beach plums that grow along the sands here (early Dutch settlers called the area Priume Hoek, meaning "Plum Point"), Prime Hook is open to birders and forest bathers year-round. Four walking trails depart from the visitors center, one of which—the half-mile (0.8 km) Boardwalk Trail—is fully

Delaware big blue hen

wheelchair-accessible. Four state highways run through the refuge too, passing wetlands that snow geese frequent and beaches where you can spot great egrets wading into the surf each summer.

Part of the "wild" factor at Prime Hook is the lack of obvious signage or park infrastructure when you approach the refuge on Broadkill Road. Adding to the sense that you've entered a zone of pure ecology is the seasonal variability of the local "residents." Look for yellow perch, pintail ducks, and Canada geese in fall and winter. Summering in Delaware? You might spot a baby eagle or detect the call of songbirds. And if you time your visit for dusk or dawn, you'll see the refuge's feathered guests at their most active.

Milton, DE | **Season:** Year-round

Hit the JAM Trail

The environmental barriers that divide town and country are being broken down by multiuse trails, and one of Delaware's coolest city-to-sticks journeys is the Jack A. Markell Trail. Named for the former governor who helped create a statewide fund for cleaning and managing Delaware's labyrinthine waterways, the "JAM Trail" connects the city of New Castle (the state's colonial capital) to the buzzing marshlands on the Wilmington riverfront.

With the exception of one short on-road portion, the 7.9-mile-long (12.7 km) trail consists of paved paths and breezy boardwalks that traverse wild spaces like the Russell W. Peterson Urban Wildlife Refuge, where eastern painted turtles and American beaver go about their business within the Wilmington city limits. The midsection of the JAM Trail follows an abandoned freight rail line connecting Wilmington to New Castle. Here, industrial-era infrastructure like railroad bridges and underpasses are the dominant landscape features. But for many trail visitors, the journey leads to Historic New Castle, where preserved early American architecture like the Amstel House (a gorgeous Georgian-style mansion) offers a colorful taste of colonial living. Or stop for a historical lunch: There's colonial fare on the menu at Jessop's Tavern in town.

Although entry points to the JAM Trail are numerous, you may have an easier time setting off from the DuPont Environmental Education Center, located on the edge of the Russell W. Peterson Urban Wildlife Refuge. On-site parking here will be less competitive than at New Castle Battery Park (the southern terminus of the JAM Trail) or at the trail's Wilmington end point, the Riverfront Wilmington (a reliable outpost for savory grub, ice-cold suds, or rental bikes if you need one.)

Wilmington, DE | **Season:** Spring to fall

Surf's Up in Fenwick

Steps away from the Maryland state line, Fenwick Island State Park is home of Delaware's southernmost beach. A three-mile (5 km) expanse of smooth sand, dunes, and winding wooden slat fences, Fenwick Island once featured a lifesaving station that offered aid to distressed boats in the Atlantic. A storm destroyed the station in 1962, but the power of the surf remains—a boon for surfers.

For consistent, rideable waves, the best time to visit Fenwick Island is summer (July is especially popular). Plan to arrive near low tide, as the tide starts to come back in, and if that window happens to be in the early morning, keep an eye out for ghost crabs as you enter the surf. These spidery little crabs spend most of the day buried in the sand to avoid the heat of the sun, but toward dusk, dawn, or on overcast days, Fenwick Island can be skittering with them.

You can surf or splash in the waters of Fenwick Island.

Fenwick Island, DE | **Season:** Summer

> "EXPLORE THE GRASSY
> SLOPES, PONDS, AND
> WOODLAND TRAILS HERE."

Botanical Wonders

❀ In a region replete with public gardens—there are 30 within a 30-mile (48 km) radius of Philadelphia!—Hockessin's Mt. Cuba Center offers an extraordinary window into the ecology of northern Delaware's rolling foothills (the Piedmont). Once the family estate of two du Pont heirs who happened to be practicing horticulturists, Mt. Cuba Center's 1,000 combined acres (405 ha) of hilltop gardens and natural forest are the result of decades of landscape architecture. But it wasn't until 2013 that general admission to the botanical gardens was offered to the public, making Mt. Cuba Center something of a new obsession for local and visiting flora fans.

Spring, late summer, and fall are the opportune times to explore the grassy slopes, ponds, and woodland trails here. Your visit begins at the center's Colonial Revival manor house, where redbrick terraces offer gorgeous views of the nearby forest, looking east. Walled formal gardens beside the house feature native plants like oakleaf hydrangea, golden star, and white azaleas.

From the manor, Mt. Cuba Center's gentle meandering paths beckon. The easy Pollinator Trail passes gardens in which bees and butterflies bounce from flower to flower, and restored wetlands where one can hear the unmistakable banjo twang of frogs. The Bluebird Loop ascends to one of Delaware's highest points, at 400 feet (120 m) above sea level, where grassland birds like American kestrel can be seen against a vista of the Piedmont hills. And the short Chestnut Trail visits hybridized trees, cultivated in partnership with the American Chestnut Foundation.

Hockessin, DE | **Season:** Spring to fall

Take a rest among
the blooming dogwoods
at Mt. Cuba Center.

The Nemours Estate, with its French-inspired gardens, is the former family home of Alfred I. du Pont.

1. CRUISE THE MICHAEL CASTLE TRAIL

Running 12.1 miles (19.5 km) on the banks of the Chesapeake and Delaware Canal, this popular biking and hiking path traverses sunny marshlands and woods where turkey, raccoons, and even peregrine falcons make seasonal appearances. Just as striking are the gargantuan freight ships chugging along the canal to the Port of Baltimore.

2. ZIP-LINE AT LUMS POND STATE PARK

Many visitors travel here to gaze at the largest freshwater pond in Delaware, but the park's overstory contains its own offerings. A 700-foot-long (210 m) zip line, tree-to-tree ropes courses, and "Tarzan swings" are just a couple of the canopy-level challenges maintained here by the Go Ape! adventure company.

3. PADDLE BRANDYWINE CREEK

The meandering flow of Brandywine Creek is perfect for beginner paddlers, but even seasoned canoers will find deep quietude as the creek winds through the hills of Brandywine Valley. Try putting in at Shaw's Bridge Park in West Chester, Pennsylvania, just across the state line, and glide for 11 miles (18 km) to Brandywine Creek State Park.

4. TAKE REFUGE AT RUSSELL W. PETERSON URBAN WILDLIFE REFUGE

The Russell W. Peterson sanctuary is right in the heart of Wilmington. The 212 acres (86 ha) of wetlands on the Wilmington riverfront are surrounded by city and railroad infrastructure, making it easy to stroll or bike right into the refuge and visit the resident herons and frogs.

5. BIKE AMISH COUNTRY

West of Dover, horse-and-buggy carriages rule the roads winding through Delaware's Amish community, and each year, cyclists link up to explore these villages on the Amish Country Bike Tour. But the peaceful fields of Amish country are ideal for cycling throughout most of the year, and the Amish farm stands and furniture shops sweeten the deal.

6. OWL AT FORK BRANCH NATURE PRESERVE

This mature floodplain woods only became accessible to hikers in 2018, with the opening of a one-mile (1.6 km) loop trail that passes vernal pools and immense green ferns. But the stars of the show in this forest are the local barred owls, which nest in the trees here.

7. SPOT DOLPHINS OFF CAPE HENLOPEN

It's not unheard of for visitors at Cape Henlopen State Park to spot Atlantic bottlenose dolphins cresting the surf of Delaware Bay. But why settle for a distant glimpse when you can witness these maritime mammals up close from a boat? Each summer, Cape Water Tours and Taxi offers narrated dolphin cruises across the bay.

8. MEANDER THROUGH NEMOURS ESTATE GARDENS

The 300-acre (120 ha) country estate of industrialist Alfred I. du Pont boasts some of the most sprawling French neoclassical gardens in the United States. It's rather ironic, given the DuPont corporation's history of environmental destruction, but strolling and picnicking amid the estate's flowering horse chestnut trees and reflecting pools speak for themselves.

9. EXPLORE BARNES WOODS NATURE PRESERVE

Delaware is a collage of woodlands and tidal waterways, and at this 23-acre (9 ha) preserve, old-growth oak forest flanks creeks and swamplands where wood ducks and beavers thrive. Per the wishes of the former landowner, the woods here are undisturbed and minimally cultivated, making for a more pristine hike.

10. CAMP AT THE CHARLES W. CULLEN BRIDGE

Beach camping is a pillar of Delaware's summertime lifestyle, but few campsites allow you to get as close to the water as the Indian River inlet, which empties into the Atlantic. The bridge-side tent and RV sites are located in Delaware Seashore State Park, minutes away from the bacchanalian nightlife at Rehoboth Beach.

Barred owl

Everglades National Park (page 131) is home to more than 1.5 million acres (607,000 ha) of coastal mangroves, marshes, and flatwoods.

FLORIDA

The Sunshine State boasts everything from epic
waterways and wetlands to wild animal encounters.

MISSISSIPPI

ALABAMA

Gulf of Mexico

"THE SEA, ONCE IT
CASTS ITS SPELLS,
HOLDS ONE IN ITS NET
OF WONDER FOREVER."
—JACQUES COUSTEAU

GEORGIA

Amelia Island

Timucuan Ecological &
Historic Preserve

Ichetucknee Springs
State Park

Devil's Den

FLORIDA

Crystal River
Preserve State Park

Lake
Dora

Brooker Creek
Preserve

Alafia River
State Park

Palma
Sola Bay

Myakka River
State Park

Eagle
Bay

Snook Haven
Park

Lake Okeechobee
Scenic Trail

Stump Pass Beach
State Park

The Great
Calusa Blueway

Shark Valley
Tram Road

Ten Thousand Islands
National Wildlife Refuge

John Pennekamp
Coral Reef State Park

Florida Keys Overseas
Heritage Trail

Dry Tortugas
National Park

ATLANTIC OCEAN

Wild-Caught Amelia

There's nothing like the taste of wild-caught shrimp, and there's no better place to experience it than Fernandina Beach on Amelia Island—the birthplace of the modern shrimping industry.

Local guides, like Amelia River Cruises, offer interactive shrimping ecotours on the backwaters and tidal creeks of Tiger Basin, west of the island. You'll learn how to deploy and retrieve an otter trawl shrimp net, which was developed in Fernandina Beach and inspired modern commercial nets. The catch of the day is displayed in an onboard aquarium for identification before they're released.

Visit during the annual Shrimp Festival, the first weekend in May, to celebrate the crustacean that put this place on the map. The streets fill with pirates, a nod to the town's history as a safe harbor for maritime thieves, and a parade of giant shrimp floats. On the water, local shrimpers compete in a decorated shrimp boat contest.

Fernandina Beach, FL | **Season:** Spring and summer

See what you can catch aboard a working shrimp boat.

Ancient Treasures

Six thousand years of natural and cultural history come to life in one of the last unspoiled coastal wetlands on the Atlantic coast. Named for the Timucua who once lived here, Timucuan Ecological and Historic Preserve is a treasure trove of unforgettable stories and species.

Great egrets gather at Simpson Creek.

Pedal the Timucan Trail south from Amelia Island State Park to Spoonbill Pond on Big Talbot Island. Stop at a covered lookout to search for the namesake bird. Continue south through the cool shade of a maritime hammock for four miles (6.4 km) and explore the side trails. Try Black Rock Trail—a half-mile (0.8 km) path through the forest leads to the shoreline where Blackbeard allegedly buried treasure. Don't miss Boneyard Beach to see scattered skeletons of giant oak and cedar trees. For a different view, rent a kayak from Kayak Amelia and paddle south on Simpson Creek to Fort George River.

Luxury found its way to the island's eastern shore in 1928, when the Ribault Club was built as a winter resort for wealthy families. Named after French explorer Jean Ribault, who claimed the island in 1562, the club sits atop a shell midden formed by the Timucua's discarded oyster shells.

Jacksonville, FL | **Season:** Year-round

Snorkeling With a Side of Stargazing

Seventy miles (110 km) west of Key West, seven small islands form the Dry Tortugas but represent only one percent of this national park. The rest is underwater and includes shipwrecks and the western end of the Florida Reef System. Dry Tortugas, as it is now known, was dedicated as Fort Jefferson National Monument in 1935. It protects 100 square miles (260 km²) of open water and coral reef, as well as aquatic species. Given its remote location in the Gulf, access to Dry Tortugas is limited—you can catch a ride on the *Yankee Freedom* ferry, book a flight on a seaplane, hire a private boat, or captain your own.

Once you reach the main island, Garden Key, the park is yours to explore. Enter the water from the southern beach and snorkel around the moat wall to see colorful coral and reef fish. Check out the Bird Key wreck, southwest of the island, where a steamboat thought to be transporting some of the 16 million bricks needed to build Fort Jefferson ran aground and sank in the mid-1800s.

If you have your own boat, head over to Loggerhead Key, which is open to day visitors, and check out the Windjammer wreck, a mile (1.6 km) off the southwest shore, where a Norwegian sailing vessel, the *Avanti*, struck the reef and sank.

After dark, you'll find unparalleled stargazing with no light pollution. But the only way to see it is to spend the night at one of 10 primitive campsites on Garden Key's southern shore. The *Yankee Freedom* can transport up to 10 campers a day for a maximum three-night stay. You must bring all supplies, including freshwater, fuel, ice, and food. Book early; reservations fill up months in advance.

Monroe County, FL | Season: Year-round

The switchbacks are epic on Alfalfa's mountain biking trails.

Two-Wheel Mecca

Central Florida's flat topography might not evoke images of mountain biking, but a century of phosphate mining carved small lakes and steep grades into its rugged terrain, which volunteers have repurposed into a mountain biking mecca at Alafia River State Park.

More than 20 miles (32 km) of single-track trails snake through a junglelike setting, offering rides for cyclists of all ages and skill levels. Beginners can start with the Easy Loop's three interconnected green trails, which feature wide tracks and gentle rolling hills. More experienced bikers can challenge themselves on steep drops and berm turns found on intermediate blue trails, like Roller Coaster and Lost Meadow. Advanced and expert riders can test their skills on technical climbs and jumps found on black and double-black-diamond trails, like Thunder Ridge and Gravitron.

Lithia, FL | Season: Year-round

Myakka River State Park features tropical old-growth forests.

> "A FINE BALANCE OF PRESERVATION AND RECREATION CREATES AN AUTHENTIC WINDOW INTO FLORIDA'S MOST TREASURED INHABITANTS."

Wild and Scenic Florida

To see great white egrets flapping across unspoiled wetlands, lesser yellowlegs foraging a marsh, and American alligators sunbathing on riverbanks is to witness wild Florida as early Native Americans and Spanish explorers once did. These rare views are abundant at Myakka River State Park, where a fine balance of preservation and recreation creates an authentic window into the wild world of Florida's most treasured inhabitants.

More than half the park's 38,000 acres (15,380 ha) are made up of dry prairie, a globally imperiled ecosystem and habitat for at-risk species, like sandhill cranes, burrowing owls, crested caracaras, and grasshopper sparrows. Nearly 40 miles (64 km) of backcountry trails cross the park, as well as an American Disabilities Act (ADA)–accessible tram.

The Birdwalk, an ADA-accessible boardwalk, invites you into the wetlands where great blue herons and glossy ibis wade the shallows in hunt. The Canopy Walkway, suspended 25 feet (8 m) in the air, offers a glimpse of life in a live oak canopy. Climb the 74-foot (22 m) viewing tower at the end to see Myakka's wetlands and prairies through the eyes of its resident bald eagles.

Step aboard the *Myakka River Queen* for an hour-long narrated boat tour of the Upper Myakka Lake and the chance to observe American alligators in their natural habitat. In the winter dry season, the gators follow the receding Myakka River to Deep Hole, a naturally occurring sinkhole southwest of Lower Lake. For a view inside their secret world, arrive early to get one of 30 free wilderness permits granted daily by the ranger's station.

Sarasota, FL · **Season:** Year-round

Shark Tooth Treasure Hunt

At the southern end of Manasota Key is a quiet stretch of beach where Gulf treasures wash ashore with each crashing wave and wait to be discovered.

Here, 15 miles (24 km) south of Venice (aka the shark tooth capital of the world), shark tooth hunters use hand-held sifters and floating screens (available for purchase at nearby sundry shops) to dig in the surf and sort through soggy sand for shark teeth. The most prized is a giant tooth from the extinct megalodon, the largest shark that ever lived. More common are small, fossilized teeth that are thousands of years old and easily identified by their dark color and Y shape.

Coral, fossils, and bone are among the other goodies that might surface. Not to mention beautiful shells, like tiny, butterfly-shaped coquina and the elaborate spiral shells of fighting conch and lightning whelk.

The park is open daily from 8 a.m. until sundown.

> **"THE MOST PRIZED IS A GIANT TOOTH FROM THE EXTINCT MEGALODON, THE LARGEST SHARK THAT EVER LIVED."**

Englewood, FL | **Season:** Year-round

You'll find loads of beachcombing treasures at Stump Pass Beach State Park, from prehistoric shark teeth to shells.

Airboat through Eagle Bay for a chance to spot Florida's unique wildlife.

Air of Adventure

Airboats are built for adventure. With flat bottoms and powerful airplane engines, they can blast through walls of marsh grass and skim the shallowest waterways, impassable by boats with submerged propellers. Their sleek design gives them (and you) unfettered access to some of the most remote areas in Florida's Everglades. (Just try to forget they don't have brakes.)

Though most people think of southern Florida when they think of the Everglades, its headwaters, Lake Okeechobee in the center of the state, offer an equally rewarding, ecologically rich experience. Fondly known as the "Big O," Okeechobee is the state's largest freshwater lake and home to lesser known Eagle Bay and Lemkin Creek at the northern end. Book a tour with Eagle Bay

Adventures for a thrilling ride into the heart of Eagle Bay's marshlands and down cypress-lined Lemkin Creek.

Because the airboat's engine creates a thunderous roar, you'll wear noise-canceling earmuffs while on board, creating a tranquil journey as you glide over fields of water lilies and carve new paths through dense reeds.

Little blue dragonflies, known as blue dashers, lead the way down Lemkin Creek, skimming its glassy surface like winged tour guides, zipping past a hobbling of chocolate brown limpkins taking cover in cypress trees. Don't be surprised if you see cows from a neighboring farm standing shoulder-deep in cool swamp water, enjoying a patch of shade.

When the boat slows, search the shallows for bluegill, sunfish, orangish oscar, longnose gar, and everyone's favorite, the American alligator.

Okeechobee, FL | Season: Year-round

American alligators sun themselves on the shore.

Not for the Faint of Heart

At Myakka River, you can't miss the alligator warning signs at Snook Haven's boat launch. And it's not uncommon to be greeted by a passing 10-footer as you push off into the dark water.

Though these intimidating predators should be given space, they need not be feared . . . too much. Most will ignore you as you pass. The camera-shy will disappear beneath the surface, sending a tingle down your spine.

If paddling is too close for comfort, book a one-hour narrated tour with Logan River Tours, which operates from November through May, to learn about the Hollywood jungle films shot here and the Prohibition-era moonshine smugglers that once frequented these waterways.

Snook Haven offers canoe and kayak rentals daily from 9 a.m. to 5 p.m.

Venice, FL | **Season:** Year-round

Swim With Horses

Go horseback riding—Florida style. Trade hard trails for soft surf and swim across Palma Sola Bay on horseback as dolphins play beside you.

C Ponies, a local horse rescue and tour operator, adopts abandoned and neglected Drum and Gypsy Vanner horses and uses the Gulf of Mexico to rehabilitate their injuries and heal their souls. Once the horses have completed their training, which can take up to four months, they become C Ponies and are ready to work with people.

Mounted guides provide safety instruction before each tour and take photos during your ride that are available for purchase afterward. You'll quickly get to know each horse's personality—like Coral, the youngest of the group, who likes to dip her nose in the water and blow bubbles.

Depending on the tide, the horses will swim across sections of Palma Sola Bay. You'll grab hold of their manes (it doesn't hurt them) as their hooves leave the ground and they soar through the water. Don't forget to look around. Palma Sola Bay is a habitat for manatees, dolphins, wading birds, and fish, so there's always something interesting to see.

For a different experience—one perfect for romantic adventurers—consider booking the sunset ride, where you'll embark on a 90-minute ride to watch the setting sun turn the sky—and reflecting waters—various shades of pink and orange. This is also a good time to have a manatee or dolphin sighting when they come out for an evening feed.

The horses are never forced to work or swim, as evidenced by their calm demeanor, and they appreciate it when riders bring them carrots to reward a job well done.

Beach-only rides with no swimming are available north in St. Petersburg. Trail rides are available northeast at Alafia River State Park in Lithia or south at Deer Prairie Creek Preserve in Venice.

Bradenton, FL | **Season:** Year-round

Although Everglades National Park is known for its waterways, cycling paths offer unique views.

A Wild Ride

🐾 You'll feel you like you've stepped inside a wildlife magazine on the Shark Valley's Tram Road, a 15-mile (24 km) paved loop in the heart of Everglades National Park. You won't see sharks (the trail is named after nearby Shark River), but you will see plenty of alligators and other native species.

Whether you bike or walk the trail, go during dry season, November through March, for the best wildlife viewing and most comfortable temperatures. You'll find anhingas drying their onyx feathers on tree branches, herons and egrets stalking through saw grass, turtles sunbathing on logs, gators napping in the grass (or in the middle of the path), and so much more. An observation tower at the halfway point offers a bird's-eye view of the "River of Grass."

Bike rentals are available at the concessionaire. Or book a seat on the tram for a two-hour tour narrated by a park-trained naturalist.

Miami, FL | **Season:** November to March

Seven Mile Bridge connects Florida's Middle Keys to the Lower Keys.

1. SWIM WITH MANATEES

From mid-November to late March, Crystal River and its headwaters, Kings Bay, become a winter refuge for threatened West Indian manatees looking to trade the cold Gulf for warmer, spring-fed water. Hire a local guide, like River Ventures, to swim alongside these gentle "sea cows" and observe them in their natural habitat.

2. DIVE THE DEVIL'S DEN

Set inside a prehistoric cave, Devil's Den is home to a spring-fed subterranean river. Sunlight pours in through a moss-covered karst window overhead, illuminating the water so snorkelers and scuba divers can explore the cavern's limestone walls and ledges, where bluegill fish and turtles love to hide. Cave-certified divers can go deeper into the underwater cave system.

3. LAZE IN THE BLAZE

Beat the Florida heat with a float down a natural lazy river beneath a shady canopy. Eight springs feed the six-mile (10 km) Ichetucknee River, creating clear, 72°F (22°C) waters. The park offers tube rentals, tram service, and two launch points for floats that last from 45 minutes to two hours.

4. TAKE A CRAIGCAT RIDE IN OLD FLORIDA

If a personal watercraft and a catamaran had a baby, you'd get a CraigCat. Gas-powered and built for two, it's perfect for zipping across Lake Dora and exploring a slice of Old Florida jungle on the Dora Canal. CatBoat Adventures

offers two-hour narrated tours. No boating experience is required.

5. GET LOST IN LAKE OKEECHOBEE

Bordering the state's largest freshwater lake, Lake Okeechobee Scenic Trail is a 109-mile (175 km) multiuse recreation trail that spans five counties, offering a tranquil place to bike, hike, or jog, especially at sunrise or sunset. Although there are more than a dozen access points, there's no shade, so bring water and sunscreen.

6. VIEW WILDLIFE ON THE MARSH

Mix and match six trails to explore Brooker Creek Preserve in Tarpon Springs. Interpretive signs guide you through forested wetlands, oak hammocks, pine flatwoods, and cypress swamps, revealing the hidden mysteries of their enchanting ecosystems. Take Bird Path to a viewing blind overlooking a freshwater marsh inhabited by 159 species of birds. Free entry.

7. MAKE YOUR WAY TO TEN THOUSAND ISLANDS

To cast a line in the westernmost Everglades is to fish like the Calusa once did. Launch a fishing kayak from the Gulf Coast Visitor Center and paddle across Chokoloskee Bay to the Ten Thousand Islands, where something is biting year-round, including tarpon, snook, redfish, sea trout, and mangrove snapper. A state saltwater fishing license is required.

8. PADDLE THE GREAT CALUSA BLUEWAY

Paddle to the 2,000-year-old Calusa cultural center on Mound Key. Venture down secluded mangrove trails in Pine Island Sound. Explore the creeks and coves of the Caloosahatchee. Camp at Cayo Costa State Park, Picnic Island, or Caloosahatchee Regional Park. These are among the many adventures you'll find along the 190-mile (305 km) Great Calusa Blueway.

9. CRUISE IN KEY LARGO

To cover the most distance around Florida's largest key, rent a watercraft and explore the natural side of Key Largo. Head to John Pennekamp Coral Reef State Park on the northeastern side of the island. It's the country's first undersea park and home to an expansive network of mangrove trails.

10. RIDE THE OVERSEAS HERITAGE TRAIL

Arguably the most scenic bike ride in the state, the Overseas Heritage Trail is a 90-mile (145 km) rail trail that flanks the Overseas Highway from Key Largo to Key West. Park at Knight's Key (mm 47) and ride the old Seven Mile Bridge 2.2 miles (3.5 km) to historic Pigeon Key to see where the railway workers once lived.

Orange blossom

Autumn colors consume
Cloudland Canyon (page 143)
at dusk.

GEORGIA

You'll find peachy keen ways to spend your days
in this haven of parks, lakes, and shorelines.

TENNESSEE

NORTH CAROLINA

Rock City

Blue Ridge
Lake

Lake Chatuge
Recreation Area

Willis Knob
Horse Camp

Cloudland Canyon
State Park

Tallulah Gorge
State Park

Springer
Mountain

Amicalola Falls
State Park

Silver Comet
Trail

Kennesaw Mountain
National Battlefield Park

SOUTH
CAROLINA

Sweetwater Creek
State Park

Stone Mountain
Park

High Falls
State Park

GEORGIA

ALABAMA

Ebenezer
Creek

Providence Canyon
State Park

Skidaway Island
State Park

Fort King George
State Historic Site

Marshes of
Glynn

ATLANTIC OCEAN

Jekyll Island

Okefenokee National
Wildlife Refuge

FLORIDA

Providence Canyon State Park offers one-of-a-kind views and colors in its "Little Grand Canyon."

Grand Camping in the Lesser Known Grand Canyon

You don't need to travel to Arizona to see a grand canyon. In southwestern Georgia, Providence Canyon is a natural wonder born of a natural disaster. Deforestation and poor soil management practices of the early 1800s set the stage for rainwater runoff from nearby cotton fields to erode the soft earth. Small gullies became deep ditches and eventually carved 16 canyons into the landscape, exposing colorful sands and minerals deposited by ancient seas.

You can peer over the edge of these rust-colored crevices from the 2.4-mile (3.9 km) Canyon Loop Trail that traces the canyon rim. To fully appreciate its grandeur, hike down to the canyon floor and follow the black trail to wander through a labyrinth of towering pinnacles

to nine different canyons. Pink, green, and purple striations hint at the 80-million-year-old history encased within these ever changing walls.

For the full canyon experience, spend the night (or several) sleeping beneath the stars. Follow the red trail southwest along the stream to six backcountry campsites scattered throughout the forest. These tent sites can accommodate up to 10 people for 14 nights. Dogs are allowed. Only a fire ring is provided, so you'll need to pack in/pack out all your supplies. All sites require at least a two-mile (3.2 km) hike in, so carefully consider the weight you pack in. And be sure to wear waterproof footwear, as sections of the trail may be wet.

Two pioneer sites are also available and include an open shelter, barbecue, fire ring, two picnic tables, pit privy, and parking.

Lumpkin, GA   Season: Year-round

Zip-line across Amicalola Falls.

Practice Your Survival Skills

It's nearly impossible to get bored at Amicalola Falls State Park and Lodge. On any given day, you can soar through the Chattahoochee canopy at the aerial adventure park, choosing from three zip-line courses. Test your aim at the outdoor archery range, where you'll learn how to use a compound bow and practice shooting 3D targets. Hunt for hidden treasures using a handheld GPS device to scavenge the woods for eight mountainside coordinates. Hone your fire-building skills and learn primitive camping techniques at Survivalist Camp.

Whatever you do, don't miss Amicalola Falls, the tallest waterfall in the state. Follow the Creek Trail up a series of wooden staircases and walkways to feel the mist on your face and enjoy VIP views. It's 600 steps to the top, but the payoff is a stunning vista across miles of rolling hills.

Dawsonville, GA | **Season:** Year-round

A Black-Water Beauty

At Ebenezer Creek, 1,000-year-old bald cypress trees rise from the black water, their buttressed trunks and stumplike "knees" providing stability, and the creek's calm surface mirroring the Spanish moss and resurrection ferns cradled in their branches.

The National Park Service designated Ebenezer Creek a national natural landmark, and the state named it a Georgia Wild and Scenic River, illustrating the beauty and value of this unspoiled environment. To access this otherworldly paradise, launch a kayak at the Tommy Long Boat Ramp and head north. If the water level is high, you can gently weave your boat through the bottomland forests for a rare view of old growth.

Paddle slowly, allowing Ebenezer to reveal itself. Watch for black- and white-winged wood storks sailing above the canopy or bright yellow prothonotary warblers flitting across your path in a teasing game of hide-and-seek.

Rincon, GA | **Season:** Spring to fall

Giant ancient cypresses dot the waters of Ebenezer Creek.

Hike to the summit of Blood Mountain for sweeping views of Chattahoochee National Forest.

Hike the Appalachian Trail for a Day

Every year, between March 1 and April 15, thousands of hikers arrive at Springer Mountain's summit to test their endurance on the Appalachian Trail (AT), hoping to complete all 2,190 miles (3,525 km) and make it to Mount Katahdin in Maine by fall.

You don't have to be a thru-hiker to tackle the AT. You can follow in their footsteps by hiking the 8.8-mile (14 km) AT Approach, which begins at Amicalola Falls State Park, home to the state's tallest waterfall, and ends at the AT's southern terminus on Springer Mountain.

A scenic alternative is the 4.1-mile (6.6 km) Benton MacKaye Springer Mountain Loop. Access the trailhead via a long, bumpy drive down Forest Service Road 42. Where the Benton MacKaye and Appalachian Trails intersect, a short detour south leads to the famous Georgia AT Club plaque at the southern terminus, where thru-hikers may be beginning (or ending) their journeys.

Benton, GA **Season:** Spring to fall

"TWISTED REMAINS OF AN ANCIENT MARITIME FOREST LINE THE SHORE."

Jekyll and Ride

Once an exclusive winter playground for the rich and famous, today Jekyll Island has a laid-back vibe that welcomes everyone to explore its history and charm.

The best way to see it is to bike it—via the 14.8-mile (23.8 km) loop around the island. Park for free at Ocean-view Beach Park and pedal north to Driftwood Beach, where twisted remains of an ancient maritime forest line the shore. A colorful sunset makes it a romantic backdrop, while overcast gray transforms it into a haunted boneyard.

Go during low or outgoing tide when the compressed sand makes for easy riding and the surf is strewn with treasures from the deep, like starfish, sand dollars, and hermit crabs. Rejoin the bike path near Clam Creek fishing pier and wind beneath towering oaks until you spot the tabby remains of Horton House, one of the oldest surviving buildings in Georgia, dating back to 1743.

Past the airport, you'll find Jekyll Island Club National Historic Landmark District, where the winter estates of the nation's most prominent families are preserved. At its heart is the sprawling Jekyll Island Club with its famous turret and even more famous members—the Morgans, Rockefellers, Vanderbilts, and the like. "Club season" was January through April, and although intended for relaxation and sport, many history-shaping achievements happened here, like the drafting of the federal banking system in 1910.

Follow the trail south to St. Andrews Park, where the Wanderer Memory Trail recounts the history of America's last known slave ship, the *Wanderer*, which illegally smuggled 409 West African captives to these shores in 1858.

If tide permits, ride back on the beach and exit via ramp #38 to access Beach Village's shops and restaurants. The trail flanks the beach and eventually returns you to your car.

Jekyll Island, GA | **Season:** Spring to fall

The historic Jekyll Island Club, now a hotel, was once a vacation retreat for the American elite.

The Call of the Wild

🦆 Tidal estuaries, salt marshes, maritime forests—with habitats as diverse as these, it's no surprise that Skidaway Island State Park is one of 17 prime bird-watching sites on Georgia's Colonial Coast Birding Trail.

Grab your binoculars and checklist (available online) and take the one-mile (1.6 km) Sandpiper Trail Loop through a salt marsh, where you might glimpse an elusive clapper rail or marsh wren hiding in the cattails. Halfway through, pick up and follow the one-mile (1.6 km) Avian Loop Trail out to Skidaway Narrows, a tidal creek where feathered beauties, like yellow-crowned night herons and black-necked stilts, forage for crabs. Don't forget to look up. Painted buntings love high perches. And with their brilliant splashes of red, blue, green, and yellow, they're a popular chase.

No two visits to Skidaway are the same. Each day has its own rhythm, and new species arrive and depart with the changing seasons and shifting tides.

Savannah, GA | **Season:** Year-round

A red-bellied woodpecker makes work of a pine tree.

Into the Blue

⛵ Once called "Switzerland of the South," the town of Blue Ridge, in northern Georgia, has it all—mountains, lakes, and four seasons all within an hour-and-a-half drive of Atlanta.

At the heart of it all is Lake Blue Ridge, technically a reservoir, courtesy of the eponymous dam at the northern end. Chattahoochee National Forest hugs most of its 60-mile (97 km) shoreline, creating a tranquil mountain lake.

To get on the water, rent a pontoon boat from Lake Blue Ridge Marina on the northwestern shore and cruise from end to end, about 11 miles (18 km), or add a splash of fun by towing a tube. Paddlecraft are also available and perfect for exploring countless coves and inlets along the jagged shoreline.

Because Lake Blue Ridge is one of the few lakes in Georgia with smallmouth bass, it's a sought-after fishing destination. Hire a local guide to learn the best spots and techniques for catching them. Largemouth bass, bluegill, and walleye are also common in these pristine waters.

On the northeastern shore, Morganton Point Recreation Area has a family-friendly pebble-sand beach with a swimming area and nearby conveniences like concessions, restrooms, showers, a picnic pavilion, boat ramp, and kayak and paddleboard rentals. It is the only spot on the shoreline with a campground, offering more than 40 sites for tent campers and RVers.

The outflowing Toccoa River, at the northern end of the lake, is a hot spot for kayakers, especially during seasonal dam releases, which create Class I to II rapids for several miles downstream. The Toccoa River Canoe Trail stretches 13.8 miles (22.2 km) from Deep Hole to Sandy Bottoms and offers stunning views of rhododendron thickets and wildlife, as well as prime fishing spots.

Blue Ridge, GA | **Season:** Late spring to early fall

Yurt Camp, Bike, and Hike

One of the oldest shelters used by ancient civilizations, yurts are popping up—literally—as a modern-day glamping option at parks across the country. With a sturdy wooden frame, insulating canvas walls, and round shape, they are designed to withstand wind and harsh climates. Compared to other lodging options, a yurt falls somewhere between a tent and a cabin, keeping you close to nature with some comforts of home.

Yurt Village, in the center of Cloudland Canyon State Park, offers 10 furnished yurts that sleep up to six people and have heating/air-conditioning, hardwood floors, a futon/bunk bed, couch, small dining table, outdoor deck, and nearby fire pit and picnic table. They are a comfortable, convenient jumping-off point for exploring Georgia's deepest canyon and surrounding state park.

Simply walk out your front door and pick up the West Rim Loop, a five-mile (8 km) loop and top-rated day hike in the United States, with sweeping canyon views.

Southeast of Yurt Village, you'll find the aptly named Waterfalls Trail, a strenuous (but totally worth it) 1.8-mile (2.9 km) out-and-back that descends into the thousand-foot (305 m) canyon via a 600-step metal staircase. It delivers on its name with up-close views of Cherokee and Hemlock Falls.

For mountain biking and horse-riding trails, head to the park's southern end and pick up the Cloudland Connector Trail, a 14-mile (23 km) multiuse path. It connects to Five Points Recreation Area, a network of single-track mountain bike trails ranging from moderate to technical with jumps. The purpose-built trails, opened in 2011, wind through a revegetated coal mine that was active from 1850 to 1922.

Rising Fawn, GA | Season: Spring to fall

Climbs and Currents

One of the most scenic canyons in the eastern United States, Tallulah Gorge is a climber's paradise. Two miles long (3.2 km) and 1,000 feet deep (305 m), this quartzite canyon has multi-pitch and mixed-aid traditional routes best suited to experienced climbers. A south-facing crag, its conditions are best in spring or fall, but check the park's website for closures.

Down below, experienced kayakers run Tallulah River's raging rapids. Dam releases during the first two weekends in April and first three weekends in November supercharge the current to Class V. Launch below Hurricane Falls.

If death-defying climbs and currents aren't your jam, get one of 100 free daily permits to access the gorge floor. Hike the boulder-strewn river trail to Bridal Veil Falls (aka Sliding Rock) and slide down the smooth rock face into the refreshing pool below.

Kayakers enjoy a high release day on the Toccoa River.

Tallulah Falls, GA | Season: Spring to fall

Enjoy the ethereal
scenery as you paddle
the Okefenokee Swamp.

> "TOUR THE VAST MARSH COVERED IN WATER LILIES AND GOLDEN CLUB."

Find Refuge in the Wetlands

Southern Georgia is home to the largest blackwater swamp in North America. A national natural landmark, Okefenokee Swamp spans more than 400,000 acres (161,870 ha) and provides diverse habitats for hundreds of species.

There are countless ways to explore the swamp's beauty and biodiversity. At the main entrance, in Folkston, you'll find Okefenokee Adventures. Take a 90-minute narrated tour down the serene, cypress-lined Suwanee Canal to the Chesser Prairie, a vast marsh covered in water lilies and golden club. You'll see examples of peat batteries (small peat islands) that tremble when you jump on them, which inspired native Choctaw to name this place Okefenokee, or "Land of Trembling Earth."

At the northern entrance, in Waycross, you'll find Okefenokee Swamp Park. Sign up for the "3-Hour Swamp Experience," a unique boat/train/nature show combo. You'll boat through narrow Seminole waterways as your guide points out popular alligator caves. You'll board the *Lady Suwannee* for a 1.5-mile (2.4 km) train ride through the wetlands. It stops at Pioneer Island, where you'll visit a re-created homestead and the Wilde's Cabin Museum, a tribute to the family that was massacred here during the Second Seminole War. The "Eye on Nature" program will introduce you to the swamp's snakes and gators (literally).

At the western entrance, in Fargo, is Stephen Foster State Park. Rent a kayak or johnboat to explore 15 miles (24 km) of day-use trails. Head east to Billy's Island to visit a former cypress logging camp once inhabited by several hundred residents and an overwater railroad that transported timber.

Folkston, GA | **Season:** Year-round

See the cascade views from Lover's Leap in Rock City Gardens on Lookout Mountain.

LOVER'S LEAP

1. FIND MAGIC IN ROCK CITY GARDENS

High atop Lookout Mountain, a storybook village of gnomes, fairyland caverns, and lush gardens has sprung up as if by magic between massive prehistoric boulders. Cross Swing-A-Long Bridge to Lover's Leap to see seven states at once. Sit beneath a 1,000-ton balanced rock and stop at Observation Point to marvel at the waterfall.

2. BLAZE THE SILVER COMET TRAIL

Blaze across northwestern Georgia on a 61.5-mile (99 km) fully accessible paved path on the former rail bed of the Silver Comet passenger train. Start at Coot's Lake Trailhead in Rockmart and ride east through forests, fields, and prehistoric rock formations to the 800-foot-long (240 m) historic Brushy Mountain Tunnel.

3. VISIT KENNESAW MOUNTAIN NATIONAL BATTLEFIELD

Travel back to 1864 and relive Major General Sherman's Union frontal assault against the Confederate Army of Tennessee. Twenty-two miles (35 km) of trails highlight the 24-Gun Battery that bombarded Confederate forces for 10 days, Confederate entrenchments on Pigeon Hill, and the "Dead Angle" defensive line at Cheatham Hill. Cannon and musket firing demonstrations are offered on peak weekends.

4. UNEARTH SOME FUN

At one of the largest granite formations in the eastern United States, just outside Atlanta, hike to Stone Mountain's summit via the one-mile (1.6 km) Walk-Up Trail or follow the five-mile (8 km) Cherokee Trail around its base. The Songbird Habitat Trail or Nature Gardens make scenic side trips.

5. PADDLE AND HIKE A PENINSULA

Sitting on the Georgia-North Carolina border, Lake Chatuge is surrounded by the Appalachian Mountains. Its 132-mile (212 km) shoreline invites you to paddle its coves, drop a line, or pitch a tent along the water's edge. Don't miss the scenic two-mile (3.2 km) peninsula hike at Lake Chatuge Recreation Area.

6. EXPERIENCE WILD AND SCENIC

Equestrians can camp with their four-legged companions in the North Georgia Mountains at Willis Knob Horse Camp in Clayton. You'll find everything you need, from equine-friendly campsites with water and electric hookups to scenic rides. Try Willis Knob Horse Trail, a 15-mile (24 km) loop in the Chattooga Wild and Scenic River corridor.

7. FALL FOR HIGH FALLS

Sunrise over High Falls electrifies the morning mist and sets the world aglow. You can recharge at this former power plant by starting your day with a peaceful paddle on High Falls Lake or a riverside trail run on the 1.1-mile (1.8 km) High Falls Loop Trail. For full effect, spend the night in a quiet lakeside yurt.

8. STEP INTO HISTORY

Built in 1721, Fort King George is the oldest remaining English fort on Georgia's coast. To learn what life was like, take a tour led by a redcoat soldier or attend a musket firing or metalworking demonstration. Primitive campouts on the bluff are available for groups and include a 30-minute nighttime walk to the fort.

9. CATCH THE CATCH OF THE DAY

Step aboard an authentic shrimp boat in Brunswick, with Coastal Tide Excursions, to learn how to trawl Glynn County's marshes for Georgia's most valuable seafood crop. All catch will be displayed in shallow tanks so the onboard marine naturalist can explain the different species of fish that live in this protected estuary.

10. SEE WHAT'S BITING AT SWEETWATER

For a sweet escape from bustling Atlanta, rent an aquabike to explore East Point Reservoir at Sweetwater Creek State Park, or cast a line to see if the bass are biting. Nearby hiking trails link hardwood forests, white-water creek, and the towering remains of the New Manchester Mill brick factory, where scenes from *The Hunger Games: Mockingjay—Part 1* were filmed.

Diamond Head, a volcanic cone, stands tall over the coast of Oahu.

HAWAII

You won't be wanting for adventure on the islands of Hawaii, which promise surf and sand among other ocean treasures.

Nāpali Coast State Wilderness Park

Waimea Canyon State Park

Wailua River

Ni'ihau

H

Kuale Ranc

Waikīkī

P A C I F I C

O C E A N

"HAWAII IS A PARADISE
BORN OF FIRE."
—RAND McNALLY

PACIFIC OCEAN

Moloka'i

Kapalua
Ziplines

Kā'anapali

Ho'okipa
Beach Park

Lāna'i

Ka'eleku Cave
(Hana Lava Tube)

Maalaea
Bay

Lāna'i
Cathedrals

Haleakalā
National Park

Waioka
Pond

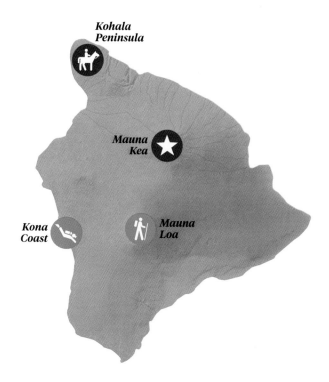

Kohala
Peninsula

Mauna
Kea

Kona
Coast

Mauna
Loa

Manta Ray Rendezvous

Have you ever looked a manta ray in the eye and felt a preternatural, cross-species connection? That's the ultimate thrill of snorkeling or scuba diving with the graceful creatures off the Kona coast.

This close encounter between humans and rays started in the 1970s, when a resort hotel on Keauhou Bay installed floodlights so guests could view the surf at night. The lights lured plankton, which in turn attracted plankton-eating *Mobula birostris*. It wasn't long before people were leaping into the bay to swim with them.

Using double-hulled canoes rather than motorized boats, Anelakai Adventures is the most eco-friendly of the outfitters offering manta ray encounters along the Kona coast. Slipping into the water, snorkelers clutch handlebars fixed to the bottom of a canoe and watch the creatures glide and somersault through the water as they draw plankton into their huge mouths—sometimes coming close enough for a look straight in the eye.

Kailua-Kona, HI   Season: Year-round

The Kona coast offers big coral and big fish for divers and snorkelers.

Trek Along an Active Volcano

From its underwater base beneath the Pacific Ocean to its sky-high summit above the Big Island, Mauna Loa is actually taller than Mount Everest—an astonishing 30,000 feet (9,144 m) from top to bottom. It's also the world's largest active volcano.

Mauna Loa is the largest subaerial volcano on Earth.

The name gives a hint to the trekking conditions. Mauna Loa means "Long Mountain" in the Hawaiian language. Reaching the summit is mostly a matter of walking across long, gently rising slopes rather than dreaded switchbacks. To answer the most obvious question: Mauna Loa erupted in November 2022—volcanic activity stopped in early 2023.

There are two ways to reach the top. From the end of Mauna Loa Road in Hawai'i Volcanoes National Park, it's just over 19 miles (31 km) to the summit with a total elevation gain of around 7,300 feet (2,225 m). From Mauna Loa Observatory on the northern flank, it's 12.3 miles (19.8 km) with an elevation gain of around 3,000 feet (910 m).

Pu'u Ula'ula (Red Hill) Cabin and Summit Cabin are the only overnight options on the mountain; national park backcountry permits are required for staying at both.

Waimea, HI   Season: Spring and summer

Camp Along Hawaii's Emerald Coast

With rust-colored and jungle-shrouded walls rising nearly straight up from the ocean, it's easy to see why ancient Hawaiians decided the stunning north shore of Kauai should be called Nā Pali ("The Cliffs").

Thank goodness, this is one part of the Hawaiian Islands that will never have resorts or fancy vacation rentals. The only way to experience the Nā Pali over multiple days is camping on remote beaches or lava-rock farming terraces built by the Native Hawaiians who lived along the coast until the early 20th century.

The only way to reach the overnight spots is hiking the rugged, 11-mile (18 km) Kalalau Trail along the cliff tops or paddling along the coast to places where it's safe to beach.

Hanakoa Campground lies beside a freshwater stream in a lush tropical valley about halfway along the trail. There's an outhouse and plenty of shade on a side trail leading to a waterfall with a swimming hole at the bottom. However, the towering cliffs make it impossible to reach the ocean from Hanakoa.

On the other hand, Kalalau Campground at the end of the trail is tucked into trees right behind the beach. Once again, there's freshwater and an outhouse, as well as side trails that rise into the mile-wide (1.6 km) Kalalau Valley. Farther west along the coast, Miloli'i Beach is only accessible by boat and is a popular place for kayak camping.

A camping permit from Hawaii State Parks is mandatory for all overnight stays. Although you may be tempted to linger for weeks, camping is restricted to five nights along the Kalalau Trail and three nights at Miloli'i Beach.

Kauai, HI | **Season:** May to October

Tour Movie History

Drive a speedy Raptor ATV across the primeval terrain on the backside of Oahu, where cinematic raptors once roamed. More than 300 movies and television shows have been filmed on Kualoa Ranch since the 1940s, including key scenes from *Jurassic Park*.

Participants pilot their own vehicles around a network of dirt trails and roads through the lush Hakipu'u and Ka'a'awa Valleys. There are plenty of chances to get wet while speeding across jungle streams.

Kualoa offers more than a dozen other outdoor adventures ranging from zip-lining, horseback riding, and mountain biking to a catamaran voyage and an immersive "malama experience" harvesting taro plants.

In addition to various film locations—*Jumanji, 50 First Dates*, and *Pearl Harbor* were also shot here—ATV tours include a sprawling WWII bunker with wartime artifacts.

Ride ATVs through Kualoa Ranch to see movie film sites on Oahu.

Kaneohe, HI | **Season:** Year-round

Horseback ride around
Kohala Mountain on the
Big Island.

> "THE KOHALA PENINSULA HAS ALWAYS BEEN THE HEART OF HAWAIIAN CATTLE COUNTRY."

Live Like a Cowboy

The quirky story of Hawaiian cattle ranching begins in 1793, when British sea captain George Vancouver landed eight cows on the Big Island. King Kamehameha placed a taboo on the slaughter of the previously unknown beasts and they were allowed to roam free. By the 1830s when the taboo was removed, the bovine population had exploded and vaqueros came from Mexico to round up the feral herds and teach Native Hawaiians the basics of riding and roping.

Nearly 200 years later, that legacy has evolved into one of the Big Island's unexpected adventures: riding the range with local *paniolo* (cowboys and cowgirls). The Kohala Peninsula near the island's northern tip has always been the heart of Hawaiian cattle country as well as one of the few places in the islands that looks decidedly un-Hawaiian. Forget black-sand beaches and tropical rainforest. The Kohala's grassy, windswept highlands look more like Scotland than anything one expects to find in Polynesia.

Most of the spreads that raise beef and dairy cows—and that offer trail rides and other equestrian activities—are located around the town of Waimea. Na'alapa Stables at Kahua Ranch offers several horseback options, including rides across the open range and around volcanic cinder cones on the 12,000-acre (4,860 ha) spread and Waipi'o Valley rides along jungle trails. Rather than nose to tail (horses strictly following one another), riders are free to trot or canter.

Back in town, the Paniolo Heritage Center at historic Parker Ranch spins tales of the paniolo and female *pa'u* riders. It's thought the name paniolo derives from the language of the Mexican vaqueros who came to Hawaii. Those same vaqueros also brought and taught guitar to the local cowboys, who composed unique Western-style paniolo songs about life on the Hawaiian range.

Waimea, HI | **Season:** Year-round

Gutsy Climbs, Epic Walls, and Deep Canyons

The lower slopes of Haleakalā volcano in East Maui are hung with waterfalls and dense vegetation and cleaved by scores of deep canyons—which means ideal terrain for rappelling, canyoning, rock climbing, and other vertiginous sports that require helmets, harnesses, ropes, carabiners, and a good amount of hutzpah.

Local climbers carefully guard the location of some of their favorite spots. But some of the most epic walls are already well known—like Venus Pond or Waioka Pond off the coast road between Hana and Kipahulu.

Given East Maui's remote and rugged terrain, hiring a local guide or booking a canyon excursion with an experienced outfitter is highly recommended over trying to conquer these vertical surfaces on your own. Rappel Maui offers a group tour that revolves around a classic drop down a jungle waterfall as well as private tours for more experienced climbers that feature a greater degree of difficulty at a more remote location.

> "LOCAL CLIMBERS CAREFULLY GUARD THE LOCATION OF SOME OF THEIR FAVORITE SPOTS. BUT SOME OF THE MOST EPIC WALLS ARE ALREADY WELL KNOWN."

Maui, HI | **Season:** Year-round

Waterfalls and the Seven Sacred Pools await visitors on the southern end of Haleakalā National Park.

On a cycle down the slopes of Haleakalā, you'll descend 6,500 feet (1,980 m) and at times be above the clouds.

Bike a Volcano

Cycling *up* a volcano is one thing, only for the ultra-fit. Cycling *down* a volcano is quite another, an outdoor adventure that can be relished by just about anyone. Haleakalā on Maui and Kilauea on the Big Island lend their slopes to the state's best volcano rides.

The Haleakalā downhill starts at around 6,500 feet (1,980 m) near Haleakalā National Park and finishes in Paia town on Maui's north shore. Between are 27 miles (43 km) of road biking through the forests, farmland, and flower gardens of up-country Maui. The ride kicks off in spectacular fashion with a series of switchbacks and hairpin turns along Crater Road before leveling off along Highway 377 through an area flush with tropical vegetation. Historic Makawao village offers trendy eateries, art galleries, and fashion boutiques before the final leg into Paia, an old sugarcane town on the Hana Highway, where riders can cool down with a shave ice.

Maui, HI   Season: Year-round

Over on the big island, bikers can undertake a 21-mile (34 km) ride in Hawai'i Volcanoes National Park between the visitors center and the Pacific coast. Multiuse hiking/biking trails are vehicle-free routes around the edge of smoldering Kilauea volcano, while Chain of Craters Road provides a spectacular descent through the lava-ravished wilderness to Hōlei Sea Arch at the end of the paved highway.

Independent-minded cyclists can ride on their own, and bike rentals are available. Guided downhill rides are available through outfitters like Maui Sunriders and Bike Volcano. Guided rides usually include snack breaks and breakfast or lunch and are self-paced, which means riders can choose their speed and stop whenever they like.

Yellow hibiscus

Night Lights

⭐ The crest of Hawaii's highest peak (13,803 feet/ 4,207 m) offers a heavenly place to watch sunset over the Pacific and the billions of stars that sparkle after dark. Given its lofty altitude, impeccably clear air, and almost a total lack of cloud cover and ambient light—not to mention much less oxygen than at sea level—the view from Mauna Kea is always breathtaking.

Visitors can reach the summit in their own four-wheel-drive vehicle, by joining a guided tour, or hiking a steep six-mile (10 km) trail that starts from the Visitor Information Station (VIS). No matter which method you choose, be sure to acclimate yourself to the altitude by pausing at the VIS before continuing to the top.

Because the summit road closes half an hour after dark, the VIS is also the place for a popular nightly stargazing program organized by the adjacent Onizuka Center for International Astronomy (Hale Pōhaku).

Hilo, HI | Season: Year-round

See the Milky Way in the clear skies above Mauna Kea.

Road-Tripping in Lanai

🚴 Privately owned since the late 19th century, Lanai has morphed from the world's largest pineapple producer into a sprawling, privately owned nature reserve with a quaint village, a single resort, and an adventurous road network best explored by four-wheel drive.

Every 4x4 foray across the island should include several iconic stops. Shipwreck Beach on the north shore gets its name from the rusty hulk of a U.S. Navy fuel barge that beached right after World War II. But a stroll along the eight-mile (13 km) beach also reveals ancient Hawaiian petroglyphs. Near the island's highest point, the boulder-strewn Garden of the Gods offers views across the water to Maui and Molokai. And no one should miss the excellent Lanai Culture and Heritage Center (ask the curator to speak a few lines of Native Hawaiian).

Road-trippers spending multiple days can also reach uber-remote Polihua Beach on the island's northwest side and the lofty Pali Kaholo cliffs, which rise nearly 900 feet (275 m) straight up from the sea. Perched along the palisades is the Kaunolu archaeological park, which preserves 160 structures at Hawaii's largest surviving ancient village site. The road to the ruins also features the quirky Lanai Cat Sanctuary, where hundreds of feral felines live out their days without threatening indigenous wildlife.

Lanai Jeep & Truck rents Wrangler and Gladiator 4x4s that can be delivered to vacation rentals in Lanai City, either of the island's two hotels, or Manele Bay ferry pier to meet passenger boats arriving from Maui.

Lanai, HI | Season: Year-round

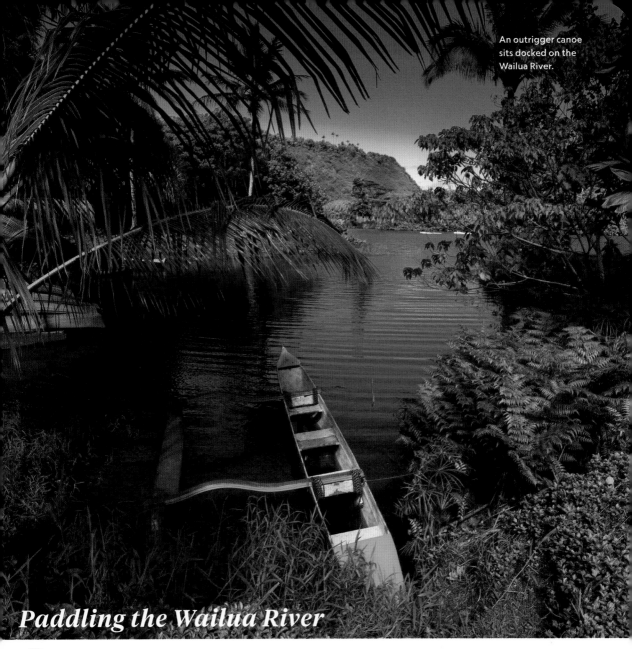

An outrigger canoe sits docked on the Wailua River.

Paddling the Wailua River

The Wailua River tumbles down from the Kauai highlands on a meandering 20-mile (32 km) journey to its rendezvous with the sea along the island's east coast. With much of its watershed protected in nature preserves, the river offers the state's best freshwater canoeing, kayaking, and paddleboarding.

With giant rainforest trees shading much of the river and its tributaries, the paddle feels like a journey into an ancient primeval jungle. Scattered along the banks are ancient religious sites (heiau) and other archaeological relics, dating from the 18th and early 19th centuries when the lower Wailua Valley was a bastion of royal power under King Kaumuali'i and his predecessors.

Just upstream from Kamokila village, the river splits into two branches. The South Fork continues to Fern Grotto and 140-foot (40 m) Wailua Falls. The longer North Fork flows through the backwoods of Wailua River State Park to the foothills of Mount Waialeale, the rainiest place on Earth.

Kapa'a, HI   Season: Year-round

Waikiki Beach is a popular spot for sunbathers and swimmers.

1. SWIM WITH SEA TURTLES

The coral garland around little-visited Molokai—the longest continuous fringing reef in the Hawaiian Islands at 28 miles (45 km)—offers safe harbor to hundreds of green and hawksbill sea turtles. Watch the graceful aquatic reptiles rise from their overnight hideaways in crevices along the reef during an early morning snorkel tour with Molokai Fish and Dive.

2. KAYAK-SNORKEL MAUI

Get to know the coral gardens and underwater denizens of the Hawaiian Islands Humpback Whale National Marine Sanctuary on a kayak-snorkel trip across Maalaea Bay on Maui's western shore. Hawaiian Ocean Sports also offers outrigger canoe tours and kayak whale-watching during the annual humpback migration (December to April).

3. TREK THE WAIMEA CANYON TRAILS

Stretching more than 10 miles (16 km), the "Grand Canyon of the Pacific" dives 3,000 feet (910 m) into Kauai's central highlands. Trails along the rim lead to acrophobic overlooks. Hard-core hikers trek the 11.5-mile (18.5 km) Waimea Canyon Trail through the gorge bottom or the six-mile (10 km) Koai'e Canyon Trail to super-secluded rainforest swimming holes.

4. ZIP OVER MAUI

Soar down the slope of an ancient volcano on the dual-track Kapalua Ziplines in the lush Pu'u Kukui Watershed Preserve on Maui's west side. The adventure features eight individual ziplines, including one that stretches 2,300 feet (700 m) across a deep jungle gorge. Spike your fear factor again by walking a vertiginous suspension bridge across the same canyon.

5. LEARN TO HANG TEN

You may not be ready for the Banzai Pipeline or 50-foot (15 m) waves at "Jaws" by the time you graduate, but Hawaiian-style surf schools on Waikiki Beach in Honolulu, Poipu Beach in Kauai, or Kihei Beach in Maui will at the very least help you ride your first ever wave.

6. DESCEND KA'ELEKU LAVA TUBE

Into the depths of the largest known lava cave on Maui, a cavern formed around 30,000 years ago during an eruption of Haleakalā volcano. It takes around 45 minutes to hike an underground trail past stalactites, stalagmites, lavacicles, strange formations like the Moray Eel and Bowling Alley, and a super-narrow passage called the Claustrophobia Check.

7. DIVE THE LANAI CATHEDRALS

Every bit as impressive as the churches of medieval Europe, these rock formations off Lanai's south coast derive their name from the way that light filters through cracks in massive, submerged lava tubes. Reef sharks, manta rays, moray eels, and octopuses are among the creatures that "prey" in the cathedrals.

8. DARE TO VISIT HAWAII'S "FORBIDDEN ISLAND"

The only way to visit little Niihau—the state's smallest and least developed inhabited island—is on helicopter day trips sanctioned by the family that has owned the island since 1864. The chopper sets down beside a beach where passengers can swim, snorkel, birdwatch, and possibly spot a rare and endangered Hawaiian monk seal.

9. LEARN OUTRIGGER 101

Paddle down Maui's scenic west coast with the folks from Ali'i Maui Outrigger Canoes in Ka'anapali. The half-day ocean adventure blends local history, traditions, and marine wildlife—as well as a crash course in how to pilot an outrigger and a chance to leap into the sea from fabled Black Rock.

10. CATCH WIND IN MAUI

With its monster waves and steady breeze, Ho'okipa Beach on Maui's north shore is one of the holy grails of global wind sports. But you don't have to be a hard-core surfer. Other beaches are ideal for novices learning or honing their skills through HST Windsurfing and Kitesurfing School.

Hawaiian monk seal

An abandoned homestead sits
in Grays Lake National Wildlife
Refuge (page 175).

IDAHO

From stargazing in a dark sky preserve to hiking and biking historic lands, Idaho is for those with an adventurous spirit.

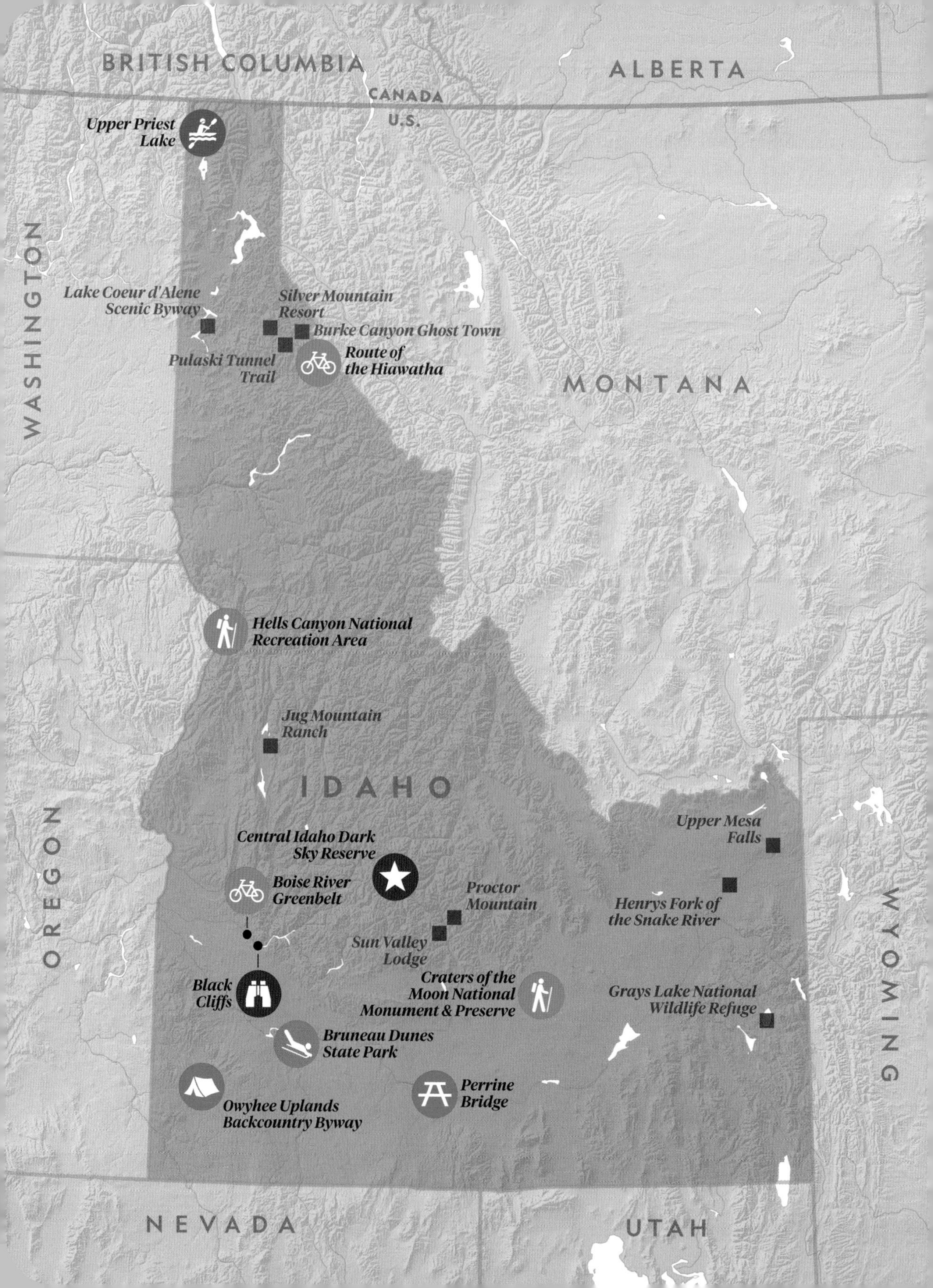

BRITISH COLUMBIA   ALBERTA

CANADA
U.S.

Upper Priest Lake

WASHINGTON

Lake Coeur d'Alene Scenic Byway   **Silver Mountain Resort**
                              Burke Canyon Ghost Town
                 Pulaski Tunnel Trail   **Route of the Hiawatha**

MONTANA

Hells Canyon National Recreation Area

Jug Mountain Ranch

I D A H O

Central Idaho Dark Sky Reserve   *Upper Mesa Falls*

Boise River Greenbelt   ☆   *Proctor Mountain*   *Henrys Fork of the Snake River*

OREGON

Black Cliffs   *Sun Valley Lodge*

Craters of the Moon National Monument & Preserve   *Grays Lake National Wildlife Refuge*

WYOMING

Bruneau Dunes State Park

Owyhee Uplands Backcountry Byway   **Perrine Bridge**

NEVADA   UTAH

Thanks to low light pollution, central Idaho boasts clear skies and stunning starry views.

Stargazing Central

⭐ Viewing a robust night sky has become a rarity for most Americans—nearly 80 percent of people in the United States can no longer view the Milky Way from their homes. Thankfully, Central Idaho is home to the clearest night skies in North America, a distinction that earned the area a designation by the International Dark-Sky Association as the United States' first dark sky reserve in 2017 (it's one of just 20 internationally). At 906,000 acres (366,645 ha), it's also one of the largest such reserves in the world. (Wilderness areas in Quebec, Canada, and on New Zealand's South Island, for example, are larger.)

In short: It's a bucket-list destination for stargazers. Excellent cosmos viewing can be found off State High-way 75 north of Ketchum through the Wood River Valley, with several vehicle pull-off points. Camping options are abundant, too, because the reserve is situated in the stunning scenery of Sawtooth National Recreation Area. (Many of the area's campgrounds—from tent sites to RV hookups—require advance reservations, so be sure to book ahead.)

Summer is a popular time to visit, especially during August, when the annual Perseid meteor showers treat viewers to stunning celestial shows. New moons are also good times to plan a visit, when skies are especially dark. But the Milky Way—a celestial wonder that an estimated third of the world's total population cannot see because of light pollution—can be seen almost any clear night.

Ketchum, Sun Valley, and Stanley, ID Season: Summer and fall

Take a ride on the sandy side at Bruneau Dunes.

A Sandboarding Sensation

Sandboarding, sand surfing, sand sledding: Whatever you prefer to call it, bombing down the giant Bruneau Dunes—one of which is the tallest single-structured dune in North America—is the main draw at this 4,800-acre (1,940 ha) state park about 64 miles (103 km) from Boise. Visitors can explore these sweeping formations on foot, but for a more adrenaline-amped adventure, grab a sandboard and get ripping. (Both stand-up and sled-style models are available to rent.) It's harder than it looks: Prepare for plenty of soft but sandy crashes, and no lift means you're on your own to reach the summit for another run.

The park's location in southwestern Idaho also makes it a prime spot for stargazing, with an on-site observatory that's home to one of the world's largest public telescopes.

Bruneau, ID **Season:** March to November

BASE Jumping Bragging Rights

Want to earn some serious bragging rights on your Idaho adventure? Join the adrenaline junkies who flock to the I. B. Perrine Bridge for BASE jumping. BASE is an acronym for fixed points (buildings; antennas, like radio towers; spans or bridges; or earth, such as cliffs) from which recreational jumpers leap into a controlled free fall before deploying a parachute or using a wingsuit.

Stretching some 486 feet (148 m) over the Snake River Canyon, the Perrine Bridge is the only place in the United States where year-round BASE jumping is allowed without a permit; just watching the free-falling daredevils in action as they soar with billowing parachutes over the rushing river far below is an adrenaline rush in itself. But those who want to jump into the high-flying action themselves can check out the Tandem BASE company, a highly rated outfitter that offers tandem jumps with an experienced instructor.

Twin Falls, ID **Season:** Year-round

A BASE jumper does a backflip from Perrine Bridge.

The views of Boise make a climb up the Black Cliffs worth the effort.

Climb the Cliffs

Known as the Black Cliffs, these towering formations of rock feel worlds away from the nearby state capital of Boise. The cliffs are made from volcanic columnar basalt and beckon adventurous climbers from Boise and beyond who have been coming to the area for decades. Thanks to their efforts, hundreds of well-established routes now offer something to climbers of all levels, from traditional to sport climbing.

Most routes are open year-round, but some are occasionally closed for raptor nesting. Spring and fall are ideal times for climbing the cliffs, as the basalt rock gets especially hot during summer (however, local climbers also say finding a sun-exposed slab is a great way to enjoy some climbing during the winter months). For more intel on specific routes, check out the Boise Climbers Alliance, a local climbing advocacy group that provides updates on the area.

Boise, ID   **Season:** Year-round

The Snake River flows
through Hells Canyon.

"THE SPECTACULAR LANDSCAPE AND GEOLOGICAL FORMATIONS ARE SURE TO IMPRESS."

A Hike to Hell and Back

Straddling the border of Oregon and Idaho for more than 100 miles (160 km), Hells Canyon is North America's deepest river gorge—at its lowest point, the roaring Snake River flows nearly 8,000 feet (2,440 m) below the canyon rim. Grand as it is, the canyon is far less well known than its Arizona counterpart, which means paradise for hikers and backpackers craving rugged, remote adventures where there's a good chance the only encounters along the way will be with wildlife. Along with the Snake River Trail, the spectacular landscape and geological formations—steep cliffs, jagged granite outcroppings, and Idaho's snowcapped Seven Devils Mountains—are sure to impress even the most seasoned outdoors enthusiasts.

Remote as the canyon feels, trailheads are accessible by roads that are open year-round, and hikers can choose a range of outings, from weekend adventures to day hikes to short, kid-friendly treks. One recommended starting point for overnight hikes is the U.S. Forest Service's historic Kirkwood Ranch, a restored 19th-century cattle ranch where amenities like restrooms (with flush toilets, natch!), picnic tables, and a water supply make roughing it a little less rough. It's about a six-mile (10 km) hike to reach the ranch campsite from Pittsburg Landing, a popular launch site for boaters and rafters. For longer treks, the Snake River National Recreation Trail #102 winds through some of the area's most breathtaking scenery. Meanwhile, the Hells Canyon National Recreation Area Visitor Center marks the starting point for several shorter trails.

Keep in mind that spring and fall are ideal seasons for planning a trip, as summer brings soaring temperatures and rattlesnakes in full force. And don't forget your fishing pole, as the Snake River is a prime spot for snagging smallmouth bass, rainbow trout, and steelhead trout.

Council, ID | **Season:** Year-round

River Ride

🚲 One of the first projects of its kind in the United States, the Boise River Greenbelt—a tree-lined, 25-mile (40 km) bike and pedestrian trail project first started in the 1960s—winds along both sides of its namesake river. Popular with pedestrians, bike commuters, and recreational riders, the mostly paved path offers easy access to 850 acres (340 ha) of parks, Boise's business district, and bars and restaurants, as well as access to Lucky Peak State Park.

Cultural landmarks also dot the route, including the Idaho Anne Frank Human Rights Memorial, located at the 8th Street Footbridge, which offers an insightful look at Frank's life and contributions to human rights. You'll also swing past Julia Davis Park—the city's oldest park, opened in 1897—home to Zoo Boise, the Idaho Black History Museum, and the Boise Art Museum. Wildlife is abundant, too: Keep an eye out for ducks, Canada geese, great blue herons, and during winter, bald eagles.

Boise, ID | Season: Year-round

Bike or walk the tree-lined Boise River Greenbelt.

Route of the Hiawatha

🚲 There are rails-to-trails rides, and then there's the Route of the Hiawatha: a showstopping adventure that takes cyclists across majestic trestles, through dramatic tunnels, and among a bird's-eye view of the treetops in the Bitterroot Mountains. And because it's all downhill, with just a 1.6 percent average grade, it's an ideal fun family ride for cyclists of all ages and skill levels—nary a grueling climb or gnarly descent at any point along the route.

Following the scenic route of the former Milwaukee Railroad, the 15-mile (24 km) route starts at Lookout Pass Ski and Recreation Area, where bike rentals, including helmets and lights, are available (as well as an optional return shuttle service). The route kicks off with the St. Paul Pass (also known as the Taft Tunnel), which dips for nearly 1.7 miles (2.7 km) underneath the Bitterroot Mountains at the Idaho–Montana border. From there, it's near-perfect pedaling, with seven trestle bridges—the highest of which soars 230 feet (70 m) into the treetops—and nine more tunnels along the way (though none are quite as long as the first). Plan for a half day to allow plenty of time to stop and savor the views.

When you reach the end of the ride, you can take the shuttle back to the start of the route or hop in the saddle and ride (uphill) back. The shuttle is, not surprisingly, the choice for most families and groups with seniors, but keep in mind that during the summer, the wait can be lengthy. (To avoid long lines, plan to start the ride early.)

Mountain bluebird

Wallace, ID | Season: Summer and early fall

High Desert Road Trip

With dramatic, river-sliced canyons, sprawling high-desert vistas, and desolate remnants of bygone-era outposts, the Owyhee Canyonlands boast approximately 517,000 acres (209,220 ha) of some of the most spectacular and off-the-beaten-path swaths of wilderness in the state, if not the West. And Owyhee Uplands Backcountry Byway, which runs from Jordan Creek, Oregon, to its eastern terminus near Grand View, Idaho, beckons with a highlight reel of the raw rugged beauty. The byway can be reached one of two ways: through Jordan Valley, Oregon (80 miles/130 km) southwest of Boise) or from Highway 78 near Grand View, Idaho (70 miles/110 km southeast of Boise); the route includes 92 miles (148 km) within Idaho and 12 miles (19 km) within Oregon. Whichever direction you're traveling, all-wheel drive is recommended, as it's primarily a gravel road that's just one and a half car lanes wide. Be sure to pack plenty of provisions and start with a full tank of gas, as there are no services along the way. The byway is closed between roughly November and March, when snowfall makes it impassible.

The route can be done in a full day. But to really savor the scenery, plan to spend at least one night car camping along the way. At Mile 81.1 (130.5 km) heading east from Oregon (Mile 21.6; 34.8 km heading west), the Little Jacks Creek Wilderness is a popular spot for hiking, backpacking, fishing, and camping. The Owyhee River also is featured prominently along the way, with several forks that offer boundless opportunity for fishing, rafting, and kayaking; the North Fork gorge is especially stunning. And don't skip the short side trip off the byway to check out Wickahoney, a former outpost whose lonely remnants offer a glimpse into the bygone boomtown era of the West.

Owyhee County, ID | Season: Late spring to early fall

Another World

Craters of the Moon, a mesmerizing volcano field in central Idaho, beckons backpackers for an otherworldly adventure. By day, visitors can explore lava tubes, cinder cones, and caves (a free permit is required to protect sensitive bat populations). By night, the shimmering celestial landscape is just as awe-inspiring, thanks to its certification as an International Dark Sky Park.

The park features eight short trails up to 1.8 miles (2.9 km) long. The three most popular—Caves Trail, North Crater Flow Trail, and Spatter Cones Trail—are paved (and a good option for anyone with mobility issues). For a more ambitious outing, check out the eight-mile (13 km) backcountry Wilderness Trail. The park's 42 first-come, first-served campsites are a convenient home base for exploring. In addition, free wilderness permits are required for overnight camping beyond the campsites.

Arco, ID | Season: Spring to fall

Unique rock formations dot Craters of the Moon National Monument.

> **"SUMMER IS PRIME TIME TO INDULGE IN THE REGION'S SIGNATURE TREAT: HUCKLEBERRIES."**

Kayak the Thorofare

Priest Lake, a popular spot for powerboaters, is the starting point for this leisurely paddle, but the backdrop soon shifts into a more serene route to the 1,300-acre (525 ha) Upper Priest Lake, with stunning mountain scenery and fewer crowds. Campsites there can be reached only by boat or backpacking, adding to the sense of solitude (and sense of accomplishment, too).

Beloved by paddlers as a premier route in the West, the 2.5-mile (4 km) Thorofare to the upper lake is ideal for beginners and families. To launch, head to the sandy beaches of the Lionhead Unit of Priest Lake State Park or to the U.S. Forest Service's Beaver Creek Campground. From there, it's a short paddle on the lake to enter the channel. Try to launch in the morning to savor the calm, glassy waters with minimal current before ski boats arrive at the lake. Along the way, keep an eye out for wildlife like moose, bald eagles, and even grizzly bears.

Should you choose to spend the night, there are a handful of campsites at Upper Priest Lake and 151 campsites around Priest Lake, as well as five cabins. Large groups can stay at Lionhead, which also has 12 RV sites.

Summer is high season, which means more crowds, of course, but it's also prime time to indulge in the region's signature treat: huckleberries. The berries flourish around Priest Lake, and visitors are allowed to pick them (just keep in mind that bears love them too!). Or you can dig into huckleberry pie, milkshakes, ice cream, and other tasty creations in local restaurants and eateries—a fitting way to cap off any paddling adventure.

Bonner County, ID | **Season:** Spring to fall

The sandy shores of Priest Lake are the perfect launching point for a kayak trip.

The road to Sun Valley is almost as fun as the skiing.

1. LEARN CRANE TECHNIQUE

Every fall and spring, migrating sandhill cranes—which can stand four feet (1.2 m) tall with a wing-span of six feet (2 km)—create a magnificent show at Grays Lake National Wildlife Refuge, the largest marsh of its kind in North America. It also hosts the largest nesting population of greater sandhill cranes in the world; more than 200 nesting pairs have been counted in some years.

2. TAKE A GONDOLA JOURNEY

This 3.1-mile (5 km) stretch from Kellogg to the Mountain House at the top of Silver Mountain is the longest gondola in North America, offering sublime lift-served mountain biking, or for a more leisurely outing, hikes to a nearby fire tower and access to a summit restaurant.

3. EXPERIENCE MINING DAYS

The eerie skeleton of Burke Canyon in Wallace, Idaho, is worth a visit. Circa 1880, the mining settlement was built across a narrow canyon and now offers a testament to its boomtown era. Remnants include deserted mining equipment and cave-like holes dug into the canyon walls, indicating where residents once had homes.

4. VIEW WINTER WATERFALLS

The namesake landmark on the Mesa Falls Scenic Byway, thunderous, 10-story Upper Mesa Falls is a main draw of Caribou-Targhee National Forest during summers. But in winter, crowds thin, and you just might have the spectacular view of the partially frozen falls all to yourself. It is accessible only via snowmobile or skis.

5. HUG THE SHORELINE

The 35.8-mile (57.6 km) route of the Lake Coeur d'Alene Scenic Byway starts at the junction of Interstate 90 and Idaho Route 97 and travels south along the eastern shoreline of Lake Coeur d'Alene, a popular recreation spot for Pacific Northwest–style adventures like alpine hikes and camping. The Mineral Ridge Trail is a perfect spot to take a break and soak up gorgeous lake views.

6. HAVE FUN IN SUN VALLEY

Once known primarily as a ritzy ski hot spot for celebs and A-listers, Sun Valley Resort in Ketchum now draws adventure-minded travelers year-round. In addition to its world-class slopes, the property features 400 miles (640 km) of single-track and 30 miles (48 km) of vehicle-free trails, plus seasonal activities like sleigh rides, sport shooting, and cross-country skiing.

7. LOOP AROUND LIFTS

The 4.5-mile (7.2 km) Proctor Mountain Loop delivers with sprawling views of the Sun Valley area and iconic Bald Mountain as it skirts its namesake peak. On the descent, look for the remnants of two chairlifts originally built in the 1930s, one of which was the world's first operating lift.

8. HAVE FUN FAT BIKING

Fat biking—featuring burly bikes with bigger, lower-pressure tires—is booming, and many outdoor destinations are adapting their cross-country trails to accommodate the increasingly popular winter pastime. At Jug Mountain Ranch, cyclists of all skill levels can hit 14 miles (22.5 km) of snowy trails (rentals are available, and a day pass is required for winter trail use).

9. FLY-FISHING NIRVANA

Anglers from all over the world travel to Idaho for its world-class fly-fishing, and Henrys Fork of the Snake River is especially epic. One of three blue-ribbon trout streams in eastern Idaho, the dry fly fishery is brimming with many species of trout, including large wild rainbows and brown. Several outfitters offer customized trips for all skill levels.

10. HIKE THE PULASKI TUNNEL TRAIL

This four-mile (6.4 km) round-trip to the Pulaski Tunnel Overlook is named after Edward "Big Ed" Pulaski. When a deadly wildfire ravaged the area in 1910, the ranger saved all but six of his 45-person firefighting crew by bringing them to safety in a mine tunnel, which hikers can see from a lookout spot at the terminus of the trail.

Lincoln Park (page 187) is a green escape nestled in Chicago's urban sprawl.

ILLINOIS

State parks abound throughout Illinois, offering green spaces, river runs, and mountain getaways.

WISCONSIN

Lake
Michigan

Galena ★

Chestnut Mountain Resort 🏃

Chain O' Lakes
State Park

North Branch
Chicago River

IOWA

❋

Nicholas Conservatory & Gardens, Anderson Japanese Gardens

Waterfall Glen
Forest Preserve

🦆 **Montrose Point Bird Sanctuary**

Maggie Daley
Park

MICHIGAN

Starved Rock State Park ⛺

Matthiessen
State Park

ILLINOIS

Lake
Shelbyville 🚲

Fox Ridge
State Park

INDIANA

Great River Road

Pere Marquette State Park 🧗

Rend Lake State Fish
and Wildlife Area

MISSOURI

Kinkaid Lake
Spillway

Giant City State Park

 Shawnee National Forest

Cache River State
Natural Area

Cave-in-Rock
State Park

KENTUCKY

See historic buildings and the Pomona Natural Bridge near the Alto Pass of Shawnee National Forest.

Take a Ride in the Forest

Change up your trail exploration and travel by horseback through miles of Shawnee National Forest's sprawling oak and hickory trees. Spanning between the Ohio and Mississippi Rivers, this ecologically diverse park calls more than a million visitors—many from the nearby urban centers—to its natural wonders each year. With the help of your equine companion, your route can take you from green to blue in minutes—riding under green canopies, across wetlands full of wildlife, and through river-run canyons.

Multiple outfitters offer horseback riding lessons, guided tours, and overnight trips for visitors, and the national forest keeps a list of groups permitted to operate in the region.

Once you're on your horse and in the park, you'll have plenty of options. Navigate around One Horse Gap Lake, where you'll have to manage the narrow rock crevices just as the name implies: one horse at a time. Search for unique rock formations at the Garden of the Gods Wilderness area, where bulbous boulders pop out from between trees to welcome hikers and riders of varying experience levels. Take to the River to River Trail to search for bald eagles, red-tailed hawks, bobcats, armadillos, and red foxes.

If an afternoon just isn't enough, stop for the evening at Camp Cadiz Campground or Johnson Creek Recreation Area for horse camping under the stars. Both campgrounds have first-come, first-served sites with vault toilets and picnic areas. Camp Cadiz is a mostly quiet spot, and a boat launch, easy hiking access, and lake kayaking make it an excellent home base for families.

Herod, IL | **Season:** Spring to fall

Autumn is a beautiful time to visit Pere Marquette State Park.

Climb New Routes

You'll need your GPS to find the newly developed rock-climbing routes at Pere Marquette State Park, but once you make your way to the coordinates, you'll be rewarded with recently built trails, natural rock steps, and distinct routes set in striking limestone bluffs. The Illinois Climbers Association worked closely with the Illinois Department of Natural Resources to push the project forward, prioritizing preservation of the landscape.

Currently 65 routes are available to visitors, with more coming as the development grows. Most of the routes are bolted and built for sport climbing, while some have top anchors for traditional leads. At Jenga Disaster Boulders, climbers can tackle bouldering problems in the park's limestone formations.

The largest state park in Illinois has long been known as a nature lover's haven, but the rock-climbing spots have brought new visitors to its forests.

Grafton, IL | **Season:** Spring to fall

Up Your Photo Game

Working on your nature photography skills doesn't have to require a trek into the wilderness. Find bounds of natural beauty ready for capture at the Nicholas Conservatory and Gardens, a community space that brings tropics to the banks of the Rock River. The conservatory hosts seasonal events, showcasing temporary plant life and nature-centered art alongside its permanent exhibits.

Down the road, the Anderson Japanese Gardens offer meticulously maintained natural spaces, and the flora isn't the only possible subject for photographers. Greenery at the gardens surrounds a 16th-century sukiya-style guesthouse and the Laurent House, the only home designed by Frank Lloyd Wright for a client with a physical disability.

Both locations have restrictions on professional or posed photography, but visitors are welcome to document their experiences in the gardens for their own personal use.

Rockford, IL | **Season:** Year-round

Find indoor and outdoor green spaces at the Nicholas Conservatory.

The sunset glows on Lake Shelbyville.

Biking for Views

Lake Shelbyville has plenty of water, but adventurous mountain bikers will find thrills away from the waves and between the trees.

The General Dacey Trail bends and twists through the forest, and bikers will get an extra boost as they ride up and down hills that roll through the region. The route con-nects to the rest of the extended trail system through the creek crossing, eventually leading to a series of loops, from Split Rock to Boulder Loop.

Mountain bikers looking to cover more miles can jump on the Camp Camfield Trail, recently converted into a multiuse path, with the option of speeding down the path or moseying along at a leisurely pace. As the trail weaves through the forest and along the banks of the lake's many enclaves, visitors will catch views of the water as they pedal.

Shelbyville, IL | **Season:** Spring to fall

> "THOUGH THE FALLS SHIFT
> WITH THE SEASONS, THEY'RE
> STRIKING ANY TIME OF YEAR."

Waterfall Hop

Vertical sandstone walls carved by glacial waters rise over the 18 canyons that run through Starved Rock State Park. The park's trails lead hikers through these canyons, around lofty bluffs, and along the rolling Illinois River, where oak, maple, hickory, and pine trees grow above the mossy-filled canyons. River trails lead to photo-worthy overlooks, while interior canyon trails bring travelers to the French, Wildcat, LaSalle, Ottawa, Kaskaskia, Aurora, and St. Louis Canyons, all home to the park's famous waterfalls.

Though the falls shift with the seasons, depending on rainfall and snowmelt, they're striking any time of year. Winter visitors will find ice towers stuck in frozen time, while hikers in the spring will get the gift of flowing streams, full pools, and rolling cascades. Even during dry periods, the rock formations showcase layers of history in the park, which was home to thriving Native American communities from as early as 8000 B.C. and was named a national historic landmark in 1966. Starved Rock is a popular meeting place for naturalists in the area, bringing the public together for free guided tours, family story times, art shows, and animal displays.

No swimming is permitted in the park's natural pools, but a picnic by the water provides a quiet and refreshing break from the trekking it takes to get there. If a dip is a necessity for your trip, Starved Rock Lodge's indoor pool is open to visitors all year. The lodge, which offers luxury suites and television-free cabins, is the perfect spot to extend your time in the park. A tall stone fireplace warms the central space, where families, couples, and friends join together for a meal at one of the restaurants, a drink at the lounge, or a dance at a show on the veranda. The pet-friendly space even shares a menu for dogs at their outdoor dining spots.

Oglesby, IL | Season: Year-round

See the cascades of
St. Louis Canyon at
Starved Rock State Park.

Ski in Midwest Country

Tucked away in the northwest corner of the state, Chestnut Mountain Resort calls skiers and snowboarders of all levels to its slopes. With most of its runs set at a beginner or intermediate level, the mountain is also a welcome space for snow-loving athletes just starting out. After riding to the top of the mountain's 475-foot (145 m) vertical drop, visitors will look out over the Mississippi River.

Those looking for an extra adrenaline kick or a spot to test out their tricks can find space at the resort's seven-acre (2.8 ha) terrain park—filled with a quarter-pipe, two half-pipes, and a series of rails and jumps. After a day of riding the lifts and carving the snow, visitors can take a break at The Summit or Sunset Grille or book an evening at the slope-side lodge.

For those who prefer warm-weather adventures, the resort offers a variety of activities once the snow melts, from zip-lining to miniature golf to river cruises.

Galena, IL | Season: Winter

Chestnut Mountain Resort boasts 19 ski and snowboard runs.

Stargaze in the Country

Galena has been a popular stargazing site for decades, but it earned the title of a Dark Sky Friendly Development of Distinction by the International Dark-Sky Association in 2021. The region boasts a consistent monthly ranking of 3 on the Bortle scale—a measurement that ranges from the blackest nights at 1 to bright inner-city skies at 9. With only slight light pollution at the horizon, rural sky ratings of 3 typically showcase summer views of the Milky Way and bright zodiacal lights in the spring and fall.

Find a spot before dusk to enhance your evening with sunset views and a meal. Pack a picnic to enjoy at Grant Park Gazebo or along the bluffs of the Mississippi River at Gramercy Park. Bring a star chart that shows constellations and moon phases to make the most of your adventure. For those looking for celebration and a community of night-sky lovers, Galena hosts stargazer-friendly events throughout the year, such as Bonfire on the Bluff in February and the Great Galena Balloon Race in June.

For the full Galena experience, you'll need to stay the night. You'll get uninterrupted views forgoing a roof at the family-friendly campsites in Blanding Landing Recreation Area. (Electric hookups, showers, and a playground are among the amenities.) You could lay your head at the historic Inn at Irish Hollow, with its miles of winding country trails. Or, if you prefer more luxury, you can book a stay and a massage at the Eagle Ridge Resort and Spa.

Galena, IL | Season: Spring to fall

Take a "Road" Trip on Your Kayak

The Great River Road winds along the Mississippi River, and in the section that travels through Illinois, you'll find several launches to get your kayak in the water. Start at the Rock River National Water Trail, which runs for 320 miles (515 km) from Wisconsin to Illinois. The trail is accessible for all, with 50 of its 155 access sites—marked by the logo—available for people with disabilities. Twelve of 16 river-access campsites along the trail are in Illinois, offering boaters the chance to stop at the water's edge for the evening and journey on at the break of dawn—or after a big camp breakfast, whatever you prefer.

Although the road follows the river, it's not the only option for aquatic adventure. Cypress trees rise from the water in Horseshoe Lake State Fish and Wildlife Area, and kayakers and canoers can paddle their way through scenes that call to mind visions of the South. Farther down the road, human-made Kinkaid Lake

Rock Island, IL | Season: Spring to fall

offers visitors 2,750 acres (1,110 ha) of water-focused fun. Sandstone bluffs and prairie grass fields line the water's edge, and boaters can throw a line for largemouth bass, bluegill, catfish, or walleye.

If you prefer to let someone else do the work on the water, trade your kayak for a ticket to the *Celebration Belle*. The old-fashioned paddle-wheel boat, which has been plying these waters for 40 years, cruises along the Mississippi from Moline, Illinois, and can hold 750 passengers for its fall foliage trips, overnight excursions, and dance parties. The boat offers themed musical cruises, including "Holiday & the Classics," "Oktoberfest," and "Broadway & Movies." Or book your passage for a narrated sightseeing cruise or fireworks dinner cruise.

A boardwalk crosses a crevasse in Giant City State Park.

Camping With Giants

Sandstone structures rise from the forest floor at Giant City State Park, towering over acres of lush mossy land. Although hiking, biking, and climbing through the woods provide a magical experience, staying overnight in the park brings the adventure to another level.

There are options for every type of park guest at Giant City. Visitors who prefer a homier stay can check out the Giant City Lodge, where cabins with modern amenities line the property and a historic lodge provides meals at its restaurant and lounge.

Those who want to sleep under the stars can reserve a spot at the park's state-run campground. With spaces for tents and trailers, the park welcomes walk-in hikers, horseback riders, and drive-up guests. No matter the overnight choice, Giant City will live up to its name with massive sandstone bluffs, deep ravines, and towering trees.

Makanda, IL | Season: Early spring to late fall

Stop to marvel at the Alfred Caldwell Lily Pool inside the Lincoln Park Conservancy.

> "MORE THAN 300 AVIAN SPECIES TRAVEL THROUGH THIS PROTECTED SPACE."

Accessible Birding in the City

Nestled between Chicago and Lake Michigan, Montrose Point Bird Sanctuary offers birding options to those who make their way through the city and through its wooden threshold. The sanctuary rests within Lincoln Park, a natural lakefront park that houses museums, gardens, an archery range, beaches, sports fields, and playgrounds.

At Montrose, you'll find accessible parking near the main entrance and the lake, along with eight-foot-wide (2.4 m) paved pathways that loop through grasses, shrubs, and trees. Tens of thousands of migratory birds spend time at the sanctuary, and "The Magic Hedge," a 150-yard (140 m) stretch of greenery formed on honeysuckle left over from a mid-20th-century Army lease of the land, attracts many of them. More than 300 avian species travel through this protected space and the Montrose Beach Dunes Natural Area, earning it international recognition.

Travel a few miles toward the southern end of the park and you'll find another oasis ringing with bird-songs: the Alfred Caldwell Lily Pool. This national historic landmark has a rocky history. It started as a Victorian garden in 1889 and was pulled out of disrepair by Alfred Caldwell when he redesigned the pool to resemble a meandering midwestern river. After the Lincoln Park Zoo took it over in the 1950s and turned it into "The Rookery," it languished and eventually closed, eroded and ravished. The Lincoln Park Conservatory finally rescued it and reopened it in 2002, as the accessible natural space it is today. Reach it and the wildlife that calls it home by car, bike, or public transportation.

Chicago, IL | **Season:** Year-round

Take your turn on the climbing wall at Maggie Daley Park in Chicago.

1. BOAT THE WETLANDS AT CACHE RIVER STATE NATURAL AREA

Visitors can explore this natural glacial-carved floodplain by foot or boat, hiking or paddling around the wetland's massive cypress trees—some more than 1,000 years old. Plan your trip around waterfowl and shorebird migration patterns to see why the region was designated as a wetland of international importance.

2. SWIM AT KINKAID LAKE SPILLWAY FALLS

Hiking to this human-made water hole, fed by a cascading waterfall, can be a challenge, but the payoff is worth it. While fishers will find bass, bluegill, and catfish in the dammed lake, swimmers can dip into the tranquil pool beyond the grass-lined barrier.

3. TAKE ON WATER SPORTS AT REND LAKE STATE FISH AND WILDLIFE AREA

These 18,900 acres (7,650 ha) of freshwater are all about fun, and there's plenty of space for paddlers, boaters, and water-sport enthusiasts of all types. Beaches and picnic sites around the lake add another layer of entertainment, while the South Sandusky Campground provides an excellent family-friendly home base for visitors.

4. EXPLORE THE FALLS AT MATTHIESSEN STATE PARK

Operated privately by its namesake in the 19th century, this park became a public space once it was donated to the state in 1918.

Exposed sandstone drops draw Deer Creek into a series of stunning waterfalls. Cascade Falls plummets 45 feet (14 m), while Giant's Bathtub drops into a wide, aptly named pool.

5. KAYAK CHICAGO'S RIVERWALK

Drop your kayak or paddleboard into the North Branch Chicago River for an experience that merges natural and urban landscapes. Rental spots line the water, making this adventure easily accessible to city dwellers, and guided tours are available for those who want more details on the scenery.

6. FISH AT FOX RIDGE STATE PARK

This freshwater lake is stocked with bluegill, bass, and catfish, but being a research facility, reservations are required to drop in a line. However, a small fishing pond at the park is home to an accessible fishing pier and one of the park's two accessible trails.

7. GEOCACHE AT CAVE-IN-ROCK STATE PARK

Though the rumors of this tremendous cave on the Ohio River sheltering criminals and pirates haven't been proven, the lore lends an extra layer of intrigue for explorers and geocachers. Navigate its high hills, dark depths, and expansive waterway by GPS to write your own version of the mystery.

8. CAMP CHAIN O' LAKES STATE PARK

Made up of a string of boater-friendly lakes and nearly 500 miles (805 km) of shoreline, this park is the ideal location for campers who want easy access to water-centered exploits. With 151 sites, including some accessible spots, there's a good chance you'll be able to snag one when adventure calls.

9. CROSS-COUNTRY SKI IN WATERFALL GLEN FOREST PRESERVE

The trails that cross the gently rolling hills of this section of DuPage County's Forest Preserve District are groomed in the winter, when weather allows, for cross-country skiers. Cold-weather warriors will be rewarded with views of iced and frozen waterfalls.

10. ROCK CLIMB IN THE CENTER OF THE CITY

Maggie Daley Park hosts two massive rock-climbing walls in the center of Chicago, where beginner and advanced climbers can catch skyline views on warm-weather days. In winter, you can trade in your climbing shoes for ice skates and glide along the quarter-mile (0.4 km) ice ribbon in the same park.

Midland painted turtle

A lupine meadow blooms at West Beach in Indiana Dunes National Park (page 197).

INDIANA

Art, nature, and unique landscapes combine to
make Indiana a go-to hub for outdoor enthusiasts.

Lake Michigan

MICHIGAN

Indiana Dunes State and National Parks

St. Joseph River

Gabis Arboretum and Railway Garden at Purdue Northwest

Tippecanoe River State Park (Go Further site as well)

France Park

Indiana-Michigan River Valley Trail

OHIO

INDIANA

ILLINOIS

Virginia B. Fairbanks Art & Nature Park

Indiana Birding Trail

Turkey Run State Park

Indianapolis

Brown County

Clifty Falls State Park

Bluespring Caverns

Knobstone Trail

Hoosier National Forest

Charlestown State Park

Adventure Hiking Trail

New Harmony

KENTUCKY

Twin Swamps Nature Preserve

This isn't your ordinary cave tour; you'll be navigating by boat through the subterranean landscape.

Subterranean Kayaking

First discovered in the 19th century, Bluespring Caverns houses the longest known navigable underground river in the United States. Today, navigating the Myst'ry River at 100 feet (30 m) below surface in a kayak is an unforgettable experience for paddlers. Reservations are required for the approximately three-hour guided tour, with small groups between four and eight participants. With no currents, the leisurely two-mile (3.2 km) round-trip paddle winds through dripstone passageways, allowing kayakers to take in the dramatic formations while keeping an eye out for albino creatures like salamanders and crayfish, translucent white because of the humidity and lack of light in the crystal clear water. Visitors can also take a one-hour guided tour on an electric boat (with a descent and ascent of about 400 feet/120 m to the dock). Light jackets are recommended for all offerings, as the caverns remain a constant 53°F (12°C).

For a longer adventure, consider an "Overnight Adventure" offered during early winter through spring. You'll arrive in the evening and walk, crawl, and climb on ladders through the caverns' undeveloped passages before snuggling into your sleeping bag in a shared bunk. (It's a popular offering, so be sure to make reservations as far in advance as possible.)

Before or after your cave adventure, be sure to check out the Karst Natural Area Trail, a half-mile (0.8 km) loop around Indiana's largest karst sinkhole plain, which is more than 90 feet (27 m) deep and covers 10 acres (4 ha). Also on-site is a gemstone mine, where you can try your hand at prospecting for semiprecious stone and minerals.

Bedford, IN | **Season:** March to October

More than 400 species of birds have been documented on the trail.

Make Your Way Through a Birding Trail

Bring the binoculars to fully appreciate the beauty of the Indiana Birding Trail, which the Indiana Audubon Society launched in 2020 and features 64 prime viewing locations across five regions of the Hoosier State. Spots along the trail include the Jasper-Pulaski Fish & Wildlife Area, home to the largest gathering of sandhill cranes east of the Mississippi River, and Indiana Dunes National Park, where more than 350 bird species have been spotted. Indiana is a prime bird migratory zone thanks to its location within the Mississippi Flyway, as birds travel between the northern Arctic on their way through Central America to their final destination in South America. Indiana's unique geography, with its wetlands, prairies, and forests—diverse habitats that have attracted more than 400 species—offers birds resources for refueling along their journey.

Multicity, IN Season: Year-round

South Bend Adventure

South Bend takes its name directly from the bend in the St. Joseph River as it turns north toward Michigan. The waterway is a beloved spot for outdoor adventure—and especially pursuits that involve paddles. For some splashy Class II white-water action, head to the East Race Waterway: a Civil War–era channel that became the first human-made white-water rafting course in North America. The attraction is open from mid-June through early September; reservations are recommended, and the $20 all-day pass is the best bang for your buck.

For more leisurely outings, Ferrettie/Baugo Creek and St. Patrick's County Parks are good options for putting in (you can rent kayaks, canoes, and stand-up paddleboards during the summer at St. Patrick's). An urban route links St. Pat's with nearby Keller Park; with about 4.5 miles (7.2 km) between them, most paddlers can complete it in about an hour.

South Bend, IN Season: June to September

Reel in smallmouth bass on the St. Joseph River.

The University of Notre Dame sits along the Indiana-Michigan River Valley Trail.

Ride Along the River

🚴 For a two-wheeled riverside adventure, the Indiana-Michigan River Valley Trail spans 17 miles (27 km) from Niles, Michigan, to Mishawaka, Indiana. Connecting four universities, four downtowns, and 16 parks, the trail serves as an umbrella name for several shorter routes that together make the route, most of which runs along the river. Near the University of Notre Dame, the East Bank Trail runs for about 3.5 miles (5.6 km), eventually connecting with the 1.7-mile (2.7 km) Northside Trail and then the Mishawaka Loop, which utilizes both sides of the river and multiple city parks over another 2.5 miles (4 km). This section includes the Mishawaka Riverwalk, one of the best showcases of the river, with beautifully landscaped walkways and pedestrian bridges.

Niles, MI, to Mishawaka, IN | **Season:** Spring to fall

Mount Baldy, Indiana Dunes National Park's most famous dune, is particularly stunning at sunset.

> "THE NATIONAL PARK TRAILS WIND THROUGH SWAMPS, BLACK OAK SAVANNAS, AND, OF COURSE, OPEN DUNES."

All in Dune Fun

In Indiana's northwest corner are sweeping acres of sand dunes in the state's only national park and its smaller, park-within-a-park cousin. Together, they feature some 15,000 acres (6,070 ha) and more than 56 miles (90 km) of trails along 15 miles (24 km) of Lake Michigan's southern shoreline.

The national park trails wind through habitats including swamps, black oak savannas, and, of course, open dunes. Hikers can choose from a variety of distances, from short, wheelchair-accessible Calumet Dunes Trail to the short but steep Mount Baldy Summit Trail, accessible only certain weekends on free ranger-guided hikes. Another noteworthy hike is known as the new Diana Dunes, starting at West Beach. The 0.8-mile (1.3 km) loop has interpretive signs that tell the story of Alice Mabel Gray, also known as Diana of the Dunes, who lived in an abandoned shanty in the dune for nearly a decade in the early 1900s and was a strong advocate for dune conservation.

Meanwhile, in the neighboring state park, seven numbered trails cover more than 16 miles (26 km). Rugged Trail 8 crosses the summits of the three highest dunes, collectively totaling 552 vertical feet (168 m). In the summer months, popular beach areas along Lake Michigan offer the perfect finish to any hike.

The adventure continues in winter, too: The parks are popular for snowshoeing and sledding. Borrow free snowshoes at the Paul H. Douglas Center in Indiana Dunes National Park (call first to check on trail conditions), then set out on the three-mile (5 km) Miller Woods trail system, which winds through serene oak savanna and dune habitats.

Porter, IN | **Season:** Year-round

A Hoosier Horseback Ride

Also known as the Hoosier, Indiana's only national forest spans 204,000 acres (82,560 ha) of pristine wilderness in the state's south-central region. An excellent way to explore the scenic landscape is via horseback. Approximately 200 miles (320 km) of national forest trails are open for equestrian use, but an area especially suited for riders is the congressional-designated Charles C. Deam Wilderness Area in Hoosier National Forest, which spans nearly 13,000 acres (5,260 ha) within the forest and has 36 miles (58 km) of multiuse trails. Horse riders are required to have a permit, and owners should take care to remain on trails designated for equestrian use.

In addition, the forest also has six designated horse campgrounds (reservations are recommended). A good one-stop resource for out-of-town equestrians is Midwest Trail Ride, a privately owned campground with campsites, cabins, and horse stables. Guests can use the property's 100-mile (160 km) trail network without a permit.

Bedford, IN | **Season:** Spring to fall

Riders can enjoy Hoosier National Forest all year long.

Make a Challenge of the Backcountry

The approximately 44-mile (71 km) backcountry Knobstone Trail is easily Indiana's most challenging hike. Its name and rugged character come from the ridge of bluffs and hills, or knobs, known as the Knobstone Escarpment, a sloping stretch distinctive for its high, flat, and narrow ridges and steep sides. Although the hills are relatively low in elevation, the diverse terrain amps up the challenge, making the Knobstone Trail, or KT, an excellent training ground for more mountainous areas. Not surprisingly, because of its difficult terrain and significant elevation changes, many long-distance hikers use the KT to train for the Appalachian Trail. But the Knobstone Trail offers a unique adventure on its own. Its high-ridge sections serve up sweeping views across the wooded hills of southern Indiana; on clear days, hikers may even see Louisville, Kentucky, and the Ohio River.

Much of the trail runs through Clark and Jackson-Washington State Forests. Many hikers opt to travel from north to south to develop their "trail legs," as the hills get steeper heading south. The route itself is well blazed, with its northern terminus at Spurgeon Hollow Lake; from there, it's 43.5 miles (70 km) to the southern terminus at Deam Lake. Highlights along the way include beautiful camping around Elk Creek Lake (also a popular fishing spot) and the tough but worth-the-effort views along the New Chapel–Jackson Road section, where exposed ridgelines offer occasional vistas all the way to Louisville.

The trail is managed by the Indiana Department of Natural Resources, which also sells detailed topographic maps and trail guides.

Jackson County, IN | **Season:** Spring to fall

Midwest Mountain Biking

Indiana's Brown County boasts a highly coveted accolade in mountain biking circles: designated as a Bronze Level Ride Center by the International Mountain Bicycling Association, which means it's among the world's top places to ride. Indeed, thanks to the work of the Hoosier Mountain Bike Association, the volunteer group that builds and maintains the trails, this network is a bucket-list mountain bike destination. About 25 miles (40 km) of flowy, single-track trails, most intermediate to advanced, feature diverse terrain like switchbacks, tabletops, berms, rock gardens, and more. The intermediate Green Valley Trail is the park's longest, offering five roller-coaster miles (8 km), while the 3.4-mile (5.5 km) Aynes Loop is a rooty quad killer. Advanced riders can savor the best views in the park from the overlook on the 2.1-mile (3.4 km) Hesitation Point Trail, which also passes the ruins of an old brick shelter. The expert-only Bobcat Bowl (3.5 miles/5.6 km) and Schooner Trace (4.1 miles/6.6 km) have tight switchbacks, gnarly rock gardens, and other challenges

Or consider tackling the Walnut Trail, a difficult two-mile (3.2 km) narrow single-track where you'll have to navigate rocks, strewn logs and roots, and off-camber turns. You can enter the experts-only Schooner Trace Trail from the Walnut Trail—but be warned, it is for skilled riders only. The four-mile (6.4 km) trail is remote, but it winds through the most beautiful part of the park.

Newbies, meanwhile, will find plenty to keep them busy on the Limekiln, Pine Loop, North Gate Connector, and North Tower Loop Trails. With exposed roots and fallen logs, North Tower Loop is the most technical of the beginner routes, offering a good challenge for beginners and a nice warm-up for experienced ones.

After your adventure, head to the nearby mountain biking hub of Nashville for a pint or two at Big Woods Brewing Company, a longtime favorite among mountain bikers, or Big Woods Pizza Company, for a hearty pie.

Nashville, IN   Season: Spring to fall

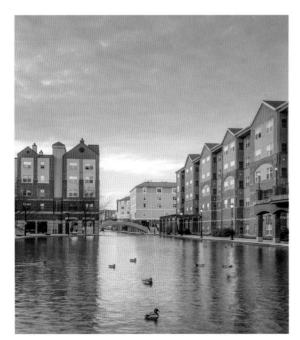

Take to the waters to explore downtown Indianapolis.

Italy in Indy

You don't need to travel to Italy for the famous gondolier experience of Venice. Instead, get a taste of la dolce vita in downtown Indianapolis, as the iconic curved boats of Old World Gondoliers transport guests on private tours through the city's canals. The outfitter's talented guides evoke the romance and tradition of their Italian counterparts, right down to the black-and-white-striped shirts, red sashes, and singing.

Private tours are available for groups of up to eight per boat; bookings for larger groups are also available. Feel free to bring your own cocktails and refreshments aboard. And if you're looking for a touch of romance on your ride, you're on the right track: The company claims to be the top destination for engagements in the state of Indiana.

Indianapolis, IN   Season: Year-round

> "THESE SOARING STRUCTURES PROVIDE A WAY TO TAKE ADVENTURE TO NEW HEIGHTS."

High Above the Watchtower

By 1952, Indiana had 33 fire towers in operation around the state, with watchmen keeping an eye out for forest fires from a vantage point way above the treetops, some as high as 100 feet (30 m) or more. Today, these soaring structures are mostly defunct of their original purpose, but they also provide a way for outdoor enthusiasts looking to take their adventure to (literal) new heights. Around the state, 13 fire towers still remain, and most of them are open to the public to climb. (However, it's always advisable to check prior to your trip, as they can be closed for various safety reasons.)

Perhaps the most adventurous to climb is the tower at Tippecanoe River State Park, a nearly 90-year-old structure that rises 90 feet (27 m) off the ground, with an elevation of 756 feet (230 m) and a superb panoramic view. At McCormick's Creek State Park, the McCormick fire tower, which was built in 1935 and used through 1967, is a mere 86 feet (26 m) tall but boasts an elevation of 770 feet (235 m).

If the heights themselves don't scare you but the idea of scaling a decades-old structure does, consider checking out one of the towers that have been renovated in recent years. At Morgan-Monroe State Forest, the newly renovated Mason Ridge Fire Tower, which saw plenty of use in 1964, is a popular attraction. Meanwhile, at Bluffton's Ouabache State Park (pronounced Wabash), the 100-foot-tall (30 m) Ouabache fire tower, originally built in the 1930s, also received a recent renovation.

Multicity, IN | **Season:** Year-round

A lily pond in Tippecanoe
River State Park

Walk through a gorge at Turkey Run State Park.

1. CHECK OUT A BACK-COUNTRY ADVENTURE

From sinkholes to remnants of pioneer homesteads to deep ravines, Adventure Hiking Trail has plenty of highlights on the 25 miles (40 km) between O'Bannon Woods State Park and Harrison-Crawford State Forest, adjacent to the Ohio River. Hikers can sleep in four shelter houses or enjoy backcountry camping.

2. WALK A LABYRINTH

A restored feature of a 19th-century religious group, this shrub labyrinth in New Harmony offers a calming way to spend the afternoon. Admission is free to walk the concentric circles of manicured hedges (but as the attraction is popular for weddings, check availability beforehand).

3. LAUNCH YOUR CANOE IN TIPPECANOE RIVER STATE PARK

The name of this popular state park is all but guaranteed to prompt some jokes and smiles among the paddlers it attracts (especially canoeists). Beyond the river, outdoor lovers can hike 23 miles (37 km) of trails or camp at a variety of sites along the waterway.

4. INTERACT WITH ART AT FAIRBANKS ART AND NATURE PARK

No "Stay Off the Art" signs here: Visitors to this free Indianapolis park are encouraged to interact with—and, yes, climb on—the whimsical structures.

5. CLIMB A NATURAL OBSTACLE COURSE

Dramatic limestone canyons, a wooden suspension bridge, ladders, and hundreds of human-made steps are just a few of the highlights on 14 various trails at Turkey Run State Park. The six-mile (10 km) Ladders Trail is a hands-down hit: As its name suggests, there are several ladders to climb, along with stream crossings.

6. FIND AMUSEMENT AT THIS ABANDONED PARK

The usual outdoor activities—hiking, birding, and paddling—are on offer at Charlestown State Park in southern Indiana. But those who relish the eerie atmosphere of abandoned places should check out Trail 7, which winds past the eerie remnants of Rose Island amusement park, built in the 1920s, scattered around the dense woods.

7. SWAMP YOURSELF IN SWAMPS

At Twin Swamps Nature Preserve, visitors can explore the mysterious, brooding atmosphere of landscapes often associated with way farther south. A long, winding loop with an elevated boardwalk traverses the diverse ecosystem of two swamps, Overcup Oak and Cypress.

8. TREK A TRAIN ROUTE

With 300 acres (120 ha) of forest, prairie, and wetlands, Gabis Arboretum and Railway Garden has plenty to explore. And train lovers of all ages will delight in the outdoor Railway Garden, which features an acre (0.4 ha) of model trains that tell the story of the area's steam engine heritage.

9. FIND FOSSILS

In addition to waterfalls and year-round hiking, Clifty Falls State Park is also packed with fossils. Clifty Creek's stony bed brims with ancient remnants from a millennia-old marine ecosystem. Fossil collecting within the park isn't allowed, but amateur archaeologists can try their skills at several nearby collecting stations.

10. DIVE A LAKE

This flooded stone quarry has been transformed into one of the area's most popular swimming spots in summer, and France Park's clear waters are also popular with divers. Indy Dive Center provides guided diving opportunities on weekends; divers must be registered to dive at France Park.

Peony flower

Iowa's landscape of woodlands
and pastures is picture perfect.

IOWA

Bike, hike, climb, snowshoe, paddle,
and more in the Hawkeye State.

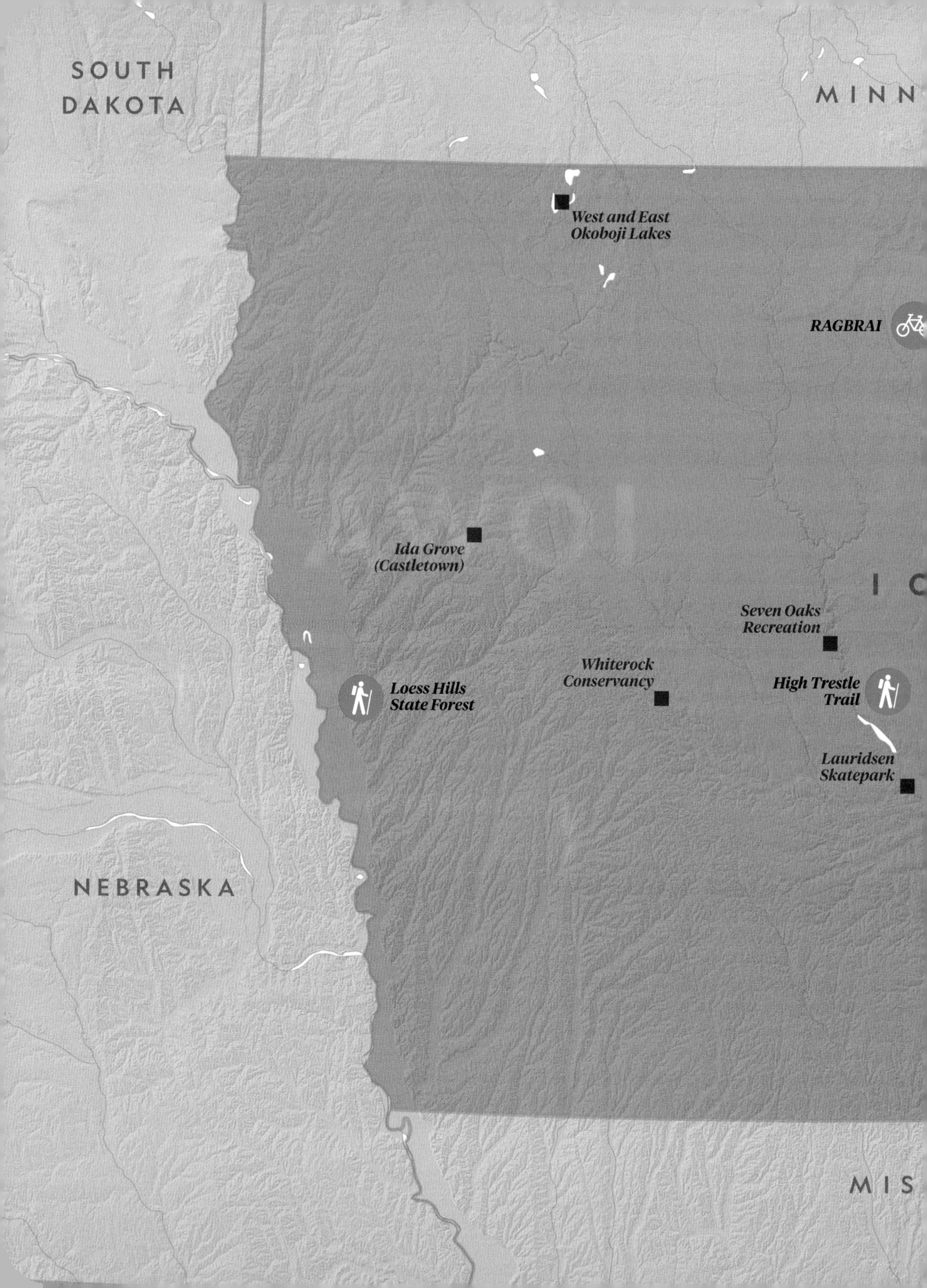

SOUTH
DAKOTA

MINN

West and East
Okoboji Lakes

RAGBRAI

Ida Grove
(Castletown)

Seven Oaks
Recreation

IO

Whiterock
Conservancy

High Trestle
Trail

Loess Hills
State Forest

Lauridsen
Skatepark

NEBRASKA

MIS

OTA

WISCONSIN

Upper Iowa

Driftless
Area

Upper Iowa
River

Clear
Lake

Effigy Mounds
National Monument

Backbone State
Park

Union Park

Field of Dreams
Movie Site

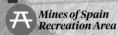

Mines of Spain
Recreation Area

I O W A

Maquoketa
Caves
State Park

Riverboat
Twilight

Pella

ILLINOIS

Shimek
State Forest

OURI

Cave Dwell at Maquoketa Caves State Park

Caves are cool, literally and in the hipster sense of the word, and this 370-acre (150 ha) state park invites amateur spelunkers and hikers to explore one of Iowa's most unique state parks. A six-mile (10 km) trail system connects a labyrinth of caverns, 13 in all, through a setting freckled with verdant forests, limestone bluffs, and scenic overlooks, as well as some curious geological formations such as Natural Bridge curving 50 feet (15 m) over Raccoon Creek, and the 17-ton (15 metric ton) Balanced Rock.

Some caves sport fun names such as Shinbone Cave, Fat Man's Misery, and the biggest in the park, the 800-foot-long (240 m) Dancehall Cave, which is large enough to walk into. Others require a headlamp and hands-and-knees entry. Trail surfaces range from wooden boardwalks and stairs to dirt trails that can get muddy. The Maquoketa Caves were first discovered in the 1830s, and became a state park in 1921, making it one of the state's earliest.

Explore the caves and greenery of Maquoketa.

Maquoketa, IA | Season: Year-round

Cheer It or Two-Wheel It During RAGBRAI

France has its famous bike race each summer, and Iowa has its cross-state ride. Started as a ride with friends in 1973 by two *Des Moines Register* newspaper columnists, John Karras and Donald Kaul, RAGBRAI (*Register*'s Annual Great Bike Ride Across Iowa) has ballooned into what is now the oldest, largest, and longest recreational bicycle touring event in the world. Around 15,000 bikers arrive in the Hawkeye State for an eight-day, 450-plus-mile (724 km) pedalpalooza that takes place the last full week of July.

Each year covers a new route across the state, but the ride always begins along Iowa's western border on the Missouri River and ends along the eastern border on the Mississippi River. One thing stays consistent, however, and that's Iowan hospitality as eight Iowa communities along the route are chosen to serve as "host" communities for riders, offering overnight stays, hot food, and warm welcomes. For those who don't stay in private homes along the route, camping areas are set up on school grounds and fairgrounds.

RAGBRAI cyclists head down Main Street in Des Moines.

Multicity, IA | Season: July

Fall in Love With Loess

Many have claimed Iowa to be as flat as a pancake. However, rising hundreds of feet above the plains, and undulating for 220 miles (350 km) along the Missouri River in western Iowa, the Loess (rhymes with bus) Hills region easily proves these breakfast-food theorists wrong.

The area was formed from thousands of years of wind-blown sediment (loess) created when receding ice age glaciers ground underlying rock into fine, dustlike drift, which was eventually swept up by strong westerly winds and deposited layer by layer, forming the steep drifts and rolling hills. The thickness of the loess, up to 200 feet (60 m) in some places, makes Iowa's hills unique in North America. In fact, only in Shaanxi, China, does an equally large and intricate landform exist.

Stretching from Council Bluffs to around Sioux City, the Loess Hills are traversed by an eponymous scenic byway. However, plenty of diversions entice outdoor exploration,

Council Bluffs to Sioux City, IA | **Season:** Year-round

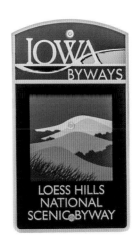

including miles of hiking trails scattered up and down the byway. The Hitchcock Nature Center explains the area's unique ecosystem, and its 45-foot-tall (14 m) observation tower boasts mesmerizing views. It's especially nice in the fall, when colors are in peak bloom, and hawks, eagles, and other birds of prey are migrating south.

A tour and chèvre cheese tasting at Doe's and Diva's Dairy, complete with resident goat and sheep herds, are good family fun. Loess Hills Lavender Farm is a scented and scenic stop, with magnificent fields of purple flowers ablaze during summer. Or drop by Small's Fruit Farm and pick strawberries, apples, and pumpkins during their seasons, and enjoy a piece of homemade pie in their pie parlor.

Fall is a colorful time to climb Devil's Backbone.

Be a Daredevil

Iowa's first state park, dedicated in 1920, Backbone State Park gets its name from a steep and narrow limestone ridge with an ominous name, "Devil's Backbone." The ridge divides the park, and at its narrowest, is 15 feet (5 m) wide, with sides between 50 and 80 feet (15 to 24 m) tall, making it one of the most popular climbing spots in the state.

Not only does the park have dozens more thrilling routes to climb, the varied landscape across its 2,000 heavily wooded acres (810 ha) includes a cave, unusual rock formations, a natural spring, a lake where visitors can rent electric boats, kayaks, and canoes, and 21 miles (34 km) of twisting trails that are especially lovely when fall colors light up the leaves. After a day of climbing, modern four-season cabins and campsites are available for rent and can be reserved ahead online.

Dundee, IA | **Season:** Year-round

A sundial sits among the tulips in Pella.

> **"IN PELLA, DUTCH HISTORY AND CULTURE ARE ALIVE AND WELL."**

Tiptoe Through the Tulips

Everyone's heard of the Pennsylvania Dutch, but how about the Iowa Dutch? Less than a one-hour drive from Des Moines is Pella, a charming slice of Holland, complete with a typical main square and a canal.

Immigrants from the Netherlands founded the town of roughly 10,000 in 1847. Many descendants of those original settlers still live in Pella, where Dutch history and culture are alive and well. Some residents even speak Pella Dutch, or Iowa Dutch, a derivative dialect of South Guelderish.

The town's most recognizable landmark is the 124-foot-tall (38 m) Vermeer Windmill, the largest working grain mill in the country, which was built in the Netherlands and shipped to Iowa in 2002. From its observation deck, take a gander over the Historical Village, a collection of 22 buildings that walk visitors through Pella history and Dutch traditions, including a church, log cabin, meat and cheese shop, wooden shoe cobbler, and the childhood home of the infamous Wyatt Earp. Drop by Jaarsma Bakery, family owned and operated since 1898, and try made-from-scratch specialties such as Dutch letters, almond-filled pastries shaped like an S.

Pella's signature event, the Tulip Time festival, unfurls through the charming streets at the beginning of May, and features parades, traditional food, clothing, and music, and a 5K run. The festival's namesake flowers strut their stuff by the thousands, with colorful tulips on dazzling display in flower beds, parade floats, and just about everywhere a bulb can be planted.

An added bonus of a Pella visit? Just a few miles away is Iowa's largest lake, Lake Red Rock, popular for water sports and camping in summer, and snowshoeing and watching bald eagles roost from the Horn's Ferry Bridge in winter.

Pella, IA | **Season:** May

Float on the Upper Iowa River

Named one of the top 100 adventures in the United States by *National Geographic Adventure* magazine, a mellow paddle around U-shaped bends and through astonishing scenery on the Upper Iowa River is a bucket-list topper for kayakers, canoeists, and tubers.

The 136-mile (219 km) river originates in LeRoy, Minnesota, and flows through the Driftless Area, eventually emptying into the Mississippi River near New Albin. The pace is leisurely, which is just the right speed to admire eagles flying overhead and the varied scenery that changes from a narrow river carving through grassy plains to a wider waterway flanked by pine tree–capped limestone bluffs 200 to 300 feet (60 to 90 m) high.

The river is especially gorgeous when fall unleashes dazzling display of yellow, orange, and red leaves. The river also meanders through the welcoming town of Decorah, and campgrounds are scattered along the Upper Iowa River's shores, making an easy rest stop for the night.

> "THE UPPER IOWA RIVER IS A BUCKET-LIST TOPPER FOR KAYAKERS, CANOEISTS, AND TUBERS."

Northeast IA | Season: Spring to fall

Chimney Rock Campground sits on the river bluffs of northeast Iowa.

Barneløpet is a children's ski and walk event along the cross-country trails in Decorah.

Daydream in the Driftless

Although most of the Hawkeye State can thank glaciers for its good looks (see the Loess Hills), one corner of Iowa was left untouched by the ice, and is called the Driftless, a name that nods to the lack of drift (ground-down land and rock) deposited when glaciers recede. What outdoor lovers will find are hills and rivers, limestone bluffs and pine groves, eagles, and European-settled towns whose friendly residents bolster the Midwest's amicable reputation.

Covering 24,000 square miles (62,160 km²) in northeast Iowa, as well as parts of Wisconsin and Minnesota, the Driftless is as dreamy as it gets in Iowa. Although summer draws people to the region's wandering rivers and streams for tubing, canoeing, and trout fishing, winter brings out cross-country skiers to the trails around

the Norwegian town of Decorah, including the 11-mile (18 km) Trout Run Trail that loops through town, and serves bikers and walkers in warmer weather.

Pikes Peak State Park is considered one of the most photographed places in Iowa, especially in October when trees blaze with gold, red, and orange leaves. The park's most majestic view of the Mississippi River comes from a 500-foot (150 m) bluff that gives the park its name.

A strenuous hike to Point Ann offers scenic views of the town of McGregor and the Mississippi River. A few miles north of the park, explore Effigy Mounds National Monument.

For a stroll through history, check out McGregor and Lansing, whose Main Streets are now National Register-listed historic districts, or wander the two-mile-long (3.2 km) Riverwalk in Guttenberg, known for its stone buildings and German heritage.

Decorah, IA | Season: Year-round

The Julien Dubuque Monument

Where Iowa Began

The stunning 1,437-acre (582 ha) Mines of Spain is directly linked to Iowa's beginnings and French-Canadian fur trader Julien Dubuque.

Dubuque arrived in 1785 and established a relationship with Native Mesquakie, who granted permission for him to mine the lead deposits in the area. In 1796, Spain, who owned the land, granted Dubuque a 189-square-mile (490 km²) tract, and he named it the Mines of Spain. Under the Black Hawk Purchase in 1832, the U.S. government opened the area to settlement, and it came to be called Dubuque.

Today, the Mines of Spain offers prime wildlife viewing of bobcats, flying squirrels, red-shouldered hawks, and bald eagles. There are interpretive nature trails, and miles of trails for cross-country skiing, hiking, and biking twist through prairies and woods, and meander down to the Mississippi River.

Dubuque, IA   **Season:** Year-round

Walk or Bike the High Trestle Trail and Bridge

Cutting through farmland and five Iowa towns (Woodward, Madrid, Slater, Sheldahl, and Ankeny), the 25-mile (40 km) trail was a former train corridor serving two different railroads: the Iowa and Minnesota Railway and the Milwaukee Road. But since opening in 2011, the pedestrian-friendly High Trestle Trail has become a go-to for bikers, walkers, runners, and families, thanks to its flat and paved surface, and connection to the larger 670-plus-mile (1,080 km) Central Iowa Trail network.

There are plenty of deviations and diversions along the trail too, such as Firetrucker Brewery in Ankeny, and the Flat Tire Lounge, a bar and grill with an 800-square-foot (75 m²) outdoor deck in Madrid. However, the highlight of the trail is unquestionably its namesake, the 13-story-tall, half-mile-long (0.8 km) High Trestle Bridge that spans the Des Moines River.

American goldfinch

Although the bridge's six viewing platforms offer expansive Des Moines River Valley vistas, the bridge itself has become the real scene stealer and a focal point along the trail for visitors and locals. Paying homage to the area's coal-mining history, 41 steel square frames at varying angles span the bridge and represent the interior of a historic mine shaft and its support cribs. The changing geometry of the abstract structures around the path creates a sensation of moving through a mine shaft.

Come dusk, the experience gets even better thanks to blue LED bulbs that stay on until midnight and give the historic bridge some futuristic flair.

Ankeny to Woodward, IA   **Season:** Year-round

Watch Iceboaters on Clear Lake

Though well known as a summertime haven for water sports, when temperatures drop to single digits and the wind howls over the frozen surface, Clear Lake brings out a heartier breed—iceboaters. Entirely wind-powered, iceboats are constructed of a lightweight shallow hull that sits on a wooden plank with three runners, or blades, attached. A mast and boom support a sail, which boat captains—often sailors sitting just inches from the ice's surface—know just how to optimize to harness the wind. At seven miles (11 km) long, 2.5 miles (4 km) wide, and with consistent "fuel" blowing across its 3,684 acres (1,491 ha), Clear Lake is ground zero for Iowa iceboaters, and made for picking up speed. Although participating requires years of experience, watching these vessels whip over the ice at speeds up to 100 miles an hour (160 km/h) gives new meaning to the phrase "Let's chill by the lake."

Clear Lake, IA | **Season:** Winter

Effigy Mounds National Monument sits on the bank of the Mississippi River.

1. TAKE A SWING AT THE FIELD OF DREAMS

Thanks to the 1989 blockbuster film *Field of Dreams*, Dyersville, Iowa, and baseball are forever linked, and the ball field that appeared on-screen is now a tourist magnet for fans, Little League games, and even major league meetups. Tour the historic farmhouse, which is also rentable.

2. DROP IN AT THE LAURIDSEN SKATEPARK

Skateboarding made its Olympic debut at the 2020 Summer Olympic Games in Tokyo, and this 88,000-square-foot (8,180 m²) skate park, the largest in the country and opened in 2021, sets the training bar for future athletes thanks to competition-caliber course features located right on the river in downtown Des Moines.

3. STEP BACK IN TIME ON A RIVERBOAT

Relive the days when the most sophisticated and relaxing way to travel the Mighty Mississippi was via riverboat. The *Twilight,* a replica of the lavish Victorian-era steamboat, offers one- and two-day journeys within Upper Mississippi River National Wildlife and Fish Refuge, a sanctuary for nearly 200 bird species.

4. STARGAZE AT WHITE-ROCK CONSERVANCY

Coon Rapids boasts some of the darkest skies in the state, far removed from big city lights, making the Whiterock Conservancy a perfect spot for stargazers to point

their telescopes toward the Milky Way. For overnight viewing, pitch a tent at one of 13 nearby campsites.

5. CLIP, GRIP, AND ZIP

Adrenaline junkies looking for the best zip-line canopy tour in Iowa will find their thrills at Sky Tours of YMCA Union Park Camp in Dubuque, soaring over tree-lined ridges and threading towering trees on nine different lines, ranging from 300 to 1,000 feet (90 to 305 m) long, some up to 75 feet (23 m) high.

6. LEAF PEEP ON HORSEBACK

Spend an autumn in Iowa and you'll be pleasantly surprised at the Technicolor peep show Mother Nature puts on around the state. Gazing from a car window is just fine, but a 2.5-hour horseback ride through Shimek State Forest, near the town of Farmington, is unforgettable.

7. EXPLORE THE FOUR SEASONS IN OKOBOJI

The glacier-carved Great Lakes region referred to simply as Okoboji is Iowa's resort region and is made up of nine natural lakes, five of which are interconnected, granting four seasons of outdoor fun to lovers of fishing, sailing, swimming, leaf peeping, snowmobiling, and cross-country skiing, as well as families who've been vacationing here for generations.

8. CONTEMPLATE THE MYSTERY OF EFFIGY MOUNDS NATIONAL MONUMENT

More than 200 mounds built by Native Americans sit on a bluff

overlooking the Upper Mississippi River Valley in Iowa's Driftless Area. Considered sacred by many Native American tribes, these ancient mounds are mostly conical in shape, but around 30 are effigies in the shape of bears and birds.

9. GET OUT YEAR-ROUND AT SEVEN OAKS

Whether you're slapping on skis or a snowboard, racing in snow tubes, or dipping into the Des Moines River in a kayak or inner tube for a float under a 185-foot-tall (56 m) bridge, this family-owned, one-stop shop for outdoor fun is open year-round.

10. VISIT A TOWN FIT FOR A KING

Looking for curiosities in Iowa? The small town of Ida Grove, self-proclaimed Castletown, U.S.A., nears the top of the list thanks to castle-style buildings scattered around its 2.1 square miles (5 km²). Conceived and built during the 1970s and '80s, they house a roller rink, the local newspaper office, and even welcome visitors at the entrance to town.

The Eye of the Needle rock
formation at Monument Rocks

KANSAS

Make your way east to west across the Sunflower State
for outdoor recreation as diverse as its landscapes.

NEBRA

COLORADO

Prairie Dog
State Park ■

Wilson
State Park

Little Jerusalem
Badlands State Park 🥾

Cheyenne Bottoms
Wildlife Area 🦆

K A N

Dorothy's House and the Land of Oz
(Wizard of Oz museum) ■

OKL

TEXAS

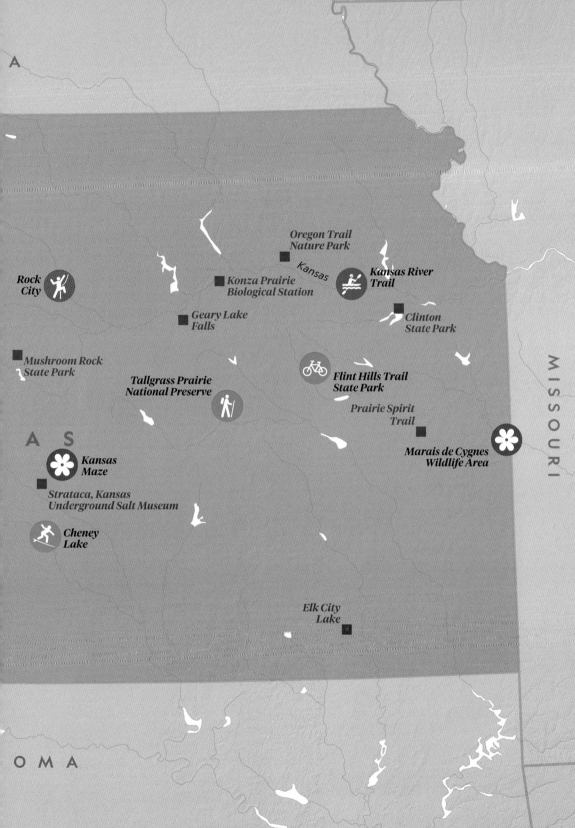

A

Rock
City

Mushroom Rock
State Park

Oregon Trail
Nature Park

Kansas

Konza Prairie
Biological Station

Kansas River
Trail

Geary Lake
Falls

Clinton
State Park

Tallgrass Prairie
National Preserve

Flint Hills Trail
State Park

Prairie Spirit
Trail

A   S

Kansas
Maze

Marais de Cygnes
Wildlife Area

Strataca, Kansas
Underground Salt Museum

Cheney
Lake

Elk City
Lake

M I S S O U R I

O M A

Kansas-Style Kitesurfing

Kitesurfing has enjoyed explosive growth over the last few years, and Cheney Lake, with its windy conditions and shallow, sandy bottom, is just the spot for beginners to give it a whirl. Located in Cheney State Park about 25 miles (40 km) from Wichita, the lake is an ideal spot for newbie kiters (as well as beginner windsurfers), thanks to several shallow areas with knee- to waist-deep water that makes it much easier to maneuver your equipment while learning the ropes. M&M Point is a recommended launch point, with a nearby cove that's well situated to "catch" kiters who may get blown downwind. Keep in mind that you'll need a wet suit except during the warm summer months.

If you're wiped out after a long session on the water, consider an overnighter. Cheney State Park has several campsites perched at the edge of the lake, so you can easily scope out the water for the next day's adventure.

Cheney, KS | **Season:** Summer

Need an alternate to kitesurfing? Set sail on Cheney Lake.

Prairie Paddling

Kansas isn't all prairies and flatlands: It's also home to scenic waterways like the Kansas River, which offers adventurers an especially memorable way to explore the state. The 173-mile (278 km) river is a vital natural resource, providing drinking water, irrigation, and electricity to many communities. But the east-flowing Kaw, as it's known among locals, also beckons paddling enthusiasts. Depending on the route, visitors can expect to see sweeping views of pastures, farmland, the Flint Hills prairie, and dramatic limestone hills in eastern Kansas. Wildlife abounds, too: Bald eagles, beavers, blue herons, and deer are spottable year-round, while migratory bird species such as gulls and pelicans pop in during spring and fall. And endangered species like least terns and piping plovers like to nest on the sandbars.

The Kaw is an excellent option for beginner and novice paddlers, as it's usually relatively calm. Depending on water levels, sandbars are perfect spots for rests and picnics. Outfitters that rent canoes, kayaks, and even stand-up paddleboards are found at most access points, especially in urban areas such as Manhattan and Lawrence.

Take a paddling adventure on the Kansas River Trail.

Multicity, KS | **Season:** Summer and fall

A Birding Paradise

Designated as a Globally Important Bird Area by the American Bird Conservancy, 41,000-acre (16,590 ha) Cheyenne Bottoms is the largest marsh in the interior United States. It is a big deal for birding enthusiasts: The majority of bird species observed in Kansas—to date, some 356 of 471—have been seen here. No matter when they stop by, visitors are all but guaranteed a mesmerizing display of feathered creatures, as well as other wildlife. Eagles are a dramatic sight during winter, followed in the spring by more than half a million ducks and geese, along with sandhill and whooping cranes. The summer months mean the arrival of tens of thousands of shorebirds, as well as a quarter million (or more!) migratory birds stopping here on their way south to warmer climates. Cheyenne Bottoms represents a critical stopover in these countless journeys: According to the Nature Conservancy, which oversees the nearly 8,000-acre (3,240 ha) preserve adjacent to the wildlife

Western meadowlark

area, birds migrate from the refuge north as far as western Alaska and the edge of the Arctic, and south to Louisiana, Texas, and Central and South America.

The Kansas Wetlands Education Center, located near one of the entrances to the wildlife area and managed by Fort Hays State University in cooperation with the Kansas Department of Wildlife Parks and Tourism, offers a wealth of resources, including educational programs and guided tours (reservations required on weekdays; first come, first served on weekends). Self-guided expeditions are also available via walking paths that crisscross the wetlands. Sunset is an especially magical time to visit, with silhouettes of countless birds against the backdrop of a darkening sky.

Great Bend, KS | **Season:** Year-round

Leavenworth's eryngoes bloom at Marais des Cygnes Wildlife Area.

Foraging Fun

Nature-made snacks are ripe for the picking at the 7,654-acre (3,097 ha) Marais des Cygnes Wildlife Area, whose mix of managed wetlands and bottomland hardwood forest draws a range of migratory waterfowl and other wetland species. But it also beckons foraging enthusiasts who take advantage of year round opportunities to taste nature's bounty. Morel and oyster mushrooms pop up in the spring and summer, while wild strawberries and blackberries are popular pickings during the summer. In the fall, persimmons and nuts like pecans and black walnuts are ready for harvest. Nuts are commonly found at abandoned farming sites and in the floodplains of the Marais des Cygnes River and other streams (though some years are more fruitful than others). Pickers should also keep in mind that foraging is only allowed for personal use.

Lyon County, KS | **Season:** Year-round

"IT'S THE LONGEST TRAIL IN KANSAS, AND THE BEST WAY TO EXPERIENCE IT IS ON TWO WHEELS."

Ride the Former Santa Fe Trail Route

In the 1880s, transcontinental train lines, including the Missouri Pacific Railroad that ran through Kansas on its way west, crisscrossed the country. Such railways are no longer in operation, but their routes have paved the way for modern-day explorers via remarkable rail-to-trail conservancy efforts like the 117-mile (188 km) Flint Hills Trail State Park that runs through east-central Kansas. It's the longest trail in Kansas, and the best way to experience it is on two wheels.

The trail is traversable for nearly 100 miles (160 km) from Osawatomie in the east to Council Grove in the west. Its most westward stretch, 24 miles (39 km) from Council Grove to Herington, is still under construction. Experienced cyclists can knock out the trail's total distance in a day. But recreational riders, as well as families with kids, can choose from several out-and-back or point-to-point routes for a more casual outing or weekend overnighter, thanks to small towns and campgrounds along the route.

Towns along the way are located approximately 10 to 15 miles (16 to 24 km) apart, with plenty of options for pit stops. Heading west, riders can enjoy several notable trailside attractions. Among them: an airplane graveyard in Rantoul (permission is required to enter); the shady, 490-acre (200 ha) Pomona State Park, one of several camping sites along the trail and perfect for an overnight pit stop; and historic sites and landmarks, several located in Council Grove.

Just west of Council Grove, the Trail Days Cafe and Museum is a fitting end to any ride. Built in 1860–61, the historic home offers an immersive experience with artifacts and home-cooked meals.

Multicity, KS | **Season:** Year-round

The Flint Hills are a playground for hiking and cycling.

Rock On

Rock climbing in Kansas? Yes, although techni-cally, it's called bouldering, as scrambling up and around these egg-shaped concretions doesn't require bolts, ropes, or harnesses. About a 10-minute drive from the town of Minneapolis, Kansas, Rock City is a boulder field that is also a national natural landmark that draws many curious onlookers, as well as occa-sional experienced climbers (some hoisting a mattress-like crash pad placed on the ground to protect them from falls). It's also a great spot for kiddos who love climbing to burn off some energy, and the boulders themselves, which resemble dinosaur eggs, make for a fantastic photo backdrop. On the hillside overlooking the Solomon River, Rock City boasts about 200 boulder formations across five acres (2 ha). Some of the boul-ders stretch up to 30 feet (9 m) wide. A small fee is required to enter the park, and the boulders are located near the parking lot.

Dakota, KS | **Season:** Year-round

> "SCRAMBLING UP
> AND AROUND THESE
> EGG-SHAPED CONCRETIONS
> DOESN'T REQUIRE BOLTS,
> ROPES, OR HARNESSES."

Rock City offers family fun for boulderers.

Little Jerusalem Badlands State Park is known for its iconic rock formations.

Ancient Landscapes

Named for the way its dramatic rock formations mimic the distant view of the ancient walled city, Little Jerusalem Badlands State Park is a newly designated, 332-acre (134 ha) state park that offers a fascinating contrast to the sweeping flatlands of the state. Its towering rock formations, deep canyons, and mysterious spires make up the state's largest Niobrara chalk formation. The landscape provides critical habitat for wildlife, including ferruginous hawks, cliff swallows, and rock wrens, as well as many native amphibians and reptiles. The park also is home to the single largest population of Great Plains wild buckwheat, an endemic plant found nowhere else in the world. In addition, fossils of flying and swimming reptiles dating back some 85 million years ago, as well as ancient clams and oysters, also have been found here (though if you happen to stumble across any, a strict no-collection policy applies for all finds in the park).

Oakley, KS | **Season:** Year-round

Two crushed-rock, minimal-grade trails offer access to overlooks of the dramatic landscape. The quarter-mile (0.4 km) Overlook Trail is a short walk from the parking lot, while the approximately 1.2-mile (2 km) Life on the Rocks Trail features two overlook spots. Along the way, keep an eye out for cliff swallows frolicking around their hive-shaped mud nests, hawks circling above, and pronghorn (also called antelope) on the landscape. For a deeper dive into the fascinating landscape and its history, consider a naturalist-guided hike into the outcroppings led by the Kansas Department of Wildlife and Parks.

Celebrate sunflowers at an annual festival.

A Sunflower Stroll

Every year during sunflower season, typically mid-August through early September, farms and attractions across Kansas burst to life with its cheerful state flower. At the family-owned Kansas Maze, which several years ago pivoted from its long-standing corn maze attraction into all things sunflower, visitors can get close to these showstopping blooms via trails among its 16 acres (6 ha)—and some 600,000 flowers! You'll also find a sunflower festival, a market, and an annual trail run through the fields, with distances of 3.1 miles (5 km) and a mile (1.6 km); just beware the pollinating bees!

Elsewhere around the state, opportunities abound to experience sunflower season. A few general rules of thumb: Plan early, as sunflower season is short and sweet; be respectful of fields and make sure you're on public property; check out social media pages for information on visiting hours and peak blooming times.

Buhler, KS   **Season:** August and September

Explore the Open Prairie

These vistas of rolling plains and rippling prairie grass haven't changed much over the centuries, meaning that the views seen today reflect what greeted Meriwether Lewis and William Clark on their journey west in 1803. Today, Tallgrass Prairie National Preserve protects 11,000 acres (4,450 ha) of the prairie that once stretched across central North America. It is now the only remaining remnant of this kind of ecosystem in the world. It's also home to another American icon: an approximately 100-member herd of bison. In addition to unique natural resources, a historic ranch house, limestone barn, and schoolhouse can also be found on the preserve.

Visitors can explore it via 40 miles (64 km) of moderately difficult backcountry hiking trails ranging from 3.8 to 13 miles (6 to 21 km). Close to the visitors center, the Southwind Nature Trail (1.75-mile/2.8-km loop) and Bottomland Nature Trail (half- to three-quarter-mile/0.8- to 1.2-km loop) are easy options for a quick hike, while the 3.8-mile (6 km) Three Pasture Loop follows ranch roads and a mowed path through upland prairie. For longer outings, the six-mile (10 km) Red House Trail and Scenic Overlook Trail (6.4 miles/10 km round-trip) showcase cultural features of the historic ranching area, such as remnants of stone fences and more than two dozen human-made ponds.

Maps are available in the visitors center, but limestone markers along the trails guide the way. Hikers also need to take care to properly open and close cattle gates, avoid walking on cattle guards, and maintain a safe distance (at least a football field) from bison. Camping isn't allowed, but you can explore the vast prairie landscapes on day hikes (camping options are about eight miles/13 km away).

Strong City, KS   **Season:** Year-round

Take the challenge of the mountain biking trails at Wilson State Park.

Send It on Sandstone

The trail system at Wilson State Park features about 25 miles (40 km) beloved by local mountain bikers, even earning the coveted "Epic" status from the International Mountain Bicycling Association. No surprise why: Three six- to eight-mile (10 to 13 km), single-track loops wind through ancient landscapes of red sandstone rock formations, with stunning views of nearby Wilson Lake reservoir and plenty of flowy dips, drops, bridges, and other challenges. Most of the trail is designated as moderate to easy, but there are several short technical sections (case in point: one named Brokebike Mountain).

The three loops—Golden Belt, Hell Creek, and Marina—should be ridden in succession in a clockwise direction, with 12 individual forks throughout the system. To ride the entire Epic route as one continuous loop, you'll stay left at all forks; if you want a shorter option, head right ("cutoff"). And if you hit a section that's above your skills, don't forget the mountain biking mantra "When in doubt, walk it out."

Sylvan Grove, KS | **Season:** Spring to fall

Blooming flowers surround
Kansas' Mushroom Rock.

1. GET SALTY

The two-hour tour at Strataca kicks off with a 90-second descent some 650 feet (200 m) to a working salt mine, which is part of a vast network of 150 miles (240 km) of tunnels that extend all the way to New Mexico. The stars of the subterranean show are the 250-million-year-old salt crystals.

2. TAKE SOME SNOW DAYS

Kansas's relatively mild winters still allow for some cold-weather adventure: Think snowy hikes and cross-country skiing. On the north shore of Clinton Lake in Clinton State Park is the state's only designated cross-country ski trail, which starts near the park office and runs for about five miles (8 km).

3. SPOT PRAIRIE DOGS

The prairie dog sculpture at the entrance to Prairie Dog State Park is a good indicator of the curious creatures usually scampering around. Camping options include a reservable cabin and primitive/hookup-enabled sites. A 1.4-mile (2.3 km) nature trail is a fun way to explore the park and observe wildlife (beyond the prairie dogs, too).

4. HAVE FUN AMONG FUNGI ROCKS

Designated as one of the Eight Wonders of Kansas Geography, the five-acre (2 ha) Mushroom Rock State Park gets its name from massive, fungi-shaped rock formations, the largest of which is 27 feet (8 m) across. Made of cemented calcium carbonate dating as far back as 144 million years, the unique rocks once served as meeting points for Native Americans and early pioneers.

5. TAKE A SUMMERTIME DIP

In scenic Elk City Lake, a 4,500-acre (1,820 ha) reservoir, amenities include a boat ramp and swim beach. Ambitious types can work up a sweat beforehand on a vast network of nearby trails in the surrounding state park.

6. RIDE AMID WILDFLOWERS AND WILDLIFE

Nature and quaint small towns make the 52-mile (84 km) Prairie Spirit Trail in eastern Kansas wildly popular among cyclists and hikers. Built on a former rail bed, the trail is mostly paved and flat, running from the Flint Hills Nature Trail in the north to the Southwind Rail Trail in the south.

7. TREK PRAIRIE VISTAS

Three trails ranging from 2.6 to 6.2 miles (4.2 km to 10 km) allow hikers (no bikes or dogs) to explore the mostly protected landscape of lowland gallery forest, ancient limestone outcroppings, and native tallgrass prairie in Konza Prairie with sweeping vistas of the Flint Hills and Kansas River Valley at the highest points.

8. FOLLOW THE YELLOW BRICK ROAD

No trip to Kansas is complete without a *Wizard of Oz* reference, and Dorothy's House and Land of Oz bring the perennial classic to life with numerous exhibits and activities, including a restored 1907 farmhouse just like Dorothy's, a yellow brick road to follow, and movie scene displays.

9. WALK IN PIONEER FOOTSTEPS

Centuries ago, pioneer wagons traversed the plains on the way west through Oregon Trail Nature Park; in fact, the road that leads to the park is part of the original Oregon Trail. Modern-day explorers can choose from several short loop trails (with some steep sections) that offer sweeping views of the surrounding landscape.

10. STRETCH TO REACH FANTASTIC WATERFALLS

Reaching the 35-foot (11 m) cascades of Geary Falls requires some effort, as there's no signage or official trail, but it's well worth it to see the powerful flows. Follow the route worn by previous visitors to see the view from the top; a steep, rocky trail leads to the base of the falls.

American buffalo

Big South Fork National River and Recreational Area is home to the tallest waterfall in Kentucky.

KENTUCKY

With plentiful waterways, unique biking trails, and high-soaring adventures, you'll find yourself with plenty to do in this sporty state.

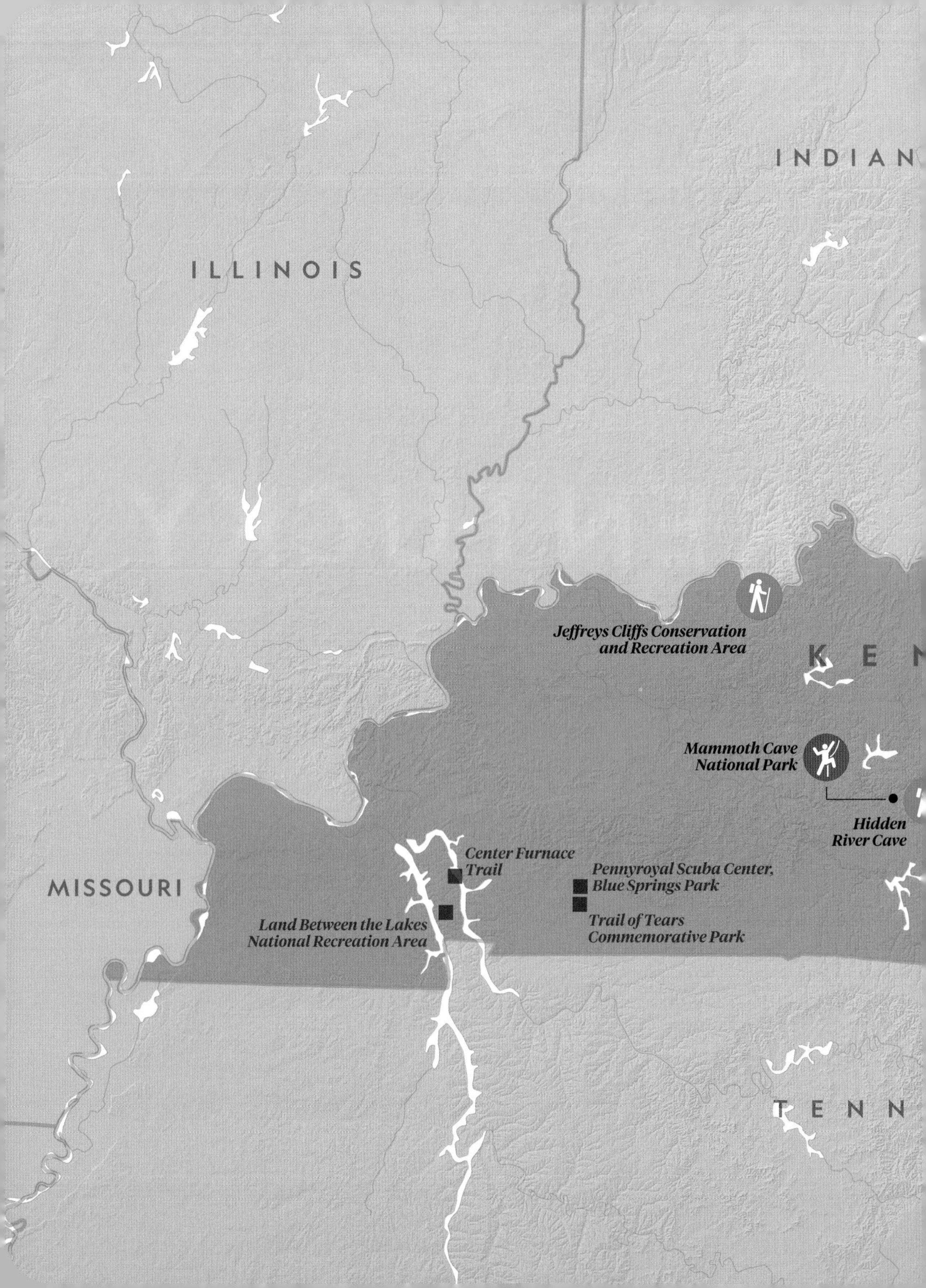

INDIAN

ILLINOIS

KEN

Jeffreys Cliffs Conservation
and Recreation Area

Mammoth Cave
National Park

Hidden
River Cave

MISSOURI

Center Furnace
Trail

Pennyroyal Scuba Center,
Blue Springs Park

Land Between the Lakes
National Recreation Area

Trail of Tears
Commemorative Park

TENN

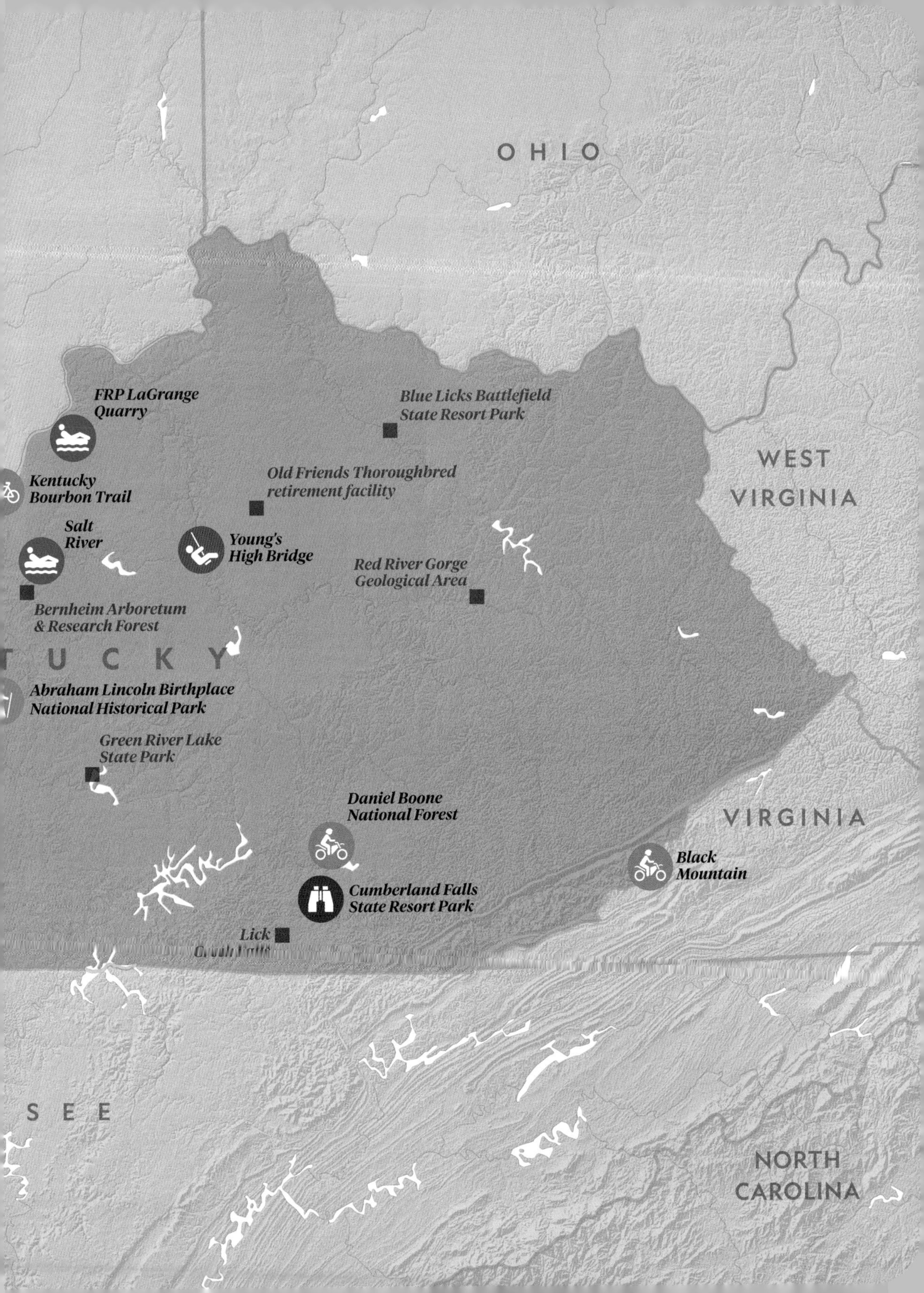

OHIO

WEST
VIRGINIA

FRP LaGrange
Quarry

Blue Licks Battlefield
State Resort Park

Kentucky
Bourbon Trail

Old Friends Thoroughbred
retirement facility

Salt
River

Young's
High Bridge

Red River Gorge
Geological Area

Bernheim Arboretum
& Research Forest

TUCKY

Abraham Lincoln Birthplace
National Historical Park

Green River Lake
State Park

Daniel Boone
National Forest

VIRGINIA

Black
Mountain

Cumberland Falls
State Resort Park

Lick
Creek Falls

SEE

NORTH
CAROLINA

Float Down the Salt River

The family that operates the Awesome Flea Market, an indoor-outdoor flea market in Shepherdsville, also runs the adjacent Awesome Lazy River, 15 miles (24 km) south of Louisville on Interstate 65. Follow the signs directing you to the parking lot. After paying at the stand, pick up a single or double tube, grab some paddles, and head to the Salt River, named after a historic salt lick in 1779. A refreshing summer tradition, tubing down the cool tree-flanked river takes about two hours. The current is gentle, so expect a leisurely ride. At the end point near a railroad bridge, guests drop off the tube and hop on a shuttle back to the starting point. The Awesome Lazy River is open Saturdays and Sundays from Memorial Day to Labor Day weekends.

The Salt River is also a prime fishing hole. Anglers come to its shores seeking various bass—but it's the annual white bass spawning that brings fishers from far and wide to these waters.

Shepherdsville, KY | Season: Summer

Laze your way along the Salt River.

Spelunking America's Greatest Cave System

As a UNESCO World Heritage site, an international biosphere reserve, and a dark sky park, Mammoth Cave National Park has a lot to offer. You can spend days exploring 52,830 acres (21,380 ha) of rolling hills, rivers, valleys, and cedars, pines, and oak trees.

Follow a guide on a historic tour route through the caves.

Thousands of years ago, the park's earliest residents, the prehistoric people from the Late Archaic and Early Woodland periods, moved from the forests and plains of Kentucky to the caves. By around 1200 B.C., early explorers discovered more than 19 miles (31 km) of cave passageways. Today, more than 400 miles (640 km) of the underground limestone rock labyrinth have been uncovered, making it the world's largest known cave system.

Mammoth offers a variety of guided cave tours, including a two-hour accessible experience that provides elevator access to the cave and 0.5 mile (0.8 km) of paved passage. Those up to the challenge should opt for the Wild Cave Tour, where adventurers hike over uneven terrain, squeeze though 10-inch-tall (25 cm), three-foot-wide (0.9 m) passages, duck jutting rocks, and even wade through water.

Mammoth Cave, KY | Season: Year-round

Greetings, Mr. President

Abraham Lincoln was born in 1809 in a one-room log cabin in Sinking Spring Farm near Hodgenville, Kentucky. Thomas Lincoln, Abe's father, bought the 300-acre (120 ha) farm in 1808. From humble beginnings, Lincoln went on to become one of the nation's greatest presidents. To learn about his early life and family, head to the Abraham Lincoln Birthplace National Historical Park, the country's first memorial to Lincoln.

Designed by prominent architect John Russell Pope, the neoclassical building resembles a smaller-scale version of the Lincoln Memorial in Washington, D.C. The cornerstone was laid by then president Theodore Roosevelt. The 56 steps leading up to the building represent the number of years Lincoln lived. Within the grand structure made with Connecticut pink granite and Tennessee marble lies a symbolic birth cabin.

Viceroy butterfly

The park has two wheelchair-accessible routes: Pathway of a President and the Boundary Oak Trail. In 1928, the War Department built stone steps and railings down to the Sinking Spring, which supplied water for baby Lincoln and his family. Ranger-led guided walking tours are available in the summer. In the fall, the hardwood trees display an assortment of autumn leaves, and the park hosts a night sky event.

Ten miles (16 km) away, the Boyhood Home Unit at Knob Creek features a replica log cabin, similar to the one where Lincoln lived from age two to seven. The three-mile (4.8 km) round-trip Overlook Trail heads to a field the Lincoln family once farmed, a steep climb to the ridgetop above the farm, a pond, and an overlook with views of the valley.

Hodgenville, KY | Season: Year-round

Stairways help you climb the elevation at Jeffreys Cliffs.

Hiking at Jeffreys Cliffs

Jeffreys Cliffs Conservation and Recreation Area is a new 230-acre (90 ha) nature preserve in Hancock County, just east of Hawesville. The preserve features near-vertical 100-foot-tall (30 m) sandstone cliffs and peaceful woodlands and has two trails. The lower 2.1-mile (3.4 km) trail takes hikers to the dramatic Morgan's Cave, which Confederate guerrillas used as a rendezvous point and hideout during the Civil War. At Tobacco Cave, find a tobacco-curing structure where Indigenous people used to dry their tobacco.

To get to the upper trail, follow the sign to Mossy Gap, head up two flights of wooden stairs, and climb to the top of the sandstone plateau. The upper trail is a flat 3.5-mile (5.6 km) path with several lookout points that offer expansive treetop views. During fall, the leaves change from emerald green to bursts of orange, yellow, and red.

Hancock County, KS | Season: Year-round

Catch a moonbow at
Cumberland Falls.

"MOONBOWS ARE
ESPECIALLY PRONOUNCED
IN WINTER MONTHS."

Catch a Rainbow

In southeastern Kentucky, visitors can photograph the rare "moonbow" at Cumberland Falls State Resort Park. During full moon on a cloudless night, the light from the moon hits the mist at the base of the gushing waterfall, and the refraction creates a lunar rainbow. Cumberland Falls is the only place in the Western Hemisphere where you can capture this enchanting phenomenon with your camera. Faint and barely visible to the naked eye, the moonlit rainbow will show up in your pictures if photographed using a slow shutter speed. Moonbows are especially pronounced in winter months when the sky gets dark earlier.

At 125 feet (38 m) wide and 68 feet (21 m) tall, Cumberland Falls is one of the largest waterfalls in the region, earning the moniker of the Niagara of the South. Indigenous people inhabited the area around the waterfall more than 10,000 years ago. Chickasaw and Creek people were said to have used the area for temporary hunting camps. Virginia explorer Thomas Walker rediscovered the falls in 1750 and named it after the Duke of Cumberland.

Today, this popular tourist attraction is open 24 hours a day and is free to visit; the paved walkway to the observation deck is wheelchair accessible. When day breaks, adventurers who want to take in the views of the rugged Appalachian Mountains can explore the scenic 10.0-mile (17.4 km) Moonbow Trail that begins at Cumberland Falls and runs adjacent to the Cumberland River, ending at the mouth of the Laurel River. Those short on time can embark on the three-mile (4.8 km) round-trip Eagle Falls Trail that starts alongside the Cumberland River, offering dramatic views of Cumberland Falls. The trail wraps around the cliffs, ascends steep steps, and routes through large boulders that eventually lead to a cascading 44-foot (13 m) waterfall.

Corbin, KY | **Season:** Year-round

Bungee Jump Off a Bridge

 The historic Young's High Bridge hovers 283 feet (86 m) above the Kentucky River, making it the highest platform bridge jump in North America. Built in 1889, the 1,659-foot (506 m) Pratt deck truss bridge originally carried the Louisville Southern Railroad and Norfolk and Western Railway across the Ohio River. The line was abandoned after the last train crossed in 1985.

In 2013, Vertigo Bungee purchased the bridge and transformed it into a bungee jumping attraction—the only bridge jump site in the eastern United States. On one weekend a month, from May to October, tethered members of the Vertigo Club take a leap off the steel bridge and plunge down toward the calm Kentucky River.

Annual membership is $10, and registration is required online. For a different view of the bridge, take the Bluegrass Scenic Railroad from nearby Bluegrass Railroad and Museum, which operates antique passenger cars from West Versailles to the eastern end of Young's High Bridge.

> "TETHERED MEMBERS OF THE VERTIGO CLUB TAKE A LEAP OFF THE STEEL BRIDGE AND PLUNGE DOWN TOWARD THE CALM KENTUCKY RIVER."

Versailles, KY **Season:** May to October

Take the plunge: Bungee jump from Young's High Bridge over the Kentucky River.

Hidden River Cave's Sunset Dome is one of the largest freestanding cave domes in the United States.

Hidden in Plain Sight

The mouth of Hidden River Cave is found in the heart of the city of Horse Cave in south-central Kentucky. For centuries, the cave supplied water and cool air to Native Americans and settlers who built a community around these vital resources. It became a popular tourist destination in the early 20th century. However, the growing town didn't have a sewer system, and all the waste ended up flushed into sinkholes and pumped underground. Pollution nearly killed Hidden River Cave, which closed in 1943. In the mid-1980s, the American Cave Conservation Association helped restore the cave. You can learn about the continued preservation effort at the American Cave Museum, built directly on top of the cave. The museum's self-guided, wheelchair-friendly tour includes an elevator ride down to the cave's observation deck. Or you can opt for the guided walking tour, where you descend into the sinkhole via steep stairs and a wooden walkway, then cross the world's longest in-cave swinging bridge.

Though the cave does not have any stalactites or stalagmites, its most distinctive feature is the 250-foot-wide (75 m), 100-foot-tall (30 m) Sunset Dome, the largest single cave room in the Mammoth Cave region. The cave is 58°F (14°C) year-round.

Hidden River Cave also offers an adventure tour where you'll be crawling through tight spaces and scrambling over rocks. There are also options to zip-line or rappel down the cave. The museum is open daily, from 9 a.m. to 5 p.m., with tours available each hour.

Horse Cave, KY | Season: Year-round

Cycle your way along the Kentucky Bourbon Trail.

Taste Bourbon by Bike

Discover the spirit of Kentucky bourbon with a bicycle trip through its birthplace. As part of the Kentucky Bourbon Trail, cyclists can embark on a one- to three-day trek from Louisville to Lexington.

The one-day itinerary is a 55-mile (90 km) loop through Woodford County that begins and ends at the historic 1812 Woodford Reserve Distillery, with stops at Wild Turkey and Four Roses.

The strenuous three-day plan begins in Lexington at Town Branch Distillery and ends in Louisville at Angel's Envy Distillery, traversing 188 miles (302 km) with 9,000 feet (2,740 m) of climbing and stops at eight additional distilleries, including Jim Beam and Maker's Mark.

Book ahead for distillery tours to guarantee a spot. In total, the Kentucky Bourbon Trail features more than 40 distilleries, and other routes are accessible via Ride with GPS, a cycling navigation app.

Louisville to Lexington, KY **Season:** Year-round

Off-Road in the Bluegrass State

The rugged terrains in the verdant forests of Kentucky make for the perfect playground for off-roading adventurers. You can find ATV trails all over the Bluegrass State.

Daniel Boone National Forest has more than 150 miles (240 km) of multiuse trails that allow off-highway vehicles (OHVs), and two designated OHV trail systems: the Redbird Crest and White Sulphur.

At Land Between the Lakes National Recreation Area, the Turkey Bay OHV Area provides 100 miles (160 km) and 2,500 acres (1,010 ha) of rolling, rocky, and steep OHV trails.

Along the Mississippi River, the Carlisle County River Trails are open year-round to OHVs. And Wright's Area 252 Riding Park has 12 miles (19 km) of hills and valley trails over a 252-acre (102 ha) farm that appeals to beginners as well as extreme riders.

Some of the most popular off-road destinations are found in eastern Kentucky. Rush Off-Road in Rush is a 7,000-acre (2,830 ha) tract of land with more than 100 miles (160 km) of wooded trails and open fields. Located in Harlan County, the 7,000-acre (2,830 ha) Black Mountain Off-Road Adventure in Evarts has more than 150 miles (240 km) of easy, moderate, and extreme trails that were repurposed from old strip mining and logging roads. The trails are open all day and year-round. While there, thrill seekers can also zip-line hundreds of feet off the ground at Black Mountain's Thunder Zipline. Each site has different permit requirements, so check before bringing your ATV to the trails, or sign up with an off-roading outfitter.

Multicity, KY **Season:** Year-round

Take a float in the FRP LaGrange Quarry.

Cool Off at the Quarry

 FRP LaGrange Quarry, an expansive rainwater-filled former rock quarry, is a favorite place for locals to cool off in La Grange, around 25 miles (40 km) east of Louisville. Open June through Labor Day weekend, the four-acre (1.6 ha), 55-foot-deep (17 m) quarry is a refreshing spot to float on a tube, kayak, or stand-up paddleboard.

There is no lifeguard on duty, and swimming is not allowed. Guests must use flotation devices at all times. For safety, the quarry is only open to adults.

Four pebble beaches provide easy access to the water. Certified scuba divers with their own gear can dive on the weekends from 11 a.m.

to 7 p.m. Dive into the clear blue water and you might come across primitive-looking paddlefish, bass, and catfish, as well as a submerged telephone booth and police car.

The quarry also has a food truck, surf shack, changing room, and portable bathrooms. Tickets are available online.

La Grange, KY | Season: Summer

See the giants of the Bernheim Arboretum in Clermont.

1. CLIMB THE RED RIVER GORGE

Nicknamed "the Red" by rock climbers, the east-central Kentucky gorge boasts an estimated 150 arches, geological formations carved out by the Red River. A national natural landmark, the gorge's rugged sandstone cliffs within Daniel Boone National Forest have a number of bolted lines for climbers of all levels.

2. NESTLE INTO THE LAND BETWEEN THE LAKES

Tucked between Kentucky Lake and Lake Barkley, Wranglers Campground at the aptly named Land Between the Lakes has 100 miles (160 km) of dedicated horse and wagon trails. Trot along single-track trails that wrap around the shoreline and wooded ridges or double-track roadbeds through mature bottomland hardwood stands. In addition to the horse trails, check out an elk and bison prairie, a planetarium, and an 1850s working farm and living history museum.

3. STROLL THE BERNHEIM ARBORETUM AND RESEARCH FOREST

Philanthropist Isaac W. Bernheim envisioned an art-filled arboretum and forested areas when he endowed 16,000 acres (6,475 ha) of land to the state of Kentucky in 1929. Modern sculptures created by Bernheim's artists in residence, as well as three whimsical wooden Forest Giants by Danish sculptor Thomas Dambo, stand prominently amid more than 8,000 varieties of trees, shrubs, hollies, and perennials.

4. GET HOT ON CENTER FURNACE TRAIL

Along this 0.3-mile (0.5 km) trail at Land Between the Lakes, you can see one of the last remaining brick furnaces, built in the 1840s during the region's flourishing iron ore industry. The loop also includes a replica of a charcoal hearth, a 150-year-old white oak tree, and a cistern that was an important water source for the community.

5. FOLLOW THE TRAIL OF TEARS

One of Kentucky's nine stops along the historic trail, the Trail of Tears Commemorative Park in Hopkinsville marks a portion of the campground the Cherokee Indians used during the trek, as well as grave sites of Chiefs White Path and Fly Smith. Other routes trace the steps of the Cherokee, Muscogee, Seminole, Chickasaw, and Choctaw people, forced to relocate from southeast U.S. to Indian Territory between 1830 and 1850.

6. VISIT THE OLD FRIENDS THOROUGHBRED RETIREMENT FARM

Visit the retirement home of former Kentucky Derby and Preakness champions on a sprawling farm in Georgetown that is a refuge for more than 200 retired Thoroughbred horses. The living museum offers a chance to meet 1997 Kentucky Derby winner Silver Charm.

7. HIKE THE LICK CREEK FALLS TRAIL

In southern Kentucky near Whitley City, this six-mile (10 km) out-and-back passes craggy sandstone bluffs, moss-covered trees, and emerald ferns. Along the way, you'll climb several short steel staircases and cross a few streams before reaching the horseshoe–shaped rock shelter where the Lick Creek Falls pours 78 feet (24 m) down into a pool.

8. MOUNTAIN BIKE AT GREEN RIVER LAKE

This state park opened in 1969 after the U.S. Army Corps of Engineers built a dam to control floods in the region. While swimming, boating, and fishing in the lake are highlights for many visitors, mountain biking enthusiasts exult in the park's 28 miles (45 km) of all-purpose trails.

9. SCUBA DIVE AT BLUE SPRINGS RESORT

Scuba dive in turquoise water at the Pennyroyal Scuba Center at this Hopkinsville resort. The spring-fed quarry is a freshwater dive site featuring more than 40 sunken treasures, including a 1941 Dodge fire truck, a bus, a yacht, a quarry lion, and a basketball hoop.

10. FIND RARE BLOOMS AT BLUE LICKS BATTLEFIELD

One of the rarest plants in the world, the federally endangered Short's goldenrod is found in Carlisle, Kentucky, along an ancient buffalo path. The plant is protected in the nature preserve at Blue Licks, which is also the site of the last Revolutionary War battle in 1782. The yellow flowers bloom from mid-August to November.

Paddle through the landscapes of Atchafalaya National Wildlife Refuge (page 250).

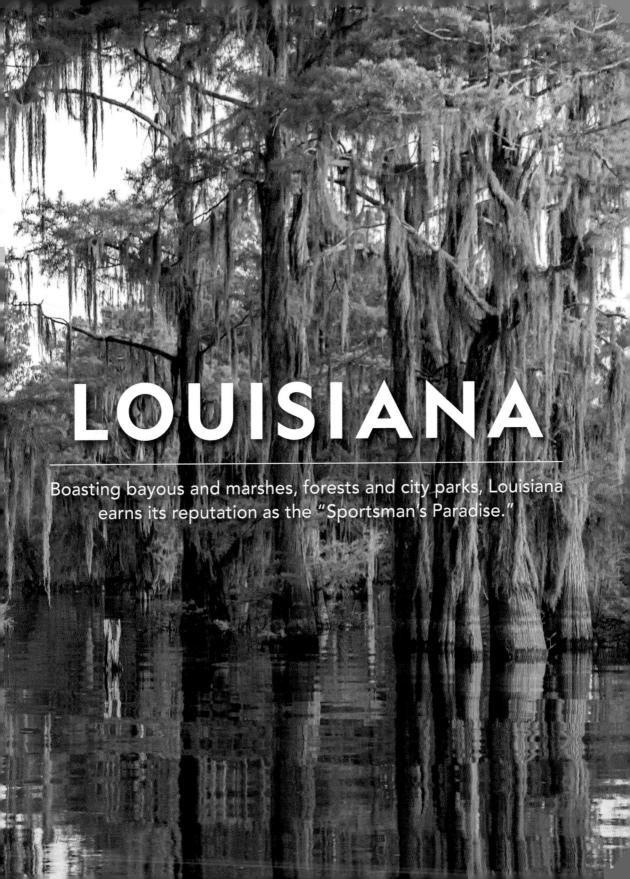

LOUISIANA

Boasting bayous and marshes, forests and city parks, Louisiana earns its reputation as the "Sportsman's Paradise."

ARKANSAS

Upper Ouachite
National Wildlife Refuge

Lake Claiborne

Lincoln Parish
Park

Restoration
Park Trail

Driskill
Mountain

LOUISIANA

Kisatchie
National Forest

Sabine

T E X A S

Gulf of Mexico

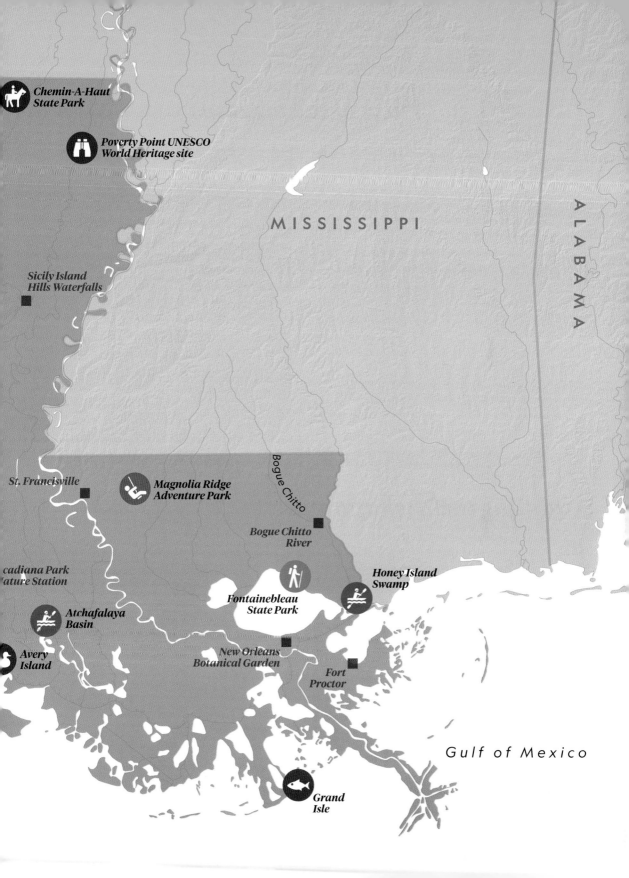

Chemin-A-Haut State Park

Poverty Point UNESCO World Heritage site

Sicily Island Hills Waterfalls

MISSISSIPPI

ALABAMA

St. Francisville

Magnolia Ridge Adventure Park

Bogue Chitto

Bogue Chitto River

cadiana Park ature Station

Honey Island Swamp

Fontainebleau State Park

Atchafalaya Basin

Avery Island

New Orleans Botanical Garden

Fort Proctor

Gulf of Mexico

Grand Isle

Take a Night Cruise of the Swamps

Up the spookiness by gliding in the dark through a murky swamp surrounded by sinister-looking moss-covered bald cypress trees. Several outfitters offer night excursions on flat-bottom boats at Honey Island Swamp, a popular swamp tour destination.

About an hour northeast of New Orleans, Honey Island earned its moniker because honeybees were once spotted on a nearby island. The 250-square-mile (650 km²) marshland is one of America's most pristine and least altered swamps. It is also alleged habitat of the mythical Honey Island Swamp Monster, an apelike creature that's said to lurk in the swamp.

Even if you don't spot the Cajun Sasquatch, there is wildlife aplenty, from toothy alligators to wild boars and raccoons. Along the way, the guides will impart their knowledge about the swamp's ecology, its natural history, and the wildlife and native plants that live there.

Pearl River, LA   Season: Year-round

A barred owl perches at Honey Island Swamp.

Paddling the Atchafalaya

Larger than the Florida Everglades, Louisiana's Atchafalaya Basin stretches across 1.2 million acres (485,620 ha) from Simmesport to the Gulf of Mexico. The basin is home to 65 species of reptiles and amphibians and more than 100 species of fish and aquatic life, and it contains the largest contiguous bottomland hardwood forest in North America. More than 300 species of resident and migratory birds, from the bald eagle to Bachman's warbler, have been spotted at the basin.

Paddling through the basin's lakes, bayous, creeks, and swamps surrounded by towering, moss-covered cypress trees is an otherworldly experience. North of Lake Dauterive, Bayou Benoit is a great option for beginners who want quick access to the cypress forest. Just west of Henderson, Indian Bayou is owned by the Army Corps of Engineers, who partnered with state, local, and federal agencies to map out a network of 24 miles (39 km) of paddling trails throughout the bayou.

If you prefer guided tours, McGee's Swamp Tours takes photography enthusiasts on a 3.6-mile (5.8 km) journey through the Big Cypress Loop.

Kayakers paddle among the Spanish moss of the Atchafalaya Basin.

Multicity, LA   Season: Year-round

Mountain Biking in Ruston

Louisiana's best rated mountain biking trail is located at Lincoln Parish Park in Ruston, about an hour east of Shreveport. At this 280-acre (115 ha) park, 11 miles (18 km) of single-track trails weave through the shaded forest and around the 25-acre (10 ha) lake. Created with the help of Louisiana Tech University's cycling club, the trail opened in 1993 and has consistently drawn mountain bikers from across the state.

The trailhead starts behind the park's playground and forks off into beginner (follow the brown signs) and intermediate (blue signs) trails. The beginner trail, which spans about four miles (6.4 km), goes through paths with wider corridors and milder terrain and follows the perimeter of the park. The intermediate trail cuts through the forest and has short spurts of climbs followed by a good downward flow over switchbacks, wooden bridges, and rolling mounds. The trail also passes by the lake and a cascading human-made waterfall.

Ruston, LA | **Season:** Year-round

Magnolia flower

One of the trail's highlights is Tomac Hill, an adrenaline-pumping 120-foot (40 m) drop. Although it has no dramatic jumps, rock gardens, or berms, mountain bikers can still catch a bit of air. In total, the trails include more than 1,000 feet (305 m) of elevation gain.

In addition to bike trails, the park also has a 1.25-mile (2 km) walking path around the lake, docks for fishing (the lake is stocked with bass), a playground for children, and a swimming beach to cool off during hot summer days. Kayaks and paddleboards are also welcome on the lake. There's a bike wash station near the beach. Day rate is $3 per person. The park is open daily from 9 a.m. to 5 p.m.

Avian Spotting on Avery Island

Avery Island is known as the home of Tabasco sauce, but its reputation as a nature preserve is also gaining traction. A hidden gem on the island, the Jungle Gardens was founded by Edward Avery McIlhenny, son of Tabasco sauce inventor Edmund McIlhenny. By the turn of the century, Edward had turned his private estate into a wholesale plant nursery. The site evolved into a drive-through tourism attraction in the 1930s.

The 170-acre (70 ha) nature preserve features several varieties of bamboo, palms, perennial grass, and century-old live oaks covered with Spanish moss and resurrection ferns. Edward also created a pond and set up a rookery to help revive the snowy egret population. It was a success. The egrets are now thriving, along with herons and songbirds.

Avery Island is an egret habitat worth visiting.

Avery Island, LA | **Season:** Year-round

> "KISATCHIE NATIONAL FOREST
> IS MADE UP OF LONGLEAF PINE
> FORESTS AND BOTTOMLAND
> HARDWOODS."

Explore Kisatchie National Forest

Louisiana's only national forest is made up of 604,000 acres (244,430 ha) of longleaf pine forests and bottomland hardwoods. The national forest is divided into five districts—Calcasieu, Caney, Catahoula, Kisatchie, and Winn—with more than 400 miles (640 km) of hiking, biking, horseback riding, and ATV trails.

Trail routes range from a half mile (0.8 km) to more than 30 miles (48 km) across rolling hills, creeks, and swamps. The well-maintained 31-mile (50 km) Wild Azalea Trail—the longest hiking trail in Louisiana and a designated National Recreation Trail—is named for the wild azaleas that bloom along the trail from March through early April.

Kisatchie National Forest is also home to Wolf Rock Cave, the only known cave in the entire state. In the Vernon Unit of Calcasieu, Wolf Rock Cave is made up of two small rock overhangs, which at one time provided shelter to the Archaic people who lived in the area from 2500 to 1000 B.C. Archaeologists discovered fishhooks, beads, and axes inside the cave, while arrowheads were found in the surrounding forest.

During the Civil War, the Union Army was said to have hidden supplies and horses in Wolf Rock Cave. Famed outlaw Jesse James was also rumored to have sought shelter at the cave, and the "Great Western Land Pirate" John Murrell was said to have hidden gold in the cave.

In the 1970s, the U.S. Forest Service cleaned up the cave and sealed off two of the back rooms. Today, hikers can access Wolf Rock Cave by going on a five-minute trek from the parking lot, on a scenic trail along Bundick Creek.

Rapides Parish, LA   Season: Year-round

Follow the trail to
Wolf Rock Cave.

Cast Off on Grand Isle

Near the southern tip of Louisiana, the eight-square-mile (21 km²) Grand Isle is the only inhabited barrier island in the state. Its unique geography between Caminada Bay and the Gulf of Mexico makes the region a prime kayak fishing spot for bull redfish, which can get up to 26 inches (66 cm) in length. Although it's possible to fish on the Gulf side, most kayak fishing takes place on the bay side of the island—where a rock jetty structure, marsh islands, and artificial reef are a short paddle distance from the launch at the end of Ludwig Lane. A prized experience for fishermen is catching a large enough bull red that the fish tows their kayaks along the water like a "Cajun sleigh ride." Several companies on the island rent out kayaks and fishing gear. The best time to fish bull reds is from October through December. You can also find northern pike, bass, and trout around Grand Isle.

> "A PRIZED EXPERIENCE FOR FISHERMEN IS CATCHING A LARGE ENOUGH BULL RED THAT THE FISH TOWS THEIR KAYAKS ALONG THE WATER LIKE A 'CAJUN SLEIGH RIDE.'"

Grand Isle, LA | **Season:** October to December

The sun sets on a row of houses along the shore of Grand Isle.

Trees and swamps pepper the landscape of Chemin-A-Haut State Park.

Ride Your Way Across the State

Although the Bayou State's swamps and marshes may draw visitors from all over the world, the state's parks and forests also beckon with equally alluring landscape, towering trees, diverse wildlife, and miles of scenic trails. And one of the best ways to explore is on horseback.

In Bastrop, near the Arkansas border, Chemin-A-Haut State Park is a popular yet secluded park with eight miles (13 km) of hilltop equestrian trails overlooking Bayou Bartholomew. The trails are shaded by pine, bald cypress, and oak trees.

At Kisatchie National Forest in Alexandria, the well-maintained Caroline Dormon Trail has nearly 11 miles (18 km) of hilly, tree-shaded trails for horseback riding, as well as parking for horse trailers.

If you're looking for a guided experience, nearby Hayes E. Daze Ranch offers one-, two-, and three-hour rides through the national forest. Located just six miles (10 km) from downtown Baton Rouge, the BREC Farr Park Equestrian Center has a network of equestrian trails. On select Saturdays and Sundays, BREC offers hour-long guided trail rides through the park, adjacent to the Mississippi River. About 30 miles (48 km) northeast of BREC, the center's newest Sandy Creek Community Park has trails that are open to horses, mountain bikers, and hikers.

Saddle up at Bogue Chitto State Park, near Franklinton, and ride through 14 miles (23 km) of forested hillsides and river lowlands. And there's no better way to discover Louisiana's Northshore than with a Splendor Farms–guided ride through a beautiful countryside of creeks and woods, and across fields and lakes.

Multicity, LA   Season: Year-round

Zip through the woods of Magnolia Ridge.

Zip for the Record

Soar through 34 acres (14 ha) of hardwood forest at the Magnolia Ridge Adventure Park in East Feliciana Parish, located about 30 miles (48 km) north of Baton Rouge. The newly opened aerial adventure park features eight zip lines that fly over rolling hills dotted with ancient magnolia trees, oaks, and elms. Guests climb onto the towers perched in treetops and zip between platforms, with each zip line getting progressively longer. The course culminates with the 900-foot-long (270 m), 70-foot-high (20 m) zip line, the longest of its kind in the state. As you zip over the flowing Comite River, your speed can reach up to 25 miles an hour (40 km/h). The adventure park also offers a Ninja Obstacle course with bridge crossings, tower climbs, and river landing. Evening flights are available on select nights during October and December holiday season. The park is open Thursday through Tuesday, from 8 a.m. to 3 p.m. Reservations are required.

East Feliciana Parish, LA   Season: Year-round

Visit a Local World Heritage Site

The biggest community of hunter-gatherers in North America once resided in northeast Louisiana. Named after a plantation that was constructed in the 1800s, the 400-acre (162 ha) Poverty Point is a UNESCO World Heritage site where Indigenous people built earthen monuments more than 3,400 years ago.

Overlooking the Mississippi River floodplain, the complex of six mounds and six semicircular ridges is a communal engineering feat as it required moving as many as 53 million cubic feet (1.5 million m³) of soil from a different location. During the Late Archaic period, when most people lived in small groups, Poverty Point was home to hundreds of residents. Yet, no written records, crop remains, or even human remains have been found. The site was abandoned around 1100 B.C., and in about A.D. 700, another group of Native people occupied a small portion of the area for a brief period. During that

time, they added another mound. Decorated rocks, ceramic human figurines, and more than 8,000 spear points were uncovered at the site, leading archaeologists to theorize that Poverty Point was once an ancient residential, trade, and ceremonial center.

You can explore the site on a self-driving tour or hike the 2.6-mile (4.2 km) loop trail to a boardwalk that takes visitors to the top of one of the biggest ancient mounds in the country. At 72 feet tall (22 m), 710 feet long (216 m), and 660 feet (201 m) wide, Mound A (also known as the Bird Mound) is made up of 400,000 tons (362,875 metric tons) of soil, brought 50 pounds (23 kg) at a time in baskets.

Tram tours are available from March through October, Wednesdays to Sundays; admission is $4.

Pioneer, LA   Season: Spring to fall

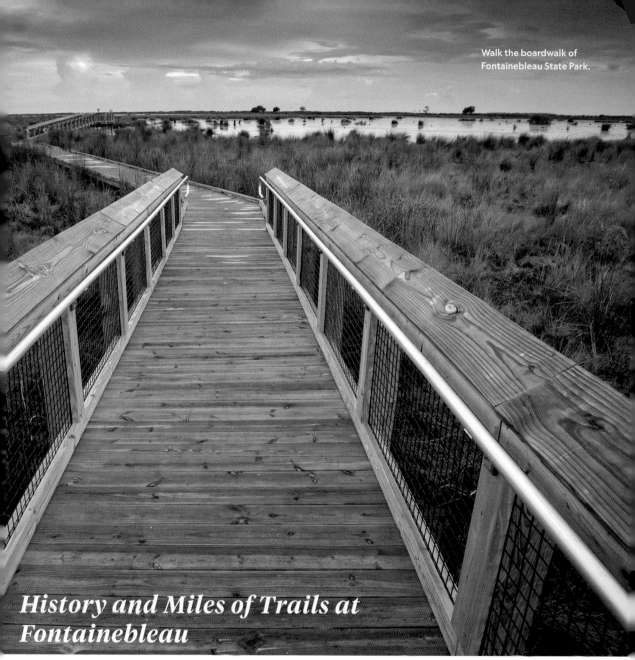

Walk the boardwalk of Fontainebleau State Park.

History and Miles of Trails at Fontainebleau

To get to Fontainebleau State Park, you'll have to drive 24 miles (39 km) from New Orleans over Lake Pontchartrain Causeway, the world's longest continuous bridge over water. A former sugar plantation, the 2,800-acre (1,130 ha) park is now home to miles of trails, lakefront cabins, and dramatic centuries-old live oak trees draped in Spanish moss.

Fontainebleau has a diverse ecosystem and a protected habitat for the more than 400 species of birds and animals that live there. A historic marker notes the location of cabins housing enslaved people on the plantation grounds; another honors the memory of Indigenous people

who lived in the area. An old railroad track has been converted into a 2.8-mile (4.5 km) paved hiking and biking trail across the park. The white-sand beach has a cluster of cypress knees, distinct for their web of gnarly roots that emerge from the sand.

Mandeville, LA | **Season:** Year-round

Enter the New Orleans
Botanical Garden through the
Pavilion of the Two Sisters.

1. BIKE THE BEAST

True to its moniker, the Beast in St. Francisville is one of the most challenging mountain hiking trails in Louisiana. The six-mile (10 km) single-track trail has steep drops, twisty turns, and grueling uphill climbs. It's an intermediate tree-shaded course that requires skillful maneuvering through protruding roots, wooden bridges, and swampy puddles.

2. BEHOLD SICILY ISLAND HILLS WATERFALLS

The tallest waterfall in Louisiana is only 17 feet (5 m) tall, but it's still an impressive sight as water cascades over a series of rocks into a pool and creek. Nearby, St. Mary's Falls flows 10 feet (3 m) into a large pool. The Rock Falls and St. Mary's Falls Trails are both located in the J. C. "Sonny" Gilbert Wildlife Management Area.

3. FIND RESTORATION IN AN URBAN PARK

Once the site of an illegal dump, Restoration Park is now a 70-acre (28 ha) urban wetland park that doubles as a floodwater detention basin. A stone trail goes around the park perimeter and has a few lookout points, while a wooden boardwalk crosses over a serene lily lake. Keep an eye out for beavers, great blue herons, and red-tailed hawks.

4. STROLL ACADIANA PARK NATURE STATION

This 40-acre (16 ha) park in Lafayette features a two-story nature center and 2.5 miles (4 km) of trails, including a wide dirt path and raised wooden walkway over swampy marshes and forest beds.

5. BIRD-WATCH AT UPPER OUACHITA NATIONAL WILDLIFE REFUGE

Established in 1978 to provide habitat for migratory birds, this refuge is made up of more than 53,000 acres (21,445 ha) of cypress swamps, creeks, sloughs, oxbow lakes, bottomland hardwood forest, and upland pine flatwood forest. Birders can try to spot or photograph bald eagles, the federally endangered red-cockaded woodpecker that lives in the southern pine forest, and migrating waterfowl like green-winged teals and mallards.

6. FLOAT DOWN THE BOGUE CHITTO RIVER

Relax as you leisurely float on a tube down the tree-flanked Bogue Chitto River, a spring-fed stream that flows through Louisiana and Mississippi. Franklinton's Louisiana River Adventures and Bogalusa's Bogue Chitto Tubing offer two- and four-hour floats and provide life jackets upon request. You can hop off the river anytime to rest on sandy beaches and sandbars.

7. HIKE UP DRISKILL MOUNTAIN

Climb 535 feet (163 m) above sea level to the top of the highest point in Louisiana. You can reach the summit on a trail that's less than a mile (1.6 km) long. You'll notice a rock pile indicating that you've arrived at the peak. This may be the easiest hike for those who are participating in the 50-state High Points Challenge.

8. STROLL THROUGH NEW ORLEANS BOTANICAL GARDEN

This well-manicured garden at City Park is New Orleans' first public classical garden, created in 1936 with funding from the Works Progress Administration. Highlights at the serene 10-acre (4 ha) park include artful sculptures, fountains, a kaleidoscope of flowers, a water lily reflecting pond, and the nation's largest collection of mature live oaks.

9. SWIM IN LAKE CLAIBORNE

At Lake Claiborne State Park in the tiny town of Homer, a popular summer activity is swimming in the fresh clear waters of the eponymous lake. A sandy beach on an inlet is tucked away from the bustle of speeding watercraft.

10. PADDLE TO SEE A FORTRESS

Built in the 1850s, the brick Fort Proctor, built to protect water routes toward New Orleans from enemies, is on the National Register of Historic Places. However, due to damage from hurricanes and the start of the Civil War, the fort was never garrisoned. There's no land access to the fort, but you can kayak across the canal to explore the crumbling but impressive structure.

Black bear

The sun rises over the Portland
Head Light in Cape Elizabeth.

MAINE

Known for its scenic coastline, Maine is also home to robust woodlands and mountains for hikers and winter adventurers.

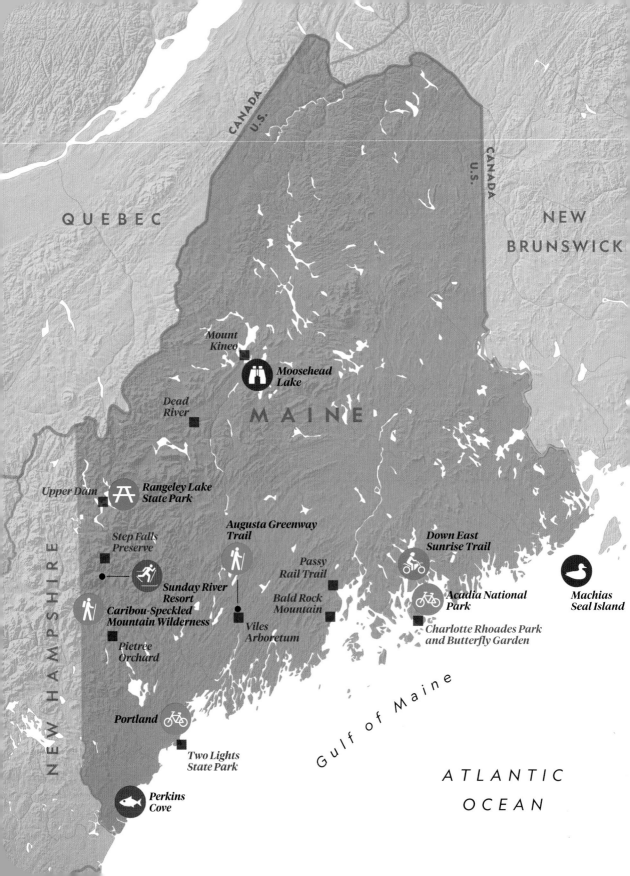

CANADA
U.S.

CANADA
U.S.

QUEBEC

NEW
BRUNSWICK

NEW HAMPSHIRE

MAINE

Mount
Kineo

Moosehead
Lake

Dead
River

Upper Dam

Rangeley Lake
State Park

Step Falls
Preserve

Augusta Greenway
Trail

Passy
Rail Trail

Down East
Sunrise Trail

Sunday River
Resort

Caribou-Speckled
Mountain Wilderness

Bald Rock
Mountain

Acadia National
Park

Machias
Seal Island

Viles
Arboretum

Pietree
Orchard

Charlotte Rhoades Park
and Butterfly Garden

Portland

Gulf of Maine

Two Lights
State Park

ATLANTIC

OCEAN

Perkins
Cove

Bike the carriage roads near Jordan Pond in Maine's Acadia National Park.

Another Side of Acadia National Park

Acadia's 26 impressive peaks and soul-stirring coastline views often overshadow one of the park's most captivating features: 45 miles (72 km) of carriage roads adorned with 17 stone arch bridges that wind through pristine valleys and lakes. Built in the early 1900s by financier and philanthropist John D. Rockefeller, Jr., the carriage roads were designed to enable motor-free travel by horse and carriage into Mount Desert Island. Today, these 16-foot-wide (5 m) "broken rock" byways are multiuse trails that reveal a down-to-earth side of the park's personality.

Soar around Eagle Lake via a 5.9-mile (9.5 km) loop that challenges cyclists with a moderate grade while offering wooded lake views. Triple your view on Tri Lakes Loop, a 10.9-mile (17.5 km) loop that skirts Eagle Lake, Bubble Pond, and Jordan Pond. The parking areas at Eagle Lake and Bubble Pond have wheelchair-accessible restrooms and parking and provide entry to two of the most accessible carriage roads in the park.

To experience the carriage roads as Rockefeller did, book a horse-drawn carriage tour with Wildwood Stables. If you have time, opt for the two-hour Day Mountain Summit Tour for a narrated history of the park and peak views of the Cranberry Isles.

During winter, snowfall blankets the carriage trails and careful grooming creates a vast network to explore by ski or snowshoe. The 4.3-mile (6.9 km) Witch Hole Loop casts a spell with charming views of ponds, marsh, and ocean. Or follow the 5.6-mile (9 km) Aunt Betty Loop to see Eagle Lake, Sargent Mountain, and six stone bridges.

Mount Desert Island, ME   Season: Spring to fall

Make fresh tracks on the slopes of Sunday River.

Peak Your Interest

With eight peaks, 135 trails and glades, and five terrain parks with jumps and jibs for all experience levels, Sunday River is a western Maine favorite among skiers and snowboarders. To carve a different path, try renting a SNO-GO ski bike, which combines skiing and mountain biking for an exhilarating downhill.

The fun doesn't end when the snow melts. From early July through mid-October, the mountain is open to weekend hikers. Ride the high-speed "Chondola" (chairlift/gondola) from South Ridge Lodge to North Peak and choose from a network of 10 hiking trails to explore the mountains' eight interconnected peaks. The moderate Summit Traverse rewards a two-mile (3.2 km) ridgeline climb with sweeping vistas overlooking the Mahoosuc Mountains and Sunday River Valley from the peaks of Barker, Locke, and Whitecap Mountains. Hike the Kids' Adventure Trail down or catch the last ride on the Chondola by 4:15 p.m.

Newry, ME | **Season:** Winter

Museum in the Streets

Augusta's history comes to life through Museum in the Streets, a self-guided, seasonal tour to 38 historical sites around the capital. Start on the eastern bank of the Kennebec River to see the oldest wooden fort in America, Old Fort Western (stop #3), where Benedict Arnold and 1,100 Continental Army troops spent six days during the American Revolution before their infamous march to Quebec City. Nearby is the former site of the 17th-century Cushnoc Trading Post (#1), where the Pilgrims of Plymouth traded fur with local Abenaki.

The tour continues across the river, where many headline-worthy 19th-century events unfolded, like the Great Augusta Bank Robbery of a burglarproof vault (#13) and the Great Fire that consumed 81 buildings (#14). A second, shorter tour follows Canal Street, highlighting the city's industrial history and disastrous attempts to harness the river to power the city's growth.

Augusta, ME | **Season:** Year-round

The riverfront bicycle path offers views of Augusta.

Take in Screw Auger Falls at Grafton Notch State Park.

Birding Bucket-List Destination

Birding in Maine is an all-season activity. Follow the Maine Birding Trail to 82 bucket-list-worthy habitats across the state, using the weather as your guide.

Although the arrival of black fly season in spring can be annoying, the flies are an essential food source for migratory warblers. Maine Audubon leads free morning Warbler Walks during peak migration in May at Evergreen Cemetery in Portland.

Summer brings the largest nesting colony of puffins to Machias Seal Island, off the northern coast. Boat tours are available through Bold Coast Charter Company from June to early August. (Book early; they sell out fast.) By September, Mount Agamenticus in York is the place to watch the fall hawk migration. Don't overlook winter. It's the only time Marginal Way in Ogunquit isn't crowded, and you might spot the dramatic plumage of a harlequin duck.

Multicity, ME | **Season:** Year-round

> ## "FEW PLACES ARE BETTER TO SEARCH FOR THESE BROWN BEAUTIES."

Take a Moose Soar-fari

A trip to Maine isn't complete without spotting the state mammal—the moose. It is estimated that between 60,000 and 75,000 moose live in Maine, making it the second largest population in the United States after Alaska. And few places are better to search for these brown beauties than in the Maine Highlands.

Because much of northern Maine is a vast expanse of undeveloped frontier land, finding a moose can take hours by car and not yield any results. Increase your odds by opting for an aerial moose safari. Currier's Flying Service and Fletcher Mountain Aviation, both in Greenville, offer seaplane tours of Moosehead Lake, Lobster Lake, Mount Kineo, and Big Squaw and Big Spencer Mountains. Longer tours travel as far north as Baxter State Park, home of Mount Katahdin, Maine's tallest mountain and the northern terminus of the Appalachian Trail.

With such a large population of moose living in Maine, your odds of spotting one are high. Although moose are active year-round, September and October are the best months to see an antlered bull, especially at dawn and dusk. They shed their antlers for winter to conserve energy and spend spring regenerating them. Summer can prove more challenging when searching for these creatures by air, as they tend to seek shade from the hot sun.

As you glide across the landscape, look closely. Moose are independent creatures, so you won't see them traveling in herds. But you can often find them at water's edge, munching on horsetails and other aquatic plants. Don't be surprised if you see one swimming across Moosehead Lake. Despite their massive bodies and skinny legs, they are adept swimmers and can easily cover 10 miles (16 km).

Greenville, ME | Season: Fall

On a "safari" in Moosehead Lake, look out for bull moose.

Go Lobsterin'

Tucked away at the southern end of Marginal Way, Maine's most famous (and scenic) cliff walk, you'll find the picturesque fishing village of Perkins Cove. Stand atop the wooden pedestrian drawbridge for a gull's-eye view of the lobster boats chugging into harbor with their catch—or book a trip aboard *Finest-kind* to experience the artistry that delivers this delicacy to your plate.

With written accounts dating back to 1605, lobstering is one of the oldest continuously operated industries in North America. Despite technological advances, lobstering hasn't changed much since the first traps were laid. You'll have a front-row seat as a Maine lobster fisher hooks wire traps with a gaff and hauls them on board to examine their contents.

To ensure sustainability of Maine's most valuable species, fishers check each lobster's gender and size, keeping only males that measure 3.25 to 5 inches (8.3 to 12.7 cm).

Ogunquit, ME | **Season:** Year-round

Fishing buoys hang outside a fisherman's shack in Perkins Cove.

All-Season Adventure

Don't be surprised if you find yourself spinning in circles atop Bald Mountain's fire tower. With 360-degree views of Rangeley's lakes and mountains, the scale and beauty of this unspoiled watery wonderland are almost too much to absorb.

To see it, hike the 2.3-mile (3.7 km) out-and-back summit trail to the top of Bald Mountain and climb the three-story metal fire tower. People of all abilities can enjoy an equally impressive view from Height of Land, a famous overlook on Route 17.

Brook trout

Rangeley's seven lakes are connected by the Northern Forest Canoe Trail, a 740-mile (1,190 km) water trail that begins in Old Forge, New York, and extends to Fort Kent, Maine, offering paddlers a chance to explore the ancient waterway Native Americans traveled 11,000 years ago. Today's anglers can troll for salmon and brook trout in five

of its lakes—Rangeley, Mooselookmeguntic, Richardson, Aziscohos, and Beaver Mountain.

By night, sleep beneath the stars at Rangeley Lake State Park, which has 50 tent and campsites. Stargazing is best from August to October when you're most likely to see the northern lights. Winter brings more than 200 inches (500 cm) of snow each year. Rangeley Lakes Trail Center, on Saddleback Mountain's western side, grooms and maintains more than 30 miles (48 km) of trails for backcountry and Nordic skiing, snowshoeing, and fat-tire biking. Dog owners can try "skijoring" with their four-legged friends. It's a Norwegian-inspired mushing sport that combines cross-country skiing and dog-sledding. Rental equipment is available.

Rangeley, ME | **Season:** Year-round

Go on a Search for the Wild Whites

Most people think of New Hampshire when they think of White Mountain National Forest, but nearly 6 percent of its 750,852 acres (303,859 ha) lies in western Maine.

Within the forest, the Caribou and Speckled Mountains form the Caribou-Speckled Mountain Wilderness, one of Maine's few officially designated wilderness areas, named for the combination of conifers and deciduous trees that add specks of color to the landscape each fall. Caribou Mountain arguably has some of the best views of the Whites. To see for yourself, park at the trailhead off Route 113 and take Mud Brook Trail to the top. The nearly 2,000-foot (610 m) ascent begins with a gradual uphill and becomes increasingly steeper. Several rocky ledges offer scenic rest stops with inspiring views.

At the summit, a 360-degree panorama unfolds across the Mahoosuc, Carter, and Presidential Ranges.

White Mountains, ME | **Season:** Year-round

Visit in autumn to see the brilliant red, orange, and yellow-speckled canopy that inspired the area's name. On your way down, take the Caribou Trail. It flanks Morrison Creek, which creates Kees Falls and a network of small waterfalls and stream crossings. You'll appreciate the tranquil soundtrack as you descend.

You can spend the night in Maine's White Mountains, though public campgrounds are limited. Hastings Campground near Gilead has 24 well-shaded tent sites and 22 RV sites near the shore of Evans Brook. Crocker Pond Campground near Bethel has seven tent sites beneath towering white pines at the northern edge of the pond, which can be used for nonmotorized boating and fishing by day.

Rev up on an ATV ride through the Down East Sunrise Trail.

Take an Epic Ride

With the longest interconnected ATV trail system in the country, there's no better place than Maine to get a little mud on your tires. More than 6,000 miles (9,650 km) of trails crisscross the state. The Down East Sunrise Trail is a Maine classic. The 87-mile (140 km) inactive rail corridor is divided into three equidistant sections. The western trail begins at Washington Junction, home to the restored railcars of Downeast Scenic Railroad. It passes through wetland and remote forests, crossing Tunk Stream and Narraguagus River on the way to Cherryfield. Here, the central trail begins, crossing the Harrington River and passing blueberry barrens, remote streams, beaver ponds, and a historic schoolhouse turned library before reaching Machias. The eastern trail picks up in Machias and rumbles through salt marshes, forests, and streams on the way to the end point at Ayers Junction.

Multicity, ME | **Season:** Year-round

Downtown Portland looks
over Back Cove.

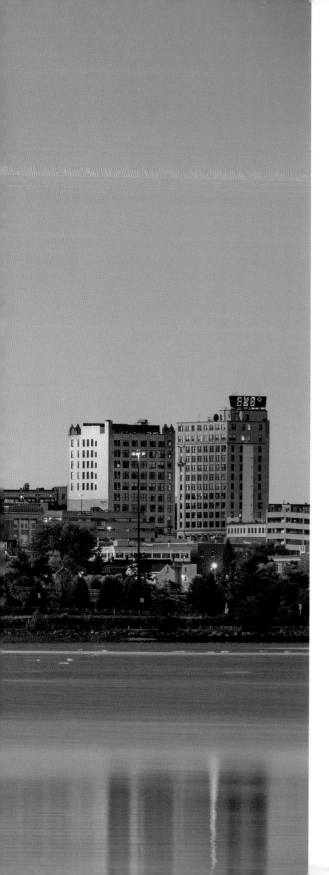

> "THE GRASSY HILLSIDE OVERLOOKS BRILLIANT BLUE WATER DOTTED WITH WHITE SAILBOATS."

Pedal Portland

Since Maine is one of the country's most bike-able states, a great way to see Portland is to pedal it. Grab your bike and head to Forest City Landing to board the ferry that crosses Casco Bay to Peaks Island. On the voyage, abandoned island fortresses reveal the area's military history. Look north to see Fort Gorges, which became obsolete before construction was completed in 1858. To the south is Fort Scammel, a three-bastion granite fort that protected the harbor during the War of 1812.

Once on Peaks Island, head south on Island Avenue and pick up the four-mile (6.4 km) Scenic Peaks Island Loop on Whitehead Street, which turns into Seashore Avenue, a wildflower-lined roadway that skirts the coast. Off the southern shore stands historic Ram Island Ledge Light Station, built in 1905 to warn sailors of dangerous underwater ledges. On the island's eastern shore, historic Battery Steele is built into the hillside overlooking the Atlantic. Constructed in 1942 to protect Portland from German naval attack, it was considered the most important fortification in Casco Bay.

Back in Portland, pick up the Eastern Promenade Trail (aka "East Prom") and ride northeast to an idyllic green space designed by the same firm that created New York's Central Park and the Boston Common. Food trucks line the street as people picnic on the grassy hillside overlooking brilliant blue water dotted with white sailboats. Continue to Back Cove Trail, which traces a 3.6-mile (5.8 km) loop around Back Cove and delivers a sweeping panoramic view of the skyline.

Portland and Casco Bay, ME | **Season:** Year-round

Flowering gardens line
the pathways of Charlotte
Rhoades Park.

1. FISH IN FAMOUS FOOTSTEPS

To cast a Gray Ghost Streamer in the pool below Upper Dam is to fish in the footsteps of Carrie Stevens, the lure's legendary inventor. The Gray Ghost imitates smelt to attract trophy-size landlocked salmon. Try to beat Stevens's record-setting brook trout— 6 pounds, 13 ounces (3 kg) and 24.75 inches (62.9 cm).

2. FLUTTER YOUR WINGS

From mid-May to mid-October, Charlotte Rhoades Park and Butterfly Garden on Norwood Cove is a magical "must-see" along the Downeast coast. The garden beds are shaped like butterfly wings and feature organically grown shrubs and flowers that feed hungry caterpillars and supply nectar for butterflies. Come in late July to participate in the annual butterfly release.

3. COOL OFF IN A CASCADE

At Step Falls, the second tallest waterfall in the state, Wight Brook flows over smooth ledges, creating natural waterslides and swimming holes perfect for cooling off on a hot summer day—or after hiking the 1.1-mile (1.8 km) out-and-back trail beside it, which leads to lush mountain views.

4. PICK FROM THE BEST

Maine's state fruit—the blueberry— is abundant, along with strawberries, peaches, and apples, at Pietree, a pick-your-own orchard folded into the mountains. A family favorite of authors Tabitha and Stephen King, they scooped it up in 2007 to preserve its delicious legacy. Mix in a stop by the farm stand to taste fresh-pressed cider, brick-oven pizza, and other local products.

5. ESCAPE TO THE WOODS

For an agricultural escape, wander through Viles Arboretum's fragrant lilac garden, heirloom apple orchard, and the largest hosta collection in the state. See white pines whose seeds traveled on the space shuttle *Atlantis* in 1991. Join a winter bird walk to spot cardinals, migratory finches, and black-capped chickadees, the state bird.

6. EXPLORE MAINE'S BELOVED COAST

Don't be fooled by its name: Two Lights State Park may honor the state's first twin lighthouses, but they aren't located here (they're nearby on Two Lights Road and not open to the public). The park's real treasure is its unspoiled views of Maine's craggy coastline and benches to enjoy them.

7. HIKE FOR EPIC VIEWS

For a coastal hike that rivals Acadia without the crowds, take Bald Rock Mountain Trail, a 3.4-mile (5.5 km) lollipop loop, to the summit for 180-degree views over Penobscot Bay. On a clear day, you can see Belfast in the north, Rockport in the south, Acadia in the east, and dozens of islands in between.

8. PEDAL THROUGH HISTORY

Pedal through the past on the 2.2-mile (3.5 km) riverside Passy Rail Trail in Belfast. At Upper Bridge, you'll find remains of a 19th-century drawbridge that cost three cents to cross on foot. Trestle Bridge is a modern version of the original that bolstered trains across the Passagassawaukeag River. City Point displays vintage railroad cars from a bygone era.

9. TAKE A ONE-OF-A-KIND CLIMB

Mount Kineo presents a unique challenge for rock climbers: It's only accessible by boat. Catch the Kineo Shuttle in Rockwood or paddle across Moosehead Lake to the 800-foot-tall (240 m), mile-wide (1.6 km) granite rock face rising from the depths. Four trad climbing routes await. Ice climbers can get there by skiing or snowmobiling across the frozen lake.

10. RIDE THE RAPIDS

Central Maine is home to the longest continuous track of white water on the East Coast. Book a rafting trip with Magic Falls Rafting Company to ride 15 miles (24 km) of Class II to V rapids along the Dead River. Go during spring melt or a scheduled water release when the Dead's water comes to life.

Black-capped chickadee

The sunrise is reflected in water at Blackwater National Wildlife Refuge (page 285).

MARYLAND

This diverse state has everything from urban green spaces to harbor towns, beaches to woodland campsites.

Upper Youghiogheny
River

 **Wisp
Resort**

Western Maryland
Rail Trail and
Chesapeake & Ohio Canal

Savage
River

Magnolia Meadow
Farms

Chesapeake & Ohio Canal

**Potomac
River**

Potomac

W E S T   V I R G I N I A

V I R G I N I A

 **Mallows
Bay**

"NO STATE CAN MATCH THE
BEAUTY OF THE CHESAPEAKE
BAY, OUR BEACHES AND
FARMS, OR THE MOUNTAINS
OF WESTERN MARYLAND, THE
PORT OF BALTIMORE, OR THE
HISTORIC CHARM OF EVERY
CORNER OF OUR STATE."
—LARRY HOGAN

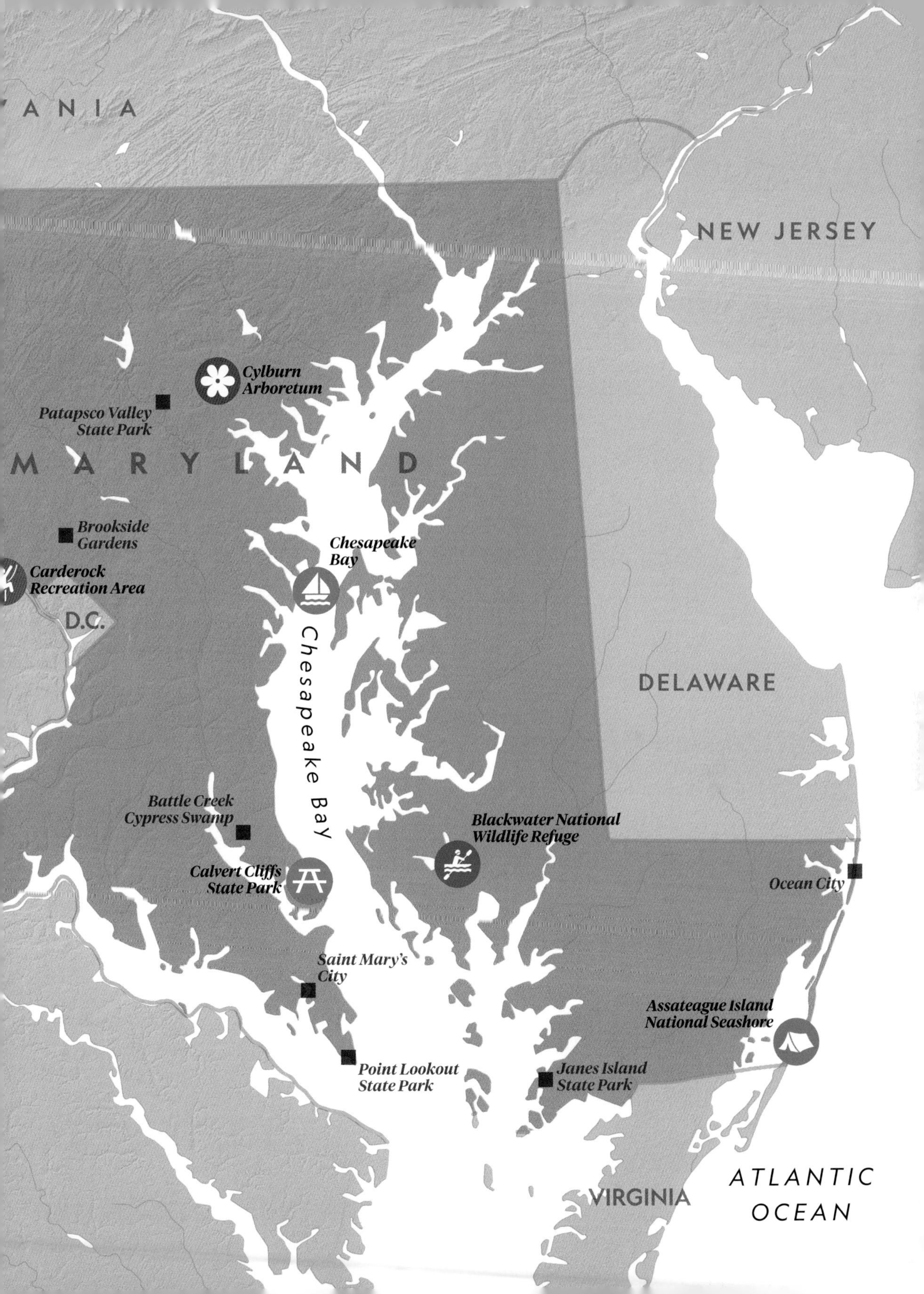

PENNSYLVANIA

NEW JERSEY

Cylburn
Arboretum

Patapsco Valley
State Park

MARYLAND

Brookside
Gardens

Carderock
Recreation Area

D.C.

Chesapeake
Bay

Chesapeake Bay

DELAWARE

Battle Creek
Cypress Swamp

Blackwater National
Wildlife Refuge

Calvert Cliffs
State Park

Ocean City

Saint Mary's
City

Assateague Island
National Seashore

Point Lookout
State Park

Janes Island
State Park

VIRGINIA

ATLANTIC
OCEAN

Get Wet and Wild on the Potomac

This is no leisurely float down a lazy river. White-water tubing on the Upper Potomac is filled with fast-moving thrills, and you're guaranteed to get wet—making it a terrific way to beat the sizzling summer heat.

The adventure begins near the historic town of Harpers Ferry (in West Virginia, near the Maryland border), where the Potomac and Shenandoah Rivers meet. Multiple out-fitters bus participants upstream for tubing trips on Class II to III rapids that surge through the tumbled river rocks and islets. While bouncing through the white water, tubers spin around in eddies, slip through narrow chutes, and plunge over mini-waterfalls—sometimes backward.

Between rapids, gentle sections allow time to take in the striking Appalachian scenery, as the river flows beneath railroad bridges and past the soaring slopes of Loudoun Heights and Maryland Heights. Bring a floating cooler with snacks and drinks for a picnic on a sandy beach or on the rocks in the midst of the rushing water.

Harpers Ferry National Park, MD | Season: Summer

Tube the Potomac near Harpers Ferry.

Climb to New Heights

Just outside Washington, D.C., Carderock is a rock climber's dream. Dramatic cliffs up to 80 feet (24 m) high overlook the Potomac River and feature doz-ens of well-established routes of all types and difficulty levels, from beginner up to a formidable 5.13b rating.

Scale Beginner's Crack, one route option at Carderock.

Primarily a top-roping area, most of the routes are 40- to 50-foot (12 to 15 m) face climbs and require tal-ented footwork. The hard schist rock is studded with quartz crystals, but it's slick from decades of climbing. Carderock was one of the first eastern crags to be devel-oped in the mid-20th century. Many climbing legends made first ascents here, including Herb and Jan Conn, whose names grace some classic routes: Herbie's Horror, the country's first 5.9, and Jan's Face, a long wall that ranges from 5.3 to 5.11d.

Those wanting a less vertical experience can head to the nearby Billy Goat Trail, which runs along the cliff tops and entails scrambling over boulders high above the Potomac. The Billy Goat Trail is a one-way route to reduce hiker jam-ups. At the exit points, take the canal towpath back to your starting point.

Potomac, MD | Season: Year-round

Family Fun All Winter Long

For perfect powder, Marylanders don't need to travel out of state. Located among the forested peaks of the Western Maryland mountains, Wisp Resort has welcomed skiers and snowboarders for decades, along with offering snow tubing, cross-country skiing, and snowshoeing. The state's only ski resort, Wisp boasts more than 30 groomed slopes for all skill levels, totaling 11 miles (18 km) of trails and a vertical drop of 700 feet (210 m).

Wisp's summit elevation reaches 3,115 feet (950 m) and overlooks shimmering Deep Creek Lake, which snowmobilers and ice fishermen traverse when it freezes solid in winter. The area receives on average more than a hundred inches (250 cm) of snowfall annually. But when Mother Nature doesn't cooperate, the resort's energy-efficient snowmaking systems make sure every slope is ready for action.

While adults study their slaloms, kids gear up too. The

Wisp Kids program teaches children ages three to 14 how to build their confidence on the slopes while they try skiing or snowboarding. The fun doesn't stop when the sun goes down—nearly all the trails are lit for night skiing, making it possible to glide under the stars.

When you want a break from skis, hop on a tube and whisk down 750-foot-long (230 m) snow-tubing chutes. Or take a ride on the Mountain Coaster: Open year-round, the coaster's two-seater carts crank uphill more than a thousand feet (305 m), before flying 3,500 feet (1,070 m) downhill over a series of twists, rolls, dips, and corkscrews at speeds up to 28 miles an hour (45 km/h).

Deep Creek, MD | **Season:** Winter

Find shark and crocodile teeth in the sand at Calvert Cliffs State Park.

Look for Fossils in the Cliffs

Between 10 and 20 million years ago, a warm, shallow sea covered southern Maryland. Prehistoric creatures such as crocodiles, mastodons, and megalodon sharks roamed the waters. Their fossilized remains were entombed in the geologic formation of the Calvert Cliffs.

More than 600 species of fossilized plants and animals have been found on these 100-foot (30 m) cliffs facing the Chesapeake. Budding archaeologists can try their hand at discovery by heading to Calvert Cliffs State Park. Hike to the beach, where fossil hunting is permitted, and bring a shovel and sieve to sift through the sand (best at low tide and after a storm). You might find prehistoric oyster shells, mollusks, shark and crocodile teeth, or—if you're lucky—a megalodon tooth.

Lusby, MD | **Season:** Year-round

"ON THE MARYLAND SIDE, THE HORSES ROAM FREE."

Camp With Wild Horses

Legend says that the wild horses of Assateague Island first arrived on a ship-wrecked Spanish galleon, and the brave creatures battled through the surf to reach shore. The less dramatic yet more likely explanation: Late-17th century colonists brought them to the barrier island trying to avoid taxes. Either way, the sturdy, shaggy animals are now an integral part of Assateague Island National Seashore. Nearly 300 horses wander the island's 37 miles (60 km) of beaches, salt marsh, and pine forest. Over the centuries, they've adapted to the harsh ecosystem, surviving scorching heat and howling storms.

The herd on the Virginia side of the island is owned by the Chincoteague Volunteer Fire Department, which coordinates their annual pony swim (made famous in Marguerite Henry's book *Misty of Chincoteague*). But on the Maryland side, the horses roam free—this is also the only area on the seashore where camping is permitted.

Choose a bayside or oceanside campsite (open year-round) and explore the pristine sands and trails lined with wild blueberry bushes. Search for seashells—Assateague is renowned for its beachcombing—or take a dip in the Atlantic as seabirds wheel overhead (the refuge is vital for migratory birds). You'll quickly be reminded that this isn't any beach vacation, as the island's equine inhabitants appear atop the dunes and amble down the trails to nibble on marsh grasses. As with all wildlife, keep your distance, and follow all campground guidelines to protect these herds, including locking food in provided safe boxes. And, of course, enjoy seeing these magnificent seashore horses in their natural habitat.

Assateague Island, MD | **Season:** Year-round

A herd of wild horses rests on the beaches of Assateague Island.

Ghosts on the Water of Mallows Bay

In Maryland, ghosts really do exist. Recently designated Maryland's first national marine sanctuary, Mallows Bay, a shallow cove in the Potomac River, protects one of the largest ship graveyards in the Western Hemisphere. Shipwrecks here date back to the Revolutionary War, but the majority are wooden steamships that were built to transport supplies to Europe during World War I. The war ended before the ships could be used, and they were scuttled in the Potomac River to salvage the scrap metal from their engines and boilers. Largely submerged at high tide, they slowly materialize as the water falls—and the Ghost Fleet appears to sail again.

Windblown seeds have covered the upper decks in greenery, where ospreys and herons build their nests, while largemouth bass and carp find shelter in the artificial reef below. Kayaking among the wrecks—best between May and September—offers sightings of bald eagles, double-crested cormorants, and river otters.

> "A SHALLOW COVE IN THE POTOMAC RIVER PROTECTS ONE OF THE LARGEST SHIP GRAVEYARDS IN THE WESTERN HEMISPHERE."

Charles County, MD **Season:** May to September

Paddle Mallows Bay in the Potomac, where you'll make your way through a ship graveyard.

The towpath of the Chesapeake and Ohio Canal runs from Cumberland, Maryland, to Georgetown in Washington, D.C.

Bike the Western Maryland Rail Trail and the C&O Canal

For more than a century, the Western Maryland Railway carried coal, other freight, and passengers from Baltimore into Pennsylvania and West Virginia. After the railroad closed in the 1970s, the tracks were abandoned—but some 20 years later, Maryland transformed a nearly 30-mile (48 km) section into the Western Maryland Rail Trail (WMRT), one of the finest in the country.

The paved trail—a favorite of bikers, runners, in-line skaters, and even cross-country skiers and snowshoers in the winter—follows the Potomac River from Fort Frederick State Park to the town of Little Orleans. Its entire length parallels the Chesapeake and Ohio Canal towpath, and numerous access points make it easy to form round-trip loops. Best of all, the ADA-accessible trail is almost completely flat, making it ideal for families, novice bikers, and wheelchair users.

Multicity, MD | **Season:** Year-round

The picturesque town of Hancock, at the midpoint of the WMRT, makes an excellent base of operations to spend several days exploring the trail in both directions. Expect peaceful wooded corridors, dramatic railway tunnels, and historic C&O canal locks and structures, such as the Licking Creek Aqueduct.

The western section really showcases the most jaw-dropping scenery though. The path cuts through rugged terrain with spectacular river views and passes the looming ruins of the Round Top Cement Mill, Hancock's largest employer during the Civil War. The noise of civilization falls away and wildlife comes out to play—look for deer, wild turkeys, and even the occasional black bear.

Black-eyed Susans

Cylburn Arboretum is a green oasis in downtown Baltimore.

A Green Urban Oasis

✸ The 200-acre (80 ha) Cylburn Arboretum is Baltimore's largest public garden, with hundreds of specimen trees and artfully designed green spaces that surround a historic mansion and offer a respite from city life.

Three and a half miles (5.6 km) of trails, including the ADA-accessible Buckeye Trail, wander through woodlands filled with American beech, northern red oak, and tulip trees. The landscaped gardens are just as inviting. Developed since the late 1800s, Cylburn's collections include summer sweet shrubs, Palibin lilacs, and weeping cherry trees. A star attraction: The hundred-year-old Japanese Maple Grove is spectacular in autumn.

During the arboretum's weeklong Summer Nature Camps, children ages five to 10 learn respect for nature through lessons on trees, flowers, and animal habitats, enlivened with eco-oriented games and crafts.

Baltimore, MD | **Season:** Year-round

Sail and Crab Your Way Through the Bay

⛵ The largest estuary in the United States, the Chesapeake Bay's nearly 12,000 miles (19,310 km) of shoreline support a rich diversity of plant and animal life. Generations of watermen have lived off the bounty of the bay, harvesting millions of bushels of crabs, oysters, and clams annually. Skipjacks—Maryland's state boat, and the last working boats under sail in the United States—still ply the waters over oyster beds.

The best way to experience the bay is a guided tour with a Chesapeake Bay Storyteller, learning about the estuary's history and ecology and the watermen way of life. Out of Annapolis, take sail on the 74-foot (23 m) wooden schooner *Woodwind*. As the yacht cruises past the United States Naval Academy, Chesapeake Bay Bridge, and Thomas Point Lighthouse, you can help hoist the sails or even take a turn at the wheel. Special history-

Ammonite fossil

themed sunset sails cover topics such as schooner construction, women in colonial Annapolis, and pirates of the Chesapeake.

Those wanting to get their hands dirty can tong for oysters and pull crab pots alongside real watermen. Near the tip of St. Mary's County, Captain Phil Langley leads Watermen Heritage Tours aboard the *Lisa S*. While hauling up crab pots and teaching the difference between Sallys (females) and Jimmys (males), Langley speaks about the Chesapeake environment and conservation efforts. On Solomons Island, Captains Rachel and Simon Dean welcome kids to become part of their watermen crew for a day. Learn how to dredge for oysters and dip net for blue crabs, then steam your crabs back at the dock.

Multicity, MD | **Season:** Spring to fall

Since 1933, Blackwater National Wildlife Refuge has been a sanctuary for waterfowl migrating along the Atlantic Flyway.

Paddle Through the
Blackwater National Wildlife Refuge

Established in 1933 as a sanctuary for migrating birds, the 30,000-acre (12,140 ha) Blackwater National Wildlife Refuge contains a third of Maryland's tidal wetlands. It's home to the largest natural population of Delmarva fox squirrels, as well as one of the highest concentrations of nesting bald eagles on the East Coast. Bird-watchers can spot tundra swans, snow geese, and ospreys among the cordgrass and water lilies that line the waterways.

Paddling the refuge's 17 miles (27 km) of water trails is also a journey into the past: The forests and marshes are largely unchanged from when Harriet Tubman lived here.

Born in 1822, Tubman trapped muskrats in the refuge and learned how to navigate by the stars and travel through the difficult terrain of the wetlands—skills that allowed her to escape slavery and return to free dozens of others as a conductor on the Underground Railroad.

Cambridge, MD   **Season:** Spring to fall

You can paddle the rapids of the Youghiogheny River or play in its mellow waters.

1. EXPLORE HISTORIC ST. MARY'S CITY

This outdoor archaeological park and living history museum recaptures Maryland's first European settlement and colonial capital, founded in 1634 by English Catholics seeking religious freedom. Visit the reconstructed 17th-century statehouse, step aboard a full-size replica of a tall ship, and explore ADA-accessible exhibits that detail colonial and Native American life.

2. FLY-FISH THE SAVAGE RIVER

Serious anglers can test their fly-fishing skills in the swift-moving tailwater of the lower Savage River, the only water in Maryland designated a "trophy trout" area. Brook, brown, and rainbow trout flourish in the deep pools of the river, which flows through the thickly wooded hills of Savage River State Forest.

3. WANDER THE BOARDWALK OF BATTLE CREEK CYPRESS SWAMP

An elevated, ADA-accessible boardwalk winds through this ecological sanctuary, which protects the northernmost naturally occurring stand of bald cypress in the United States. Listen for trilling tree frogs and warbling songbirds while walking among the hundred-foot-tall (30 m) cypress trees, which can live for more than 1,500 years.

4. RAFT THE YOUGHIOGHENY RIVER

Rafting the Upper "Yough" (pronounced Yock) in Swallow Falls State Park isn't for the faint of heart: The Class IV to V river tumbles through the mountains of Western Maryland, featuring nonstop white water. For 11 adrenaline-pumping miles (18 km), rafters battle intensely technical passages with tight slots, blind chutes, and ledge drops.

5. SURF IN OCEAN CITY

In Ocean City, you can snack on saltwater taffy, ride the Ferris wheel, wander the famed boardwalk—and hang ten. The seaside town's coastline creates an excellent beach break and has three designated surfing areas. Consistent swells year-round produce glassy head-high sets that are perfect for beginners and pros alike.

6. MOUNTAIN BIKE IN PATAPSCO VALLEY STATE PARK

Only 30 minutes outside Baltimore, this 16,000-acre (6,475 ha) park is a thrilling playground for avid mountain bikers, with some 220 miles (350 km) of challenging trails that traverse rough wooded terrain and include hilly single-tracks and river crossings.

7. PADDLE AROUND JANES ISLAND STATE PARK

More than 30 miles (48 km) of marked water trails meander through the salt marsh of Janes Island. Once the home of Paleo-Indians, this Chesapeake Bay island in Tangier Sound is now a haven for birds and other wildlife that roam its wetlands and white-sand beaches.

8. ENJOY BROOKSIDE GARDENS

Named for the winding brooks that surround its 50 acres (20 ha) within Wheaton Regional Park, Brookside hosts 20,000-plus plants woven into intricately designed displays. ADA-accessible walking trails feature benches and shady gazebos. In winter, more than a million twinkling LED bulbs transform the gardens into a luminous holiday wonderland.

9. ENCOUNTER HISTORY AT POINT LOOKOUT

This tranquil park on a Chesapeake peninsula has a storied history: During the Civil War, it was a stop on the Underground Railroad, the site of a hospital for wounded Union troops, and later a prison camp for more than 50,000 Confederate soldiers. A museum, re-created barracks, and the remains of Civil War fortifications bring the past to life.

10. GET LOST IN MAGNOLIA MEADOW'S CORN MAZE

Kids can go wild at Magnolia Meadow Farms, home to Maryland's largest corn maze. The family farm hosts an annual fall festival stuffed with kid-friendly activities, from pumpkin picking and hayrides to pedal karts and apple cannons, along with the challenging corn maze and campfires with live music.

Fox cub

Cape Cod's sandy shores (page 293) form the easternmost portion of Massachusetts.

MASSACHUSETTS

The Bay State is an all-seasons destination boasting city escapes, woodsy retreats, and river canyons.

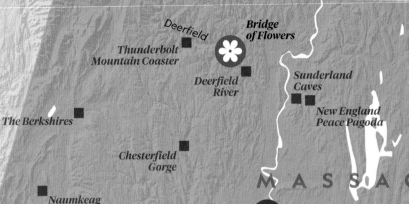

VERMONT

NEW HA

NEW YORK

Deerfield

Bridge of Flowers

Thunderbolt Mountain Coaster

Deerfield River

Sunderland Caves

New England Peace Pagoda

The Berkshires

Chesterfield Gorge

MASSACHUSE

Naumkeag

Dinosaur Footprints

Auburn Ice Canyon

Bash Bish Falls State Park

CONNECTICUT

"I WENT TO THE WOODS BECAUSE I WISHED TO LIVE DELIBERATELY, TO FRONT ONLY THE ESSENTIAL FACTS OF LIFE, AND SEE IF I COULD NOT LEARN WHAT IT HAD TO TEACH, AND NOT, WHEN I CAME TO DIE, DIS-COVER THAT I HAD NOT LIVED."
—HENRY DAVID THOREAU, *WALDEN*

Long Island Sound

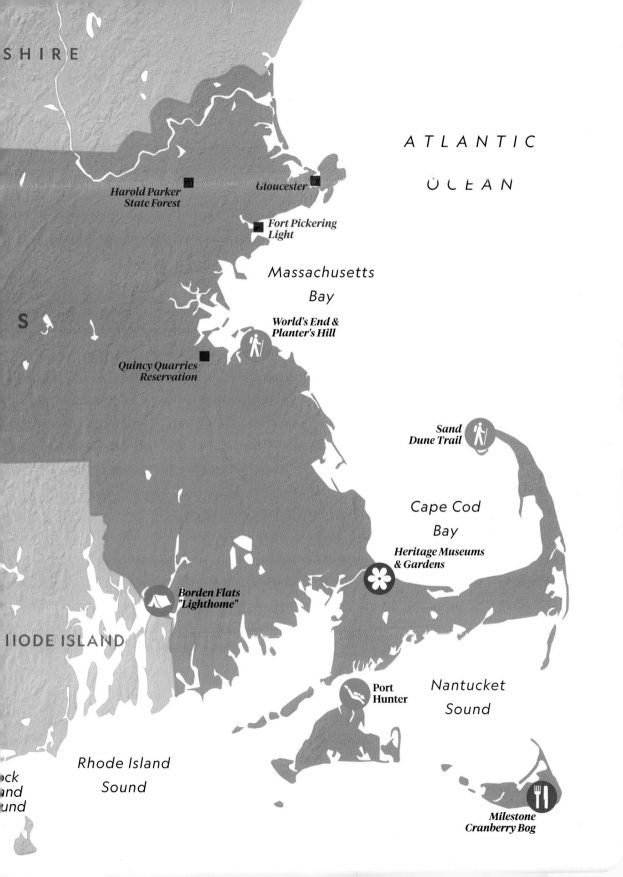

SHIRE

ATLANTIC

OCEAN

Harold Parker
State Forest

Gloucester

Fort Pickering
Light

Massachusetts

Bay

World's End &
Planter's Hill

S

Quincy Quarries
Reservation

Sand
Dune Trail

Cape Cod

Bay

Heritage Museums
& Gardens

Borden Flats
"Lighthome"

IIODE ISLAND

Port
Hunter

Nantucket

Sound

Rhode Island

Sound

ock
nd
und

Milestone
Cranberry Bog

A Walk in the Park

The landscape architect Frederick Law Olmsted, renowned for his work at New York's Central Park, also left his mark in Hingham, Massachusetts. A seaside park, World's End was originally designed to complement a planned residential neighborhood. Olmsted designed a British countryside estate theme garden with tree-lined carriage roads that meander around the peninsula, including four spoon-shaped hills formed by glaciers.

The 4.5-mile (7.2 km) loop around the peninsula varies from wide gravel roads and wooden boardwalks to narrow dirt paths and a route up to the top of Planter's Hill. At the peak, you can sit on a bench and take in the distant Boston skyline. Along the way, you'll pass American elm, English oak, and chestnut trees, as well as meadows, marsh, a pond, and views of the rocky shorelines. In winter when snow blankets the ground, explore the 251-acre (102 ha) park on cross-country skis. Equestrians with an annual horseback riding permit can take their horses on the trail.

Hingham, MA | **Season:** Year-round

Walk through World's End park to Hingham Harbor.

Wreck Diving

In 1918, a fully loaded freighter, the *Port Hunter*, collided with tug *Covington* in Vineyard Sound. The quick-thinking skipper of the *Covington* used the tug to push the *Port Hunter* 85 feet (26 m) to the sandy bottom of the water, on the edge of Hedge Fence Shoal.

The mammoth 380.5-foot (116 m) British World War I freighter was on passage from Boston to New York before meeting its demise. The freighter was carrying $5 million in clothing, $3 million in railroad car parts, and war supplies, including three million rounds of ammunition, motorcycles, and machine guns.

The top of the ship's bow lies 20 feet (6 m) below the surface, while the stern is found about 80 feet (24 m) deep. The ship's rudder and propeller shaft are still intact, but the midsection is engulfed by drifting sand.

Over the years, local fishermen and divers removed most of the materials aboard the ship, from leather jackets to the propeller.

Angelfish and groupers swim alongside jellyfish and cunners. The site's currents are strong, so it's recommended to dive at slack tide when the water is relatively still.

Just off Nauset Beach lies a barge wreck for divers to explore.

Falmouth or Martha's Vineyard, MA | **Season:** Summer

Get Inspired by the Dunes

The coastal dunes on Cape Cod were formed by a combination of glacial retreat, erosion, and deposition. The ground was further destabilized when early European settlers removed vegetation in the area and cleared the land for agriculture. The dunes, which range from a few dozen feet to more than 100 feet (30 m) tall, cover a third of Cape Cod National Seashore along the Outer Cape, from Chatham to Provincetown.

For more than a century, Cape Cod National Seashore has inspired artists like Jackson Pollock and literary legends like Tennessee Williams and Henry David Thoreau. Some of their iconic works were created during their stays at the dune shacks scattered across Peaked Hill Bars. The first shack on the dunes was built in 1882 as a lifesaving station, providing shelter and supplies to shipwrecked sailors. The original shack is gone, but 19 new shacks were built in the 1920s using shipwreck scraps washed up from the beach. The shacks are mostly primitive, with no electricity or running water. Added to the Register of Historic Places in 2012, the Dune Shacks now house artists, musicians, and writers who apply for weeklong artist and writer in residence programs.

To explore the sand dunes and the shacks, you can hike the 2.4-mile (3.8 km) looped Sand Dune Trail, a moderately challenging route that takes you to the water's edge. It's best to visit March through October, when the weather is mild, but be prepared for crowds. Dogs are not permitted on the trail, and Cape Cod National Sea Shore has an entrance fee.

For more thrills, go on a four-wheel-drive excursion with Art's Dune Tours. Experiences include a sunset tour with a clambake dinner on the beach or a trip combining a dune drive and kayaking.

You can also experience the dunes on two wheels by following the Province Lands Bike Trail, and 5.5-mile (8.8 km) loop that winds through trees, dunes, and bogs.

Provincetown, MA Season: Year-round

The museum sits on 100 acres (40 ha) of spectacular gardens.

Flower River in Cape Cod

The Heritage Museums & Gardens in historic Sandwich, Massachusetts, is situated on 100 acres (40 ha) of manicured botanical gardens, with easy-to-navigate nature trails and spots for peaceful respites. In May, 35,000 blooming purplish blue grape hyacinths create the illusion of a river as they wind through the green garden.

Although the Bulb River steals the show for a week in May, the wide variety of hydrangeas and rhododendrons are the highlight for visitors the rest of the year. The museum's Hydrangea Display Garden showcases thousands of blue, pink, purple, white, and fuchsia flowers in an English garden setting.

Another draw at the park is the Hidden Hollow, an outdoor nature-inspired play area spread over two acres (0.8 ha), and the first certified Nature Explore outdoor classroom in New England.

Sandwich, MA Season: Year-round

Spend the night at the
Borden Flats "Lighthome."

"GUESTS WILL HAVE TO PERFORM LIGHT KEEPER DUTIES."

Spend the Night in a Lighthouse

You don't have to marry a lighthouse keeper to live by the sea. Near the city of Fall River, Massachusetts, you can stay overnight at a historic sparkplug-style lighthouse on the Taunton River. The 50-foot-tall (15 m) Borden Flats "Lighthome" was built in 1881 to help guide ships through the relatively shallow Mount Hope Bay. After decades of deterioration, the red-and-white-striped lighthouse was put up for auction and sold to Oregonian James Nick Korstad in 2010.

Korstad rehabbed the five-story structure and updated it with a nautical-themed living room, a TV room, and a bedroom that sleeps two, as well as a fully equipped kitchenette with a microwave and stove. In 2018, Korstad sold the lighthouse to Kevin Ferias, a former guest, who continued Korstad's Overnight Keepers Program.

Marine history buffs can experience the life of a lighthouse keeper and stay at the brick and cast-iron tower, one of the few offshore lighthouses remaining in the world and a National Register of Historic Places site. The structure is completely off-grid, with no electricity, Wi-Fi, or running water. Everything is powered by solar panels and batteries, and bottled water is provided.

It's also not a typical Airbnb or hotel. The lighthouse is a fully active U.S. Coast Guard Aid to Navigation, with the lantern room still operated by the U.S. Coast Guard. Guests will have to stick to a strict check-in and checkout schedule and have to perform light keeper duties to keep the facility in the same clean condition.

The Overnight Keepers Program is very popular and books up fast. Overnights are from mid-April to November. Bookings include boat rides to and from the lighthouse.

Somerset, MA I **Season:** April to November

Bogged Down

Cranberries in Massachusetts are grown in natural bogs, which evolved from deposits left by glaciers more than 10,000 years ago. Records of cranberry farms in Nantucket date back to 1857.

During the annual Nantucket Cranberry Festival, the Nantucket Conservation Foundation offers scheduled guided tours through the 234-acre (95 ha) Milestone Cranberry Bog, the island's oldest continuously working farm and one of the world's largest cranberry bogs. Visitors can see millions of shiny red "rubies" bobbing in the water, watch the harvest, and learn about the history of cranberry production.

You also have the option of going on a quarter-mile (0.4 km) self-guided tour. Even if it's not cranberry season, you can still hike the public trails around the property. The 6.2-mile (9.9 km) Milestone and Middle Moors loop goes through hills and sandy roads to Altar Rock and back to the Milestone Cranberry Bog.

> "SEE MILLIONS OF SHINY RED 'RUBIES' BOBBING IN THE WATER, WATCH THE HARVEST, AND LEARN ABOUT THE HISTORY OF CRANBERRY PRODUCTION."

Nantucket, MA | **Season:** October

During the autumn harvest, Nantucket puts on a show with cranberry bog demos, family games, and musicians.

Bash Bish Falls cascades nearly 200 feet (60 m).

The Tallest Falls in the State

The honor of highest single-drop waterfall in the state belongs to Bash Bish Falls in the Taconic Mountains of Berkshire County, near the New York–Connecticut border. There are two hiking routes to see the giant cascade: The longer 1.5-mile (2.4 km) out-and-back route starts from New York's Taconic State Park, whereas a shorter trail (0.6 mile/0.9 km round-trip) leads off from Bash Bish Falls State Park in Mount Washington, Massachusetts.

Park at the free, lower parking area off Falls Road. The steep path follows the trickling Bash Bish brook through maple, oak, and beech forest, and over boulders, pro-truding tree roots, stone stairs, and wooden steps. Keep an eye out for peregrine falcons, bobcats, and black bears. From the viewing deck, you can see the 80-foot-tall (25 m) waterfall splash down to a massive triangle-shaped rock and split into two streams.

Berkshire County, MA | Season: Spring to fall

For a closer look at the waterfall, head down the stone steps toward the turquoise plunge pool. The trail is slick so wear shoes with good traction. Swimming and diving are forbidden, but you can rest at the boulders strewn around the pool.

Adjacent to Bash Bish Falls State Park is 4,169-acre (1,687 ha) Mount Washington State Forest, which has an additional 30 miles (48 km) of trails. Join up with the South Taconic Trail for a challenging 3.4-mile (5.5 km) hike through a northern hardwood forest to the peak of Alander Mountain. At 2,250 feet (685 m), Alander is a grassy plateau with sprawling views of the southern por-tion of the Taconic Mountains and the Hudson River Val-ley. The trails close at dusk.

Cross the border into New York for a jaunt in Taconic State Park, where you'll find, among hikes and swimming holes, the Bash Bish Cabins overlooking the Bash Bish Brook (fed by the falls). Spend the night in a cabin and hike directly to the falls.

You can now stroll the Bridge of Flowers, once a trolley span.

Cross the Bridge of Flowers

✺ In 1908, the Shelburne Falls and Colrain Street Railway built a concrete trolley bridge that connected to Buckland across the Deerfield River in northwest Massachusetts. After automobiles replaced trains as people's main mode of transport, the bridge became obsolete.

The abandoned weed-covered bridge was revived in 1929, when the Shelburne Falls Area Women's Club raised $1,000 to transform the structure into a flower garden. They planted flowers and shrubs, and the bridge blossomed into a popular tourist attraction. The bridge underwent a half-million-dollar renovation in the 1980s.

The Bridge of Flowers is open from April through October, 24 hours a day, and is free to visit. The path is wheelchair and walker accessible. Donations welcome.

Shelburne Falls, MA | **Season:** April to October

Walk in the Footsteps of Giants

🔭 Two-legged carnivorous dinosaurs from the early Jurassic period once roamed the banks of the Connecticut River, Mount Tom Range, and East Mountain in Holyoke. When Pangaea broke apart, the region was turned into a valley with a subtropical landscape of lakes and swamps where dinosaurs lived. The dinosaurs' footprints in the mudflats were covered in sediment, which protected them from erosion. When the last glacial period ended 15,000 years ago, the glaciers receded, scoured the valley of debris, and exposed the footprints.

In the mid-1800s, Massachusetts state geologist Edward Hitchcock discovered more than 100 tracks made by three different dinosaurs. No bones were found at the site, so the dinosaurs were not identified. Instead, Hitchcock gave the tracks their own species name: 15-foot-long (5 m) *Eubrontes giganteus;* a lion-size three-toed *Anchisauripus sillimani;* and a small *Grallator*. The site also uncovered fossilized plants, fish, and insects, as well as prehistoric ripple marks. The tracks were forgotten until workmen constructing Route 5 unearthed them in 1929. In the 1960s, Yale professor John Ostrom observed that the tracks had 28 trackways moving in the same direction, indicating that the dinosaurs might have traveled in packs.

Now you can see the prints for yourself—some of Ostrom's are outlined in chalk—at Dinosaur Footprints, an eight-acre (3 ha) wilderness just off Route 5. Free to the public, Dinosaur Footprints is a short trek from the parking turnout.

Holyoke, MA | **Season:** Year-round

Winter climbs await at the frozen walls of Auburn Ice Canyon.

Ice Climb Just Outside the Big City

Although its neighbors to the north may boast better ice-climbing sites, western Massachusetts' Auburn Ice Canyon is conveniently located just an hour west of Boston.

Auburn Ice Canyon, sometimes called Ice Box Canyon, is a flood diversion channel for the greater Worcester area. The channel's melting snow ices over, creating thick walls of ice that are ideal for steep ice climbs. Routes can reach 100 feet (30 m) tall, and are on the concrete walls as well as natural, jagged rock walls.

Several top-rope options make the canyon a great spot for beginners. And the steep routes are a huge draw for stronger climbers. After a prolonged cold spell, plenty of ice freezes over, drawing huge crowds on the weekends.

Auburn Ice Canyon is located off Route 20 in Auburn, and parking is available at the Dr. Arthur and Dr. Martha Pappas Recreation Complex.

Auburn, MA | **Season:** Winter

Harold Parker State Forest boasts 11 ponds and miles of hiking trails.

1. HIKE TO WATERFALLS AND CANYONS IN THE GORGE

Dubbed the "Grand Canyon of Massachusetts," the Chesterfield Gorge is a natural formation of glacial meltwater-carved ancient rock that emerged from the seabed a half billion years ago. You can reach the dramatic rock canyon by hiking through the wide, four-mile-long (6.4 km) Chesterfield Gorge Trail that runs along the Westfield River and passes by several mini-waterfalls.

2. EXPLORE THE SUBTERRANEAN

Hidden in Mount Toby State Forest is Sunderland Caves, a full cave system that runs about 50 yards (46 m) underground in central Massachusetts. Geology buffs can reach the cave through a 3.2-mile (5.1 km) portion of the Robert Frost Trail. Along the way, you'll pass waterfalls, cave overhangs, and a fire tower.

3. GO WHALE-WATCHING

Spot majestic humpback whales, stately finback whales, and elegant minke whales off the cold waters of Gloucester, a charming fishing village in northeastern Massachusetts. From April through October, several Gloucester companies take travelers out on naturalist-led whale-watching boat trips to witness whales breach and feed on mackerel, herring, and krill.

4. RIDE A CLASS III TO IV RIVER

Go white-water rafting on the Deerfield River, which originates in the Berkshire Mountains in Vermont and flows south into Massachusetts. Several outfitters have guided trips that start at Monroe Bridge and paddle through the Class III and IV rapids. For beginners and children, the milder Zoar Gap section features Class II and III rapids.

5. MOUNTAIN BIKE SINGLE-TRACK

Harold Parker State Forest is a 3,295-acre (1,333 ha) preserve with more than 30 miles (48 km) of mountain biking trails maintained by the New England Mountain Bike Association. The multiple single-track trails are easy to navigate and weave through mixed oak and white pine forests on rocky paths alongside ponds.

6. FIND THRILLS ON AN ALPINE COASTER

With 3,870 feet (1,180 m) of track, the Thunderbolt Mountain Roller Coaster at Berkshire East Mountain Resort is North America's second longest mountain coaster. The single-rider glides downhill through wide turns and rolling drops. Riders can adjust the speed of the cart using the braking system.

7. ROCK CLIMB THE QUARRY

The graffiti-strewn Quincy Quarries in Quincy, Massachusetts, is a haven for rock climbers. Nicknamed the "Birthplace of the Granite Industry," the quarry operated from 1825 to 1963 and supplied granite to homes and businesses, including the Bunker Hill Monument. A number of routes are spread over 21 small crags, with dozens of moderate top-rope and traditional climbing lines.

8. FIND ZEN AT THE NEW ENGLAND PEACE PAGODA

The dome-shaped New England Peace Pagoda is a Buddhist stupa, built as a symbol of peace in 1985. Guests are welcome to visit the pagoda, temple, Zen rock garden, and a water lily pond with a stone bridge walkway and colorful prayer flags.

9. TIPTOE THROUGH THE TULIP FESTIVAL

Each April and May, tens of thousands of candy-colored tulips, yellow daffodils, and other minor bulbs carpet the public gardens at Naumkeag in Stockbridge. Visit the 44-acre (18 ha) country estate during the annual Daffodil and Tulip Festival to see the spring bloom, take an art class, and attend horticultural workshops.

10. SEE SALEM'S HISTORIC LIGHTHOUSE

Built in 1871, the historic Fort Pickering Light in Salem was part of a three-lighthouse system that includes Derby Wharf Light in Salem, and Hospital Point Light in Beverly. Though the iron-and-brick lighthouse itself is closed to the public, you can still photograph the iconic building from Winter Island Park.

Pink rhodonite

The Lake of the Clouds is nestled in Porcupine Mountains Wilderness State Park, in Michigan's Upper Peninsula.

MICHIGAN

Bordered by four Great Lakes, this is a water lover's paradise—
with plenty to see and do inland, too.

CANADA
U.S.

MINNESOTA

Isle Royale
National Park

Lake Superior

ONTARIO

Copper Harbor
Trails

Pictured Rocks
National Lakeshore

Whitefish Point
Light Station

Tahquamenon
Falls

Kitch-iti-kipi

Mackinac
Island

CANADA
U.S.

MICHIGAN

Grand
Traverse Bay

Petoskey
State Park

Thunder Bay National
Marine Sanctuary

Lake Huron

Sleeping Bear Dunes
National Lakeshore

WISCONSIN

Lake Michigan

Manistee National
Forest

Tawas
Bay

Ludington

Silver Lake
State Park

Sanilac Petroglyphs
Historic State Park

TreeRunner
Adventure Park

Matthaei Botanical Gardens
& Nichols Arboretum

ONTARIO

Belle Isle Park and
Detroit RiverWalk

Warren Dunes
State Park

ILLINOIS

INDIANA

OHIO

Belle Isle, in the Detroit River on the U.S. and Canada border, was developed in the 19th century.

Wander Belle Isle Park and Stroll the Detroit RiverWalk

Metro Detroiters don't have to leave the city for a green getaway: Located downtown, Belle Isle beckons in the middle of the Detroit River. Designed in the 1880s by Frederick Law Olmsted, the architect of New York City's Central Park, the nearly thousand-acre (405 ha) island features three lakes, 150 acres (60 ha) of woodlands, walking and biking trails, and glittering views of the Detroit skyline.

The ADA-accessible paths lead to historic nature attractions. Opened in 1904, the Belle Isle Aquarium is the oldest aquarium in the United States. Along with tropical species, the aquarium shows off native fish like perch and bluegill. The Belle Isle Nature Center also focuses on Michigan wildlife and hosts nature walks around the island. For a more global bent, the glass-domed Anna Scripps Whitcomb Conservatory displays a diverse assortment of exotic plants in five sections, including a Palm House and a sunken Fernery.

The Belle Isle Bridge connects to the mainland at the eastern end of the Detroit RiverWalk, the city's celebrated waterfront restoration. Currently running 3.5 miles (5.6 km) from Joe Louis Arena to Gabriel Richard Park—with plans for more—the RiverWalk transformed dilapidated parking lots and industrial sites into artfully designed plazas and glorious gardens. Enjoy the beautifully landscaped and meditative Garden Rooms between GM Plaza and Cullen Plaza, then stroll along the river to Hart Plaza, where the landmark "Monument to Joe Louis" honors the Detroit boxer with an 8,000-pound (3,630 kg) bronze sculpture of his fist.

Detroit, MI | **Season:** Year-round

See the *F. T. Barney* wreck on a dive in Thunder Bay.

Dive Thunder Bay Sanctuary

Thunder Bay is known as "Shipwreck Alley" for good reason: More than a hundred wrecks lie within the boundaries of the national marine sanctuary. The cold, freshwater of Lake Huron has left them among the best preserved in the world.

Known wrecks date from 1849 to 1966, ranging from wooden schooners to steel-hulled freighters. Best dives include the 296-foot-long (90 m) steamer *Grecian*, with intact bow and stern 75 feet (23 m) underwater, and the wooden barge *Monohansett*, resting in clear waters only 20 feet (7 m) deep. Experienced divers can float over the eerie *Cornelia B. Windiate*, lost in 1875. Sitting upright in 185 feet (56 m) of water, the schooner is frozen in time, with its masts still standing and the crew's lifeboat resting nearby—a haunting reminder that all hands were lost.

Alpena, MI | **Season:** Spring to fall

Let's Go Fly a Kite

As large as a sea, Lake Huron generates powerful wind and waves—the perfect combo for superb kitesurfing. A blend of windsurfing, wakeboarding, and paragliding, kitesurfing sends riders flying over the water, harnessed to large hand-controlled kites. Soaring jumps can easily reach 80 feet (24 m) in height; the record is more than 100 feet (30 m).

Tawas Bay, in northern lower Michigan, is one of the world's top kitesurfing spots. Consistent winds, shallow water, and the long, sandy beaches of Tawas Point State Park, a curving two-mile (3.2 km) peninsula, draw hordes of kitesurfers in summer to ride waves and try out stunts. The beaches are key: As the sun warms the sand each day, it creates robust thermals that bear riders aloft. Local outfitters such as Great Lakes Kiteboarding and Motor City Kite & Surf offer lessons for all ages to learn their first jumps, rolls, S-bends, and loops.

East Tawas, MI | **Season:** Summer

Tawas Bay offers myriad ways to enjoy the water.

Take an autumn ride on the On the Edge Mountain Bike Trail in Copper Harbor.

Get Your Adrenaline Pumping on the Copper Harbor Trails

Situated at the tip of the Keweenaw Peninsula, Michigan's northernmost town offers action aplenty—including one of the top mountain biking trail systems in the world. The Copper Harbor Trails challenge extreme riders with nearly 40 miles (64 km) of single-tracks that emphasize tough-fought climbs and technical descents. Best of all, they're free to use and open year-round.

Trails with imaginative names like Raptor Ridge, Flying Squirrel, and West Woopidy Woo rumble over rugged bedrock through old-growth forest and lead to sweeping vistas above Lake Superior. Most of the routes are rated intermediate or expert level, but beginners will find gentle loops and all are welcome on the trails, from dog walkers to bird-watchers to berry pickers.

Come in September for the Copper Harbor Trails Fest, held every Labor Day weekend. Arduous cross-country, endurance, and downhill races attract world-class riders, and there's even a kids' race for young hellions on wheels.

Copper Harbor, MI | **Season:** Year-round

> ## "WITH NO MOTOR VEHICLES TO WORRY ABOUT, BICYCLES REIGN."

Bike Legendary Mackinac Island

Time seems to stand still on Mackinac Island, a 3.8-square-mile (9.8 km²) jewel in northern Lake Huron near the Straits of Mackinac. Once the domain of Anishinaabe Indians, French fur traders, and British soldiers, the popular destination isle sports centuries-old forts and Victorian homes, and the primary modes of transportation are foot, bicycle, or horse-drawn carriage. Forget about cars: They've been banned since 1898.

With no motor vehicles to worry about, bicycles reign. A must for any Mackinac visit is pedaling around the island's perimeter on Lake Shore Boulevard. The 8.2-mile (13.2 km) paved loop runs alongside the vivid blue waters of Lake Huron and provides easy access to iconic sights. Stop for photo ops at fascinating geologic formations such as Arch Rock, a 146-foot-tall (45 m) limestone bridge, and the eerie cave of Devil's Kitchen. Near the halfway point around the island, take a break at British Landing. The historic site, still marked by a cannon, is where British soldiers first invaded and eventually captured the island during the War of 1812. For much of the ride, the Mackinac Bridge forms a monumental backdrop. One of the longest suspension bridges in the world, it links Michigan's Upper and Lower Peninsulas.

There's more to Mackinac than its edges, however. Strike into the interior on the island's more than 70 miles (110 km) of trails. Wind through cedar and spruce forest to the central heights, where you'll find Fort Holmes, at the highest point, and Sugar Loaf, a 75-foot (23 m) limestone pillar sacred to early Native Americans. There's even mountain biking on this little island. After a full day on two wheels, roll to aptly named Sunset Rock and watch the sun sink behind the Mackinac Bridge.

Mackinac Island, MI · **Season:** May to October

Mackinac Island's downtown is bustling during the summer season.

Explore a Remote Wilderness

Calling adventure seekers: You can't get much more remote than Isle Royale, the least visited national park in the lower 48 states. Accessible only by boat, the 45-mile-long (72 km) island in the northwestern corner of Lake Superior is a primordial wilderness of deep forest, basalt ridges, and peat bogs, with hundreds of smaller islands nearby. Once you head into the backcountry on the park's 165 miles (266 km) of trails, you're on your own.

The island's isolation has formed an ecosystem so unique that it was designated an international biosphere reserve. Only 19 mammal species can be found here (compared to more than 40 on the mainland), many descended from hardy creatures that were able to cross the frozen lake in winter. The stars: wolves and moose, frequently spotted by backpackers and canoeists throughout the park. For more than 60 years, scientists have observed the large mammals in the world's longest-running predator-prey study.

Isle Royale, MI | Season: April to October

Hike the Indian Portage Trail across Isle Royale's wilderness.

A Fast-Moving Ride in the Snowbelt

There's a benefit to being in the middle of the snowbelt. Some 80 to 100 inches (200 to 250 cm) fall annually in northern mid-Michigan, creating the perfect powder base for snowmobiling. Cadillac is the hub: With more than 200 miles (320 km) of groomed trails that run through the Huron-Manistee National Forests and connect to additional networks, it boasts some of the best snowmobile trails in the state.

The routes meander through majestic red pine forest past white-blanketed fields and winding rivers. Snow clings to pine boughs that meet overhead, creating a dazzling winter wonderland while riders zoom through serpentine turns, hilly spurs, and flat railroad beds. Hop on the White Pine Trail, which stretches 92 miles (148 km) from Cadillac to Grand Rapids, to experience a local favorite. Michigan's second longest rail trail, it crosses 14 open-deck bridges and passes through charming small towns that welcome snowmobile riders.

Outfitters in the area offer snowmobile rentals for single and double riders, plus equipment, such as helmets, for those looking to take a self-guided ride. For a guided tour, look to K&R Outfitters. Choose between one of two full-day tours they offer: the South Run, which is a leisurely 100-mile (160 km) ride along the White Pine Trail to Reed City, or the North Run, a 150-mile (240 km) trip through Manistee National Forest. Both packages include lunch.

Multicity, MI | Season: Winter

Ice Climb Along the Lakeshore

Ready your crampons. Climbing a frozen waterfall of ice is challenging, chilly, and exhilarating—and there's no better place to try it in Michigan than Pictured Rocks National Lakeshore.

Named for the glorious, mineral-formed ribbons of color that adorn the park's sandstone cliffs facing Lake Superior, Pictured Rocks is a wonder of geology, with sedimentary rocks dating to 800 million years ago. Streams and waterfalls are abundant here, tumbling over cliffs and escarpments surrounded by hardwood forests of maple and beech.

Winter brings luminous beauty and the deep hush of heavy snow and ice. The area's annual snowfall averages 140 inches (355 cm); some winters see more than 200 inches (500 cm). From mid-December to early April, waterfalls and the water that seeps out of porous sandstone bluffs freeze into curtains and columns of brilliant ice, inviting intrepid climbers.

Munising, MI | **Season:** Winter

A top attraction is Miners Falls. The Miners River is the longest and largest river that drains into the lakeshore, and its cascade forms a 40-foot-high (12 m) pillar of ice. Getting to the falls takes some determination: The only way in requires three miles (5 km) of skiing or snowshoeing. Additional extraordinary columns can be found at Miners Basin 1.2 miles (2 km) north, while the more accessible azure ice curtains of Sand Point glitter 20 to 50 feet (6 to 15 m) high.

Layer up and conquer these frozen fortresses with guided excursions from Down Wind Sports, which also organizes the Michigan Ice Fest every February. During the week-long festival, learn how to use those crampons, set your ice ax, and inch your way up a shimmering wall of ice. You can also take courses and clinics, and meet celebrated climbers.

Sail the Great Lakes

The northwestern corner of Michigan's Lower Peninsula is a sailor's paradise. Its captivating coastline is dotted with safe harbors, quiet coves, delightful towns, and secluded islands.

The boating mecca of Traverse City has plentiful options to charter sailboats, including the award-winning sailing school, Great Lakes Sailing Co. Begin by practicing boat handling in the protected twin arms of Grand Traverse Bay. Sandy beaches, vineyards, and cherry orchards line the water, tempting sailors to come ashore.

For a longer journey, strike north along the coast to Charlevoix and Petoskey, the childhood haunts of Ernest Hemingway. Ready to face open water? Adventurous sailors can make the 30-mile (48 km) journey from Charlevoix to Beaver Island, the largest island in Lake Michigan. The island offers numerous trails for hiking, biking, and birding.

Multicity, MI | **Season:** Spring to fall

Set sail in Michigan's Upper Peninsula.

From the top of Sleeping Bear Dunes, look out to Lake Michigan.

> "AS NIGHT FALLS, THE PARK'S ENDLESS VISTAS BECOME A DAZZLING DISPLAY OF STARRY SKIES."

A Family-Friendly Trip to the Dunes

The towering sand formations of Sleeping Bear Dunes are no ordinary beach dunes. Perched atop glacial moraines, the shifting sands blow ever higher as wind and waves erode the headlands below. The result: immense sandy bluffs that reach a staggering 450 feet (135 m) over Lake Michigan.

The dune field of Sleeping Bear Plateau extends five miles (8 km) long and three miles (5 km) wide, encompassing the soaring headlands of Empire Bluffs, Sleeping Bear Bluffs, and Pyramid Point. Those up for a challenge can tackle the Dune Climb. It's only 3.5 miles (5.6 km) round-trip, but the trail is all sand, up and over multiple dunes. Climbing through the powdery grains is very strenuous, but rocketing down the steep slopes is a thrill for all ages.

The awe-inspiring dunes are only one part of Sleeping Bear Dunes National Lakeshore, which protects 65 miles (105 km) of pristine Lake Michigan coastline. More than 100 miles (160 km) of trails wind past inland lakes, breezy meadows, and northern hardwood and conifer forest that's carpeted with jack-in-the-pulpit and Canada violets in spring. Further explorations lie offshore on the Manitou Islands, reached by ferry. North Manitou is 15,000 acres (6,070 ha) of wilderness with a single village of 19th-century cottages—now the domain of park rangers—while South Manitou has 500-year-old white cedar trees and a historic lighthouse that marked a vital natural harbor.

Stay for the ranger-led astronomy programs after dark. As night falls, the park's endless vistas become a dazzling display of starry skies, showcasing twinkling constellations, the Milky Way, and meteor showers.

Empire, MI : **Season:** Late spring to early fall

Kitch-iti-kipi is also
known as the Big Spring.

GO FURTHER

1. VISIT A LIGHTHOUSE
With 3,200 miles (5,150 km) of shoreline, it's no surprise that Michigan has more lighthouses than any other state. See the salvaged ship's bell from the Edmund Fitzgerald at Whitefish Point Light Station, climb the 112-foot-tall (34 m) Big Sable Point Lighthouse, or volunteer to be a Mission Point Lighthouse keeper for a week.

2. SPOT PETROGLYPHS AT SANILAC PETROGLYPHS HISTORIC STATE PARK
Called Ezhibiigaadek Asin, or "written on stone" in the Anishinaabemowin language, the Sanilac Petroglyphs are Michigan's largest known group of ancient rock carvings. Kids can discern archers and animals as they study dozens of etchings dating to the Late Woodland period a thousand years ago.

3. MARVEL AT THE BIG SPRING
An emerald gem in the Upper Peninsula, Kitch-iti-kipi—considered a place of magic and legend by early Native Americans—is Michigan's largest natural freshwater spring. An ADA-accessible observation raft glides across the 200-foot-wide (60 m) bubbling pool, revealing ancient tree trunks, curious trout, and swirling sand formations in the crystal clear waters.

4. LOOK FOR PETOSKEY STONES
Budding fossil hunters can seek Michigan's state stone at Petoskey State Park and other rocky beaches on the northern Lower Peninsula. Unique to the Great Lakes, Petoskey stones have intricate hexagonal patterns left from prehistoric coral colonies. Sharp-eyed rock hounds might even score a rarer honeycomb-patterned Charlevoix stone.

5. ENJOY NICHOLS ARBORETUM
Affectionately called the "Arb" by locals and students, the University of Michigan's Nichols Arboretum presents a rich landscape of broad valleys, secluded glens, open prairie, and enchanting woodlands along the Huron River. Come in June to experience 10,000 flowers in peak bloom at the Peony Garden, the largest collection of heirloom peonies in North America.

6. CHALLENGE YOURSELF AT TREERUNNER ADVENTURE PARK
In Metro Detroit, you can still take to the trees. TreeRunner Adventure Park, in West Bloomfield, provides more than 250 suspended challenge obstacles to test the mettle of daredevils, including 45 zip lines and 14 different aerial trails. The excitement keeps going after dark: Themed glow nights illuminate the park with lights and music.

7. RIDE ATVS ON THE SAND DUNES OF SILVER LAKE STATE PARK
Are you "dune ready"? Strap in for a thrilling ride along the Lake Michigan shore at the only sand dunes east of the Mississippi that permit off-road vehicles (ORVs). The shifting sands of the 450-acre (180 ha) ORV scramble area promise different terrain with every visit, from long glides to dramatic drop-offs.

8. SOAK UP THE SUN
Michigan has a multitude of spectacular beaches, especially on the shores of Lake Michigan. One of the best: Warren Dunes. The state park has three miles (4.8 km) of soft white sand that beckon beachgoers. For a break from sunbathing, trek to the top of the dune formations, where hang gliders take flight.

9. GO DEEPWATER FISHING
Big lakes mean big fish—and Michigan's deep waters are a dream for anglers. The outstanding offshore fisheries of Lakes Michigan and Huron host a wide range of sport fish, including lake trout, salmon, walleye, perch, and steelhead. Take a charter fishing trip out of Ludington or Rogers City to try to land a trophy catch (that's also delicious).

10. SNOWSHOE TO TAHQUAMENON FALLS
These amber-colored falls are breathtaking in all seasons, but winter reveals a special beauty. Follow lantern-lit snowshoe paths to view the ice sculptures edging the roaring Upper Falls, one of the largest waterfalls east of the Mississippi, and the five lovely cascades of the Lower Falls four miles (6.4 km) downstream.

Big Sable Point Lighthouse

Cross Bay Lake in the Boundary
Waters Canoe Area Wilderness
(page 323)

MINNESOTA

Outdoor recreation is in Minnesota's DNA, with bike trails, thousands of lakes, and stunning rivers to explore.

MANITOBA

CANADA
U.S.

ONTARIO

Lake of
the Woods

Voyageurs
National Park

Arrowhead 135

CANADA
U.S.

Pine to Prairie
International
Birding Trail

Boundary Waters
Canoe Area Wilderness

Superior
Hiking
Trail

Lost 40 Scientific
and Natural Area

Lutsen Mountains Ski
and Summer Resort

NORTH
DAKOTA

Redhead Mountain
Bike Park

Lake Superior

Itasca State
Park

MICHIGAN

Hawk Ridge
Bird Observatory

Cuyuna Country State
Recreation Area

St. Louis River Estuary
National Water Trail

MINNESOTA

Grand Rounds
Scenic
Byway

WISCONSIN

SOUTH
DAKOTA

Luminary
Loppet

Mississippi National
River & Recreation Area

Winona
Ice Park

Blue Mounds
State Park

Root River
State Trail

Niagara Cave

IOWA

Scenic trails circle Bde Maka Ska with the Minneapolis skyline in the distance.

Cycle the Grand Rounds of Minneapolis

An 1899 map of Minneapolis and neighboring St. Paul highlights 43.5 miles (70 km) of interconnected bike routes. In the decades since, the Twin Cities have expanded their two-wheeled legacy, creating a cycling infrastructure that is unmatched for a metro area with more than four million residents. The crowning glory of Minneapolis's cycling network is the Grand Rounds, a 51-mile (82 km) loop that nearly circles the entire city.

Accessible from almost every part of Minneapolis, the Grand Rounds Scenic Byway circumnavigates the city by following its green spaces, lakes, and rivers in a rough circle. One 13.3-mile (21.4 km) stretch traverses the Chain of Lakes in southwest Minneapolis. That flows into 12.6 miles (20.3 km) along Minnehaha Parkway, which is home to a legendary 53-foot (16 m) waterfall that freezes into a curtain of ice every winter. From there, the Grand

Rounds follows the Mississippi River north for 9.2 miles (14.8 km) until it hits a 1.2-mile (1.9 km) downtown section, an excellent spot to view the twinkling lights of the city skyline at night. From downtown, the trail winds through a six-mile (9.7 km) urban stretch in northeast Minneapolis before following Victory Memorial Parkway, a leafy boulevard commemorating the war veterans of Hennepin County, for 3.8 miles (6.1 km), which leads to a four-mile (6.4 km) stretch along Theodore Wirth Park, the largest park in Minneapolis that was named after a Swiss immigrant and icon of the urban park movement in the United States.

The one "missing link" in the Grand Rounds' 130-year-long history is a segment in north Minneapolis, expected to be complete within the next 20 years. Until then, enjoy the nearly full circle by downloading the Nice Ride Minnesota app and renting traditional or e-bikes located at neon stations around the city and pedal away.

Minneapolis, MN | Season: Year-round

Cross-country ski past brilliant luminarias.

Celebrate the Cold

Just when it feels like winter may never end, the two-day City of Lakes Loppet Winter Festival begins in early February, giving new life to a long season in Minnesota. The hearty event, based out of Minneapolis's Theodore Wirth Park, includes competitive Nordic skiing, fat biking, skijoring, and snowshoe races, plus more laid-back fun like "Captain Ken's Kubb Tournament" (a nod to the iconic lawn game) and orienteering with a map and compass while on cross-country skis.

The festival's marquee event is the Luminary Loppet, a brisk nighttime walk around 109-acre (44 ha) Lake of the Isles that is lit with the fiery glow of 1,200 luminaries and backlit by the sparkling downtown skyline. Along the route are ice sculptures, fire dancers, bonfires, cookies, hot chocolate, and s'mores. The walk culminates at a tent with food trucks, local Surly beer, and live music, all of which add festive light to a dark time of year.

Minneapolis, MN | **Season:** February

Climb on Ice

It may come as a surprise that the country's second largest human-made ice park is on the site of an old dolomite limestone quarry that sits in the Mississippi River Valley 650 feet (200 m) above the town of Winona in southeastern Minnesota. The *Field of Dreams* adage "build it and they will come" has proven as true for ice climbing as it was for baseball, with visitors from as far as Texas flocking to Winona Ice Park to climb from New Year's Day well into March.

The ice is made by attaching a fire hydrant to thousands of feet of pipe, then letting the water spray over 1,500 horizontal feet (460 m), forming five different walls, the highest of which is 100 feet (30 m). With free access, beginner to expert routes, climbing instruction available from Big River Climbing Guides, and gear rental from Winona State University's outdoor education department, there's no reason not to try this winter sport.

Winona, MN | **Season:** January to March

Winona Ice Park is free and open to climbers.

The Superior Hiking Trail stretches through the woods in Tettegouche State Park.

The Superior Hiking Trail

🚶 With its rugged terrain, steep inclines, and sharp descents, not to mention the presence of black bears and biting mosquitoes, as well as quick-changing weather, this 310-mile-long (500 km) trail is as challenging as any in the country.

The southern section heads north, bisecting Duluth and providing urban skyline views to the Aerial Lift Bridge, where 1,000-foot (305 m) "lakers" enter the Duluth Harbor. Farther north, the trail heads deep into the boreal forest, traversing the Sawtooth Range, crossing swift-flowing rivers with frothy waterfalls, and rising 1,829 feet (557 m) before ending at the Canadian border.

With 93 backcountry campsites, the trail can be done as a backpacking trip or be easily sliced into smaller day hikes—the distance between trailheads ranges from three miles (4.8 km) to 11 miles (17.7 km). For the most comprehensive, detailed maps and information, purchase the *Guide to the Superior Hiking Trail* from the Superior Hiking Trail Association.

Multicity, MN | **Season:** Spring to fall

Set up camp in a
winter wonderland.

> **"THE SEASON IS MAGICAL . . . THE AIR IS SO CRISP IT TAKES YOUR BREATH AWAY."**

Winter Camp by the Water

The Anishinaabe and other Indigenous peoples have used what is now the Boundary Waters Canoe Area Wilderness as part of their waterborne transportation superhighway for centuries. Today, a quarter million annual visitors use this wilderness to paddle the thousand-plus lakes, fish for walleye, swim in the freshwater, and sleep under the stars.

The Boundary Waters is primarily a summer destination, but for those who want even more solitude and an opportunity to hone survival skills, winter is the time to be here. The season is magical—a white blanket of snow covers the landscape, the air is so crisp it takes your breath away, and wolves howl in the distance. But surviving winter in northern Minnesota requires skill. Temperatures can remain below zero for days; lakes and portages can be difficult to navigate in deep snow; and staying warm and dry is an around-the-clock exercise.

For the uninitiated, it's wise to take advantage of the local experts. Piragis Northwoods Company, in conjunction with Cast Outdoor Adventures, has the gear and expertise that can help a rank beginner turn into a confident, self-sufficient winter camper. In addition to fully guided custom trips, they offer a unique "Quick Start" program: Before the trip, they help groups plan a route and advise on the kind of clothing to pack and how to prepare food. When the group arrives in Ely, they load up with needed rental gear, and then a guide heads out into the wilderness with the group to help set up the first night's camp, gather firewood, and give a five-hour shakedown of winter camping survival skills. This proven system provides campers the support they need, but also encourages them to become self-sufficient.

Ely and Grand Marais, MN | **Season:** Winter

Hike and Bike Through the Trees

In a state with thousands of acres of forests, some trees still stand out, like the majestic old-growth red and white pines that occupy the Lost 40 Scenic and Natural Area. The trees still exist in this once heavily logged region of northern Minnesota due to an error made during an 1882 Public Land Survey that accidentally mapped the trees as Coddington Lake, which sits a half mile (0.8 km) to the southeast.

The mistake is a boon for today's tree lovers. The site, co-managed by the National Forest Service and the Minnesota Department of Natural Resources (DNR), contains the state's co-champion red pine, which stands 120 feet (37 m) tall. Don't expect signs pointing to this particular red pine on the site's one-mile-long (1.6 km) loop trail. Note to warbler lovers: This mature northern forest is a designated Audubon Important Bird Area, with 91 species of birds recorded, 21 of which are warblers that send up a delightful dawn chorus.

Northhome, MN | Season: Spring to fall

Visit the Lost 40 in the fall for spectacular colors.

Pick Your Tire in Cuyuna Country State Recreation Area

This once scarred region of open-pit iron-ore mines in central Minnesota abandoned in the 1980s has found new life as one of the best mountain biking destinations in the Midwest. The ugly pits have been transformed into deep, clear lakes, and the mountains of rock deposits surrounding them are now topped with lush vegetation through which a 70-mile (110 km) network of purpose-built single-track winds.

The 5,000-acre (2,020 ha) recreation area has five major "units" of trails throughout. In addition to upgrades on existing trails, like four new challenging gravity flow trails in the park's Mahnomen Unit, the most exciting recent addition is the fifth Sagamore Unit.

In the southwest corner of Cuyuna, it includes seven miles (11 km) designed specifically for adaptive riders who use three- or four-wheeled handcycles. In the winter, the trail system contracts to 45 groomed miles (72 km) of trails, but that's still quite a workout. Fat-tire biking is an exercise in slowing down. Cuyuna's rejuvenation isn't only about the trails. The entire area has blossomed: Cyclists can camp, glamp, or rent a luxurious cabin. At Cuyuna Cove, the tiny Scandinavian-themed cabins are a few blocks from the historic town of Crosby, home of Red Raven bike and coffee shop.

Ironton, MN | Season: Year-round

Try Your Hand at Ice Fishing

Rule number one of ice fishing: Ice is never 100 percent safe. But anglers on Lake of the Woods between December and March have greatly increased odds that they won't fall into the water because the behemoth 1,679-square-mile (4,349 km²) lake demarcates the farthest point north in the contiguous United States. Temperatures in these parts often plunge well below zero.

Ice fishing here is a cultural experience like no other: Imagine a vast network of ice roads, one of which stretches 37 miles (60 km), that spider off in all directions and are meticulously checked daily for cracks and other roadblocks by the resort owners who plow them. The ice is carefully monitored, and once it is thick enough, anglers with ATVs and snowmobiles are allowed to traffic it and set up collapsible houses. Later in the season, when the ice has thickened further, small day houses and pickups are also allowed.

Lake of the Woods County, MN | **Season:** December to March

Spaced along the roads are fancy fish houses, many of which have televisions, bunk beds, heaters, and a matrix of electronic fish finders. There are also a number of resorts, hotels, and motels in the area. If cabin fever sets in, anglers can drive to the Igloo Bar, a seasonal restaurant three miles (4.8 km) from shore. Yes, that's right, this bar is on the ice. Outfitted with big screen TVs, running water, and a hot-food menu (think sandwiches and pizza), it may be the only spot in the world where patrons can order a burger, sip a beer, and simultaneously fish for walleye. If one is caught, the entire place erupts in celebration.

Because Lake of the Woods is so massive, it has a diverse fishery. The tastiest catch is a 14- to 18-inch (36 to 46 cm) walleye. For those who want to reel in a trophy, there are also northern pike and muskie, a prehistoric-looking toothed monster that often tips the scales at 40 pounds (18 kg).

Roll or Walk the Root River State Trail System

We have the Chicago, Milwaukee, St. Paul, and Pacific Railroad to thank for abandoning their track through Bluff Country in southeastern Minnesota, which led to the development of a paved 60-mile (97 km) trail system used by cyclists, runners, walkers, in-line skaters, and in the wintertime, cross-country skiers. Connecting 10 small, thriving towns, the forked trail system parallels in part the Root River, a recreational hot spot for paddlers and anglers.

The trail's centerpiece is Lanesboro, a delightfully restored 19th-century town with art galleries, museums, and the renowned Commonweal Theatre Company. Ride the entire trail system, then kick back and float the Root River.

Cross the historic Root River State Trail railroad bridge.

Multicity, MN | **Season:** Year-round

> ## "UPWARDS OF 75,000 RAPTORS FLY THROUGH, FROM BALD EAGLES TO THE RARE GYRFALCON."

Watch the Migration

Few places in the world are better to perch with a pair of binoculars and watch the annual southern raptor migration than the Hawk Ridge Bird Observatory, a bluff 550 feet (170 m) above the western tip of Lake Superior in the city of Duluth. Once a primary site for shooting birds of prey, Hawk Ridge has transformed over the past half century into a world-renowned center for ornithological research, one of the primary places in the country for counting and banding raptors. It's also where thousands of bird-watchers from all around the globe gravitate every autumn to see upwards of 75,000 raptors fly through, from bald eagles to buteos to broad-winged hawks to peregrine falcons to the rare gyrfalcon.

How many birds and what species you'll see on any given day during the two-month window depends on many factors: Raptors like to keep "bankers' hours," meaning that they tend to fly through between 10 a.m. and 2 p.m. They also like days when the wind is coming from the northwest so that they can ride the thermals rather than fight against them. Arctic peregrines flying all the way to Antarctica tend to arrive at Hawk Ridge earlier in the fall while broad-winged hawks flying to Central and South America arrive en masse and rarely stop.

Why and how the birds migrate is fascinating and varied. The excellent educational staff at Hawk Ridge fields questions, and offers in-person outings, as well as a growing number of online resources and opportunities.

Duluth, MN | Season: Fall

A sharp-shinned hawk migrates through the Hawk Ridge Bird Observatory.

Walk the rocks in the headwaters of the Mississippi
River on Lake Itasca.

1. PADDLE THE MISSISSIPPI NATIONAL RIVER

This 72-mile-long (116 km) stretch of the Mighty Mississippi starts north of the Twin Cities in the town of Ramsey before splitting St. Paul and Minneapolis in half, offering views of the metro skyline bookended by peaceful stretches of wooded shoreline. It's an ideal urban wilderness escape for anglers, paddlers, and bird-watchers.

2. SEE BISON AT BLUE MOUNDS STATE PARK

All American bison alive today are descendants of 100 survivors from full-scale slaughter in the 1800s. The 130-strong Minnesota bison herd, most of which live at Blue Mounds in the southwestern corner of the state, is a partnership between the Minnesota DNR and the Minnesota Zoo to preserve a genetically diverse population.

3. HOUSEBOAT IN VOYAGEURS NATIONAL PARK

This water-based park that shares a border with Canada covers 218,055 acres (88,244 ha) and sprawls across four massive lakes (plus 26 smaller lakes), a good reason to explore it with a houseboat. Be sure to rent one with plenty of outdoor sleeping space—Voyageurs was recently designated an International Dark Sky Park.

4. BIRD ON THE PINE TO PRAIRIE INTERNATIONAL BIRDING TRAIL

Running north to south through northwestern Minnesota, this 200-mile (320 km) drive traverses multiple unique habitats, from pine forests to native tallgrass prairie. Along the way it offers 51 different sites to spot 275 species of birds, including life listers like snowy owls, chestnut-collared longspurs, northern goshawk, and golden-winged warblers.

5. RIDE REDHEAD MOUNTAIN BIKE PARK

Built at the site of a half dozen abandoned open-pit iron-ore mines dating back to 1898, this mountain bike haven near the northern town of Chisholm offers 25 miles (40 km) of purpose-built single-track that traverse rugged bedrock and deep red iron-stained dirt, passing rusty relics of its hard-working past—from mining lanterns to hard hats.

6. RACE THE ARROWHEAD 135

Only the toughest cyclists, runners, and skiers contend in this 135-mile (217 km) January race across the frozen landscape of northern Minnesota, where temperatures dip well below zero and howling wolf packs are heard in the distance.

7. CROSS THE HEADWATERS AT ITASCA STATE PARK

The legendary Mississippi River begins with a mere trickle here in northern Minnesota before it winds 2,552 miles (4,107 km) south to the Gulf of Mexico. Step across the stones that demarcate the river from Lake Itasca, then check out fascinating facts about the Old Man River inside the nearby visitors center.

8. EXPLORE SUBTERRANEAN NIAGARA CAVE

This limestone cave system outside of Harmony, sculpted millions of years ago by water seeping through the karst formation, looks like a scene from *Star Wars*. On the mile-long (1.6 km) hike 200 feet (60 m) below the earth's surface, visitors will see a 60-foot-long (18 m) waterfall, 450-year-old fossils of sea-dwelling life-forms, and a subterranean wedding chapel.

9. SKI FRESH POWDER AT LUTSEN MOUNTAINS

Rising to a height of 1,688 feet (515 m) in the Sawtooth Mountains overlooking Lake Superior, the four interconnected peaks that comprise Lutsen offer big-mountain skiing in the Midwest. Founded in the 1880s by Swedish immigrant C.A.A. Nelson, the resort now has 62 primary trails, 32 side-country trails, and two terrain parks.

10. PADDLE THE ST. LOUIS RIVER ESTUARY NATIONAL WATER TRAIL

The St. Louis River, which flows into Lake Superior, was once heavily polluted by big industry. Painstaking efforts to clean up North America's largest freshwater estuary have resulted in a new water trail that provides 11 loops for paddlers to enjoy the river's stunning, rejuvenated beauty and its bountiful wildlife.

Find plenty of wide-open road and green spaces throughout Mississippi.

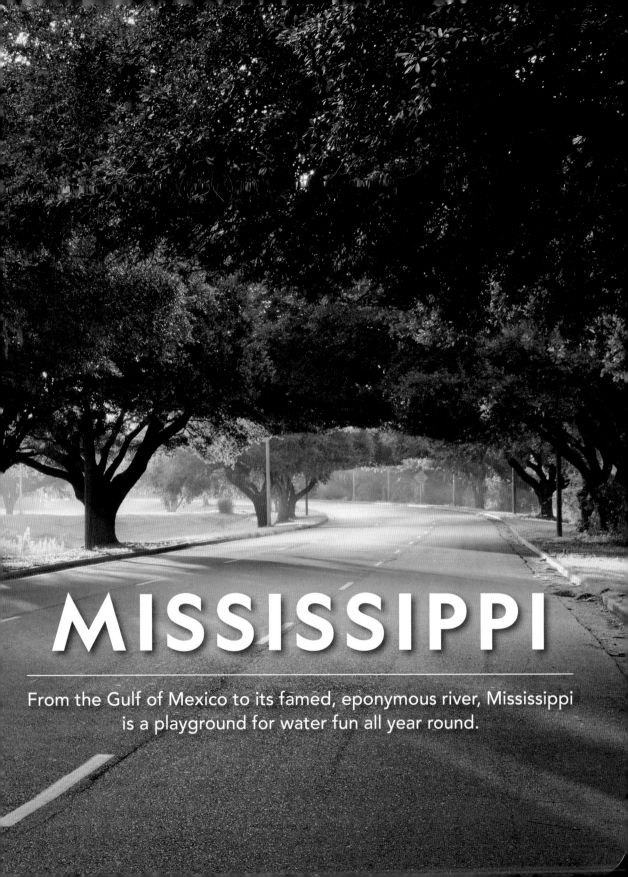

MISSISSIPPI

From the Gulf of Mexico to its famed, eponymous river, Mississippi is a playground for water fun all year round.

TENNESSEE

ARKANSAS

Woodall
Mountain

Mississippi

 Lower Mississippi
River

Old Mountain
Outdoor Adventures

Natchez Trace
Parkway

MISSISSIPPI

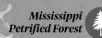 Mississippi
Petrified Forest

 Barnett
Reservoir

Chunky

Chunky
River

Mississippi

ALABAMA

Brookhaven

 Longleaf
Horse Trail

Red
Bluff

Clark Creek
Natural Area

Pascagoula Historic
Bike Trail

Mississippi Sandhill Crane
National Wildlife Refuge

Gulf Coast
Gator Ranch

LOUISIANA

Harrison County
Beach Loop

Biloxi

Grand Bay
National Estuarine
Research Reserve

Jourdan River
Blueway Trail

Gulf Islands
National Seashore

Gulf of Mexico

Chandeleur Islands

A rainbow stretches over the beaches along Gulf Islands National Seashore.

Barrier Island Camping

Stretching for 160 miles (260 km) all the way to Florida, Gulf Islands National Seashore boasts some of the most pristine beaches in the country, with white-sand shores, a 19th-century fort, and diverse maritime forests and habitats. Six of the barrier islands fall within the Mississippi border, and all are open to the public but accessible only by boat—which is a big part of the adventure.

Farthest to the west, Cat Island is completely undeveloped (as are Horn and Petit Bois Islands, which are also designated as wilderness areas). Davis Bayou, meanwhile, has a visitors center, a wooden pier perfect for dropping in a fishing line, and several developed campsites. History buffs shouldn't miss visiting 85-acre (34 ha) Ship Island, home to Fort Massachusetts, a coastal fortress completed by the Army Corps of Engineers in 1866. The fort stands as the only remnant from the Civil War–era of Ship Island, when the island served as a bustling port for supply ships and housed nearly 5,000 captured Confederate soldiers. Ferries normally run from mid-March through October, and dolphin sightings are all but guaranteed during the one-hour ride across the Mississippi Sound.

Backcountry camping is allowed on all islands (except, at the time of writing, Ship Island), and campers arriving via boat don't need a permit: Just pitch your tent on a flat stretch of sand and savor the sublime experience of falling asleep to the crashing waves. Be sure to follow the strict rules (no campfires, glass bottles, or camping on sand dunes) and Leave No Trace guidelines (packing out everything you bring in).

Multicity, MS | Season: Spring to fall

Take a hike through and up Mississippi's Red Bluff.

Hike Mississippi's Little Grand Canyon

A tucked-away treasure near the town of Foxworth, Red Bluff, also known as the Little Grand Canyon, requires some effort to find. But it's well worth it to explore the rugged, red-orange landscape, which was created by still active erosion; in fact, look for the now closed highway that's partially washed away. But don't be deceived by the short distance (approximately 3 miles/ 4.8 km): The hike down to the ravine is fairly steep, slick in parts, and will certainly be challenging for novice hikers. The payoff is worth it, though, as the route crosses a working railroad track and winds past multiple bluffs that serve as stunning lookout points of Pearl River, the trail's unofficial terminus. You'll likely do some wading at that point, so waterproof hiking boots, as well as trekking poles, are recommended.

Foxworth, MS | **Season:** Year-round

An Equine Adventure

One of the best equestrian trails in the state, the 26-mile (42 km) Longleaf Horse Trail invites a leisurely day of riding through Mississippi's piney woods landscape. The trail is wide (between 15 and 25 feet/4.6 and 7.6 m), well maintained, and rarely crowded, with many amenities for riders, including a large trailer parking and staging area at the trail's northern end in Carson and another large trailer parking area at the Sumrall Station.

The equestrian trail also shares restrooms and other facilities with the parallel-running Longleaf Trace Trail, a 44-mile (71 km) rail trail from Hattiesburg to Prentiss that's popular with cyclists, pedestrians, and in-line skaters. Beginning at the University of Southern Mississippi in Hattiesburg (bike rentals are available at the visitors center), the trail features eight restrooms and three covered rest areas along the way.

Multicity, MS | **Season:** Year-round

Longleaf Trace has miles of trails for a ride.

Look to the skies while birding on Horn Island.

Leave the Beach to the Birds

Originally constructed for beachgoers, the 26 miles (42 km) of beaches along the Harrison County Loop south of U.S. Highway 90, with their rock jetties and sand beaches, are a big-time draw for birds, too, offering prime habitat for dozens of species of shorebirds and migrating waterbirds.

Maximize the experience by driving west to east along U.S. Highway 90, stopping at the six key viewing points along the way without having to make repeated U-turns across the divided highway. (The westernmost access point is in Pass Christian Harbor; the easternmost one is in Biloxi.) During migration and winter, the first few hours of a falling tide are ideal for viewing, when freshly exposed mudflats draw shorebirds and waters are still deep enough for other species like gulls, ducks, and terns to feed fairly close to shore.

And don't forget to scan the rock jetties, where you're likely to see American oystercatchers, and if you're super lucky, perhaps even a glimpse of the rare purple sandpiper.

Pass Christian Harbor to Biloxi, MS | **Season:** Year-round

Make camp and wake up to the sunrise on the banks of the Mississippi River.

"CHOOSE FROM SEVERAL OPTIONS FOR A PADDLING TRIP."

Paddle the Lower Mississippi

There's no more iconic waterway on the continent than the Mississippi River. Beyond its economic impact, the Mighty Miss, which divides the continental U.S. from its northern source at Lake Itasca to its terminus in the Gulf of Mexico, has over the centuries inspired literature, music, and of course, recreation. But the heart of this 2,350-mile (3,780 km) river lies in the region known as the Mississippi Delta. Outdoor enthusiasts craving their own Huck Finn–inspired Mississippi River adventure can choose from several options for a paddling trip, from a leisurely day paddle to more ambitious, multiday journeys.

But running the river isn't nearly as simple as grabbing your gear and putting in. In short, the Lower Miss, as this stretch is often known, isn't the place to learn how to paddle: It's part of a major commercial waterway with nearly nonstop traffic, a system of 29 locks, and serious currents. But for intermediate-level paddlers, running the Miss means experiencing this world-famous river in a way that few ever do, especially during an overnight trip: navigating her challenges firsthand by day, falling asleep in a tent pitched on her banks at night. An excellent resource to start planning any adventure is Rivergator.org, which is run by world-renowned paddling guide John Ruskey and provides a wealth of information on prepping for a trip, put-in and takeout spots, river conditions, and overall considerations.

For customized trips, Ruskey's Quapaw Canoe Company is by far in a class of its own. With locations in Vicksburg and Clarksdale, the outfitter specializes in trips ranging from a one-day run to a three-week expedition. A popular option is the Muddy Waters Wilderness, a 101-mile (162.5 km) adventure through the Mississippi Delta landscape that inspired McKinley Morganfield, the blues legend better known as Muddy Waters.

Multicity, MS | **Season:** Spring to fall

Sail a Schooner

In the 1800s, Biloxi oyster schooners dominated the Gulf Coast horizon, their billowing sails an unmistakable symbol of the seafaring culture of the Mississippi Gulf Coast. Step on board a reproduction of these "white-winged queens," as they were also known, for a firsthand look into this centuries-old heritage and the history of Biloxi, which traces its roots to the arrival of the French in 1699. Two model schooner vessels at the Biloxi Maritime and Seafood Industry Museum are available for half- and full-day charters, as well as walk-up sailings. Trusty captains offer tales of the area's maritime history, and passengers are welcome to bring their own food and refreshments (ice and coolers are provided). Sunset, if you can time your sailing accordingly, offers an especially sublime experience. The two-story museum is itself worth a visit, with a well-curated display of original artifacts that tell the story of the local seafood industry.

Biloxi, MS | **Season:** Spring to fall

Shrimp boats dock in Biloxi Bay.

Relax at the Rez

The 33,000-acre (13,355 ha) Barnett Reservoir, more commonly known as "the Rez," is beloved by Mississippians for its abundant recreation opportunities, from high-octane pursuits like waterskiing to more tranquil lakeside hikes, bird-watching, and picnics. Many nearby parks, trails, restaurants, and viewpoints around the reservoir round out an outdoorsy itinerary, and with nearly two dozen hotels in the area, it's easy to extend the fun into the next day or over a long weekend.

Old Trace Park is a popular spot for lakeside strolls or bike rides along a paved trail; the park also has an 18-hole disc golf course. For boat rentals and fishing supplies, head to Main Harbor Marina. A pontoon boat is the preferred way to explore the reservoir, which boasts a sprawling surface area of 16 miles long (26 km) and seven miles (11 km) wide. Plan to anchor and linger at "The Cove," a lively locals' gathering spot at the Reservoir Overlook. For a more low-key adventure, several local outfitters rent kayaks and offer guided tours. And don't miss soaking up the sunset at the Reservoir Outlook at Milepost 105.6; the Chisha Foka Multi-Use Trail lets you get there by walking or cycling.

A bounty of restaurants fuel appetites after an active day on the water. Shaggy's on the Rez serves up heaping portions of seafood-centric dishes like po'boys and fried fish platters. Cock of the Walk is a longtime favorite for hearty southern fare like fried catfish, and servers wearing period clothing reflecting the region's bygone riverboat heyday flip cornbread in the skillet right in front of hungry diners' eyes.

Spicebush swallowtail butterfly

Ridgeland, MS | **Season:** Spring to fall

Ride the Trace

🚲 Partially tracing the Old Natchez Trace corridor Indigenous peoples and European settlers once traveled, this 444-mile (715 km) historic route cuts diagonally through the Magnolia State before eventually reaching Alabama and then Tennessee. A coveted ride for many cyclists, it's designated by the National Park Service as a bicycle route, meaning no commercial traffic and a maximum speed limit for cars of 50 miles an hour (80 km/h). The Trace also offers an experience that's uniquely Mississippian—rich with antebellum history, the blues, and of course, southern hospitality around every bend.

The parkway winds through eight Mississippi communities, including Natchez, Jackson, and Tupelo. Find multiple options for overnight lodging along the way, from chain hotels to cycling-friendly B&Bs. In addition, five separate campgrounds are designated as cyclists-only. One of those, located at Milepost 234 in the town of Houston, is called Witch Dance Campground after an old legend that claims witches once gathered in the wooded area to dance. Campgrounds, as well as hotels and B&Bs, are spaced so cyclists can plan their routes in 30- to 60-mile (48 to 97 km) stretches.

A few pro tips on riding the Trace: Be sure to wear high-visibility gear; spring or fall offer the most optimal weather (not during the infamously sticky summers); ride single file as far to the right as possible (commercial groups and riders 10 and older will need a permit from the National Park Service beforehand). For thru-riders, the Chisha Foka Multi-Use Trail, running from Milepost 95.8 to Milepost 105.6, is an ideal option for avoiding the traffic around Jackson.

Multicity, MS | Season: Year-round

Lake Lincoln State Park offers MTB trails and so much more.

Mississippi MTB

🚲 Plenty of flowy fun awaits riders of all skill levels at this volunteer-maintained trail near Brookhaven. In Lake Lincoln State Park, beginner-friendly loops are ideal for newbies, including the family-friendly one-mile (1.6 km) Kids Loop. Or try the original Mt. Zion trail, an intermediate 8-mile (13 km) single-track loop for longer adventures. Intermediate cyclists, meanwhile, will love ripping through the nine-mile (14.5 km) RC loop, which features plenty of tight, technical action, including climbs and descents, and more than 40 wooden features: walls, bridges, and even a seesaw (all jumps have ride-around options). You'll also find fun things to look at along the trail, including "Blue Jean Alley," several pairs of jeans hanging among the trees, and even a boneyard with several cattle skulls nailed to trees.

Brookhaven, MS | Season: Year-round

Forests border the banks of
the Mississippi.

> "ENORMOUS FIRS AND MAPLES LIVED FOR MORE THAN 1,000 YEARS AND SOARED SOME 100 FEET (30 M) HIGH."

See Fossilized Trees

A relatively unknown fun fact about Mississippi: Its state rock is petrified wood, which is the star of the show at the Mississippi Petrified Forest. One of just a handful of petrified forests in the United States—and the only one in the Southeast—the privately owned property is maintained as a national natural landmark, offering a fascinating look into the powerful forces that fossilized massive trees into stone giants some 36 million years ago. These enormous firs and maples, which lived for more than 1,000 years and soared some 100 feet (30 m) high, clogged an ancient river, were covered with sediment, and eventually fossilized.

Stroll among the ancient remnants along the Nature Walk, which winds through the peaceful, primeval landscape, then sit for a spell on the mighty "Caveman's Bench": a hefty bench-shaped petrified log that is just the spot to snap a photo.

Rock hounds shouldn't miss perusing the rocks and minerals from all over the world in the small but impressive Earth Science Museum. Inside the museum, you'll find examples of petrified wood from every state, plus images of plant life in the park throughout the ages. There are also fossil displays, including dinosaur footprints, whale bones, and turtle shells. Little ones will delight in trying their hands at gem fluming. Grab a bag of "mine muck" for washing and screening; you keep what you find. Camping is also available, with full-hookup and primitive sites.

Flora, MS | Season: Year-round

Look for gators on an
airboat swamp tour.

1. PADDLE A BLUEWAY TRAIL

The longest free-flowing (undammed) waterway in the lower 48 is one of several state-designated Blueway Trails. The approximately six-hour route of the Pascagoula River Jackson County Blueway is ideal for experienced paddlers (additional entry points offer shorter trips for beginning paddlers). The river hosts some 22 threatened and endangered species, as well as more than 300 plant species.

2. STALK COASTAL CREATURES

With an interpretive center, trails, and a boardwalk, Grand Bay National Estuarine Research Reserve makes Gulf Coast nature easily accessible. Visitors can enjoy fishing, kayaking (it's BYOB—bring your own boat), birding, and more across 18,000 acres (7,285 ha) of natural habitats like salt marshes, pine forest, and bayous rich with carnivorous plants, shorebirds, and the occasional alligator.

3. FISH AT THE CHUNKY RIVER

Ranked by fly-fishing enthusiasts as one of the top spots in the state, the Chunky River also boasts a 65-foot (20 m) waterfall created in the mid-1800s to power a gristmill, which is now open to visitors as a park. Also on-site are 27 campsites and a Trading Post with kayak rentals.

4. BAG A MISSISSIPPI HIGH POINT

Highpointers, as they're known, can check off the Mississippi high point at 806 feet (246 m) on Woodall Mountain near Iuka, in the state's northeast corner. It's a privately owned, 0.1-mile (0.2 km) trail, but the owners of the property encourage respectful hikers.

5. CYCLE THROUGH HISTORY

The flat Pascagoula Historic Bike Trail offers 15 points of interest through the coastal city of Pascagoula, including several historic districts, a circa 19th-century lighthouse that was rebuilt after a hurricane destroyed it, Jimmy Buffett's childhood home, the site where William Faulkner penned two of his works, and of course, the beautiful Gulf Coast shoreline.

6. ZIP AROUND

In addition to zip lines and aerial obstacles, Old Mountain Outdoor Adventures also offers unique experiences like treetop net dodgeball and even a free fall. Choose from several package options; one of the most popular is the self-guided canopy tour, which allows harnessed participants to move at their own pace among the trees.

7. AIRBOAT AMONG ALLIGATORS

Alligators own this swampland at the edge of the Grand Bay Estuary. But brave visitors can venture into their terrain at the Gulf Coast Gator Ranch. Zoom through 105 acres (43 ha) of generally untouched wilderness on a high-speed airboat for an up close—but safe—interaction.

8. VISIT A CRANE REFUGE

Home to approximately 100 Mississippi sandhill cranes, one of the world's rarest bird populations, Mississippi Sandhill Crane National Wildlife Refuge also boasts 10 varieties of carnivorous plants in the last remaining wet pine savanna habitat in the United States. Two short trails, each less than a mile (1.6 km) long, wind through the landscape; the visitors center also has an observation deck.

9. ISLAND FISHING

The Chandeleur Islands are an uninhabited, 50-mile (80 km) chain in the Gulf of Mexico and part of Breton National Wildlife Refuge, which Theodore Roosevelt established in 1904. Today it's a top fishing destination for redfish and trout, with chartered trips available via several outfitters.

10. WALK AMONG WATERFALLS

The 700-acre (280 ha) forested expanse of Clark Creek Natural Area is brimming with scenic falls, some as high as 30 feet (9 m). The property features approximately 4.6 miles (7 km) of maintained and primitive trails crossing creeks and tributaries and passing several falls.

Honeybee

Branson Landing and historic
downtown Branson offer
sweeping river views.

MISSOURI

From zipping down ski trails to paddling in the Ozarks, Missouri's outdoor recreation is as diverse as it is fun.

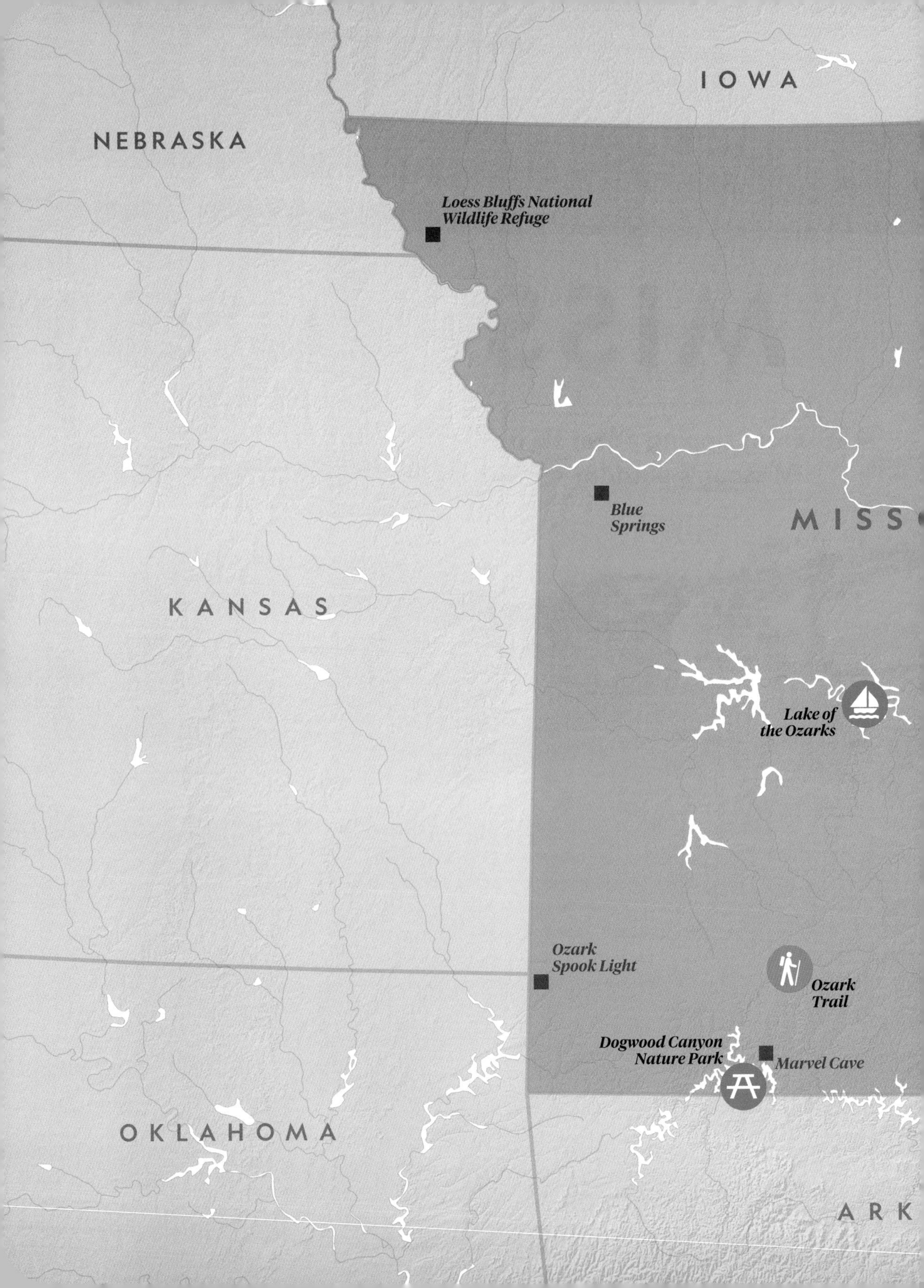

IOWA

NEBRASKA

Loess Bluffs National
Wildlife Refuge

Blue
Springs

MISS0

KANSAS

Lake of
the Ozarks

Ozark
Spook Light

Ozark
Trail

Dogwood Canyon
Nature Park

Marvel Cave

OKLAHOMA

ARK

ILLINOIS

INDIANA

Mark Twain
Cave

Go Ape Zipline &
Adventure Park

Katy Trail
State Park

Hidden
Valley

Canoehenge

Bonne Terre
Mine

Portuguese Point
Scenic Overlook

Pickle Springs
Natural Area

Braille
Trail

Johnson's Shut-Ins
State Park

Welch Spring
Hospital Ruins

Ozark National
Scenic Riverways

KENTUCKY

Saint Francis
River

Saint Francis

SAS

TENNESSEE

Hike the Braille Trail

Designed in 1981 especially for people with visual or physical disabilities, the Braille Trail is the first of its kind in Missouri state parks and is also designated as a national recreation trail. The 0.9-mile (1.4 km) route offers access to the 7.5-acre (3 ha) Elephant Rocks State Park, whose name belies its star features: pachyderm-shaped granite boulders that stand end to end, just like their circus counterparts. The mostly asphalt trail varies in slope. To help those who are visually impaired, interpretive stations have Braille text and carpet patches, as well as hand-rope-lined trails to mark changes on the path. A short spur off the trail leads hikers to the top of the granite outcrop, where they can explore this section. Another spur off the trail leads back to the ruins of an old railroad engine house, a remnant of the area's quarrying and railroad history from the 1860s to the early 1900s. There are 30 picnic sites around the elephant rock, with a few tables that have been modified to be mobility friendly with extended-end tables.

Iron, MO | **Season:** Year-round

Giant, billion-year-old boulders sit end to end at Elephant Rocks State Park.

Backpack the Katy

Built on the former corridor of the Missouri-Kansas-Texas Railroad, the 237-mile (381 km) Katy Trail is the longest rail trail in the country—and one of the most historic. More than half the trail's length traces Lewis and Clark's path up the Missouri River, an especially scenic stretch where cyclists can pedal under dramatic river bluffs as eagles circle overhead. After leaving the river, the trail winds through bucolic farmland and small towns, with 26 trailheads and four fully restored railroad depots between its end points in Clinton (west) and Machens (east).

Not surprisingly, many cyclists incorporate the Katy on their cross-country tours. Small towns along the way provide cozy accommodations after a long day in the saddle, not to mention a peek into the region's railroad days and heritage as the gateway to the West. Multiple campgrounds also offer a more rustic experience.

Multiple outfitters and rental shops offer bikes and gear along the way. One worth noting is the St. Charles–based Bike Stop, which owns a cycling-friendly café, bakery, and bike shop all located in the area. The company also provides shuttle service for riders on the Katy.

Cycle across old railroad bridges.

Multicity, MO | **Season:** Year-round

Dive the Mines

Once the world's largest producer of lead ore, Bonne Terre Mine is the Show Me State's real-life version of Atlantis—and a must-do for divers. Those who have open water certification will delight in visibility of more than 100 feet (30 m), which provides prime viewing of the well-preserved machinery and mining equipment. It's an ethereal reminder of a flood that occurred in the 1960s, when an underground water source was struck. In fact, enough water flowed to form what's now known as the Billion Gallon Lake. Divers can explore the unusual underwater world via guided tours among 24 dive trails between 40 and 60 feet deep (12 and 18 m); reservations and scuba certification are required for divers. The attraction's roster of famous visitors includes Jacques Cousteau, who spent several days filming at the site in 1983. Indeed, the mine's spectacular setting—dramatic rock pillars and mining artifacts scattered about—make for sensational underwater photography.

Bonne Terre, MO | **Season:** Year-round

But the fun isn't restricted just to divers: The subterranean site also offers guided boat and walking tours. Pontoon boats leisurely float passengers atop the crystal clear waters, with remarkable views of the shafts and mining equipment below, thanks to the 500,000 watts of stadium lighting above the water's surface. The one-hour walking tours, meanwhile, follow old mule trails on the mine's two upper levels (tours require navigating a 65-step staircase in and out). And with a year-round air temperature of 62°F (16.7°C), the mine offers a sweet reprieve from sticky summer weather. Reservations are required for diving the mines. Larger groups should also make reservations for boat and walking tours.

The St. Francis River is surrounded by autumn foliage.

Run the Saint

As savvy paddlers know, the Midwest boasts its fair share of top-notch white water; you just have to know where to find it. One of its most beloved waterways is the St. Francis River, a tributary of the Mississippi. Known as the Saint in local paddling circles, the waterway is a coveted white-water destination, which depending on levels ranges from Class II to IV. Every spring, the Saint also hosts the Missouri Whitewater Championship.

Beginner and intermediate paddlers should start at the 3.3-mile (5.3 km), Class II upper run. Experienced paddlers, meanwhile, flock to the 2.3-mile (3.7 km) lower run, where Class II+/III rapids (and even IV, depending on water levels) put skills to the test. If you're looking to step up your game, check out the spring clinic offered by the Missouri Whitewater Association, which is recommended for paddlers with at least some experience on moving water.

Fredericktown, MO | **Season:** Spring to fall

> "DIPPING A PADDLE INTO THIS STRETCH OF WATER IS ONE OF THE STATE'S MOST SUBLIME ADVENTURES."

A Paddler's Paradise

Whether on a lazy afternoon float or a multiday trip, dipping a paddle into this stretch of water in the southeastern Ozark Highlands is one of the state's most sublime adventures. As the first national park to protect a river system, the 134-mile (216 km) waterway is made up of the Current River and its major tributary, the Jacks Fork, as well as the surrounding 80,000 acres (32,345 ha) of natural wonders (massive springs, underground streams, and caves), hiking trails, and historic landmarks.

Six major freshwater springs feed the rivers—including one of the largest in the world, Big Spring, in Van Buren. Both the Current and the Jacks Fork below Alley Spring are runnable all year long, and with mostly Class I and occasional Class II spots, they're doable (and enjoyable) for almost all skill levels. The Jacks Fork above Alley Spring is better suited for more experienced paddlers, as it's a wilder stretch with limited access.

Depending on paddlers' skill and water levels, completing about 10 miles (16 km) a day is a safe bet, but up to 20 miles (32 km) also is doable. Depending on water levels, Baptist Camp access is a recommended put-in spot for the upper Current; Cedar Grove and Akers Ferry are solid options, too. At mile 25, the Pulltite Campground provides an excellent stopping point. Stretch your legs with a short hike to the Pulltite Spring and Pulltite Cabin, a Creole-style vacation lodge built in 1913.

Nine miles (14.5 km) below Pulltite, Round Spring is a convenient takeout point for floats on the upper Current. (Look for a short path from the parking lot near the lower access leading to the spring.) Expect less overall boat traffic below Round Spring; many trips end at the area known as Two Rivers, where the Jacks Fork flows into the Current.

Ozark Highlands, MO | **Season:** Spring to fall

Canoe down the Current
River of the Ozarks.

Wildlife Escape

When you're craving time in nature but dreading the task of planning the adventure, Dogwood Canyon Nature Park is an excellent option. The 10,000-acre (4,050 ha) reserve feels worlds away from the kitschy attractions of nearby Branson, with beautifully maintained trails for hiking, biking, and horseback riding.

One especially popular option is the open-air Wildlife Tram Tour, a year-round offering that takes guests on a two-hour guided ride through the canyon and onto the ridgetops of neighboring Arkansas to see herds of bison, elk, and deer. If you're lucky, you may even catch a glimpse of the park's rare white American bison, whose name is Takoda, a Sioux word that means "friend to everyone." The canyon also is a winter habitat for migrating bald eagles; the reserve's Eagle Watching Tours, starting in January, offer the chance to see them in their natural habitat.

> "THE RESERVE FEELS WORLDS AWAY FROM KITSCHY ATTRACTIONS, WITH BEAUTIFULLY MAINTAINED TRAILS FOR HIKING, BIKING, AND HORSEBACK RIDING."

Lampe, MO | **Season:** Year-round

Dogwood Canyon Nature Park boasts 10,000 acres (4,050 ha) of conserved land and protected wildlife.

Tiny islands dot the coastline of Lake Ouachita.

Lake Life

A premier boating recreation spot of the Midwest, the Lake of the Ozarks is actually an enormous reservoir with more than 1,100 miles (1,770 km) of coastline and an unusual serpentine shape, which inspired the nickname "The Magic Dragon." The 92-mile (148 km) main channel of the lake, also known as the Osage Arm as it was formed by damming the Osage River, and the four arms that branch off it (Gravois, Grand Glaize, Little Niangua, and Big Niangua) form the lively heart of the boating and entertainment scene. Dozens of lakeside restaurants and bars draw both locals and visitors, and boats are the preferred means of transport for many. Away from the action, tranquil coves and tributaries beckon kayakers and canoers for a peaceful paddle or float trip.

There are plenty of land-based options for fun, too: The entire area is a sprawling playground, with campgrounds, hundreds of miles of hiking trails, and caves open to visitors. In addition, two state parks fall within the area. At 17,441 acres (7,058 ha), Lake of the Ozarks State Park, just south of Osage Beach, is Missouri's largest, with 89 miles (143 km) of shoreline, marinas and boat-launching areas, two public swimming beaches, campgrounds, and trails galore, including an aquatic trail. Another highlight is Ozark Caverns, with lantern-lit tours into the caves, which stay at 56°F (13.3°C) year-round. Tours include a walk past Angel Showers, a feature of the cave system where it seems water is coming out of the rock ceiling. The cavern is also home to four species of salamanders, four species of bats, and 16 species of invertebrates. Aboveground, the Coakley Hollow interpretive trail is an easy loop from the parking lot. More than 3,600 acres (1,455 ha) of Ha Ha Tonka State Park, meanwhile, include 16 miles (26 km) of trails, eight known caves, and the ruins of a privately owned castle dating back to 1905, which was destroyed by fire in the 1940s.

Multicity, MO | **Season:** Year-round

You can ski the slopes of Hidden Valley at sunset.

Midwest Ski Resort

The Hidden Valley ski resort offers Missouri powder seekers the chance to hit the slopes without having to hop on a plane. Hidden Valley falls under the Vail Resorts umbrella, but the property doesn't boast the dizzying stats of its western cousins: Here, vertical drop is a moderate 320 feet (100 m), with 65 skiable acres (26 ha), 17 trails across two peaks, and almost exclusively machine-made snow. Even so, the resort, which opened in 1982, is a beloved local hill among winter sports enthusiasts. About a third of Hidden Valley's runs are beginner-friendly, and 60 percent are intermediate. Experts can show off their aerial tricks at the off-run terrain park for experts.

Nonskiers can also get in on the winter fun at the Polar Plunge Tubing Park. Sixteen separate tubing lanes wind down a 1,200-foot (365 m) hill, with two conveyor carpets transporting riders back to the top.

Wildwood, MO | Season: Winter

Shut-In Swimming

Don't be fooled by their deceptive moniker: Shut-ins are another name for the chutes and pools created by fast-moving streams flowing around dense volcanic rock, effectively "shut off" from the surrounding landscape. A uniquely Midwest adventure, these natural water features are found across the Show Me State, but some of the most spectacular are located at Johnson's Shut-Ins State Park, which is entirely dedicated to them.

To get to the shut-ins, which are carved into rock by the Black River, you can stroll along a boardwalk, which also offers beautiful views and provides easy access to the water. Scrambling over the boulders to reach the shut-ins is another option (one that kids love; just be careful of sprained ankles). Swimmers must stay out of restricted areas,

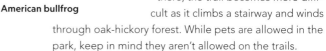
American bullfrog

and fishing is not allowed where swimmers can go in the water.

If you want to extend your daytime dip into an overnight outing, the park also offers tent and RV camping and cabins, a general store, visitors center, and hiking, biking, and equestrian trails. The 2.4-mile (3.9 km) Shut-Ins Trail is a great loop for a moderate challenge. The first portion of the trail is wheelchair-accessible and leads to an observation deck overlooking the water. From there, the trail becomes more difficult as it climbs a stairway and winds through oak-hickory forest. While pets are allowed in the park, keep in mind they aren't allowed on the trails.

Middlebrook, MO | Season: Summer

Hike a trail through Alley Spring.

Backpack the Ozark Trail

Missouri was named Best Trails State at the International Trails Symposium in 2013, thanks in large part to the increasing popularity of the 390-mile (630 km) Ozark Trail, which is poised to become one of the best long-distance trails in the country. The vision is to connect the trail, which runs from the St. Louis metropolitan area southwest to the Arkansas border, with the Ozark Highlands Trail to create a 700-mile (1,130 km) thru trail. (To date, almost 550 miles/ 885 km have been completed.)

For now, though, the Ozark Trail provides more than enough opportunities to keep backpackers busy, with 14 total sections that are mostly connected. Adventurers now have access to a 200-mile (320 km) continuous trail, including through the St. Francois Mountains—one of the best trail destinations between the Rockies and the Appalachians.

Multicity, MO | **Season:** Year-round

Marvel Cave in
Silver Dollar City

1. SEEK EERIE ORBS

For a spine-tingling nighttime adventure, grab a flashlight and head down a gravel road that locals call the Devil's Promenade to try to spot a phenomenon known as the Ozark Spook Light, which has sparked legends and mysteries for decades. The Spook Light is said to originate in Oklahoma, but it's best seen from Joplin, Missouri.

2. SEE CANOEHENGE

The town of Leasburg is home to the paddlers' version of Stonehenge. Canoehenge boasts canoes stacked to resemble their English counterparts across the Atlantic. The quirky structure is part of the Ozark Outdoors Resort, which also features a campground.

3. TAKE REFUGE WITH WILDLIFE

Pronounced "Luss," Loess Bluffs National Wildlife Refuge, along the eastern side of the Missouri River floodplain, spans wetlands, old hickory forests, and sweeping grasslands. It's also home to wild geese, bald eagles, and 300 other bird species, as well as white-tailed deer and other wildlife. Don't miss the trail to the 200-foot (60 m) summit, which is popular with photographers.

4. WONDER AT GEOLOGICAL STARS

Hoodoos, spires, and slot canyons are the stars of the show at Pickle Springs Natural Area, which is decidedly off the tourist track. The two-mile (3.2 km) Trail Through Time lives up to its name, winding through rock formations that feel lifted from another epoch.

5. MONKEY AROUND

Swing through the treetops and maneuver obstacles like ladders, bridges, and tunnels up to 35 feet (11 m) off the ground at Go Ape Zipline & Adventure Park in two Missouri locations. Several packages are available, but gloves are required for all participants, so bring your own pair (or buy them on-site).

6. BREATHE IN THE HEALING WATERS

Is the water in Welch Spring Hospital Ruins healing? A doctor in 1913 thought so: He even built a health spa centered around it to help asthma patients. Nature has reclaimed the property and covered its stone facade in lush, green overgrowth. Hiking trails take adventurers up close, but swimming in the spring itself is banned.

7. SPELUNK INTO A LITERARY LEGACY

The Mark Twain Cave may not have spectacular stalactites or other jaw-dropping formations. But, as its name suggests, it boasts precious literary history as the inspiration for many scenes in Mark Twain's *The Adventures of Tom Sawyer*. Bookworms in the bunch will especially love the guided tour, which is well suited for explorers of all ages and skill levels.

8. TAKE IN MISSOURI VISTAS

An easy, five-minute trek yields huge payoffs at Portuguese Point Scenic Overlook. A Gasconade dolomite slab hundreds of feet above awaits hikers, who are treated to generous vistas of Gasconade River—the longest river within the state at 280 miles (450 km).

9. GO SPELUNKING IN THE OZARKS

Opened in 1894 as a Lake of the Ozarks tourist attraction, Marvel Cave, which was originally mined for marble, still draws adventurous visitors today. A tour kicks off with a 300-foot (90 m) descent into the largest cave entrance room in the United States before taking visitors to nearly 500 feet (150 m) below the surface; a train ride transports them back to the surface.

10. REFLECT ON BLUE SPRING

Among the most famous of Mississippi's springs, Blue Spring on the Ozark National Scenic Riverways (several others have the same name) sparkles with a vibrant blue believed to have inspired the Native American name "Spring of the Summer Sky"; its 310-foot (95 m) pool is one of the deepest in the country. It's easy to reach—just a half-mile (0.8 km) round-trip—but you'll go just for a look, as swimming is strictly prohibited.

Hidden Lake Trail in Glacier
National Park (page 364)

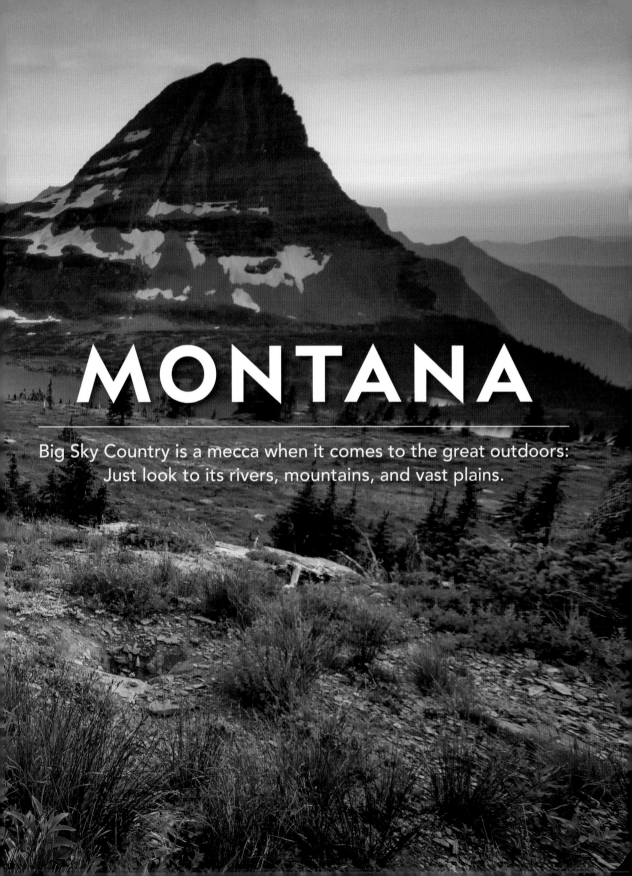

MONTANA

Big Sky Country is a mecca when it comes to the great outdoors:
Just look to its rivers, mountains, and vast plains.

BRITISH
COLUMBIA

ALBERTA

CANADA
U.S.

Whitefish Mountain
Resort

■

Bar W
Guest Ranch

 Going-to-the-
Sun Road

Middle Fork of the
Flathead River

Middle
Fork
Flathead

National Bison
Range

■

Clearwater River
Canoe Trail

Brennan's
Wave

■

Great Divide Mountain
Bike Route

■

Helena

M O N

Lewis & Clark
Caverns State Park

■

Beehive
Basin Trail

Hyalite Canyon
Recreation Are

Storm Castle
Creek

Big Sky
Resort

Lone Mountain
Ranch

IDAHO

Yellowstone
National Park

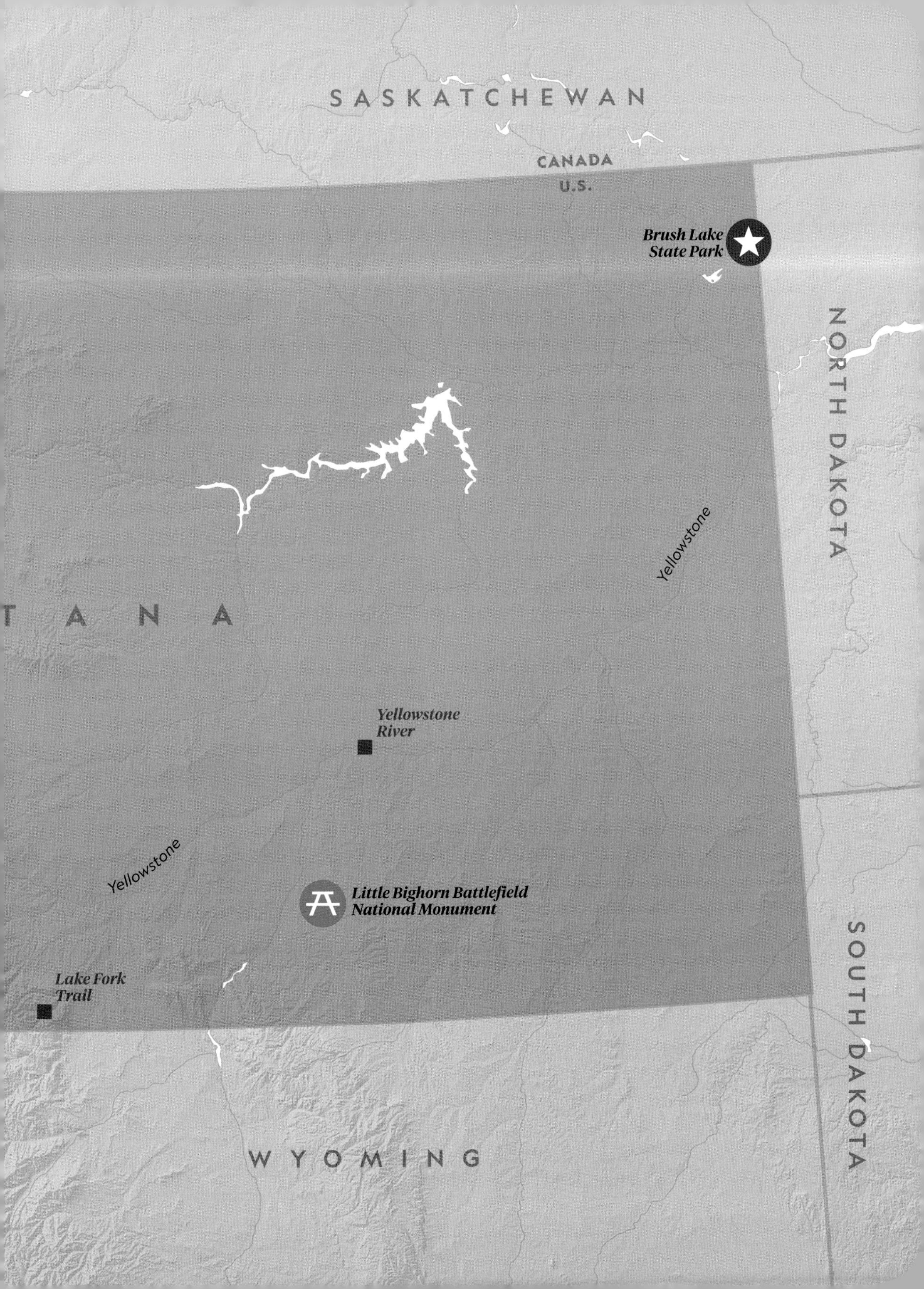
SASKATCHEWAN
CANADA
U.S.
Brush Lake
State Park
NORTH DAKOTA
Yellowstone
TANA
Yellowstone
River
Yellowstone
Little Bighorn Battlefield
National Monument
Lake Fork
Trail
SOUTH DAKOTA
WYOMING

Paddle the Clearwater River Canoe Trail

The antithesis of a frothy white-water trip, this slowly meandering 3.5-mile (5.6 km) paddle in a canoe or touring kayak starts upstream from Seeley Lake on the Clearwater River. It's for bird and wildlife lovers who want up close views of great blue herons, common loons, mink, muskrat, beaver, and otter. Early morning is an excellent time to get out and observe. The 1.5-mile-long (2.4 km) hiking trail that parallels the river allows paddlers to loop back to their car at the end of the route. Be forewarned that grizzly bears also use the trail as a migration corridor—carry bear spray at all times.

To access the put-in, drive 3.7 miles (6 km) north on Montana Highway 83 from the town of Seeley Lake. Take Forest Service Road 17597 on the highway's west side and drive 0.7 mile (1.1 km) to the trailhead. Heritage Outdoors in Seeley Lake offers boat rentals and shuttle services.

Seeley Lake, MT | Season: Spring to fall

The Clearwater River Canoe Trail passes through mountain vistas.

Mountain Bike Along the Continental Divide

Montana's laid-back state capital of 32,000 residents is often overlooked by out-of-state travelers. But Helena, at 3,875 feet (1,181 m) on the eastern slope of the Continental Divide, is a mountain biker's dream, with a 75-mile (121 km) trail system.

Helena offers miles of rugged mountain bike trails.

Roll out of bed at the rehabbed Lamplighter Cabins and Suites on the west side, roll over to leisurely sip a freshly ground espresso at Fire Tower Coffee House and Roasters, then ride the Mount Helena Ridge Trail, a 7.9-mile (12.7 km) one-way ridgetop traverse where you can lose yourself in the magic flow of the trail, stopping every so often to enjoy alpine wildflowers, big views of the Helena Valley, and possible sightings of a black bear or elk. After a few hours, descend back into town for an IPA on the rooftop bar of Mt. Ascension Brewing Company.

Helena also has direct access to the 2,808-mile-long (4,519 km) Continental Divide Trail, which starts in Banff, Alberta, and finishes in Antelope Wells at the Mexico border, making it an ideal rest stop for ultra-endurance cyclists. And gravel heads can grind out miles on Helena's seemingly endless universe of scenic Forest Service roads.

Helena, MT | Season: Spring to fall

Contemplate U.S. History at Little Bighorn

This memorial on the desolate windswept plains of southeastern Montana is easily accessible off I 90. It's an ideal place to take a break, turn off modern distractions, and tune in to the enormity of the battle that took place here in 1876.

On June 25, Gen. George Custer and the 640 men of the Seventh Cavalry entered the Little Bighorn Valley, where 8,000 Northern Cheyenne and Lakota Sioux had gathered. Custer had planned a surprise attack for dawn of June 26, but his Crow and Arikara Indian scouts sensed that the camp had detected the regiment's presence. Instead, Custer divided his troops and ordered Maj. Marcus Reno and his 140-man battalion to cross the river and lead a direct attack.

"Soldiers came at us like thunderbolts," recounted Sioux chief Low Dog of Reno's attack. The fighting was fierce, and Reno's forces were eventually outnumbered by the estimated 1,500 to 1,800 warriors who pushed them back into the surrounding ridges. Finally, on what is today known as Last Stand Hill, Sioux and Lakota warriors overpowered General Custer and roughly 210 of his soldiers, killing them all. The victory was short-lived. Within a year, the tribes were forced to surrender to the U.S. government, their Great Plains way of life forever lost.

The Seventh U.S. Calvary Memorial

In June 2024, the park will open a new visitors center and museum. Until then, wander Custer National Cemetery among the graves of named and unnamed war veterans, Medal of Honor recipients, Native American scouts, and frontier women and children.

Crow Agency, MT | **Season:** Year-round

Stargaze by the Lake

Montana isn't all mountains. The eastern third of the state is Great Plains grassland and in its far northeastern corner sits 280-acre (110 ha) Brush Lake State Park. Surrounded by rolling fields of wheat, the mile-long, spring-fed lake is surprisingly deep—60 feet (18 m)—and crystal clear, making it an excellent spot to swim or water-ski from the park's day use area, which has a dock, a boat ramp, and a lakeside hiking trail. Adjacent to that is a 12-site campground open from May to November.

Because the park is so remote (the closest town, Dagmar, is more than 8 miles/13 km away), it's an excellent spot to view the night sky. Pitch a tent at the campground and, around 9 p.m. in the summertime, watch stars fill the sky with constellations like Lyra the Harp, Cygnus the Swan, and Aquila the Eagle. Later in the fall, the aurora borealis might pulse in shades of emerald green.

See stars in the clear skies above Brush Lake State Park.

Dagmar, MT | **Season:** Summer

> "THIS DRAMATIC, GLACIATED ALPINE LANDSCAPE IS UNLIKE ANY OTHER IN THE LOWER 48."

Going-to-the-Sun Road

Within Glacier National Park are 26 glaciers, 762 lakes, 2,865 miles (4,610 km) of streams, and 175 mountains, the tallest of which rises to a height of 10,448 feet (3,185 m). This dramatic, glaciated alpine landscape supports abundant wildlife, from golden eagles to grizzly bears, and is unlike any other in the lower 48. The 50-mile-long (80 km) Going-to-the-Sun Road starts in the town of West Glacier, climbs to 6,646-foot (2,026 m) Logan Pass along the Continental Divide, and finally descends into the town of St. Mary on the eastern side of the park, making it one of the most beloved roads in the country. On the busiest summer days, as many as 975 cars an hour pass any given viewpoint.

To alleviate the gridlock, park officials recently implemented a ticketed entry system between June and October, when the road is open. But avoid carbon-emitting congestion altogether by cycling Going-to-the-Sun Road in May or June before it opens to motorized vehicles. You will still be sharing the road with hundreds of other cyclists, piles of snow along the shoulders, and construction and clearing crews working hard to open it for the season, but nothing beats the sweaty thrill of climbing a steady 6 percent grade while surrounded by one of the most majestic landscapes on Earth.

How far you can ride depends on how far the road is plowed. Most solo cyclists park at the iconic Swiss Chalet–style Lake McDonald Lodge on the shoreline of nearly 10-mile-long (16 km) Lake McDonald near the park's west entrance, and cycle 21.2 miles (34 km) up to Logan Pass, the turnaround point. Glacier Guides, about 1.5 miles (2.4 km) outside of the park's western entrance, rents hybrid road/mountain bikes and e-bikes and offers guided trips. From their headquarters, the one-way ascent to Logan Pass is 32 miles (51.5 km).

Multicity, MT | **Season:** May or June

Going-to-the-Sun Road offers cyclists a ride through the Rockies.

Rip Through Rapids of the Middle Fork

There are a lot of western rivers, but few offer as much easy access, stunning alpine scenery, potential for wildlife sightings, and crystal clear glacier-fed water as the Middle Fork of the Flathead River. Designated a Wild and Scenic River in 1976, this protected water originates deep in the heart of the Bob Marshall Wilderness and flows along the southwestern border of Glacier National Park.

The classic full-day Middle Fork raft trip covers 15 river miles (24 km), starting with a mellow float through Class I to II rapids, an excellent opportunity to spot bear, moose, osprey, eagle, and even cutthroat trout darting through the water. After a picnic lunch, the pace picks up with eight miles (13 km) of Class II to III white water through rapids like Bone Crusher and Jaws. On the hottest summer days, a dunk into the icy river is refreshing. Book a full- or half-day trip with Glacier Raft Company in the town of West Glacier.

> "AFTER A PICNIC LUNCH, THE PACE PICKS UP WITH EIGHT MILES (13 KM) OF CLASS II TO III WHITE WATER THROUGH RAPIDS LIKE BONE CRUSHER AND JAWS."

West Glacier, MT | **Season:** Summer

A raft trip down the Middle Fork of the Flathead River takes paddlers along the border of Glacier National Park.

Miles of cross-country trails take skiers through snow globe–like scenes at Lone Mountain Ranch.

Ski Your Way Through a Winter Playground

It's difficult to conjure up a more idyllic western winter playground than Lone Mountain Ranch. Sitting at 6,600 feet (2,010 m) on 148 wilderness acres (60 ha), just 18 miles (29 km) northwest of Yellowstone National Park and seven miles (11 km) east of Big Sky Resort, Lone Mountain was homesteaded in 1915 and has been providing western hospitality to guests ever since.

Scattered around the main lodge are more than 20 luxury log cabins with wood-burning fireplaces, luxury showers, and hot coffee served every morning to the door. The most challenging part of the stay is deciding whether to sleep in and read by the cozy fire or to venture out to ice-skate, fly-fish a blue-ribbon trout stream, alpine ski at nearby Big Sky, or take a backcountry guided tour into Yellowstone National Park.

Big Sky, MT : **Season:** Winter

For Nordic skiers, the lodge has more than 50 miles (80 km) of groomed ski trails, climbing through Douglas fir forests to high-alpine meadows with views of Lone Peak. The skiing here isn't easy, but it is exhilarating. For beginners, the lodge offers ski lessons, rentals, and access to easier terrain on an adjacent golf course.

No matter what the activity, guests work up an enormous appetite—the reason Horn and Cantle restaurant in the main lodge serves three locally sourced meals a day. For lunch, guests can choose a bagged option to refuel on-trail. For dinner, take a horse-drawn sleigh ride to the North Fork log cabin for a hearty prime-rib feast while being serenaded by a cowboy guitarist.

The walls of Hyalite Canyon freeze over for ice climbers.

The Epicenter of Ice Climbing

Hyalite Canyon Recreation Area, within Custer Gallatin National Forest, is the ancestral land of the Crow, Blackfeet, Flathead, Shoshone Bannock, and Cheyenne peoples. Today, it's the most heavily accessed recreation area in Montana.

In winter, Hyalite Canyon transforms into the epicenter of American ice climbing. With more than 150 routes in less than a three-square-mile (8 km^2) area, Hyalite offers the most consistent, concentrated, and easily accessible ice climbing in the country. Alpine legends like Conrad Anker hone their skills here. For those new to the sport, a great place to start is at the annual Bozeman Ice Festival every December. This more than a quarter-century-old celebration of ice offers films, speakers, and gear swaps around town, plus expert-led clinics in Hyalite Canyon.

Bozeman, MT | **Season:** Winter

Hike or Run Beehive Basin

Ask locals what their favorite season is and even the most devoted skier may surprisingly answer "summer." As sublime as snow can be, winter can also be long, dark, and bitter cold in the northern Rockies, making summer feel especially ethereal.

That's why, in a state with thousands of hiking trails, most with stunning views, the 6.4-mile (10.3 km) out-and-back Beehive Basin Trail in Gallatin National Forest's Lee Metcalf Wilderness stands out: From mid-July to mid-August, the basin blooms with every shade of color in the rainbow. Almost 300 species of wildflowers grow here, including sticky geranium, glacier lily, purple lupine, yellow columbine, and monkey flower. The abundance of buds is largely thanks to the varied topography and a healthy ecosystem with ample water from snowmelt and summer rains. Beyond the flower show, the hike offers an opportunity to see mountain goats, bighorn sheep, black bear, and moose.

To access the trailhead, drive north from the Big Sky's Mountain Village to the end of Beehive Basin Road. The hike starts at 7,900 feet (2,410 m), zigzags through a few switchbacks to reach a relatively flat section before climbing again along a creek and ending above tree line at 10,700 feet (2,360 m) at a lake nestled in a cirque surrounded by jagged peaks. It's an excellent spot to break out the picnic and feast on panoramic views of majestic Lone Peak to the south. Because this is a well-loved wilderness area, heed especially the seventh principle of Leave No Trace: "Be considerate of other visitors."

Western meadowlark

Big Sky, MT | **Season:** Late spring to early fall

Ski past Yellowstone's famous geysers and hot springs.

Ski Yellowstone National Park's Backcountry

In winter, Yellowstone National Park takes on an ethereal, empty beauty. Visitation drops exponentially from roughly one million people a month at the height of summer to 25,000 a month in the depths of winter. This off-peak season is the ideal time to see snow-covered bison gathering near open water, watch geysers shooting off with few solitary witnesses, and hear wolves howling under the night sky.

Most park roads are closed to wheeled vehicles in the winter season, so travel is via snow coach, snowmobile, skis, fat bikes, or snowshoes. Two park lodges, Old Faithful Snow Lodge and Mammoth Hot Springs Hotel, are open in winter, and both offer a roster of winter adventures. Choose between a daylong backcountry ski tour from the rim of the Grand Canyon of the Yellowstone, a snowshoe tour of Old Faithful and the surrounding forest, or staying warm on a snow coach wildlife tour through the Lamar Valley.

Yellowstone National Park, MT · Season: Winter

Bison graze beneath
snow-covered mountains.

1. ZIP-LINE WHITEFISH MOUNTAIN RESORT

Soar like an eagle through the trees, over ski slopes, and across ravines on this mile-long (1.6 km) zip-line descent. The 2.5-hour-long thrill ride is spread across six lines, some of which take you 300 feet (90 m) above the forest floor. Moderate hiking is required, and two expert guides lead the way.

2. VIEW A COMEBACK AT THE NATIONAL BISON RANGE

By the end of the 19th century, mass slaughter had driven the bison to near extinction. In the 1870s, a visionary named Little Falcon Robe brought six orphaned bison calves to the Flathead Indian Reservation to regenerate the herd. Today the 18,766-acre (7,594 ha) range, managed by the U.S. Fish and Wildlife Service, supports up to 500 bison.

3. SPELUNK AT LEWIS AND CLARK CAVERNS STATE PARK

Explore otherworldly underground formations like stalactites and stalagmites in this limestone cave system in southwest Montana. The Classic Tour requires navigating 600 stairs and "duck waddling." The Paradise Tour allows small kids and those with mobility issues to view the marquee attraction, Paradise Room. Stay at the park's 40-site campground.

4. SURF BRENNAN'S WAVE IN MISSOULA

Kayakers, surfers, and SUPers play year-round on this human-made wave on the Clark Fork River in downtown Missoula. Built in memory of local Brennan Guth, who died while kayaking in Chile, the two-part wave is suitable for beginners to experts, depending on flows.

5. FLY-FISH THE YELLOWSTONE RIVER

Bring your A game or hire a guide to fish for native cutthroat, rainbow, and brown trout along 200 miles (320 km) of one of the longest free-flowing rivers in the United States. Because of the size of the river and its variable conditions, most guiding companies, like Montana Angler, prefer fishing from rafts or drift boats.

6. ROCK CLIMB AT STORM CASTLE

This limestone climbing hub features dozens of bolted, mostly single-pitch, sport-climbing routes ranging in difficulty from 5.5 to 5.13s. It sits on the east side of Gallatin Canyon south of Bozeman off U.S. 191. Montana Alpine Guides in Bozeman offers private and group guided instruction—beginners welcome.

7. MOUNTAIN BIKE THE GREAT DIVIDE

More than 3,000 miles (4,830 km) of single-track, double-track, and pavement following the contour of the Continental Divide connect Canada to Mexico via the Great Divide Mountain Bike Route. Roughly a third of this mountainous route is in Montana. It's an epic undertaking, especially if you decide to race the route in the Tour Divide.

8. HIKE LAKE FORK TRAIL NEAR RED LODGE

This 9.5-mile-long (15.3 km) out-and-back trail in the Beartooth Mountains sits off U.S. 212, the famed Beartooth Highway between Red Lodge and Yellowstone National Park. The hike promises all the grandeur of Montana, with lodgepole pine forests leading to alpine lakes and, eventually, 11,047-foot (3,367 m) Sundance Pass. Watch for bears and moose.

9. ALPINE SKI AT BIG SKY RESORT

With 5,850 acres (2,365 ha) of skiable terrain, from gentle corduroy groomers to some of the most aggressive, exposed, expert-only lines in the country off the 11,166-foot (3,403 m) summit of Lone Mountain, Big Sky is truly a mountain for every level skier and snowboarder. The resort also offers snowshoeing, winter zip-line tours, Nordic skiing, and dogsledding.

10. RIDE HORSES AT BAR W GUEST RANCH

A week is never enough at the Bar W, a ranch at the base of Spencer Mountain, 40 minutes away from the west entrance of Glacier National Park. With horseback riding instruction, daily trail rides, cattle roundups, and rodeos, as well as childcare for toddlers, this traditional dude ranch is the ultimate Western family vacation.

Camberwell beauty butterfly

Dismal River meanders through
Nebraska Sandhills (page 376).

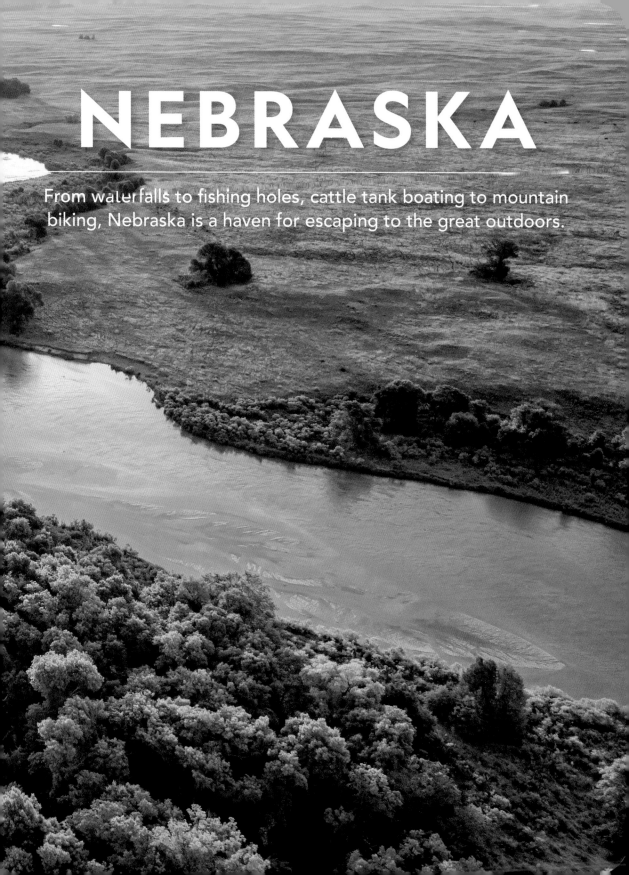

NEBRASKA

From waterfalls to fishing holes, cattle tank boating to mountain biking, Nebraska is a haven for escaping to the great outdoors.

SOUTH

WYOMING

Toadstool Geological Park and Campground

Whitney Lake

Smith Falls State Park

Fort Robinson State Park

Chadron State Park

Merritt Reservoir

Calam

Carhenge

Sandhills

Chimney Rock National Monument

N E B R

Lake McConaughy State Recreation Area (Big Mac)

Buffalo Bill Ranch State Historical Par

Prairie Chicken Dance Tours

Platte

C O L O R A D O

MINNESOTA

DAKOTA

Ponca
State Park

IOWA

 Chicago & North
Western Cowboy Line

Calamus
River

Harvest
Moon ■

ASKA

Lauritzen
Gardens
■

 Sherman
Reservoir

Fontenelle
Forest ■

Platte

Platte River
State Park

Arbor Day
Farm ■

MISSOURI

Indian Cave
State Park ■

Red Cloud ■

KANSAS

A Surprise in the Hills

Given that Nebraska's Sandhills region is the largest sand dune formation in the Western Hemisphere, one might expect to find a dry and arid landscape. But this seemingly endless and endlessly beautiful wilderness hides many surprises, including its size, which at 19,000 square miles (49,210 km²), covers more than a quarter of the state. The Sandhills area sits on one of the world's largest underground water sources, the Ogallala Aquifer, which enables lush green meadows, grasses, and 720 different varieties of plants to grow between undulating hills. With tens of thousands of lakes, ponds, and wetlands, the Sandhills are one of the last large intact grasslands on Earth, and are rich in animal diversity too, including migrating birds and waterfowl as well as deer, antelope, and bison.

Most of the land is privately owned, but book a safari-style ecotour at Switzer Ranch and learn about the unique flora and fauna and local cattle ranching history.

Sheridan County, NE | Season: Year-round

A windmill stands tall in the prairie landscape of the Sandhills.

Travel Back in Time

If a trip to another planet is on the bucket list, take a journey to Toadstool Geological Park in the northwest, sometimes referred to as Nebraska's "badlands," where a walk through an otherworldly landscape reveals some of the state's most diverse and unique scenery.

Located in the Oglala National Grasslands, the fantastical, mushroom-shaped sandstone and clay hoodoos were carved by wind and water erosion from a river that ran through the area 30 million years ago. Hiking is the best way to get up close to the rocks, and the park has two main trails, one a one-mile (1.6 km) interpretive loop that departs from the picnic area. Visitors can tread gently over the weathered-stone sculptures and keep their eyes peeled for (but don't remove) fossilized remnants of ancient saber-toothed cats, rhinos, birds, tortoises, and other critters.

The loop trail accesses the three-mile (5 km) Bison Trail, connecting hikers to the Hudson-Meng Education and Research Center. The often empty path meanders through tall native grasses. During spring and summer, wildflowers bloom along the paths, and various songbirds, mule deer, and other mammals can often be spotted.

Harrison, NE | Season: Year-round

The sun rises over Toadstool Geological Park.

Meet Big Mac

Everything about Lake McConaughy is big. Not only is it Nebraska's biggest reservoir, created by the Kingsley Dam along the North Platte River, but it's also a place for outdoor fun on the beloved "Big Mac" with its 30,000 watery acres (12,140 ha).

Lake Mac is popular with weekend warriors as well as summer vacationing families who come in droves to enjoy miles of white sandy beaches, clear blue waters, and lakeside dining and recreation. The annual Kites and Castles sandcastle building contest and kite flying event in July are also popular. Swimmers, boaters, windsurfers, beach campers, and anglers won't be disappointed either, and even scuba divers have found a reason to love Lake Mac, especially around the dam, the most popular dive site. Winter is much less crowded but no less enjoyable, especially for birders, thanks to Lake McConaughy's position on the Central Flyway.

Ogallala, NE | Season: Year-round

The area around Lake Mac is one of the top birding spots in the country, with more than 360 species identified. Visit in the spring and fall to see migrating birds, in particular white pelicans, ducks, geese, and shorebirds. Come March and April, more than 20,000 sandhill cranes stop in the area on their route north for nesting season. Spot them roosting on sandbars and islands. Birders can use the Lake McConaughy Birding Trails Map (available online) to find the best places to look for feathered friends.

On the east side of Kingsley Dam, Lake Ogallala is often called the "little lake," with only 320 acres (130 ha). What it lacks in size and sandy shoreline, it makes up for as a calm place to camp, bird-watch, and fish. The nearby town of Ogallala was once a stop on the Pony Express and the transcontinental railroad. Its Front Street is a reproduction of an Old West town and made for selfies.

Mountain bikers cycle a single-track near Scottsbluff.

Mountain Bike Buttes and Pines

Across Nebraska, mountain biking is alive and well. Among the best places to two-wheel is Chadron State Park. Not only is it Nebraska's oldest state park, designated in 1921, it's also arguably one of its most beautiful.

Located in Nebraska National Forest at an elevation of nearly 5,000 feet (1,525 m), Chadron State Park is surrounded by ponderosa pines, distinctive buttes, ridges, and rocky canyons. Hiking and biking trails for various skill levels crisscross the park and the surrounding Nebraska National Forest, totaling more than 100 miles (160 km) of picturesque exploration opportunities. The park's two main canyons (north and south canyons) have several trails, including the Black Hills Overlook Trail and the Steamboat Loop Trail.

Chadron, NE | Season: Year-round

"THE VARIETY OF FISH
SWIMMING IN CORNHUSKER
STATE WATERWAYS MAKES IT
FUN FOR FISHERMEN."

Get Hooked

Despite its landlocked location, Nebraska is a wonderland for water sports thanks to more than two dozen natural and human-made lakes and reservoirs, as well as hundreds of ponds, creeks, streams, and nearly 80,000 miles (128,750 km) of rivers, including the legendary Missouri and Platte. The variety of fish swimming in Cornhusker State waterways also makes it fun for fishermen, and the large reservoirs are a good place to start.

McConaughy, Merritt, and Davis Creek are known for their walleye, while white bass can be found at Harlan, Swanson, Medicine Creek, and Enders. Spanning a border with South Dakota, Lewis and Clark Lake teems with walleye and sauger alongside largemouth bass, smallmouth bass, bluegill, and catfish.

Calamus Reservoir in the beautiful Sandhills is popular for all kinds of outdoor action, including fishing for perch, catfish, carp, northern pike, and more, while Whitney Reservoir is a perennial favorite for crappies, a panfish found throughout Nebraska. Sherman Reservoir is yet another popular fishing area that has great walleye, northern pike, crappie, catfish, and white bass. The picturesque Sutherland Reservoir is loaded with smallmouth bass, white bass, and striped bass along with trout and walleye.

Fly fisherman might enjoy a trip to Elm Creek, in the south-central part of the state or to the scenic Niobrara River. The Missouri River flows for about 400 miles (640 km) along the state's eastern border, and its banks and open lands offer excellent fishing spots, as does the Upper Snake River in the Sandhills, a good spot for trout.

The Nebraska Game and Parks Commission regularly hosts community fishing nights and tournaments aimed at recruiting newbies. In January, they organize ice fishing clinics.

Multicity, NE | **Season:** Year-round

Wade into and fly-fish the waters of the South Platte River.

Get Tanked

Spend a summer in Nebraska and it's only a matter of time before an invitation to tank is proffered. So, what exactly is tanking? Somewhere at the nexus of ingenuity and good clean fun, the idea to use cattle tanks as boats was born. The buoyant, round vessels typically used to provide drinking water to livestock and horses were historically made of steel, though plastic tanks are everywhere nowadays.

During hot summer months, tanking is practically a state sport, and sun-drenched rivers are full of round tubs of four to six people drifting at the speed of fun, no paddling required. Dozens of outfitters near rivers rent tanks, so stock up on snacks and sunscreen, and grab your family or besties. Some popular rivers include the Middle Loup, Calamus, Elkhorn, North Platte, Niobrara, and Republican, all of which supply calm currents, beautiful scenery, and an entertaining, only-in-Nebraska experience.

> "SOMEWHERE AT THE NEXUS OF INGENUITY AND GOOD CLEAN FUN, THE IDEA TO USE CATTLE TANKS AS BOATS WAS BORN."

Multicity, NE | Season: Summer

A one-of-a-kind experience: Paddle and relax down the river in a cattle tank.

Cowboys herd their cattle on a family-owned ranch.

Ride Through Nebraska History

There's something about exploring the great outdoors the way ranchers, pioneers, cowboys, and Native Americans did it that ratchets up the experience to epic levels. Nebraska's state parks are not just places to soak up irresistible scenery; they also offer a chance to saddle up and ride through the area's local history too.

Among the state's most popular horseback riding destinations is the stunning Fort Robinson State Park, a former U.S. Army fort whose 22,000 acres (8,900 ha) of rolling hills, buttes, and Pine Ridge scenery are as stunning as they are historic. The park has 20 miles (32 km) of trails, with more riding opportunities in nearby Nebraska National Forest. Fort Robinson's historic buildings once housed soldiers and officers, but now invite travelers to bunk. During summer months, memories are made by taking horse-drawn wagon and stagecoach tours of the park, or via guided tail rides.

For a real glimpse into the Wild West, head to Buffalo Bill Ranch State Historical Park, whose namesake William Frederick Cody, was a U.S. Army scout, Pony Express rider, and showman who produced Buffalo Bill's Wild West Show and Congress of Rough Riders of the World, a traveling open-air show that romanticized stereotypes of the American West. Visitors can take a horse-drawn wagon ride or saddle up and trot across Buffalo Bill's historic ranch, where a restored mansion and barn display his memorabilia. The adjacent Buffalo Bill State Recreation Area offers easy access to the North Platte River, where you can cast a line after your ride for largemouth bass, bluegill, and northern pike.

At Ponca State Park, experienced wranglers organize guided rides through forested hills and bluffs along the Missouri River that are part of the Lewis and Clark National Historic Trail. The guided rides are available from Memorial Day through Labor Day.

Multicity, NE | **Season:** Year-round

Half a million sandhill cranes roost on the Platte River.

Get a Crane's-Eye View

🦆 Keep heading east from beautiful Platte River State Park to a stretch of river that has gone to the birds in the best possible way. From late February to early April, 80 percent of the planet's crane population, close to a million cranes, gathers to fatten up and rest before continuing their journey to their Arctic and subarctic nesting grounds. Platte River Valley is the most important stopover on the annual journey, with nearby farmlands and wet meadows supplying abundant food, and the Platte's shallow sandbars providing a place to rest at night, and protection from predators such as coyotes.

This feathery pit stop is considered one of Earth's great animal migrations, and the Iain Nicolson Audubon Center at Rowe Sanctuary has strategically placed viewing stations along the Platte River. Guided opportunities are also available and invite nature lovers to watch cranes fly at dusk and take off at dawn.

Louisville, NE | **Season:** February to April

Follow the Cowboy Trail

🥾 Built in the 1880s, the historic Chicago and North Western Railroad's Cowboy Line hauled people, gold, and livestock for more than a hundred years. Abandoned in the 1990s, a 195-mile (314 km) portion of tracks between Norfolk and Valentine has been transformed into the state's first recreational trail, the Cowboy Trail. Still a work in progress, the path will eventually make its way to Chadron, where it can then claim its title as the nation's longest rail-to-trail conversion.

Loved by walkers, bikers, and runners, the Cowboy Trail rewards users with views of river valleys, forests, and prairies, as well as 221 bridges, one of which is a quarter-mile-long (0.4 km) trestle spanning the Niobrara River. Take a cool-down dip in the creek at the 153-acre (62 ha) Long Pine State Recreation Area or rest and recharge at

Bassett Lodge and Range Café, a classic 1950s diner with hearty meals and hot coffee. Look out for relics of railroad history along the corridor, including weathered mile markers and buildings such as Neligh Mill, a water-powered flour mill that's now a national historic site. It's open to the public so duck inside to check out some original 1880s equipment.

With around 20 connected communities along its trajectory, the Cowboy Trail is easy to access for an evening stroll or multiday odyssey. And don't think it's only for warm summer months. Fall reveals a flourish of gold and red leaves, while horseback riders, dogsledders, snowshoers, and cross-country skiers take advantage of the popular scenic trail in the winter too.

Multicity, NE | **Season:** Year-round

Smith Falls cascades 63 vertical feet (19 m).

Make Your Way to Nebraska's Tallest Falls

Who doesn't love a good twofer? Visitors to Nebraska's newest state park, Smith Falls State Park, dedicated in 1992, can also take a gander at its splashy namesake. At 70 feet (21 m), the spring-fed cascade plunges into a narrow and sunlight-sheltered canyon on the south side of the Niobrara River, allowing flora to grow that is atypical for the region. The state's tallest falls are reachable on a one-mile (1.6 km), out-and-back trail.

The park sits on a 76-mile (122 km) stretch of the Niobrara River designated as a National Wild and Scenic River by the National Park Service, in part for the quantity of fossils buried along its banks and the western and eastern flora and fauna that flourish in the region's microclimates. Floaters and paddlers adore the Niobrara's mellow currents and easy-on-the-eyes scenery, while waterfall chasers can find more than 200 smaller versions around the area.

Valentine, NE | **Season:** Year-round

Not as old as its inspiration from across the pond, Carhenge is still an installation to behold.

1. DANCE WITH PRAIRIE CHICKENS

Spring means one thing: the annual mating dance of the greater prairie chicken, a member of the grouse family. Join a dawn tour to watch the flirty fowl stomp their feet, the males inflating their bright orange air sacs and booming their bubbling trill, all to attract the ladies.

2. ESCAPE TO NATURE AT FONTENELLE FOREST

Just 10 minutes from downtown Omaha, one of Nebraska's five national natural landmarks immerses visitors in the wonders of the 2,100-acre (850 ha) forest. There you'll find 24 miles (39 km) of hiking trails, a one-mile (1.6 km), ADA-accessible boardwalk, and Raptor Woodland Refuge, where rescued birds of prey thrive 30 feet (9 m) above the forest floor.

3. REV UP YOUR INSTA-GRAM AT CARHENGE

Guaranteed to garner a few likes, and questions, this humorous reproduction of England's Stonehenge is made of 38 American cars rescued from nearby farms and dumps. What Jim Reinders's family started in 1987 is now a year-round draw for anyone looking for something unexpected in the Cornhusker State.

4. STARGAZE AT MERRITT RESERVOIR

Beloved for fishing, boating, and camping, Merritt Reservoir also ranks tops in the state for admiring the Milky Way and other celestial beauties. So minimal is the light pollution, the annual Nebraska Star Party is held here, bringing out experts and beginners alike to gaze at dark skies.

5. SHOW SOME LEAFY LOVE AT ARBOR DAY FARM

Families can hike forested trails, cross timber bridges, explore tree houses in the forest canopy, and walk nature trails around Arbor Lodge, the historic home where the idea of Arbor Day took root (celebrated nationally on the last Friday of April).

6. HIKE INDIAN CAVE STATE PARK

Located in far southeastern Nebraska, this 3,052-acre (1,235 ha) wooded park along the Missouri River has 22 miles (35 km) of hiking and biking trails, as well as a wide sandstone cave estimated to be around 12,000 years old. There's no bad view from the Missouri River Overlook, which is especially colorful in the fall.

7. STROLL THROUGH "AMERICA'S MOST FAMOUS SMALL TOWN"

Author Willa Cather's novels introduced the world to Nebraska's prairies and to her hometown of Red Cloud (population 962). Here, historic homes and brick buildings house bookshops and restaurants, and recreational opportunities include hikes on the Willa Cather Memorial Prairie and a nine-hole golf course ranked among the best in the state.

8. TEST YOUR NAVIGATION SKILLS IN A CORN MAZE

It's called the Cornhusker State after all, and fall means apple picking, pumpkin carving, and corn mazes, some more elaborate, scary, and difficult than others, but always a traditional autumn activity and a popular way to spend a day on the farm before the long winter arrives.

9. HIKE TO CHIMNEY ROCK

The one-mile (1.6 km) out-and-back trail might be easy, but it's packed with hard-core history and spectacular views. The imposing formation rises 470 feet (140 m) above the North Platte River Valley and was one of the most recognizable landmarks for pioneers on the Oregon, California, and Mormon Trails during the great western migration.

10. STOP AND SMELL THE ROSES

What started with a rose garden in 1995 is now the 100-acre (40 ha) Lauritzen Gardens, a treasured Omaha botanical garden and arboretum offering four seasons of stunning floral and plant displays across 20 different styles of garden, including a butterfly garden, rose garden, Japanese garden, and a model railroad garden, where model trains chug through miniature landscapes.

The sun rises over Valley of Fire State Park (page 396).

NEVADA

Nevada boasts more than Sin City—including red rock canyons, rapids-filled rivers, and adventures that take you to new heights.

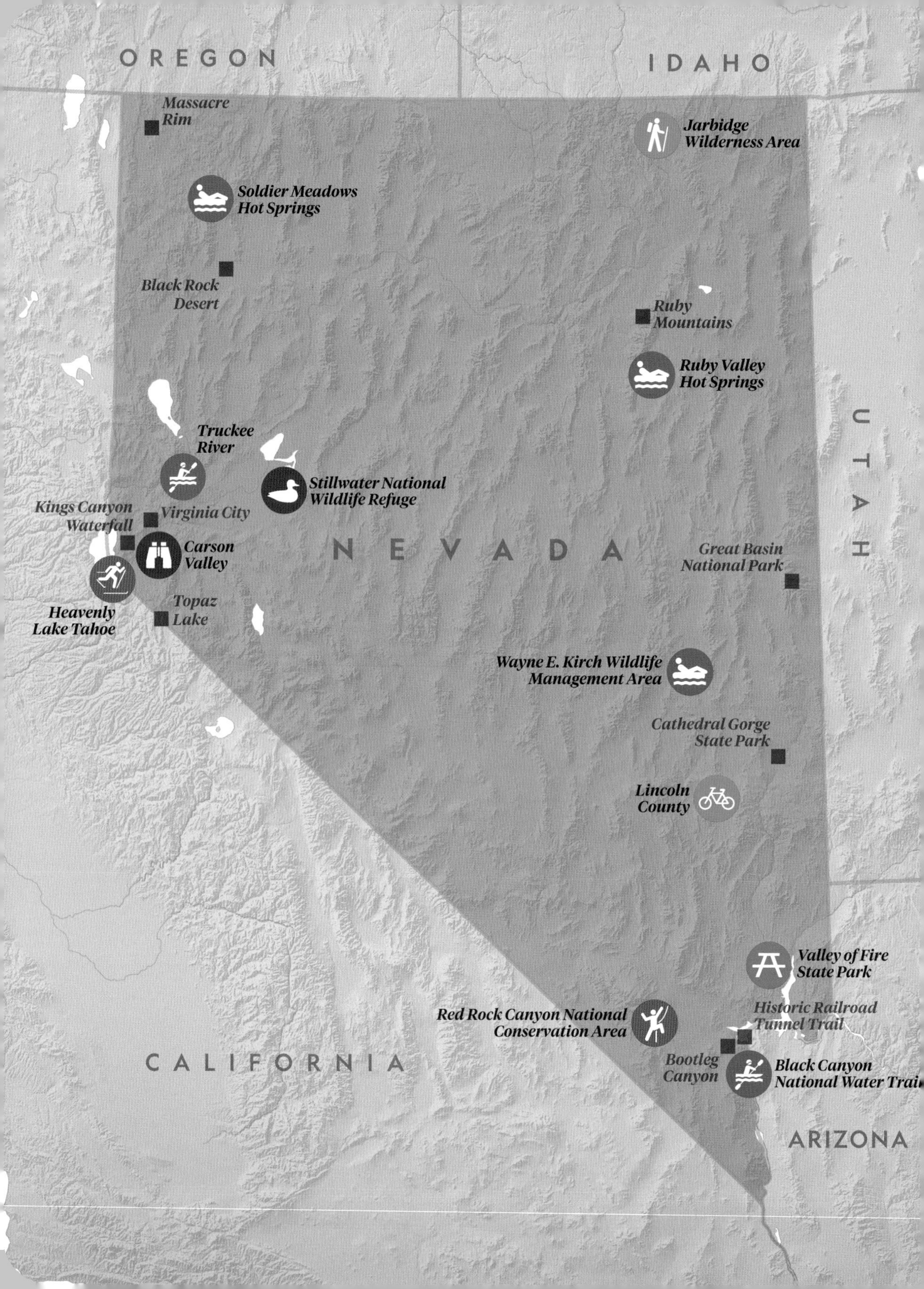

OREGON

IDAHO

Massacre
Rim

Jarbidge
Wilderness Area

Soldier Meadows
Hot Springs

Ruby
Mountains

Black Rock
Desert

Ruby Valley
Hot Springs

Truckee
River

Stillwater National
Wildlife Refuge

Kings Canyon
Waterfall

Virginia City

NEVADA

Great Basin
National Park

UTAH

Carson
Valley

Heavenly
Lake Tahoe

Topaz
Lake

Wayne E. Kirch Wildlife
Management Area

Cathedral Gorge
State Park

Lincoln
County

Valley of Fire
State Park

Historic Railroad
Tunnel Trail

Red Rock Canyon National
Conservation Area

Bootleg
Canyon

Black Canyon
National Water Trail

CALIFORNIA

ARIZONA

Mountain bike trails lead riders past rock formations at Cathedral Gorge State Park.

Mountain Bike Lincoln County

Billed as the hottest new mountain bike destination in the West, the town of Caliente in Lincoln County is a hub for mountain biking fans in search of technical descents, single-track, dirt jumps, and gravel grinding in scenery that's easy fodder for rhapsody. Just four miles (6.4 km) from Caliente, Barnes Canyon has chunky rock garden trails as well as a network of more than 13 miles (21 km) of single-track for riders of all levels, with construction under way on an 11-mile (18 km) connector to Kershaw-Ryan State Park, an oasis for riders just minutes from town.

Springs feed the landscape dotted with oak, elm, and cottonwood trees that are a beautiful contrast to the towering volcanic walls of Rainbow Canyon. Bikers will find both long and short loop trails, with views for days. New to the park in 2020 is a black diamond downhill trail. Suitable for more intermediate and advanced riders, a 24-mile (39 km) descent from the Ella Mountain fire lookout at 7,400 feet (2,255 m) will link with the connector trail between Barnes Canyon and Kershaw-Ryan State Park. As of October 2021, the upper eight miles (13 km) are complete, with some challenging slickrock and boulder areas. Several annual mountain bike festivals and races celebrate the sport too, including the Beaver Dam Gravel Grinder, held in Beaver Dam State Park, and the renowned Park to Park Pedal–Extreme Nevada 100 Bicycle Tour that rolls riders through Caliente and the historic mining town of Pioche and then through four scenic state parks: Kershaw-Ryan, Cathedral Gorge, Spring Valley, and Echo Canyon.

Caliente, NV | Season: Year-round

Both climbers and boulderers enjoy Red Rock Canyon.

Climb the Red Rocks

Betting on red might be the name of the game on the Strip, but for a guaranteed win, check out the crimson found 20 miles (32 km) away at Red Rock Canyon National Conservation Area. Simply called Red Rocks by those in the know, the vast 195,819 acres (79,245 ha) of Mojave Desert are full of geological formations and Aztec sandstone canyon walls colored by the presence of iron oxide that when exposed to the elements oxidizes, or "rusts." The result is desert eye candy in shades of red and orange. Set against a bluebird sky, there's nothing prettier. Red Rocks is ideal for climbers of all levels who will find endless opportunities to learn and be challenged on thousands of named and unnamed routes and crags, made for traditional climbing, sport climbing, and bouldering. For gear or route recommendations from experienced climbers, check out Desert Rock Sports, just 15 minutes from Red Rocks.

Las Vegas, NV | **Season:** Year-round

Ski Nevada's Heavenly Slopes

If ever a place lives up to its name, it's Heavenly, the state's largest ski resort, spanning 4,800 glorious acres (1,940 ha) on the California-Nevada border at the southeast end of stunning Lake Tahoe. With miles of wide-open bowls, groomed cruisers, black diamond plunges, and plenty of easy slopes for new learners and families, it's one of the most diverse ski areas on the lake, and popular for good reason.

It's also home to the Olympic Downhill, a 5.5-mile (8.8 km) thigh burner of a run that drops nearly 2,000 vertical feet (610 m). The postcard views of the deep blue lake framed by Sierra Nevada peaks are the best around and can be enjoyed on skis or off with a ride up the Heavenly Mountain Gondola, a 2.4-mile (3.9 km) glide to 10,000 feet (3,050 m). For something different, hop on the Ridge Rider, a gravity-powered alpine roller coaster that winds through rocks and forests.

Stateline, NV | **Season:** Winter

Fresh powder and epic views await at Heavenly Mountain.

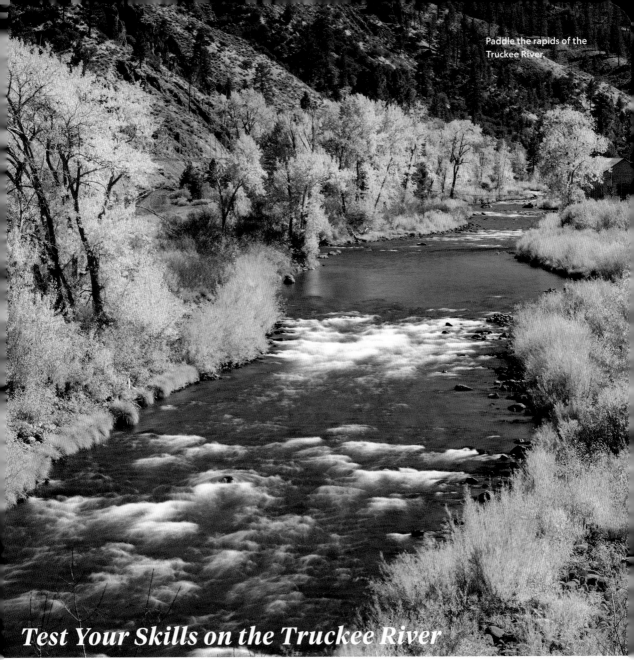

Paddle the rapids of the Truckee River.

Test Your Skills on the Truckee River

Flowing from Lake Tahoe in California and winding through the Sierra Nevada mountains and Reno, before pouring into Pyramid Lake, the Truckee River snakes for 121 scenic miles (195 km), with numerous ways to thrill or chill. One of the most easily accessible is the human-made section in downtown Reno that has been transformed into the fun-for-all Truckee River Whitewater Park. Here, Class II and III rapids spread over half a mile (0.8 km) and cascade through 11 pools. It's a great place to practice basic strokes and important navigation skills, such as turning.

The rapids are situated in the hotel-casino district and surround Wingfield Park, an island with an amphitheater, green space, and footbridges that link to the Riverwalk District. The popular Reno River Festival, held each May, sees the world's top white-water athletes maneuver the Truckee River Whitewater Park and is a blast to watch.

Reno, NV | **Season:** Year-round

Soak in mineral-rich
hot springs.

> **"SOAKING IN THEM IS PRACTICALLY A RITE OF PASSAGE."**

Soak in Hot Springs

Mother Nature did Nevada a solid when she decked it out with hundreds of mineral hot springs. In fact, the Silver State has more than any other state in the country, counting more than 300 occurring naturally. Soaking in them is practically a rite of passage, though it's important to pay attention and heed warning signs, as some are scalding and can cause serious injury. However, when safe, the steaming beauties are as soothing to the body as they are the soul thanks to their settings in Nevada's most pristine wilderness.

At Wayne E. Kirch Wildlife Management Area, the Kirch Hot Springs, also known as Sunnyside, are among the most beautiful, with crystal clear waters and views of the surrounding Nevada desert. About an hour south of Elko, bordering Ruby Lake National Wildlife Refuge, the Ruby Valley Hot Springs have a main pool, about 30 feet (9 m) deep, surrounded by smaller ones. Most springs reach around 100°F (38°C), but some are too hot to safely enter.

A collection of six pools near Gerlach is known as Soldier Meadows Hot Springs, surrounded by marshy vegetation with distant mountain views. Water temps range from the mid-90s to low 100s, but check before dipping in. The area is remote, so it may be worthwhile to spend the night at one of the BLM-managed campsites. Or try your luck with the free cabin on the property. Available on a first-come, first-served basis, it offers a wood-burning stove, a pit toilet, and a roof over your head.

If the pools of the Las Vegas Strip aren't enough, head 45 minutes away to the Colorado River. Goldstrike Hot Springs requires a four-mile (6.4 km) hike through a narrow canyon, but the steamy pools and waterfalls are worth it.

Multicity, NV **Season:** Year-round

Wings of a Feather

🦆 The United States has more than 562 wildlife refuges and sanctuaries, and Nevada is home to several, including Stillwater National Wildlife Refuge, with beavers, mountain lions, mule deer, coyotes, bats, tree frogs, and turtles. But it's the hundreds of thousands of shorebirds that use the more than 79,000 acres (31,970 ha) as a stopping place on their annual migrations that rank it of global importance by the Western Hemisphere Shorebird Reserve Network. An estimated 280 species of birds reside here on any given day. Shorebirds and wading birds are abundant spring through fall, including American white pelican, white-faced ibis, and Wilson's and red-necked phalaropes. Winter welcomes bald eagles, rough-legged hawks, prairie falcons, and golden eagles. Stillwater is an easy day trip from Reno and has numerous walking trails and nonmotorized boating opportunities too. For free guided tours, drop by the Stillwater visitors center in nearby Fallon.

Fallon, NV | Season: Year-round

Foxtail Lake in Stillwater National Wildlife Refuge

Soar Above a Scenic Valley

🔭 Cradled between the Sierra Nevada and Pine Nut Ranges, Carson Valley is speckled with farms and ranches, rivers and snowcapped mountain peaks, and vistas that shimmer gold come fall. The best part for travelers is the sheer variety of outdoor adventure and relaxing activities from which to choose, including one that combines them both—hot-air ballooning. Soaring into bluebird skies with Balloon Nevada on a morning or evening float is hands down the best way to take in the 400-mile-long (640 km) northern Nevada beauty. On an hour-long flight, experienced pilots and guides point out historical and natural highlights, such as Job's Peak, rising 10,633 feet (3,241 m) in the Eastern Sierra, and on a clear day, stunning Lake Tahoe, just 20 minutes away. Wildlife such as the bald and golden eagles, hawks, falcons, and deer have also been spotted.

Held every September, the Great Reno Balloon Race—the world's largest free hot-air ballooning event—is a reason to look to the skies. Up to 100 hot-air balloons take part in the race, which started in 1982 with just 20 balloons. Today, it's a beloved tradition that includes a special Glow Show, during which balloons light their flames as the sun sets. It's worth sticking around for this spectacular display. Local kids can take part in the fun, too, with the E.L. Cord Tissue Paper Balloon Launch, which has regional fifth graders use various materials to design model hot-air balloons that soar into the skies.

Gardnerville, NV | Season: Year-round

Paddle the Black Canyon

For a fun-filled river trip a mere 45 minutes from the Las Vegas Strip, the 26-mile (42 km) Black Canyon National Water Trail invites guests for a leisurely float down a green ribbon of the Colorado River, beginning at the Hoover Dam. Board a motorized inflatable raft for an easy cruise through the scenic waterway and a dive into history, shared by knowledgeable guides. Along the way, plenty of desert landscape will turn a day out into an epic adventure, as guides point out swimming holes and beaches, hiking trails and narrow slot canyons, as well as some muscle-soothing hot springs. Keep your eyes open for resident wildlife along the way, including big horn sheep, falcons, coyotes, bald eagles, and red-tailed hawks. The water moves but rapids are nonexistent, which means this lollygag is mellow enough for the whole family and first-timers.

Hoover Dam is a site to see, and a limited number of outfitters provide an exclusive launch from the dam.

Clark County, NV | Season: Year-round

The water trail ends at Eldorado Canyon, though guided day tours stop at Willow Beach. Some suppliers are happy to arrange multiday odysseys that overnight on the river's sandy banks. Check out companies like Desert Adventures, Evolution Expeditions, and Jerkwater Canoe Co. that handle gear, lunch, permits, pickup, guiding expertise, and more to create a unique no-hassle adventure on the Colorado River. Self-guided tours are also possible at different launch points.

At the end of the tour in Willow Beach, outfitters will shuttle you back to the starting point. En route, you'll travel over the Mike O'Callaghan–Pat Tillman Memorial Bridge, which stretches across the Colorado River between Arizona and Nevada.

Mountain bluebird

A hiker and pack llamas wind through a meadow of lupine and mule's ears.

High-Elevation Hike

Nevada's first wilderness area, designated in 1964, Jarbidge has expanded over the decades and now covers 113,000 jaw-dropping acres (45,730 ha) that include pristine lakes, rivers, and streams, not to mention desert, towering mountains, and carved-out canyons. One of the most celebrated peaks is Matterhorn, and a difficult, 12-mile (19 km) loop trail offers stellar views from a perch of 10,839 feet (3,304 m). The Hummingbird Springs Wilderness Trail starts at 9,200 feet (2,800 m), and winds around Gods Pocket Peak and Divide Peak. With more than 100 miles (160 km) of trails to explore along with diverse animals and vegetation, Jarbidge surprises at every curve. Fall pops with magnificent golden displays of aspen trees, while during spring and summer, the area's 60 varieties of wildflowers turn many trails and meadows into a colorful natural kaleidoscope.

Jarbidge, NV | Season: Spring to fall

"VALLEY OF FIRE STATE PARK SPARKLES AS A MUSE."

Capture the Ultimate Desert Gram

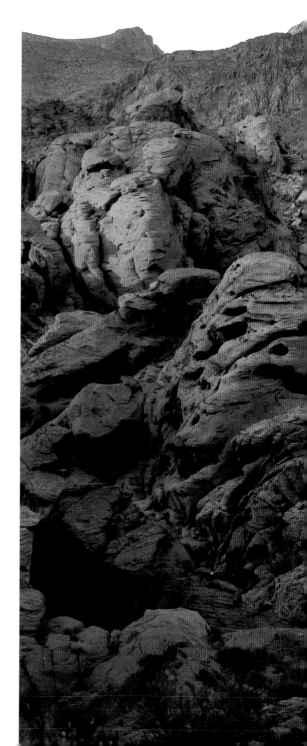

They say a picture is worth a thousand words, but snapping photos around Nevada's oldest and largest state park might be worth 10,000. Just an hour from the neon lights of downtown Las Vegas, Valley of Fire State Park sparkles as a muse for photographers and outdoor lovers, thanks to 46,000 acres (18,615 ha) of swirling red sandstone, surreal rock formations, slot canyons, wildflowers, and mind-blowing desert serenity accessible via hiking trails. Sunset is a sublime time to visit and discover how the geological wonderland reportedly found its name in 1920, when an AAA official traveling through the park saw the red stone at the end of the day and said the valley looked like it was on fire.

One of the park's most photographed sites, and a backdrop to inspire lots of Instagram love, is Fire Wave, a bowl-shaped depression that appears to be painted with beige and red-orange stripes that curve around the ancient rocks. Getting there is an easy 1.5-mile (2.4 km) round-trip walk. For maximum bang for photo buck, the easy one-mile (1.6 km) loop known as the White Domes Trail offers diverse scenery to pose with including intriguing rock formations, the ruins of a 1965 movie set, a shallow slot canyon, and white sandstone cliffs that give the trail its name.

Although the Natural Arches Trail's largest arch collapsed in 2010, the nearly five-mile (8 km) out-and-back route on the park's eastern edge near Elephant Rock still dishes out tons of desert color and serenity, as well as smaller arches and a massive balancing rock that looks designed for funny "perspective" shots.

The first part of the 4.5-mile (7 km) Pinnacles Loop Trail takes walkers across dry and sandy open desert and gets more Instagram-worthy when the otherworldly red-rock pinnacles come into view.

Overton, NV | **Season:** Year-round

Drive through the red rocks of Valley of Fire State Park.

A bristlecone pine tree grows in Wheeler Peak Grove in Great Basin National Park.

1. COMMUNE IN THE VASTNESS

Although the Black Rock Desert's claim to fame is the eight-day cultural phenomenon known as Burning Man, it's also a vast conservation and wilderness area of rugged canyons and mountains, bubbling hot springs, expansive dry lake beds, spewing geysers, wild horses, and historic and unblazed trails, and is pure gold for outdoor fans.

2. EXPLORE GREAT BASIN NATIONAL PARK

From colossal underground caverns to Snake Mountain peaks to the oldest trees on Earth (the Great Basin bristlecone pine—more than 5,000 years old), this park on the Utah border shows off Mother Nature's extreme side better than most. Winter snowshoeing and cross-country skiing are especially peaceful here.

3. HELI-SKI IN THE ALPS OF NEVADA

This pinch-me heli-skiing trip to the Ruby Mountains is not for everyone, but if you can swing it, "the Rubies," with 15 peaks above 11,000 feet (3,350 m) and off-the-beaten-path acreage, are the stuff of backcountry skiing legend, and family-owned Ruby Mountain Heli has been turning off-piste dreams into mountain-high reality for nearly 50 years.

4. CAMP NEAR A GEOLOGICAL CATHEDRAL

The carved bentonite clay spires found in the 1,600-acre (650 ha) Cathedral Gorge State Park were formed by erosion tens of millions of years ago, making this eastern Nevada marvel just right for pitching a tent at one of the 22 campsites, and exploring the unique creations, caverns, and slot canyons.

5. STROLL ALONG THE RAILROAD TUNNEL TRAIL

The easy two-mile-long (3.2 km) level lollygag retraces an old railroad route used during the construction of the Hoover Dam. Walkers enjoy sweeping views of Lake Mead, the country's largest human-made reservoir, and pass through five tunnels cut from the surrounding mountainside. Just 1.5 miles (2.4 km) beyond the last tunnel is the remarkable dam.

6. ZIP-LINE OVER BOOTLEG CANYON

Mountain bikers come from all over to explore its 36 miles (58 km) of beginner and advanced trails, but for those hankering for height and speed, strap in and cruise 8,000 feet (2,440 m) over Bootleg Canyon. The starting line is the top of Red Mountain, with views of Boulder City, Lake Mead, and the El Dorado Valley.

7. CATCH IT AT TOPAZ LAKE

Like its more well-known alpine cousin to the north, Topaz Lake also straddles the California-Nevada border, though its setting leans stark desert rather than pine-covered peaks. But anglers (as well as boaters and campers) love the year-round scene for trophy rainbow and brown trout and smallmouth bass.

8. RELIVE IT IN VIRGINIA CITY

Everyone in the family will enjoy a day out in this preserved Victorian-era town, complete with wooden boardwalks, swinging door saloons, museums, and year-round cultural events that take visitors deep into Nevada's Old West roots. Virginia City might be touristy, but it's also 100 percent original and a must when in the Silver State.

9. UNPLUG AT MASSACRE RIM

Tucked between Sheldon National Wildlife Refuge and the Black Rock Desert, the Massacre Rim Wilderness Study Area is far from civilization and cell service, and experienced backcountry campers will find limitless solitude. The area was recently designated an International Dark Sky Sanctuary, making the stargazing here some of the best in the world.

10. GET A NATURE FIX AT KINGS CANYON

When visiting the state's capital, Carson City, take the five-minute drive west of downtown to the Kings Canyon trailhead. The walk isn't far or steep, but the 25-foot (8 m) cascading waterfall, especially beautiful during spring's snowmelt, brings a perfect midday Mother Nature pick-me-up to those in need.

Tortoise

New Hampshire offers picturesque rivers for fly-fishing.

NEW HAMPSHIRE

From sandy coasts to snowy peaks, New Hampshire is a four-season destination calling all nature lovers.

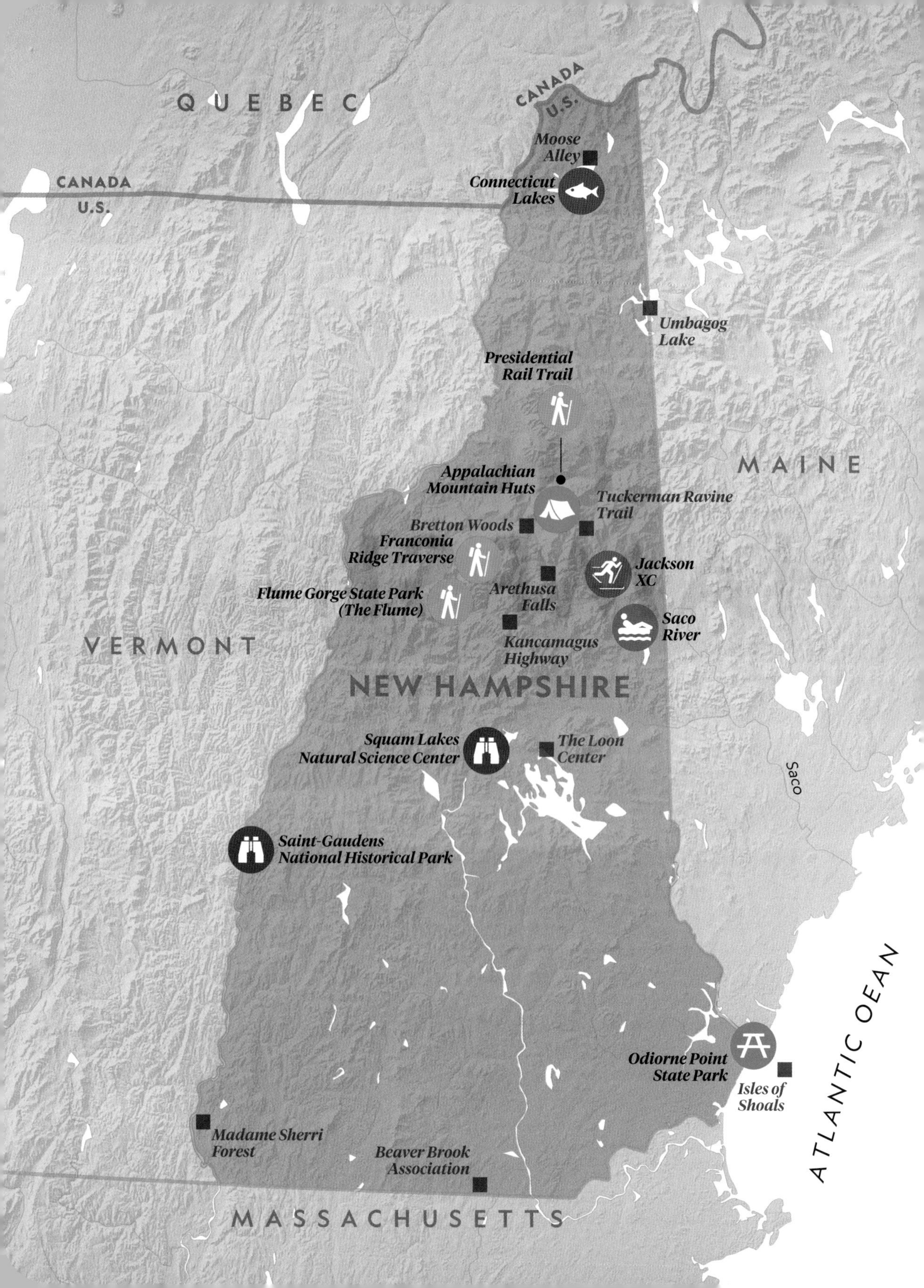

QUEBEC

CANADA
U.S.

CANADA
U.S.

Moose
Alley

Connecticut
Lakes

Umbagog
Lake

MAINE

Presidential
Rail Trail

Appalachian
Mountain Huts

Tuckerman Ravine
Trail

Bretton Woods

Franconia
Ridge Traverse

Jackson
XC

Flume Gorge State Park
(The Flume)

Arethusa
Falls

Saco
River

VERMONT

Kancamagus
Highway

NEW HAMPSHIRE

Squam Lakes
Natural Science Center

The Loon
Center

Saco

Saint-Gaudens
National Historical Park

ATLANTIC OEAN

Odiorne Point
State Park

Isles of
Shoals

Madame Sherri
Forest

Beaver Brook
Association

MASSACHUSETTS

Take a peek at Cherry Mountain from the Silvio O. Conte National Fish and Wildlife Refuge along the Presidential Rail Trail.

The Presidential Rail Trail

You don't always have to climb thousands of feet for a killer mountain vista. New Hampshire's Presidential Rail Trail demonstrates this with quiet beauty. Running 18 miles (29 km) east from the Mount Washington Regional Airport access road to the town of Gorham, this expansive and well-maintained gravel path for both cyclists and pedestrians features a painting-worthy view of Mount Adams, Mount Madison, and Mount Jefferson (the northern citadels of the Presidential Range). But these mountains are the tip of the iceberg.

The rail trail cruises through a patchwork of landscapes that speak to the ecological diversity of northern New Hampshire. You'll traverse corridors of eastern hemlocks, cross rippling waterways like the Israel and Moose Rivers, and experience birdsong-filled wetlands in the Silvio O. Conte National Fish and Wildlife Refuge. The observation platform at Cherry Pond (at the 1.5-mile/2.4-km mark, heading east) is an opportune place for spotting northern harriers, mourning warblers, and black-backed woodpeckers. Keep an eye on the glassy waters, too. Moose and black bears roam the shores of this secluded pond.

Parking is available at both ends of the trail, along with two mid-trail parking areas in Jefferson and Randolph. The Presidential Rail Trail can be undertaken as a piecemeal or marathon ride, and you can also use the rail trail to connect with other popular trails in the region, such as the Fallsway Trail to cascades along Snyder Brook, or the Cohos Trail, a relatively new 162-mile (261 km) trail from the White Mountains to the Canadian border.

Whitefield to Gorham, NH | **Season:** Spring to fall

Cast your line on the Connecticut River.

An Angler's Delight

Most visitors venture to the Great North Woods, the mysterious realm north of the White Mountains. But those who bring their rods and reels to these highlands are rewarded with some of New England's most bounteous fishing.

The Connecticut Lakes, near the Canadian border, are a destination for wizened anglers. Of four lakes in total, three offer public boat launches. For landlocked salmon and trout, enter the glassy expanse of First and Second Connecticut Lakes. Looking to fry some rainbow trout? Try the quieter waters of Third Connecticut Lake. The forested shoreline here is more rustic.

The fourth, northernmost lake is little more than a glacial tarn where fishing isn't allowed. But the Nature Conservancy maintains a beautiful trail to the lake that begins at the U.S. Customs and Border Protection station on Route 3. It's worth the side trek.

Multicity, NH | **Season:** Spring to fall

Hike the Flume

In 1808, 93-year-old Jess Guernsey was searching the woods near Mount Flume for a place to fish. Instead, she found an 800-foot (240 m) granite gorge festooned with waterfalls and moss. Covered by a glacier during the Ice Age, the gorge became the cradle of Flume Brook. New Hampshire State Parks built twisting boardwalks through the misty gorge, and the Flume was born.

The two-mile (3.2 km) loop hike through the Flume begins in a forest riddled with glacial boulders before following Flume Brook to reach the mouth of the gorge and the start of the boardwalk, which climbs alongside the moist walls to 45-foot-tall (14 m) Avalanche Falls.

The return journey to the visitors center has its own treats: Sentinel Pine Bridge, a classic New England covered bridge, crosses the mighty Pemigewasset River. And just beyond here, aspiring spelunkers can shimmy through the Wolf Den, a real squeezer of a cave.

Lincoln, NH | **Season:** Spring to fall

Avalanche Falls drops 45 feet (14 m) into the gorge.

The cross-country tracks in Jackson cross through White Mountain National Forest.

Cross Country Ski on the Jackson XC Trail

Half the beauty of cross-country skiing is the simplicity. You clip into your skis and set off into the woods on whatever local trails are available. In the hills near Jackson village, next door to Pinkham Notch, the Jackson Ski Touring Foundation maintains nearly 100 miles (160 km) of Nordic ski trails. These groomed and rustic paths offer access to the boreal woodlands, exposed mountain summits, and frozen bogs where moose occasionally appear.

The Jackson XC trail network has something for everyone. A gentle glide on the Ellis Falls Trail will take you along the peaceful waterway fed by Glen Ellis Falls. The Eleventh Hole trail features White Mountain views at the Wentworth golf course. But the most formidable trail is the 10.2-mile-long (16.4 km) Wildcat Valley Trail. Start by taking the lift at Wildcat Mountain to its 4,062-foot (1,238 m) summit and ski to Jackson village.

Jackson, NH | Season: Winter

"EIGHT BACKCOUNTRY
HOSTELS SPREAD ACROSS
THE WHITE MOUNTAINS."

High Mountain Huts

Imagine, after a long hike, resting in a cozy bunk bed and listening to 70-mile-an-hour (112 km/h) winds rattle the windows. You're not out of the woods yet, but you're not camping either. You've shacked up at one of the Appalachian Mountain Club's high mountain huts: eight backcountry hostels spread across the White Mountains from Franconia Notch State Park to the slopes of Mount Washington and the Carter-Moriah Range.

After humble beginnings as bare-bones hiker shelters and inspired by the Swiss Alps hut system, the AMC huts have now operated for more than a century. First, hikers reserve bunks at the hut(s) of their choosing. (Summer reservations for weekends should be made a few months in advance at *outdoors.org*.) After clomping into White Mountain National Forest and reaching the hut, guests are greeted with a hearty family-style dinner prepared by the "croo" of live-in hut staff: young rapscallions who carry more than 60 pounds (27 kg) of perishable food up to their huts twice a week, using wooden packboards. A breakfast of pancakes and eggs is dished up at 7 a.m. and from there, you either return to the valley or continue onward to the next hut.

The huts offer a gateway overnight backpacking experience for the uninitiated, and an alternative for anyone cringing at the thought of unfurling a musky Coleman tent and choking down rehydrated chili. For a family-friendly expedition with waterfalls and beaver lodges, Zealand Falls Hut and Lonesome Lake Hut are the ticket. The quad-quaking climb to Madison Spring Hut in the northern Presidentials, or Greenleaf Hut on the shoulder of Mount Lafayette, will allow you to spend a night amid the tundra of the alpine zone. And for isolation amid boreal spruce and peat moss deep in the Pemigewasset Wilderness, Galehead Hut is the most remote of the huts.

Multicity, NH | **Season:** Year-round

Madison Spring Hut is a shelter for hikers.

Coast on the Coast

New Hampshire's compact seacoast is where mountains and woodlands meet the surf, with curious results. Take Odiorne Point State Park. At this coastal preserve, hermit crabs, groundhogs, and red-tailed hawks share the white pine forest, salt marshes, and gusty beaches. The park also contains abandoned World War II–era gun batteries and bunkers. These relics of the era when Americans feared an Axis powers attack on the Atlantic coast are now decorated with impressive graffiti.

Simply wandering the park's immense network of trails will lead you to gems like the Frost Point Breakwater jetty or lively tide pools along the park's midsection. But pay special attention to the pebbly shores of Periwinkle Cove. Near low tide, the waterlogged tree stumps of a "sunken forest" reveal themselves. The cove is also bypassed by the Route 1A bike trail, which continues south of the park past decadent seaside mansions and barnacle-encrusted rocks.

Rye, NH | Season: Year-round

Odiorne Point State Park has scenic rocky coasts.

From Peak to Peak

If you're traveling to the White Mountains up I-93 North, the regional gateway is Franconia Notch, and its high point is Mount Lafayette, a granite giant that towers 5,249 feet (1,600 m) above sea level. But Lafayette is merely the pinnacle of a much bigger behemoth—the Franconia Ridge. A stony spine of krummholz and alpine flowers such as diapensias, the ridge consists of multiple 4,000-foot (1,220 m) summits. Connected by a single trail with panoramic views of the White Mountains, three of these peaks—Lafayette, Lincoln, and Little Haystack—can be summited in a single day. This challenging loop hike is the Franconia Ridge Traverse.

In 8.4 miles (13.5 km), you'll climb (and descend) some 3,800 vertical feet (1,160 m). Arrive before dawn at the Lafayette Place Campground parking area. Pick up the Old Bridle Path and turn right on the Falling Waters Trail, which bypasses splendorous cascades like the Cloudland Falls while climbing at a punishing grade to break through the tree line atop Little Haystack. From here, the Franconia Ridge Trail continues north to Lincoln and Lafayette, passing gusty alpine gardens and tuffets of green sphagnum moss.

A gradual descent from Lafayette leads to Greenleaf Hut—one of the Appalachian Mountain Club's high mountain huts—where hikers can refuel with a bowl of soup. The final descent down the Old Bridle Path includes "The Three Agonies," a trilogy of difficult rocky scrambles. But the views into Franconia Notch are more than enough to alleviate your aching soles.

Lilac flowers

Multicity, NH | Season: Spring to fall

Historic Sights

When Augustus Saint-Gaudens wasn't busy cutting sculptures of Abraham Lincoln or the Black soldiers of the 54th Massachusetts Volunteer Infantry Regiment, he wandered the forests of Cornish, New Hampshire. One of the beaux arts generation of sculptors, Saint-Gaudens built his home on a sunny hill with enviable views of Mount Ascutney, across the Vermont state line. Saint-Gaudens lived in the home seasonally beginning in 1885; he lived there year-round from 1900 until his death in 1907. Visit the grounds where he conceived and created Civil War–era sculptures that would become landmarks in cities like Chicago and Boston.

Saint-Gaudens's restored federal-style house and gardens (designed with the help of landscape architect Ellen Shipman) are the centerpieces of Saint-Gaudens National Historical Park. One of the most arresting sculptures in the park is the Col. Robert Gould Shaw and

Cornish, NH | Season: Year-round

Choose your vessel: Tube, canoe, or kayak on the Saco River.

54th Massachusetts Infantry Regiment Memorial. Unveiled in 1897, the sculpture honors the first federally raised African American regiment from a Union state during the Civil War, as well as its white commander.

Even within this stunning home, the natural world seeps in. The atrium pairs a golden relief sculpture with a black pond where green frogs swim beneath lily pads. The sprawling lawn of the homestead features sculptures of Adm. David Farragut and Col. Robert Gould Shaw. A modest blue cabin in the nearby woods is Saint-Gaudens' ravine studio, where his assistants spent hours cutting stone.

The studio is the gateway to the short Ravine Trail, one of the estate's lush and deeply quiet footpaths. Descend wooden stairs to the ravine floor, where rivulets of water ripple beside a winding path to the swimming hole where Saint-Gaudens used to cool off. Back on the lawn, you can also pick up the Blow-Me-Down Trail (2 miles/3 km) that visits a historic pondside gristmill at the edge of the estate.

Float Away

Summer in the Mount Washington Valley can be frightfully broiling, but the Saco River retains its enlivening chill year-round. Flowing southeast from Saco Lake (located in the depths of Crawford Notch), the river passes the towns of Bartlett and Conway, New Hampshire, and Fryeburg, Maine—all of which offer river access points where swimmers and paddlers can cool off. But to *really* take in the beauty of the Saco, try cruising it on a tube.

Outfitters in the Conway area such as Saco River Tubing Center and Saco Bound rent sturdy inner tubes that you can ride across the New Hampshire-Maine state line. The mountains and their foothills fade to farmlands as you pass sandy beaches and brave occasional rapids. In summer, the average depth of the Saco is only three feet (0.9 m), making it easy to dismount and explore the wooded banks.

Conway, NH | Season: Summer

"SQUAM LAKE IS AN OASIS OF CALM."

Wildlife on the Lake

Directly north of Lake Winnipesaukee's heavily developed shoreline, Squam Lake is an oasis of calm. Katharine Hepburn and Henry Fonda traveled here to film *On Golden Pond*. But the waters and woodlands of the lake are home to more than just fortunate landowners. The region is rustling with wildlife, and the Squam Lakes Natural Science Center offers a direct window to Squam's resident animals, as well as mountain trails and guided boat tours.

Bringing visitors "Nearer to Nature" since 1966, the Science Center is tucked away in the woods outside of Holderness, just a couple steps away from the lakeshore. A twisting loop trail from the visitors center will introduce you to some of Squam Lake's denizens: black bears, river otters, white-tailed deer, red-tailed hawks, coyotes, and even mountain lions. Most of the mammals and birds here were injured or orphaned in the wild, with low odds of survival on their own. As residents of the Science Center, these animals receive care and lots of space to roam.

From the live animal exhibits, you can explore the transitional zone between woods and wetland on the brief Ecotone Trail or ascend to a stunning view of Squam Lake on the Mount Fayal Trail (1 mile/1.6 km). But many visitors head for the water and hop aboard a Squam Lake Cruise. From a canopied pontoon boat, you'll search for New Hampshire's iconic common loons and bald eagles, while your guide tells the story of Squam's ecological history.

Back on shore, stroll the one-acre (0.4 km) Kirkwood Gardens, on the grounds of the Holderness Inn. A stroll through this purposefully designed landscape will take you by a variety of trees, shrubs, ferns, and flowers that have adapted to the New England climate, along with the birds, bees, and butterflies the plants attract. A beautiful patio offers a resting spot to take in the views, or rest under the vine-covered pagoda at the west end of the lower garden.

Holderness, NH | **Season:** Spring to fall

See Squam Lake stretch before you from Rattlesnake Mountain Overlook.

A lighthouse sits on
Isles of Shoals.

1. TAKE ON THE TUCKERMAN RAVINE TRAIL

Of all the paths to New England's highest peak—where the fastest surface wind in the Northern and Western Hemispheres was measured—the Tuckerman Ravine Trail offers the most grandeur. Scale the cascade-swathed walls of a glacial cirque to reach a moonscape of alpine tundra and mossy rocks before you arrive at the gusty summit.

2. SKI OR ZIP-LINE AT BRETTON WOODS

Bretton Woods is known as one of the ritziest ski resorts in the Whites—fancy enough for hosting the Bretton Woods Conference of 1944. The ski trails are worth the splurge, but summer and fall visitors can take treetop zip-line tours of the woodlands against the epic backdrop of Mount Washington and the Presidential Range.

3. DRIVE THE KANCAMAGUS HIGHWAY

Roller-coasting across 34.5 miles (55.5 km) of White Mountain National Forest, the Kancamagus Highway is the most scenic way to get from Lincoln to Conway. From its vistas of the Pemigewasset Wilderness and the Sandwich Range to the adjacent trailheads for hikes like Mount Chocorua and Sabbaday Falls, the amenities of "the Kanc" are abundant.

4. CANOE OR KAYAK UMBAGOG LAKE

The name Umbagog is Abenaki for "shallow water," and as you paddle your canoe or kayak across this remote lake at the nexus of Maine and New Hampshire's northern timberlands, you'll notice that it's only 12 to 14 feet (3.6 to 4.2 m) deep in many places, offering glimpses of fish like smallmouth bass and white perch.

5. SPOT MOOSE ON MOOSE ALLEY

The northernmost segment of NH-3, connecting Pittsburg with the Canadian border, is nicknamed "Moose Alley" because of the frequency with which moose lumber out of the pine forest that flanks this desolately beautiful highland road. Hit the byway just before dawn to boost your odds of spotting a moose, and drive slowly.

6. HIKE TO ARETHUSA FALLS

Crashing 140 feet (43 m) down a sun-splashed granite cliff, Arethusa Falls is New Hampshire's tallest waterfall, and the 2.8-mile (4.5 km) ascent to the cascade through Crawford Notch State Park offers its own treats. Veer left onto the Bemis Brook Trail cutoff to visit two "taster" waterfalls—Coliseum Falls and Bemis Brook Falls— before continuing to Arethusa.

7. BIRDING AT THE LOON CENTER

The cry of the loon is one of the state's iconic sounds, and a gentle walk through the woods and marshlands of the Loon Center might be your best bet for seeing one of these birds up close. The mossy trail offers views into active loon nesting areas on Lake Winnipesaukee's northeastern coves.

8. RIDE A STEAMSHIP TO THE ISLES OF SHOALS

The grassy Isles of Shoals have hosted anglers, marine scientists, and—according to legend—the pirate Blackbeard, who allegedly spent his honeymoon here. Hop aboard an Isles of Shoals Steamship Company cruise and explore flowering footpaths and seaside cottages on Star Island.

9. FOREST BATHE AT BEAVER BROOK ASSOCIATION

A 40-mile (64 km) labyrinth of trails connects forests, bogs, ponds, and meadows at this preserve in the Merrimack River Valley. Deer, rabbits, raptors, and of course, the titular beavers are frequently spotted from the paths that offer access to charming villages such as Hollis and Brookline, as well as several popular rail trails.

10. STRUT THE MADAME SHERRI FOREST

Madame Sherri was a Roaring Twenties fashion designer from New York who threw Gatsby-worthy parties at her mansion in southwestern New Hampshire. Explore the ruins of her castlelike stronghold, and then hop on the nearby woodland trails to reach unsung landmarks like Moon Ledge, an overlook with views of the Connecticut River.

Eastern newts

The sun sets over Seaside Park
on the New Jersey shore.

NEW JERSEY

Known for its sandy shores, New Jersey offers plenty more, from historic village jaunts to trails through the pinelands.

NEW YORK

High Point State Park & New Jersey Veterans' Memorial

Wawayanda State Park

Tillman Ravine

Melick's Town Farm

Spruce Run Reservoir **NEW JERSEY**

Duke Farms

Delaware & Raritan Canal State Park

Terhune Orchards

Bulls Island

Delaware & Raritan Canal

Washington Crossing State Park

Grounds for Sculpture

PENNSYLVANIA

Allaire State Park and Historic Village at Allaire

Holland Ridge Farms

Point Pleasant

Jersey Shore

Silver Bay and Cattus Island

Whitesbog Historic Village

Pine Barrens

Skydive Cross Keys

ATLANTIC OCEAN

Atlantic City

MARYLAND

Delaware Bay

DELAWARE

Stone Harbor

Visit East Point Lighthouse in the fall for fewer crowds.

Offseason at the Shore—and More

There's more to "the Shore" than beaches, boardwalks, and bars. When the temperatures drop and crowds disperse, its off-season personality emerges.

The transformation begins in September. As the last vacationers pack their suitcases and head home, new visitors descend on Cape May: monarch butterflies. The annual migration ushers tens of thousands of amber-winged beauties to the southernmost shore point, where they rest before continuing their 2,000-mile (3,220 km) journey south to Mexico for the winter. The Garrett Family Preserve is a prime viewing spot in September and October.

Another unlikely visitor shows its face (or muzzle) from October through March, when horseback riding is permitted on Brigantine Beach and along the southern six miles (10 km) of Island Beach State Park in Seaside Park. (Bring your own horse. Permits are available from City Hall.)

Horses are among the many surprises you'll find on Long Beach Island, but they won't be riding on the sand. Every Columbus Day weekend, the sky over Ship Bottom fills with colorful creatures, like neon squid, rainbow dragons, and of course, sea horses. It's LBI Fly, a three-day international kite festival with flying demonstrations, races, trick kite shoot-outs, and a glow-in-the-dark night fly.

Also illuminating the night are New Jersey's lighthouses. There are 23 up and down the coast (11 are open to the public). Visit on the third weekend in October to compete in the annual Lighthouse Challenge—visit 10 land-based lighthouses, three lifesaving stations, one museum, one virtual site, and the NJ Lighthouse Society—over the two-day weekend.

Multicity, NJ | Season: Fall to spring

Walk through the conservatory and greenhouse at Duke Farms.

A Conservation Ride

In the late 1800s, tobacco magnate J. B. Duke purchased a gentleman's farm and harvested award-winning produce. But it was his visionary daughter, Doris, who transformed the property into the innovative, conservation-minded oasis it is today.

You can see the sustainability efforts in action via 18 miles (29 km) of fully accessible paved paths. (Bike rentals are available for a fee, or you can bring your own.) Stop by the Great Meadows, where native grasses and wildflowers enhance biodiversity and help absorb carbon dioxide from the atmosphere. On the southern loop trail, a former stone well house has been repurposed into a birding platform overlooking restored wetlands, farm fields, and forests—habitats for great blue herons, bald eagles, and the threatened American kestrel. Don't miss the solar array, which has more than 3,000 solar panels that generate electricity for all the farm's buildings and electric vehicles.

Bridgewater, NJ | **Season:** Year-round

Go With the Flow

What happens when you combine the calming energy of a lake with the restorative power of yoga? You get SUP (stand-up paddleboard) yoga, a transformative outdoor experience.

Nestled among the rolling hills of Hunterdon County in Central Jersey, Spruce Run Reservoir is an oasis of natural beauty enjoyed by hikers, campers, and paddlers alike. Local yoga studio Wildflower transcends classroom walls to bring ancient practice to this peaceful place.

You can bring your own paddleboard and anchor or rent gear from Yellow Dog Paddle stationed at the boat launch. The instructor will help you launch your board into the lake and lead the class to a quiet cove, where you'll drop anchor for 30 minutes of Vinyasa Flow beneath the open sky. Each pose is designed to challenge your balance, strengthen your core, and foster connection with nature as your fingers and toes graze the water.

Spruce Run, NJ | **Season:** Late spring to early fall

Test your balance while doing yoga on a paddleboard.

Charter a fishing boat from the docks at Point Pleasant.

Wicked Tuna

For some of the best sport fishing in the Northeast, take an overnight trip to "the canyons," a popular fishing destination about 80 miles (130 km) off New Jersey's coast. Comprising several submarine canyons, like Hudson, Toms, and Lindenkohl, it's *the* place to troll for tuna—bluefin, yellowfin, bigeye, and albacore. In the fall, local guides, like Voyager Fishing, offer overnight tuna/mahi-mahi trips with 12 to 15 hours of fishing time for tuna alone. (A sleeping bunk is included in the fare, but bring your own sleeping bag and pillow.)

Full- and half-day inshore trips are available year-round and are suitable for all skill levels. Within an hour of departing the dock, your captain will find productive fishing holes with saltwater favorites, like ling, cod, tilefish, sea bass, striped bass, bluefish, jumbo porgy, and more. Bring your own rod and reel or rent the equipment you need. Bait is always free.

Point Pleasant, NJ | **Season:** Spring to fall

Washington Crossing Bridge was built in 1904 over the Delaware River.

> ## "THEIR VICTORY BOLSTERED THE AMERICAN TROOPS AND FUELED FURTHER TRIUMPHS."

Revolution Revisited

On a stormy Christmas night in 1776, Gen. George Washington crossed the icy Delaware River from Pennsylvania to New Jersey with 2,400 soldiers, 200 horses, and 18 cannons to mount a surprise attack on Hessian mercenaries downriver in Trenton. Their victory bolstered the American troops' waning confidence and fueled further triumphs over the British Army at Assunpink Creek and Princeton, a turning point of the American Revolution known as the "Ten Crucial Days."

Today, that cold, stormy river crossing may be a distant memory, but Washington Crossing State Park ensures its legacy lives on. Every year, thousands gather on the riverbanks and memorial bridge to watch historical reenactors dressed in blue coats, beige breeches, and black tricornes climb into Durham boats and row across the river, re-creating the brave voyage that saved the Revolution. The Christmas Day Crossing takes place every December 25 from noon to 3 p.m. and is free to the public.

Visit Washington Crossing any day of the year to take a self-guided walking tour. You'll see Johnson Ferry House, the red-and-white gambrel-roof farmhouse and tavern believed to have been used by Washington and his officers that fateful night. Behind Nelson House, you'll find a full-scale reproduction of a ferryboat used to transport cannons across the river. Twice a month, the park offers free historian-led tours. On Saturdays in October and November, you can learn how muskets were used in the Battle of Trenton and see a firing demonstration at the Nature Interpretive Center. Groups can also overnight at the park at one of four primitive campsites in the Phillips Farm area.

Titusville, NJ | **Season:** Year-round

Into the Bogs

Dating back to 1857, Whitesbog Village was once the largest cranberry farm in the state. Here, Elizabeth White, the farmer's eldest daughter and a self-taught agriculturalist, experimented with farming techniques that produced the highbush blueberry.

Today, Whitesbog is a preserved historic village with free trails open daily from sunrise to sunset. The best way to explore its fruitful history and vast grounds is by bike. Park in front of the general store, which is open on Saturdays from 10 a.m. to 2 p.m. (and sells cranberry *everything*). Workers' cottages, the barrel factory, and the old water tower are located just down the road. Stop by Suningive, Elizabeth White's former home, where blueberries still grow in the garden. Follow the sandy roads out to the cranberry bogs where red beauties grow just beneath the water's surface. To see how they make the journey from bog to table, visit during the annual harvest in late September or early October.

Browns Mills, NJ · Season: Fall

Bright berries fill the bogs during cranberry harvest season.

A High Note

Hike to the highest point in New Jersey at the aptly named High Point State Park. Here you'll have a clear view of the tripoint—the spot where New Jersey, Pennsylvania, and New York are connected by the Delaware River. To get there, take the Monument Trail, a 3.5-mile (5.6 km) loop from Lake Marcia. At the top, you'll find New Jersey Veterans' Memorial, a towering obelisk monument standing guard over the rolling hills and mountains below. With the American, New Jersey, and POW/MIA flags flapping in the wind, it's a moving tribute to the men and women who've served.

On your way down, take a detour on the Cedar Swamp Trail to see a rare mountaintop Atlantic white cedar bog. Because these trees are usually found near sea level, this bog may be one of the highest of its kind in the world, sitting at an elevation of 1,500 feet (460 m).

The parkland below contains more than 50 miles (80 km) of multiuse trails for hiking, mountain biking, and horseback riding. During winter, you can use them for skiing, snowshoeing, dogsledding, and snowmobiling. A popular, family-friendly hike is the 2.6-mile (4.2 km) White Cedar Swamp Trail. The easy loop borders the bog, where you might see wildlife. For a bigger challenge, tackle the 3.5-mile (5.6 km) Monument Trail Loop, which is also a popular winter snowshoeing route.

The park also has three lakes, each with its own draw. Lifeguards and a sand beach make Lake Marcia ideal for swimming and for families. With a boat ramp and well-stocked waters, Steenykill is the place to launch your electric-motor boat or paddlecraft and fish for trout and largemouth bass. And with 50 lakeside tent and RV sites, Sawmill Lake is ideal for spending the night. There are also a number of hiking trails in and around the camping area, as well as a playground.

Sussex, NJ   Season: Year-round

Jersey Fresh

April showers bring May flowers, but in the Garden State, they bring strawberries in mid-May, blueberries in July, apples throughout the fall, and a veritable cornucopia of fruits and vegetables all season long. With more than 100 pick-your-own (PYO) farms throughout the state, you can hand-select your favorite to get taste of what "Jersey Fresh" means.

U-pick season kicks off in mid-May with asparagus followed by strawberries. Terhune Orchards, a sustainable family farm and vineyard in Princeton, has both. It's one of the few in the state that also has a winery, tasting room, and a variety of wines crafted from their own vineyards and orchards.

Blueberries, the state fruit, are usually at their juiciest from mid-June through July. Visit Emery's Berry Farm, in New Egypt, to explore rows of organic highbush blueberries and pick from five varieties. Kids love petting the resident goats, sheep, and miniature donkey. Stop by their Farm Market and Country Bakery for homemade pies, pastries, and jams.

Apple season runs from late July through December. Melick's Town Farm, in Califon, is the largest apple orchard in the state, and it has been farmed by the same family for three centuries. Nearly 20,000 apple trees—with 20 varieties—await. Visit the Oldwick Cider Mill, at Melick's Town Farm, to taste fresh, unfiltered apple cider or try an award-winning hard cider. Apple wine is on the menu, too. (At other times of the year, you can also pick strawberries, peaches, pumpkins, and flowers.)

No matter where you are in the Garden State, farmers markets and roadside farm stands ensure that homegrown taste is never far from reach. Just look for the "Jersey Fresh" label.

Multicity, NJ | **Season:** Spring to fall

Paddle the Pines

The largest remaining Atlantic coastal pine barren ecosystem can be found in southern New Jersey. With more than a million acres (404,685 ha), pine barren covers more than 20 percent of the state's land area but represents only a tenth of its original size—once stretching from North Carolina to Nova Scotia.

Explore it by kayak or canoe for up close views of its pitch pines, Atlantic white cedars, trademark rust-colored water, cranberry bogs, and the turtles, wading birds, and tree frogs that live here. Pinelands Adventures offers self- and naturalist-guided hikes and paddle trips, ranging from 1.5 to 8 hours. Try the trail from Quaker Bridge for a 4- to 5-hour paddle that follows the narrow, winding Batsto River through Wharton State Forest to Batsto Lake at historic Batsto Village. Or opt for the 11-mile (18 km) overnight paddle down the Mullica River.

The Mullica River cuts through the New Jersey Pine Barrens.

Multicity, NJ | **Season:** Spring to fall

> ## "TRY TO REMEMBER TO TAKE IT ALL IN BECAUSE THE SCENERY AND SENSATION ARE UNMATCHED."

Free-Fall Fun

If you're looking for adrenaline-pumping adventure, Cross Keys, in southern New Jersey, is the place to dive in (literally). Known for its full-service drop zone, happy staff, and fun "boogies"—like the mid-February Freezefest and costumed Halloween jumps—it's a happy gathering place for amateurs and experts alike (as illustrated by the giant smiley face on the ground outside the hangar). With more than 10,000 jumps under their belt, plus certified and highly trained instructors, it's a great place to take your first jump.

Unlicensed divers fly tandem with an experienced instructor attached via harness. You'll receive safety training to learn how to position your body during free fall, read the altimeter on your hand to monitor your altitude, deploy the parachute, and land safely. Because the first time jumping out of a plane can be a tad mind-blowing, the instructor will help you remember important things, like pulling the rip cord.

When it's time to go, you'll board a 900-horsepower Super Grand Caravan turbine plane, which holds up to 17 people, and climb to 13,500 feet (4,115 m). When the door opens, you'll jump out and experience 60 exhilarating seconds of free fall. Try to remember to take it all in because the scenery and sensation are unmatched. When you reach 5,500 feet (1,676 m), you'll yank the rip cord and release your parachute. The sound of wind ripping by your ears will be replaced by quiet solitude as you float back to drop zone, soaking in South Jersey's patchwork landscape and Philadelphia's glimmering skyline. It may go without saying, but the extra fee to catch it all on video? Totally worth it.

Williamstown, NJ | Season: Year-round

Take to the skies on
a thrilling skydive.

Ride the Ferris wheel on
Atlantic City's Boardwalk.

1. CLIMB THE STAIRWAY TO HEAVEN

With more than 60 miles (97 km) of multiuse trails and several lakes and ponds for boating and fishing, Wawayanda State Park is a peaceful reprieve from northern Jersey's urban landscape. Climb Stairway to Heaven, a 1.3-mile (2.1 km) section of the Appalachian Trail, to Pinwheels Vista for *WOW*-ayanda views across Vernon Valley's rolling hills.

2. ROAM BENEATH THE HEMLOCKS

Legend has it, the cascading brook in Tillman Ravine was a favorite Lenape meeting place because the sound of rushing water prevented eavesdropping. Take the upper route to enjoy those serene sounds as you roam beneath the hemlocks. Return on the lower route, which skirts and crosses the brook's falling water and swimming holes.

3. BIRD-WATCH ON THE BAY

Cattus Island County Park is a hidden gem along the Central Jersey coast. A sliver of land dividing Silver and Barnegat Bays, it cradles six miles (10 km) of nature trails that meander through coastal woods, marshland, and beach. Bring binoculars to see osprey, herons, and egrets, and visit the small butterfly garden for colorful blooms and wings.

4. RIDE THE LOCKS

Once a hub for transporting coal and freight from Pennsylvania to New York, the historic Delaware and Raritan (D&R) Canal is now a 70-mile (110 km) recreation trail.

For an especially scenic stretch, ride north from Kingston Lock to Millstone Aqueduct, which hugs Carnegie Lake, where Princeton University's crew team practices.

5. CROSS MONET BRIDGE

Step through Damascus Gate at Grounds for Sculpture and follow your curiosity through the 42-acre (17 ha), fully accessible open-air museum where hands reach up through the earth, bronze bulls loll in the shade, stone monoliths invite reflection, and intimate human moments are frozen in metal. Cross Monet Bridge to see his water-lily pond come to life.

6. TRAVEL BACK IN HISTORY

In the 19th century, historic Allaire Village was Howell Iron Works, Co., a self-sufficient iron-producing town. Today, it's an outdoor living history museum with nature trails, interpreters in period costumes, and hands-on activities that provide a glimpse into the lives of the iron men and their families.

7. BIKE OR WALK ALONG THE RIVERSIDE

Historic locks and bridges link history and natural beauty along the 15.8-mile (25.4 km) riverside rail trail from Frenchtown to Lambertville. Explore the charm on bike or foot, stopping to picnic beneath sycamore shade at Bulls Island, browse local artwork at 19th-century Prallsville Mills, and visit shops and cafés in the historic bookend towns.

8. WALK THE ATLANTIC CITY BOARDWALK

Built in 1870, Atlantic City's five-mile (8 km) boardwalk is the oldest and longest in the world. It's open to cyclists daily from 6 to 10 a.m., so you can ride the boards as the sun rises over the Atlantic. Or sit back and enjoy the view from an iconic Royal Rolling Chair, a throwback to 1887.

9. CELEBRATE THE TULIPS

You don't need to travel to Holland for world-class tulips. Every April, millions of them burst into bloom at Holland Ridge Farms in Cream Ridge, and fall brings a sea of yellow sunflowers. Grab free pruning shears and a bucket and stroll down row after colorful row, clipping your favorites for $1 per stem.

10. SEE THE GULLS OF STONE HARBOR

Don't let Stone Harbor's golden sand beaches distract you from its stunning back bays and creeks. Four boat ramps provide access to this often overlooked salt marsh, which is home to the world's largest nesting colony of laughing gulls. Visit Wetlands Institute to experience this important habitat and meet its resident creatures.

Eastern black swallowtail butterfly

Williams Lake sits below
Wheeler Peak (page 441).

NEW MEXICO

From a relaxing soak in the hot springs to zipping down snowy
slopes, the Land of Enchantment has something for everyone.

UTAH

COLORADO

Rio Grande

San Juan

OKLAHOMA

Cumbres & Toltec
Scenic Railroad

Enchanted Forest
Cross Country Ski Area

Taos Ski
Valley

San Juan
River

Wheeler
Peak

Angel Fire
Bike Park

Georgia O'Keeffe
driving tour

Sangre de
Cristo Mountains

Jemez
Springs

Bandelier National
Monument

Galisteo Basin
Preserve

Paseo del
Bosque Trail

Sandia Peak
Tramway

Albuquerque

A R I Z O N A

Rio Grande
River

N E W   M E X I C O

Bosque del
Apache National
Wildlife Refuge
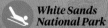

Cosmic Campground
International Dark Sky Sanctuary

Gila
Wilderness

Rio Grande

White Sands
National Park

Carlsbad Caverns
National Park

U.S.
MEXICO

Rio Grande

T E X A S

SONORA

CHIHUAHUA

The Enchanted Forest offers a network of backcountry trails for both cross-country skiers and snowshoers.

Glide Through the Enchanted Forest

The Enchanted Forest Cross Country Ski Area is just what the name implies: an otherworldly oasis of ponderosa pines and high-alpine meadows through which more than 31 miles (50 km) of groomed cross-country ski, snowshoe, and mixed-use trails meander.

Owned by Geoff and Ellen Miller Goins, the daughter of John and Judy Miller, who founded the Nordic area in 1985, Enchanted Forest is a no-frills throwback to a simpler era that sits at 9,800 feet (2,990 m) in the Sangre de Cristo Mountains on a plateau atop Bobcat Pass above the resort town of Red River. The warming hut is just that—a place to warm chilly toes and fingers and eat hot soup, perhaps alongside the University of New Mexico Nordic team that often trains here. On bluebird days, which are most days in New Mexico, the outside deck has Adirondack chairs perpetually pointed toward the sun.

Because of the high altitude, the skiing here is challenging. It requires strong cardio to ski 3.1 miles (5 km) to the summit of the Long John Hike and its pièce de résistance, the majestic view of 13,167-foot (4,013 m) Wheeler Peak, the highest point in New Mexico. For those who want to slow down and focus more on the views, four yurts are scattered throughout the 1,400-acre (565 ha) ski area. Each accommodates six to eight people, and comes equipped with a propane cookstove, wood fireplace, bunks, and a fire pit outside to stay warm while gazing at the stars after an invigorating day.

Red River, NM | Season: Winter

Natural hot springs pool high in the Jemez Mountains.

Soak It All In

For an off-the-beaten-path village in the Jemez Mountains, Jemez Springs has a rich history. Seven hundred years ago, it was Gíusewa Pueblo, home to the Walatowa, ancestors of the present-day residents of nearby Jemez Pueblo. In the 1500s the Spanish arrived and established a Catholic mission, the remains of which are still here. In 1860, a bubbling hot spring erupted into a geyser and Jemez Springs has been a spa destination ever since.

Jemez Springs Bath House, the village-owned, century-old, site on the National Register of Historic Places still offers four massage rooms, eight soaking tubs, and a free soak on your birthday. Jemez Hot Springs was renovated in 2016 and offers four outdoor pools that contain 17 healing minerals. For a more primitive setting, visitors can hike to Spence Hot Springs, a popular rocky pool seven miles (11 km) north of town that maintains a consistent 95°F (35°C) temperature spring through fall.

Jemez Springs, NM Season: Year-round

Mountain Bike Angel Fire Bike Park

Mountain biking is all about pushing boundaries. There's no better place to do that than at Angel Fire Bike Park. From May through early October, this year-round resort is a mecca for mountain bikers who pilgrimage to its 2,000 vertical feet (610 m) of lift-served trails.

More than 30 mostly downhill trails are designed and built specifically for mountain biking and carve through aspens and ponderosas; around large bermed corners; over rollers, rock gardens, and human-made wooden features; and, on some trails, over gap jumps and tabletops.

Brush up at the skills park at the base, then take the lift up to the 10,650-foot (3,250 m) summit and pick your thrill, from one of three easy green runs to a plethora of intermediate, advanced, and expert-only runs. The pinnacle of achievement is the mountain's one "Pro Line," a trail that requires high speed and even higher skill to clear the massive, mandatory gap jumps.

Angel Fire, NM Season: Late spring to early fall

There are mountain bike trails for riders of all levels.

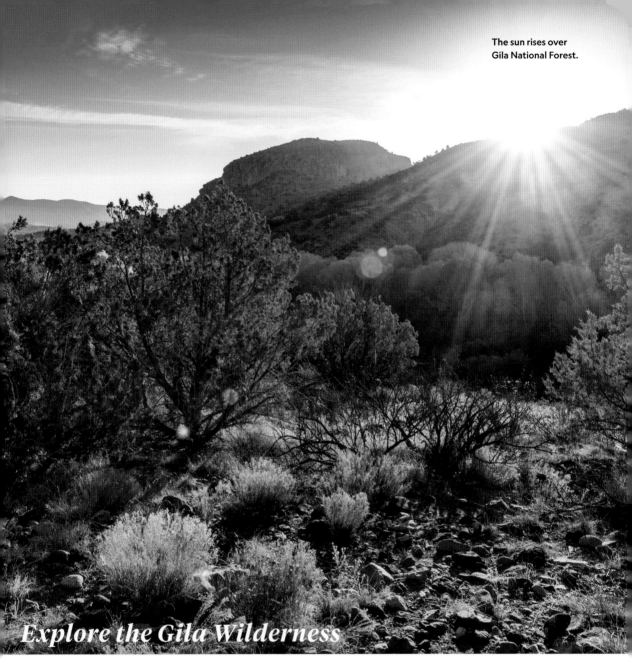

The sun rises over Gila National Forest.

Explore the Gila Wilderness

The Gila Wilderness, an 874-square-mile (2,264 km²) swath of mountains and desert surrounding southwest New Mexico's Gila River, has been home to humans for more than 10,000 years. In 1924, the "Gila," as it is known, became the first federally recognized wilderness in the country, "an area where the earth and its community of life are untrammeled by man, where man himself is a visitor who does not remain."

Today the Gila is still rugged, hard-to-navigate country where the peaks of the Mogollon Mountains, the southernmost terminus of the Rockies, converge with the Chihuahuan and Sonoran Desert landscapes. Visitors can enjoy hundreds of miles of hiking and horseback trails, fly-fish for cutthroat trout, bask in the silence of this vast wilderness, or try to imagine life as it was in the 13th century by visiting the 1,533-acre (620 ha) Gila Cliff Dwellings built by the Mogollon culture around 1280.

Silver City, NM | **Season:** Year-round

> ## "IT'S EASY TO BE INTIMIDATED BY TAOS'S FAMOUSLY STEEP TERRAIN."

Ski Taos

Taos Ski Valley is where traditions of the European Alps meet bluebird sky, champagne powder, and the laid-back vibe of the Southwest. This unlikely convergence at 9,200 feet (2,800 m) in the southern Rockies' Sangre de Cristo Mountains, is thanks to a legendary German immigrant named Ernie Blake.

Blake, who grew up skiing in Switzerland, immigrated to the United States in 1939. He eventually moved to New Mexico, where he, his wife, Rhoda, and their growing family lived in an 11-foot (3 m) RV for months in the shadow of 13,161-foot (4,012 m) Mount Wheeler, the state's highest peak, to realize their dream of creating an Alps-style ski area.

The Blake family sold the resort in 2013, but today's skiers and snowboarders still reap the rewards of their vision and tireless work. A local favorite is boot packing with skis and boards slung over shoulders to the top of Highline Ridge to ski powdery tree runs like Tresckow or lounging slopeside while eating Wiener schnitzel at the Bavarian restaurant at the mountain's base.

It's easy to be intimidated by Taos's famously steep terrain, especially looking straight up at Al's Run, a bumpy, narrow, black diamond, one of the only slopes visible from the base. But Taos is equally world renowned for its Ski Week program in which instructors teach the most weak-kneed beginners how to safely ride any slope.

On days when the legs are too rubbery to slide downhill, head 20 miles (32 km) down the mountain to Taos, a free-spirited high-desert village of 6,000 residents. It offers galleries and fascinating museums, like the former home of legendary frontiersman Kit Carson. Look for restaurants tucked away in centuries-old adobes with organic northern New Mexico cuisine. Nearby Taos Pueblo, a UNESCO World Heritage site, is a Native American community that has been continuously inhabited for almost 1,000 years.

Taos Ski Valley, NM | **Season:** Winter

Taos Ski Valley offers more than 100 trails off its peaks.

Hike Through Ancestral Grounds

Peaceful solitude emanates from Frijoles Canyon, the centerpiece of Bandelier National Monument that sits at 6,000 feet (1,830 m) in the Jemez Mountains. It's easy to see why the ancestral Puebloan people settled here in 1150: Its 500-foot-high (150 m) canyon walls offered protection, and Frijoles Creek provided irrigation for corn, beans, and squash.

Around 1550, the ancestral Puebloans moved on to communities near the Rio Grande, most of which are still thriving today. It's fascinating to see the structures they left behind: dwellings dug from volcanic tuff of canyon walls, underground kivas that served as spiritual centers of the community, and the remains of Tyuonyi, once a two-story pueblo that housed 100 people—all of which can be viewed by walking the 1.4-mile (2.3 km) Pueblo Loop Trail from the visitors center. Farther afield are miles of back-country trails that lead to ancient pictographs and expansive views of the mountains of northern New Mexico.

Los Alamos, NM | Season: Year-round

Ancient cliff dwellings are preserved at Bandelier National Monument.

Bird-Watching at Bosque del Apache National Wildlife Refuge

This unassuming 57,331-acre (23,201 ha) refuge along the Rio Grande is bisected by I-25. It's easy to whiz by on the interstate, mesmerized by the wide-open spaces bordering the Chupadera Mountains to the west and the San Pascual Mountains to the east. Starting in late October, however, this oasis of cottonwood and willow trees hugging the river becomes a critical stopover site for tens of thousands of cranes, geese, and ducks migrating south every year.

Into January, Bosque del Apache is a world-class bird-watching destination, especially for those who love sandhill cranes. These slender, long-legged, slate-colored birds put on a lively performance with at least 10 different calls, multiple threatening postures, and elaborate dances.

Western kingbird

In spring, wildflowers start to bloom, and the cranes, geese, and ducks fly north, leaving room in the waterway for smaller migrating birds like sandpipers, plovers, avocets, and a dozen species of warblers.

Each season brings its own rich scenery and wildlife sightings. The refuge offers 11 hiking trails and one bike path to explore the varied habitats—from the bosque to a desert arboretum to distant peaks. One great way to stretch the legs is to hike the 9.5-mile (15.3 km) round-trip trail to the summit of Chupadera Peak.

San Antonio, NM | Season: Year-round

Balloon Over Albuquerque

Pigs do fly. You will likely see one (along with monkeys, giant babies, and other inflated objects) soaring across a cerulean sky at the world's largest balloon festival. The Albuquerque International Balloon Fiesta, which takes place over nine days every October at the aptly named 360-acre (145 ha) Balloon Fiesta Park directly north of Albuquerque, attracts more than 500 brilliantly colored balloons from around the world.

Visitors can watch the action while eating their way through green chile cheeseburgers, burritos, and other New Mexican fare offered on-site, or sign up to soar with Rainbow Ryders, the only concession authorized to take the public up in the sky. Two events not to miss: The morning Special Shape Rodeo features 100-odd, oddly shaped balloons, like an octopus, honeybee, Uncle Sam, or Darth Vader. The showstopper, however, is the Mass Ascension, a two-stage launch of all partici-pating bal-loons at 7 a.m. rising into the sky as "The Star-Spangled Ban-ner" reverberates from below.

Balloons aren't the only things in the sky. Come dark, watch the night light up with an aerial light show during which drones make pictures in the sky. Skydivers also put on a perfor-mance on select nights. Stay for the closing night's "AfterGlow" firework display.

Back on solid ground, festivalgoers can watch carvers in a chain saw exhibition turn logs of wood into sculptures of bears, eagles, and other animals. And bring your camera: The Fiesta hosts a photo competition from the events.

Albuquerque, NM | Season: October

White Sands is a one-of-a-kind national park with plenty to explore.

Sled the White Sands

Sprawling across 275 miles (443 km) of the Chihuahuan Desert in south-central New Mexico, the world's largest gypsum sand dunes make up one of our nation's newest national parks. From a distance, these shifting mounds could easily be mistaken for snow-covered hills, which is a good reason to sled down them.

Before your first descent, take a ranger-guided hike to Lake Lucero, offered between November and April, to understand how the dunes form. At this dry lake bed, wind-deposited gypsum precipitates into crystals of impure brown selenite found on mudflats of the shore-line. These crystals eventually erode into sand grains that ultimately blow into towering dunes.

At the park gift store, buy a waxed, plastic flying saucer, find a gently sloping dune with a level landing spot, sit or lie feet facing downhill, and take off.

White Sands, NM | Season: Year-round

The Rio Grande offers thrill
seekers wild rapids.

> "WITH NINE RAFTABLE SECTIONS, PADDLERS CAN CHOOSE THEIR LEVEL OF 'STOKE.'"

White-Water Raft the Rio Grande

In 1968, Congress designated a 55.7-mile (89.6 km) northern New Mexico section of the 1,900-mile-long (3,060 km) Rio Grande as one of the original eight National Wild and Scenic River sections in the United States. The designation, which protects "rivers with outstanding natural, cultural, and recreational values in a free-flowing condition," is well deserved.

From above, the path of the river looks like a hot butter knife sliced through the stunning Rio Grande Gorge, a box canyon with imposing 800-foot-high (240 m) walls. Within the gorge are hot springs, ancestral Puebloan petroglyphs, and an exploding population of bighorn sheep that perch in seemingly impossible places. Farther downstream, along the Race Course section, paddlers often unwittingly pass 1.4-billion-year-old granite and quartzite.

Unlike many other western rivers, where water flows have decreased to the point of being unrunnable, this northern section of the Rio Grande is never too low to run, thanks to downstream irrigation water rights. And because the river is so far south, the season is seven months long, from March through September. With nine raftable sections between the Upper and Lower Gorges, paddlers can choose their level of "stoke," from placid, gentle Class I moving flat water that's ideal for swimming and bird-watching to gripping Class IV+ white water in the iconic Taos Box section in the heart of the gorge.

New Mexico River Adventures, in the village of Embudo, offers half- to full-day to 24-hour adventures on this stunning river. Their well-trained guides, renowned as the region's swift-water safety specialists, train other companies' white-water guides.

Embudo, NM | **Season:** March to September

Colorful meadows sit in the valley of Wheeler Peak.

1. CAMP AT THE COSMIC CAMPGROUND

This primitive site with four concrete observation pads designed for telescopes in Gila National Forest has the unique distinction of being one of only 15 certified International Dark Sky Sanctuaries in the world. Pitch a tent here and have unfettered, 360-degree views of the night sky. The nearest significant source of light is more than 40 miles (64 km) away across the state line in Arizona.

2. CYCLE THE PASEO DEL BOSQUE TRAIL

Albuquerque's 16-mile-long (26 km), paved, multiuse trail follows the meandering Rio Grande from Alameda Boulevard in the north through the heart of downtown all the way south to the Rio Bravo Riverside Picnic Area. Its crowning glories are the enormous cottonwood trees that provide shade along the river.

3. HORSEBACK RIDE THE GALISTEO BASIN PRESERVE

This former 10,000-acre (4,050 ha) ranch south of Santa Fe offers 25 miles (40 km) of trails for equestrians. Ride through wide-open savanna grasslands bisected by sandy arroyos and craggy sandstone formations. Two of three trailheads have designated spaces for horse trailers. Nearby Galisteo Creek Stables offers trail rides for beginners.

4. WATCH BATS AT CARLSBAD CAVERNS NATIONAL PARK

Every evening from May to October, thousands of Brazilian free-tailed bats take leave from the Natural Entrance to Carlsbad Caverns, spiraling outward always in a counterclockwise direction to search for food. Watch this exhilarating mass ascension from the Bat Flight Amphitheater near the entrance, where a ranger explains other fascinating bat behavior.

5. RIDE SANDIA PEAK AERIAL TRAMWAY

This 15-minute ride ascends from the hustle of Albuquerque to the 10,378-foot (3,163 m) summit of Sandia Peak. In addition to stunning 11,000-square-mile (28,490 km^2) views, the tramway accesses the peaceful Cibola National Forest, home to 100 miles (160 km) of hiking trails and the now defunct Sandia Peak Ski Area. It's open year-round, save for two weeks in April and November.

6. RIDE THE CUMBRES AND TOLTEC SCENIC RAILROAD

This restored 1880s steam train chugs for 64 stunning miles (103 km) along the longest and highest narrow-gauge railroad in the country. Starting in the northern New Mexico village of Chama, it climbs over 10,015-foot-high (3,053 m) Cumbres Pass and zigzags across the state border 11 times before descending to Antonito, Colorado.

7. SUMMIT WHEELER PEAK

At 13,161 feet (4,011 m), New Mexico's highest mountain may be slightly lower than its Colorado neighbors, but standing at its exposed summit is still a thrill. There's more than one way to reach the top, but the 6.3-mile (10.1 km) one-way Williams Lake to Wheeler Peak Summit Trail is the most beautiful.

8. DRIVE GEORGIA O'KEEFFE COUNTRY

The legendary 20th-century artist painted 9,866-foot (3,007 m) Cerro Pedernal at least 29 times. View the real flat-topped landmark and O'Keeffe's many other muses by driving 48 miles (77 km) northwest of Santa Fe to take the wildly popular tour of her home and studio in the village of Abiquiú, which sits in the shadow of her beloved mountain.

9. FLY-FISH THE SAN JUAN RIVER

The four-mile (6 km) stretch of the San Juan River below Navajo Lake Dam in the state's northwest corner is one of the most hallowed and productive trout streams in the country, producing rainbows and browns that average 16 to 18 inches (41 to 46 cm). Fish it year-round with Orvis-endorsed outfitter Fisheads San Juan River Lodge.

10. LLAMA TREK THE SANGRE DE CRISTOS

Let a sure-footed ungulate shoulder the load on a multiday family trek exploring the thick woods and high-alpine tundra of northern New Mexico's Carson National Forest. Wild Earth Llama Adventures will design a safe, educational, age-appropriate itinerary, with guides who understand kids and provide meals that even your pickiest eater will love.

Autumn colors take over
upstate New York.

NEW YORK

There's so much more to the Empire State than the Big Apple—from skiing upstate to sandy shores on the coast to a robust wine region in the Finger Lakes.

ONTARIO

Wellesley Island
State Park

CANADA
U.S.

Lake Ontario

Sandy Island Beach
State Park

Selkirk Shores
State Park

NEW

Canalside

Finger
Lakes

Bristol
Mountain

Taughannock Fall
State Park

Lake Erie

PENNSYLVANIA

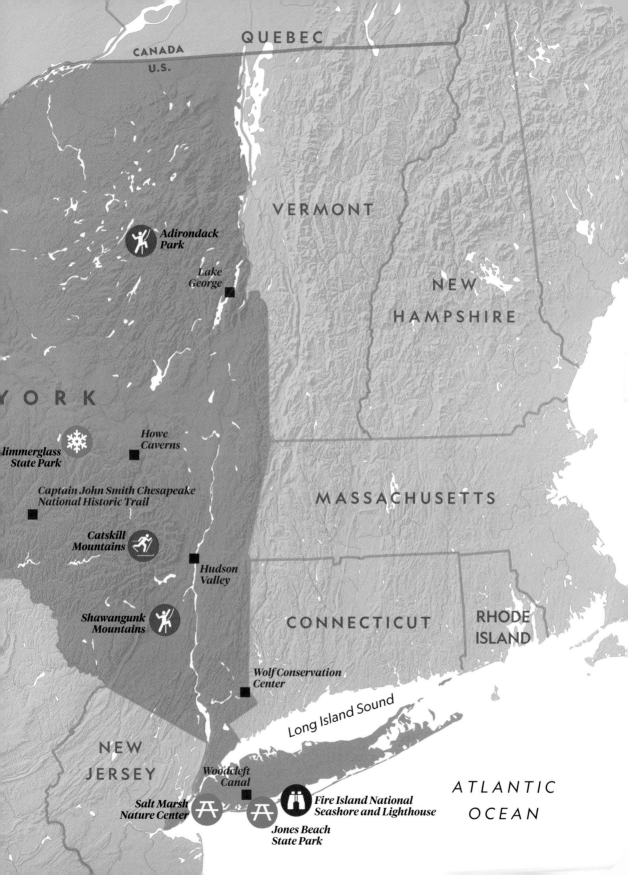

QUEBEC

CANADA
U.S.

VERMONT

NEW
HAMPSHIRE

*Adirondack
Park*

*Lake
George*

YORK

*Howe
Caverns*

*limmerglass
State Park*

MASSACHUSETTS

*Captain John Smith Chesapeake
National Historic Trail*

*Catskill
Mountains*

*Hudson
Valley*

*Shawangunk
Mountains*

CONNECTICUT

RHODE
ISLAND

*Wolf Conservation
Center*

Long Island Sound

NEW
JERSEY

*Woodcleft
Canal*

ATLANTIC
OCEAN

*Salt Marsh
Nature Center*

*Fire Island National
Seashore and Lighthouse*

*Jones Beach
State Park*

Get in the Groove at Jones Beach State Park

The 6.5 miles (10.5 km) of bright white sand in Jones Beach State Park welcome six million visitors each year, making it an extra lively spot to catch some sun. After swimming in the Atlantic, you can head to the boardwalk to try your hand at miniature golf, work on your shuffleboard game, or get adventurous at Wild-Play's zip-line park and ropes course.

The water brings many New Yorkers out in summer, but not everyone comes to the park for a day on the beach. Northwell Health at Jones Beach Theater brings big names to its stage and 15,000 guests to enjoy performances under the stars. Hundreds of shows have echoed across the theater and into the park since it first started presenting musicals in the 1950s. (Jimmy Buffett, James Taylor, and Aerosmith have played here more than 20 times.) Seats at the outdoor amphitheater look out over the ocean, and at the right time of year, concertgoers can pair their show with a fiery seaside sunset.

Jones Beach Island, NY | **Season:** Year-round

See live performances at the boardwalk band shell.

World-Class Skiing in the Catskills

Natural snowfalls and towering mountains provide a winter wonderland in the Catskills for skiers and snowboarders. With snowy runs all over the range and lodges scattered at the base of the mountains, the area is perfect for beginners and experts, families and solo riders, downhill and cross-country skiers—everyone has a place at this world-class ski spot.

The range at Hunter Mountain Resort reflects that inclusivity. The resort boasts wide cruising lanes for new skiers and boarders. Experts also flock to the resort, and one of its three mountains, Hunter West, hosts only black and double black diamond trails.

Windham Mountain combines excellent skiing with small-town charm. Boarders and skiers can kick off their boots after a day on the slopes and relax at the resort's spa or sit down for a meal at its Tavern 23 restaurant. If the priority is catching as many runs as possible, you can instead opt to grab a bite at one of its on-mountain food trucks.

Cross-country skiers and snowshoers can follow the 26-mile (42 km) Catskill Scenic Trail. The mostly flat path will glide visitors through snowy scenes out of a film.

Scenic views greet skiers below challenging slopes.

Catskills, NY | **Season:** Winter

Make Your Way Up the Gunks

This renowned climbing epicenter, one of the oldest in the country, is only 85 miles (137 km) from New York City. Even with that accessibility, it feels a million miles away from the hustle and bustle. The Trapps, the most popular cliff on the mountain, is accessible by a gravel road and a series of trails—and the cliff ranges in height from 30 to 250 feet (9 to 76 m).

Weekend climbing warriors make their way to the Shawangunks, affectionately known as the Gunks, in the spring, summer, and fall—but the mountain really shines in September and October. Climbers will have to book early to beat out the foliage folks for hotel and restaurant reservations—like those at the iconic castle-like Mohonk Mountain House—but planning ahead will ensure you don't miss out on the best season of the year. If you're up for more rustic digs, The American Alpine Club and the Mohonk Preserve operate and manage a campground with 50 campsites and six vehi-

cle sites with a bathhouse and covered pavilion. If you find your way to the walls in the summer, you can escape the stifling heat at the nearby swimming hole.

The quartz conglomerate on the mountain makes for solid routes, and the cracks run horizontally up the walls, rather than vertically. The routes are traditional, with plenty of traverses, roofs, and jugs to be tackled. Although you'll find a few bolted climbs, you won't find any sport climbs. Overall, climbers should be thoughtful about their skill level and wary of + ratings. Experts suggest dropping down a few grades while you get comfortable in the space. Climbers will be rewarded tenfold for their patience and persistence.

Multicity, NY | **Season:** Spring to fall

The Fire Island Lighthouse stands above grassy sand dunes.

Blaze the Way on Fire Island

At 168 feet (51 m) high, the Fire Island Lighthouse is the tallest on Long Island. To reach the top, with its New York City skyline views, you'll have to climb 182 steps—and stepping is something you'll be doing a lot of on your visit. You can arrive at the island by ferry, public transportation, or car, but although bridges connect either end with the mainland, the roads stop there. You'll have to rely on water taxis, bicycles, and your feet to get around.

Hikers searching for a unique way to experience the lighthouse can join the guided Fall Twilight Trek, a nine-mile (14.5 km) walk that starts at Fire Island Pines and ends at the landmark. This registration-required hike takes seven hours and is not for the faint of heart.

Fire Island, NY | **Season:** Year-round

The Finger Lakes region boasts
more than 100 wineries.

> "BIKING ADDS A LEVEL OF ADVENTURE TO THE CHARM OF THE LAKES."

Pedal to Vines

America's first wine trail was born in the Finger Lakes. Five wineries came together in 1983 to establish the Cayuga Lake Wine Trail, declaring that visitors would find "a variety that is unmatched in wine tasting and touring." The claim still stands—and it's grown. The Cayuga Trail now travels between 13 wineries, and it's not the only route to take. Eight wineries have joined the Keuka Lake Wine Trail, and the Seneca Lake Wine Trail will bring guests to more than 30 wineries.

Guests can book a driver to visit any of the region's 100 or so wineries, but ditching four wheels for two will give you a deeper feel for this idyllic land. Biking adds a level of adventure to the charm of the lakes, where wineries are open year-round and consistently produce award-winning bottles.

Intrepid cyclists can plan their own trips through New York's wine country, mapping out routes on country roads that connect the lakes and marking their chosen stops along the way. If you're doing it on your own, it's a good idea to pop into one of the area's long-standing bike shops for local insights and to be sure your bike is up for the task. Corning Bike Works and Wheels Unlimited have been serving cyclists at Finger Lakes for decades.

For those who prefer to have someone else guide the trip, multiple outfitters will do the hard work—besides the pedaling. The New York Finger Lakes Bike Tour from Wilderness Voyageurs will have cyclists rolling to wineries, restaurants, ice cream shops, waterfalls, and inns at the shores of the wine region's three major lakes. Carolina Tailwinds hosts a NY Finger Lakes Tour that starts just outside Ithaca and spends six days winding through small towns, lakeshore inns, and countryside wineries.

Finger Lakes Region, NY | **Season:** Spring to fall

Winter at the Beach

Although Glimmerglass State Park draws visitors in the summer months to its clear waters and sandy beaches, winter guests will find a different type of joy in a snow-covered landscape. The trails that showcase wildflowers and grassy fields in warm weather become perfect paths for snowshoers.

Take your snowshoes out on the Sleeping Lion Trail, which runs for about 2.5 miles (4 km) through hemlock woods and around the shoulder of Mount Wellington. You'll catch views of Otsego Lake on the way down until you finally reach the road and follow it to Hyde Hall, a restored neoclassical country mansion constructed in the early 19th century.

To avoid the strain of the mountain but still enjoy the snowy scenery, snowshoe your way to Hyde Hall Covered Bridge, the only one still standing in the county. Built in 1825, the 53-foot (16 m) bridge is the oldest existing wooden covered bridge in the United States.

Cooperstown, NY | **Season:** Winter

> "WINTER GUESTS WILL FIND A DIFFERENT TYPE OF JOY IN A SNOW-COVERED LANDSCAPE: WILDFLOWERS AND GRASSY FIELDS BECOME PERFECT PATHS FOR SNOWSHOERS."

Winter visitors to Glimmerglass State Park can snowshoe, cross-country ski, ice-skate, take winter hikes, or go ice fishing.

Salt Marsh Nature Center is the largest of five New York City nature centers and overlooks Marine Park Alliance's Forever Wild Preserve.

Big Nature in the Big City

New York City's urbanites needn't go far to find immersive natural experiences. Brooklyn's Salt Marsh Nature Center, with its focus on education and ecology, is a community gathering place for admirers of all things green.

The best way to discover the marsh is across its still water. Drop into Wheel Fun Rentals across the street from the center to borrow a kayak, double kayak, or stand-up paddleboard to ply marsh waters. They'll even rent you a dry bag to pack your picnic lunch. From your board, you can navigate the wetlands and take in the native flora and fauna. Venturing just beyond the center, you can paddle around Mau Mau Island and meet the ducks and geese that home in the open waters of nearby Gerritsen Creek.

These birds aren't the only wildlife in the marsh, which welcomes cormorants, sandpipers, herons, egrets, black-birds, and hawks, and protects young fish, shrimp, and crabs before they venture out to sea. Children can learn more about the creatures, along with the city's environmental and cultural history, in the center's natural classroom.

There are also opportunities for exploration by foot, and the center makes an excellent starting point for wandering Marine Park, the borough's biggest park at 530 acres (215 ha) of protected space, including grassland and salt marsh. Protected as a Forever Wild Preserve, the park is worth exploring by self-guided tour on the Salt Marsh Nature Trail. The loop trail will lead you through this distinct ecosystem and to nearby outdoor activities, including the Lenape Playground, bocce courts, bicycle greenways, cricket fields, and Marine Park golf course. The park also has a launch and landing site for kayakers to use at Gerritsen Inlet. On the other side of the water, you'll find Seba Skate Park, a series of sports fields, and a model aircraft field.

Brooklyn, NY   Season: Year-round

The state park protects both dunes and birdlife.

Birds, Dunes, and More

 The sand dunes of the 17-mile (27 km) Eastern Lake Ontario Barrier Beach and Wetland Complex serve as a buffer to protect the wetlands at Sandy Island Beach State Park from the winds and waves of the ocean. This uncommon ecosystem provides a remarkable defensive space for rare migratory birds, and sandpipers, plovers, killdeer, and gulls all make their way onto the island each year.

Birders can walk the beach, portions of which are only accessible by boat, and use the island's raised viewing platforms to protect the dunes—and its rare plants, including the dune willow, dune grass, and sand cherry—while they search for the park's unique wildlife.

Although Sandy Island Beach is open for swimmers and boaters, its purpose is preservation. The park's small bird sanctuary at Sandy Pond Beach is closed during nesting season, allowing the best chance at breeding.

Pulaski, NY | **Season:** Year-round

Get the Adrenaline Soaring

Build your confidence while soaring through the sky at Bristol Mountain. Reserve time at Bristol Mountain Aerial Adventures' Aerial Adventure Park and challenge yourself on the course's zip lines, tightrope walks, rope ladders, and bridges. With seven courses, there's truly something to test everyone's grit. You'll bond with the other bold guests as you wiggle and wobble through your lofty journey. If you prefer to adventure without onlookers, however, you can avoid the group session and book a private one.

At the Kids Adventure Park, children between the ages of four and seven can tackle the same kind of course, but closer to the ground. With harnesses meant for kids, they'll climb over unsteady caterpillars, hang onto rock walls, and glide along kid-size zip lines—all under the supervision of a Bristol Mountain staff member.

For views of the forest canopy along with your circuslike thrills, join the Zipline Canopy Tour. You'll strap your harness into seven zip lines that cover 5,000 feet (1,525 m) across the sky, with the longest one running for 1,600 feet (490 m). To get the lines, you'll hike through the woods, take an off-road ride, and cross swinging bridges over green ravines.

If you can't make it to the mountain or want to bring the fun to your own backyard, the company will transport its Mobile Park to you. The system is meant for children and contains eight elements to test balance and bravery, from rope nets to balance beams.

Canandaigua, NY | **Season:** Year-round

Ausable Chasm is a two-mile (3.2 km) gorge in upstate New York.

Ice Climb the Adirondacks

When temperatures drop in the Adirondacks, flowing waterfalls freeze, creating massive ice walls that tempt cold-weather climbers. One of the earliest in the season to form and last to go, Cascade Pass is a popular, though windy, roadside route at Pitchoff Mountain. The North Face of Pitchoff, on the other hand, is a quiet, more remote spot where climbers will be rewarded for withstanding its exposure with remarkable views over the mountains. Determined climbers can search for a crevice along Route 86 near Whiteface Mountain Ski Resort to find Multiplication Gully, a hidden ice chute framed by rock walls.

Unless you're an experienced climber with the gear to get up these walls, you'll need a guide to ensure a safe and successful trip. High Peaks Mountain Guides provides lessons to level up your winter climbing.

Lake Placid, NY   **Season:** Winter

Fall is the perfect time for fishing the Selkirk Shores on Lake Ontario.

1. SPELUNK BY LANTERN AT HOWE CAVERNS

Explore limestone caverns carved millions of years ago and discovered just before the Civil War at this popular upstate attraction. Howe Caverns offers walking and boat tours, evening tours by lantern, and family flashlight tours—or put on a pair of coveralls and a headlamp and spelunk your way through these underground passages.

2. HIKE FROZEN WATERFALLS

The cascades at Taughannock Falls State Park are spectacular when they're flowing, but the 215-foot (66 m) falls send a barrage of ice across the gorge in winter. You can typically hike the 1.5-mile (2.4 km) out-and-back trail to the base year-round, and guided hikes are held even in the coldest months.

3. FOLLOW THE CAPTAIN JOHN SMITH

Nearly 15,000 years of culture are packed into the 3,000-mile (4,830 km) Captain John Smith Chesapeake National Historic Trail. The route combines the paths of John Smith's voyages through the Chesapeake Bay and its tributaries, and the northernmost portion runs through the state to New York's Otsego Lake. Follow the yellow "smart buoys" to explore the cultural and ecological significance of the trail.

4. SNOWMOBILE UPSTATE

Winter wilderness abounds at Lake George during the snowy season, and snowmobilers will find long straightaways and wooded corridors that wind up mountains and across frozen rivers. These well-maintained trails run past bars and restaurants, making it easy for riders to stop for sustenance along the way.

5. ICE-SKATE BUFFALO'S CANALSIDE

Downtown Buffalo's waterfront is booming, and the Ice at Canalside keeps the fun going through winter. Guests can rent skates and hit the ice, or for those who want to go bladeless, there are sections for curling and bumper cars. To stay warm, groups can rent igloos with complimentary hot cocoa.

6. SNOW TUBE THE HUDSON VALLEY

With its tremendous snowfall, consistent cold, and mountainous landscapes, the Hudson Valley is a prime spot for winter adventures. With little skill required, tubing is a mostly inclusive cold-weather activity. Even little ones won't be left out at Mount Peter, where its Little Tikes Tubing section ensures fun for the whole family.

7. HAVE A WINTER CAMP-SITE TO YOURSELF

Spend a winter evening at one of the secluded, rustic cabins at Wellesley Island State Park. Cross-country ski your way to the Minna Anthony Common Nature Center, where you can warm up by the fireplace and search for bald eagles soaring in the sky.

8. CALL OF THE WILD

The focus of the Wolf Conservation Center is solely to protect critically endangered wolves, boost the population, and provide public education. Guests can observe the three ambassador wolves that reside at the educational exhibit, while the rest are supported through carefully managed breeding and wild reintroduction.

9. BLUFF CAMPING ON THE BORDER

Wake up to sunrise views over Lake Ontario after spending the night camping at Selkirk Shores State Park's bluffs. Bring your binoculars to spot the region's migratory birds and time your hike on the Selkirk Lakeshore and Buck Alley Trail Loop to catch sunset views on the lakeside portion.

10. GO FISHING IN FREEPORT

Once an oystering community, Freeport lives on as a popular fishing hub. The Nautical Mile along the Woodcleft Canal is packed with seafood restaurants, boat rental spots, and charter outfitters. Book a trip out of the marina with one of the many groups offering shoreline and offshore expeditions.

North American beaver

Rosebay rhododendrons bloom
on Mount Mitchell (page 469).

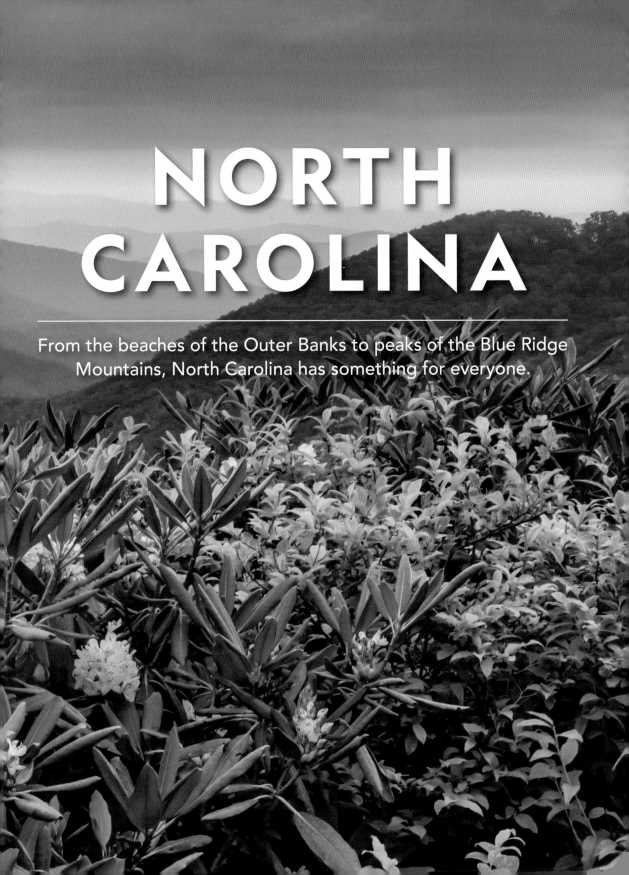

NORTH CAROLINA

From the beaches of the Outer Banks to peaks of the Blue Ridge Mountains, North Carolina has something for everyone.

KENTUCKY

TENNESSEE

Sugar Mountain
Resort

Hanging Rock
State Park

Mile High
Swinging Bridge

Linville Gorge
Wilderness

Table Rock
Mountain

Mount
Mitchell

Blue Ridge
Mountains

NORTH

Biltmore
Forest

Pisgah
Inn

Green
River

Uwharrie National
Forest

Whiteside
Mountain

DuPont State
Recreational Forest

SOUTH CAROLINA

GEORGIA

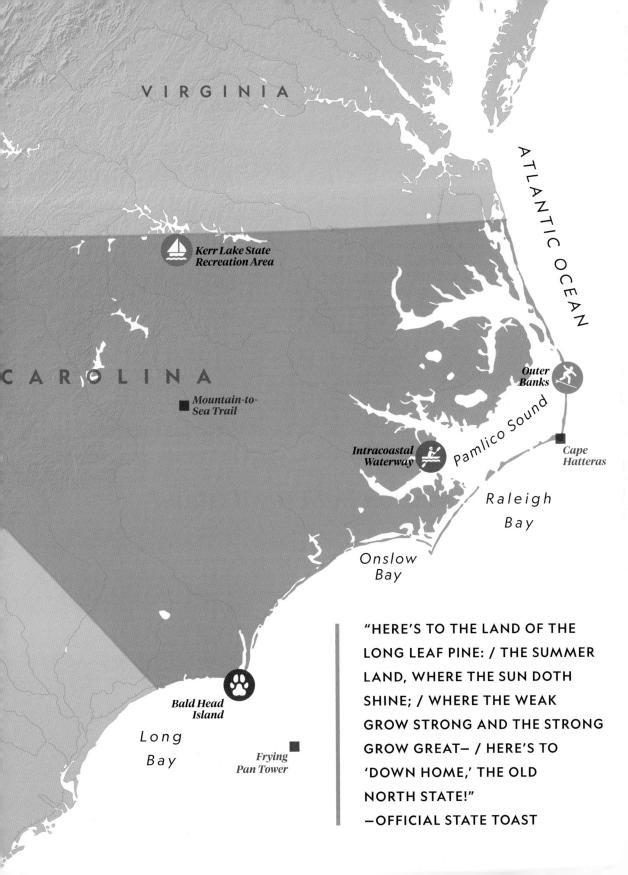

VIRGINIA

ATLANTIC OCEAN

Kerr Lake State
Recreation Area

CAROLINA

Mountain-to-
Sea Trail

Outer
Banks

Pamlico Sound

Intracoastal
Waterway

Cape
Hatteras

Raleigh
Bay

Onslow
Bay

Bald Head
Island

Long
Bay

Frying
Pan Tower

"HERE'S TO THE LAND OF THE
LONG LEAF PINE: / THE SUMMER
LAND, WHERE THE SUN DOTH
SHINE; / WHERE THE WEAK
GROW STRONG AND THE STRONG
GROW GREAT— / HERE'S TO
'DOWN HOME,' THE OLD
NORTH STATE!"
—OFFICIAL STATE TOAST

Winter and Summer in the Mountains

Skiers and snowboarders will find 21 slopes on Sugar Mountain Resort's 125 acres (50 ha) of skiable terrain, which gets increasingly more challenging as you rise up the mountain. Most of these runs are available at night when striking sunsets warm the cold sky.

Beyond downhill snow sports, guests can ice-skate at the outdoor rink or take a guided snowshoe tour. Tubing down 700-foot (210 m) lanes is made even better by the Magic Carpet that quickly and easily takes you back up the hill. Winter events, like a New Year's Eve alpine torchlight parade or the mountain's winter music series, provide entertainment for visitors willing to bear the cold.

Although the resort was built for snow sports, you'll find plenty of mountain activity when it's warm. Chairlifts take bikers to either trails or its terrain park, while the annual Sugar Mountain Resort Summit Crawl calls hikers to reach the 5,300-foot (1,615 m) peak by foot.

Sugar Mountain, NC | Season: Summer and winter

Look out to Tyne Castle from the top of Sugar Mountain.

Ditch the Wheels on Bald Head Island

Leave your car behind and board the 20-minute ferry across Cape Fear River to Bald Head Island. Out of the island's 12,000 acres (4,860 ha), 10,000 acres (4,050 ha) are untouched and preserved beaches, marsh, or maritime forests. This protection makes it a safe harbor for marine wildlife, including the loggerhead sea turtles who return to the island each summer to lay their eggs. The Bald Head Island Conservancy ensures the animals safely make their way into the ocean. You can join its efforts by participating in a Turtle Walk and volunteering to monitor the nests on the beach.

At summer's start, volunteers watch out for the nesting mothers. In mid-August, they begin paying close attention to nests under the sand, looking for the moment when they begin to "boil," or churn, as hatchlings dig their way out of the sand. If you're lucky enough to catch these tiny turtles as they rear their heads and scuttle toward the sea, you'll be part of a magical moment like no other.

Turtles aren't the only wildlife that calls the island home. Offshore fishers with a valid North Carolina fishing license will find tuna, grouper, and mackerel.

Spot turtles from sandbars on Bald Head Island.

Bald Head Island, NC | Season: Summer

Extreme Paddling on the Green River

Tree-lined and thrilling, the Green River Gorge has made its mark on white-water paddling. A dam-released flow, Green River is essentially split into three sections for aquatic adventurers. The Upper Green is best for moderate paddlers looking to up their game. This section winds for miles and shifts between Class II and III rapids, with two Class IV drops in the mix.

Next comes the Narrows, which might be the world's most famous spot for steep creeking, a movement that requires drastically lowering into low-level white water. Only the most experienced kayakers should tackle this section. The Green River Narrows Race—the world's largest extreme kayak race—draws more than 2,000 spectators each year.

The Lower Green releases the intensity built above it and becomes the perfect spot for beginners. Those looking to leisurely paddle down a slow-flowing river will find an afternoon well spent in this section, and plenty of outfitters will help make rafting trips a breeze.

Paddling isn't the only wet and wild adventure in the gorge. If you want to stay in the water but ditch the paddles, rappel down Big Bradley Waterfall, a 200-foot (60 m) drop covered in splashing water and salamanders. If you prefer to stay dry, book a zip-line adventure over the gorge. The Gorge offers a canopy tour that includes a section called the steepest and fastest zipline in America. Brave visitors can strap in to descend 1,100 vertical feet (335 m) over 1.25 miles (2 km) and 11 ziplines. Along with the thrilling speed of the ziplines, the canopy tour also includes traversing a sky bridge and descending with three huge rappels. It's not just about the thrills here; the tour works its way from the rim of the gorge through stunning old-growth forests with sweeping views of the Green River game lands.

Multicity, NC | Season: Spring to fall

Make your way to Triple Falls in DuPont State Recreational Forest.

Blue Ridge Biking

Bike trails weave through the Blue Ridge Mountains in DuPont State Recreational Forest, where ecological national resource management reigns king. Bikers should be ready for a rugged experience and should keep a map for their own navigation. The park has limited options for drinking water, no food services, and restricted cell service, but knowledgeable staff at the visitors center can help you plan your routes.

Choosing from 86 trails, cyclists can ride easy forest roads or rip-roar through riveting single-track. Routes will cross large granite domes, weave through forests, and travel along sandy paths. Because the park was developed with the goal of serving all its guests, mountain bikers are expected to stick to established trails. These all-are-welcome roads and trails run past waterfalls, lakes, and woodlands.

Cedar Mountain, NC | Season: Spring to fall

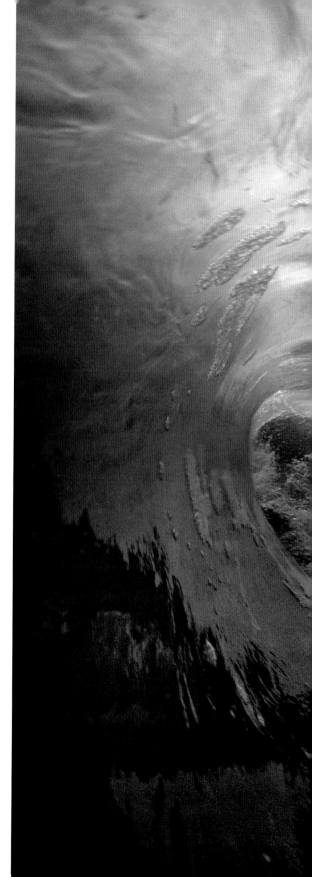

"NEWCOMERS CAN ENJOY WAVES ALONGSIDE EXPERTS."

Make Waves at the Outer Banks

The Outer Banks, a chain of islands off the coast of mainland North Carolina, have more than 100 miles (160 km) of shoreline, and much of it showcases perfect surfing swells. From Carova at the north end of the islands to Ocracoke at the southernmost tip, surfers can find the right Atlantic waves.

With a breadth of options, newcomers can enjoy waves alongside experts. Many outfitters offer lessons to beginners. Outer Banks Surf School is on a mission to spread the love of the sport through safe, joyful workshops, and Kitty Hawk Kites teaches students in four convenient locations. If you have the time, joining a camp will give you a stronger foundation to grow as a surfer.

Even with all the preparation possible, riding waves requires just that: riding the waves. At times, the swells will rise in your favor, and at others, they just won't roll quite right. Lucky for you, on the Outer Banks, a new set of conditions is just a short drive north or south. Depending on the weather, season, and crowds, surfers might find better luck at another of the 17 surfing spots.

At Nags Head, professionals ride waves for thousands in prize money during competitions near Jennette's Pier. The Eastern Surfing Association Mid-Atlantic Regional Surfing Championship, a qualifier for the USA Surfing Championships, is often held in the same spot, and spectators can sit in the sand to watch experts during the multiday events.

Still, not all the action on the island is in the water. The winds that bring perfect swells for surfers also make for perfect kite-flying weather. Stunt kite pilots and kite enthusiasts flock to Jockey's Ridge State Park for the Outer Banks Kite Festival in September.

Multicity, NC | **Season:** Spring to fall

Get barreled during prime surfing conditions on the Outer Banks.

Off-Roading Through the Woods

Green and rugged, Uwharrie National Forest spans three North Carolina counties, and on its western edge is Badin Lake Recreation Area, where off-highway vehicles (OHVs) are welcome on trails. Riders can bring all-terrain vehicles, four-wheel drives, and trail bikes to explore miles of rough forest terrain.

Although riding OHVs is anything but peaceful, the park continues to prioritize conservation amid the raucous pursuit: Driving these trails requires a pass from the park, going off-trail or creating shortcuts is strictly forbidden, and OHV-permitted routes are marked with an orange diamond to avoid confusion.

Turn your adventure into an overnight stay by either camping along the trails or booking a site at the Art Lilley Campground, which rests within the OHV trail complex and is free with a trail pass. RVs and campers are allowed at the sites, but no water or electricity hookups are available.

> "ALTHOUGH RIDING OHVS IS ANYTHING BUT PEACEFUL, THE PARK CONTINUES TO PRIORITIZE CONSERVATION AMID THE RAUCOUS PURSUIT."

Multicity, NC | **Season:** Year-round

The rugged, rocky terrain of Uwharrie National Forest makes it ideal for OHVs.

Enjoy the views from a lookout on Hanging Rock.

Make a Daring Climb

When the Civilian Conservation Corps started its work on Hanging Rock State Park in the 1930s, the space had been a haven for campers, swimmers, and hikers. It now draws rock climbers to the boulders and cliffs that have carved through the Dan River Basin.

The first of Hanging Rock's two major climbing spots, Moore's Wall, houses multiple routes and is not for the faint of heart. Rappelling down the complex wall can require a complicated search for stations, and quartzite rock and overhanging lines lend themselves to plenty of scrambles. The shady pitches make this wall an excellent choice for summer climbing.

The second spot, Cook's Wall, is less popular and takes more effort to find. The routes on this part of the mountain are steep, and their lack of traffic has meant they aren't always perfectly cleared. Experts suggest a

helmet and a weather check before you head to the rock, as the wind can pick up. Regardless of which wall you decide to scale, you'll need to get a permit before you don your harness.

If you want to make your trip a weekend adventure, book one of the 73 sites at the park's campground. After climbing, you can grill under the stars or follow the 20-plus miles (32 km) of hiking, biking, and horse trails from camp to plummeting waterfalls and scenic overlooks. Swimming (in season) and fishing (year-round) is available on the lake. Six-person cabins with kitchens and bathrooms are also available for visitors who'd prefer a bit more creature comfort.

Pinkish white dogwood blossoms

Danbury, NC | **Spring to fall**

Kerr Lake has more than 800 miles (1,290 km) of shoreline.

Set Sail

The Kerr Lake State Recreation Area is all about the water: camping by it, sailing on it, swimming around it, fishing in it, and boating across it. This protected area at the border of North Carolina and Virginia covers seven access points around the shore of the reservoir and hundreds of wooded campsites, from RV spots to group camping sites. Unsurprisingly, many of these sites sit on the water's edge, and campers can wake up to the sound of waves gently falling against shore.

The park's multiple ramps and private marinas provide launch points for boaters looking for wide-open spaces, and some access points, including Nutbush Bridge, are open 24 hours a day, seven days a week. Beyond personal boating trips, the waters welcome competitive sailors during competitions from the Carolina Sailing Club, which promotes and organizes small sailboat racing events in North Carolina.

Henderson, NC | **Season:** Spring to fall

Hit the Blue Mountain Trails in Style

The Biltmore Estate merges luxury and adventure in the heart of North Carolina's Blue Ridge Mountains. Guided horseback riding tours will take you through meadows either as a group or privately, and if you'd rather your equine travel be even more effortless, you can choose to hop in a horse-drawn carriage instead.

For visitors set on heart-pumping exploration, there are miles of trails to trek. Start at the Outdoor Adventure Center, where you can either grab a map to find your own way or join a guided hike. The technical Westover Woods Hike will take you over uneven, often muddy terrain, while the Sensory Journey Hike encourages a deep and peaceful connection to the landscape through sight, sound, smell, touch, and—yes—taste.

Those who prefer to pedal can borrow a bike from the Biltmore's Bike Barn and take advantage of the more than 20 miles (32 km) of trails. Challenge yourself on single-track dirt trails or opt for a leisurely roll along the flat, paved trail near French Broad River. The exclusive West Range of the estate is accessible by bicycle only on the West Range Loop Guided Bike Ride, when a support vehicle will accompany you for safety and snacks along an eight-mile (13 km) gravel route.

If you're looking for a high-end place to lay your head after a day of adventure, book a stay at the Inn on Biltmore Estate (the former home of the Vanderbilts), where mountain views will follow you to your bedroom window and spa treatments will help you relax weary muscles.

Asheville, NC | **Season:** Year-round

In eastern North Carolina, paddle through Alligator River.

Paddle America's Great Loop

The Intracoastal Waterway was developed out of a late 18th-century push to improve transportation across the country. Through the early 19th century, a series of canals were built to improve economic growth. Today, the waterway stretches from New York to the Gulf of Mexico—and it makes up a major piece of "America's Great Loop," an extensive aquatic system that winds through the country's central states, and moves through the Great Lakes region.

This stretch of waterway is still used for commercial traffic, but it's also a popular spot for paddlers. Multiple outfitters rent kayaks, paddleboards, and surfboards, along with guided tours. Join a Twilight Tour with Summertide Adventure Tours to leave at dusk and watch the sun fall behind the marshes, or paddle around Sheep's Island with the Adventure Kayak Company to experience a salt marsh creek.

Ocean Isle Beach, NC | Season: Spring to fall

Linville Falls pours over a rock face in Linville Gorge.

1. HIKE THE STATE'S HIGHEST PEAK

Reach the highest summit east of the Mississippi by hiking through spruce-fir forests to the top of Mount Mitchell. The views from the observation deck are accessible to all. Visitors can drive nearly to the top of the mountain and then travel the paved trail to the summit.

2. SEE ASHEVILLE FROM ABOVE

Get a unique view of the Blue Ridge Mountains by booking a hot-air balloon ride over the region. Outfitters run trips year-round, but high-flying guests will catch the best views in spring or in fall when the foliage blooms and turns. With geographic limitations, balloons often fly adjacent to protected spaces.

3. TRAVERSE THE MILE-HIGH SWINGING BRIDGE

After hiking or taking an accessible elevator to the heights of Grandfather Mountain, brave walkers travel the country's highest suspension footbridge over an 80-foot (24 m) chasm filled with green spruce and rock formations. As an extra bonus, if you visit on a windy day, you might just hear the bridge sing.

4. SEARCH FOR FALLS AT LINVILLE GORGE

Hike Linville Gorge, with its towering cliffs and river-carved ravines, to search for Linville Falls. From the Parkway visitors center, hike the short Erwin's View Trail to the overlook for a distant view of the falls. Tackle the stairs on the more challenging Linville Gorge Trail for a closer look.

5. KITESURF CAPE HATTERAS

Whether you're trying the sport for the first time or are a seasoned expert, this cape has the wind and waves needed to ride these world-class waters upwind. Take a lesson from an outfitter, which will provide boat support, spot selection, and camps to hopeful kitesurfers.

6. TAKE IN THE BLUE RIDGE VIEWS

At the newly built deck at Pisgah Inn, the reengineered outdoor space is fully accessible with its wide platforms and sloping ramps. Grab sandwiches and salads from the restaurant for a panoramic picnic—or dine in to stay warm without sacrificing the views.

7. CLIMB WHITESIDE MOUNTAIN

Offering both mountaineering and rock-climbing routes, depending on the face you choose to tackle, these sheer cliffs rise above the Mississippi River, providing bold climbing adventures for those courageous enough to navigate the mountain landscape. Time your trek to ensure your preferred path isn't closed for peregrine nesting.

8. TREK FROM MOUNTAIN TO SEA

The Mountain-to-Sea Trail runs from inland mountains to Outer Banks shorelines. If you plan to travel the full 1,200 miles (1,930 km)—700 miles (1,130 km) of which are already completed—you'd walk past farms, small towns, streams, swamps, and forests. Even a day trip provides a peek into the state's diverse landscape.

9. CATCH MUSIC ON THE MOUNTAIN

Match an afternoon of hiking the Linville Gorge with the monthly "Music on the Mountain" event at the Table Rock Lodge. Evenings are full of traditional bluegrass tunes from local musicians, and guests are invited to bring their own acoustic instruments to participate in the jam sessions.

10. SLEEP IN A LIGHT STATION

Arrive by helicopter and spend a one-of-a-kind evening at the Frying Pan Tower (built in 1964 and retired in 1992), which sits high above the water. Once you've made it there, you can swing at biodegradable golf balls, skeet shoot, fish from the walkways, sway from a hammock at the helipad, and scuba in the protected reef below.

GRANDFATHER MOUNTAIN NORTH CAROLINA MILE HIGH SWINGING BRIDGE ELEV. 5278

Take a sunset sail on
Lake Sakakawea (page 483).

NORTH DAKOTA

Fish, paddle, hike, backpack, cycle, and so much more
through this vast state full of adventure at every turn.

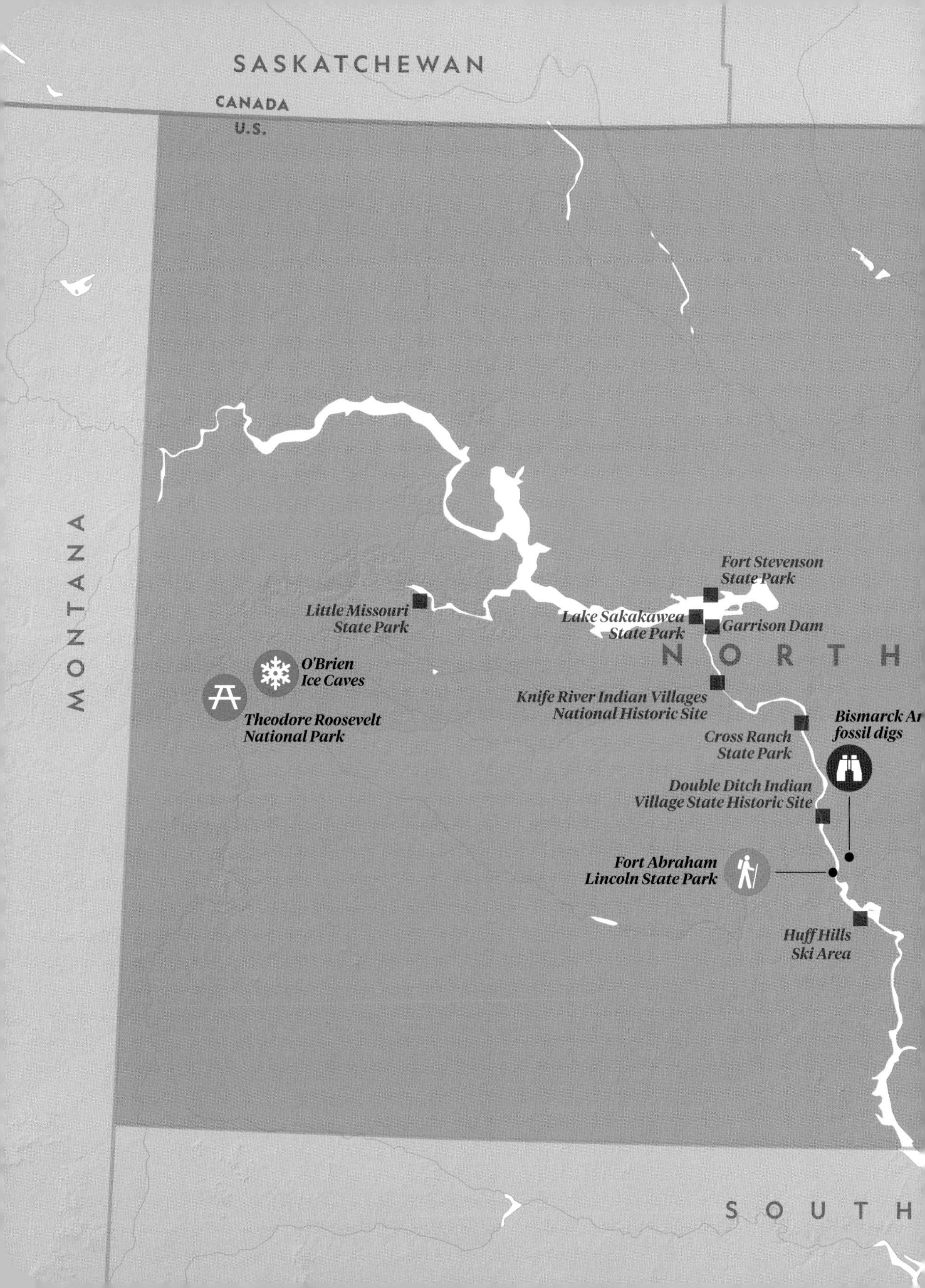

SASKATCHEWAN

CANADA
U.S.

MONTANA

Little Missouri
State Park

O'Brien
Ice Caves

Theodore Roosevelt
National Park

Lake Sakakawea
State Park

Fort Stevenson
State Park

Garrison Dam

N O R T H

Knife River Indian Villages
National Historic Site

Cross Ranch
State Park

Bismarck Ar
fossil digs

Double Ditch Indian
Village State Historic Site

Fort Abraham
Lincoln State Park

Huff Hills
Ski Area

S O U T H

MANITOBA

CANADA
U.S.

International
Peace Garden

Pembina Gorge State
Recreation Area

Lake Metigoshe
State Park

Red

Red
River

Turtle River
State Park

White Horse Hill
National Game Preserve

MINNESOTA

DAKOTA

Arrowwood National
Wildlife Refuge

Fort Ransom
State Park

Sheyenne National
Grassland

DAKOTA

Dig for Dinosaurs

If you dream of long-gone days when mighty dinosaurs ruled Earth, you're not limited to books, movies, and museums. Every day, paleontologists uncover remains of prehistoric life among the pristine, lonely landscape that nature has preserved as one of North Dakota's greatest treasures. Nearly the entire surface of the state is sedimentary rock, making it ideal for fossil preservation. And you don't have to be a scientist to participate.

Die-hard dino fans come to the Bismarck Area fossil digs to assist paleontologists during summer months. Each year, the specific site work may vary, but registration for half- and full-day volunteer work generally opens in February. You may end up working on a site that preserves 67-million-year-old creatures and uncover teeth from *Tyrannosaurus* or bones from *Triceratops*. Children 15 and up are welcome. There are few better ways to touch the ancient past and learn about history.

Bismarck, ND | **Season:** Year-round

See what giants you may uncover on a fossil dig.

Earthen Lodges and Dwellings

The oldest state park in North Dakota, Fort Abraham Lincoln State Park was established in 1907 to preserve the area's history and natural beauty. A Mandan village here, named On-A-Slant after its location on a sloping plain, dates to 1575 and once con-

Earthen lodges of On-A-Slant village, built by the Mandan tribe

tained about 85 earth lodges. Today, the village is a state historic site and has six reconstructed earth lodges for visitors to get insight into the lives of the Mandan peoples.

Fort Abraham Lincoln was among the largest and most important forts on the Northern Plains, and George Armstrong Custer served here from 1873 until the 1876 Battle of the Little Big Horn.

About 19 miles (31 km) of hiking trails along grass, dirt, or hard-packed single-track surfaces are mostly on the easy to moderate side, with only a few steep sections. The Young Hawk Interpretive Trail has numbered posts and a trail guide that describes the plant and animal life, as well as the history of the area. The short Little Sioux Trail loops through native prairie and ash woodland habitat in the farthest reaches of the park.

Morton County, ND | **Season:** Year-round

Ice, Ice Baby

❄️ Because North Dakota has few places where carbonate rocks exist at or near the surface of the earth for groundwater to flow through and create cave systems, the state's few caves are a result of erosion or slope failure. The O'Brien Ice Caves are named for a nearby family that has ranched the area for generations.

The Ice Caves trailhead is located southwest of Grassy Butte, and the easy 1.5-mile (2.4 km) trail accesses the large blocks of sandstone that have detached from a ridge cap and slid down the southern slope. Many of the blocks have come to rest at various angles against others, creating insulated chambers with restricted airflow where water from melting snow and early spring rain drips and freezes well into late spring and summer. Even if you visit late in the season when little ice remains, the caves' cool temperatures offer respite from the sun.

The ice caves are among the highlights of the Maah Daah Hey Trail, a 144-mile (232 km) single-track trail through the Badlands, Medora, and Theodore Roosevelt National Park. The trail system showcases large expanses of rolling prairie punctuated by jagged peaks, winding rivers, and plateaus for adventurous mountain bikers. The trail's name fits the scenery. Translated simply from the Mandan language, it means "an area that will be around for a long time." The Ice Caves Trail leaves the Maah Daah Hey between Mile Post 108 and 109, and bikers can explore the caves by foot. Or, if you want to do a shortened version of the Maah Daah Hey Trail, this spot is a great starting (or ending) point. For those taking on a longer trek, choose from 10 campgrounds along the trail. The horse-friendly Magpie Campground offers easy access to the Ice Caves and Devils Pass.

Western meadowlark

Billings County, ND | **Season:** Winter

Try your luck from the docks of Woodland Resort.

Perch Capital of the U.S.A.

🐟 The largest natural body of water in North Dakota, Devils Lake covers more than 160,000 acres (64,750 ha) and is known as the Perch Capital of the World, as well as being one of the best fisheries in the country for walleye, northern pike, and white bass. Anglers spend time here in all seasons to catch fish worth telling stories about.

White Horse Hill National Game Preserve on the south shore of the lake consists of 1,674 acres (677 ha) ranging from prairie to forested hills. Bird-watchers have spotted up to 270 bird species, including the common yellowthroat, eastern wood peewee, hairy woodpecker, least flycatcher, ovenbird, pileated woodpecker, red-eyed vireo, and yellow warbler.

Fargo, ND | **Season:** Year-round

The sunrise matches the colors of the hills at Theodore Roosevelt National Park.

> **"MANY OF THE PARK'S TRAILS
> ARE SHORT NATURE STROLLS."**

A Rugged Landscape to Explore

The more than 70,000 acres (28,330 ha) of Theodore Roosevelt National Park preserve three areas of North Dakota's rugged yet scenic Badlands linked by the Little Missouri River, where the Badlands meet the Great Plains. The South Unit, where the Painted Canyon resides, is the most popular part of the park. Elkhorn Ranch was the location of Theodore Roosevelt's second ranch and principal home in the Badlands. Adventurous travelers prefer the North Unit, where backcountry trails open up to spectacular views.

The bizarre multicolored rock formations, dramatic canyons, and sweeping plains were formed by 65 million years of geological turmoil. Today, the landscape is home to elk, white-tailed and mule deer, pronghorn, prairie dogs, more then 186 types of birds, and about 700 bison—increased from the reintroduction of an initial 29 in 1956, after bison disappeared from the area in the late 1800s.

Many of the park's trails are short nature strolls, and the number of signed miles is a little more than 100 (160 km). The easy Wind Canyon Trail climbs to a spot with the best view of the Little Missouri River in the South Unit and is also beloved for sunset views. The Coal Vein Trail takes hikers along butte edges and through small gorges, where hikers feel far away from everything. The 10.3-mile (16.6 km) Petrified Forest Loop traverses Badlands wilderness and ancient petrified forests.

In winter, curious visitors opting for a different adventure can don snowshoes and wander through the park, which does not groom trails. Best places to start are on the frozen Little Missouri River and on closed park roads. While the 144-mile (232 km) Maah Daah Hey Trail is one of the top mountain biking trails in the United States, bicycles aren't permitted on the trail as it passes through the North and South Units of the park.

Billings and McKenzie Counties, ND Season: Year-round

Go Into the Red

The slow-moving Red River of the North forms the boundary between North Dakota and Minnesota, flowing north through the Red River Valley and emptying into Lake Winnipeg in Manitoba, Canada. The river contains more than 70 species of fish (and is internationally known for its trophy channel catfish), and the large variety of birds that rest in the narrow strip of trees along its banks have lured dedicated bird-watchers.

The river is a recreational paradise, with canoers and kayakers preferring spring and summer months to journey down its 550 miles (885 km). Bring your own craft or rent a kayak at Lindenwood Park in Fargo, where a fully ADA-compliant kayak launch lets you access the river without traversing through the riverbank's claylike mud. River Keepers, a local nonprofit that advocates for the river's stewardship, holds an annual Race the Red canoe and kayak race.

Fargo, ND Season: Spring to fall

> "THE RIVER CONTAINS MORE THAN 70 SPECIES OF FISH, AND THE LARGE VARIETY OF BIRDS THAT REST IN THE NARROW STRIP OF TREES ALONG ITS BANKS HAVE LURED DEDICATED BIRD-WATCHERS."

Cruise easily on the calmer stretches of the Red River just outside Fargo.

Pembina Gorge cuts through lush forest just west of Walhalla.

Paddle Pembina

The Pembina Gorge has one of the largest uninterrupted blocks of woodland in North Dakota and the longest segment of unaltered river valley in the state. Three different biogeographical regions come together here: boreal forest, central grassland, and eastern deciduous forest. Surging waters eroded through glacial till and underlying beds of shale to carve the gorge, making one of the deepest and steepest river valleys in North Dakota. The Pembina Gorge exemplifies natural diversity, with at least 30 plant and 21 animal species categorized as rare in the state, like the American woodcock, alder flycatcher, and orange-crowned warbler.

The 2,800-acre (1,130 ha) Pembina Gorge State Recreation Area within the gorge has more than 30 miles (48 km) of trails for hiking, horseback riding, mountain biking, and off-highway vehicles (OHVs). Some of the trails are designated for nonmotorized use only, and others are multiuse—although restrictions may apply.

The Pembina River, which runs through the gorge, attracts canoe and kayak enthusiasts to the only white water in North Dakota. Near Walhalla, the river flows fairly rapidly over many small rapids. Access points with floating docks exist at Vang Bridge, Brick Mine Bridge, and White Bridge—all maintained by Pembina River Keepers, a local group of canoe and kayak activists dedicated to conservation of the waterway. Pembina Gorge State Recreation Area offers kayak rentals at hourly and daily rates, including paddles and life jackets. For an additional fee, the recreation area also offers transportation for paddlers from Walhalla or the Brick Mine Bridge.

Cavalier County, ND | **Season:** Year-round

Hike the tallgrass prairie at Sheyenne National Grassland.

Prairie Escape

Take a trip into the past, when the Great Plains stretched to the horizon and the vast prairie grasses rippled like water in the wind. Sheyenne National Grassland is the only national tallgrass prairie region of the United States, providing essential habitat for the western prairie fringed orchid and the greater prairie chicken. Nearly 300 other bird species have been seen here, and daily feathered visitors during migration seasons include cranes, ducks, geese, and swans.

If you've never considered backpacking across grassland, this place may inspire you. There are no designated backcountry campsites here, but dispersed camping is permitted. A graveled, marked 30-mile (48 km) segment of the North Country National Scenic Trail winds through Sheyenne National Grassland, and those in search of a shorter route may choose the four-mile (6.4 km) Oak Leaf Trail, a loop attached to the northeast end of the longer trail.

Ransom and Richland Counties, ND | **Season:** Year-round

Go Wild at a Clear Lake

Lake Metigoshe in the Turtle Mountains may straddle the border between North Dakota and Manitoba, Canada—but the majority of the lake is located in North Dakota. The rolling hills, aspen forests, and small lakes here attract nature lovers seeking a serene escape from the stress of everyday life. The landscape also attracts deer, moose, beavers, and more than 174 species of birds—37 of which are on the Natural Heritage Program's state rare species list, including the LeConte's and Baird's sparrow, bufflehead duck, and cinnamon teal. If you sit still enough, you may be lucky and spy them.

With its clear water (the lake's name is derived from the Chippewa language meaning "clear water lake surrounded by oaks"), Lake Metigoshe is among the state's most popular year-round vacation spots. The Old Oak

Trail, certified in 1976 as a national recreation trail (making it the state's first nationally recognized trail), winds for three miles (4.8 km) through aspen, birch, and oak forests with interpretive markers and a corresponding brochure to identify standout natural wonders.

In winter, two of the park's trail systems through forest, grass, and wetland areas accommodate cross-country skiers and snowshoers. The East Side Multi-Use Trails consist of Antelope, Beaver, Coyote, and Deer Trails for a combined total of eight miles (13 km). The West Side Multi-Use Trails consist of Cub, Tenderfoot, Scout, and Eagle Trails for a combined total of four miles (6.4 km). The park has a collection of snowshoes and cross-country skis for day rental rates.

Bottineau County, ND | **Season:** Year-round

From Fort Ransom, take in sweeping views of the Sheyenne River Valley.

Explore the River Valley

In the wooded Sheyenne River Valley, Fort Ransom State Park is accessible via the Sheyenne River Valley National Scenic Byway, which leads through the tree-lined rolling hills of the Red River Valley. The park takes its name from a military fort dating to the 1860s. The Sunne Farm, a farmstead within the park, is a tribute to the homesteading days in North Dakota, and hosts Sodbusters Days twice each year—in spring and fall.

Canoeing and kayaking are popular on the Sheyenne River during summer months, and on-site boat rentals are available (both hourly and daily rates apply). The boat launch is next to the visitors center, and park staff can pick up paddlers at the Fort Ransom Sportsmans Club boat ramp for an additional fee. The park's 20 miles (32 km) of nonmotorized trails are mostly multiuse, allowing for hiking, biking, horseback riding, cross-country skiing, and snowshoeing.

Fort Ransom, ND | **Season:** Spring to fall

Red Cliffs tower above the
Little Missouri River.

1. BE LURED BY MILES OF LAKESHORE

Lake Sakakawea State Park, on the south shore of its namesake lake and adjacent to Garrison Dam, is 739 acres (299 ha) of water fun—and for good reason, as the lake is the third largest human-made reservoir in the country. Anglers, in particular, are lured here for wonderful walleye fishing, as well as the chance to reel in northern pike and Chinook salmon.

2. APPRECIATE BADLAND BEAUTY

If you don't think badlands can be beautiful, Little Missouri State Park will change your mind. With some of the most rugged, picturesque Badlands terrain, the park has more than 45 miles (72 km) of trails best accessed on foot or horseback.

3. FOLLOW WALLEYE DREAMS

On the north shore of Lake Sakakawea, Fort Stevenson State Park takes its name from a 19th-century frontier military fort, now underwater. The park is three miles (5 km) south of Garrison, the Walleye Capital of North Dakota, so fishers flock here with boats and hopes of catching a big one.

4. FLOCK TO FIND FEATHERED FRIENDS

Established in 1935 as a refuge and breeding ground for migratory birds, Arrowwood National Wildlife Refuge is tucked along a 14-mile (23 km) stretch of the James River, so migratory waterfowl are especially abundant. Stay among like-minded birders nearby at Pipestem Creek Bed and Birding, a small grains farm with comfortable cabins and birding activities.

5. BE A CITIZEN SCIENTIST

Knife River Indian Villages National Historic Site preserves the remains of several Hidatsa and Mandan settlement sites and is a significant stop on the Lewis and Clark National Historic Trail. Participate in research on the area's biodiversity by using the iNaturalist app to take photos of plants and animals in the park. It's citizen science in action.

6. FIND PEACE IN FLOWERS

The International Peace Garden is on the border of the United States and Canada. With nearly 2,400 acres (970 ha) of gardens and trails, biking is among the best way to get to know the landscape, which runs through Dunseith, North Dakota. Visit in spring, when the wildflower bloom boosts the already rich floral scenery.

7. SKI THE HUFF

Located along the western slope of the Missouri River, Huff Hills is the state's largest ski area, with 16 runs and a solid mix of terrain for skiers and riders of all levels. A dedicated terrain park area accessed via the Green Lift includes ramps, kickers, rails, barrels, boxes, walls, and more. The Country Kitchen at the base of the mountain is the perfect stop for an après-ski meal, with burgers, sandwiches, pizza, and hot and cold drinks (from hot cocoa to beer) on offer.

8. EXPLORE UNTOUCHED RIVERLAND

Along an undeveloped stretch of the Missouri River, Cross Ranch State Park has nearly 17 miles (27 km) of trails for year-round use, making them ideal for cross-country skiing in winter and hiking the rest of the year. Lodging options include yurts, cabins, and tent campsites.

9. LOOP A RECREATIONAL OASIS

Tucked into a wooded valley along the Turtle River, the eponymous state park's more than 12 miles (19 km) of trails wind through the forested hills and along the river. Hikers and bikers share all but two of the trails, with the Eco Loop and Cattail Loop reserved for visitors on foot.

10. WALK IN INDIGENOUS FOOTSTEPS

Double Ditch Indian Village State Historic site on the east bank of the Missouri River features evidence of concentric ditches, part of defensive perimeters for a large earth lodge village the Mandan peoples inhabited for nearly 300 years. Missouri Kayak Adventures offers rentals and a river shuttle for a Double Ditch Route on the river.

Ash Cave (page 493) is adorned
with a beautiful waterfall after
spring rains.

OHIO

The Buckeye State has a lot to brag about, from majestic waterfalls and forests to stunning lakes and parks.

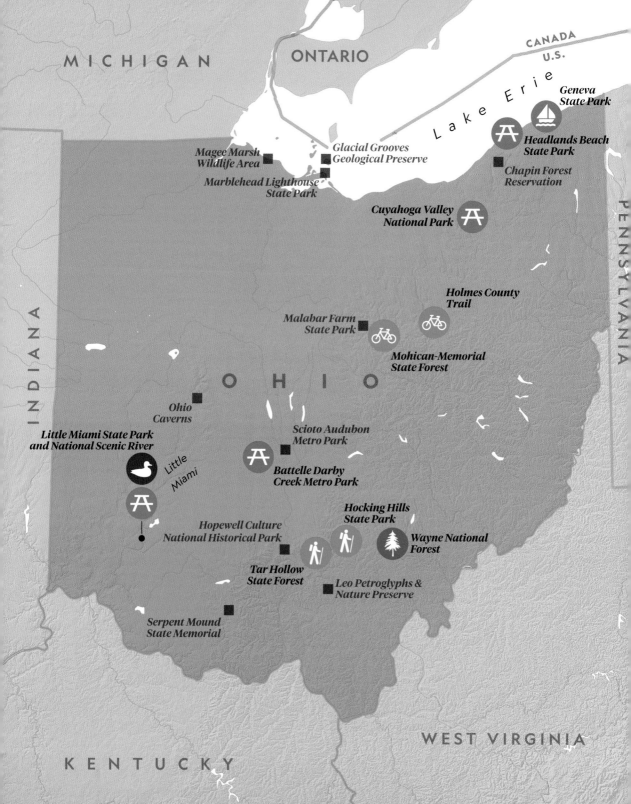

MICHIGAN

ONTARIO

CANADA
U.S.

Lake Erie

Geneva
State Park

Magee Marsh
Wildlife Area

Glacial Grooves
Geological Preserve

Headlands Beach
State Park

Marblehead Lighthouse
State Park

Chapin Forest
Reservation

PENNSYLVANIA

Cuyahoga Valley
National Park

Holmes County
Trail

Malabar Farm
State Park

Mohican-Memorial
State Forest

O H I O

Ohio
Caverns

Scioto Audubon
Metro Park

Little Miami State Park
and National Scenic River

Little
Miami

Battelle Darby
Creek Metro Park

Hocking Hills
State Park

Wayne National
Forest

Hopewell Culture
National Historical Park

Tar Hollow
State Forest

Leo Petroglyphs &
Nature Preserve

Serpent Mound
State Memorial

INDIANA

KENTUCKY

WEST VIRGINIA

Autumn colors come in full force at Wayne National Forest.

The Forested Foothills

The only national forest in Ohio, Wayne National Forest occupies 244,265 acres (98,850 ha) in three units (Athens, Ironton, Marietta) across 12 counties in the forested Appalachian foothills of the southeast portion of the state. Despite its appearance as an untouched wilderness, countless Indigenous archaeological sites dot the forest, and remnants of the iron industry abound. The premier developed site is the Vesuvius Recreation Area, named after the Vesuvius Iron Furnace, one of 46 charcoal iron furnaces located in the six county Hanging Rock Iron region of southern Ohio.

Though visitors enjoy Wayne National Forest year-round, it's especially popular for leaf peeping in fall months. The color spectrum of autumn leaves ranges from the American elm's pale yellow to brilliant reds of sumac and dark purple of ash. Drivers try to find a favorite spot along the National Forest Covered Bridge Scenic Byway, a self-guided 35-mile (56 km) tour on State Route 26 from Marietta to Woodsfield, paralleling the Little Muskingum River.

Hikers and horseback riders who want to venture deep into the forest can choose from more than 300 miles (480 km) of trails. The Lake Vesuvius Horse Trail System, with nine trails along rock cliffs and streams, is among the most popular for both riders and those on foot. Hiking here is open throughout the year, and horseback riding is allowed during open season, which runs from mid-April through mid-December. The Wildcat Hollow Hiking Trail can be enjoyed two ways: a five-mile (8 km) loop for day hikes, or a 17.2-mile (27.7 km) loop along ridgetops and stream bottoms for backpackers.

Multicity, OH | **Season:** Year-round

Pick your fun: Paddle through or zip above Lake Erie.

Retreat to the Lake

⛵ Lake Erie looms large at this park that spans 698 acres (282 ha) of its shoreline, within the village of Geneva-on-the-Lake. Some visitors include Geneva State Park in their Ohio Wine Country itinerary as a spot to enjoy relaxing on the sand beach with meditative lake views between winery visits. The breezes off the lake and the rich soil left behind by glaciers that carved out the Great Lakes make this area prime for grape growing.

The lake's nearly unlimited opportunities for boaters include facilities at Geneva Marina, a six-lane boat ramp that provides easy access to Lake Erie's central basin, and kayak rentals (for use on Cowles Creek) from Lake Erie Canopy Tours. Lake Erie fishing, especially for walleye and perch (as well as channel catfish, steelhead trout, and coho salmon), is some of the most prized angling in the United States and the best fishing in Ohio.

Geneva, OH | **Season:** Spring to fall

Bike Wild Woodlands

🚲 The wild landscape of this park and the surrounding Mohican-Memorial State Forest are thanks to the last glaciers to enter Ohio more than 14,000 years ago. The narrow Clear Fork Gorge follows the Clear Fork of the Mohican River and cuts more than 300 feet (90 m) deep into sandstone bedrock, creating steep cliff walls and rock outcroppings among the towering hemlocks and stands of old-growth white pine.

The 25.5-mile (41 km) single-track Mohican Mountain Bike Trail loops through the gorge on its journey through both the state park and state forest and is also open to hikers. Additional hiking trails range from easy to difficult for distances of anywhere from less than a mile to 2.5 miles (1.6 to 4 km). One of the more beloved hiking trails is the Lyons Falls Trail, a two-mile (3.2 km) moderate to difficult journey that includes views of two waterfalls—25-foot (8 m) Little Lyons Falls and 80-foot (24 m) Big Lyons Falls.

Ashland County, OH | **Season:** Year-round

Bike or hike along covered wood bridges within the state forest.

Farmland abounds in the Big Prairie of Holmes County.

Ride a Rail to Trail

This former railroad route now multipurpose recreational trail is the first in the United States to accommodate Amish buggies. Ultimately to run for 29 miles (47 km), the trail is currently open in two paved sections (15 miles/24 km from Fredericksburg to Killbuck and 7.5 miles/12 km from Glenmont to Brinkhaven). One lane is paved for biking, running, and wheelchairs while the other is used for horseback riding and horse-drawn buggies.

The trail runs along farm fields and tree-lined streams, and walkers and bikers can choose a segment based on the length you'd like to travel. At Hipp Station in Millersburg, a restored train depot serves as the trail's headquarters and features information and wildlife displays. The Holmes County Trail is a component of the 326-mile (525 km) Ohio to Erie Trail developed to connect the shores of Lake Erie in Cleveland and the Ohio River in Cincinnati.

Holmes County, OH | **Season:** Year-round

"WHEREVER YOU ARE, YOU'RE SURROUNDED BY A WATER SOUNDTRACK."

The Power of Water

With 268 acres (109 ha) of dolomite and limestone gorge, this nature preserve is a testament to the power of glaciation and the Little Miami State and National Scenic River, which stretches through two miles (3.2 km) of the preserve. The waters of the Little Miami flow through deep and narrow channels and cliff overhangs, and the three miles (5 km) of hiking trails give visitors a tranquil introduction to the forces of nature among slopes of hemlock, Canada yew, and mountain maple forest. Once through the narrow limestone reaches of the gorge, the river slows to a calmer pace, and meanders downstream. Wherever you are, you're surrounded by a water soundtrack.

Migration periods in the spring and fall attract a diversity of neotropical birds in the heavily wooded gorge—a welcome retreat in an area that's heavily agricultural. Birders swarm the area to observe the flocks in their migratory patterns. Many of Ohio's more common and widespread breeding populations are easily found in summer, from Louisiana waterthrush and yellow-throated warbler along the river to yellow-breasted chat and prairie warbler in the upland region.

In spring, the valley floor is covered with wildflowers, including the rare snow trillium, native to the Ohio Valley. This early bloomer thrives in the shallow, limestone gravel soils at the base of the cliff faces. Among the first wildflowers to appear in Clifton Gorge are the appropriately named harbingers of spring with dainty white petals and purple-black anthers. An abundance of sharp-lobed hepatica pops up in spring as well, painting the floor in colorful pink, purple, and blue hues as winter's browns and grays give way to spring pastels.

Greene County, OH | **Season:** Spring to fall

The Little Miami River winds its way through lush and steep canyon.

Dune Habitat

The 35-acre (14 ha) natural sand beach on Lake Erie at Headlands Beach State Park is the largest beach in Ohio. Initially deposited by the lake, the sand here (and at the adjacent Headlands Dunes State Nature Preserve) has been piled into dunes by prevailing winds. Plant species more commonly found on the Atlantic coastal plain—like beach grass, beach pea, purple sand grass, sea rocket, and seaside spurge—grow well in the dunes.

In summer, swimmers seek fun and refreshment in the cool lake water, while beachcombers prefer to wander among the dunes in search of colorful sea-glass treasures. Headlands is also one of Ohio's premier birding locations, where lake birds, raptors, and shorebirds are all at home in the park's mix of habitats along the Lake Erie shoreline. The area has an impressive list of 334 bird species, with more than 130 species spotted on single days during spring migration.

Lake County, OH | Season: Spring to fall

The Fairport Harbor West Breakwater Lighthouse at Headlands Beach

Where the Buffalo Roam

Battelle Darby Creek is the largest of the Columbus and Franklin County Metro Parks, with more than 7,000 acres (2,830 ha) along 13 miles (21 km) of Big Darby Creek and Little Darby Creek. The park offers a wide diversity of natural and restored habitats, including tallgrass prairie, floodplain forest, oak savanna, wet prairie, wetland, upland forest, and ravines. A trail network of nearly 26 miles (42 km) runs through Battelle Darby Creek, leading hikers through deep forests and lush meadows, past scenic overlooks, and near Native American sites.

Big and Little Darby Creeks have both state and federal Scenic River designations. Access points are available for floating down either creek in a canoe or kayak, and for those who don't have their own, nearby Trapper Johns Canoe Livery offers rentals with

shuttle service to the put-in. Paddlers are bound to see ospreys and bald eagles flying the river corridor, more than 100 different species of songbirds in the trees, as well as beavers and river otters along the banks or in the water.

Among the park's highlights are the bison that call the restored prairies home. As part of a comprehensive effort to restore the park's tallgrass prairie ecosystem, the first six bison were reintroduced in 2011—the first time in more than 200 years the animals have lived on the Darby Plains. The herd now numbers 12. The best places to get a glimpse of the bison are from the Darby Creek Greenway Trail and the overlook deck at the Nature Center.

Large-flowered trillium

Franklin County, OH | Season: Year-round

Geological Wonders

Hocking Hills State Park encompasses distinctly different natural areas, ranging from rocky cliffs to lush waterfalls to forested gorges, ensuring that visitors have a variety of choices. The scenic features are carved in Black Hand sandstone, a bedrock deposited more than 350 million years ago, when a delta in the warm shallow sea covered Ohio. The recess caves at Ash Cave, Old Man's Cave, Whispering Cave, and Cantwell Cliff are all carved into the softer sandstone composition.

The park has seven major hiking areas, all one-way trail systems. The easiest path is the half-mile (0.8 km) Ash Cave Trail, the first half consisting of an accessible asphalt trail lined by hemlocks and cliff walls to a recess cave and seasonal waterfall. From there, a set of stairs continues to a rim trail leading back to the trailhead. The most challenging path is the Whispering Cave Trail, a 4.5-mile (7.2 km) loop that includes the swinging Hemlock Bridge, a seasonal waterfall, and the second largest cave in the region. For those following the Buckeye Trail, it joins with the Grandma Gatewood Trail for six miles (10 km) through the park.

Extend your Hocking Hills immersive experience by glamping in a geodesic dome in nearby Logan's Inn and Spa at Cedar Falls, a green-certified property surrounded on three sides by the state park. With towering ceilings and sweeping forest views through a picture window, a stay here is like having your own oasis in the woods. Along with domes, the inn also offers cabins with whirlpool hot tubs, luxurious yurts, cozy cottages in the woods, and large lodges fit for big families or group retreats. If your feet are tired from the hiking, indulge in some R&R at the full-service spa. Kindred Spirits Restaurant offers casual fine dining in an original log cabin, built in the 1840s.

For a more rustic experience, Hocking Hills State Park offers primitive campsites, as well as camper cabins. There are non-electric and electric sites, as well as 30 walk-in family sites with pit latrines.

Logan, OH | **Season:** Year-round

Country roads lead through Tar Hollow State Forest.

An Ancient Wilderness

Ohio's third largest state forest at 16,446 acres (6,656 ha), Tar Hollow is named for the pine tar early settlers acquired from scattered shortleaf and pitch pines growing on the forest ridges. The landscape here is characteristic of the Ohio wilderness of early settlement. The forestland here and in Tar Hollow State Park was acquired for conservation purposes as the Ross-Hocking Land Utilization Project, a Depression-era project.

The forest has a 22-mile (35 km) network of hiking trails, most notably the Logan Trail, a figure eight with double loops roughly eight miles (13 km) each in length. The Logan meets up with the 1,444-mile (2,324 km) Buckeye Trail—the longest circular loop trail in the United States. A 46-site horse camp for riders and their equine friends is located at the south end of the forest on Poe Run Road, and 33 miles (53 km) of bridle trails radiate out from the camp.

Laurelville, OH | **Season:** Spring to summer

Visit majestic Brandywine
Falls in Cuyahoga Valley.

> ## "THE RIVER HELPED SPUR THE ENVIRONMENTAL MOVEMENT IN THE UNITED STATES."

A River Reborn

The winding Cuyahoga River has been a transportation route, a boundary marker, a power source, and a dumping place. It's also been the birthplace of oil, rubber, and petroleum industries. The river is infamous for having burned in 1969, an event that helped spur the environmental movement in the United States. Today, it's been reborn as Cuyahoga Valley National Park, preserving around 33,000 acres (13,355 ha) of forests, meadows, and waterfalls where the Appalachian Plateau and the Central Lowlands come together. That rehabilitation has allowed the park's habitats—from deciduous forests to cultivated agricultural lands to wetlands—to flourish, providing a home for a wealth of plant and animal species.

The park is home to more than 125 miles (200 km) of hiking and biking trails, including the historic route of the Ohio and Erie Canal, the country's first inland waterway between the Great Lakes and the Gulf of Mexico. After its construction, from 1825 to 1832, mules walked this trail towing canal boats loaded with goods and passengers. Today, the multipurpose Towpath Trail runs for 87 miles (140 km), 20 miles (32 km) of which are within the national park. Portions of the Buckeye Trail, a 1,444-mile (2,324 km) trail that loops the state, also pass through the national park. For mountain bikers, the East Rim Trail System has varied terrain and exciting obstacles for intermediate bikers, and a short technical trail for those in search of a challenge.

Don't leave the park without a stop at 60-foot (18 m) Brandywine Falls, one of the most popular attractions. To get up close, hike the 1.5-mile (2.4 km) Brandywine Gorge Loop, which includes sections of several trails. For more time in this section of the park, stay at the Inn at Brandywine Falls, a restored Greek Revival farmhouse built in 1848 and included on the National Register of Historic Places.

Cuyahoga and Summit Counties, OH | **Season:** Year-round

From above, it's easy to see the shape of Serpent Mound State Memorial.

1. FOLLOW THE LIGHT TO A STORIED HISTORY

The oldest lighthouse in continuous operation on the Great Lakes, Marblehead Lighthouse rests on Marblehead Peninsula, a headland of Columbus limestone that juts into Lake Erie. Spend time visiting the lighthouse and its museum, where exhibits include a Fresnel lens and fossils found in the bedrock exposed along the lakeshore.

2. STOP OVER ON THE SONGBIRD SHORELINE

On the southern shore of Lake Erie, Magee Marsh Wildlife Area is a prime stopover for North American warblers during their migration. Spring and fall migrations here are spectacular, and more than 300 bird species have been recorded in the area. The annual birding festival runs approximately 10 days in early May.

3. FOLLOW THE KING OF SERPENTS

Serpent Mound is one of the most widely recognized effigy mounds in the world. (Effigy mounds are human-made mounds in the shape of animals.) Take your time along the walkway that surrounds the representation of a snake with a curled tail, thought to have been made by the Adena culture around 300 B.C.

4. VISIT AN URBAN GREENWAY

Scioto Audubon Metro Park in Columbus, along the banks of the Scioto River, was once an industrial area dominated by factories, warehouses, and railroad yards. Today, it's home to wetlands, one of the nation's largest outdoor climbing walls, and the 10-mile (16 km) Scioto Greenway Trail that's ideal for leisurely walks or long bike rides.

5. WALK THROUGH ROCK ART

Along a half-mile (0.8 km) walking trail in the Leo Petroglyphs and Nature Preserve, among unglaciated Mississippian sandstone cliffs, are small waterfalls and a slab of rock that preserves the traces of nearly 40 figurative drawings of humans, birds, a fish, snake, animal and human footprints, and other figures attributed to Fort Ancient culture.

6. STUDY SUSTAINABLE AGRICULTURE

The dream of Pulitzer Prize–winning author, farmer, and conservationist Louis Bromfield, Malabar Farm State Park welcomes visitors year-round. Take advantage of quiet winter months to snowshoe or cross-country ski along park trails with a variety of terrain for beginner to advanced skiers. Don't miss the annual Maple Syrup Festival in March.

7. GET GROOVY SOUVENIRS

Walk among ancient Earth history at Glacial Grooves Geological Preserve within Kelleys Island State Park. Glacial grooves measuring up to 400 feet (120 m) long, 35 feet (11 m) wide, and 15 feet (5 m) deep were scoured into Devonian limestone nearly 18,000 years ago by a great ice sheet that covered part of North America.

8. BEHOLD A NATURAL BEAUTY

Venture deep underground through the largest cave system in Ohio, with nearly two miles (3.2 km) of passageways, chambers, and streams. Original explorations began in the Ohio Caverns in 1897, and cavers uncovered a wealth of wonderful formations, including the Crystal King—a 5-foot-long (1.5 m), 400-pound (180 kg) stalactite believed to be more than 200,000 years old.

9. VISIT PREHISTORIC MONUMENTS

Hopewell Culture National Historical Park in Chillicothe is a ceremonial center of earthen mounds along the North Fork Paint Creek and is considered the most spectacular set of Hopewell cultural remains in Ohio. Get a close glimpse on the Tri-County Triangle Trail, a paved bike trail that traverses the site for more than 30 miles (48 km).

10. FIND QUIET IN THE FOREST

Encompassing 390 acres (160 ha), Chapin Forest Reservation in Lake County is especially noteworthy for its beautiful sandstone formations. Rent cross-country skis and snowshoes at the Pine Lodge Ski Center to enjoy the wintry silence among nearly six miles (10 km) of groomed trails that wind through a thick forest of beech, hemlock, maple, oak, and tulip trees.

Elk Mountain and Post Oak
Creek in Wichita Mountains
Wildlife Refuge (page 502)

OKLAHOMA

From climbing and corn mazes in OKC to sand dunes and salt plains across the state, you'll want to explore everything the Sooner State has to offer.

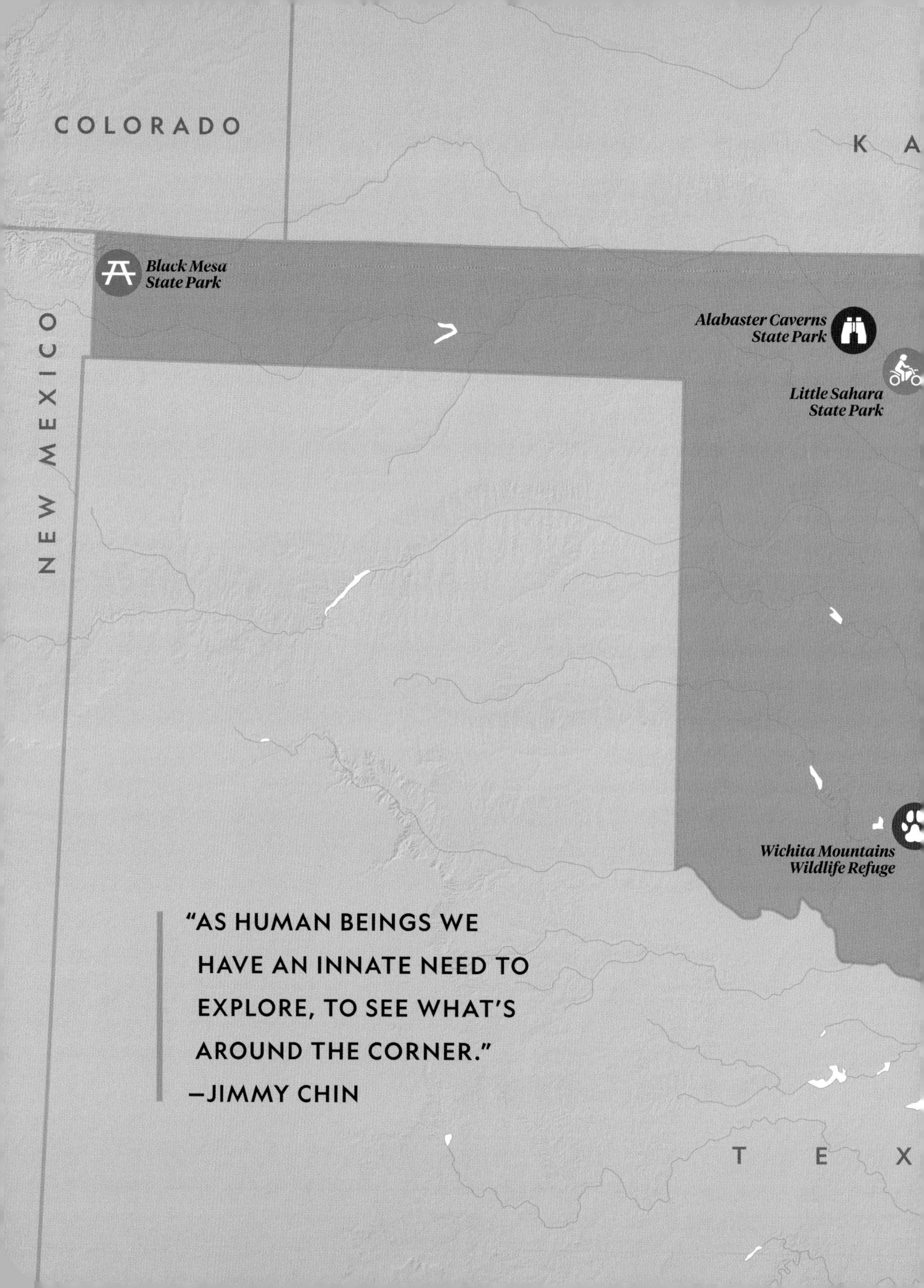

COLORADO

KA

NEW MEXICO

Black Mesa State Park

Alabaster Caverns State Park

Little Sahara State Park

Wichita Mountains Wildlife Refuge

"AS HUMAN BEINGS WE
HAVE AN INNATE NEED TO
EXPLORE, TO SEE WHAT'S
AROUND THE CORNER."
—JIMMY CHIN

TEX

MISSOURI

OKLAHOMA

Salt Plains
State Park

Philbrook
Museum of Art

Gathering
Place

Natural Falls
State Park

Illinois

Illinois
River

OKLAHOMA

Tenkiller
Ferry Lake

ARKANSAS

Oklahoma City Zoo
and Botanical Garden

P Bar
Farms

Wheeler
Ferris Wheel

Summit
OKC Silos

Lake
Thunderbird

Robbers Cave
State Park

Medicine Park

Little
Niagara Falls

Turner
Falls Park

McGee Creek
State Park

Glover
River

Beavers Bend
State Park

Endangered Ark
Foundation

Presbyterian
Falls

A S

Summit the Silos

Going to the gym doesn't usually top vacation itineraries, but for climbers, Oklahoma City's Summit OKC Silos might be worth the trip. This silo turned climbing gym offers a unique chance to ascend inside a piece of the state's agricultural history. The 90-foot-high (27 m) circular room is climate controlled and offers a 360-degree traverse dotted with climbing holds, providing diverse routes for newcomers and advanced climbers alike.

The gym's friendly and encouraging community invites guests to try top-rope, lead, and auto-belay, as well as 10 feet (3 m) of roof climbing on the silo ceiling. For anyone with a Spider-Man fantasy, the exterior silo walls have a few routes too, which are open only when weather permits, and the views of downtown OKC can't be beat.

With so many ways to try out the sport—from day and month passes and ladies' nights to private lessons and fitness classes for climbers—there's no excuse not to drop by and clip in.

Oklahoma City, OK | **Season:** Year-round

Scale new heights at Summit OKC Silos.

Visit the Old West

The 60,000-acre (24,280 ha) Wichita Mountains Wildlife Refuge is home to around 650 buffalo. And seeing these near-threatened creatures grazing in this setting is something to behold. Sharing the rugged wilderness are herds of Texas longhorn cattle, elk, and deer.

See where the buffalo roam at Wichita Mountains Wildlife Refuge.

For hikers in search of granite boulders to scramble over and easy to hard trails climbing past lakes, waterfalls, creeks, and free-roaming wildlife, the refuge also takes top prize. Intermediate to advanced hikers looking for a good workout should lace up at the out-and-back Charon's Garden Trail, an uneven landscape of massive granite boulders and a lot of heavy scrambling. The dog-friendly Bison Trail is the longest in the refuge at 6.1 miles (9.8 km) and a good park sampler, with views of French Lake, prairies, and usually some bison and longhorn sightings.

Come May and early June, local color arrives in the form of vibrant yellow Corylopsis, black-eyed Susans, and sneezeweeds that line trails and poke through granite cracks, adding even more sunshine to this already enchanted setting.

Indiahoma, OK | **Season:** Year-round

Go Beneath the Surface

Mussels

Scuba diving in Oklahoma? Don't laugh so quickly. Hemmed into the foothills of the Ozark Mountains, Tenkiller Ferry Lake (aka Lake Tenkiller) attracts kayakers, swimmers, and nature lovers to explore its forested hills and 130 miles (210 km) of spectacular lakeshore. But what's beneath the water's surface ranks Lake Tenkiller as one of the state's best underwater exploration sites.

Thanks to its clear waters and eight to 28 feet (2 to 9 m) of visibility, the human-made lake, created by damming the Illinois River, is a diving hot spot, where an underwater park hides sunken treasures such as a school bus, a U.S. Coast Guard helicopter and a plane fuselage, boats, as well as other artifacts from a town left behind when the lake was created. The lake hits depths of 165 feet (50 m), with visibility up to 35 feet (11 m) depending on the time of year. The diverse underwater terrain includes sloping hills and rock cliffs, as well as many Oklahoma fish species, including various types of bass and catfish. Several marinas dot the shoreline, and outfitters offer scuba training and certification, as well as equipment rental. Visitors can also arrange for private guided tours to sunken and natural sites around the lake.

Out of the water, two state parks—Tenkiller State Park and Cherokee Landing State Park—call Lake Tenkiller home and offer camping sites and hiking trails. Cherokee Landing holds what is left of a town that was abandoned when the lake was built. Many homes, as well as the old jailhouse, are still intact, and artifacts from horseshoes and buggies to wagon wheels and Native American pottery are on display. Make sure to take a trip to one of the lake's islands, such as Goat Island, where bleating creatures scamper over rocks and can often be seen from the water. The area also has golf courses and restaurants.

Muskogee, OK | Season: Summer

Become a Duner

Little Sahara State Park looks straight out of North Africa, which explains the name of this mini-desert, also known as Waynoka. The sandy, wind-shaped hills were formed by remnants of prehistoric times when the Cimarron River once flowed through the area. What has "duners" rolling into the northern part of the Sooner State these days is prime off-roading adventure and the chance to zip across 1,600 acres (650 ha) of open space, bowls, jumps, and hills that can reach between 25 and 75 feet (8 to 23 m) tall in certain areas.

ATVs, dune buggies, 4x4s, and side-by-sides are welcome, and duners can bring their own vehicles or rent from private vendors in the nearby town of Waynoka, aka the Little City by the Sand, which hosts numerous sand-centric events each year. Weekend and holidays can get busy, and there is a daily entrance fee to ride.

Waynoka, OK | Season: Year-round

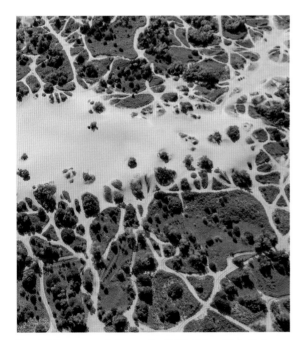

Tough foliage grows in the sands of Little Sahara State Park.

> "THE CRYSTALS ARE BELIEVED TO BE THE ONLY OF THEIR KIND IN THE WORLD."

Look Out for Birds and Crystals

Lots of places on tourist maps are referred to as "hidden gems," but only Salt Plains State Park lives up to the literal name. Although visitors can choose their favorite activity across the 820-acre (330 ha) park, including biking, hiking, canoeing, and swimming, digging for selenite crystals is the main draw. Found beneath the massive sea of salt in the adjacent Salt Plains National Wildlife Refuge, these crystals hold reddish, hourglass-shaped inclusions of sand and clay and are believed to be the only crystals of their kind in the world. An ocean once covered the barren landscape that now lures bucket- and shovel-toting treasure hunters young and old who dig up chunks of salt as well as these Oklahoma jewels. Digging in designated areas is permitted between April 1 and October 15. Beware: It's a messy task, guaranteed to cover clothes in sand, salt, and water, so plan to take a rinse in the park's partially salted lake (about half as salty as the ocean).

With its varied landscape of woods, grasslands, marshes, and salt plains on the Kansas-Oklahoma border, Salt Plains State Park is a bird-watching hot spot too, and an estimated 300 species of birds have been spotted here. The salt flats are a nesting habitat for least terns, snowy plovers, and American avocets. Tens of thousands of American white pelicans, one of the largest birds in North America, begin arriving in early September from nesting grounds in the north, en route to their winter homes in Texas and Louisiana. The lakeshore is also a preferred pit stop for migrating whooping cranes. Several of the park's nature trails offer good vantage points, as does the observation tower.

Jet, OK | Season: Spring to fall

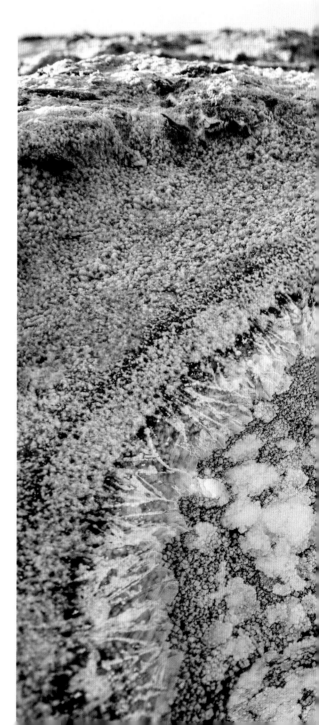

Unique salt formations form in desert puddles.

Be Ah-Mazed

Fall is a fabulous time to travel through the Sooner State, and not just because of the crimson and orange leaves that put on a show. Autumn is also corn maze season, and just an hour west of Oklahoma City, the family-owned P Bar Farms creates a new intricate cornfield design each year and has been inviting visitors to enjoy the farm life via hayrides, a pumpkin patch, and more outdoor family fun since 2011. Past corn maze designs have included a nod to *Jurassic Park*, the Route 66 road sign, and a larger-than-life replica of the 2008-issued Oklahoma quarter. Supersleuths eager to demonstrate amazing maze skills can twist and turn through 1.5 miles (2.4 km) of cornstalks. There are 10 stopping points in the maze, each with trivia questions that give hints on finding the exit. The maze is divided into two halves, and a country store between is a good spot to strategize and fuel up with a snack. For a side of spine tingle, check out the Haunted Maze in October.

> "SUPER SLEUTHS EAGER TO DEMONSTRATE AMAZING MAZE SKILLS CAN TWIST AND TURN THROUGH 1.5 MILES (2.4 KM) OF CORNSTALKS."

Hydro, OK | Season: Fall

Don't get corn-fused finding your way through the corn mazes that pop up in the fall.

Little Niagara Falls may not be as large as its big New York cousin, but it's beautiful to behold.

Fall (and Zip) for Waterfalls

Oklahoma's diverse landscape includes lakes, plains, mesas, and forests, as well as several waterfalls. Chasing them takes nature lovers on a scavenger hunt to some of picturesque corners.

Little Niagara Falls in Chickasaw National Recreation Area is nothing like the famous falls on the Canadian-American border, but unlike at *those* Niagara Falls, visitors here can dive into the swimming hole of these cool and crystal clear waters.

Located inside the state park of the same name close to the Arkansas border, stunning Natural Falls, sometimes called Dripping Springs, plummets 77 feet (24 m) over a cliff. Though visitors can't swim at the falls, other cooling-off spots are close by, and an observation deck above the falls is accessible via an easy hiking trail. Shorter but no less pretty, Presbyterian Falls tumbles through a section of the Lower Mountain Fork River, a popular destination for canoeing, kayaking, and year-round fishing that is especially eye-catching in October, when surrounding trees ignite with fall color.

Honey Creek falls over rocks into a natural swimming pool inside Turner Falls Park in the Arbuckle Mountains. For a different perspective, check out the nearby 777 Zip, an exhilarating two-person ride that takes guests to a 777-foot (237 m) tower high above the park's Collings Castle, where unparalleled views of Turner Falls await.

Near the historic and pretty town of Pawhuska, Bluestem Lake spillway cascades over shale and rocks to create the mesmerizing contemplation spot of Bluestem Falls. The 325-acre (130 ha) lake is also a big draw for anglers seeking to catch largemouth bass, bluegill, channel catfish, walleye, crappie, and other local fish. Three boat ramps and four docks surround the lake for personal watercraft.

Spend a sunny day rafting the Illinois River.

Float on the Illinois River

For a calm day out on the water with family and friends, or a solo paddle full of self-reflection, the Illinois River offers calm currents and serenity in the Oklahoma Ozarks. Especially popular is the stretch northeast of Tahlequah, where the river has plenty of cooling swimming holes and scenery accented by steep bluffs and leafy shoreline, and animals and birds, including the occasional bald eagle, can often be spotted. A leisurely float is the most popular way to experience the Illinois River's splendor, and with more than a dozen resorts and launching locations, visitors have a pick of places from which to rent tubes, rafts, kayaks, and canoes, whether for an hour or a full day. If a multiday river adventure calls, Elephant Rock Nature Park is a good place to overnight, thanks to shady campsites and a few air-conditioned yurts.

Tahlequah, OK | **Season:** Summer

Get Thee to a Bat Cave

The grand dame of Alabaster Caverns State Park is, as the name suggests, a cavern formed of alabaster, a rare form of gypsum. The only other places in the world with similar caves are China and Italy.

Guided tours take visitors into Mother Nature's ultimate art gallery, where the air cools to around 50°F (10°C) and the walls seem to twinkle like stars. Colorful selenite crystal formations poke from small crevices and grooves, and a slow-moving stream trickles through the length of the cavern. Guided tours are offered six months a year, April through October, to protect hibernating bats. For spelunkers, Alabaster Caverns has four "wild" caves to explore, though permits are required. The spelunking adventure takes you through caves that range in length from 550 to 1,600 feet (170 to 480 m).

Brazilian free-tailed bat

Of note, the park is the starting point for an unusual encounter with the flying mammals at nearby Selman Bat Cave where a handful of visitors each summer witness hundreds of thousands of Mexican free-tailed bats pour from their den and feed on insects at dusk. Preregistration is required and begins in May, and 75 lucky winners are chosen through a random drawing to participate in one of only eight viewing sessions offered each July. The bats travel more than 1,400 miles (2,250 km) every year to give birth to their young and care for them in this protected area in Oklahoma. The bat cave is closed to the public except for this special event.

For overnighters, the park has both tent and RV campsites.

Freedom, OK | **Season:** Spring to fall

Stand on Top of Oklahoma

Debunking any myth that Oklahoma's topography is boring, Black Mesa State Park and its distinctive 45-mile-long (72 km) volcanic mesa rises like a mirage from the plains and prairies in the state's panhandle. An 8.5-mile (13.6 km) out-and-back trail beckons hikers to follow to the park's summit at 4,973 feet (1,516 m), the Sooner State's highest point. At the elevation indicator, take in the 360-degree vast views, a great spot to twirl, arms out, *Sound of Music* style.

Black Mesa takes its name from the layer of black lava rock that coated the area about 30 million years ago. Also dwelling around here millions of years ago were dinosaurs, and near the east end of the park, next to Carrizo Creek, tracks have been preserved in sandstone. For stargazers, the park is also a front-row seat to the annual Perseid meteor shower, between mid-July and mid-August.

Kenton, OK | **Season:** Spring to fall

Take a stroll through the gardens outside the Philbrook Museum of Art.

1. STROLL THROUGH OKLAHOMA'S FIRST RESORT TOWN

Known for its distinct round red stones found on buildings and walls, the picturesque city of Medicine Park was the state's first resort town and invites easy strolls along its streets dotted with restaurants and shops. On hot days, locals head to Bath Lake, a swimming hole located right in the heart of downtown.

2. RIDE THE WHEEL IN OKC

Overlooking the Oklahoma City skyline, the 100-foot (30 m) Wheeler Ferris wheel, in the neighborhood of the same name, used to thrill riders at the pier in Santa Monica, California. It now stands above the south bank of the Oklahoma River, with pedestrian and bike access to the Oklahoma River Trail network.

3. GATHER AT THE GATHERING PLACE

The 66-acre (27 ha) Gathering Place is more than a park along the Arkansas River; it's a mind-blowing place to climb, play, and enjoy the outside at the adventure playground, ponds and water features, towering slides, walking trails and rock sculptures, and sprawling lawns that invite humanity to gather on common ground.

4. KAYAK THE GLOVER RIVER

Oklahoma isn't especially known for its river rapids, but the remote and uncommercialized Glover is an exception. Meant for advanced paddlers, the pristine river flows out of the Ouachita Mountains through dense and secluded forests lined by steep bluffs and towering pines, making it the ultimate getaway.

5. PICTURE THE FALL FOLIAGE

Hikers and anglers love Beavers Bend State Park year-round, but when leaves turn vibrant ruby red, burnt orange, and honey yellow, leaf peeping turns ordinary nature shots extraordinary. Soak up the colorful setting by hiking trails, pitching a tent at a campground, or canoeing on Broken Bow Lake.

6. CAMP AT MCGEE CREEK STATE PARK

On the south side of McGee Creek Reservoir, this park offers year-round camping, including eight rustic lake hut rentals for those who prefer a roof over their heads. The park also has 64 miles (103 km) of shoreline and beaches, and miles of forested hiking and biking trails to discover.

7. MOUNTAIN BIKE AT LAKE THUNDERBIRD

There's a lot here for serious trail warriors, whether on foot or horseback, but mountain bikers swoon over long rides and single-track trails with steep climbs, drops, and rock gardens, as well as some short and easy runs too, all well marked for maximum enjoyment of this beautiful 1,874-acre (758 ha) outdoor lover's haven.

8. WANDER THE GARDENS AT PHILBROOK MUSEUM OF ART

A little piece of Tuscany in Tulsa, this pink villa sits on 25 acres (10 ha) of gorgeous gardens filled with flowers, manicured lawns, serene ponds, and an herb and produce garden that feeds the on-site restaurant and local food banks. Keep your eyes open for the roaming resident cats too. Much of the garden is wheelchair accessible.

9. ROCK CLIMB AT ROBBERS CAVE

A favorite in the San Bois Mountains thanks to sandstone cliffs with great routes for beginner and intermediate level climbers, the park is open year-round, but fall leaves make it especially scenic. Make time to see the cave where outlaws Jesse James and Belle Starr hid out.

10. VISIT THE OKC ZOO

The whole family will enjoy a visit to the Oklahoma City Zoo, where you'll find not only live animals of all sizes but also a diverse botanical garden and statues of endangered species made with more than one million toy bricks.

Indian blanket flower

Salt Creek Waterfall spills 286 feet (87 m) into Willamette National Forest.

OREGON

Known as an outdoor oasis, this Pacific Northwest destination
doesn't disappoint when it comes to adventure and exploration.

Fort Stevens State Park,
Shipwreck of Peter Iredale

W A S H

*Historic Columbia River
Highway State Trail*

*Horsetail Falls
Trail*

*Portland Japanese
Garden*

*Ponytail
Falls*

Deschutes

P A C I F I C   O C E A N

**Neskowin
Ghost Forest**

*Wooden Shoe
Tulip Farm*

*Deschutes
River*

*McDonald
State Forest*

**Cape
Perpetua**

**Sea Lion
Caves**

*Tamolitch
Falls*

**Maple Avenue
Bridge**

O   R   E

**Oregon Dunes National
Recreation Area**

*Newberry National
Volcanic Monument*

*Summer Lak
Hot Spring*

*Swinging
Bridge*

**Rogue Valley
ZipLine Adventure**

*Redwood
Nature Trail*

*Oregon Redwoods
Trail*

C A L I F O R N I A

GTON

Painted
Hills

GON

Crane Hot
Springs

Alvord
Desert

IDAHO

NEVADA

See the Sea Lions of Oregon's Coast

Watch Steller sea lions growl, bark, and grunt while perched on rocks at Sea Lion Caves, the largest sea cave in America. Located 11 miles (18 km) north of Florence on the Oregon coast, just off Highway 101, the caves are a privately owned wildlife preserve and bird sanctuary that's part of Cape Perpetua Marine Reserve. Between December and March, a couple hundred sea lions congregate in the 12-story-tall cave.

The cave is accessible via a short walk from the gift shop, through an elevator that descends 208 feet (63 m) down to an observation area. You can also see the 56-foot-tall (17 m) Heceta Head in the distance, one of the most photographed lighthouses on the coast.

Gray whales are known to pass by the Sea Lion Caves region during their northward migratory journey. Bring your binoculars to catch a glimpse of marine birds like pigeon guillemots, rhinoceros auklets, and oystercatchers flying over the water.

Florence, OR | **Season:** December to March

Steller sea lions make their homes in the caves along Oregon's coast.

Bike Through the Desert

The desolate-looking Alvord Desert in southeastern Oregon is a stark contrast to the state's lush, evergreen landscape. Once a 200-foot-deep (60 m) lake that extended more than 100 miles (160 km), the area has since dried due to low precipitation in a region that receives an average of 7 inches (18 cm) of rain each year. The dry lake bed spans 12 miles (19 km) long and seven miles (11 km) wide and is popular with campers, photographers, and cyclists.

One of the largest playas in Oregon, the desert and its remoteness make it a good candidate for a bikepacking trip. It's quite a surreal experience biking across the flat cracked alkali desert floor, with the Steens Mountain range, which runs the length of the playa, towering 5,000 feet (1,525 m) above. The Alvord Desert butts up to the Steens fault zone, which explains the region's plentiful hot springs. On the western edge of the desert, you'll find a privately owned hot springs, where $5 (cash) will get you a soak in therapeutic thermal waters.

Set up camp before the sun sets, then sit back and gaze at the Milky Way glittering above.

Cracked mud and mineral deposits on a dry lake bed in Alvord Desert

Princeton, OR | **Season:** July to November

The Coast's Nature Show

Along the Oregon coast, visitors will come across a few spectacular nature shows near Cape Perpetua. During high tide, ocean water shoots up from the Spouting Horn like a whale's blowhole. The phenomenon is caused when pressure builds inside the cave and funnel water and air into it. A short trail leads to views of the Spouting Horn and the tide pools, which are brimming with sea life during low tide.

Resembling a bottomless sinkhole, Thor's Well is a 20-foot-deep (6 m) hole in the basalt rocks. Also known as the ominous "Gate to Hell," it appears to drain and fill up repeatedly during high tide.

Cook's Chasm is a sheer-sided inlet on ancient volcanic rock that's constantly being pounded by the ocean. The three-quarter-mile (1.2 km) Captain Cook Trail is a round-trip out-and-back path that offers views of Cook's Chasm, Spouting Horn, and Thor's Well.

Two miles (3 km) north of Cook's Chasm, you'll find

Devil's Churn, a narrow inlet that started as a small fracture and evolved over time, as waves from the Pacific Ocean crashed into the ancient volcanic rock. Cape Cove Trail is a paved path that leads to Devil's Churn.

Chinook salmon

If you have more time, drive about 10 miles (16 km) south to the Hobbit Trail, and a short hike to Hobbit Beach. On this trek, you'll feel like you've journeyed into Middle-earth as the trail takes you through an emerald green fern-covered forest filled with Sitka spruce and rhododendrons. Follow the trail signs closely to reach the aptly named Hobbit Beach. On the edge of this tucked-away cove you'll find tide pools to explore and have a chance to search the sand for seashells and crabs. A two-mile (3.2 km) trail from the beach leads to Heceta Head Lighthouse State Scenic Viewpoint.

See the Ruins

When the *Peter Iredale* ran aground near Fort Stevens in 1906, it became an immediate tourist sensation. People flocked to see the shipwreck ruin wedged into the sand. Originally owned by British shipping firm Iredale & Porter, the four-masted steel bark was built in Maryport, England, in 1890. *Peter Iredale* was en route from Salina Cruz, Mexico, to Portland to pick up cargo for the U.K. when it met its unfortunate demise. Strong winds grounded the ship on Clatsop Sands, and thank goodness, all the crew survived. But the barnacle-covered wreckage remains there to this day. Now, as part of Fort Stevens State Park, *Peter Iredale* is one of the most accessible shipwrecks on the West Coast. During low tide, you can walk up to the shipwreck, which has been slowly decaying over the last century. It's also a great place to beachcomb for sand dollars.

Remains of the *Peter Iredale* rest in an abandoned Clatsop pit.

Watch the sun set over the Columbia River Gorge from Vista House.

> "THE FIRST SCENIC HIGHWAY IN THE UNITED STATES, THE ROUTE WEAVED THROUGH OREGON'S DREAMY LANDSCAPE."

Historic Columbia River Highway State Trail

Constructed between 1913 and 1922, the Historic Columbia River Highway was the first scenic highway in the United States, with a route that weaved through Oregon's dreamy landscape, cascading waterfalls, and picturesque viewpoints. Abandoned in 1960, it was reopened as a national historic landmark in 2000. Two years later, it was named a national recreation trail. Today, 68 miles (109 km) of the original 73 miles (117 km) are open to hikers and cyclists.

The Historic Columbia River Highway State Trail is made up of three segments: Bonneville, Mitchell Point, and Twin Tunnels. The 11-mile (18 km) out-and-back Bonneville segment starts at the Bridge of the Gods trailhead in Cascade Locks and ends at the John B. Yeon State Scenic Corridor. The car-free trail crosses under the interstate and past a small waterfall. After it passes the Eagle Creek Day Use Area, the trail goes up a 40-foot (12 m) staircase, which is equipped with a bike-wheel grove. Along the way, marvel at the historic Bonneville Dam, the Tooth Rock Tunnel, and the Columbia River.

The Twin Tunnels segment is a car-free 4.5-mile (7.2 km) trail that connects Hood River and Mosier through the restored Mosier Twin Tunnels. From the Mark O. Hatfield West trailhead, the path winds through rolling hills of firs and ponderosa pines. The newest paved section, the Mitchell Point segment is a nearly six-mile (10 km) path from Wyeth State trailhead to Viento State Park. Bike to Shellrock Mountain before passing the Columbia River Gorge and four waterfalls, including Starvation Creek and Lancaster Falls. Bicycles and e-bikes are allowed on the trail.

Multicity, OR   **Season:** Year-round

Somewhere Over the Bridge

Inspired by Utah's Pipe Dream Cave, local rock-climbing expert Ian Caldwell wanted to replicate the experience of climbing the cave's steep overhanging routes at a site closer to home in Redmond, Oregon. In 2014, he convinced the Redmond city staff to let him create a rock-climbing course under the Maple Avenue Bridge. The 70-foot-tall (21 m) and 780-foot-long (238 m) concrete bridge is built over Dry Canyon, its floor covered with dirt, grass, sagebrush, and junipers. Along one of the concrete bridge's three 210-foot (64 m) arches, Caldwell created a path of bolts, holds, and permadraws. Climbers start at the 45-degree overhang and complete the route at 75 degrees, before rappelling down to the canyon floor.

The versatile route appeals to beginners, endurance builders, and those in training. The Maple Avenue Bridge is located within Dry Canyon Park, which has four miles (6.4 km) of trails, mountain bike single-track, playgrounds, an amphitheater, and sports fields.

> "THE CONCRETE BRIDGE IS BUILT OVER DRY CANYON, ITS FLOOR COVERED IN DIRT, GRASS, SAGEBRUSH, AND JUNIPERS."

Redmond, OR | **Season:** Year-round

Climb the underside of 70-foot-tall (21 m) Maple Avenue Bridge, which has three 210-foot (64 m) arch spans to conquer.

Tamolitch Falls spills into the McKenzie Wild and Scenic River.

Hike to the Blue Pool

People from all over the world hike to see if Tamolitch Falls (also known as Blue Pool) in Willamette National Forest is really *that* blue. The answer is: Yes. Depending on the time, the Tamolitch Falls' colors range from sapphire blue to turquoise to a light iridescent blue.

The pool was formed more than 1,600 years ago, when lava flow from the Belknap Crater buried a three-mile (5 km) stretch of the McKenzie River between Carmen Reservoir and Tamolitch Falls. The water from the river seeps through underground lava fields, resurfacing up the cliff-rimmed basin and forming the deep blue pool. In 1933, Willamette National Forest recreational engineer William Parke renamed the basin "Tamolitch," which means "bucket" in the Chinook language.

You can reach Tamolitch Falls in two ways: a two-mile (3.2 km) hike up from the Trail Bridge Reservoir or a three-mile (5 km) hike down from Carmen Reservoir. The trek from the reservoir traverses through a portion of the famed McKenzie River Trail, the 26-mile (42 km) route popular with mountain bikers. (If you opt for a day on the McKenzie River Trail, the path is equally stunning, crossing the river and passing two worthwhile scenic overlooks: one to Sahalie Falls and one to Koosah Falls.) The moderate trail goes through old-growth forest of large Douglas fir, western hemlock, western red cedar, and maples. Along the whimsical walk, you'll pass the gushing river, moss-covered rocks, and ferns that blanket the forest floor.

During autumn, the forest becomes more magical when leaves turn brilliant shades of gold and red. Year-round, the 30-foot-deep (9 m) pool stays at a cool 40°F (4°C)—much too cold to swim in, so stay dry and just enjoy the views. Weekends are packed, so opt for early morning or late afternoon hikes during the week. Parking is free.

Rev up the ATVs for a thrilling adventure on the Oregon Dunes.

OHV on the Dunes

 Extending 40 miles (64 km) along the Oregon coast from Florence to Coos Bay, Oregon Dunes National Recreation Area has one of the largest expanses of temperate coastal sand dunes in the world. Designated as a national recreation area in 1972, Oregon Dunes is a natural playground for ATVs and has several areas that allow off-highway vehicles (OHVs). Drive through hilly dunes along the 5.5-mile (8.9 km) Coast Guard North OHV Trail, which starts north at the South Jetty OHV Trail and heads south, ending at Siltcoos Beach Day Use. Along the way, it links to the Breach OHV Trail, Chapman's OHV Trail, and Goosepasture OHV Trail. Those who want to explore the dunes on foot should head to the Oregon Dunes Day Use Area. Or hike the Tahkenitch Dunes National Recreation Trail, through a mile of conifer forest and shore pines to reach the ocean.

Reedsport, OR | Season: Spring to fall

Zip-Line the Mining Hills

On a clear day, you can see some of Oregon's greatest natural wonders—Upper and Lower Table Rocks, snowcapped Mount McLoughlin, and even the rim of Crater Lake—as you fly across the zip line at Rogue Valley ZipLine Adventure, the longest zip line in the Pacific Northwest. Nestled in 83 acres (34 ha) of a historic gold mining hill in southern Oregon, the aerial adventure park offers 2,700 feet (820 m) of zipping on five zip-line courses.

Guests gear up at the main office with a gold mining town facade—an homage to its rich past. From there, a steep hike goes to the first course. During the three-hour tour, guests will zip on lines that get progressively longer and higher off the ground. The pièce de résistance is the final course, which runs a quarter-mile (0.4 km) across scrub oak and pine treetops. Speeds can get up to 50 miles an hour (80 km/h).

The park is ADA accessible, and staff members will make an effort to help differently abled people navigate the course. You can also rent a helmet equipped with a camera to record your experience. Zip-line riders must be at least eight years old. Rogue Valley ZipLine Adventure also offers a "Zip, Dip, and Sip" tour that combines a zip-line adventure with lunch at the Laurel Hill Golf Course, white-water rafting at Rogue River, and wine tasting at the charming Del Rio Vineyards and Winery.

Zip-line guests are picked up and dropped off via shuttle from Laurel Hill Golf Course. After a day of high-flying thrills, families can opt to keep the excitement going by stopping at the nearby Rogue Valley Family Fun Center. The outdoor entertainment hub features a go-kart track, batting cages, two 18-hole miniature golf courses, and a bumper boat pool with a "tropical" island and rock waterfall, in addition to an indoor arcade and play area. The park is open year-round.

Central Point, OR | Season: Spring to fall

Tree stumps stick out of the Pacific Ocean during low tide at the Neskowin Ghost Forest.

Visit a Ghost Forest

It's quite an eerie sight when you first witness the Neskowin Ghost Forest as it emerges from the surf during negative tide. Shrouded in fog, hundreds of ancient stumps jut up across Oregon's Tillamook coast. They're the remnants of what was once a nearly 2,000-year-old Sitka spruce forest that was likely buried in sand after a major earthquake dropped the forested land into the tidal zone. In the 1990s, a series of powerful winter storms unearthed the petrified tree stubs that had been buried for several centuries. Exposed to the elements, the trees have been eroded down to headstone-size stumps, covered with barnacles, sea stars, and sea anemones. The low tide also allows you to circumvent or scramble up Proposal Rock, one of the most accessible sea stacks along the Oregon coast. To get to the ghost forest, you'll have to cross a shallow creek, so wear waterproof boots.

Neskowin, OR | **Season:** Year-round

See the waterfall at the
Portland Japanese Garden.

1. RIDE HORSEBACK THROUGH THE FOREST

Operated by Oregon State University College of Forestry, McDonald State Forest in Corvallis has more than 17 miles (27 km) of single-track trails and 40 miles (64 km) of gravel and dirt road through fields of wildflowers and over wooden bridges. The forest is open to the public for day use recreation, and the trails are well signed and easy to follow.

2. CROSS THE SWINGING BRIDGE

Built in 1963, the aptly named Swinging Bridge is a narrow wood-deck suspension footbridge that crosses the Illinois River. Hike the short trail to the wooden stairs, then head up 60 feet (18 m) to take in the views of Selma and the clear, blue water from above.

3. SEE THE OREGON REDWOODS

Oregon has two old-growth redwood groves within a 30-minute drive of each other. Old-growth redwood trees tower like giants over the Redwood Nature Trail at Alfred A. Loeb State Park near the California-Oregon border. Although the redwoods along Rogue River–Siskiyou National Forest's Oregon Redwoods Trail are smaller than the ones at Alfred A. Loeb, this trail stands out because it includes a wheelchair-accessible ridgetop portion.

4. SEE THE PAINTED HILLS

The most visited unit of John Day Fossil Beds National Monument in central Oregon's high desert, the Painted Hills are nature's masterpiece. The hills' tie-dye hues of golds, reds, yellows, and blacks change throughout the day, based on the sun's position and moisture level. The park has five trails that offer a range of panoramic views to close-up looks.

5. WALK BEHIND THE WATERFALL

The Horsetail Falls Trail is a short hike with huge rewards. The easy-to-navigate trail in the Columbia River Gorge is less than half a mile (0.8 km) through trees and into a clearing where you'll witness the cascading Ponytail Falls, which drops into a creek and feeds into the 176-foot (54 m) Horsetail Falls below. Keep going on the trail, and you'll arrive at the caverns behind the waterfall for a completely different perspective.

6. RAFT THE DESCHUTES RIVER

White-water raft down the lower Deschutes River on sections between the mouth of the Deschutes and Pelton Dam. Navigate the beginner-friendly Class II and Class III rapids through fast-moving water, while taking in views of the desert canyon, dramatic basalt rock formations, and blooming native plants.

7. EXPLORE NEWBERRY NATIONAL VOLCANIC MONUMENT

Technically a caldera, the Newberry Crater stretches across 17 square miles (27 km²) inside an active volcano. During winter, the only way you can reach the caldera is by snowshoeing, cross-country skiing, or snowmobiling. Two Nordic trails originate from Newberry's Sno-Park: the Paulina View Trail that leads to the waterfall and the Ponderosa Rim Trail.

8. REFLECT AT THE PORTLAND JAPANESE GARDEN

Spend your afternoon in quiet reflection at downtown Portland's Japanese Garden. The tranquil oasis is made up of eight garden styles, including a tea garden, a sand-and-stone garden, and a natural garden. Cross Moon Bridge or Zig-Zag Bridge surrounded by blue Japanese irises.

9. SOAR OVER THE TULIP AND DAFFODIL FESTIVAL

Each spring, thousands of tulips and daffodils cover the fields at the Wooden Shoe Tulip Farm, with snow-covered Mount Hood in the background. During the Tulip Fest, you can stroll the rows of yellow, purple, orange, and pink flowers, and pose for a picture in front of the windmill. For an aerial view of the floral canvas, hop on a tethered hot-air balloon ride.

10. HOT SPRING IN OREGON

Oregon is home to several hot springs, thanks to its volcanic activity and converging fault lines. The historic Summer Lake Hot Springs in southern Oregon is a 145-acre (59 ha) resort with indoor and outdoor pools filled with natural artesian hot mineral springs. Soak in therapeutic waters at the outdoor rock pool and enjoy the views.

Visit charming Kunkletown in the Poconos.

PENNSYLVANIA

Visit majestic forests, raft beautiful waterways, find winter thrills, or spot wildlife in this robust and diverse state.

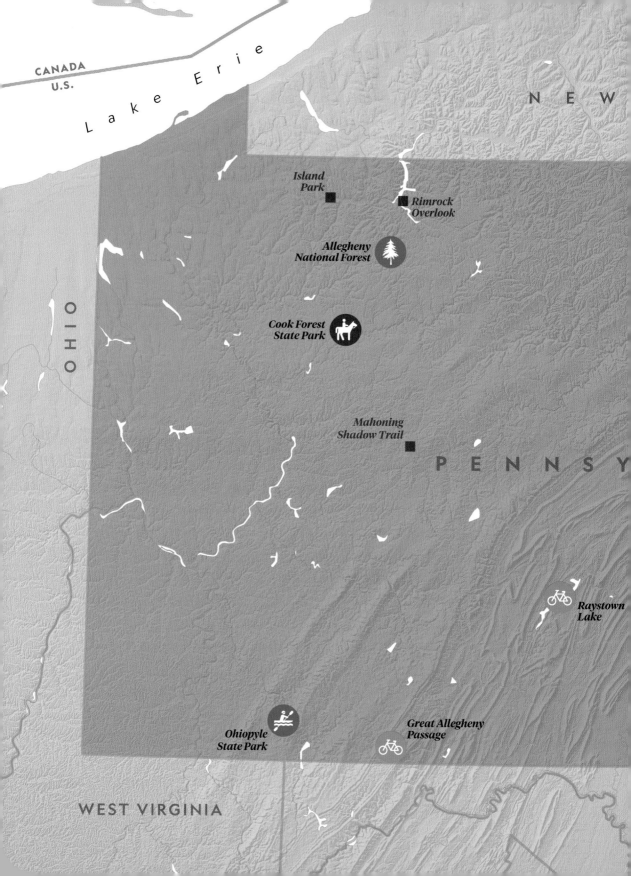

CANADA
U.S.

Lake Erie

OHIO

NEW

Island
Park

Rimrock
Overlook

Allegheny
National Forest

Cook Forest
State Park

Mahoning
Shadow Trail

PENNSY

Raystown
Lake

Ohiopyle
State Park

Great Allegheny
Passage

WEST VIRGINIA

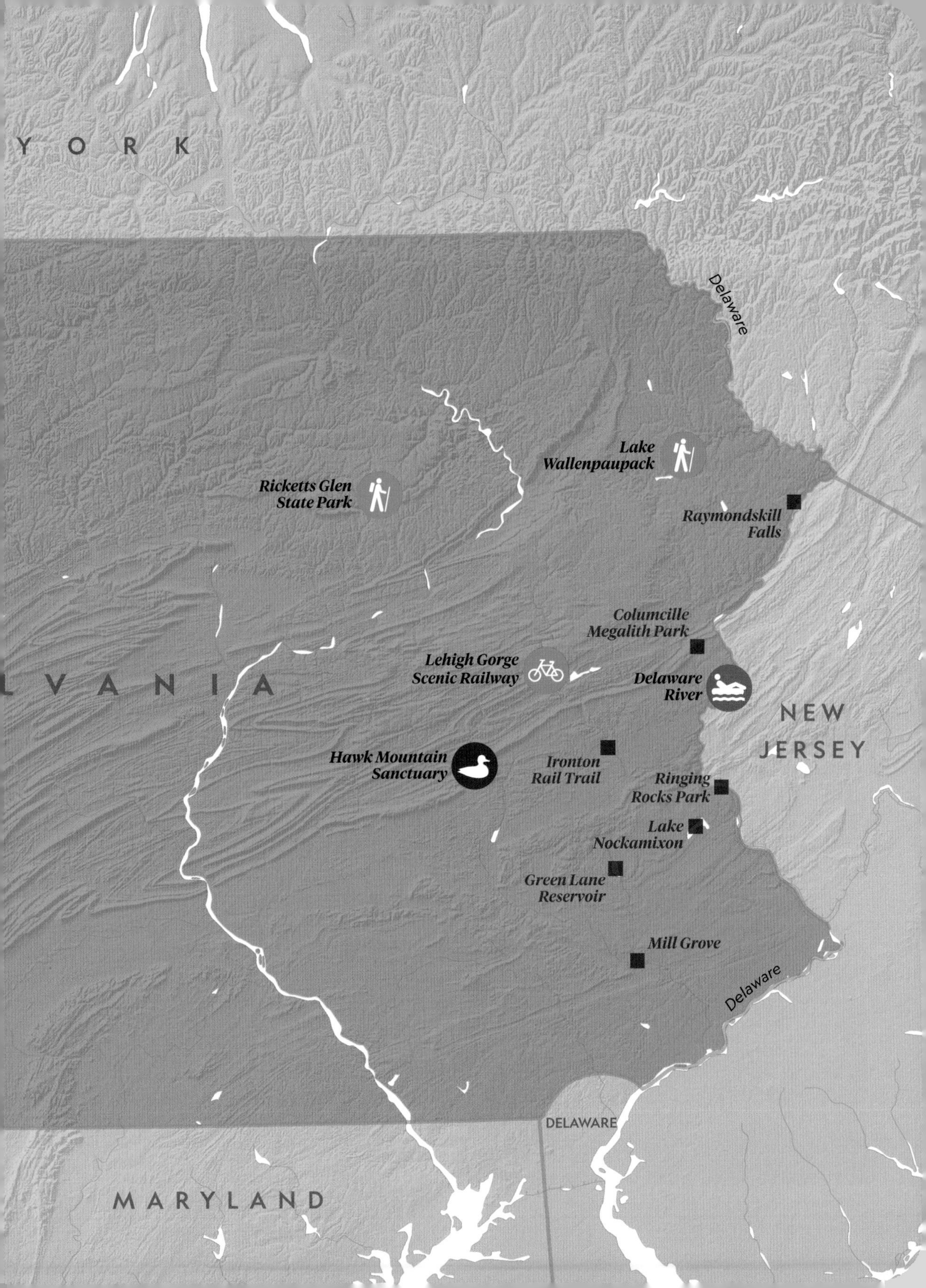

YORK

NEW

JERSEY

Delaware

L V A N I A

DELAWARE

MARYLAND

Delaware

Ricketts Glen
State Park

Lake
Wallenpaupack

Raymondskill
Falls

Columcille
Megalith Park

Lehigh Gorge
Scenic Railway

Delaware
River

Hawk Mountain
Sanctuary

Ironton
Rail Trail

Ringing
Rocks Park

Lake
Nockamixon

Green Lane
Reservoir

Mill Grove

Happy Trails to You

Often overshadowed by northern neighbor Allegheny National Forest, Cook Forest is a national treasure in its own right, with multiuse trails, river-front campsites, and some of the finest examples of the country's vanishing old growth. In the heart of the park stands Forest Cathedral, an ancient forest where 300-year-old white pines and hemlocks are preserved. To see this national natural landmark, follow the 1.2-mile (1.9 km) Longfellow Trail. The trees stand nearly 200 feet (60 m) tall, so you'll have to crane your neck to glimpse their crowns.

Multiuse trails like Hefren Run are open to horses. Try the Equestrian Trail, which skirts the northern edge of Forest Cathedral, or Bridle Trail along its eastern boundary. If you arrive at Cook Forest by kayak or canoe via the Wild and Scenic Clarion River, Thompson Eddy has three one-night sites waiting for you. Rustic riverside cabins, full hookups, and primitive campsites are available for longer stays.

Cooksburg, PA | Season: Spring to fall

Take a crisp fall ride through Cook Forest State Park.

Laze on the River

A classic Pennsylvania way to spend a hot summer day is tubing on a river. In eastern Pennsylvania, it all goes down on the Delaware, the longest free-flowing river in the eastern United States.

For a scenic stretch, rent a tube from Bucks County River Country, catch the shuttle six miles (10 km) north to the launch point, and let the river carry you back on its calm current. If you're tubing with a group, bring a rope or rent a tether ($2 to $3) to connect you.

A typical float takes two to four hours, depending on river conditions, and relaxation comes easy among the bucolic beauty of the state's forests and farms. For a more active experience, rent a kayak, canoe, or raft (also available from Bucks County River Country) and explore the shoreline and river islands. Open daily from 9 a.m. to 5 p.m. in season (Memorial Day to Labor Day); reservations are required. Expect additional fees for parking ($7/car) and key check ($2).

Spending the day on the water can build up an appetite. Back at base camp, the Red Mushroom Cafe offers burgers, hot dogs, and homemade ice cream.

Spend the day tubing down the Delaware River.

Point Pleasant, PA | Season: Summer

Scenic Bike Ride on the Lehigh Gorge Rail Trail

Bring your bike and step aboard the Lehigh Gorge Scenic Railway, named one of the "50 Best Rides in the Country" by *Outside* magazine. During select weekends from April through November, the bike train departs historic Jim Thorpe Station, located in the center of a charming mountain town that was a prosperous coal-shipping center in the early 1800s. The bike train travels 25 miles (40 km) north through the lush Lehigh Gorge. When it arrives at White Haven, find the trailhead and follow the rail trail south along the Lehigh River back to Jim Thorpe. Along the way, you'll pass over railroad trestles and see remains of locks and dams that once regulated the canal's water levels to transport coal downstream. Stop for photos at Buttermilk and Luke's Falls. During the autumn months, you'll cycle past more than 127 species of trees glowing in various shades of gold, orange, and red.

Lehigh Township, PA | **Season:** Spring to fall

Should you not have the time (or the stamina) to ride the whole trail, you can choose between three trails to break up the route: the 10-mile (16 km) D&L Black Diamond Trail from Glen Summit to White Haven, the 10-mile (16 km) Upper Gorge Trail from White Haven to Rockport, or the 15-mile (24 km) Lower Gorge Trail from Rockport to Jim Thorpe.

Ruffed grouse

Bike train reservations are required and can be made by calling the railway directly. Pocono Biking offers bike rentals and daily one-way shuttles to five trailheads located 10 to 36 miles (16 to 58 km) upriver.

Have a different ride in mind? After a visit to the No. 9 Coal Mine & Museum, you can ride by rail into the mountain to see the mine's original 900-foot (270 m) elevator shaft.

Take in Lake Wallenpaupack from the shores of Wilsonville Recreation Area.

Big Day on the Big Lake

There are many ways to spend a day at Lake Wallenpaupack. You can hike it—try the 5.2-mile (8.4 km) Blue Loop at Shuman Point for unspoiled lake views. You can fish it—hire a guide, like Ray's or Troll On, to take you to the most productive fishing holes for landing small- and largemouth bass, walleye, and brown trout. You can boat it—rent a pontoon or deck boat from Pine Crest Marina or try a six- to eight-person paddleboard or pedal pontoon. Bring binoculars and head to Kipp Island to glimpse the pair of bald eagles that return to nest and raise their young every year. Or you can kick back and tour it—take a 50-minute narrated tour with Lake Wallenpaupack Boat Tours to learn about the lake's hydroelectric history. The fun doesn't stop when temperatures drop. In winter, "Big Lake" becomes a frozen playground for ice fishing, ice hockey, and ice tee golf.

Hawley, PA | **Season:** Year-round

"EVERY INCH OF THIS PLACE IS COURSING WITH BEAUTY."

Waterfall Wonderland

Virgin woodlands. Raging waterfalls. Watchable wildlife. Quintessential Pennsylvania is on full display at Ricketts Glen State Park. Home to the Glens Natural Area, a Y-shaped gorge carved by Kitchen Creek, this national natural landmark is arguably the best waterfall hike in the state, if not the entire Northeast.

Experience the wonder via the Falls Trail System, a 7.2-mile (11.6 km) steep, rocky lollipop loop that visits 21 free-flowing waterfalls, ranging in size from the staggered ledges of 11-foot (3.4 m) Cayuga to the towering tumbling staircase of 94-foot (28.7 m) Ganoga. Natural nooks and crannies invite you to stop at your favorites to soak in misty views (and snap a selfie).

To access the trail, park at Glens Lot trailhead and hike northeast through an ancient forest of virgin pine, hemlock, and oak. Follow Kitchen Creek, where the welcoming committee—a cascading trio of Murray Reynolds, Sheldon Reynolds, and Harrison Wright—pours a sample of the beauty you're about to behold.

Waters Meet is where Kitchen Creek's east and west branches converge and the trail loop begins. Take the eastern Glen Leigh branch and follow the stone staircase as it winds past moss-draped boulders to eight waterfalls. Fifteen-foot (4.6 m) Wyandot and Onondaga Falls bookend this section, with Ozone Falls, a twisty 60-foot (18.3 m) giant, in between.

At the top, follow the Highland Trail through the woods and Midway Crevasse boulder field to connect to the western Ganoga Glen branch. You'll see 10 waterfalls as you descend, including its namesake, Ganoga, the tallest in the park. Climb out to the rocks at Ganoga's base to fully absorb its size and splendor.

If you can't do the full loop, take the Evergreen Trail, a one-mile (1.6 km) loop to Adams Falls and a sleek chute plunging into a swimming hole—further proof that every inch of this place is coursing with beauty.

Benton, PA | **Season:** Spring to fall

Three separate cascades make up Ozone Falls.

Pedaler's Paradise

Pedal the Great Allegheny Passage (GAP), a 150-mile (240 km) rail trail with stopovers in welcoming towns—such as the state's maple syrup hub, Meyersdale (Mile 31.9)—where you'll find charming cafés and B&Bs.

The GAP starts at Point State Park in Pittsburgh, where the Allegheny, Ohio, and Monongahela Rivers converge. Pedaling east, you'll see hints of the region's industrial past, like the Red Waterfall (Mile 119), where iron-rich runoff from coal mining stained the soil red.

When you reach Ohiopyle State Park (Mile 71.9), take a photo-worthy detour to Cucumber Falls. You'll cross the Casselman River farther east at Salisbury Viaduct (Mile 33.7), a 101-foot (31 m) trestle bridge with panoramic views. Stop for a photo at the Eastern Continental Divide (Mile 23.7), the highest point on the GAP. The illuminated Big Savage Tunnel (Mile 22) is one of the last highlights on the Pennsylvania side.

> "PEDALING EAST, YOU'LL SEE HINTS OF THE REGION'S INDUSTRIAL PAST, LIKE THE RED WATERFALL, WHERE IRON-RICH RUNOFF FROM COAL MINING STAINED THE SOIL RED."

Pittsburgh, PA **Season:** Spring to fall

Make your way across the pedestrian- and cyclist-only bridges on the Great Allegheny Passage.

Take on Class II to IV rapids on a paddling trip down the Youghiogheny River.

Wild Water Everywhere

In the heart of Pennsylvania's Laurel Highlands, Ohiopyle State Park is home to some of the state's most scenic and thrilling white water.

The Youghiogheny River, aka "the Yough" (pronounced "Yawk"), is a 75-mile (120 km) water trail that flows north from the base of the dam in Confluence to the mouth of the Monongahela River in McKeesport. You'll find the tamest water (Class I and II rapids) along the Middle Yough, between Confluence and Ohiopyle. To ride it, put in at the Ramcat launch in Confluence (river mile 2.9) and paddle until you see the takeout on the river right under the Route 381 bridge.

Experienced paddlers can challenge their skills on the Lower Yough "loop," a 1.5-mile (2.4 km) stretch with Class III to IV rapids that begins below Ohiopyle Falls, makes a U-turn around the Ferncliff Peninsula, and ends at the Great Allegheny Passage Bridge.

Ohiopyle, PA | **Season:** Summer

Wilderness Voyageurs offers fully guided and guide-escorted trips to help less experienced paddlers safely navigate the Yough's wild waters. Daily trips run April to October. Options include a family-friendly adventure on the Middle Yough plying Class I–II rapids and a "Pedal and Paddle" trip, where you'll cycle nine miles (14.5 km) of the Great Allegheny Passage (page 534) to the Ramcat Launch, and then trade your wheels for a raft and tackle the mild rapids of the Middle Yough. If you need equipment, you can rent a four- to six-person raft, a two-person cataraft "shredder," or a solo or tandem inflatable kayak "ducky."

If you prefer to enjoy raging rapids from the safety of the shoreline, hike the Ferncliff Trail, a relatively flat 1.8-mile (2.9 km) loop that follows the peninsula's perimeter beneath virgin hemlocks and giant pines, set against the sound of rushing white water. Follow the rhododendron-lined cliffside trail to Ohiopyle Falls, where you can hike on river boulders to see the frothy falls up close.

Raystown Lake is a mecca for boaters, bird-watchers, and cyclists.

Get Active at Raystown Lake

 Raystown Lake snakes through state game lands, its serpentine curves and lush shoreline inviting you to discover adventure around each bend.

For fast access to its 28 miles (45 km), rent a pontoon boat from Seven Points Marina. The shoreline is full of secret coves and inlets, perfect for spotting resident bald eagles and osprey. Or you can drop a line to land local favorites, like big striper, muskie, and lake trout. Keep an eye out for Ray, the Raystown version of the Loch Ness monster.

Back on land, Allegrippis Trails is a lakeside mountain biking mecca with 24 scenic single-track trails that span 36 miles (58 km). The trailhead at Seven Points Road connects to the Mountain Bike Skills Park, where you'll find banked turns, jumps, and drop-ins.

Hesston, PA | **Season:** Spring to fall

Four Seasons of Fun

Spring, summer, and fall draw hikers to explore more than 200 miles (320 km) of trails in Allegheny National Forest (ANF). For a hike with otherworldly views, try the Minister Creek Trail. From the trailhead at Minister Creek Campground, take the Middle Loop to the Minister Valley Overlook and follow the South Loop back to wander through fields of gigantic moss-covered boulders. Come winter, snowfall transforms many of these trails into cross-country ski and snowshoe routes. Visit Hearts Content, a national natural landmark, to ski or trek beneath 300-year-old white pines.

In warm weather, mountain bikers love to shred trails at places like Buzzard Swamp, where you'll pass by 15 human-made ponds. By winter, snowmobilers are sledding more than 365 miles (585 km) of groomed, interconnected snowmobile trails that form a giant loop around the forest.

Warm days lure anglers to ANF's crystal clear streams, which are stocked with brook, brown, and rainbow trout. The Allegheny Reservoir has been called the "best walleye water in the Northeast outside of the Great Lakes." It also contains smallmouth bass, muskellunge, northern pike, and yellow perch. Midwinter, the reservoir becomes a frozen slice of solitude for ice fishing. (A Pennsylvania fishing license is required.)

ANF is the only national forest in Pennsylvania, and with countless opportunities to enjoy the great outdoors any day of the year, it truly is one of a kind.

Allegheny National Forest, PA | **Season:** Year-round

A handler holds a great horned owl at Hawk Mountain Sanctuary.

Hawk Eye

🦆 The rocky ledges at Hawk Mountain's North Lookout are some of the best seats in the country for watching the annual autumn hawk migration. From August 15 through December 15, staff and volunteers monitor the flyway, tracking eagles, hawks, falcons, and vultures on their annual voyage south.

Hawk Mountain's tradition as the world's first sanctuary for birds of prey began in 1934, making it the longest-running raptor migration count in the world. An estimated 18,000 raptors pass through this area each fall. Hiking trails connect 10 lookouts where observer-interpreters are stationed daily to help visitors identify different species. The Silhouette Trail is an ADA-accessible route to South Lookout. Broad-winged hawks and American kestrels are likely to be spotted earlier in the season, while rough-legged hawks and goshawks tend to arrive later. Sharp-shinned and Cooper's hawks usually appear mid-season. Windy days tend to be most productive, with birds flying from dawn to dusk.

Kempton, PA | **Season:** August to December

St. Oran Bell Tower at
Columcille in Bangor

1. HIKE TO THE RIMROCK OVERLOOK

About 450 million years ago, shallow inland seas created massive boulders that today form Rimrock Overlook. Take the 2.6-mile (4.2 km) out-and-back trail from Kinzua Beach to explore these behemoths and climb the narrow stone staircase between them for sweeping views of the Allegheny River calmly carving an elegant path through an endless expanse of dense forest.

2. BIKE FOR SIGHTS IN COAL COUNTRY

Sunrise on the Mahoning Shadow Trail almost guarantees you'll see your shadow—and more. Chase this 15-mile (24 km) fully accessible rail trail along the Mahoning Creek through the farms and forests of former coal country. When you reach town, detour through Barclay Square to Phil's Burrow to see Punxsutawney Phil and Phyllis.

3. GET A THREE-FOR-ONE

Get three waterfalls in one at Raymondskill Falls, the tallest in the state at 178 feet (54 m). Well-maintained trails offer misty cascade views. Plus, there are two unnamed bonus falls—one next to Lower Falls and a 25-footer (8 m) a short hike upstream from Upper Falls.

4. FIND TRANSFORMATION IN THE WOODS

Ensconced in the Appalachian Mountains, Columcille is a Celtic-inspired outdoor sanctuary that invites you on a transformative journey through woodland trails. Prehistoric stony giants guide the way through Fairie Ring, and a meditation pond invites a moment of reflection.

5. STRIKE A HIGH NOTE

Grab a hammer and set out for a *striking* adventure at Ringing Rocks Park. Follow the Loop Trail to a massive field of diabase boulders that ring when struck. The high note is High Falls, where water pours over a tilted ledge and falls 20 feet (6 m), forming the tallest waterfall in the area.

6. ADVENTURE TO A ONE-OF-A-KIND ISLAND

Over a century ago, Island Park's roller coaster, band shell, and casino drew fun seekers from miles around. Today, that history has been swallowed by nature. Launch a kayak on the Lehigh River at Hope Road and paddle east past Turkey Island. The hidden channel on Island Park's northeastern shore leads to a water-lily pond where the park once stood.

7. VISIT RAILROAD HISTORY

Discover Eastern Pennsylvania's industrial heritage on the 9.2-mile (14.8 km) Ironton Rail Trail spur and loop. You'll see Troxell-Steckel House, a 1756 Pennsylvania German stone farmhouse, the blaze red Caboose No. 6 from Ironton Railroad's glory days, and nine towering brick kilns that once transformed local limestone into the Portland cement upon which much of the country was built.

8. EXPLORE AUDUBON'S FIRST HOME

See the world through the eyes of conservationist John James Audubon, for whom the National Audubon Society was named. Twenty-five miles (40 km) northwest of Philadelphia, Mill Grove estate, Audubon's first U.S. home, offers five miles (8 km) of hiking trails through the woodlands along Perkiomen Creek that inspired his early ornithological illustrations.

9. RIDE, PADDLE, SAIL, OR FISH

The largest lake in Southeast Pennsylvania, Nockamixon ("Nox") offers accessible activities for all. This warm-water fishery has more than 250 species and six launch areas, including an ADA-accessible dock at Tohickon. You can paddle, sail, or cast a line, and its network of nature trails is ideal for exploring the wooded shoreline on bike or horseback.

10. CHECK OFF THIS BIRDER'S PARADISE

Recognized by Audubon Pennsylvania as an Important Bird Area (IBA), Green Lane Reservoir's diverse habitats—which include three bodies of water, hardwood forests, marshlands, and more—attract more than 270 species. Pick up a checklist at the main park office and head to Hill Road Day Use Area and Church Road Bird Sanctuary.

Purple crown vetch

The coastline of Brenton Point
State Park in Newport

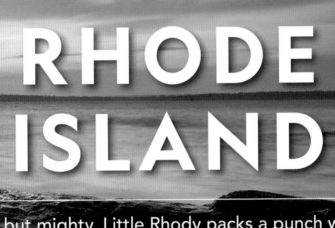

RHODE ISLAND

Small but mighty, Little Rhody packs a punch with its beautiful coastline and picturesque parks.

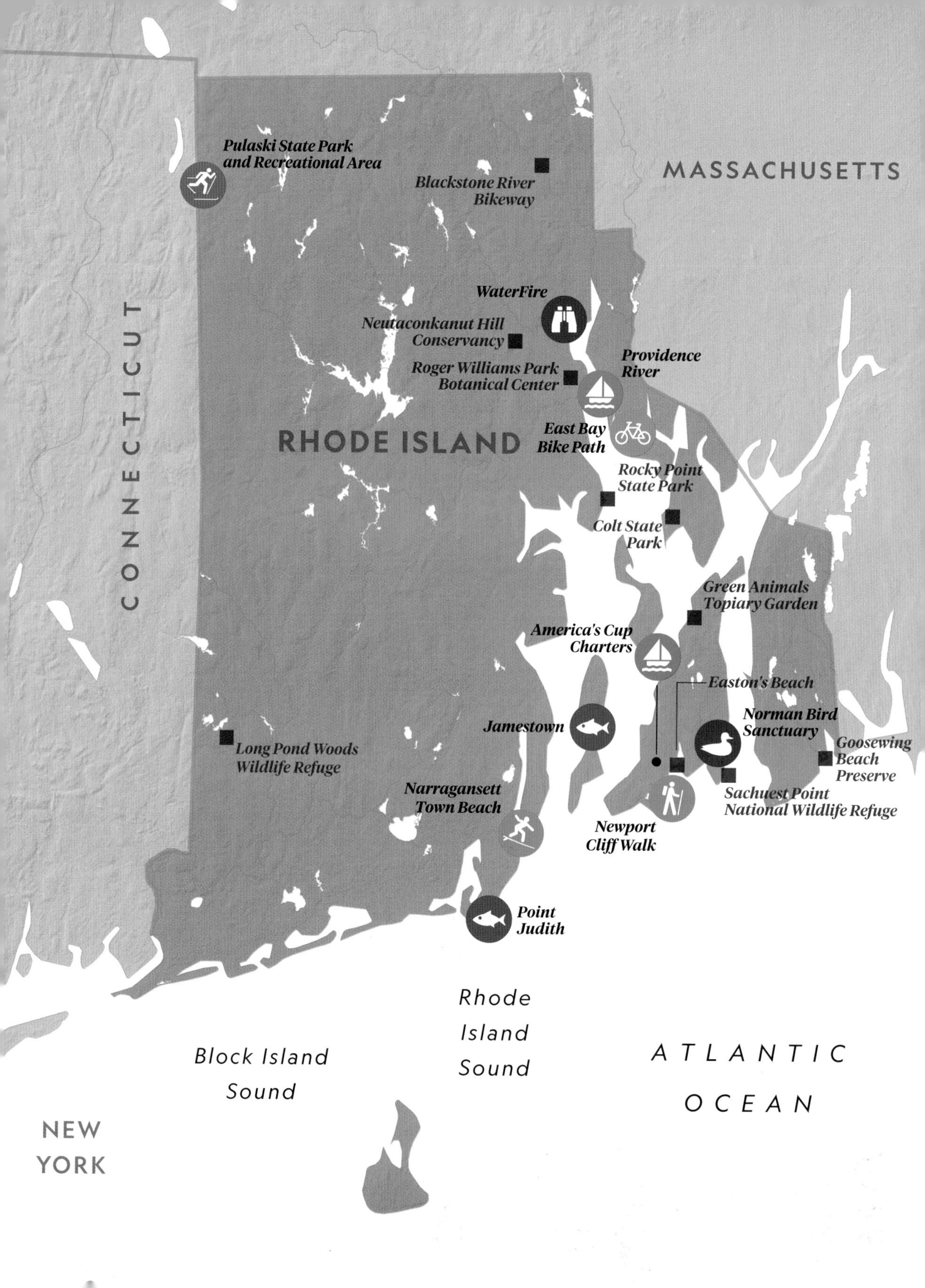

MASSACHUSETTS

Pulaski State Park and Recreational Area

Blackstone River Bikeway

WaterFire

Neutaconkanut Hill Conservancy

Providence River

Roger Williams Park Botanical Center

RHODE ISLAND

East Bay Bike Path

Rocky Point State Park

Colt State Park

CONNECTICUT

Green Animals Topiary Garden

America's Cup Charters

Easton's Beach

Jamestown

Norman Bird Sanctuary

Long Pond Woods Wildlife Refuge

Goosewing Beach Preserve

Narragansett Town Beach

Sachuest Point National Wildlife Refuge

Newport Cliff Walk

Point Judith

Rhode Island Sound

Block Island Sound

ATLANTIC OCEAN

NEW YORK

Gondoliers will take you on a tour of the Providence River in an authentic Venetian gondola.

Ride a Gondola Through Providence

Three waterways flow into Providence and coalesce to form the Providence River, which ripples south through downtown to the Fox Point Hurricane Barrier (Narragansett Bay waits on the other side). But for decades, congested roadways covered the city's namesake river. In the 1980s the city uncovered the river and added cobblestone pathways to its flanks.

This visionary decision paid off. The Providence River-Walk is one of the city's most well-trod paths for pedestrians and runners. Festivals are hosted along the water, and with several public docks, the water is easily accessible for kayakers and canoers. A boat ride along the Providence River is a lovely way to take in the city's architecture, public art, and industrial relics like the towering smokestacks of the Manchester Street Generating Sta-

tion. But if you want an extra rich taste of Providence—a city with a proud history of Italian immigration and community building—hop aboard one of the Venetian gondolas that traverse the river in summer and fall.

Operated by La Gondola, a charter that's amassed an impressive fleet of gondolas (including the first gondola believed to have been built in the United States), these romantic river voyages are best enjoyed with someone special toward the end of a summer day, when the cityscape is bathed in shades of pink and purple. The gondolas are outfitted with hand-sculpted ornaments and adorned with solid brass trim, just as you'd find in Italy. Equally authentic are the gondoliers, who dress in traditional Venetian uniforms. The crew provides blankets and umbrellas, and you're welcome to bring your own wine. It's a Rhode Island spin on an Old World classic.

Providence, RI | Season: Summer

Ski through lush forest on the XC trails of Pulaski State Park.

Hit the Trails of Pulaski

When Polish nobleman and soldier Casimir Pulaski sailed to the American colonies to fight in the Revolutionary War, New England was his port of entry, and the region still bears monuments commemorating the freedom fighter. But the finest homage might be Rhode Island's Pulaski State Park.

The park is a destination for springtime trout fishing on the shores of Peck Pond, which becomes a reliable swimming hole by June. But when snow blankets western Rhode Island, Pulaski State Park becomes the only groomed cross-country ski facility in the Ocean State.

Ten miles (16 km) of cross-country ski trails snake through the park and adjacent forests. The Pulaski Trail offers gentle terrain for beginners, while the longer, more intermediate routes like the Covered Bridge and Hemlock Glen Trails feature steeper downhill runs. You'll need to bring your own skis.

Glocester, RI | **Season:** Winter

The WaterFire Festival

Between the high-rises and murals of downtown Providence, the Moshassuck and Woonasquatucket Rivers converge to form the Providence River, which flows south to Narragansett Bay. Cobblestone paths line the waterway, and as you explore the river walk, you may notice metal pyres in the water. What are those for? The answer is clear on Saturday nights from September to December, when Providence literally becomes aglow for WaterFire.

At dusk, the pyres are filled with wood and lit by boats of torchbearers that travel up the river to Waterplace Park, a human-made lagoon near the heart of the city. New Age music reverberates from speakers, and vendors offer beer and wine to revelers as they walk the fiery river. Created by Barnaby Evans and running since 1994, WaterFire is your chance to watch a scrappy, creative city come together under the stars in the name of art.

Providence, RI | **Season:** September to December

A sculptural installation by Barnaby Evans at WaterFire in Providence

Birding Sanctuary

When Mabel Norman Cerio wasn't busy painting portraits, she spent many hours birding in the forest and meadows around her Middletown home. In her will, she declared that the property should become a sanctuary "where birds and bird life may be observed, studied, taught, and enjoyed by lovers of nature and by the public."

More than half a century since Mabel's passing, the Norman Bird Sanctuary offers visitors the chance to observe green herons, bobolinks, mute swans, and other migratory birds as they settle into the 325-acre (130 ha) sanctuary along the Atlantic Flyway. Seven miles (11 km) of on-site trails wander through wooded glens and gusty grassland.

Whichever path you set off on, don't miss the view of nearby Sachuest Bay and Second Beach from the top of Hanging Rock, a windswept goliath of stone that can also serve as an enviable picnic spot.

Middletown, RI | **Season:** Year-round

More than 50,000 spectators come to watch the nine-day America's Cup regatta.

> "IN SPRING AND SUMMER, THE CYAN EXPANSE OF NEWPORT HARBOR IS SPECK-LED WITH J-CLASS BOATS."

America's Cup

If you're wondering why Newport is often called the "Sailing Capital of the World," consider the America's Cup races. From 1930 to 1983, Newport laid claim to the coveted America's Cup trophy as sailors from across the world traveled here to race their yachts against those helmed by members of the local New York Yacht Club. By the time Australia finally usurped the prize, sailing had become a fixture of Newport recreation and culture. In spring and summer, the cyan expanse of Newport Harbor is speckled with J-class boats—including 39-foot (12 m) yachts that have competed for the America's Cup. But you can do more than admire these vessels: You can ride them.

For more than 30 years, America's Cup Charters has maintained one of the largest fleets of America's Cup yachts in the world. Winning seacraft like the US-17 *Weatherly* (1962) and the US-22 *Intrepid* (1967 and 1970) have been renovated and restored to battle-ready conditions, and visitors looking to earn their sea legs can cruise the harbor and Narragansett Bay aboard these yachts under the guidance of an experienced crew.

The two-hour cruise across the bay is a fine jumping-off point for novice sailors. You'll careen across the water past sandy coves, estuaries, and mansions along the shoreline. You can sit back and enjoy the ride or help the crew raise the sails and navigate the yacht.

If joining the crew sounds enticing, consider kicking things up a notch and trying your hand at three hours of afternoon yacht racing. You'll be assigned a crew position, with practice before setting out. From there, you'll reenact the America's Cup race—positioning your boat at a starting line, ripping across the water, and savoring the briny breeze as the other yacht nips at your stern (if you're lucky).

Newport, RI | **Season:** Spring and summer

Walk the Cliffs

The rocky coastline of Aquidneck Island is complemented by some of the most arresting cliffs in New England—so beautiful that members of Newport's gilded class built their mansions atop these oceanside overlooks. But before the rich arrived here, the Narragansett peoples broke in the footpaths atop the cliffs, and thanks to public use laws, those paths have survived. Today, they're known as the Newport Cliff Walk.

Winding 3.5 miles (5.6 km) from the sands of Easton's Beach to the quieter waters at Reject's Beach, the Cliff Walk begins as a paved path that winds past multimillion-dollar homes, wildflowers, and some stomach-plunging precipices. But as you venture farther south, the Cliff Walk becomes more rugged. Soon, you'll be scrambling from rock to rock (shoes with good grip are a must) and you'll need to be mindful of slick surfaces. But the briny sea breeze and monotone roar of the ocean keep the adventure feeling more like a meditation.

The Cliff Walk follows the shoreline past Newport mansions.

Newport, RI | Season: Year-round

Don't Clam Up

Mollusks are the key to a Rhode Islander's heart: especially quahogs. These large hard-shelled clams can travel across sand thanks to a muscular "foot" that emerges from the shell. The Narragansett peoples used quahog shells to make wampum. Today, the mighty mollusks are the baseline ingredient for "stuffies," a Rhode Island specialty consisting of chopped clam meat, peppers and onions, bread crumbs, and a savory spice mix, baked and served in quahog shells.

But instead of procuring their precious clams from seafood markets, many residents harvest them directly from the shallows of Narragansett Bay. In Jamestown—at the foot of the Newport Pell Bridge—the sandy beach and placid waters of Potter Cove make for an ideal "clamming" venue for visitors and veteran quahog connoisseurs alike.

Hard clams

First, grab a tourist clamming license from the state ($11). Next, assess your gear. Water shoes will help you walk across the muddy bay floor, and if you're serious about harvesting enough clams for dinner, a clam rake will help you dig them out of the bilge (you can buy a clam rake from online retailers or recreational equipment stores). Throw in a basket or a mesh bag to carry your clams, and you're ready to harvest.

Although there's no legal season for quahog hunting, locals often haul in their clams before July and August, when the annual quahog spawning occurs. Before adding a quahog to your stash, make sure it's at least 1 inch (2.5 cm) wide across the hinge of the shell.

Newport, RI | Season: Summer

Pedal From Park to Park

A state as intimate and compact as Rhode Island would appear to be the perfect environment for bike paths connecting town, country, and the sea. The East Bay Bike Path—the first multi-community bike trail built by the Rhode Island Department of Transportation—is a showcase of the Ocean State's natural and human-made features. The trail runs 14.5 miles (23.3 km) from India Point Park in Providence to the waterside picnic greens at Independence Park in Bristol.

Mostly flat (except for two hills in Providence) and reliably sun-kissed, the bike path will take you past urban forests like Squantum Woods State Park, old railroad infrastructure, briny wetlands such as Jacob's Point Salt Marsh, gusty coves, and curiosities like the open-air seaside chapel at Colt State Park. Ample access points make it easy to section bike, walk, or jog the East Bay trail. Sometimes it can feel like the hub of the universe for active Rhode Islanders.

Providence to Bristol, RI | **Season:** Spring to fall

If you're looking to complete the trail in one trip, consider starting near the southern terminus at Colt State Park, where more parking is available. Haines Memorial State Park in Barrington is a great place to stop for lunch along the route, with two picnic groves and ample shade. Another great stopping point along the route is Bristol, where you'll find views of Narragansett Bay. Park your bike by the boardwalk, built by the Audubon Society of Rhode Island, for the best sights and some great bird-watching. To bike the full length of the trail, plan at least three hours to make it out and back.

But if you'll be renting a bike before jumping on the trail, starting from Providence may make more sense. Local retailers like Dash Bicycle Shop and Trek Bicycle offer a nice selection of loaner models. Given the laid-back pace and atmosphere of the trail, you can even pull off a shorter ride with one of the rentable e-bikes scattered across the city at various kiosks. Simply download the Spin app, unlock a bike for an hourly rate, and pedal away.

Summer Swells

Whenever an Atlantic storm sweeps across the Rhode Island coastline, you can hear the sound of a hundred wet suits being zipped up. The aptly named Ocean State has a jagged shoreline, causing swells to rumble toward the state beaches from a variety of directions.

Shaped like a crescent moon and offering reliably gentle waves powered by groundswells, Narragansett Town Beach is one of Rhode Island's most beloved year-round surfing venues. The sandbars here have a way of relocating, which can augment the waves, and the winds are less abrasive than across Narragansett Bay in Newport. Beginner surfers will find no better place for waves.

Though the beach is packed during the summer, November is considered one of the best months for consistent swell. Just be sure to bring that wet suit—fall and winter water temperatures here are low!

Narragansett offers surfers a chance to catch big waves.

Narragansett, RI | **Season:** Spring to late fall

> "THE RHODE ISLAND
> SHORELINE IS A PROVEN
> DESTINATION FOR
> FISHERFOLK SEEKING
> STRIPED BASS, BLUEFISH,
> AND OTHER PRIZED SPECIES."

A Shore Thing

Walk the rocky, barnacle-encrusted beaches of Narragansett Bay on a summer evening and chances are, you'll find anglers standing in the gentle surf, furiously reeling in lines. The Rhode Island shoreline is a proven destination for fisherfolk seeking striped bass, bluefish, and other prized species that travel through the bay each year.

Part of the draw is the scenery itself. Imagine casting your line against a fuchsia sunset on a sultry July night, in the shadow of a 19th-century lighthouse whose whistle still guides ships through the occasional bout of fog. This is the scene at Point Judith, a tiny peninsula sitting at the nexus of Narragansett Bay and the vast Rhode Island Sound. You can set up your line and cast from the rocks beneath the light. But many visitors choose to amble over to nearby Camp Cronin, a sandier stretch of beach that's ideal for wading into the waves with your rod and lures.

The catch at Point Judith varies month to month, based on the migratory patterns of the fish. Visiting in June? Expect stripers to arrive first, followed by bluefish. Flounder, fluke, and scup join the party in July. In August, the bluefish can get swept up in feeding frenzies that are visible from shore, usually in early morning and late evening. But the best time to fish Point Judith might just be late summer and early fall, as stampedes of fish depart from Narragansett Bay to the great blue yonder of the Atlantic.

Point Judith, RI | **Season:** Summer and fall

Try your hand at ocean fishing on the shores of Point Judith.

Visit the creatures of Green Animals Topiary Garden in Portsmouth.

1. BIKE A HISTORIC CANAL

River birch trees, iron bridges, and rugged cliffs are hallmarks of the Blackstone River Bikeway. This 48-mile (77 km) pathway follows the Blackstone Canal that connects Providence to the city of Worcester, Massachusetts. In the 19th century, barges traveled between the cities, and you can still see the old locks as you pedal along the canal.

2. WALK ABOUT IN A GLASS HOUSE

The largest glass greenhouse display garden in New England is tucked away in the urban oasis of Roger Williams Park. This facility was built to accommodate trees, but as you walk beneath towering palms and cacti, you'll also find carnivorous pitcher plants and a liberally stocked koi pond.

3. TAKE IN GARBAGE TURNED TO TREASURE

A suitably gritty park for a gritty city like Providence, Neutaconkanut Hill was once an informal garbage dump, but volunteers—and nature—have reclaimed the hill (which offers a terrific view of the city). Along the forested trails here, two rusted Camaro muscle cars were left behind as a reminder of the park's past.

4. TAKE IN THE BEAUTIFUL SEASCAPE

Acres of lawns, shade trees, breezy trails, and views of Narragansett Bay make Colt State Park feel like a shrine to the beauty of the seascape. Bull statues modeled after those at the Palace of Versailles and an open-air "chapel by the sea" are the gravy for this sumptuous state park.

5. GO GREEN

In 1872, a wealthy homeowner in Newport County hired Portuguese gardener Joseph Carreiro to slice and snip his evergreen shrubs into a collection of topiary sculptures. After countless "haircuts" by a succession of gardeners, the large topiary elephants, giraffes, and bears still loom over visitors as they stroll the paths of Green Animals Topiary Garden.

6. ENJOY PRISTINE GOOSEWING BEACH PRESERVE

Protected by the Nature Conservancy since 1989, Goosewing Beach is one of the state's most pristine swimming venues—a welcome change of pace from the more crowded, developed beaches around Newport. On-site trails lead to grassy dunes and Quicksand Pond, where winter flounder and oysters thrive.

7. CATCH THE SURF

Asking Newporters to name their favorite beach is like querying a New Yorker for the best pizza joint, but for surfable swells, all roads lead to Easton's Beach. When strong northeast winds wallop this beach (located right next to Cliff Walk), the waves here can grow in excess of three to four feet (0.9 to 1.2 m).

8. CATCH THE MIGRATION

For marine waterbirds like cormorants, sea ducks, or grebes, the steep rocky shoreline, grasslands, and marshes of Sachuest Point National Wildlife Refuge are an ideal winter stopover. Set off across three miles (5 km) of trails with your best binoculars—or your fishing rod. Saltwater night fishing permits are available for purchase here.

9. HAUNT AN AMUSEMENT GHOST TOWN

Sweeping views of Narragansett Bay are paired with eerie ruins from an amusement park that used to bustle on the land where Rocky Point State Park now exists. Rusting gondola sky-ride towers and the original theme park entry archway are a few highlights amid the seaside paths and fishing piers here.

10. WORK UP A SWEAT

Wes Anderson was so smitten with Long Pond that he filmed scenes of *Moonrise Kingdom* here. But reaching the glassy pond is a roller coaster of a hike, with rock scrambling through the hemlock woods of Hopkinton. At roughly three miles (4.8 km), it's one of the most rigorous hikes on any Audubon Society land, but worth the sweat.

Burying beetle

Myrtle Beach on the
Grand Strand

SOUTH CAROLINA

Hike the trails, paddle the rivers, or walk the boardwalks of
South Carolina for an adventure to remember.

Caesars Head State Park

Jones Gap State Park

Devils Fork State Park

Mountain Bridge Wilderness Area

Table Rock State Park

Chattooga River

Jocassee Gorges

Swamp Rabbit Trail

SOUTH

Lake Murray

GEORGIA

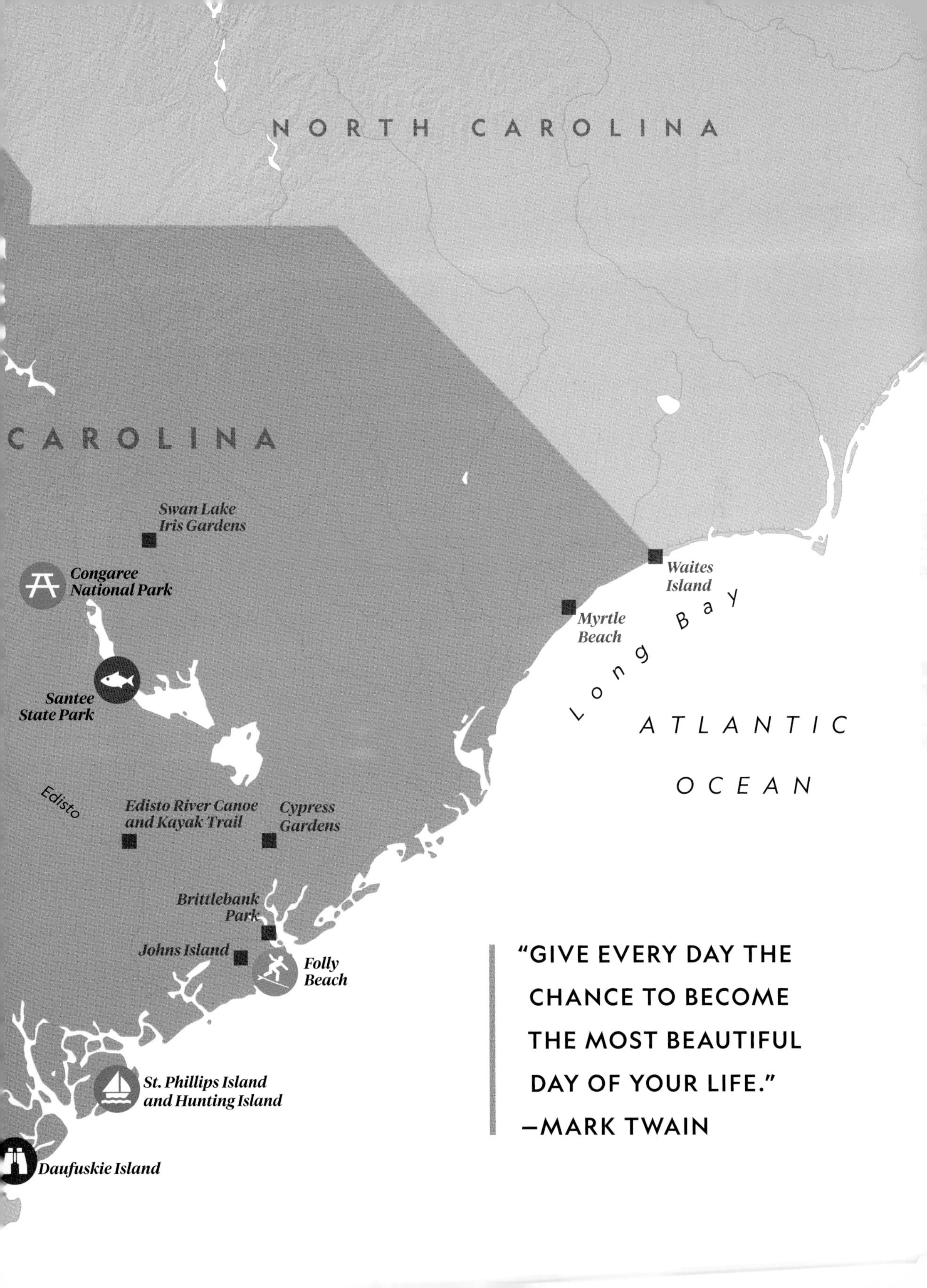

NORTH CAROLINA

CAROLINA

Swan Lake
Iris Gardens

Congaree
National Park

Santee
State Park

Waites
Island

Myrtle
Beach

Long Bay

ATLANTIC

OCEAN

Edisto

Edisto River Canoe
and Kayak Trail

Cypress
Gardens

Brittlebank
Park

Johns Island

Folly
Beach

St. Phillips Island
and Hunting Island

Daufuskie Island

"GIVE EVERY DAY THE
CHANCE TO BECOME
THE MOST BEAUTIFUL
DAY OF YOUR LIFE."
—MARK TWAIN

Dive With the Devil

The year-round, crystal clear mountain waters in 7,565-acre (3,060 ha) Lake Jocassee lure scuba divers seeking one of the top freshwater dives in the world. The human-made reservoir is formed by four clean and cold Appalachian Mountain rivers: Horsepasture, Thompson, Toxaway, and Whitewater. Lake visibility can range between 20 and 50 feet (6 and 15 m), and divers from all over the Southeast join charters with outfitters like the Scuba Shop to attain underwater bliss in sites reachable by boat or from shore.

The south end of the lake is home to Devils Fork State Park—the only public access to Lake Jocassee and the surrounding land, which includes several waterfalls, making it a cool respite in summer months and an excellent South Carolina trout fishing spot. In spring, spy the white blooms of the rare Oconee bell *(Shortia galacifolia)* along the creek that follows the 1.5-mile (2.4 km) Oconee Bell Nature Trail, looping through hardwood forest.

Salem, SC | Season: Year-round

Take a dive at Devils Fork State Park.

Fly High

The 3,266-foot (996 m) overlook at Caesars Head State Park is an ideal place to observe the fall hawk migration from September to the end of November each year, when bird-watchers can see broad-winged hawks, kestrels, osprey, sharp-shinned hawks, and peregrine falcons. During migration, the birds seek to conserve their energy for their journey to Central and South America by catching thermal winds without having to flap their wings. The Blue Ridge Escarpment is the only place in the South Carolina mountains that helps the raptors in this manner. Spring bird migration is another popular viewing time, with 167 bird species on the park checklist.

With more than 41 miles (66 km) of hiking trails, the park favorite is the moderate, 4.4-mile (7 km) round-trip Raven Cliff Falls Trail through Mountain Bridge Wilderness Area to a scenic overlook of 420-foot (128 m) Raven Cliff Falls—the tallest waterfall in South Carolina. The moderately strenuous 6.6-mile (10.6 km) Suspension Bridge Trail shares the same trailhead, yet crosses a suspension bridge above the falls, offering a view as water plunges below.

Lush greenery lines the trails of Caesars Head State Park.

Cleveland, SC | Season: Spring to fall

Catch the Big One

🐟 Santee State Park lies along the shore of Lake Marion, the largest lake in the state, covering 110,000 acres (44,515 ha). Considered South Carolina's inland sea, the lake spans five counties—Berkeley, Calhoun, Clarendon, Orangeburg, and Sumter—and was formed by damming the Santee River in the 1940s to supply hydroelectric power. The reservoir project was sped up due to World War II, and the area that became Lake Marion wasn't fully cleared. The result: Thousands of stumps, tree trunks, and cypress trees were flooded when the Lake Marion Dam was completed, creating the ultimate habitat for the crappie, bream, and catfish that live in the lake. Today, it's known for an abundant population of catfish, as well as largemouth bass, striped bass, bream, and crappie. Since 1949, the lake has held the record for the biggest largemouth bass caught in South Carolina. That record was tied 44 years later, but nobody has surpassed it. It's no wonder that fishers flock to the park with big goals.

The state park features two boat ramps to access the water, along with an accessible fishing pier next to the park store. Those who want to get an early morning start can stay in one of 20 modern cabins, 10 of which are on a pier overlooking Lake Marion—close enough to roll out of bed and cast your line moments later. The other 10 cabins are located on the lakeshore. Two additional campgrounds are available for tent camping or RV guests.

In the lake across from the park lies a flooded cypress forest. It's an ideal place for kayakers to take their time paddling among the trees and for enjoying the landscape and quietude. Pontoon boat tours into the lake's swampy headwaters are also based out of the park's marina.

Santee, SC | **Year-round**

Catch a sunset at Table Rock State Park.

To the Top of the Mountain

🥾 Towering Table Rock Mountain is South Carolina's most photographed natural wonder. The 3,100-foot-high (945 m) granite dome looms over the state park that shares its name, inspiring hikers to climb 2,000 feet (610 m) to the summit. The 7.2-mile (11.6 km) round-trip Table Rock Trail is strenuous, ascending steeply through the boulder-strewn open forest of oak, hickory, pine, and hemlock. The view makes the work worthwhile—from Table Rock Reservoir to Caesars Head State Park, Carrick Creek Falls to Pinnacle Lake.

Hikers have more than 12 miles (19 km) of trails in this park, including moderate two-mile (3.2 km) loop Carrick Creek Trail, where hikers can kick off their shoes to splash in the cool mountain water beneath Carrick Creek Falls.

Pickens, SC | **Season:** Year-round

Paddle through the trees of Cedar Creek in Congaree National Park.

> ### "SPYING A SPARKLING CARPET OF FIREFLIES MAKES FOR A MAGICAL EVENING."

Find Fireflies Among the Trees

Stand on the accessible boardwalk that skirts the edge of the floodplain forest in Congaree National Park—where floodwaters from the Congaree and Wateree Rivers regularly deposit fresh, nutrient-rich soil—and you're among the largest remaining section of old-growth bottomland forest in the United States. Encompassing more than 20,000 acres (8,090 ha), the park contains some of the tallest trees in eastern North America, with one of the highest canopies in the world.

Spying a sparkling carpet of fireflies makes for a magical evening, but imagine seeing them all flashing at once. Synchronous fireflies are common in Southeast Asian jungles, where they mate year-round, but they're harder to find in the Western Hemisphere, where mating lasts only a couple of weeks. Congaree National Park is one of the few easily accessible locations in the United States to view them.

From mid-May through mid-June, this mesmerizing event is a short distance from the park's visitors center, just off the main boardwalk. Special programs, exhibits, and Junior Ranger activities make it easy for firefly fans to get a glimpse of the glittering spectacle. Prepare in advance, however: To protect critical firefly habitat, the park uses a lottery system and charges a fee for the event.

Get a deeper look at forest life by paddling the marked Cedar Creek Canoe Trail, which winds about 15 miles (24 km) through the Congaree Wilderness from Bannister's Bridge to the Congaree River. Along the way, large bald cypress trees form a canopy over the quiet, dark-water stream. Keep your eyes open for river otters, deer, birds, turtles, snakes, and an occasional alligator. Bring your own kayak or canoe, grab a rental craft from an outfitter in nearby Columbia, or join a guided paddling tour.

Congaree National Park, SC | Season: Summer

Hike to a Rainbow

The Mountain Bridge Wilderness Area covers more than 13,000 acres (5,260 ha) of pristine woodlands on the Blue Ridge Escarpment and encompasses two state parks, Jones Gap and Caesars Head. The Middle Saluda River, South Carolina's first designated Scenic River, is the centerpiece of Jones Gap State Park and some of the most popular of the 18 trailside, hike-in campsites are within earshot of the roaring waters.

A network of easy to strenuous hiking trails link both state parks, and one of the most spectacular, Rainbow Falls Trail, begins in Jones Gap. The strenuous five-mile (8 km) round-trip hike traverses the Middle Saluda River multiple times before climbing granite and wooden steps, ascending approximately 1,000 feet (305 m) in just 1.6 miles (2.6 km). At Rainbow Falls, which drops 100 feet (30 m) over steep walls streaked with metamorphic layers of amphibolite gneiss, granitic gneiss, and mica schist. In spring, look for azalea, meadow rue, and Solomon's plume among the boulders.

> "IN SPRING, LOOK FOR AZALEA, MEADOW RUE, AND SOLOMON'S PLUME AMONG THE BOULDERS."

Cleveland, SC | **Season:** Spring to fall

Mountain Bridge Wilderness Area boasts small cascades and forests with blooming rhododendron flowers.

The Edwin S. Taylor Folly Beach Fishing Pier extends more than 1,045 feet (320 m) out into the Atlantic Ocean.

Surfside Folly

Just 11 miles (18 km) from downtown Charleston, Folly Beach is the closest beach to town, and the quickest way you can slow down and grab a few hours of laid-back beach lifestyle. Folly Beach is the largest settlement on Folly Island, one of the Sea Islands that forms a natural barrier between the Atlantic Ocean and the South Carolina mainland. Folly Beach has become a popular surf spot, with a handful of favorite sites for surfers of different skill levels.

Blame (or thank) Hurricane Hugo in 1989 for the most famous break at Folly's—the Washout. The hurricane washed away a block of beachfront homes, letting the wind blow across the shore through the wetlands to the Folly River, creating a consistent swell and an occasional 10-foot (3 m) wave. Not all breaks are as hard-core as the Washout, though. Other favorite surf spots include Clouds, Piddleys, Folly Pier, the county park, 6th Street East, 10th Street East, and the old Coast Guard base.

Folly Beach is also a prime nesting area for loggerhead sea turtles, which crawl onto the beach two to five times between May and September to lay eggs. Because female turtles often return to their own hatching place to nest, it's essential that Folly remain turtle friendly. Local groups like the Folly Beach Turtle Watch Program help protect turtles, nests, and hatchlings, and also remind visitors to refrain from shining lights on the beach or disturbing turtles so they can continue their cycle of life.

Bottlenose dolphins

Folly Beach, SC | **Season:** Spring to fall

Haig Point Lighthouse on Daufuskie Island

Gullah Life Landmarks

One of the Sea Islands—barrier islands off the coast of South Carolina—Daufuskie remains largely untouched by modern development. Without a bridge to the mainland, the island is accessible only by boat, and the few paved roads are best traversed by bike and golf cart.

Choose your wheels and follow the Rob Kennedy Trail, established by the Daufuskie Island Historical Foundation to highlight 20 historic landmarks from Indigenous residents in the 1700s to its Gullah-Geechee inhabitants—descendants of enslaved people who have farmed and fished the island and its waters for centuries. Ride below the canopy of live oaks and linger at historic cottages that emerge from lush forests, like the Frances Jones House, a Gullah home built in the late 1860s. While you wander, look for blue jewel-toned painted doors and window shutters originally tinted "haint blue" by local indigo dye to keep evil spirits at bay.

Daufuskie Island, SC | **Season:** Year-round

Urban Escape

In the heart of South Carolina just west of Columbia, Lake Murray, a 50,000-acre (20,230 ha) lower Piedmont reservoir, was constructed in the late 1920s to produce hydroelectric power. At completion, the lake's 1.6-mile (2.6 km) dam was the largest earthen dam in the world. Bordering four counties, the reservoir's proximity to Columbia makes the watery playground an easy day trip or weekend escape. Once you're there, the lake seems to stretch to the horizon in all directions. It feels like a world away from the city.

One of the best fishing spots in the nation, Lake Murray is home to a number of tournaments throughout the year that lure competitive fishers. Striped and largemouth bass are two of the most popular species, but the lake also has bluegill, crappie, catfish, and redear sunfish (also known as shellcracker). You don't have to be a pro to make a great catch. Fishing guides like Mike Glover, known as "Striper Mike," have years of knowledge of the best local practices and gear necessary for a day of successful fishing. They also have plenty of fish stories.

Eastern tiger swallowtail butterfly

In the middle of the lake, Bomb Island, formally known as Doolittle Island, was once a training site for World War II B-25 bombers (five of the planes ended up crashing in Lake Murray). But now, an estimated flock of more than a million purple martins fill the predawn and evening summer skies over the island—the oldest and largest purple martin sanctuary in North America. The flocks of this iridescent species of swallow rest here while they prepare to fly to South America for the winter months.

Columbia, SC | **Season:** Year-round

Roam the coastal dunes of Hunting Island State Park.

Barrier Breather

Travel through the "salty Eden" of St. Phillips Island and Hunting Island State Park, which count among the barrier islands of South Carolina's coast. South Carolina's most popular state park, Hunting Island was once a hunting preserve for 19th- and early 20th-century planters. The island's lighthouse, built in 1859, is the only publicly accessible lighthouse in the state. Board Coastal Expeditions' Hunting Island Dolphin Cruise to spy pods of bottlenose dolphins feeding in the salt marsh estuary, as well as native birds of prey and shorebirds who make their homes in the barrier islands. Tucked between Capers and St. Helena Islands, St. Phillips Island, where the only access is by boat, has a wild feel because it has never been colonized, timbered, or developed. Ancient sand dune ridges interspersed with swales and ponds traverse the length of the island, providing critical habitat for wildlife.

Hunting and St. Phillips Islands, SC | **Season:** Spring to fall

Take a guided boat tour at Cypress Gardens in Moncks Corner.

1. FREE-FLOW THE EDISTO

Encounter the Edisto River Canoe and Kayak Trail, a 62-mile (100 km) section of North America's longest free-flowing black-water river. With no rapids, this stretch shaded by cypress, live oak, and red cedar trees makes for a relaxing float trip. Stay overnight at the Edisto Treehouses, within the 150-acre (60 ha) Edisto River Refuge.

2. TAKE A WILDWATER ADVENTURE

A National Wild and Scenic River since 1974, the free-flowing Chattooga is considered one of South Carolina's premier white-water rivers. Adventure into its remote, deep gorge with Wildwater, the first commercial outfitter to run the Chattooga, and make a post-trip stop for U-pick fruit at Chattooga Belle Farm.

3. BOAT THROUGH HISTORY

What were once rice fields and dikes of Dean Hall Plantation built by enslaved people more than 300 years ago are now 170 acres (70 ha) of blooming gardens and wildlife-rich waterways. Wander the 3.5 miles (5.6 km) of looping trails at Cypress Gardens or paddle a swamp boat through shimmering reflections of bald cypress and tupelo trees.

4. WANDER TO WATERFALL

Saddle up for a ride through rolling hills and the rugged Jocassee Gorges, which has one of the highest concentrations of waterfalls in the eastern United States. Though Horseback Waterfall Tours offers this guided tour year-round, it's especially spectacular under the fall canopy of red and orange foliage.

5. BEACH BY HORSEBACK

Feel the ocean breeze as you ride the undeveloped shoreline of Waites Island—a short distance from the heart of Myrtle Beach. The untouched barrier island on the Atlantic coast is home to Inlet Point Plantation, offering beachfront rides where lucky riders may spy dolphins in the surf.

6. GO CASUAL CRABBING

Meals taste best when you source them yourself. Learn the fine art of crabbing with Tia Clark (host of Casual Crabbing with Tia), a Charleston native who teaches guests to catch their own from the dock at Brittlebank Park, one of the best spots to catch blue crabs in Charleston.

7. TRACK SWAMP RABBITS

Take the slow route on this 22-mile (35 km) multiuse greenway along the Reedy River connecting Travelers Rest and Greenville. Named after the indigenous swamp rabbit, the old railway corridor has options for short and long excursions. At the end of your journey, stop in at Swamp Rabbit Brewery for refreshments.

8. UNFURL THE SAILS

Pirates once ruled the Atlantic Ocean off the coast of Myrtle Beach, but now anyone can sail the 60-mile (97 km) Grand Strand coastline. Sit back and relax or take the helm on a sailing charter with Sailing Myrtle Beach to experience the Intracoastal Waterway, Little River Inlet, and the mighty Atlantic.

9. STROLL WITH SWANS

Spy seven true swan species (Bewick's, black, black-necked, mute, trumpeter, tundra, and whooper) and the small coscoroba swan on a saunter through Sumter's Swan Lake Iris Gardens. Among the seasonal blossoms in the gardens' 150 acres (60 ha) are more than 120 varieties of iris that burst into bloom in late spring.

10. LIVE ISLAND LIFE

Found along the Gullah Geechee Cultural Heritage Corridor, Johns Island is the largest island in South Carolina, separated from its border islands by the Kiawah and Stono Rivers. Its most famous resident is the sprawling Angel Oak Tree, a southern live oak estimated to be more than 400 to 500 years old.

Carolina jessamine

Cathedral Spires at
Custer State Park (page 573)

SOUTH DAKOTA

Home to two national parks and 63 state parks, the home of Mount Rushmore offers wide-open spaces and plenty to see and do.

NORTH

MONTANA

Shadehill
Recreation Area

SOUTH

Oahe Downstream
Recreation Area

Bear Butte
State Park

Spearfish
Canyon

Sylvan
Lake

Black Elk Peak
(Harney Peak)

Black Hills
National Forest

Mount Rushmore
National Memorial

George S.
Mickelson Trail

Custer
State Park

Badlands
National Park

Black Hills
Balloons

Centennial
Trail

WYOMING

The
Needles

Wind Cave
National Park

NEBR

DAKOTA

MINNESOTA

DAKOTA

Trail of
the Spirits

Glacial Lakes
region

Sanderson
Gardens

Palisades
State Park

IOWA

Lewis and
Clark Lake

ASKA

Gram-Worthy Falls

The limestone walls of Spearfish Canyon might seem like enough of a reward for driving 15 miles (24 km) south on U.S. 14A from the town of Spearfish, but the true payoff is capturing a digital triple crown of waterfalls.

From the spectacular cascade of 60-foot-high (18 m) Bridal Veil to the consistent, fanlike flow of 47-foot-high (14 m) Spearfish to the multitiered complexity of Roughlock (accessed south of the Spearfish Canyon Lodge off Roughlock Falls Road), each waterfall has its own character and beauty well worth the short hikes from the road.

Most people visit in the height of summer, peaking the first two weeks of August with thousands of bikers heading to the Sturgis Motorcycle Rally. A quieter, more counterintuitive time to see the falls is in the heart of winter, when the water freezes into daggers of ice that precariously dangle over the falls.

Spearfish, SD | Season: Year-round

Roughlock Falls pours into Spearfish Canyon.

Hike Black Elk Peak

The 7,242-foot (2,207 m) summit of Black Elk Peak is the highest peak between the American Rockies and the French Pyrenees. It got its name after a young Oglala Lakota healer named Heȟáka Sápa, or Black Elk, had a vision from atop the mountain in 1871.

The Black Elk Peak fire lookout tower in the Black Hills

Read about that vision as it was recounted to John Neihardt in the 1932 book *Black Elk Speaks*, then summit the peak. The shortest, most direct, and most populated of a dozen routes is Trail #9, which starts at the Sylvan Lake Visitor Center in Custer State Park. It's a moderately strenuous seven-mile (11 km) round-trip hike with a 1,100-foot (335 m) elevation gain. Those who prefer more solitude and additional mileage should start at Trail #3 (the Norbeck Trail) or Trail #7 (Grizzly Bear Creek Trail).

No matter how you reach the top, the summit delivers views of the fascinating geology of the Black Hills, including the rugged needles of Cathedral Spires; Mount Coolidge to the south and southwest; and Little Devils Tower and the back side of Mount Rushmore to the east. Because this is a sacred peak, it's essential hikers respect fellow seekers of the summit and heed Leave No Trace ethics.

Custer, SD | Season: Spring to fall

Thread the Needles

These granite rock formations that look custom-made for climbers in Custer State Park were discovered almost by accident. In 1937 Fritz Wiessner was on his way to climb Wyoming's Devils Tower when he stopped off to make the first known ascent of Totem Pole Rock, a pinnacle that hangs precariously over " The Needles Highway," a 14-mile-long (23 km) portion of South Dakota 87 that twists and turns around these fascinating formations.

A decade later, a couple from Connecticut named Herb and Jan Conn were driving through on their way to climb in Wyoming's Tetons and, stopping off on a whim, they made first ascents of two now iconic climbs, the Fan and Exclamation Point. The Conns became so enamored with the climbing here that they bought land in Custer, put up 200 more first ascents, and literally put South Dakota rock climbing on the map.

Today, there are close to 1,000 routes, most of which

Custer, SD | **Season:** Spring to fall

Common pheasant

are "trad" or traditional climbs, meaning that they are bolted from the ground up using hand drills. Many of the routes are only moderately difficult, but trad climbing can be precarious because the bolts are spaced farther out, meaning that if you slip, you have farther to fall. Even experienced climbers opt to go with a local guide who can safely lead climb to the top of these 120-foot-tall (37 m) pinnacles, most of which are the width of a bar stool at the summit. Sylvan Rocks in Custer offers a daily four-hour introductory group lesson, private instruction, and multiday packages. If you don't dare to climb the Needles, the route is still a worthwhile scenic drive that winds through pine, spruce, birch, and aspen forests. Look to the rock formations to see if you can spot climbers.

Take a Trail Ride

Built at the base of Mount Coolidge in the 1920s for an executive of Bell Telephone Company, the original Blue Bell Lodge remains much the same a century later, albeit with 29 additional surrounding cabins nestled in a bend along French Creek that offer modern luxuries like daily housekeeping. As the only horseback riding concession in Custer State Park, the lodge gives visitors a taste of the cowboy West with experiences like 15-minute Lil' Buckaroo rides for kids or meandering full-day trail rides through towering ponderosa pines.

The evening Chuckwagon Cookout takes visitors on a hayride along the park's 18-mile-long (29 km) Wildlife Loop to Parker Canyon, viewing wildlife like bison along the way while being serenaded by country and folk musicians. After a hearty cookout, guests can return to their cabins to gaze at the stars around an outside fire pit.

Cowboys herd bison in Custer State Park.

Custer, SD | **Season:** Spring to fall

"DISCOVER A LAND OF MIXED-GRASS PRAIRIE WHERE A BISON HERD ROAMS THE PASTEL-STRIATED BUTTES."

Explore the Badlands

In 1922 a South Dakota senator introduced legislation to establish Wonderland National Park. The park was created, but the name was changed to "Badlands," a term the Lakota people and French fur trappers used for centuries to describe the area's wide-open spaces intersected by difficult-to-navigate buttes.

Both titles are fitting for this 244,000-acre (98,740 ha) park in the southwestern corner of South Dakota, a land of mixed-grass prairie where a 1,400-strong bison herd roams the pastel-striated buttes. These buttes are the best snapshot that exists in North America of the transition between the late Eocene epoch (36.9 million years ago) through the late Oligocene epoch (26.8 million years ago).

That age is unfathomable, but visitors' imaginations kick in when an interpretive ranger explains how these windswept plains were once home to herbivores like brontotheres. Roughly the size of an overgrown rhino with blunt horns, the brontotheres inhabited the once lush, hot forest that covered the region during the late Eocene. Learn about these and dozens of other prehistoric species found here at the park's Fossil Preparation Lab near the visitors center. Paleontologists staff the lab and educate visitors about how to properly report fossils discovered in the park.

Most visitors to the Badlands drive though the park, never taking time to get out and explore the 64,000 acres (25,900 ha) of wilderness. Follow a bison or game trail to see the surreal formations up close, experience a rare native prairie (an endangered ecosystem), and wonder at majestic bison that still freely roam. The park offers rental cabins at Cedar Pass Lodge, two official campgrounds, and endless opportunities to pitch a tent under a night sky where more than 7,500 stars are visible on any given night.

Oglala Lakota, Jackson, and Pennington Counties, SD | **Season:** Year-round

Striated rock formations are just one of the draws of Badlands National Park.

Ride the Hills

Revered by local expert mountain bikers, the 111-mile (179 km) multipurpose Centennial Trail, which follows the heart of the Black Hills from the town of Sturgis in the north to Wind Cave National Park in the south, is a roller coaster of rugged climbs, loose-screed descents, tight switchbacks, and stream crossings. With more than 2,000 feet (610 m) of elevation change, there's never a dull—and rarely a flat—moment of riding.

The payoff is an epic, multiday mountain biking adventure that challenges cyclists' technical riding, bike maintenance, and wayfinding skills while taking in rolling prairie, towering ponderosa pine forests, and the storied rock formations of the Black Hills. Note that the trail isn't always easy to discern, so be sure to bring a GPS device. It's also open to hikers, which have the right-of-way over mountain bikers. Two Wheeler Dealer bike shop in Spearfish offers bike rentals, equipment, and wise advice from experts.

> "THE PAYOFF IS AN EPIC, MULTIDAY MOUNTAIN BIKING ADVENTURE THAT CHALLENGES CYCLISTS' TECHNICAL RIDING, BIKE MAINTENANCE, AND WAYFINDING SKILLS."

Fairburn, SD   Season: Spring to fall

Mountain bike through meadows on the Centennial Trail.

Cast a line in a trout stream in Spearfish Canyon in the Black Hills.

Cast a Wide Net

Envision *A River Runs Through It*–style scenes of a solitary angler fly-casting from the banks of a pristine river and South Dakota isn't the first landscape that comes to mind. But the network of creeks running through Black Hills National Forest are an unsung gold mine for sport anglers. Two main waterways, Rapid Creek and Spearfish Creek, combined with dozens of smaller streams, provide some of the best year-round fishing for wild brown, rainbow, and brook trout in the country.

Eight- to 14-inch (20 to 36 cm) wild brown trout are the predominant species here. Rapid Creek, the largest waterway of the central region of the Black Hills and a tributary of the Cheyenne River, has excellent fishing from its headwaters near Black Hawk Creek Campground, all the way to Rapid City. Some of the best is right in the city limits, where you'll find locals fly-casting at Founders Park. If the browns aren't biting, then head over to the nearby food trucks to feast on a fish taco.

Spearfish Creek, 48 miles (77 km) to the northwest, offers the highest trout per mile in the Black Hills as well as some of the most stunning scenery within the 1,000-foot-high (305 m) walls of its eponymous canyon. It is a fly-fisher's paradise. May through September are the best fishing months as well as the busiest seasons for Mount Rushmore and Badlands National Park. (During the warmer months, anglers might be interrupted by tubers looking to cool off on a relaxing ride down the swiftly moving creek.) But those who are willing to hike can always find an unpressured section of creek with fish and plenty of solitude. And if you don't mind colder weather, Spearfish Creek is fishable year-round because its fast-flowing water doesn't freeze. Dakota Angler & Outfitter in Rapid City offers all the gear as well as expert local guides.

Multicity, SD | **Season:** May to September

See blooming meadows and groves on the Trail of the Spirits.

Hike the Trail of the Spirits

Legends abound here at Sica Hollow State Park, a thickly forested woodland on the eastern slope of the Prairie Coteau Hills in the remote northeastern corner of the state. When the first Sioux arrived in the region, they named it *sica*, or "evil," because the mineral-laden, red-tinted water gushing out of a spring looked like the blood of their ancestors. Its gurgling red bogs with escaping methane gas that occasionally glows in the dark increases the eeriness along the half-mile-long (0.8 km) interpretive "Trail of the Spirits."

An anomaly to the surrounding prairie, the off-the-beaten-path state park, which encompasses two cemeteries, has an additional eight miles (13 km) of multiuse trails through hardwood forest, popular with hikers, runners, mountain bikers, and cross-country skiers.

Sisseton, SD | **Season:** Year-round

Go Deep Into Wind Cave National Park

Overshadowed by the facade of Mount Rushmore 50 miles (80 km) to the north, this ever expanding, 158-mile-long (254 km) limestone cave is one of the most culturally significant in the world. Here, the Lakota people believe they emerged from the spirit realm through a hole at the cave's entrance.

Geologically, Wind Cave is the most complex three-dimensional maze cave in the world: Crammed below just 1.2 miles (1.9 km) of surface area are miles of underground passages leading in every direction, some of which end at underground lakes. Others contain the best example on the planet of a formation known as "boxwork." Unlike stalactites and stalagmites, boxwork is made of thin blades of calcite that form rare honeycomb, boxlike patterns on the walls. It's so thick in places it's known as "cratework."

Black-footed ferret

Exploring the cave is an intimate experience. For those with claustrophobia, the park also offers beautiful aboveground hiking trails through mixed-grass prairie filled with bison, pronghorn, coyotes, and black-footed ferrets. Be sure not to miss the sublime sunset views from Rankin Ridge, the highest point in the park.

Because many people visit the cave en route to other western parks, Wind Cave's busiest days are Tuesdays and Wednesdays, so plan your visit in advance to beat the crowds and nab a reservation in time. Park visitation has dramatically increased in the past few years. To avoid standing in a line behind 200 other eager amateur speleologists, make a reservation online or arrive at the park early in the morning.

Wind Cave National Park, SD | **Season:** Year-round

White-tailed deer roam the woods after a snowstorm.

Solitude on the XC Trail

The 109-mile-long (175 km) George S. Mickelson Trail gently undulates through the heart of the Black Hills, from Deadwood to Edgemont, crossing more than 100 converted railroad bridges and through four rock tunnels, rarely exceeding a 4 percent grade. In the summer months, the crushed lime-stone and gravel path is a thorough-fare for cyclists and horseback riders of all ages and abilities.

In quiet winter months, however, it becomes a meditative spot for cross-country skiers, fat bikers, and snowshoers to explore the sublime beauty of the Black Hills in solitude, in the footsteps of Calamity Jane and Wild Bill Hickok. With 15 estab-lished trailheads, it's easy to chase the snow. The Custer State Park Visi-tor Center offers snowshoes free of charge for up to two weeks starting in January. Though the trail is open year-round, amenities are closed between October 1 and April 30.

Multicity, SD | **Season:** Year-round

The faces of Presidents Washington, Jefferson, Roosevelt, and Lincoln are carved into the face of Mount Rushmore.

1. SUMMIT SACRED HEIGHTS

Known as Mato Paha to the Dakota and Noahvose to the Cheyenne, Bear Butte State Park, which towers above the Black Hills, is a sacred place for many Indigenous groups who come here to seek visions or hold religious ceremonies. The Summit Trail rises a precipitous 900 feet (270 m) in less than two miles (3.2 km).

2. FIND THE ANGLER'S BEST BETS

The Glacial Lakes Region in the northeastern corner of South Dakota is an under-the-radar haven for boat-based anglers who want to reel in walleye, smallmouth bass, and panfish all day long. There are hundreds of bodies of water here, but the best luck will likely be on Waubay and Bitter, the two largest lakes in the region.

3. PADDLE SYLVAN LAKE

In 1891 a man named Theodore Reder dammed Sunday Gulch Creek to form 17-acre (7 ha) Sylvan Lake. Surrounded by massive granite outcrops, the stunning lake within Custer State Park is just five miles (8 km) southwest of Mount Rushmore, the perfect cooling oasis for visitors to rent kayaks, canoes, or stand-up paddleboards.

4. SOAR TO NEW HEIGHTS

Greet the rising sun as you soar over undulating hills, ponderosa pines, and eroded granite spires that make up the magical landscape of Black Hills National Forest. The one-hour flight includes a complimentary glass of champagne and an unforgettable bird's-eye view. Book a reservation through Black Hills Balloons.

5. PLAY ON LEWIS AND CLARK LAKE

This 48-square mile (124 km²) dammed reservoir on the Missouri River in the state's northeastern corner is the epicenter of South Dakota water sports. Kayaking, sailing, tubing, wakesurfing, and fishing are popular in the hot summer months. Rent a powerboat and tow tube at Lewis & Clark Marina in Yankton on the northeast shoreline.

6. CAMP ON THE PRAIRIE

Shadehill Recreation Area offers 85 campsites, a boat dock, and views to the surrounding prairie in the southeast corner of Shadehill Reservoir. There is also a memorial to Hugh Glass, the American frontiersman who survived a grizzly bear mauling here in 1823. The area is now grizzly free.

7. ROCK CLIMB AT PALISADES STATE PARK

Quartzite cliffs rise upwards of 50 feet (15 m) from both sides of Split Rock Creek in this park located minutes from the Minnesota border. They may pale in comparison to the climbing near Mount Rushmore, but their location a few miles north of Interstate 90 make them an ideal road-trip oasis.

8. SCOUT FOR EAGLES

Oahe Downstream Recreation Area is an excellent winter destination to spot bald eagles. As many as 70 birds roost along the shoreline in towering cottonwood trees and fish in the open water below the Oahe dam.

9. PICK YOUR OWN PRODUCE

A delightful throwback to a simpler era, Sanderson Gardens near Brookings is where guests can pick spring rhubarb and asparagus, summer strawberries and raspberries, or autumn pumpkins, and gourds every day of the week.

10. SEE THE PRESIDENTS

No visit to South Dakota would be complete without a visit to Presidents Washington, Jefferson, Roosevelt, and Lincoln at Mount Rushmore, expertly carved into the Black Hills by Gutzon Borglum. The sculptor started the project in 1927 and worked on it, with a team of 400 men and women, until his death in 1941. His son James Lincoln Borglum added the finishing touches and served as the park's first superintendent.

American pasqueflower

Cades Cove in Great Smoky
Mountains National Park
(page 586)

TENNESSEE

Camping, birding, paddling, hiking, and historical jaunts are just a few of the ways you can explore Tennessee.

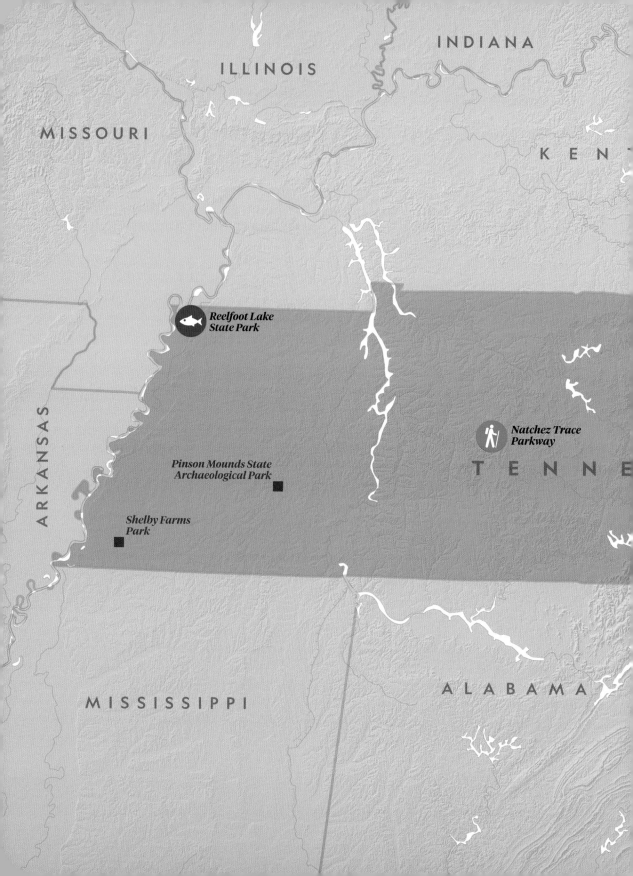

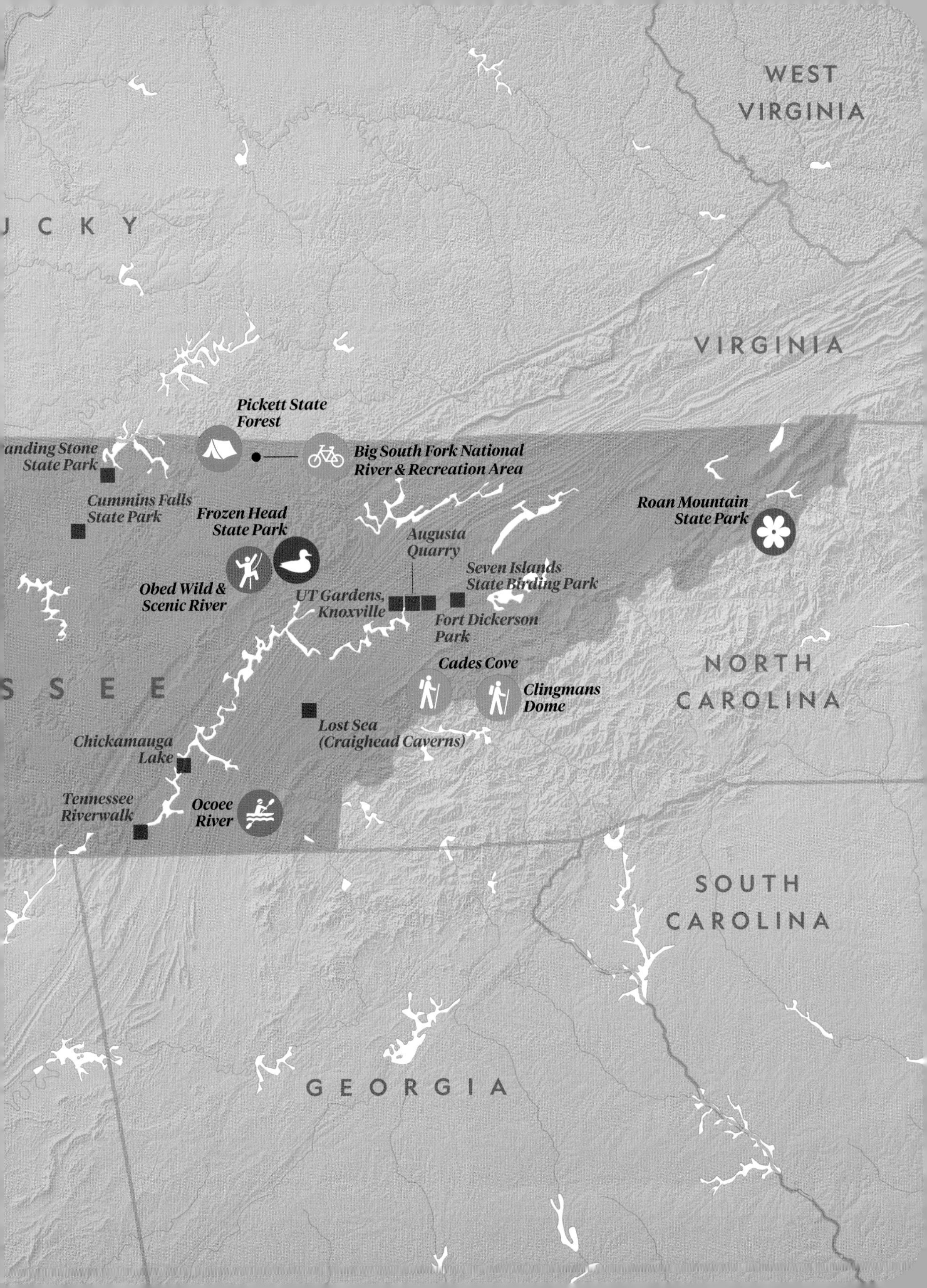

WEST
VIRGINIA

VIRGINIA

JCKY

anding Stone
State Park

**Pickett State
Forest**

🏕 ● —— 🚲 **Big South Fork National
River & Recreation Area**

*Cummins Falls
State Park*

**Frozen Head
State Park**

*Augusta
Quarry*

*Seven Islands
State Birding Park*

**Roan Mountain
State Park** ✳

**Obed Wild &
Scenic River**

*UT Gardens,
Knoxville*

*Fort Dickerson
Park*

NORTH
CAROLINA

SSEE

Cades Cove

🚶

🚶 **Clingmans
Dome**

*Chickamauga
Lake*

*Lost Sea
(Craighead Caverns)*

**Tennessee
Riverwalk**

🛶 **Ocoee
River**

SOUTH
CAROLINA

GEORGIA

Hike Through History

Starting in Nashville, Tennessee, and ending in Natchez, Mississippi, the 444-mile (715 km) Natchez Trace Parkway loosely follows the Old Natchez Trace, a travel corridor Indigenous peoples and settlers followed and used as a major thoroughfare for goods headed to and from the Mississippi River.

The two-lane roadway gives travelers an opportunity to slow down and stop at a variety of natural spots that give a little sense of what it was like to journey along the entire distance on foot. At Milepost 437.2, Timberland Park has nine different hiking trails of various lengths and activity levels that wind for five miles (8 km) through the 72-acre (29 ha) space. Baker Bluff, a popular stop at Milepost 404.7, includes a scenic overlook and one of two waterfalls along the parkway—Jackson Falls. The other waterfall at Fall Hollow can be found at Milepost 391.9, where it cascades down a sheer rock face in the lush forest.

Franklin to Columbia, TN | **Season:** Spring to fall

Find quiet spots, like Little Sandy Creek, along the Natchez Trace Parkway.

A Verdant Valley

Located in Great Smoky Mountains National Park, Cades Cove is a popular destination for wildlife spotting and hiking, and it also provides a unique look into history. For hundreds of years, Cherokee peoples hunted here, and European settlers arrived in the early 1800s. Today, the region has one of the best collections of log buildings in the eastern United States with more than 90 structures. The 11-mile (18 km) one-way Cades Cove Loop Road circles the cove through this verdant, historic landscape.

Each season brings its own beauty—from wildflowers in spring to gushing streams and waterfalls in summer, a palette of leaf colors in fall to wide-open landscape in winter. Among the most popular trails are the hike to the stone outcrop of Charlies Bunion that offers vast mountain views, the old-growth hardwood forest and log bridges of Alum Cave Trail, and the wonderland of Rainbow Falls Trail.

Take your time to traverse the area by camping in the 159-site Cades Cove Campground, open year-round. Camping here gives visitors valuable dawn and dusk hours to spot wildlife, like turkeys, raccoons, coyotes, black bears, and white-tailed deer.

See historic waterwheels and an old mill in the woods of Cades Cove.

Blount County, TN | **Season:** Year-round

Flow Into a Flooded Forest

In the northwest corner of Tennessee, Reelfoot Lake State Park is one of the greatest fishing preserves in the country. The 15,000-acre (6,070 ha) lake was formed after a series of earthquakes in 1811–12 caused the Mississippi River (3 miles/5 km away) to flow backward for a short time. The resulting flooded cypress forest is an ecosystem that's unique in the state, with a system of bayous, creeks, and swampland.

Reelfoot Lake's location along the Mississippi Flyway makes it a popular resting place for migrating birds, like bald and golden eagles, Swainson's warblers, peregrine falcons, and Mississippi kites. The park's annual Eagle Festival takes place in February, when visitors can spy bald eagles and waterfowl in their natural winter environment. Park rangers lead guided tours every day of the festival. Birders who arrive in the fall will delight in the hundreds of white pelicans who stop at the lake on their migration route.

Lake and Obion Counties, TN | **Season:** Year-round

The shallow cypress swamp waters serve as a natural fish hatchery. Though Reelfoot is considered the top bluegill fishery in the state, among the 50 species of fish that call the lake home are bream, catfish, crappie, and largemouth bass. Anglers can fish from the bank, pier, boardwalk, or boat; the park has five public boat ramps for fishing boats and small pontoon boats. Because the submerged cypress stumps require boaters to exercise caution in navigation, you'll see few large boats on Reelfoot. Kayakers who want to leisurely explore the lake's environment can bring their own craft or rent either hourly or daily from park locations. Reelfoot Lake State Park also offers deep swamp canoe tours and scenic pontoon boat tours. These tours are offered May through September. Swimming in the lake is not allowed.

Ride the rapids of the Ocoee River in Polk County.

Paddle the Rapids

The Ocoee River is one of the most popular white-water rivers in the world, creating deep gorges while running through the mountains of Cherokee National Forest. White-water racing events have been held here since 1978, and it's considered the birthplace of freestyle kayaking. In 1996, the Ocoee Whitewater Center hosted the first Olympic white-water event on a natural river.

Experience the river close up on a rafting trip with any of a handful of outfitters, like Ocoee Rafting, the oldest company on the river. You don't need white-water experience—only the desire to hang on and have fun on challenging rapids with names like Grumpy's, Table Saw, Godzilla, and Humongous. If you'd rather enjoy the beauty of the region from land, the Cherokee National Forest has two extensive mountain bike trail systems (Chilhowee and Tanasi) in the Ocoee River Zone.

Cherokee National Forest, TN | **Season:** Spring to fall

Take in the fall colors of the Obed Wild and Scenic River from the Lilly Bluff Overlook.

"THE RUGGED REGION APPEARS MUCH AS IT DID IN THE LATE 1700S."

Wild and Free

Stretching along the Cumberland Plateau, the Obed River and its tributaries pass through narrow, V-shaped gorges of horizontal Pennsylvanian and Mississippian sedimentary rock that can reach up to 500 feet (150 m) deep. The rugged region appears much as it did in the late 1700s, and its Wild and Scenic designation for 45.3 miles (72.9 km) preserves its free-flowing condition.

The Obed and its white-water streams attract experienced paddlers from all around the eastern United States to run its Class II to Class IV rapids, especially from January through April. Even when conditions are calm in river sections that are given a Class II rating, all sections are extremely remote and have potentially lethal hazards that make this Wild and Scenic River inappropriate for beginners.

The imposing expanses of rock in this region are known for their vertical faces that often seemingly become horizontal and overhang the rapids of the Obed River. The Tieranny Roofs wall is home to the longest climbing routes in the Obed, where visitors scale an inverted staircase of sandstone before it extends to the roof. Approximately 350 permanently bolted routes range in difficulty from 5.7 to 5.14—a wide variety for beginner to advanced climbers. Bouldering is also becoming one of the most popular activities in the park.

In 2017, the Obed Wild and Scenic River was designated an International Dark Sky Park, the second National Park Service unit east of Colorado and the 17th national park in the United States to earn the designation. Ranger-led activities at Lilly Overlook and Nemo Bridge include opportunities to enjoy spectacular dark sky conditions and view bright stars, star clusters, distant galaxies, and constellations with the naked eye and telescopes.

Cumberland and Morgan Counties, TN | **Season:** Year-round

Wildflower Spectacle

Famous for the largest naturally occurring garden of native Catawba rhododendrons in North America, Roan Mountain is actually not one mountain, but a high ridge about five miles (8 km) long that ranges from a height of 6,285 feet (1,916 m) at Roan High Knob to a low of 5,500 feet (1,676 m) at Carver's Gap. The park is host to the annual Roan Mountain Rhododendron Festival, held in June, when thousands of people visit the mountain and the rhododendrons are in peak bloom. In a good year, a single bush may have more than 100 clusters of flowers.

The state park's more than 2,000 acres (810 ha) of terrain among steep ridges, hardwood forest, and the Doe River include 12 miles (19 km) of day use hiking trails with difficulty levels ranging from easy to strenuous. Despite its "difficult" rating, the mile-long (1.6 km) Raven Rock Trail is one of the best places from which to watch a Roan Mountain sunset.

> "IN A GOOD YEAR, A SINGLE BUSH MAY HAVE MORE THAN 100 CLUSTERS OF FLOWERS."

Carter County, TN | **Season:** Summer

A rhododendron field blooms at sunrise in Roan Mountain State Park.

For spectacular views of the Great Smoky Mountains, walk to the lookout of Clingmans Dome.

Smoky Mountain Majesty

There are 94 miles (151 km) of the Appalachian Trail (AT) running through Tennessee, with an extra 160 miles (260 km) along the border of Tennessee and North Carolina. The AT crosses 6,643-foot-high (2,025 m) Clingmans Dome in Great Smoky Mountains National Park, the highest point in all of Tennessee and the third highest mountain east of the Mississippi, following Mount Mitchell and Mount Craig, both in North Carolina. Of course, this is only a small portion of the AT, which stretches all the way from Georgia to Maine.

Take advantage of the high perch to get sweeping spruce-fir forest and mountain views from the observation tower atop Clingmans Dome, where you can see for more than 100 miles (160 km) on clear days. The seven-mile (11 km) Clingmans Dome Road leads to the

tower, and scenic pullouts offer views of ridges and valleys as you progress to the end of the road. From there, a steep half-mile (0.8 km) paved trail leads to the 54-foot (16 m) tower. Best photo opportunities are at sunrise and sunset, when the sky glows with color above the mountains.

Hikers who want to get a taste of the AT without committing to the entire 2,190 miles (3,520 km) can test their mettle on the combined Little River Trail/ Goshen Prong Trail for a challenging distance of 13.5 miles (21.7 km). Start at the Elkmont Campground in Gatlinburg on the Little River Trail for 3.7 miles (6 km) until you come to its junction with the Goshen Prong Trail. The quiet trail with river crossings and rocky ascents meanders along fern fields, rhododendron thickets, and old stone walls. This spot is lush with wild-flowers in summer and offers ample places to take a break and admire the beauty of the Smokies.

The CCC Museum is dedicated to the Civilian Conservation Corps.

Forest Spirit

Pickett CCC Memorial State Park, within Pickett State Forest, was developed between 1934 and 1942 by the Civilian Conservation Corps (CCC), a work program to help lift the United States out of the Great Depression. The CCC workers built rustic cabins, a ranger station, a recreation lodge, and hiking trails around the 12-acre (5 ha) Arch Lake. More than 58 miles (93 km) of trails with varied lengths and difficulty levels spread through the wilderness, with views of waterfalls, natural bridges, sandstone bluffs, and diverse plant life.

In 2015, Pickett became the first state park in the Southeast to earn a Silver-tier International Dark Sky Park designation. Camping here is the best way to enjoy the night sky filled with stars. Reserve one of 26 campsites or stay in a park cabin. Although modern cabins are available, historic CCC stone and wood shingle cabins built in the 1930s are the better sentimental choice.

Pickett County, TN | **Season:** Year-round

Cumberland Plateau Immersion

Big South Fork National River and Recreation Area was established to protect the Big South Fork of the Cumberland River, as well as its tributaries. With scenic gorges and sandstone bluffs, this is some of the most rugged terrain in the Cumberland Plateau.

For great views, mountain bikers ride the Big South Fork, an IMBA Epic trail, running 34.2 miles (55 km) from Bandy Creek Visitor Center. Start out with thick creekside laurel and rhododendron forest, and work up to slick-rock-like sandstone, hardwood ridge, gravel, and clifftop single-track sections. The easy 3.5-mile (5.6 km) Middle Creek Nature Loop winds through hardwood forest and past rock shelters. The moderate Twin Arches Loop includes cliffs and rock overhangs. In the south end, the 2.9-mile (4.6 km) loop of Gentleman's Swimming Hole Trail leads to the "Meeting of the Waters" junction of the Clear Fork and White Oak Creek.

Oneida, TN | **Season:** Year-round

Wheel up some dirt on trails near the Big South Fork River.

Debord Falls is one of many cascades in Frozen Head State Park.

Feed Your Head

One of the crown jewels of Tennessee's Cumberland Mountains, Frozen Head State Park and Natural Area amounts to more than 24,000 acres (9,710 ha) of wilderness. The park's name comes from a 3,324-foot (1,013 m) peak that's often covered in ice or snow in winter months. The region is considered an excellent example of what presettle-ment conditions may have looked like in this area hundreds of years ago.

More than 130 species of birds have been observed in the park throughout the year, including several neotropical migrant birds like the cerulean warbler, as well as breeding populations of a few high-elevation species that are rare outside of the Blue Ridge Mountains. Many of the region's bird species are numerous along the park's more than 50 miles (80 km) of backpacking and day-hiking trails. There are more than 30 campsites, ranging from tent sites to backcountry sites.

Morgan County, TN | **Season:** Year-round

Walk the urban green
spaces of Chattanooga.

1. CHASE WATERFALLS

Located on the Blackburn Fork State Scenic River, Cummins Falls State Park is home to Tennessee's eighth largest waterfall, at 75 feet (23 m) high. The idyllic gorge can be seen from an overlook or accessed by a rugged hike to the base of the gushing waterfall and a refreshingly cool swimming hole.

2. WANDER THROUGH A GARDEN GETAWAY

Take your time in the official botanical gardens of the state of Tennessee, part of the UT Institute of Agriculture. The University of Tennessee Gardens function as an outdoor laboratory to evaluate the performance and landscape use of nearly 4,000 trees, shrubs, annuals, perennials, ornamental grasses, and tropical plants each year.

3. ROLL ALONG THE RIVER

Find nature in the big city on the Tennessee Riverwalk, located on the southern banks of the Tennessee River. The path runs through downtown Chattanooga and along the water for 16.1 miles (25.9 km). Slow down to enjoy the waterfront views or rent a kayak from L2 Outside, launch under the Market Street Bridge, and revel in river time.

4. LIVE THE LAKE LIFE

Tucked into the middle of the Cumberland Plateau, Standing Stone State Park covers nearly 11,000 acres (4,450 ha). The park centers around Kelly Lake, where anglers can catch bass, bluegill, catfish, and trout. Stay in cabins that overlook the lake, or pitch your tent at the park campground, which accommodates RVs.

5. STEP INTO HISTORY

Pinson Mounds State Archaeological Park has at least 15 earthen mounds, making this archaeological site the largest Middle Woodland period mound group in the United States. Hike or bike the six miles (10 km) of trails, which include a nature trail and a boardwalk with a stop overlooking the Forked Deer River bordering the park.

6. TAKE AN URBAN ADVENTURE

Shelby Farms Park, 20 minutes from downtown Memphis, is one of the largest urban parks in the country. More than 40 miles (64 km) of multiuse trails let cyclists choose between smooth pavement and undulating dirt, and stand-up paddleboard (SUP) rentals are a great way to enjoy quiet time on Hyde Lake.

7. CATCH BIG FISH

Chickamauga Lake is so close to Chattanooga that you can see most of the city from the lake's 810 miles (1,300 km) of shoreline. Launch your boat (or rent one) from the lake's handful of marinas and cast a line for record-setting bass; Chickamauga is home to the state record largemouth bass.

8. FIND THE LOST SEA

Once used as a shelter for local Cherokee peoples, the extensive and historic Craig-head Caverns features stalactites, stalagmites, anthodites, a waterfall, and the largest underground lake in North America (the second largest in the world). Guided tours include a glass-bottom boat voyage on the 4.5-acre (1.8 ha) lake called the "Lost Sea."

9. LOOK TO THE SKIES FOR FEATHERED FRIENDS

Hike eight miles (13 km) of trails in Seven Islands State Birding Park along the French Broad River. The natural landscape of aquatic and grassland habitats makes this park a premier birding destination with more than 200 species sighted, including purple martins and tree swallows.

10. FIND RESPITE AT A SWIMMING HOLE

The sparkling blue waters of the 350-foot-deep (110 m) Augusta Quarry surrounded by tall rock cliffs call to swimmers and paddleboarders looking to enjoy this serene setting within the city. Add a visit to Fort Dickerson, one of the best preserved earthen forts from the Civil War era, built overlooking the Tennessee River.

Passionflower

Agave plants grow throughout the parklands of Texas.

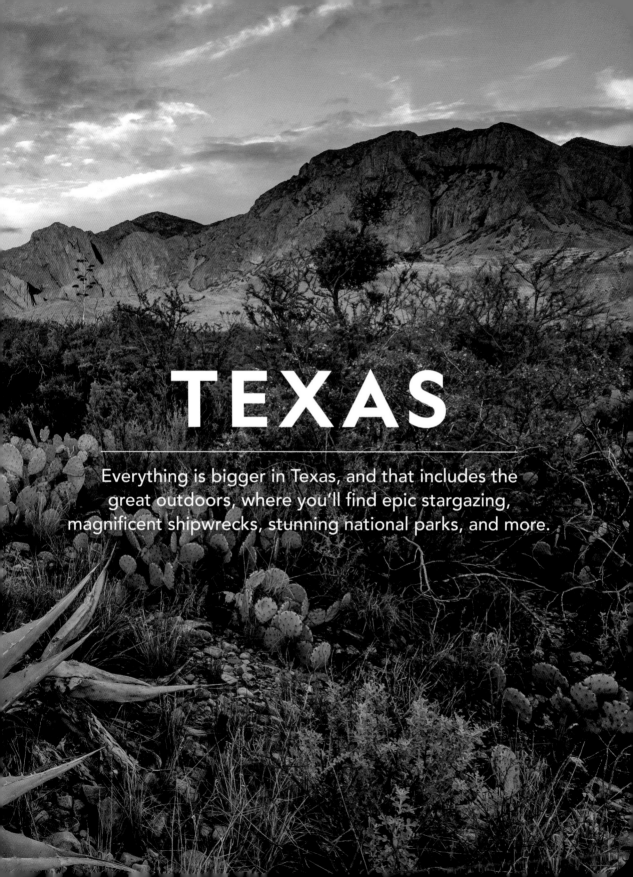

TEXAS

Everything is bigger in Texas, and that includes the great outdoors, where you'll find epic stargazing, magnificent shipwrecks, stunning national parks, and more.

ARIZONA

NEW MEXICO

Palo Duro Canyon
State Park ■

T E

Hueco Tanks State Park
and Historic Site

Balmorhea
State Park ■

SONORA

Big Bend Ranch
State Park

★ ■

Santa Elena
Canyon

CHIHUAHUA

U.S.
MEXICO

COAHUILA

Gulf of California

SINALOA   DURANGO

MISSOURI

TENNESSEE

OKLAHOMA

ARKANSAS

MISSISSIPPI

Copper Breaks
State Park

Eisenhower
State Park

X A S

LOUISIANA

Meadow View
Nature Area

Mother Neff
State Park   Waco

South Llano
River State
Park

Spider Mountain
Bike Park
        Pace Bend Park

Lady Bird Lake

Hamilton
Pool Preserve

gram
ake &
Dam

Blue Hole
Regional Park   Lagoonfest
                                  Texas

Robert L. B.
Tobin Land Bridge

Galveston

Enchanted
Rock State
Natural Area

Mission Reach
Paddling Trail

Jacob's Well
Natural Area

Gulf of
Mexico

"MAY YOUR TRAILS BE
CROOKED, WINDING,
LONESOME, DANGEROUS,
LEADING TO THE MOST
AMAZING VIEW."
—EDWARD ABBEY

Texas Clipper
wreck

NUEVO
LEÓN

TAMAULIPAS

Seeing Blue

❀ You can see Texas's beloved state flower many places, but for the best views, head to Ennis, the Official Bluebonnet City of Texas. Each April, the city's Ennis Garden Club maps out 40 miles (64 km) of drivable trails. For six weeks, the rolling hills of the Meadow View Nature Area are covered in a sea of bluebonnets and other wildflowers.

Other spots listed on the Bluebonnet Trail include Kachina Prairie Park, Veterans Memorial Park in Ennis, and Minnie McDowal Park. Texas is the only place that grows the *Lupinus texensis* and *Lupinus subcarnosus* species of bluebonnets, and the state has more bluebonnet flowers than anywhere in the world. Each year, the Texas Department of Transportation plants more than 30,000 pounds (13,600 kg) of wildflowers along the freeways. Although picking bluebonnets from the side of the road is not illegal, it's better to just snap a few pictures and leave the flowers for others to enjoy.

Multicity, TX | Season: April

Bluebonnets bloom between late March and late April.

Hole in the Well

🏊 Beat the summer heat by diving into Jacob's Well, a 12-foot-wide (4 m) artesian spring-fed sinkhole in Texas Hill Country. At more than 23 feet (7 m) deep, the sinkhole leads to the second largest fully submerged cave in Texas. According to researchers, the lowest point of the mile-long (1.6 km) cave system is nearly 140 feet (43 m) deep.

Jacob's Well was discovered in the early 1850s by William C. Winters, an early settler of the Wimberley Valley. According to local lore, it was named "Jacob's Well" because Winters said it was "like unto a well in Bible times."

The swimming hole is open from May 1 to September 30, by online reservations only. Each reserved slot guarantees two hours of swim time. The water temperature stays at a constant 68°F (20°C).

After you dry off from the swim, go for a short hike along the park's several trails to see giant cypress trees, fossils, birds like warblers and greater roadrunner, monarch butterflies, and vistas of the Wimberley Valley. Every Saturday morning from October through April, a naturalist leads an hour-long, guided tour.

Walk to Jacob's Well, a karstic spring and water hole.

San Marcos, TX | Season: Year-round

Shred Through Texas Hill Country

Take the Texas Eagle chairlift to the top of a 350-foot (110 m) hill and shred through windy single-track trails on your mountain bike at Spider Mountain Bike Park in Texas Hill Country. Located an hour north of Austin, the park has the only year-round dedicated mountain bike chairlift in the state. Spider Mountain has nine trails rated in similar fashion to ski slopes.

First-timers should start with the Itsy-Bitsy beginner's trail, which has wide turns, smooth paths, gentle rolls, and fun switchbacks. The intermediate Vipers Den is steeper, and has tighter switchbacks, jumps, and rockier paths. Another popular moderate trail is the Tarantula, which has bridges, berms, and a wall ride painted with the Lone Star flag. The advanced trail traverses under the chairlift, has steep, rocky drops, and offers views of Lake Buchanan.

There's no on-site restaurant, so bring plenty of water and snacks. Tickets include unlimited rides on the chairlift.

Burnet, TX | Season: Year-round

Bikes, helmets, and pads are available for rent. The park is open Friday through Monday. On weekdays when Spider Mountain is closed, you can pay $15 to hike or ride uphill. Those who stay at the nearby Thunderbird Lodge on Lake Buchanan are offered a free chairlift pass, bike rental, or watercraft rental and can access the hiking trails at no extra cost. The lodge has 23 units, from four-person motel-style casitas to stone cottages to villas that can host up to 20 guests. For an extra-special stay, book the Spider House. The three-bedroom house has walk-out lift access right on the mountain. There are also primitive camping sites and eight RV-hookup sites at Reveille Peak Ranch just 10 minutes from Spider Mountain. Rustic restrooms, changing rooms, and showers are available on the campgrounds.

A Dam Good Time

Channel your inner child as you slide down the Ingram Lake Dam on the Guadalupe River in Texas Hill Country. Built in 1956 for flood control, the dam has an incline of about 45 degrees and is covered with natural algae. When water overflows from the river, the slippery concrete structure is transformed into a giant waterslide into the pool below. Climb back up on the drier side of the dam and repeat for maximum fun. The rough surface of the dam can wear out your bathing suit, so be sure to bring a tube, mat, kayak, or boogie board. The pool in the area above the dam is deep and is a great swimming spot. The top part of the dam is flat, so you can camp out with your cooler and lawn chair when you need a break from the thrills. There is no entrance fee, and no lifeguard available. Paid parking is available at a lot across the street.

Ingram, TX | Season: Summer

Slide and swim at Ingram Dam.

> "FOR THE BEST VIEWS WITH THE DARKEST SKIES, HEAD TO BIG BEND NATIONAL PARK."

Bigger, Better Skies

Texas is home to six International Dark Sky Parks, two Dark Sky Sanctuaries, and even a Dark Sky Community (the quaint town of Dripping Springs). Texas's Dark Sky Parks include Big Bend Ranch State Park and the adjacent Big Bend National Park in southwest Texas; Copper Breaks State Park south of the Oklahoma border; and Enchanted Rock State Natural Area, UBarU Camp and Retreat Center, and South Llano River State Park in Texas Hill Country.

For the best views with the darkest skies, head to Big Bend National Park, which has the least light population of any national park unit in the contiguous United States. Take the Hot Springs Canyon Trail along the river for expansive views of the Chihuahuan Desert and an unobstructed sky. A wheelchair-accessible 100-yard (90 m) Rio Grande Village Nature Trail, with vistas of the Sierra del Carmen and the Chisos Mountains, is also a great stargazing spot. Situated in very remote locations, Dark Sky Sanctuaries in Texas include Black Gap Wildlife Management Area and Devils River State Natural Area at Del Norte, both administered by the Texas Parks and Wildlife Department.

Many of the parks offer star parties, self-guided constellation tours, moonlight walks, and light pollution education programs. A few parks feature campgrounds, cabins, and RV sites. Though not a Dark Sky Park, Davis Mountains State Park in West Texas is home to the McDonald Observatory, which hosts open-air constellation tours, as well as live telescope views.

The best times to stargaze are on clear nights with a new moon. The Milky Way is the most visible during summer months. Time your visit between mid-July and mid-August so you can witness the Perseid meteor shower, considered one of the best meteor showers of the year.

Multicity, TX | **Season:** Year-round

Stars shine bright over the Chisos Mountains and Rio Grande in Big Bend National Park.

Dive Into History

Before the *Texas Clipper* was sunk into the bottom of the Gulf of Mexico, 17 miles (27 km) off the coast of South Padre Island, it was a warship, a luxury liner, and a maritime training vessel. Built in 1944, the historic World War II troop transport and attack ship was one of the first to arrive at Iwo Jima in the Pacific War. After the war, it was retrofitted into a luxury liner sailing between New York City and the Mediterranean. In 1965, the ship was loaned to the Texas Maritime Academy as a training vessel. Now, as one of the country's largest artificial reefs, the coral-, barnacle-, and sponge-encrusted ship is supporting new marine life and providing fish habitats. The highest point of the 473-foot-long (144 m), 7,000-ton (6,350 t) boat lies 65 feet (20 m) beneath the surface. Suitable for intermediate divers, the recreational dive site attracts schools of Atlantic spadefish, stingrays, red snappers, groupers, and angelfish. The water is clearest from March through October.

South Padre Island, TX | **Season:** March to October

> "THE CORAL-, BARNACLE-, AND SPONGE-ENCRUSTED SHIP IS SUPPORTING NEW MARINE LIFE AND PROVIDING FISH HABITATS."

Blue angelfish swim throughout the USTS *Texas Clipper* shipwreck.

Ancient Jornada Mogollon peoples drew pictographs into the rocks.

Trace the Past

Wildlife brims at Hueco Tanks State Park and Historic Site, northeast of El Paso. The rocks at Hueco Tanks rose 34 million years ago, when an underground mass of magma entered an older limestone formation, and then cooled. Wind, sun, and rain eroded the limestone, resulting in the majestic hoodoos still standing in the park. "Huecos," natural rock basins, were formed and trapped rainwater that helped quench the thirst of animals, birds, and travelers dating back 10,000 years who crossed the Chihuahuan Desert. Early residents—the Jornada Mogollon—left pictographs, petroglyphs, and artifacts, sacred documentation of an ancient culture. The Jornada painted more than 200 "mask" designs beneath rock overhangs, within boulder shelters, and at other hidden sites.

The park has six trails, ranging from an easy stroll around the interpretive center with views of the pictographs to a more strenuous hike up the North Mountain for a sweeping view of El Paso. In addition to trails, the park is also a popular bouldering and rock-climbing destination. Hueco Tanks is also a birder's paradise, with sightings of more than 200 species of birds, including prairie falcon, burrowing owl, and white-throated swift.

Tip: Sign up for ranger-led pictograph, hiking, birding, or rock-climbing tours. The ranger typically has access to off-limits parts of the park. Only 70 people are allowed in the park at a time, and you must call in advance for a permit. Limited capacity and permit requirements remain in places to protect the sacred Hueco Tanks, which have been vandalized in the past.

Texas horned lizard

El Paso, TX | Season: Year-round

Kayak Lake Texoma at Eisenhower State Park.

Bouldering by the Lake

Named for the 34th president, who was born in the nearby town of Denison, Eisenhower State Park comprises 1,785 acres (720 ha) of tallgrass prairie, woodland, and the shores of Lake Texoma. It's located at the Texas-Oklahoma border, about 80 miles (130 km) north of Dallas. Climbers know it as "ESP," a popular bouldering site with large sandstone and limestone rocks. The park has more than 100 different climbing routes, ranging from six to 10 feet (1.8 to 3 m). Average scales are in the V0 to V3 range, which make the boulders at ESP perfect for beginners. Most of the boulders are located on the shoreline of the lake. For safety, bring a crash pad. The park has little shade, so bring plenty of water and sunscreen also, and after a rigorous workout, cool off in the refreshing lake. In additional to bouldering, Eisenhower State Park also has hiking and biking trails, campsites, and a fishing area.

Grayson County, TX | **Season:** Year-round

Mother of All Parks

When Isabella Neff died in 1921, six acres (2 ha) of land along the Leon River west of Moody was donated to "the public, for religious, educational, fraternal, and political purposes" at her behest. Two years later, in 1923, her youngest son, then governor Pat Neff, established the State Parks Board, paving the way for the creation of more than 90 state parks, historic sites, and natural systems in Texas. Governor Neff and a local resident named F. P. Smith donated additional parcels, increasing the size of the park to 259 acres (105 ha). In 1937, Mother Neff State Park became an official state park.

Nearly 3.5 miles (5.6 km) of trails connect throughout the park, with paths leading to Wash Pond, a rock tower, and a cave. Accessible year-round, the dog-friendly, shady trail is easy to navigate and has benches and stone picnic tables. You can climb the curved stone staircase to the top of the rock tower and its observation deck overlooking the valley. The tower was built by the Civilian Conservation Corps (CCC) in the 1930s. More than 200 men of the CCC lived in Mother Neff State Park from 1934 to 1938 as they built many of the park structures you can still see today. Farther along, up rock steps, you'll arrive at the overhang rock shelter, which the Tonkawa once inhabited more than 200 years ago. Finally, head to Wash Pond, a clear natural spring-fed basin that the CCC expanded. During the 1930s, people used to wash their laundry in the pond, thus its name. The 0.6-mile (0.9 km) Prairie Loop meanders through Washita Prairie to a pond and bird blind. Near the Playground Trail, a Nature Playscape has climbing logs, slides, a dig site, and a concrete armadillo.

Moody, TX | **Season:** Year-round

Swim in the limestone grotto of Hamilton Pool.

A Swimming Oasis

One of the best swimming holes in Texas, Hamilton Pool is a tropical oasis in Dripping Springs, around 25 miles (40 km) west of Austin. It was formed thousands of years ago, when the dome of an underground river collapsed due to erosion, forming a limestone grotto. Hamilton Creek flows over the limestone outcropping, creating a 50-foot (15 m) waterfall into a pool of vibrant green water, where the deepest part dips to 25 feet (8 m). Named after Morgan Hamilton, who owned the property in the 1860s, Hamilton Pool is part of Balcones Canyonlands Preserve. To get to the pool, visitors will need to hike about a quarter mile (0.4 km) from the parking lot. No lifeguards are on duty, but loaner life jackets are available. Online reservations are required. On Saturday mornings, take an hour-long guided hike to learn about the native plants and animals that reside in the canyon.

Dripping Springs, TX | **Season:** Spring to fall

Take a canoe trip down
Wimberley Creek.

1. SWIM IN SPRING POOLS

Leap off the diving board and into the world's largest spring-fed swimming pool at Balmorhea State Park in West Texas. Built by the Civilian Conservation Corps back in the 1930s, the 1.3-acre (0.5 ha) pool ranges in depth from three to 25 feet (0.9 to 8 m).

2. SURF THE GALVESTON

In winter months, you can catch some great waves in Galveston, an island city on the Texas Gulf Coast. A popular spot is around the historic Pleasure Pier, where surfers can ride waves while watching tourists speed through on a roller coaster. Several outfitters around town rent surfboards and boogie boards.

3. PADDLE UNDER A BRIDGE AND BATS

Kayak or stand-up paddleboard on the still waters of Lady Bird Lake, with the Austin skyline as a worthy backdrop. If you're paddling at dusk between April and October, watch out for the millions of bats that emerge from the concrete Ann W. Richards Congress Avenue Bridge when the sun goes down.

4. DIVE INTO BLUE HOLE IN WIMBERLEY

Swing from a rope tied to a majestic cypress tree and jump into the crystal clear Blue Hole, a Cypress Creek–fed swimming area in Wimberley. With four designated limestone slabs for swimmers to climb in and out of the water, Blue Hole is open for swimming Memorial Day through Labor Day. Reservations are required.

5. WALK IN SAN ANTONIO CANOPY

Walk among the lush treetops along the wheelchair-accessible 1,000-foot-long (305 m) Skywalk that winds through cedar elm, mesquite, and live oak trees and connects to the top of a natural land bridge. The landscaped Robert L. B. Tobin Land Bridge acts as a human and wildlife crossing over the busy Wurzbach Parkway.

6. TREK TO THE LIGHTHOUSE AT PALO DURO CANYON

Hike the nearly six-mile (10 km) round-trip trail to the iconic Lighthouse, the 310-foot-tall (95 m) hoodoo rock formation in Palo Duro Canyon State Park in the Texas Panhandle. The moderate, well-maintained trail leads hikers uphill over rocks, and rewards them with expansive views of the second largest canyon in the United States.

7. CLIFF DIVE AT PACE BEND PARK

Leap off the ragged cliff and plunge into the freshwater Lake Travis at Pace Bend Park in Spicewood. To get back to the cliff, divers can either climb up the rocks or swim to the nearby beach area. There are several prime cliff-jumping spots, including a 45-foot-tall (14 m) rock face.

8. CANOE AT SANTA ELENA CANYON

Canoe the Rio Grande through the narrow Santa Elena Canyon, at Big Bend National Park. Paddle through calm water surrounded by limestone cliff walls that jut as high as 1,500 feet (460 m). The entire navigable route is 18 miles (29 km) long, but you can rest at one of the pebbly banks before turning around.

9. LAGOON IN HOUSTON

In the heart of bustling Houston, you'll find white-sand beaches, palm trees, and the state's largest lagoon. Guests at Lagoonfest Texas can swim, float, Jet Ski, kayak, sail, and stand-up paddleboard around the 12-acre (5 ha) pool. Run through a large inflatable course or lounge by the beach with a cocktail.

10. KAYAK THE SAN ANTONIO RIVER

Connect with nature by kayaking along the eight-mile (13 km) Mission Reach Paddling Trail, from Roosevelt Park to Camino Coahuilteca, just south of downtown. Along the way, glide down more than 30 "canoe chutes," and drift past elegant egrets and herons. As part of the Ecosystem Restoration Project, more than 23,000 trees have been planted along the trail.

Nine-banded armadillo

Capitol Reef National Park (page 613) has striking rock formations and layers of golden sandstone.

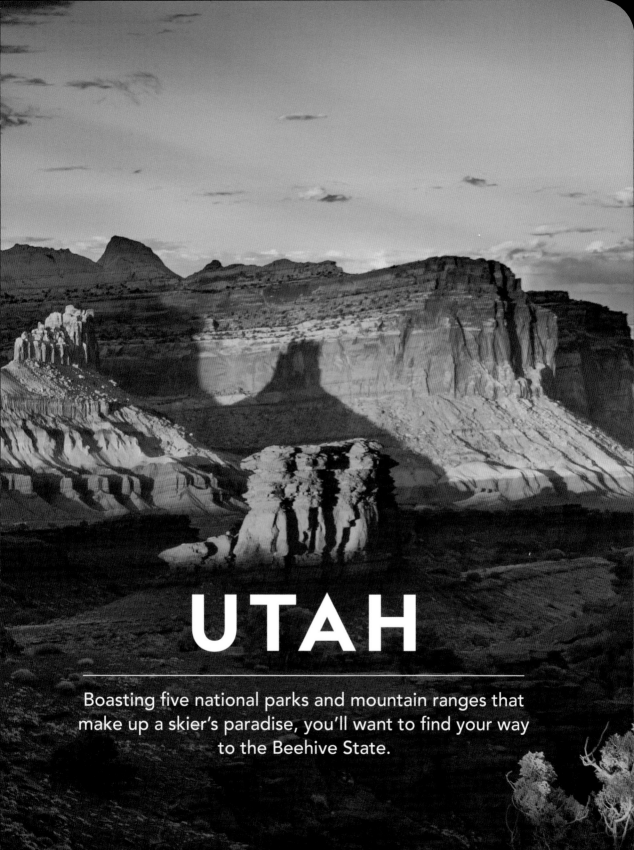

UTAH

Boasting five national parks and mountain ranges that make up a skier's paradise, you'll want to find your way to the Beehive State.

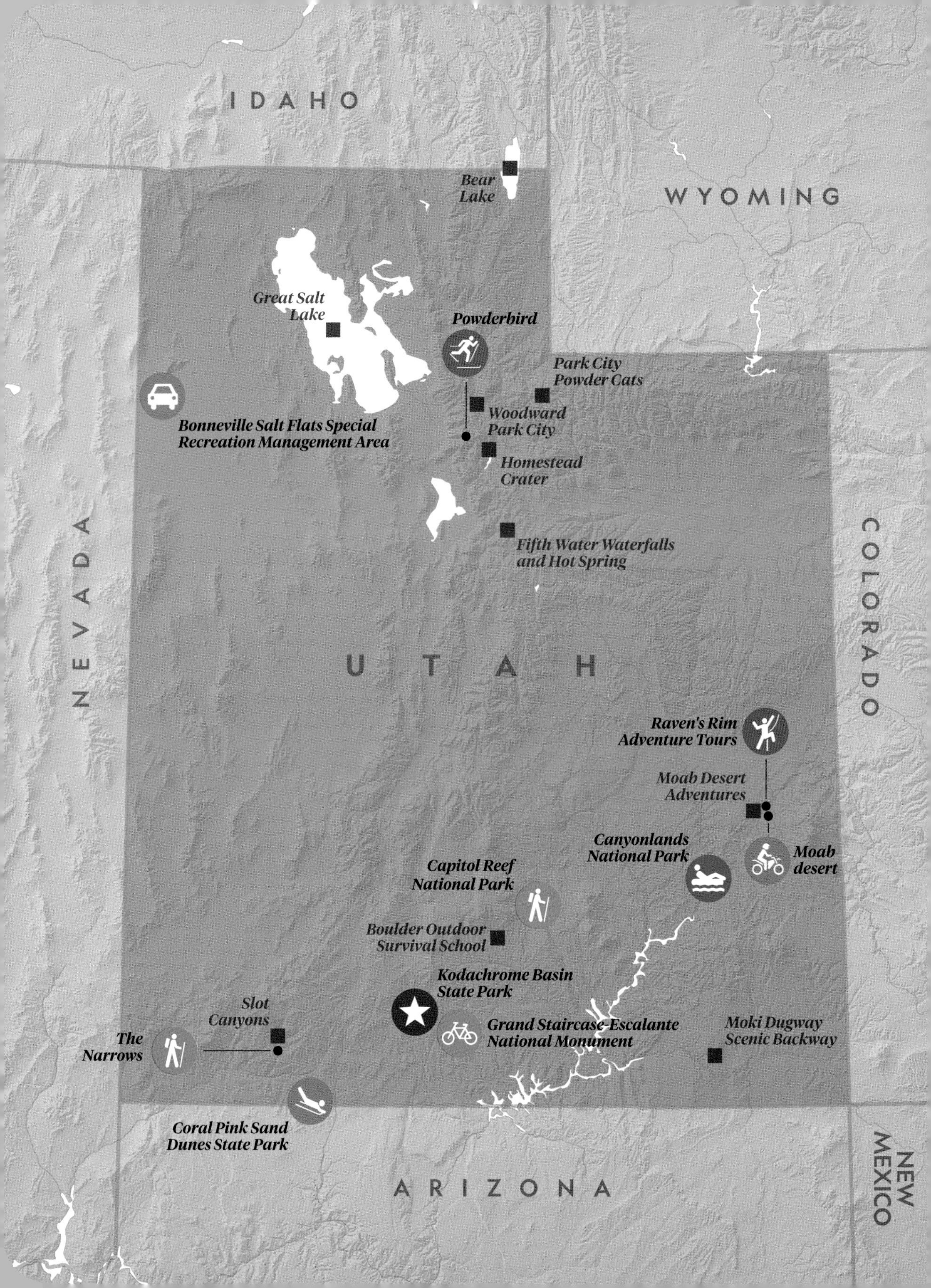

IDAHO

WYOMING

Bear
Lake

Great Salt
Lake

Powderbird

Park City
Powder Cats

Bonneville Salt Flats Special
Recreation Management Area

Woodward
Park City

NEVADA

Homestead
Crater

Fifth Water Waterfalls
and Hot Spring

COLORADO

U T A H

Raven's Rim
Adventure Tours

Moab Desert
Adventures

Canyonlands
National Park

Moab
desert

Capitol Reef
National Park

Boulder Outdoor
Survival School

Kodachrome Basin
State Park

Slot
Canyons

Grand Staircase-Escalante
National Monument

Moki Dugway
Scenic Backway

The
Narrows

Coral Pink Sand
Dunes State Park

ARIZONA

NEW
MEXICO

Dirt roads and rugged terrain await mountain bikers at Grand Staircase–Escalante.

Climb the Grand Staircase

Much of Grand Staircase–Escalante National Monument is impossible to explore unless you're willing to backpack, mountain bike, or combine both on a multiday bikepacking adventure. The terrain includes the Escalante River Canyon, lofty Kaiparowits Plateau, and a huge chunk of the Grand Staircase, a massive geological formation that descends from Bryce Canyon to the Grand Canyon.

In a park as large as Delaware and Rhode Island combined, there's plenty of room to bike and camp. However, riders need to carry everything they need—tent, sleeping bag, food, water, first aid, and bike repair kit—in saddlebags, handlebar bags, or bike panniers that easily attach to the bike frame.

The park's longest route is the Grand Staircase Loop, which rambles for 160 miles (260 km) through the national monument and adjacent Glen Canyon National Recreation Area. About halfway along, the trail reaches the shore of Lake Powell. Along the way, you'll find plenty of nature, but very few people.

Another good bikepacking route is the Burr Trail, which starts in the town of Boulder and runs across the northern part of the national monument and into Capitol Reef National Park. Combining the Burr and Wolverine Loop stretches this into a 90-mile (145 km) out-and-back from one end or the other. The Burr Trail Scenic Backway is a great option for those who want to drive rather than hike or bike the route, with various family-friendly stops along the way for picnics and short hikes.

Those who don't want to schlep their own gear can sign on for a guided group ride with Rim Tours Mountain Bike Adventures, a four-day journey along the Burr Trail corridor that includes both Grand Staircase–Escalante and Capitol Reef.

Kanab, UT | **Season:** Year-round

Hike the water-filled Narrows at Zion National Park.

The Narrows at Zion NP

One of the nation's most iconic hikes, the Narrows flows through a slot canyon in Zion National Park. At times the gorge is so narrow you can almost touch both walls at the same time. And because the trail runs right through the Virgin River, you will get wet.

Most people walk the Narrows "bottom up" from a trailhead at the north end of Zion Canyon. Though the majority never venture more than an hour upstream, hikers can splash their way all the way to Big Spring, 9.4 miles (15 km) from the start.

The other way to explore the canyon is "top down" from Chamberlain's Ranch just outside the national park. The total distance is 16 miles (26 km) with an option to camp overnight at several spots near the trail's midway point. However, a wilderness permit is required for anyone splitting the Narrows into a two-day trek.

Zion National Park, UT | Season: May to October

Take on the Dunes

Hang ten for landlubbers is an apt description of sandboarding, an outdoor sport that entails gliding down desert sands in places like Coral Pink Sand Dunes State Park in southern Utah.

Towering as high as 100 feet (30 m), the dunes actually vary between pink, orange, and ocher, trillions of quartz grains once part of a Navajo sandstone formation that also generate the intense hues at Zion, Bryce, Arches, and Canyonlands.

After each run, surfers must hike back up the dune—no lifts or towropes in this part of Utah! But you don't have to pack your own plank. The visitors center rents sandboards (for those who want to stand) and sand sleds (for those who prefer sitting) on a first-come, first-served basis at $25 a day, including wax. Novices who dig the sport can buy their own board from Slip Face Sandboards in Provo, Utah.

Kane County, UT | Season: Year-round

Pink-hued sand gives Coral Pink Sand Dunes State Park its name.

Drop into fresh powder and steep terrain in the Wasatch Range.

Heli-Skiing the Wasatch

Utah's mighty Wasatch Range is one of the spots where heli-skiing was pioneered in the early 1970s. The tradition continues at Powderbird, which delivers skiers and snowboarders to fresh powder locations just a few minutes from its heliport near Snowbird and Alta resorts in Little Cottonwood Canyon.

As the only heli-skiing operation licensed to touch down on U.S. Forest Service land, Powderbird has access to a snow-covered hinterland with more terrain than all the snow resorts in Utah combined. The higher parts of the Wasatch average more than 500 inches (1,270 cm) of snow each winter.

Located around a 30-minute drive from Salt Lake City, Powderbird offers semiprivate and private heli-skiing, single and multiday packages, and sightseeing flights for those who just want to admire the snowy mountains from above.

Alta, UT | **Season:** Winter

Take an off-road tour
through the Moab desert.

"THE REGION AROUND
MOAB BOASTS MORE THAN
100 OFFICIAL 4×4 ROUTES."

Moab Desert Dives

How rugged are the back roads and off-road routes in the desert, mountains, and canyons around Moab? So incredibly tough that Land Rover, Jeep, Hummer, and other vehicle makers venture there to test four-wheel-drive vehicles on terrain that would chew up and spit out ordinary cars. A special edition Jeep is even named for the southeast Utah town.

The region around Moab boasts more than 100 official 4x4 routes that take adventure-seeking drivers into the nether regions of Canyonlands and Arches National Parks, La Sal National Forest, several state parks, and 3.6 million acres (1.5 million ha) of desert supervised by the Bureau of Land Management (BLM).

Legendary trails like Hell's Revenge, Top of the World, Steel Bender, Fin and Things, and the Moab Rim are only for pros or very experienced amateurs in vehicles modified for crawling across slickrock and up and down steep inclines. Four-wheel-drive is a given, but many of these off-road machines are also equipped with larger tires, tougher suspensions, higher clearance, roll cages, belly armor, and winches for those rare times when you get in a jam.

Other routes around Moab are easily navigable for off-road rookies who rent a vehicle in Moab or want to test the 4x4 they recently purchased. The Potash Road/Shafer Trail route wanders along the west bank of the Colorado River below Dead Horse Point, including the jaw-dropping cliff where the famous final scene in the movie *Thelma & Louise* was shot.

The White Rim Trail loops around Island in the Sky mesa in Canyonlands National Park, a 100-mile (160 km) wander normally done as a two or three-day 4x4 camping trip. The unpaved Salt Valley Road in Arches National Park leads 8.2 miles (13.2 km) to a trailhead for the remote Tower Arch, Marching Men, and Klondike Bluffs rock formations.

Moab, UT | **Season:** Year-round

Ferrata Fear Factor

Anyone who's dreamed about scrambling across a sheer rock wall or stepping like a mountain goat across a narrow cliffside trail should try the *via ferrata*.

The Italian name means "iron path," a term that perfectly describes the fixed metal cables, steps, ladders, handholds, and footbridges that keep climbers on a slow but steady journey up and across and down an intimidating palisade. And though it does take some physical strength and a lack of acrophobia, via ferrata is designed for ordinary mortals to achieve what would otherwise be impossible.

Utah's via ferrata courses are located at Raven's Rim near Moab, the Kolob region north of Zion National Park, the Amangiri resort near Lake Powell, and Waterfall Canyon in the mountains east of Ogden. The first two offer a chance to scramble across red-rock faces, while the third offers highland forest scenery. Waterfall Canyon, which features three separate routes, is rated as one of the nation's top iron paths.

Multicity, UT | **Season:** Spring to fall

Parriott Mesa is one of the via ferrata routes in Castle Valley.

Hiking the Reef

The largest and least visited of Utah's five national parks, Capitol Reef stretches 60 miles (97 km) through the rocky wonderland of southern Utah. Its namesake is a massive chunk of Earth's crust uplifted 50 to 70 million years ago into a long, mesa-like geological structure called the Waterpocket Fold.

Nowadays the Reef is studded with countless canyons, arches, monoliths, and pale sandstone domes that 19th-century Mormon settlers compared to the Capitol Building in Washington, D.C. In a park that's largely roadless, many of these geological landmarks can only be explored by foot along more than 120 miles (190 km) of hiking trails through a variety of terrain.

The Fruita area in the heart of Capitol Reef—named after the 1880s fruit orchards that park visitors are free to harvest—offers 15 different day hikes. They range from easy jaunts like the walk through a massive gap in the Reef called the Grand Wash to fairly strenuous hikes like the steep climb to Cassidy Arch.

Cathedral Valley at the park's north end also offers a number of easy to moderate day hikes, although four-wheel-drive is often necessary to access the valley via several rough dirt roads. Heading into the park's deep south, Notom-Bullfrog Road leads to trailheads for half a dozen easy to moderate day hikes in the remote Waterpocket District.

Armed with a backcountry permit, hikers can undertake backpack camping along much more intense routes like Muley Twist Canyon, Spring Canyon, and Halls Creek Narrows (which requires considerable walking through a shallow stream).

Roosevelt elk

Capitol Reef National Park, UT | **Season:** Year-round

Float Away

Two of the most iconic rivers of the American Southwest come together in Canyonlands National Park. Though the Green and Colorado are the primary movers and shakers in creating the radically eroded terrain, they also facilitate the park's aquatic adventures.

"We glide along through a strange, weird, grand region," wrote John Wesley Powell during the first known journey down the Green River in 1869. "Ten thousand strangely carved forms . . . In long, gentle curves the river winds about these rocks."

A float trip down these rivers through Canyonlands feels exactly that way today. The Green and Colorado may be dammed elsewhere along their courses, but they remain wild and free for their entire passage through the national park.

Unlike river runs through the Grand Canyon, which always operate at breakneck speed, Canyonlands offers

two distinct possibilities. The Green and the upper reaches of the Colorado invite easygoing flat-water float trips down to the Confluence. Below Spanish Bottom, the Colorado morphs into a raging river through Cataract Canyon that takes on white-water demons like the Big Bitty, Mile Long, and Big Drops Rapids.

Anyone with national park permits can undertake their own flat-water paddle with primitive camping along the way. However, they should be sure to book a jet boat shuttle to get them back to Moab where their journey most likely started. Veteran outfitters like OARS and Western River Expedition offer guided float trips through Cataract Canyon. The trips range from four to eight days, with overnight camping. OARS also includes a scenic flight over Canyonlands National Park with each tour.

Canyonlands National Park, UT | **Season:** Spring to fall

Pedal to the Metal

Automobiles were still a novelty in 1914, when pioneering race car driver Teddy Tetzlaff set a world land speed record of 142.8 miles an hour (229.8 km/h) in a Blitzen Benz on the Bonneville Salt Flats in western Utah. Over the century that followed, the dry lake bed became *the* place for pushing vehicles to ever faster speeds.

When it hasn't been soaked by a recent rain, the ultra-flat surface and seven-mile (11 km) straightaway of the "Bonneville Salt Flats International Speedway" ensure ideal conditions for pressing the pedal to the metal.

Spectators and qualified drivers/teams are welcome at annual events like Speed Week, World of Speed, the BUB Motorcycle Speed Trials, and Mike Cook's Land Speed Shootout. Even if you don't "run whatcha brung," visitors are often free to wander the pits, snap selfies with the vehicles, or chat with drivers and crew.

Race in a streamliner car at the Bonneville Salt Flats.

Wendover, UT | **Season:** Year-round

> "MEMBERS OF A 1948 NATIONAL GEOGRAPHIC EXPEDITION WHO FOUND THE INCREDIBLY VIBRANT ROCK WALLS AND SPIRES NAMED THE BASIN FOR KODAK'S NEW COLOR FILM."

Picture-Worthy Starry Nights at Kodachrome Basin

To be declared an International Dark Sky Reserve by the international body that judges such things, a place has to boast "an exceptional or distinguished quality of starry nights" as well as an after-dark environment protected for its scientific, natural, educational, or cultural heritage, and/or public enjoyment.

Kodachrome Basin State Park in south-central Utah fits that definition to a tee. It's basically situated in the middle of nowhere—miles from the nearest town or other ambient light—one of the most isolated of the state's 22 Dark Sky Reserves. Members of a 1948 National Geographic expedition who found the incredibly vibrant rock walls and spires christened the basin for Kodak's new color film.

Visitors can camp at Kodachrome or overnight at nearby Bryce Canyon. Kodachrome has 63 campsites, including two bunkhouses and full and partial hookup sites. Bryce has backcountry camping, as well as two campgrounds: The North Campground is open year-round, with reservations required end of May through mid-October; the South Campground is open April through October on a first-come, first-served basis. Flanked by high canyon walls, the campgrounds aren't ideal for stargazing. Instead, set up your telescope in the parking lot for the Panorama Trail.

Cannonville, UT   Season: Year-round

The Milky Way is in full display above Kodachrome Basin State Park.

Soak in the mineral-rich
waters of Diamond Fork
Hot Springs.

GO FURTHER

1. SWIM IN THE GREAT SALT LAKE

With a salinity that can range up to seven times more than an ocean, the largest saltwater lake in the Western Hemisphere offers swimmers and floaters an experience close to weightlessness. Slip into the briny liquid at Antelope Island, Silver Sands Beach, or the artsy Spiral Jetty.

2. ANGLE AT BEAR LAKE

Utah's second largest natural freshwater lake is renowned for trout. However, anglers can also cast for endemic whitefish, sculpin, and cisco in their own boats or charters from Garden City. With the big water body freezing over on average seven out of every 10 years, winter ice fishing is another possibility.

3. DIVE DESERT

Scuba in Utah may sound like an oxymoron, but divers craving something totally different can plunge into the geothermal spring inside Homestead Crater. The caldera's bizarre beehive-shaped limestone dome was created more than 10,000 years ago by mineral-infused water percolating upward. Would-be frogmen and women can also scuba the spring at Bonneville Seabase near the Great Salt Lake.

4. SOAK IN NATURE'S HEATED POOLS

Tucked up a wooded canyon in Uinta National Forest, Fifth Water Hot Springs is less than two hours by road from Salt Lake City. Reaching the milky, turquoise-colored pools and their little waterfall requires a 4.5-mile (7.2 km) round-trip hike. The experience is especially cool in winter when Fifth Water is draped in snow.

5. CLIMB VERTICAL ASPIRATIONS

Maybe you've never heard of the Towers, the Priest, and the Titan, but veteran rock jocks know these daunting red-rock giants as holy grails of global climbing. All of them loom above the river road upstream from Moab, vertical challenges that can be achieved on guided climbs with Moab Desert Adventures.

6. CONQUER THE CANYONS

Utah's deeply eroded terrain is saturated with slot canyons. Some are wide enough to walk, others so narrow the only way to explore them is via canyoneering. Blending skills like rappelling and downclimbing, the sport has spread around the globe since it was pioneered in the Zion region in the late 1970s.

7. LEARN MORE AT BOULDER OUTDOOR SURVIVAL SCHOOL

"Know more, carry less" is the motto of a wilderness survival academy near Capitol Reef and Grand Staircase–Escalante that teaches students 18 and older how to survive with minimal gear in remote wild places. Lasting seven to 28 days, the courses range from basic outdoor skills to hunting/gathering, navigation, and wilderness medicine.

8. HANG WITH UINTA'S COOL CATS

The Uinta Mountains of northeast Utah offer auspicious conditions for remote off-piste skiing and snowboarding. The challenge is how to get there without hiking for hours through snow. Park City Powder Cats solves the problem by using tracked snowcats to reach 43,000 acres (17,400 ha) of private terrain in the range.

9. DRIVE THE MOKI DUGWAY

Though it's sometimes ranked among the nation's most dangerous roads, the panoramas from this series of unpaved switchbacks in southern Utah more than compensate for its vertiginous dropoffs. Officially State Route 261, the three-mile (4.8 km) ascent/descent along the edge of Cedar Mesa includes bird's-eye views of the Valley of the Gods.

10. TUBE AND RIDE AT WOODWARD

Open year-round, Woodward Park City is an action-packed outdoor sports hub. In warmer months, find lift-served mountain biking trails. Come winter, the park is transformed, with snow tubing and a terrain park for skiers and snowboarders. Throughout the year, an indoor trampoline park and skateboarding park keep tumblers and riders busy.

Colorful forests surround
Green River Reservoir.

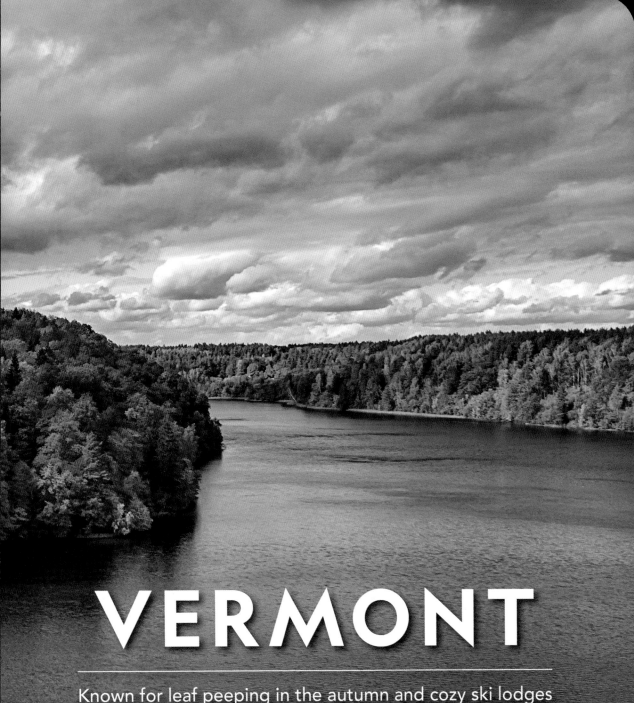

VERMONT

Known for leaf peeping in the autumn and cozy ski lodges come winter, Vermont also has loads to offer year-round.

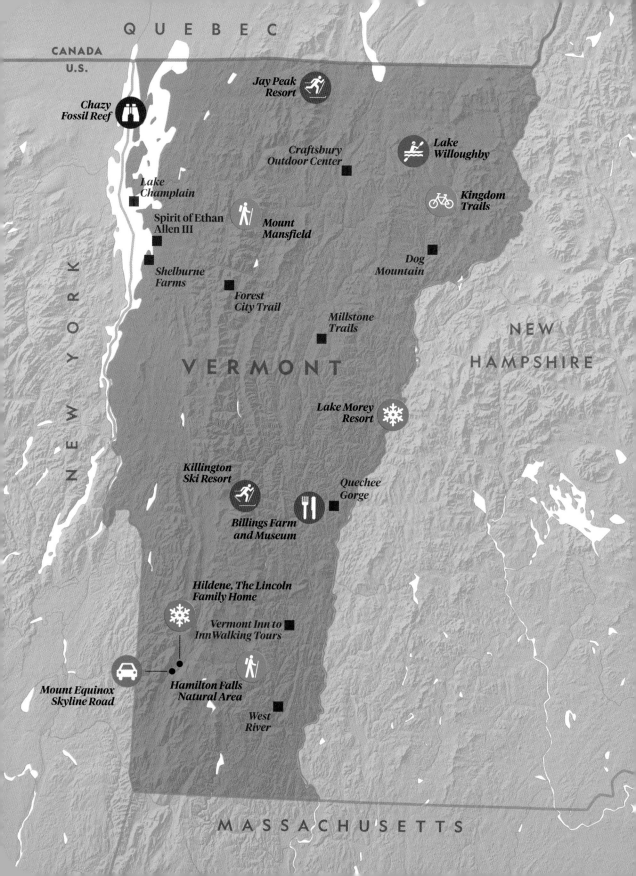

QUEBEC

CANADA
U.S.

Jay Peak
Resort

Chazy
Fossil Reef

Lake
Willoughby

Craftsbury
Outdoor Center

Lake
Champlain

Kingdom
Trails

Spirit of Ethan
Allen III

Mount
Mansfield

Shelburne
Farms

Dog
Mountain

Forest
City Trail

NEW YORK

Millstone
Trails

VERMONT

NEW
HAMPSHIRE

Lake Morey
Resort

Killington
Ski Resort

Quechee
Gorge

Billings Farm
and Museum

Hildene, The Lincoln
Family Home

Vermont Inn to
Inn Walking Tours

Mount Equinox
Skyline Road

Hamilton Falls
Natural Area

West
River

MASSACHUSETTS

Killington Resort has 155 ski runs to tackle.

Ski From Peak to Peak

Relentlessly snowy winters demand a recreational tonic, and skiing is how many Vermonters keep themselves fit. It began in the early 20th century, when Norwegian immigrants in the village of Stowe used skis to traverse snowbound roads. Bemused onlookers gave it a shot. Decades later, skiing is a pillar of Vermont living and a top draw for winter visitors.

In the heart of the Green Mountains, you'll find the Godzilla of ski areas in the eastern United States. Killington, named for the second tallest mountain in Vermont but spanning six mountains, boasts more than 1,500 acres (610 ha) and 150 miles (240 km) of downhill and cross-country skiing. Trails like the Great Northern and Superstar runs the gamut from beginner conditions to black diamond rigor, swerving and plummeting

through windswept alpine woodlands. The ski routes at Killington offer a vertical drop of 3,050 feet (930 m)—the largest in New England and the reason skiers call Killington the "Beast of the East."

But great skiing is more than just elevation and acreage. In the Northeast Kingdom, near the Canadian border, a curious meteorological phenomenon awaits skiers at Jay Peak. Through a combination of subzero winter temperatures and orthographic uplift—where air mass from the valley is forced up mountainsides to form clouds and often precipitation—Jay Peak is home to some of the most abundant and reliably fresh powder in the Northeast. Vermonters and regular visitors to Jay Peak refer to this unique climate at the "Jay Cloud" and compare the snow here to the powder found in Utah. On average, Jay Peak sees 359 inches (912 cm) of snow each year.

Multicity, VT : **Season:** Winter

Find your footing along trails up Mount Mansfield.

Mountain Views

At 4,395 feet (1,340 m) tall, Mount Mansfield is a giant, holding court over the Northeast Kingdom and Champlain Valley. But of all the trails that slab and scramble to the lichen-encrusted summit, the 2.6-mile (4.2 km) Sunset Ridge Trail might just be the most enchanting.

The Sunset Ridge Trail departs from the west in Underhill State Park. Efficient and only steep when it needs to be, the trail is a buffet of visual delights. The trail crosses chuckling streams in lush birch and beech woods.

But the ridge is the main attraction. After breaking through the tree line, the trail ascends to the Chin (Mansfield's highest summit) on a vast exposed ridgeline from which the expanse of Lake Champlain can be seen in all its deep blue beauty. If you're game for hiking with a headlamp, time your descent around dusk to watch the sun disappear behind the distant Adirondacks.

Chittenden County, VT | **Season:** Spring to fall

Prehistoric Wonders

The oldest known fossilized reef in the world runs right through Lake Champlain's islands. An obsidian ribbon of rock, the 480-million-year-old reef contains fossilized remains of ancient marine mollusks such as gastropods and cephalopods, and Vermont's finest access point is the Goodsell Ridge Fossil Preserve. Here, you can take a self-guided tour of the fossilized reef on trails that spiderweb across the 85-acre (34 ha) preserve.

For a primer on how the Chazy Fossil Reef came to be, start with the Walk Through Time Trail, which tells the story of evolution with the help of paintings and photographs staged in wildflower-speckled fields and spruce woods. The White Trail and the Blue Trail venture deeper into the forest and offer a closer look at the Precambrian creatures fossilized in the exposed reef slabs. In some spots, you'll even find yourself walking atop the reef. It has a way of sneaking up on you.

La Motte, VT | **Season:** Year-round

Along with fossils, find petroglyphs at Chazy Fossil Reef.

Seek out Hamilton Falls in the Green Mountains.

Hike to Hamilton Falls

Rivers have a way of sculpting bedrock into works of art, and Hamilton Falls—one of Vermont's tallest cascades—is a geographic wonder. The thunderous falls spill 104 feet (32 m) through glacial potholes carved into an uplifted sheet of stone by Cobb Brook. Tucked away in 772 acres (312 ha) of white pine and red oak forest at Jamaica State Park, Hamilton Falls is reachable by two linked trails along the nearby West River, which offer their own visual treats en route to the frothy pool below the falls.

Park in the lot near the end of Ball Mountain Dam and pick up the West River Trail to cross the 247-foot-tall (75 m) earthen gravity dam through which the West River rumbles. You'll descend a set of steep western-style switchbacks to the banks of the river, following it until the Hamilton Falls Trail branches left, taking you up through more shadowy woods to the cascade.

Jamaica, VT | Season: Spring to fall

Mountain bike through forests on Webs Trail at the Kingdom Trails.

"CRUISE AND SIDEWIND THROUGH THE WOODLANDS, GLENS, AND MEADOWS."

The Kingdom Trails

The Northeast Kingdom is Vermont's most sparsely populated region, but it's home to family-owned dairy farms, rolling green hills, mossy forests, and the waterfall-festooned swimming holes that many of us imagine when we think of the state. Constellations of quiet dirt roads interweave across "the Kingdom," offering direct access to its villages and wild spaces. And then, there are the Kingdom Trails.

One of the most exciting ways to discover the gems of northern Vermont is by taking a ride on this 85-mile (137 km) network of biking trails that cruise and sidewind through the woodlands, glens, and meadows near the town of East Burke. In many ways, Kingdom Trails is a labor of civic pride. Founded in 1994 by the proprietors of a local ski shop turned bike shop, the growth of the trails system is largely thanks to decades of the founders persuading more than 100 landowners to allow construction of trails across their property. Trail maintenance and expansion is funded through memberships and daily admissions ($20 adults, $12 youth 8–15) that can be purchased at the welcome center before you pedal away.

Whether you feel like floating along a gentle stream-side path or testing your bike's suspension on one of the rockier, more challenging trails spruced up with elements like narrow wooden bridges and hairpin berms (avoid attempting with a hardtail bike), the bevy of single- and double-track trail options is almost intimidating. Kingdom Trails has something for everyone—even scenic pedestrian trails that bumble across the countryside. If you're not bringing your own wheels, bike rentals are available at several shops in the East Burke vicinity. And when you've had your fill of the Kingdom landscape, award-winning craft beer from nearby breweries like Hill Farmstead and Rock Art will be waiting for you in town.

Multicity, VT | **Season:** Spring to fall

Classic Charm on the Farm

🍴 Vermont's scenic charms have a way of luring visitors back to the verdant hills and cow pastures. Take Frederick Billings. After joining the California gold rush in 1848 and running the Northern Pacific Railway, he returned to Woodstock flush with cash, bought himself a dairy farm near Mount Tom State Forest, and imported Jersey cows renowned for their high-protein milk—the origin of the state's cheddar.

Today, Billings Farm remains a working agricultural operation with oxen, draft horses, and sheep. But the farm is also a living museum showcasing the history of local farming techniques. You can get close to the animals, explore more than 200 acres (80 ha) of cropland by foot or wagon rides, and try your hand at churning fresh-milked cream into butter. Just be sure to pick up a maple ice cream cone from the on-site dairy bar (and perhaps a block of smoked cheddar) before hitting the road.

Woodstock, VT | **Season:** Year-round

Cows graze at Billings Farm and Museum in Woodstock.

Lace Up Your Skates

❄️ Most trails wind their way across permanently solid earth and stone, but each winter on Lake Morey, a different path materializes. Trail builders from nearby Lake Morey Resort shovel their way through the snow that's piled up atop the frozen water to create a sunny 4.3-mile (6.9 km) loop trail of ice. This is the Lake Morey Skate Trail, and according to the resort, it's the longest ice-skating trail in the United States.

With entry points at the resort and at Fairlee Town Beach, the skate trail skirts the Lake Morey shoreline, bypassing several small rinks carved out as features of the trail. As you glide past the pine forest flanking the lake, it's not unusual to catch sight of an occasional lone bald eagle, observing skaters from a branch (bald eagles often roost in the woods around Lake Morey during the winter). On a clear winter day, views of nearby peaks like Sawyer Mountain and Bald Top crank up the winter wonderland atmospherics.

Most years, the skate trail opens by mid-January, once the ice is thick enough for skating from shore to shore. Bring your own skates or rent a pair of Nordic skates from the resort (these flat-bladed skates are better than hockey skates for long-distance skating). For those uncomfortable on skates, the resort also rents kicksleds—standing sleds with handlebars and pontoon-like runners you can push around the lake. Admission is free, but donations are appreciated to help the volunteers who maintain the lake and the skate trail keep up the good work.

Fairlee, VT | **Season:** Winter

A Presidential Destination

❄ When the hustle of Washington, D.C., became too much for the Lincoln family, Mary Todd Lincoln and her sons would escape to the Green Mountains. Robert, the Lincolns' only son to live to adulthood, was so enamored with the area that he built a Georgian Revival mansion in 1905 on 392 acres (159 ha) of land in the hills near Manchester and dubbed it "Hildene," a derivative of the Old English words for "hill" and "valley with stream."

It was a prescient move. Robert, who was the chairman of the Pullman Company at the time the house was built, used the mansion as a summer home. Hildene remained in the family until the death of Peggy Beckwith—Robert's granddaughter—in 1975. Peggy was the last member of the Lincoln family to live in the home, and on her death, she bequeathed it to the Church of Christ, Scientist, with the directive to maintain Hildene as a memorial to the Lincoln family. Nowadays,

Manchester, VT | **Season:** Year-round

the estate includes the mansion and 14 historic buildings, as well as a formal garden, observatory, welcome center, and a museum store in what was once the carriage barn. Visitors are invited to tour the home and grounds, where they'll find an original 1903 Pullman car, an 1832 schoolhouse, a goat dairy and cheese-making facility, a greenhouse, an apple orchard, and a 600-foot (180 m) boardwalk that winds through beautiful wetlands.

A real draw to Hildene comes when the temperatures cool. Each winter, the Lincoln Family Home is an off-radar destination for cross-country skiers and snowshoers looking for something more rustic and serene than the usual ski resorts. Twelve miles (19 km) of interconnected trails dart through woods, marshes, and meadows around the preserved mansion (where rental skis are available). Because the trails aren't groomed, you may have to do some "blazing" of your own. But true to the historic nature of Hildene, Vermonters have savored the snow that way for more than a century.

Take the Skyline Drive

🚗 Looming over the town of Bennington like a slumbering dragon of spruce and stone, Equinox Mountain is a magnet for Green Mountain visitors. But the peak actually belongs to the Taconic Range, the nexus of Vermont's southern mountains and the Adirondacks in New York. From the summit, you can also see the Berkshires and the distant White Mountains in New Hampshire.

But you don't have to haul yourself over rock and root to experience this breathtaking vista. You can drive there along the Mount Equinox Skyline Drive. Open from Memorial Day through late October, the 5.2-mile (8.3 km) road climbs a staggering 3,248 feet (990 m) and features hairpin turns and open ridgeline sections that are thrillingly exposed. Carthusian monks from a nearby monastery own and maintain the road, the longest privately owned paved toll road in the United States.

The forested Equinox Mountain stands above a pond in Manchester.

Bennington, VT | **Season:** May to October

> "LAKE WILLOUGHBY HAS CAST SPELLS ON VISITORS FOR CENTURIES."

Swim, Paddle, and Fish

Tucked between Mount Pisgah and Mount Hor, Lake Willoughby has cast spells on visitors for centuries. The rippling cerulean surface, alive with swimmers and kayakers during the summer, hides a rather surprising fact. At roughly 320 feet (100 m) deep, Lake Willoughby is the deepest lake entirely within the state of Vermont. Rainbow trout, common shiner, and even landlocked Atlantic salmon call Willoughby home. It's no wonder Robert Frost alluded to the lake—now a national natural landmark—in his poem "A Servant to Servants."

Many swimmers and paddlers choose to put in at the lake's north beach, which is located just beside VT-16 (parking is available on the other side of the road). The north beach offers tempting sands and, on gustier days, waves that can be surprisingly robust. This might make launching a kayak or canoe from the north beach a little tricky, but the clarity and cool temperature of the water are heavenly on broiling summer afternoons when Vermonters crave the relief of sea breeze. At sundown, the vista of Willoughby's mountain gap from here is sublime.

The south beach (park on the side of VT-5A) boasts its own perks. The water down here is reliably calmer, and sections of the south beach are more secluded in the lakeside woodlands. As you swim or float through the water, take note of the mountains' immense sandstone cliffs. If you're lucky, you might spot a peregrine falcon taking flight from one of the crags.

Off the water, you take the out-and-back 4.1-mile (6.6 km) Mount Pisgah Trail, a challenging route through Willoughby State Forest that affords beautiful lake views from its highest point. It's particularly stunning come fall.

Orleans County, VT | **Season:** Spring to fall

Willoughby Gap is arguably at its best come fall.

Visit Shelburne Farms, a working dairy farm that offers family education and tastings.

1. SAIL ON THE *SPIRIT OF ETHAN ALLEN III*

Sprawling from Vermont to New York and even Quebec, Lake Champlain can feel vast as a sea. But a narrated cruise aboard the *Spirit of Ethan Allen III* puts the lake's craggy forested shores in historic context with the accounts of Indigenous peoples and revolutionaries (including Allen himself) whose stories unfolded along Champlain's waters.

2. SCRAMBLE FOR SIGHTS

One of the more overlooked paths to the tallest undeveloped peak in Vermont (shaped like a dromedary) is Forest City Trail. Climbing through ferns past bubbling streams, you'll link up with the epic Long Trail for thrilling rock scrambles with views of nearby Mount Ethan Allen before summiting Camel's Hump at 3.5 miles (5.6 km).

3. LIVE THE FARM LIFE

Frederick Law Olmsted, the visionary landscape architect who created Central Park, helped design the forests, vegetable fields, and footpaths that comprise 1,400-acre (565 ha) Shelburne Farms near Champlain's southern shores. Sustainable agriculture workshops are taught on-site, but many visitors come to get pleasantly lost amid the overstory and understory.

4. CROSS THE ISLAND LINE TRAIL

This trail connects the colorful, quirky neighborhoods of Burlington and Colchester to Lake Champlain's beaches and wooded shores. The 12-mile (19 km) paved bike path stretches along the lakeshore north from Oakledge Park to the Colchester Causeway, where you can pedal three miles (4.8 km) across Champlain's waters to Grand Isle.

5. MAKE TRACKS

Nordic skiing and snowshoeing are part of life in the Northeast Kingdom. The Craftsbury Outdoor Center grooms and maintains more than 100 miles (160 km) of winter trails that weave through pinewoods and connect skiers and snowshoers to the Kingdom's villages. Rentals and lessons are available, and dogs are welcome on the trails too.

6. MARK YOUR SPOT AT DOG MOUNTAIN

Founded by Vermont artists, Dog Mountain is a mountaintop mecca of hiking trails, dog ponds, and canine agility courses, covering more than 150 acres (60 ha). Odds are that your fluffy companion won't look at your local dog park the same way after gallivanting here. Visitors can even leave written messages of love on the walls at the Dog Chapel.

7. SEE THE LITTLE GRAND CANYON

Thirteen thousand years ago, glacial movement through the lands that would become Vermont formed the state's "Little Grand Canyon." The Ottauquechee River flows through the towering 168-foot (51 m) walls of Quechee Gorge, forming waterfalls and pools that you can gaze down upon from the trail that ambles along the gorge rim.

8. MILL ABOUT A MILLSTONE MECCA

The old granite quarries of Millstone Hill are some of central Vermont's unsung oddities. Thanks to the work of volunteer trail builders from the Millstone Trails Association, you can pedal past mountains of grout (granite waste) and towering cliffs on trails and boardwalks spanning 1,500 acres (610 ha) across three forests.

9. WALK INN TO INN

Each summer, four cozy inns in the southern Green Mountains offer visitors the chance to replicate the European "walking holiday" by sauntering across the countryside on the Vermont Inn-to-Inn Walking Tour. Your luggage is ferried from one lodging outpost to the next, leaving you to savor the wildflowers, swimming holes, and mountain views.

10. CANOE THE WEST RIVER

Vermont is renowned for its lakes, but there's nothing like paddling the bends of a foaming waterway like the southern West River. A tributary of the mighty Connecticut River, it courses past villages and covered bridges to the city of Brattleboro. The Vermont Canoe Touring Center offers boat rentals and guided paddles.

Red clover

Wind along Skyline Drive in
Shenandoah National Park
(page 645).

VIRGINIA

Find green spaces just outside the nation's capital, along with coveted beaches, historic landmarks, and subterranean wonders throughout the state.

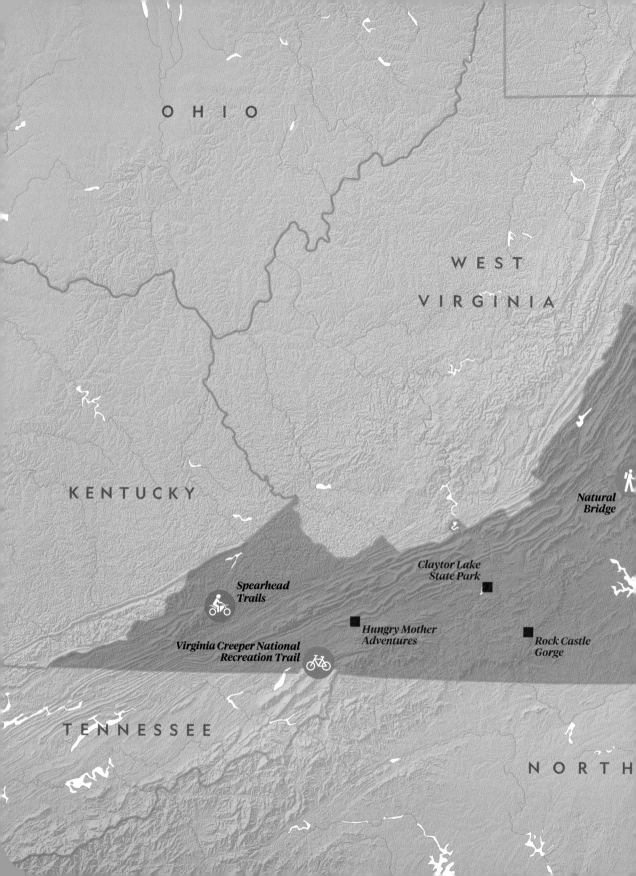

OHIO

WEST

VIRGINIA

KENTUCKY

Natural
Bridge

Claytor Lake
State Park

Spearhead
Trails

Hungry Mother
Adventures

Rock Castle
Gorge

Virginia Creeper National
Recreation Trail

TENNESSEE

NORTH

PENNSYLVANIA

NEW JERSEY

MARYLAND

DELAWARE

Great Falls
Park

D.C.

Manassas

Luray
Caverns

Prince William
Forest Park

Shenandoah
National Park

Chancellorsville

Chesapeake Bay

Fredericksburg

Albemarle
County

Monticello

Crabtree
Falls

VIRGINIA

Devil's
Marbleyard

James

James
River

Virginia's
Eastern Shore

James

Appomattox

Historic
Jamestowne

ATLANTIC
OCEAN

Staunton River
State Park

Back Bay National
Wildlife Refuge

False Cape
State Park

CAROLINA

Hear the Roar

Just 15 miles (24 km) outside Washington, D.C., is a natural wonder: the Great Falls of the Potomac. The river here drops 76 feet (23 m) in less than a mile and sharply narrows as it enters Mather Gorge, creating a thunderous, awe-inspiring cascade. Three overlooks—two of them ADA accessible—at Great Falls Park offer splendid views of the falls, which change dramatically during different seasons and water levels. Don't miss the High Water Marks pole, which shows how floods have reached incredible heights during spring melts and torrential rainstorms.

The park's River Trail traces Mather Gorge atop cliffs up to 75 feet (23 m) high, where vultures wheel overhead and great blue herons skim the fast-moving water. The trail also passes remnants of the historic Patowmack Canal, which sought to bypass the churning falls and rapids. Largely built by enslaved laborers, the canal was championed by George Washington, who dreamed of making the Potomac navigable and uniting the young country through trade.

McLean, VA | **Season:** Year-round

Great Falls rushes between the border of Virginia and Maryland.

Jaw-Dropping Natural Wonders

"Wow." That's the reaction most people have upon seeing Natural Bridge, a 215-foot-tall (66 m) limestone archway set against the Blue Ridge Mountains. Carved by Cedar Creek, the national historic landmark is estimated to be 500 million years old and was surveyed

Take a three-mile (5 km) hike to see Natural Bridge.

by a young George Washington. His initials, etched circa 1750, can still be seen beneath the arch. Thomas Jefferson later purchased the surrounding land and hired a freed African American named Patrick Henry to be the caretaker, essentially the bridge's first park ranger.

Now a state park, Natural Bridge encompasses 1,500 acres (610 ha) of forest, fields, and karst terrain in the Shenandoah Valley, with seven miles (11 km) of hiking trails. The ADA-accessible Cedar Creek Trail runs beneath the 30-story stone arch and passes the Monacan Village, a living history showcase of Native American life in the late 17th century. Beyond the village, the trail reaches Lace Falls, a 30-foot (9 m) cascade.

Special "Parks After Dark" nights take advantage of the area's designation as an International Dark Sky Park, with full moon yoga sessions and "owl prowl" hikes.

Natural Bridge, VA | **Season:** Year-round

Glide Your Way Over the Eastern Shore

The world looks different when you're a mile in the air. Silently soar over the Eastern Shore with Virginia Hang Gliding, which offers bird's-eye views of the Chesapeake Bay, Atlantic Ocean, and Virginia's barrier islands. After being towed to altitudes of 2,000 to 5,300 feet (610 to 1,615 m), the tandem glider peacefully descends over maritime forests and tidal marshes, while glittering bays and deep-sea waves stretch to the horizon. Feeling extra daring? Choose to experience adrenaline-pumping aerial acrobatics as the pilot leads the glider through barrel rolls, corkscrews, and loop-de-loops.

A native of the Eastern Shore, company founder Don Guynn knew the peninsula was the perfect spot for hang gliding due to sparse population and no major airports. Best of all: unparalleled aerial scenery that thrills the soul. "Gazing down at the world from such dizzying heights brings this amazing sense of perspective," Guynn says.

Painter, VA | Season: May to September

"It's meditative and joyous all at once."

All hang-gliding flights are done in tandem with an expert pilot with years of experience. Flights last from 12 to 30 minutes, depending on the elevation you drop in from (aerobatic flights are shorter, but the thrills are more exciting). And this can be a family affair—fliers ages 8 and older are welcome, as long as they are able to follow and adhere to pilot directions. Two mounted GoPros on each glider capture your flight so you have a keepsake video to take home. Those who aren't daring enough to take to the skies can come along for the adventure and watch your flight from the ground. Virginia Hang Gliding has a 25-acre (10 ha) property that includes a covered area with picnic tables and charcoal and gas grills for you and your guests to use, so there's (almost) as much fun on the ground as there is in the air.

A re-creation of a Powhatan Indian Village at the Jamestown Settlement museum, located near Historic Jamestowne

An Original Colony

In 1607, three ships sailed through the mouth of the Chesapeake Bay and up the James River. Their purpose: to found a colony in the New World. Named Jamestown after England's King James I, the small colony almost collapsed multiple times—but it became the first permanent English settlement in North America.

Both a national park and an active archaeological site, Historic Jamestowne is located atop the original colony. Walking tours with park rangers, archaeologists, and living history interpreters vividly bring 17th-century Jamestown to life, treading the same ground where Captain John Smith and Pocahontas stepped. After watching excavations in progress outside the rediscovered James Fort, visit the on-site archaeology museum to see more than a thousand artifacts that have been unearthed at Jamestown. Prized finds include armor, coins, and tobacco pipes.

Jamestown, VA | Season: Year-round

Shenandoah National Park extends along the Blue Ridge Mountains.

"SHENANDOAH ENCOMPASSES SUN-DAPPLED FOREST, GRANITE PINNACLES, AIRY MEADOWS, AND GLORIOUS WATERFALLS."

The Beauty of Shenandoah

Dedicated in 1936 as Virginia's first national park, Shenandoah encompasses 200,000 acres (80,940 ha) of sun-dappled forest, granite pinnacles, airy meadows, and glorious waterfalls. A visit must begin with a spin down Skyline Drive, considered one of the most scenic mountain drives in the United States. The celebrated thoroughfare runs the length of the park for more than 100 miles (160 km) along the crest of the Blue Ridge Mountains, with 70 overlooks that display magnificent vistas of endless blue-tinted peaks and misty valleys.

While driving, keep your eyes peeled for the park's resident wildlife: white-tailed deer, coyotes, wild turkeys, and maybe even a black bear—Shenandoah has one of the densest populations of black bears in the United States. They're frequently spotted climbing trees or foraging for juicy blackberries, which carpet the park in summer.

Skyline Drive provides access to most of Shenandoah's trailheads and its unparalleled hiking. The park contains more than 500 miles (800 km) of trails, including 101 miles (163 km) of the Appalachian Trail (many say it's the loveliest stretch). Hikes range from easy to very strenuous; some, such as Dark Hollow Falls or Whiteoak Canyon, descend to alluring waterfalls and forest glades, while others steeply climb to rocky outcrops with 360-degree views. Take in the sunset from the heights of Stony Man, or navigate a maze of boulders to summit Old Rag.

For a change of pace, explore Rapidan Camp, the woodland retreat of President Herbert Hoover, or relax in Big Meadows, the sprawling grassland in the heart of the park. Filled with wildflowers and butterflies by day, the peaceful meadow becomes the perfect arena for stargazing.

Shenandoah National Park, VA   **Season:** Year-round

Cycle Along the Creeper Trail

🚲 Considered one of the best rail trails in the country, the 34-mile (55 km) Virginia Creeper Trail follows a rugged mountain railroad bed as it passes through thick forests, lush pastures, and inviting small towns in southwest Virginia. Its lengthy downhill and level stretches are perfect for families and beginner bikers.

Originally a Native American footpath, the route became a line of the Virginia-Carolina Railroad. Nicknamed "Virginia Creeper" for the steam locomotives that struggled up the steep mountain grades, the line featured about a hundred bridges. Nearly 50 wooden trestles still remain.

Start at the eastern terminus and highest point at Whitetop Station. From here, an easy downhill stretch runs for 17 miles (27 km) through Christmas tree farms, towering trestles over mountain streams, and historic restored railroad depots. Those who make it to the trail's end at Abingdon are rewarded with views of South Holston Lake and rolling fields with grazing horses.

> "THE VIRGINIA CREEPER TRAIL PASSES THROUGH THICK FORESTS, LUSH PASTURES, AND INVITING SMALL TOWNS."

Multicity, VA | **Season:** Spring to fall

The Virginia Creeper Trail runs 34 miles (55 km) between Abingdon and Whitetop, near the North Carolina border.

Dream Lake is the largest body of water in Luray Caverns, but its deepest point is only 20 inches (51 cm).

Go Underground

Deep beneath the Blue Ridge Mountains, the immense chambers and intricate stone formations of Luray Caverns—the largest caves in the eastern United States—are a wonder four million centuries in the making. Soaring stalagmites, fascinating flowstone designs, and crystal clear pools fill rooms the size of cathedrals. The colors here are unsurpassed: All the structures are made from calcite, a crystalline form of limestone that's dazzlingly white in its pure form, tinged blue and green from copper, and imbued with red and yellow from iron.

Well-lit, paved walkways wind through otherworldly rooms. In the Saracen's Tent, gaze upon gracefully draped sheets of translucent calcite; in the enormous spaces of the Giant's Hall, marvel at the Double Column, a 47-foot-high (14 m) pillar created by a stalactite and a stalagmite growing into one another. The deceptive Dream Lake—it's no deeper than 20 inches (51 cm), despite being the largest body of water in the caverns—enchantingly mirrors the thickly clustered stalactites hanging above.

There's even live music deep underground. The world's only Stalacpipe Organ, the largest musical instrument on Earth, gently taps stalactites across three acres (1.2 ha) of the caverns and makes them sing in a haunting symphony.

Aboveground are additional intriguing sites included in the caverns' general admission: the Car and Carriage Caravan Museum, with an impressive collection of historic vehicles including an 1840 Conestoga wagon and a 1925 Rolls Royce, and the Shenandoah Heritage Village, a re-created 19th-century farming community with cottage-style gardens and a charming vineyard.

Luray, VA | **Season:** Year-round

Ride vineyard to vineyard in the Blue Ridge Mountains.

Ride to the Vines

First attempted by European settlers more than 400 years ago, winemaking in Virginia is now a flourishing industry. The area around Charlottesville is the heart of Virginia wine country, with dozens of wineries nestled in the rolling foothills of the Blue Ridge Mountains. What better way to experience the countryside—and raise a glass of local vintage—than on horseback?

Indian Summer Guide Service provides year-round private horseback rides through the orchards and vineyards of Albemarle County, ending at the tasting rooms of award-winning wineries. Build a flight of four wines at Keswick Vineyards' outdoor tasting bar, drink barrel-aged ciders at Castle Hill Cider, or nibble on homemade gourmet chocolates at Glass House Winery (pair the Pink Drink rosé with the Raspberry Champagne chocolate). Want more horse action? Watch a live polo match at King Family Vineyards while sipping a robust Petit Verdot.

Albemarle County, VA   **Season:** Spring to fall

A Real Experience at the False Cape

Less than 20 miles (32 km) from the crowded resort town of Virginia Beach is an unspoiled gem: False Cape State Park. One of the last remaining undeveloped areas along the East Coast, the park protects a mile-wide (1.6 km) barrier spit between the Atlantic Ocean and Back Bay.

Getting here isn't easy: Private vehicles are banned. The only way in is on foot, bicycle, boat, or the Blue Goose Tram, which enters the park through Back Bay National Wildlife Refuge. But the reward is worth it—six miles (10 km) of pristine beaches, nine miles (14.5 km) of hiking and biking trails, and unmatched solitude among the rolling dunes and wetlands.

Named because it resembled Cape Henry, the southern boundary of the Chesapeake Bay entrance, False Cape earned a reputation as a ship's graveyard in the 1800s. Shipwreck survivors founded the once thriving

Bright crimson northern cardinal

settlement of Wash Woods, one of the area's first communities. The village graveyard and the remains of the 19th-century church steeple, built using cypress wood washed ashore from a wreck, can still be seen off the Sand Ridge Trail.

After roaming the paths of False Cape, take to the waters of Back Bay and paddle in search of wildlife. The refuge's 9,000-plus acres (3,640 ha) of woodlands, marshes, and barrier islands are a sanctuary for migratory birds and waterfowl. More than 300 species can be spotted here, including piping plovers, peregrine falcons, bald eagles, and ospreys. But the park isn't just for the birds: It's also home to river otters, bobcats, white-tailed deer, red foxes, and endangered loggerhead sea turtles, which come ashore to nest every summer.

Virginia Beach, VA   **Season:** Spring to fall

Explore more than 600 miles (965 km) of ATV routes at Spearhead Trails.

Go Off the Road

The seven "coalfield counties" of far southwestern Virginia boomed during the first half of the 20th century, but by the 1950s, most of the veins were mined out. Local officials and residents resolved to create a multiuse trail system to revitalize the Heart of Appalachia region and move forward from its industrial past. The result: Spear-

head Trails, a staggering network of 600-plus miles (965 km) of mountainous off-roading.

There are activities here for any outdoor enthusiast: hiking, kayaking, horseback riding—even archery. But the ATV adventures really shine. Go wild on the endless variety of trails,

ranging from wide-open ridgelines to twisting forest routes to verdant valley tracks where elk herds wander. Try out the Original Pocahontas Trail for a family-friendly outing through deep woods, or Stone Mountain for rough riding with stunning Appalachian vistas.

Coeburn, VA | **Season:** Spring to fall

Crabtree Falls is just off the scenic Blue Ridge Parkway.

1. FIND SERENITY AT PRINCE WILLIAM FOREST PARK

Within busy, heavily populated Northern Virginia is a sylvan oasis. The fragrant woods and trickling streams of the park's 15,000 acres (6,070 ha) invite forest bathing while strolling along 37 miles (60 km) of trails. Don't miss the 150-million-year-old piece of petrified wood, one of the largest ever discovered in Virginia, displayed in front of the visitors center.

2. TAKE FLIGHT AT HUNGRY MOTHER ADVENTURES

Located just outside Hungry Mother State Park, this adventure center boasts the longest, highest, and fastest zip line course in Virginia. Nearly a mile of lines reach heights of 200 feet (60 m) and speeds over 30 miles an hour (48 km/h) while flying through the treetops and over mountain valleys. Younger kids can join the action on a mini-zip line.

3. RAFT THE JAMES RIVER

You can raft thrilling Class III and IV rapids past skyscrapers in one American city: Richmond. The challenging white water of the Lower James River runs right through the Virginia capital. Tackle spinning holes and triple drops, then pop ashore for pizza and a pint at a downtown brewery.

4. HIKE TO CRABTREE FALLS

Just off the scenic Blue Ridge Parkway in the George Washington and Jefferson National Forests, a 2.5-mile (4 km) loop leads to Crabtree Falls, the highest vertical cascade east of the Mississippi River. The rushing waters of Crabtree Creek tumble over a 60-foot (18 m) rock cliff into a hollow filled with ferns and wildflowers.

5. PADDLEBOARD AT CLAYTOR LAKE STATE PARK

Paddleboarding is a serene way to commune with the water—while also offering a full-body workout. Take a spin on the tranquil surface of Claytor Lake in southwest Virginia. The 4,500-acre (1,820 ha) lake has a marina and multiple outfitters that rent stand-up paddleboards.

6. VISIT A CIVIL WAR BATTLEFIELD

During the Civil War, more battles were fought in Virginia than any other state. See where the Union and Confederate Armies clashed for the first time at Manassas, learn about the tragic cost of the war at Fredericksburg and Chancellorsville, and visit the McLean House, where Lee surrendered to Grant at Appomattox.

7. TACKLE THE DEVIL'S MARBLEYARD

Ready for a scramble? The aptly named Devil's Marbleyard, located in James River Face Wilderness, spotlights a spectacular jumble of boulders ranging in size from coffee tables to school buses. Clambering over the radiant white quartzite rock pile requires navigating crevasses and hidden caves.

8. WANDER JEFFERSON'S GARDENS AT MONTICELLO

Thomas Jefferson's gardens at his estate were more than a showpiece: They were a botanic laboratory. In Monticello's fruit orchards, flower beds, and the vegetable garden terrace, he experimented with hundreds of European and New World plant varieties, ranging from French figs to Virginia cider apples to beans collected by the Lewis and Clark expedition.

9. HIKE ROCK CASTLE GORGE

This 11-mile (18 km) hike will get your heart pounding. The trail drops more than a thousand feet (305 m) in the first three miles (4.8 km) as it descends into the gorge before sharply rising to open meadows. The payoff: panoramic views of the Virginia Piedmont and brilliant wildflowers that carpet the gorge in spring.

10. STARGAZE AT STAUNTON RIVER STATE PARK

Located in the heart of southern Virginia near the North Carolina border, Staunton River was designated the state's first International Dark Sky Park in 2015. Check out a free telescope at the visitors center and join other celestial enthusiasts during the park's star parties.

Mount St. Helens is an active stratovolcano in southwestern Washington State (page 665).

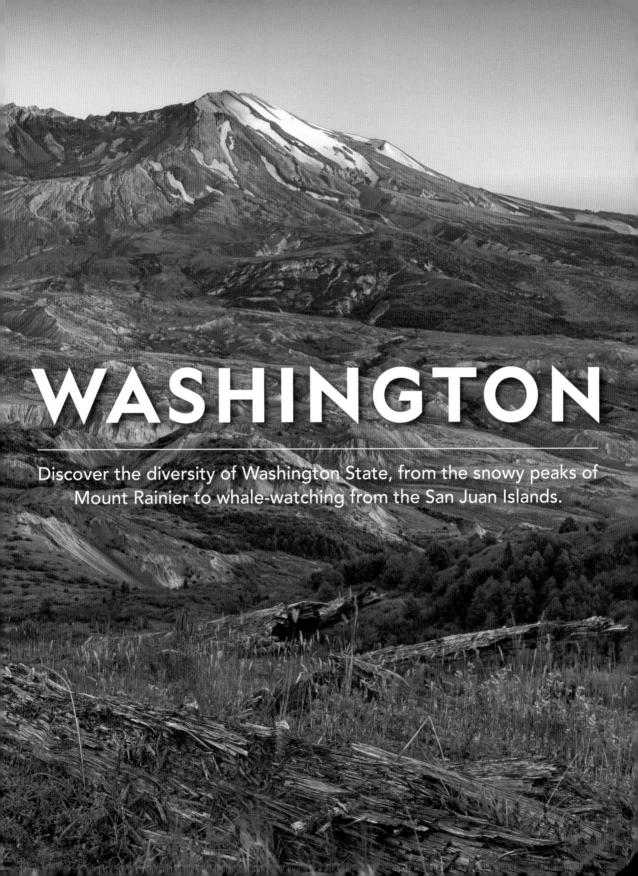

WASHINGTON

Discover the diversity of Washington State, from the snowy peaks of Mount Rainier to whale-watching from the San Juan Islands.

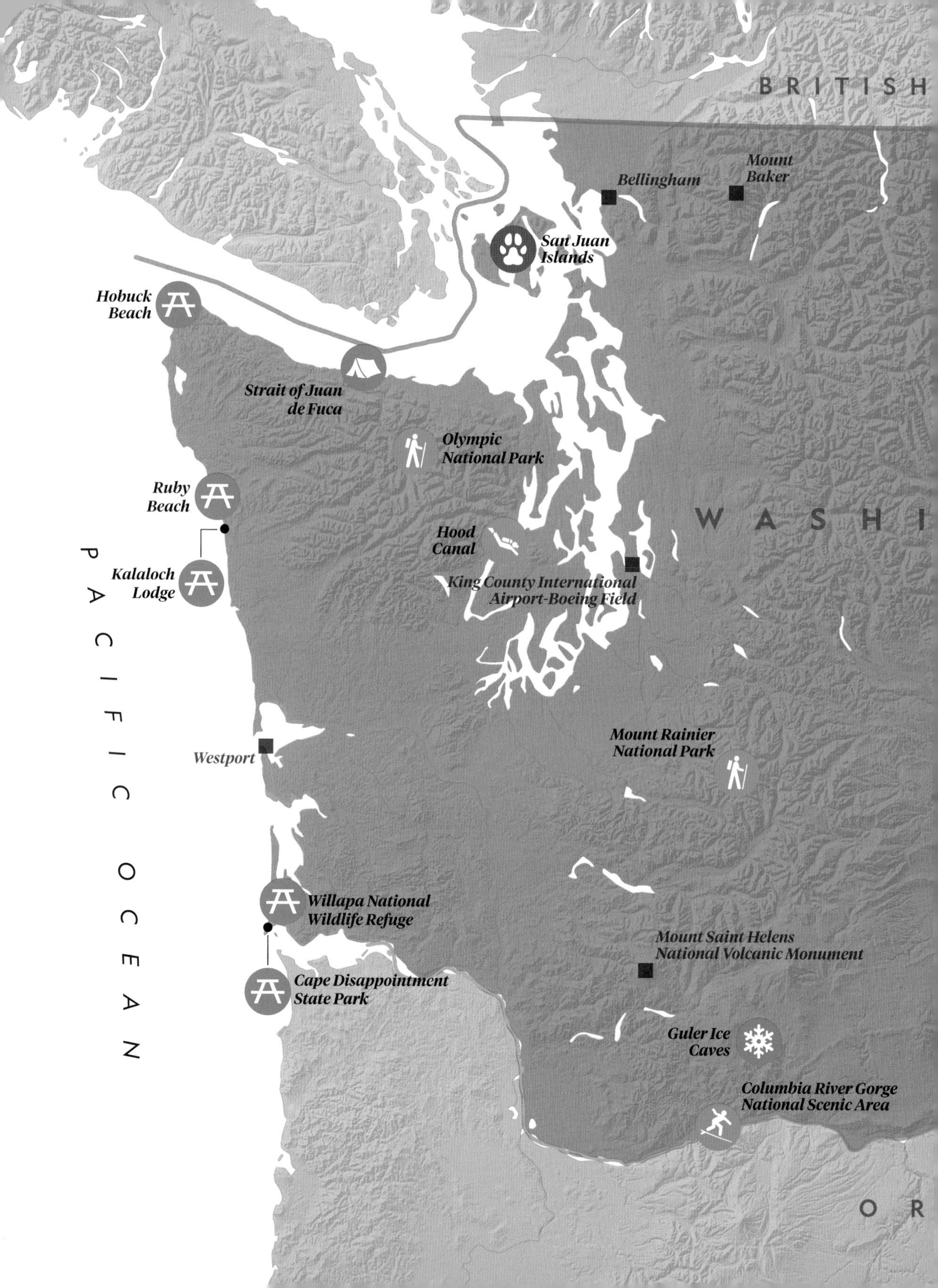

BRITISH

Bellingham

Mount
Baker

San Juan
Islands

WASHI

Hobuck
Beach

Strait of Juan
de Fuca

Olympic
National Park

Ruby
Beach

Hood
Canal

Kalaloch
Lodge

King County International
Airport-Boeing Field

PACIFIC OCEAN

Mount Rainier
National Park

Westport

Willapa National
Wildlife Refuge

Cape Disappointment
State Park

Mount Saint Helens
National Volcanic Monument

Guler Ice
Caves

Columbia River Gorge
National Scenic Area

OR

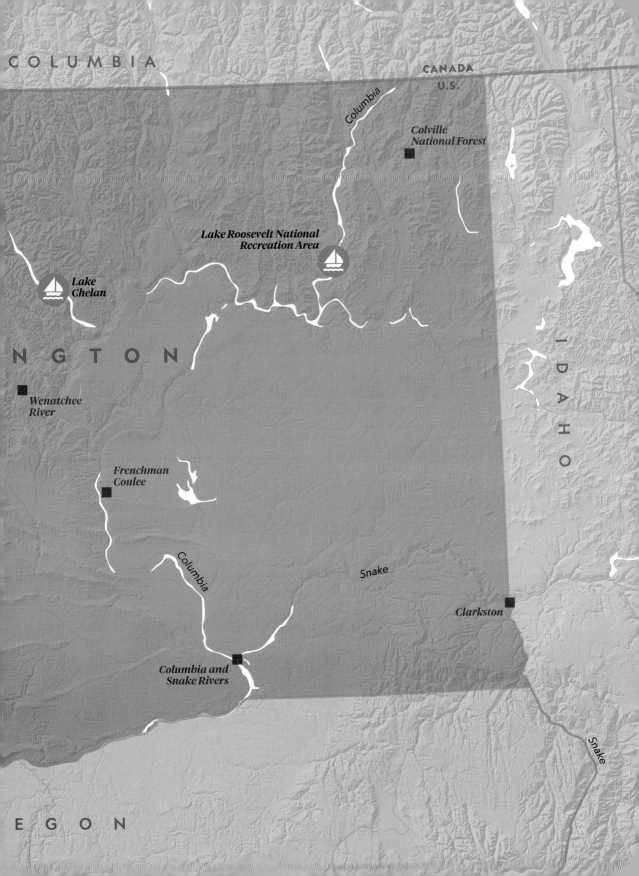

Tide Pool Camping

Stretching along the northern edge of the Olympic Peninsula, the Strait of Juan de Fuca divides Washington State from Vancouver Island in British Columbia. Those relishing dreamy views should also look down—because the rugged shore harbors an incredible array of tide pool life.

Tongue Point Marine Life Sanctuary and Salt Creek Recreation Area near Port Angeles are celebrated for the size, health, and biological variety of their contiguous tide pool area. Located beneath rocky bluffs, the area is easily accessible at low tide. Pool life runs a colorful gamut from gold and orange sea stars to purple and red urchins, green anemones, and cobalt-colored mussels as well as sea slugs, crabs, tiny fish, and even octopus.

Those who want to spread their tide pooling across multiple days can overnight at Salt Creek's seaside campground. In addition to 92 sites (about half with hookups), the campground features historic World War II bunkers.

Port Angeles, WA | Season: Year-round

A giant green anemone sits in the tide pools at Tongue Point.

Pacific Beachcombing

Beachcombers can roam the coast in Olympic National Park, four Native American nations, Willapa National Wildlife Refuge, and half a dozen state parks perched along the Pacific. Sea stacks, tide pools, and awesome sunsets make Ruby Beach the most popular place to frame an artistic photograph or stroll the sand. At low tide, about six miles (10 km) of the shore are walkable.

Farther down the coast of the park, the Kalaloch area offers half a dozen beaches where shore explorers can scramble over driftwood logs, build sandcastles, or keep an eye out for sea otters. There's even car and tent camping on bluffs above the sea.

Beachcombers can also camp at Hobuck Beach on the Makah Reservation, which hosts the annual Hobuck Hoedown Paddle Surf Festival.

At the mouth of the Columbia River, Cape Disappointment State Park features broad sandy beaches and camping in the coastal forest near the spot where the Corps of Discovery reached the Pacific Ocean in 1805. The park's Lewis and Clark Interpretive Center spins tales of their epic journey.

Driftwood timber and spruce trees line Kalaloch Beach.

Multicity, WA | Season: Year-round

Whaling the San Juans

Call it a cetacean superhighway—the Haro Strait and other channels that flow between the San Juan Islands in northwest Washington. That's the main route that thousands of whales travel each year while migrating between the open Pacific Ocean and the inland Salish Sea. In addition to a resident pod of orcas (killer whales), humpbacks, minkes, and gray whales also swim the route, along with sea lions, harbor seals, porpoises and dolphins, elephant seals, and sea otters.

Overlooking the Haro Strait, Lime Kiln Point State Park along the western edge of San Juan Island offers landlubbers several clifftop viewpoints to watch whales from the shore. An interpretive center inside the park's photogenic 19th-century lighthouse offers exhibits, whale-related swag, and an acoustic station to listen to cetaceans communicating beneath the surface.

Two other parks along the island's western shore—the American Camp unit of San Juan Island National Histori-

Orca

cal Park and San Juan County Park—also offer a chance of spotting marine mammals from the shore.

Or one can take to the sea. Local outfitters offer whale-watching via kayak, sailboat, and motorized watercraft, journeys that can last anywhere from a few hours to a couple days. Discovery Sea Kayaks organizes three-day and five-day kayak camping expeditions during summer months with overnight tenting at several state parks. The campsites are as magical as the kayaking, with hiking trails and views of ospreys and harbor seals patrolling the water. Maya's Legacy offers half- and full-day whale/wildlife tours guided by marine naturalists that also seek out bald eagles and other birdlife, as well as the exotic sheep and deer species on Spieden Island.

San Juan Islands, WA | Season: Year-round

Dive the Hood Canal

A fishhook-shaped fjord stretching for around 50 miles (80 km) between Puget Sound and the Olympic Peninsula, the Hood Canal isn't a natural choice for underwater exploration. It's extremely deep and almost always chilly, but the gentle currents and submarine sites attract a wide variety of sea creatures.

The ominous-looking wolf eel and giant Pacific octopus are among the denizens that divers can observe and photograph on Hood Canal dives. Complementing those top-shelf predators are giant codfish, sea stars, jellyfish, shellfish, nudibranchs, colorful anemones, and even harbor seals, sea otters, and other marine mammals.

Among the top spots for shore diving are Sund Rock Marine Preserve, Octopus Hole Conservation Area, and Potlatch State Park. YSS Dive in Hoodsport offers scuba equipment rentals, tank refills, and several courses.

Mason County, WA | Season: Summer

A fishing pier stretches out into the Hood Canal.

> "MOUNT RAINIER IS A
> GREAT WHITE BEAST
> OF A MOUNTAIN."

Summiting Mount Rainier

Looming high above Seattle and the rest of western Washington, 14,410-foot (4,392-m) Mount Rainier is a great white beast of a mountain. It's not especially difficult to summit—though only veteran climbers or those on guided trips should attempt the ascent. Rather, its fame derives from its status as the highest peak along the Pacific coast between California and Alaska, the most heavily glaciated mountain in the lower 48 states, and an active, potentially very dangerous volcano. It's also the nation's fourth oldest national park.

More than 20 routes to the summit start from four primary trailheads. Around three-quarters of the 10,000 people who attempt the Rainier climb each year start their trek from Paradise. Located at 5,400 feet (1,645 m) on the peak's southern slope, the area boasts a national park visitors center that can lend advice on weather, trail conditions, and other factors, as well as a cozy lodge where climbers can chill out before and after their ascent.

From Paradise, the summit is eight to nine miles (13 to 15 km) and roughly 9,000 feet (2,750 m) of elevation gain along the Disappointment Cleaver/Ingraham Glacier route. After trekking across the Muir Snowfield between Paradise and Nisqually Glaciers, most climbers overnight at Camp Muir, a cluster of stone huts built in the early 1920s. The path from there to the top varies depending on the ice conditions. Generally, it runs straight across the top of several glaciers, a danger zone with numerous crevasses and seracs, and then a final push from Disappointment Cleaver to the crater rim.

Anyone attempting the ascent must pay an annual climbing fee and obtain a climbing permit, or a solo climbing permit from the Park Service.

Mount Rainier National Park, WA | **Season:** Spring to fall

It takes endurance and the
right equipment to summit
Mount Rainier.

Kitesurfing the Columbia Gorge

American kitesurfing was born in Washington State, the brainchild of Boeing aerospace engineer Billy Roeseler and his son Cory who tested their prototypes on Seattle's Lake Washington.

The Roeselers eventually moved their experiments to the breezy Columbia River Gorge between Washington and Oregon. Forty years later, the ultra-scenic passage offers the state's best kitesurfing thanks to a steady wind created by sea breeze blowing upriver from the Pacific and dry inland air funneling downstream through the gorge.

The river's Washington shore offers a dozen kitesurfing launch sites between the towns of Stevenson in the west and Roosevelt in the east. Many are equipped with changing rooms and grassy rigging areas, and some even boast sail-drying racks. Given the sizable swells, swift current, and tricky winds, only professionals or veteran riders should attempt kitesurfing in the Columbia Gorge.

> "THE ULTRA-SCENIC PASSAGE OFFERS THE STATE'S BEST KITESURFING THANKS TO A STEADY WIND CREATED BY SEA BREEZE BLOWING UPRIVER FROM THE PACIFIC AND DRY INLAND AIR FUNNELING DOWNSTREAM THROUGH THE GORGE."

Multicity, WA | **Season:** Summer

When the wind is right, kitesurfing is a thrilling adventure in the Columbia Gorge.

Ride the *Lady of the Lake* passenger ferry across Lake Chelan.

Cruise Lake Chelan

Why bother hiking or driving into the North Cascades when you can cruise into the national park across one of the most scenic lakes in North America? Passenger boats have been crossing the lake since 1889, a service that continues aboard the *Lady of the Lake* and its sister vessels. The 50-mile (80 km) journey takes anywhere from 70 minutes on the speedy, hydrofoil-equipped *Lady Liberty* to four hours on the 285-passenger flagship *Lady of the Lake* with its open decks to view the surrounding mountains and a water body that ranks among the world's 25 deepest lakes.

Reaching rustic Stehekin village at the lake's north end, passengers have a choice of disembarking for a layover of three to six hours or staying for multiple days. Accommodation is available at North Cascades Lodge, Stehekin Valley Ranch, rental cabins, or several campgrounds. The Park Service's Golden West Visitor Center offers exhibits and information on the North Cascades and Lake Chelan, as well as advice on various activities.

The valley's main hiking route runs along the Stehekin River as far as High Bridge Ranger Station and the Pacific Crest Trail. Another trail leads down the eastern lakeshore, and a third to remote Rainbow Lake. Visitors can also rent bikes, angle for three different kinds of river trout, explore the Buckner Homestead Historic District and its apple groves, saddle up for an all-day guided horseback ride to Bridge Creek, or hop the free shuttle from the pier to the heavenly Stehekin Pastry Company.

Ornamental large-leaved shrub rhododendron

Chelan, WA | **Season:** Spring to fall

Dock your boat at the Kettle Falls Marina in Lake Roosevelt.

Live Aboard

Cast for rainbow trout and white sturgeon, watch elk dog-paddle their way to Summer Island, anchor in a remote cove where yours is the only vessel, sip organic rosé at a shoreline winery, and explore the site of old Fort Colvile and St. Paul's Mission on a houseboat journey along Lake Roosevelt.

Stretching 150 miles (240 km) along the Columbia River between Grand Coulee Dam and the Canadian border, the lake is the state's largest and easily longest. Most of the lake and its numerous coves, bays, and beaches fall within Lake Roosevelt National Recreation Area.

Marinas at Kettle Falls in the north and Keller Ferry and Seven Bays in the south rent houseboats ranging from 35 to 64 feet (10 to 20 m). Sleeping anywhere from four to 14 people, the boats are often equipped with queen beds, full kitchens, propane barbecues, washer/dryers, waterslides, hot tubs, electric fireplaces, and air-conditioning.

Multicity, WA | Season: Spring to fall

Olympic Rainforest Hikes

It's an entirely different kind of rainforest: temperate rather than tropical, squirrels instead of monkeys, and giant Sitka spruce rather than massive mahoganies. Yet that's what makes hiking the Olympic Peninsula rainforest so special: the chance to explore a primeval world like nowhere else on the planet.

Olympic National Park safeguards four large stands of temperate rainforest nurtured by 12 feet (3.6 m) of rain a year. The most easily accessible is the Hoh Rain Forest with its old-growth spruce, maple, cedar, and Douglas fir trees. Short hikes along the Hall of Mosses Trail (0.8 miles/1.3 km) and Spruce Nature Trail (1.2 miles/1.9 km) make experiencing the rainforest easy for just about anyone.

Farther south, the Quinault Rain Forest offers easy hikes like the 3.8-mile (6.1 km) Quinault Loop Trail and a

Cougar (or mountain lion)

five-minute walk from South Shore Road to the world's largest Sitka spruce—a 191-foot (58 m) behemoth that sprouted more than 1,000 years ago. Among the area's longer, more demanding treks are a 16-mile (26 km) walk through old-growth forest along the North Fork Quinault River and a 13-mile (21 km) path along the East Fork Quinault River to Enchanted Valley.

Roosevelt elk browsing the undergrowth along the trails often go unseen until hikers are practically on top of them. Among the other denizens are black bears, mountain lions, bobcats, and river otters. And with a little imagination, it's not hard to see why the dark, damp Olympic rainforest has generated so many Sasquatch sightings.

Olympic National Park, WA | Season: Year-round

Colorful lights illuminate Guler Ice Cave.

Into the Ice Caves

An ancient lava tube adorned with frozen stalagmites, stalactites, and other frosty formations, Guler Ice Cave is located near Mount Adams in Gifford Pinchot National Forest. Stretching 650 feet (200 m), the cave is accessed via the main entrance or several narrow "pit" openings along McClellan Meadows Trail.

Formed 9,000 to 12,000 years ago during the late Pleistocene era, the cave is part of the expansive Indian Heaven Volcanic Field. Its geological oddity derives from groundwater seeping through the ceiling and slowly solidifying into ice during winter temperatures.

The best times to visit Guler are during the winter or spring, although many of the formations last into early summer and some endure all the way until the following winter. Hikers should bring along a flashlight or headlamp, a jacket, and maybe even gloves and a warm hat.

Lewis County, WA | **Season:** Winter and spring

Climb the steep cliffs of
Frenchman Coulee.

1. HIKE MOUNT ST. HELENS

Few people beyond the region had even heard of this western Washington volcano until May 18, 1980, when it generated the deadliest, most devastating eruption in U.S. history. Now a national volcanic monument, the peak offers several challenging hikes, including the 32-mile (51 km) Loowit Trail around the entire mountain and the two steep summit trails up the south slope.

2. MAKE LIKE LEWIS AND CLARK

Trace the route of the Corps of Discovery along the mighty Columbia and Snake Rivers aboard the retro paddle wheelers and modern river steamers of American Cruise Lines. The 11-day voyage includes shore excursions to Mount St. Helens, Multnomah Falls in the Columbia River Gorge, and the Sacajawea Interpretive Center in Pasco, Washington.

3. RAFT THE WILD WENATCHEE RIVER

Although it flows only 53 miles (85 km) between the Cascades and the Columbia River, the Wenatchee churns up enough white water and Class III rapids to make it a major attraction for rafters and kayakers. Around a 2.5-hour drive from Seattle, the Bavarian-themed town of Leavenworth is the put-in for half-day float trips down to Cashmere.

4. CONQUER FRENCHMAN COULEE

The basalt columns and sheer cliffs of Frenchman Coulee and neigh-

boring Echo Basin attract hard-core climbers to the Columbia River Valley between Trinidad and Hanford. With more than 600 routes across the Sunshine, Zigzag, Middle East, and Vantage walls, the twin canyons offer scope for just about every level of rock jock.

5. HANG TEN OFF WESTPORT

Between the Jetty, the Cove, and the Groins, this southwest Washington town offers three gnarly breaks and consistent year-round board and bodysurfing. Four local surf shops offer board and wet suits rental, while BigFoot Surf School features group and private lessons to learn to hang ten or hone your skills.

6. SAIL PUGET SOUND

Hop aboard the two-masted schooner *Zodiac* in Bellingham harbor for a single-day or multiday journey through the storied Puget Sound and manifold islands. Built in 1924 as the posh private yacht of a Johnson & Johnson family, the 160-foot (48 m) vessel can sleep as many as 26 passengers in elegant Roaring Twenties comfort.

7. SOAR ABOVE THE CASCADES

Snatch a bird's-eye view of Mount Rainier, Mount St. Helens, and the vast Cascades forest on a flightseeing excursion with Kenmore Air. Taking off from historic Boeing Field between Seattle and Tacoma, the 90-minute flights are carried out in a nine-passenger Cessna Caravan. The company also offers

scenic flights over the San Juan Islands and Seattle.

8. CYCLE THE COLVILLE

Tucked up on the state's remote northeast corner, Colville National Forest offers some of the best mountain biking in the Pacific Northwest. Rides range from the easy Frater Lake Trail to challenging routes like the Jungle Hill Trail, Marcus Trail, and Thirteen Mile Trail. The forest boasts more than 50 dedicated biking routes.

9. DELIVER THE MAIL IN HELLS CANYON

You can experience North America's deepest river gorge—at 7,993 feet deep (2,436 m)—basically in two ways: You can undertake a rugged backcountry hike covering several days or climb aboard a speedy jet boat in Clarkston, Washington, for the Wednesday U.S. Mail run to remote ranches, resorts, and homes along the Snake River.

10. SKI OR RIDE THE "AMERICAN ALPS"

With a snowfall a snowfall average of more than 400 inches (1,020 cm), the North Cascades offer some of the nation's best skiing and snowboarding terrain. Among the cold-weather adventures are heli-skiing the backcountry while overnighting in a yurt, gliding down the double black diamonds at Mount Baker, and the 1,500-foot (460 m) descent down the Great White Express.

Harpers Ferry (page 670) sits at
the junction of the Shenandoah
and Potomac Rivers.

WEST VIRGINIA

Four seasons of fun await in West Virginia, from summer days lazing on the river to winter snow sports—and everything between.

OHIO

KENTUCKY

WEST VIR

Watters Smith
Memorial State Park ◼

Gauley
River

Summersville Lake
(Little Bahamas of the East) ◼

Cranberry Glades
Botanical Area ◼

New River
Gorge Ziplines ●

New River
Gorge Bridge ◼

New River Gorge
National Park & Preserve

Oakhurst
Links

Hatfield-
McCoy Trails ◼

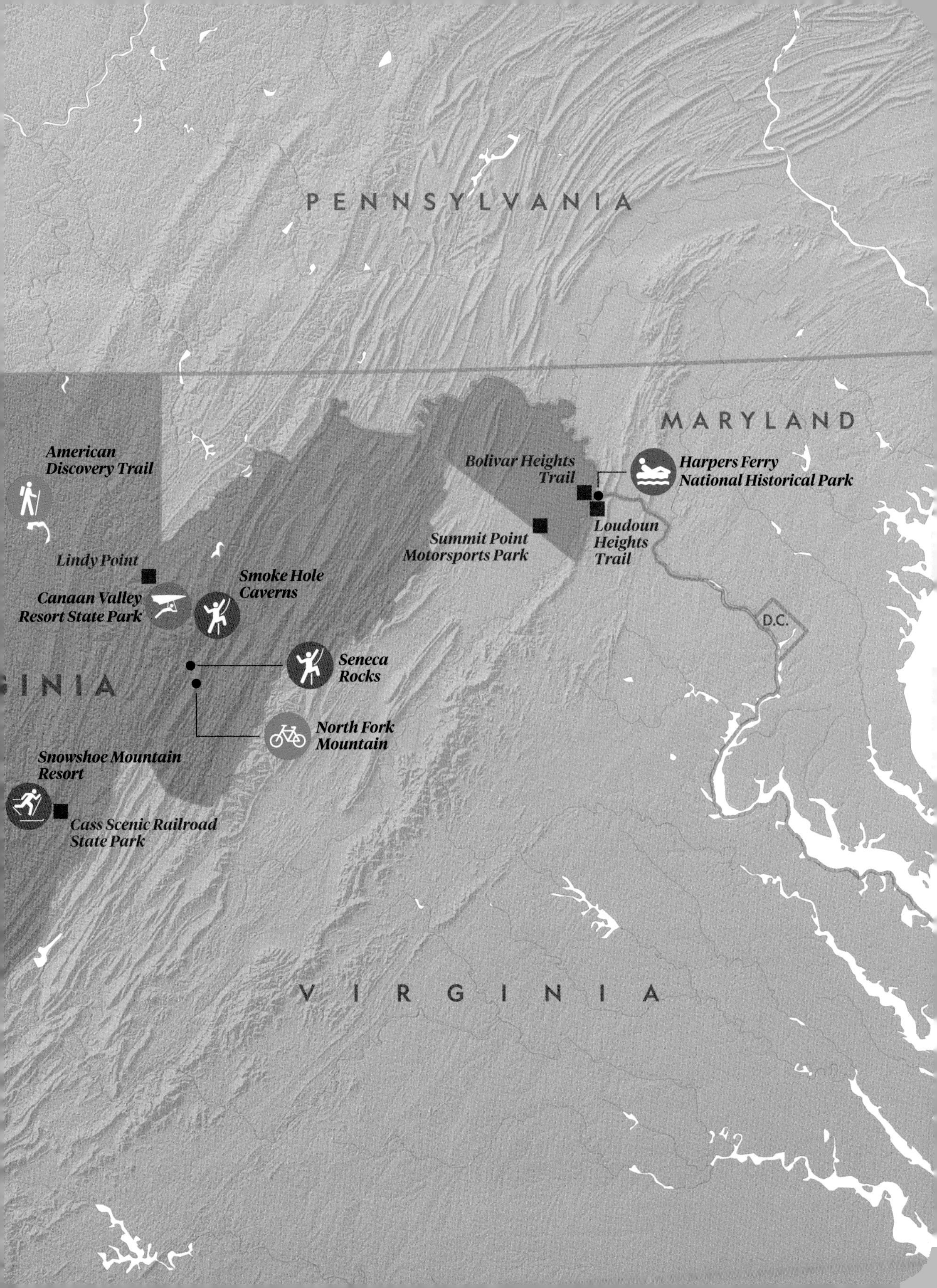

PENNSYLVANIA

MARYLAND

American
Discovery Trail

Bolivar Heights
Trail

Harpers Ferry
National Historical Park

Lindy Point

Summit Point
Motorsports Park

Loudoun
Heights
Trail

Smoke Hole
Caverns

Canaan Valley
Resort State Park

D.C.

Seneca
Rocks

GINIA

North Fork
Mountain

Snowshoe Mountain
Resort

Cass Scenic Railroad
State Park

VIRGINIA

Tube Town U.S.A.

Grab your sunscreen, pack your drinks, and put on your swimsuit. A tubing trip down the Shenandoah River gets everyone out on the water. You'll find families with young children, parties with waterproof speakers, and nature lovers all together on the river—and the shuttle service that most outfitters run makes the adventure even more accessible and carefree.

Groups such as the Harpers Ferry Adventure Center and River Riders will meet you in Harpers Ferry and drop you two or three hours (by tube) up the river. You'll drop in there and float your way to town. If you are seeking a more thrilling adventure, sign up for a white-water tubing experience with one of the many outfitters. River & Trail Outfitters will combine your aquatic escapade with a zip line through the tree canopy, an aerial adventure course, and a climbing wall.

The tubing season runs from late May through September.

Harpers Ferry, WV | Season: Summer

Take on a natural lazy river near Harpers Ferry.

Adventure Trek on the American Discovery Trail

This coast-to-coast trail stretches from Cape Henlopen State Park in Delaware to Point Reyes National Seashore in California. With some sections still under construction, the 6,800-mile (10,940 km) American Discovery Trail combines five national scenic and 12 national historic trails, 36 national recreational trails, and several local and regional trails.

This route merges nature and community. In West Virginia, that means your trip will include not only Harpers Ferry National Historical Park and Canaan Valley National Wildlife Refuge but also the cultural museums in Parkersburg and the Julia-Ann Square Historic District.

The West Virginia portion of the trail is split into four major sections: First, you'll trek through an Appalachian valley toward Monongahela National Forest. The second section, from Streby to Nestorville, requires a serious climb through the mountains, while the third, from Nestorville to Wilsonburg, will bring you back in time to when Clarksburg and Bridgeport were steeped in the Civil War. The final stretch will take you to the Ohio border by way of tunnels and bridges on the North Bend Rail Trail.

The Loop Trail winds through red spruce forest.

Multicity, WV | Season: Spring to fall

Take a Snow Day

Making good on its promise to bring both adventure and cushy comforts, Snowshoe Mountain Resort provides snowy slopes, winter activities, and first-rate accommodations.

Once you're on the snow, you can choose your own adventure. Skiing, snowboarding, tubing, cross-country skiing, and snowmobiling are all available across the resorts' three mountain sections, 60 trails, and five terrain parks. Newcomers of all ages can take advantage of the lesson options, including a "Mommy and Me" package that provides instruction to parents as well. The resort has also made significant efforts toward inclusion with its adaptive winter sports program, offering one-on-one lessons and adaptations for athletes with physical, visual, and developmental disabilities.

The mountaintop village offers dining, relaxation, and shopping options for a break from the slopes: Grab a

burger and beer at the Junction Ale House, or warm up with a street taco plate at the Sunset Cantina. Detox with a massage and body scrub at the Spa at Snowshoe. Pick up treats, clothes, and gear at one of the village shops.

There's a reason Snowshoe has been called the "crown jewel of powder skiing in the mid-Atlantic." But those still uncertain about the state's snow-sport caliber can ease their minds with Snowshoe's snow guarantee. The resort is so confident that between Mother Nature (the resort sees about 180 inches/460 cm of natural snowfall each year) and their snowmaking skills, they will always have more skiable terrain than any other mountain in the Southeast. If they're wrong, your ski day is on them.

Snowshoe, WV | Season: Winter

Take a Zip-Lining Tour

There's more than one way to get high above the New River Gorge. Outfitters have set up an array of aerial adventures over the deep valley, its rapids-filled river, and its rolling green forests. The river has cut through the Appalachian Mountains to create massive bluffs at its ridges, refuges for rare birds and animals, and an aquatic ecosystem like no other—all of which can be spotted from above. Adventures on the Gorge can guide visitors across the sky on its zip-line courses, ropes park, canopy tours, and bridge walks. The TreeTops Zipline Canopy Tour features 10 zip lines, five swinging sky bridges, short forest hikes, and a free-hanging rappel. Meanwhile, TimberTrek Adventure Park contains seven intense obstacle courses across four acres (1.6 ha) of the wooded gorge that will test your teamwork, balance, and strength.

Zip through the canopies on an aerial tour of the New River Gorge.

New River Gorge, WV | Season: Spring to fall

See America's newest national park from the summit of Hawks Nest State Park.

> "FIND A DIVERSE ASSEMBLY OF MARINE LIFE, FROM SMALLMOUTH BASS TO FLATHEAD CATFISH."

Explore the Newest National Park

The 70,000-acre (23,330 ha) New River Gorge National Park and Preserve can be explored by air, land, or water—and the best trips to this recently redesignated national park combine all three.

For adventure by foot, plan a trip along the 2.3-mile (3.7 km), point-to-point Endless Wall Trail. It crosses Fern Creek, follows the edge of the mountain's cliffs, and provides determined hikers with river views at Diamond Point—the spot where most trekkers turn around and head back to their starting point.

If you want to stay on the ground but pick up your speed, drop by Arrowhead Bike Farm. The site near the trailheads of many New River Gorge routes hosts bike clinics and tours, rents bicycles, and is home to a restaurant, bar, and campground. Challenge yourself on the New River Coal Country Trail or take it easy on the Rend Trail. Arrowhead also serves as an excellent base to climb Kaymoor Top, a wall full of steep sport climbs with big holds.

Soar above the flourishing preserve—and back in time—in a World War II Stearman biplane. Wild Blue Adventure Company will either fly you over the park on a straight sightseeing tour or twist and turn you through the sky with barrel rolls, hammerheads, and S-turns. You'll take off from Fayetteville, minutes from the New River Gorge Bridge and Nuttallburg, one of the many bygone coal towns that popped up in the late 19th century.

The river is what created the gorge here, so it's fitting to spend some time on it while in the park. On the New River, anglers will find a diverse assembly of marine life, from smallmouth bass to flathead catfish.

New River Gorge National Park, WV | **Season:** Year-round

Mountain Bike the North Fork Mountain

The 23-mile (37 km) North Fork Mountain Trail starts off on the forest floor and makes its way to the region's many rocky ridges. For mountain bikers who share the route with hikers, this technical terrain takes about five hours to traverse. Views of the towering Seneca Rocks and lush Potomac River Valley follow you along the path, and with just short breaks off your bike, you can trek to easily accessible and gorgeous mountain overlooks. Take these opportunities to hydrate with water you've brought because there isn't any available on the trail.

Ride this trail from south to north to experience the three-mile (5 km) descent that makes all the uphill efforts and boulder navigation worth it. Besides a few switchbacks and narrow tree gaps, bikers can let go and roar down the mountain in celebration of completing what the International Mountain Bicycling Association has designated as "Epic."

> "VIEWS OF THE TOWERING SENECA ROCKS AND LUSH POTOMAC RIVER VALLEY FOLLOW YOU ALONG THE PATH, AND YOU CAN TREK TO EASILY ACCESSIBLE AND GORGEOUS MOUNTAIN OVERLOOKS."

Cabins, WV | **Season:** Spring to fall

The scenery is just as good as the mountain bike trails throughout the North Fork Mountain.

Paddle your way carefully through the rock-strewn Gauley River.

White-Water Plunge

Wet and wild doesn't even begin to define the white water that plummets through West Virginia's Gauley River. In fall, this 25-mile (40 km) stretch of water features more than 100 tumultuous rapids, steep drops, technical runs, and massive waves. Riding this fast-flowing river is not a leisurely tubing trip with a cooler; it's one of the most intense, respected white-water runs in the world.

The Upper Gauley's rocky, quick-moving routes are best left to experts and those willing to take on the risks of the river. Don't let some of the rapid names, such as Meadow View and Pillow Rock, fool you. These rapids mean business, and only paddlers willing to work should attempt to navigate them.

Less experienced and younger paddlers should begin their time at the Lower Gauley. Even with that recommendation, these 13 miles (21 km) are nothing to scoff at.

Multicity, WV | Season: Spring to fall

With rapids aptly named Pure Screaming Hell and Heaven Help You, there's plenty of teeth-clenching danger to be had.

Though you can raft the river on your own, most visitors book a guided trip with a local outfitter. ACE Adventure Resort and New and Gauley River Adventures run full-day and multiday expeditions along both portions of the river.

Fall brings Gauley Season, when the river bursts and rapids grow. In summer, the rapids are inconsistent, and the water flow fluctuates, so guides will determine which section is best to explore on any particular day. Paddlers open to whatever the river brings can roll the adventure dice and join River Expeditions for one of their summer trips.

Enjoy mountain views with a summer chairlift ride.

Take to the Skies

Paragliding isn't a sport you can just *try*. It requires controlling the paraglider, or wing, in the air through only your own physical skill. However, if you've racked up the hours it takes to learn, launching from the 4,000-foot-high (1,220 m) mountain atop Canaan Valley Resort State Park, with its views of the Allegheny Front and Red Creek, is an experience without match.

After growing interest, the Mountaineer Hang Gliding Association partnered with the park to open an on-site launch. Visitors can ride the scenic chairlift with their equipment and walk a boardwalk—built to protect the endangered Cheat Mountain salamanders—to the launch site. The space is one of only two paragliding sites in the eastern U.S. accessible by lift.

The chairlift is open to all, so nonflying guests can also catch views over the Great Appalachian Valley—and, with some luck, an in-air glider.

Davis, WV | **Season:** Spring to fall

Rock Climb the Seneca Rocks

The Seneca Rocks at Monongahela National Forest will have you challenging both your rock-climbing skills and your technology addiction. Experienced climbers can reach the top of the summit from almost every one of the 375 mostly moderate and difficult routes set in the massive Tuscarora sandstone formation. However, without any cell service, you'll have to brag about it once you get back to town.

Moderate weather makes this climbing spot pleasant in spring, summer, and fall, but rain will loosen worn rock on the ledges. Wear a helmet and stay out from under drop zones and rappel routes. For more expedition tips—and stunning views of the rock wall—start your trip at the Seneca Rocks Discovery Center, open from late March to late October.

To extend your stay, book a site at the national forest's Seneca Shadows Campground, where you can drink your morning coffee with a view of the towering rocks. The campground is a mile walk to the town of Seneca Rocks, where you can step back in time at historic Harper's Olde Country Store and fuel your climb with brisket or ribs from Hoggie's Barbecue.

If you're looking to improve your climbing, the Seneca Rocks Climbing School offers beginning and advanced classes, as well as self-rescue and women's-only offerings and private lessons. Their experienced guides all have expertise in both climbing and education, ensuring you'll get the most out of your session. Seneca Rocks Mountain Guides also offer lessons on the mountain, along with three-hour personalized seminars.

Huttonsville, WV | **Season:** March to October

Smoke Hole Caverns offers guided tours through a subterranean world.

Head Into the Smoke Hole Caverns

This has long been a place of refuge and gathering. The Seneca Nation of Indians used the front sections to smoke wild meat, sending billows out into the valley and earning the caverns their name. They weren't the only ones cooking in the caverns: Early settlers used the cold stream to make corn whiskey. Visitors can see an original still on display.

Ecological history is just as prominent. As it has for millions of years, mineral water flows through the caverns, forming stalactites and stalagmites that jut from the ceiling and floor. Don a jacket and sturdy shoes plus a camera before you head below the forest floor for a tour.

This underground adventure is an easy addition to a Seneca Rocks experience; the Smoke Hole Resort, with its lodge, cabins, and RV sites, is just 13 miles (21 km) north of town. Between the caverns and the rock wall, you can experience the highs and lows of West Virginia in just one weekend.

Cabins, WV | **Season:** Year-round

Lindy Point Overlook in
Blackwater Falls

1. HIKE INTO HISTORY

Harpers Ferry National Historical Park, at the confluence of the Potomac and Shenandoah Rivers, merges history and nature at every corner—and offers plenty of hikes and ranger programs to explore both. Though Maryland Heights is the most popular trail, it can get crowded. Try the Bolivar Heights Trail for an easy alternative and Loudoun Heights for a challenge —the 7.5-mile (12.1 km) trail is part of the longer Appalachian Trail and offers multiple views of the rivers, Harpers Ferry, and even into Pleasant Valley, Maryland, to the east.

2. RIDE THE RAILS

The town of Cass was established in 1901, and it looks nearly the same now as it did at the turn of the century, including its transportation. Hop a train at Cass Scenic Railroad State Park, once used to haul lumber, then ride a restored train to Bald Knob Overlook.

3. EXPERIENCE PIONEER LIFE

Capture the pioneer spirit as you wander Watters Smith Memorial State Park. Watters and Elizabeth Smith settled the land in 1796, and built their hand-hewn log cabin, later reconstructed in 1876 by his great-grandson and now one of two museums. Bring a picnic, go for a hike, and check out West Virginian heritage.

4. TRAVERSE THE NEW RIVER GORGE BRIDGE

This bridge turned a 40-minute drive into a one-minute crossing, but the most exciting way to traverse it is by walking the catwalk beneath the cars. Outfitters such as Bridge Walk lead guided tours day and night. Plus, once a year, it's open to pedestrians to eat, dance, BASE jump, and rappel.

5. CATCH A SUNSET AT LINDY POINT

This popular out-and-back trail in Blackwater Falls State Park has major payoffs for relatively low effort. You'll reach a wooden platform with iconic views over the valley. The distance makes it easy to time your photo-worthy sunset or sunrise moment.

6. ATV INTO A HISTORIC RIVALRY

The Hatfield-McCoy Trail System runs wild through the region where that equally wild feud took place. Off-road vehicle, all-terrain vehicle, utility terrain vehicle, and dirt bike riders can speed on hundreds of trail miles through rugged forests. If you don't have your own, nearby outfitters can set you up.

7. WALK THE CRANBERRY BOGS

The acidic wetlands of the Cranberry Glades Botanical Area in Monongahela National Forest make up the state's largest bog acreage. Walk the wheelchair-accessible boardwalks to spot hummingbirds, finches, pollinators, and carnivorous plants. Start with the loop from the Cranberry Mountain Nature Center Interpretive Loop.

8. SCUBA DIVE IN THE LITTLE BAHAMAS OF THE EAST

Summersville Lake is a freshwater paradise for scuba divers. The calm, warm lake is teeming with life—full of catfish, bass, and walleye. Search for the striking rock formation beneath its surface, a small sunken boat near the winter access ramp, and Bubbles Cove, a rock wall that mimics cavern diving.

9. GOLF WITH ELITES

Bring your clubs out to the land of America's first golf course: the Greenbrier. The Oakhurst Links course was built on the grounds in 1884, but it was recently closed for damage. Still, the resort maintains four premier courses—and its namesake is the only one in the world that has hosted both the Ryder and Solheim Cups.

10. SPEED UP

Summit Point can quench any motor sport athlete's need for speed. Its first track, Summit Point Circuit, opened in 1969 and is a thrilling two-mile (3.2 km) course with 10 turns and a 2,980-foot (910 m) straight. It, along with two other circuits, is now used as a training ground for federal and security agencies.

Make camp on the beaches of
Lake Superior (page 693).

WISCONSIN

Whether you're setting sail on a Great Lake or exploring the Ice Age Trail, you won't be wanting for adventure in the Badger State.

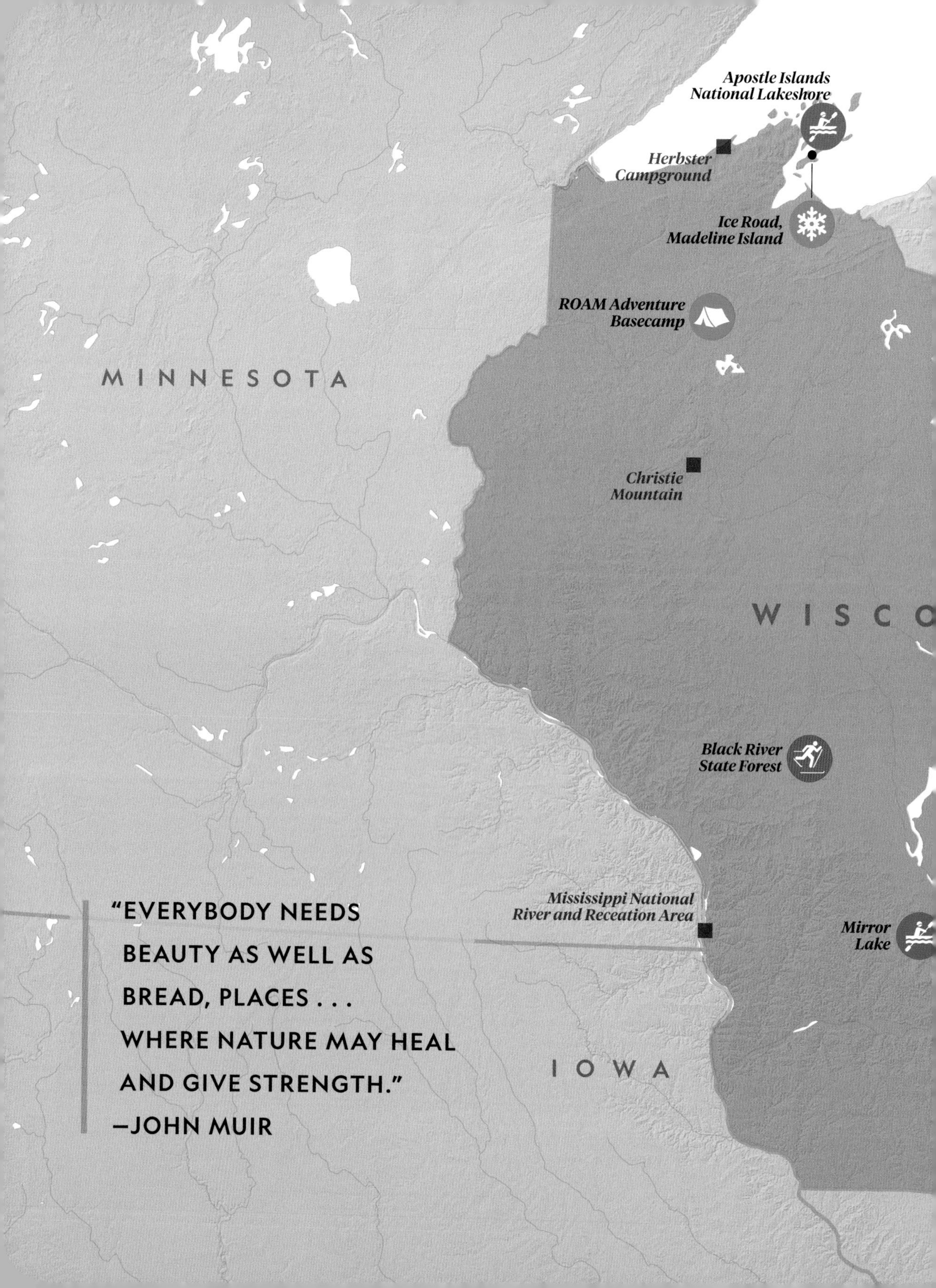

Apostle Islands
National Lakeshore

Herbster
Campground

Ice Road,
Madeline Island

ROAM Adventure
Basecamp

MINNESOTA

Christie
Mountain

WISCO

Black River
State Forest

"EVERYBODY NEEDS
BEAUTY AS WELL AS
BREAD, PLACES . . .
WHERE NATURE MAY HEAL
AND GIVE STRENGTH."
–JOHN MUIR

Mississippi National
River and Receation Area

Mirror
Lake

IOWA

Lake Superior

CANADA
U.S.

ONTARIO

MICHIGAN

Heart of Vilas County
Bike Trail System

Wildman Adventure Resort:
Menominee River Outpost

Bagley Rapids
Recreation Area

Cave Point
County Park

N S I N

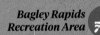

Stevens Point
Sculpture Park

Chain
O' Lakes

Siberian
Outpost

Lake
Michigan

MICHIGAN

Lake Michigan

Kohler Park Dunes
State Natural Area

Marcus Performing Arts Center:
Peck Pavilion

Ice Age National
Scenic Trail

Camp
Wandawega

ILLINOIS

Ice Road Skaters

The Ice Road isn't really a road at all, though it's used as one during the winter and is the only such route listed on official state maps. When the two miles (3.2 km) of Lake Superior between Bayfield and Madeline Island freeze solid, people start to cross. Some drive their cars, others ice-skate, and—during the Run on Water event of the Bayfield Winter Festival—people add running, walking, snowshoeing, and biking to the list of options. A water taxi ferries visitors between Madeline Island and Bayfield. Called the Windsled, it's a covered, flat-bottomed airboat that can float on water should the ice break.

It seems risky, but safety is paramount on the ice. The road is marked with discarded Christmas trees to keep cars on track, and the ice is monitored several times a day when the road is open. Once the ice melts, you can return for a Madeline Island Ferry ride to follow the course you skated.

Bayfield to Madeline Island, WI | Season: Winter

The Winter Ice Road at La Pointe on Madeline Island

Paddle Through Cave Point

Centuries of Lake Michigan waves have crashed into Cave Point to carve it into the towering, hollowed-out section of today's Door Peninsula. Though the park's half-mile (0.8 km) hiking trail offers excellent lake views and will connect you to other trails in Whitefish Dunes State Park, a secret world below the cliffs is out of sight for hikers.

Down at the waterline, kayakers will discover dozens of underwater caverns. If you have your own boat, you can launch a mile (1.6 km) north of Cave Point at Schauer Park for a small fee. If not, you can join one of the many tours run by local outfitters. Peninsula Kayak Company leaves from Sturgeon Bay and follows the shoreline to Whitefish Dunes State Park. Kayak Door County runs a similar tour. On calm days, there are two caves still open to kayakers. The crests that built the peninsula's facades are still crashing, however, so kayakers should be keenly aware of weather changes.

For a break from paddling, pull your kayak to shore at the sandy beach just north of the caves and hike to the park's picnic area. With even more time, you can stop at Whitefish Dunes for a swim at its grassy beach.

Cave Point features limestone cliffs along Lake Michigan.

Sturgeon Bay, WI | Season: Spring to fall

Walk Through the Ice Age

The entire 1,200 miles (1,930 km) of the Ice Age National Scenic Trail follow moraines, or the rocky material left behind when glaciers carved Wisconsin thousands of years ago. Following this footpath, you'll wind through the state from protected parks to Ice Age National Scientific Reserve, which are affiliated with the National Park Service and were created to protect these glacial landscapes.

Drop onto the trail for an educational and beautiful day hike or plan a multiday trip to walk a more comprehensive stretch of the glacier's path. If you choose the first, you can book campgrounds in state parks and national forests along the route. Plan ahead when booking your campgrounds, as sites vary from primitive walk-in grounds to sites with electric hookups. Reservations at campgrounds are recommended. If you choose the second, you can backpack camp along the way.

Multicity, WI | Season: Spring to fall

In the summer, hikers should be sure to keep their binoculars close to spot birds —including eastern bluebirds, sandhill cranes, and common nighthawks, after dark—that soar above the prairies and forests. In winter, visitors can ditch their hiking boots and opt for cross-country skis or snowshoes. Any time of year, those on the trail will be treated to landscape features that started to develop two billion years ago, including the rocks at Grandfather Falls and the basalt bluffs in Polk County.

The trail is supported by a group of conservation advocates, nature lovers, and scientists—and volunteers are often tasked with maintaining the route. If you're moved by the mission, join a volunteer day to give back and ensure the trail stays functional and accessible.

Visit the Headwaters Wilderness of Chequamegon-Nicolet Forest.

Rapid Fire

Listen to the rapids of the North Branch Oconto River gently roll from your campsite as you fall asleep in your tent at Bagley Rapids Recreation Area. The campground is basic—no electricity or flush toilets, but plenty of space and lots of quiet. Inside Chequamegon-Nicolet National Forest, the sites make for a great spot to practice your paddling skills at Bagley Rapids.

Most rafters and paddlers on this route are doing it on their own, and this river is best attempted by those who feel comfortable taking lead on their own adventure. If you prefer to watch the river instead, head to the nearby Mountain Fire Lookout Tower and climb the 100 feet (30 m) up to the top. The tower is open until just after sunset from May through November, so you can catch the changing sky if you time your climb right.

Mountain, WI | Season: May to November

> ### "KAYAKING AROUND THE ISLANDS IS UNLIKE MOST OTHER LAKE PADDLING."

Kayak the Apostle Islands

At the northernmost border of Wisconsin, you'll find 21 islands and a stretch of mainland that make up the distinct and serene Apostle Islands National Lakeshore, with its massive rock formations, hundreds of bird species, and crystal clear waters.

The islands are only accessible by boat, and 12 of the 21 islands have private docks. You also have the option of anchoring in bays, but Lake Superior weather can change quickly, so it's important to regularly monitor forecasts. Kayaking to and around the islands is unlike most other lake paddling. Lake Superior is cold, rough, and prone to fog and sudden squalls. Extreme weather can rapidly overtake your trip, and it's critical that you have the skills to navigate the dangers and self-rescue. If you're unsure of your skill, it's best to book a tour with an experienced guide.

Trek & Trail will take you on adventures that last anywhere from a few hours to a few days. The full-day Sand Island trip includes a visit to the island's lighthouse and lost village, while the Devils Island Rendezvous will wind you through the archipelago until you reach Devils Island sea caves, a prized notch on any island paddler's belt.

For exploration that doesn't involve crossing Lake Superior, Escape Excursion will taxi you to the islands to hike and camp—or motorboat you and your borrowed kayak to an island for deeper exploration.

If you'd rather sit back and relax, Apostle Islands Cruises books nonstop runs around the islands. On them, you can sightsee and photograph the striking rock walls and caves without a paddle in hand.

You'll find campsites on 18 of the islands. Individual and group sites are available with picnic tables, fire rings, and bear lockers, along with primitive backcountry camping.

Bayfield, WI | Season: Spring to fall

Devils Island is one of
22 Apostle Islands in
Lake Superior.

Take an Art Hike

Art and nature merge at the Stevens Point Sculpture Park, where pieces line the edges of a crushed granite trail. With the goal of providing a welcoming outdoor space for artwork, including environmental art, Stevens Point features sculptures from local, regional, and national artists. Sit on Joe Krajkiewcz's red maple leaf bench and admire the unusual bicycle-like sculpture, "Maurice's Contraption," from Paul Murphy.

Accessibility is key at the park. The trail is free and wheelchair accessible during warm and dry months. It's also close to easy parking and not far from other landmarks, connecting to the Green Circle Trail and Zenoff Park.

Also available are children's programs, including self-led scavenger hunts and instructor-led art education activities. The goal is that anyone, regardless of age, ability, or finances, can experience the park and its art.

> "ACCESSIBILITY IS KEY AT THE PARK. THE TRAIL IS FREE AND WHEELCHAIR ACCESSIBLE DURING WARM AND DRY MONTHS."

Stevens Point, WI | **Season:** Year-round

Walk the wooded trail to see the rotating art exhibits at Stevens Point Sculpture Park.

Enjoy 1.5 miles (2.4 km) of lighted ski trails at Black River State Forest, then warm up by a large bonfire.

Ski by Candlelight

It's one thing to cross-country ski through gorgeous snowy trails that weave between tall pines. It's another to glide along that same magical trail lit by glowing candles in the dark. The annual candlelight ski, hike, and snowshoe event at Black River State Forest makes the spot a necessary addition to any winter lover's bucket list. There are 24 miles (39 km) of looping and linking trails across the park, and most of them are groomed in the winter for both skate and traditional skiing.

The forest is a popular cross-country ski destination for a reason: The two forks of its river roll through the park under tremendous sandstone towers, providing a powerful combination of calm and adventure. The string of glacial mounds spread over seven miles (11 km) in the park serves as perfect overlooks for hikers, winter and summer alike.

Jackson County, WI | Season: Winter

You won't be the only one enjoying the forest while you're there. On a calm and quiet winter evening, you just might spot a transplanted elk and its young. In 2015 and 2016, the Department of Natural Resources released elk from Kentucky, after the animals' absence for 125 years.

If you're set on spending as much time in the forest as possible, its Pigeon Creek Campground is open year-round, and some sites are plowed during winter. Between November and April, these sites are first-come, first-served. If you aren't quite that brave but are looking for a place to have your lunch, hop into the warming shelter at the Smrekar Trails parking lot.

Mirror Lake reflects the surrounding fall foliage.

Paddling Reflections

It's not unusual for the only ripple on Mirror Lake to be from a kayaker's paddle. The stillness of the lake and its clear waters reflect the trees along its shoreline, giving it its name. You can bring your own boat and launch it either inside the state park or in Delton.

Dells Watersports rents kayaks, canoes, and paddleboards to guests from its Baraboo location. For people with disabilities, the park rents adaptive kayaks with adjustable outriggers, raised backs, additional side supports, and hand braces on the paddles.

Overnight guests can book an evening at the Seth Peterson Cottage, a 1958 Frank Lloyd Wright home that fell into disrepair and was restored in 1989. The tilted roof and glass walls brighten the wood and stone in this remote cottage, where you can catch uninterrupted views of the lake.

Baraboo, WI | **Season:** Summer

Set Sail on a Great Lake

Sailing can feel exclusive, limited to those with financial means and physical abilities—but not in Sheboygan. In this Lake Michigan town, sailing is for everyone; just ask the Sailing Education Association of Sheboygan (SEAS). The nonprofit is "dedicated to creating affordable pathways for the community to safely enjoy boating." SEAS provides sailing lessons, cruises, and events to support its goal of inclusivity.

The nonprofit also provides adaptive sailing opportunities for those with physical or cognitive disabilities. This unique program focuses on providing sailors with additional needs the confidence, skill, and opportunity to succeed on the water. They can lead a boat on their own or work alongside friends and family to navigate on Sonar sailboats, a popular adaptive sailing choice around the world. Because SEAS works to ensure every participant is safe and suc-

cessful, it assesses prospective students individually to determine the best path forward.

This inclusivity spread to the rest of the Sheboygan sailing community. The Sheboygan Yacht Club was built out of grit, friendship, and love of sailing—and that spirit continues. It advertises friendly sailors alongside its stunning views and delicious meals, runs sailing events in spaces where non-sailors can join, and supports a youth sailing club for anyone who wants to learn.

Sailing on Lake Michigan can range from an intense workout on the water to a relaxing float under an orange sunset. If you have your own sailboat, dock it at the Harbor Centre Marina for the afternoon to explore Deland Park and walk to the nearby downtown restaurants.

Sheboygan, WI | **Season:** Spring to fall

ROAM Adventure Basecamp is a unique camping spot and outdoor sports venue.

Adventure at ROAM Basecamp

Stay comfortable and expedition-ready at ROAM Adventure Basecamp. The four all-weather cabins look like they were plucked out of Scandinavia and dropped into Wisconsin. You won't find a television but will find in-floor heaters and adjacent restrooms. The 30 campsites don't have electricity or water hookups but do have plenty of firewood. Good thing, because the wood-fired sauna is sure to help you relax.

ROAM's biggest draw is its prime location. Its sites and cabins sit among hundreds of miles of trails, making it simple to get right to exploring when you wake up in the morning. You'll find quick and easy access to the trails of Sawyer and Bayfield County Forests, along with Chequamegon-Nicolet National Forest. It's also sandwiched between the Saint Croix National Scenic Riverway and the Spider Chain of Lakes. Bring your gear of choice—hiking boots, mountain bikes, swimsuits, kayaks, snowshoes, or cross-country skis—and jump right into the exploits.

Hayward, WI | **Season:** Year-round

A boardwalk path crosses
the dunes to Lake Michigan
at Kohler Andrae State Park.

1. GO TO SUMMER CAMP FOR ADULTS

The rustic and retro Camp Wanda-wega specifically shares a "Mani-festo of Low Expectations" with guests, covering everything from leaky tents to toad friends. It offers counselor-led activities and sports equipment of the past. Come for the nature, stay for the self-led for-est fun.

2. TAKE SIDES IN A PAINTBALL BATTLE

All-level players are welcome to test their paintball skills and challenge their opponents at the Wildman Adventure Resort. Guests move stealthily through the forest at the Menominee River Outpost, searching the terrain field and hiding in bunkers. The resort provides everything needed for the game, including safety equipment.

3. SOAK UP OPEN-AIR THEATER ON THE RIVER

The Marcus Performing Arts Center has several spaces across Milwaukee, and the Peck Pavilion is the perfect spot for a summer date night. Located on the Milwau-kee River, this 400-seat outdoor theater has been booked for movies, dance and musical con-certs, theater programs, and cul-tural celebrations.

4. BEACH CAMP ON LAKE SUPERIOR

What the Herbster Campground lacks in private campsites, it makes up for in lake views and sunsets. The mile-long (1.6 km) beach is the only one on the south shore that offers beachside tent camping. It also has a playground and lots of sandy shoreline, but no lifeguard at the beach.

5. HIKE LAKE MICHIGAN SAND DUNES

The unmarked and undesignated footpaths in Kohler Park Dunes State Natural Area are no easy task, but the wooden cordwalk provides a clear route to scenic overlooks and protected ecosys-tems. Pack a GPS unit or compass and a topographical map to explore the rest of the geography.

6. BIKE THE HEART OF VILAS COUNTY

Follow this paved national recre-ation trail for more than 52 miles (84 km)—or just tackle a portion of the route. This smooth route moves through Northern Highland-American Legion State Forest, past multiple campgrounds and picnic spots, and over scenic bridges. Its distance connects communities from St. Germain to Mercer.

7. TAKE THE RIDE OF YOUR LIFE

At Jim's Siberian Outpost in Malone, you can take a family-friendly dogsled tour that includes a visit with the happy pack of pups, a lesson on this history of the Iditarod, and insight into the training the dogs and human ath-letes go through to prepare. Then it's your turn on the sled: Learn how to ride and the com-mands to guide the dogs, then hold on tight. It's a fast-flying adventure on snow.

8. FIND BALANCE WITH STAND-UP PADDLEBOARD YOGA

Melt away stress during a SUP yoga session on the Waupaca Chain O' Lakes, created by melting glaciers more than 12,000 years ago. Natural springs uncovered during that melt keep the water clear and filtered. Multiple outfit-ters offer SUP yoga, including Yoga Hive Wisconsin.

9. SNOWBOARD ON FAMILY-FRIENDLY SLOPES

Christie Mountain is built for families who want to ski and snow-board together. The beginners' park and ski school give newcom-ers a chance to acclimate, while the back side of the mountain has more advanced runs. Stay on mountain at the seven-person Northern Boundaries cabin. A sep-arate tubing park on the mountain offers an alternative way for families to enjoy the snow.

10. ICE FISH IN GENOA

Fishing on the Mississippi River doesn't stop when winter comes. The National Park Service at the Mississippi National River and Rec-reation Area holds intermittent events for ice fishing, and you can always head to a popular spot and search for help. Try Mississippi River Pool 8 in Genoa.

The Grand Prismatic Spring at
Yellowstone National Park
(page 704)

WYOMING

Wyoming can boast wide-open spaces, lots of fresh air, plenty of sunshine, and more than a few ways to get you outside.

MONTANA

Yellowstone
National Park

Cody

Teton Wagon Train
and Horse Adventure

T. A. Moulton Barn,
Grand Teton National Park

Jackson Hole
Mountain Resort

Wyoming
Dinosaur
Center

National Museum
of Wildlife Art

Snake

Snake
River

IDAHO

Coney Classic Alpine
Skijor and Dog Party

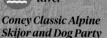
Wind River
Range

WYO

Pinedale

Killpecker
Sand Dunes

UTAH

Flaming Gorge
National Recreation Area

Eatons'
Ranch

Devils Tower
National Monument

SOUTH
DAKOTA

Ten
Sleep

M I N G

Miracle
Mile

Casper
Mountain

Register Cliff
Historic Site

NEBRASKA

Vee Bar
Guest Ranch

Snowy Range
Ski Area

Vedauwoo
Recreation Area

C O L O R A D O

Fish the Miracle Mile

When it comes to good fish tales, sometimes the reality is a little disappointing. But in the case of a stretch of the North Platte River known as the "Miracle Mile," the reality exceeds expectations. Located between Kortes Dam and Pathfinder Reservoir at the foot of the Seminoe Mountains, this prime patch of river is actually 5.5 miles (8.9 km) long and known to anglers the world over. Though the scenery is reason enough to wade in, anglers come for the steady stream of trophy rainbow, brown, and cutthroat trout that call the cold waters home. Cold water released from Kortes Dam, fed by snowmelt from mountain streams, is fertile ground for tailwater trout, earning the Miracle Mile its mythical status among anglers as the place to catch big and healthy fish that live up to exaggerated stories. If needed, expert guides, gear, lures, and other supplies can be found at shops such as the Platte River Fly Shop in nearby Casper.

Casper, WY | **Season:** Spring to fall

Catch brown trout on the North Platte River.

Discover Skijoring

Skijoring is the unofficial winter sport of Wyoming, combining two favorite pastimes: skiing and horseback riding. During the ride, one skier is pulled by a teammate on horseback or by a team of dogs. It seems simple, but in competitions around Wyoming, riders and skiers navigate slalom gates and hurl themselves over obstacles.

Skijoring is believed to have come from the Sami, Indigenous people from Norway, who skied behind reindeer. Skijoring eventually made it into Scandinavia's competitive Nordic Games in the early 1900s, and its popularity spread around Europe. When soldiers returned home from World War II to America's West, they brought the sport with them.

Saratoga's competitive Skijoring Races have $10,000 in prizes up for grabs while in Sundance, the Winter Festival takes place along Main Street, making it easy for spectators to observe the wild ride. In Alpine, the Coney Classic Alpine Skijor is a fund-raiser for the local cross-country ski trails and an animal shelter. The event brings out dogs and their human companions who are pulled, or beside them, on 5K, 3K, and 1K courses.

Skijoring races are held at Jackson Hole Mountain Resort.

Multicity, WY | **Season:** Winter

Find Your Inner Cowboy

Back in the late 1800s, "dude" was a word cowboys used when referring to city dwellers. When these urbanites discovered the wide-open plains and stunning mountain scenery made for great vacations, ranches opened to hosting them, calling their businesses "dude ranches," and there's perhaps no better state for a western adventure than the Cowboy State itself.

Dude ranches are found in some of the most majestic scenery in the country and invite couples, families, and bona fide city slickers to experience the cowboy lifestyle. The oldest dude ranch in America, Eatons' Ranch on the eastern slope of the Bighorn Mountains, is run by the fourth and fifth generations of the Eaton family who first founded their ranch in 1879. Guests stay in rustic but comfortable cabins and can try fly-fishing, learn to two-step at the Friday night dance, and explore 7,000 private acres (2,830 ha) on horseback.

Multicity, WY | **Season:** Year-round

At Vee Bar Guest Ranch, guests ride their happy horses through meadows and mountain terrain as well as get the chance to help ranch wranglers move cattle. With a backdrop of Grand Teton National Park, the daily routine at Triangle X Ranch centers around morning and evening horseback rides, as well as square dancing and float picnics on the Snake River. The Lazy L&B Ranch is anything but, and its location in the unpopulated and unspoiled Wind River's East Fork Valley makes a spectacular setting for horseback rides, campfire songs, cool-off dips in the river, and bird-watching. Fly-fishing is a must-do at the Lazy L&B, with access to a section of the Upper Wind River that is home to rainbow, cutthroat, and brown trout.

Wildflowers in the Snowies

Their high alpine scenery, including more than 100 crystalline lakes, makes the Snowy Mountain Range, aka the Snowies, a top destination any time of year. But come July and August, you'll catch wildflower season.

For an easy wildflower-hunting outing, try the relatively flat 3.2-mile (5.1 km) out-and-back Twin Lakes Trail that's often bursting with blooms in July. Among the colorful flowers are lupine, purple fringe, alpine forget-me-nots, and glacier lilies, to name just a few.

The Snowies are located around 35 miles (56 km) west of Laramie in the beautiful Medicine Bow-Routt National Forests, home to a small and welcoming ski resort, the Snowy Range Ski Area, as well as hiking and biking trails galore.

White columbines bloom in the Snowy Range.

Albany County, WY | **Season:** July and August

Sand dunes reach as tall as 100 feet (30 m) at Killpecker Sand Dunes.

> "THESE MERCURIAL MOUNTAINS ARE SCULPTED ANEW EACH DAY FOR ATV AND DIRT BIKE RIDERS."

Singing Sand

As far as pleasant and unexpected surprises go, the sprawling 109,000-acre (44,110 ha) Killpecker Sand Dunes in the Red Desert might be one of the best for visitors. In-the-know ATVers and sandboarders are on to something, and come to ride, roll, and slide up and down miles of ever shifting sand dunes that are as unusual as they are fascinating. With the help of wind, these mercurial mountains are sculpted anew each day for ATV and dirt bike riders, who have access to around 11,000 acres (4,450 ha) of dedicated dunes for off-road recreation.

But you'll find much more to explore without the need for a motor. Stretching from Green River Basin across the Continental Divide into the Great Divide Basin—which measures up to 100 miles (160 km) long and 40 miles (64 km) wide in some places—the dunes also make a superb destination for photography, stargazing, and extraordinary days of exploring the flora and fauna.

Though the desolate landscape can look lifeless at times, the Killpecker Sand Dunes are home to creatures large and small, including desert elk (the only such elk in North America) that breed in the adjacent Steamboat Mountain area. Natural ponds form at the base of some of the dunes, attracting toads and waterfowl, while desert grass adds a dash of green across the earth-toned terrain. A landmark in the dunes is Boar's Tusk, the remnants of an ancient volcano that shoots 400 feet (120 m) from the sand.

The Killpecker Sand Dunes are also one of only seven "singing" or "booming" sand dunes in the entire world. The eerie sonic phenomenon happens only when conditions (sand size and shape) are just right, causing a humming over the surface that adds even more mystery and beauty to the location.

Sweetwater County, WY | **Season:** Year-round

Slide Along the Continental Divide

❄ The authentic western mountain town of Pinedale sits at 7,200 feet (2,195 m) on the edge of the Wind River Mountain Range. Known for its generous snowfall, stunning mountains, and bluebird days, this high-altitude playground on the Continental Divide is an epicenter of snowmobiling and gives riders access to a vast network of groomed trails, frozen lakes, and backcountry powder that make some of the country's best snowmobiling terrain.

A favorite is the Continental Divide Snowmobile Trail (CDST) that follows the Wind River Mountain Range, and cuts right through Pinedale. The Wind River Mountains harbor hundreds of miles of groomed trails, too, while the Wyoming Range has groomed routes as well as thousands of acres of off-trail powder. Trails in the Gros Ventre Mountains run right to Jackson Hole, while deep amid the peaks of Bridger-Teton National Forest, the Gunsight Pass snowmobile riding area has narrow forested trails and scenic lookout points.

> "KNOWN FOR ITS GENEROUS SNOWFALL, STUNNING MOUNTAINS, AND BLUEBIRD DAYS, THIS HIGH-ALTITUDE PLAYGROUND ON THE CONTINENTAL DIVIDE IS AN EPICENTER OF SNOWMOBILING."

Multicity, WY | **Season:** Winter

From powdery valleys to ice-covered lakes, you'll find surreal beauty snowmobiling through Pinedale.

Broken Hearts is one of the ultra-classic ice-climbing routes in Cody.

Ice Climb the Falls

The South Fork of the Shoshone River, about 35 miles (56 km) southwest of Cody, is a wonderland for outdoor lovers and is especially known by winter climbing fans keen to take their skills to new heights—that is, up the face of a frozen waterfall! Boasting the largest concentration of frozen waterfalls in the country, this region offers world-class ice climbing and is Wyoming's premier hub. Thanks to the state's long, cold winters, climbers arrive from around the country to ascend icy cascades that present a variety of challenging ascents for multiple skill levels.

For newbies looking to learn, schools and guides in and around Cody teach the nuts and bolts. Wyoming Mountain Guides offers a season package that includes five two-day climbing courses to help improve your skills as well as new equipment. The outfitter's introductory course teaches the basics, from how to stay safe and warm in winter climbing conditions to the fundamentals and techniques of ice climbing. (Come warmer months, they also offer alpine and rock-climbing courses.) Each February (in non-pandemic years), the Cody Ice Festival invites curious climbers of all ages to fine-tune their skills or develop them at climbing clinics or with experienced instructors.

For those who already have ice-climbing skills under their belt, there are myriad routes to explore. For an easier challenge, take on Stringer in the Legg Creek area. One of the shorter approaches of all Cody's climbs, the route is completely bolted, which makes rappelling easy. In the Deer Creek area, Smooth Emerald Milkshake is a moderate climb that can be found off the Deer Creek Trail. There are 800 feet (240 m) to climb here, and the views are spectacular. But heed signs and pay attention to weather conditions: Avalanches can happen in this area.

Cody, WY | Season: Winter

Take in sweeping vistas at the Blacktail Ponds Overlook.

Drift Along the Snake River

At 1,078 miles (1,735 km) long, the Snake River is the longest tributary of the Columbia River, cutting across three states (Wyoming, Idaho, Washington), and it's hard to imagine a better or more pristine summertime experience than a trip along this watery highway. Whether a slow roll with Teton views or a rip-roaring Class II and III white-water churn through Snake River Canyon, each showcases breathtaking scenery. Deciding is a simple matter of desired drenching. A float trip is a near-effortless lollygag through glorious Grand Teton National Park, and the only way to get wet is to dive into the refreshing river. White-water rafting is a bumpy but no less scenic story that requires some frenzied paddling from time to time, with a 100 percent chance of getting wet. Choose one or do them both.

Multicity, WY | **Season:** Spring to fall

Explore America's First National Park

At 2.2 million acres (899,000 ha), Yellowstone astonishes for its sheer size, as well as the staggering array of attractions within its majestic borders. From spraying geysers and otherworldly thermal springs to plunging waterfalls, imposing canyons, and wildlife galore, it's easy to understand why close to 3.8 million people visit each year.

Regardless of how it's explored, Yellowstone is grand. But with crowds and cars comes traffic, and getting off the road for a human-powered journey only elevates the extraordinary allure of Yellowstone.

As one would expect from a park that is a living hyperbole, 900-plus miles (1,450 km) of hiking trails of varying difficulty levels crisscross this boundless and beautiful wilderness. Many treks lead to some of Yellowstone's top-rated highlights. Hiking to the top of Mount Washburn affords incredible views, while Lamar Valley is known as the place to spot wildlife. The Fairy Falls Trail offers the best vantage point for an elevated look at the largest hot spring in the United States, the rainbow-hued Grand Prismatic.

No trip is complete without a gander at Yellowstone's Grand Canyon and its two waterfalls, which can be appreciated from the North Rim Trail. Day hiking doesn't require a permit, but multiday treks and camping do. Many adventure outfitters offer guided hiking tours of Yellowstone National Park, but whether you go for a day or spend a week, always take plenty of water, stay aware, and leave nothing but footsteps behind to help preserve this special place and the animals within.

Bison

Yellowstone National Park, WY | **Season:** Year-round

Climb the limestone pillars at Ten Sleep Canyon.

Don't Plan to Sleep in Ten Sleep

A cowboy town with a curious name, Ten Sleep is also one of the state's premier climbing areas, thanks to a massive eponymous canyon that draws outdoorsy folk to its unspoiled beauty. The stunning blue- and gold-hued limestone and dolomite cliff walls have been etched by millennia of wind and water, and to observe them is enough to be amazed by Mother Nature yet again.

For rock climbers, the thrill is an up-close encounter with the cliff faces via hundreds of climbing routes. The terrain is good enough to put the blip of a town (population 300) on outdoor adventurer maps, but don't expect big-city amenities, hotels, or even a grocery store. However, what Ten Sleep lacks in size, it makes up for in authentic western charm, including a saloon and general store. U.S. Highway 16, appropriately referred to as the Sweet 16, cuts through the impressive canyon.

Ten Sleep, WY | **Season:** Spring to fall

An abandoned barn sits in Mormon Row with the Grand Tetons in the background.

1. PARAGLIDE OFF RENDEZVOUS MOUNTAIN

Jackson Hole Mountain Resort is consistently rated one of the country's top ski and snowboard destinations, but summer brings different adventures, including a tandem leap from the top of the resort's Rendezvous Mountain and aerial views of Teton Village, Jackson Hole, and the Teton Range.

2. JOIN A DINO DIG

Wyoming has one of the richest fossil records in the United States, and the Wyoming Dinosaur Center invites budding paleontologists to dig for a day at an active site. Whatever is found stays at the museum, along with the name of the discoverer, and is used to support other scientific studies.

3. CROSS-COUNTRY IN CASPER

Gliding through Wyoming's pristine winter scenery is tranquility personified. Casper Mountain boasts 26 miles (42 km) of groomed Nordic trails, a mile of which is lit at night. The trails have been used in biathlon competitions for cross-country skiing and rifle marksmanship.

4. STARGAZE WITH THE DEVIL

In Wyoming, it's easy to get to the middle of nowhere, where inky dark skies make stargazing nothing short of bewitching, including at Devils Tower National Monument, sacred site for the area's Native American tribes, and popular with night sky photographers and the constellation curious. Park rangers sometimes host after-dark programming.

5. MOUNTAIN BIKE IN VEDAUWOO

Vedauwoo is notable for its granite rock formations. Climbers love it, as do mountain bikers who can pedal around the rocky outcroppings. The Turtle Rock Loop circles Turtle Rock, while the Box Canyon Trail leads to Glen Dome and panoramic views of the area.

6. CAMP AT FLAMING GORGE

This massive human-made reservoir is 91 miles (146 km) long and has more than 360 miles (580 km) of shoreline, making it heaven for swimmers, boaters, and anglers who come for big trout. Hikers and bikers are treated to astonishing vistas, while the remote location means overnight campers can view wide-open skies filled with stars.

7. SNAP A GRAM AT MOULTON BARN

Every influencer knows a picture is worth a thousand likes. One of the most frequent photos taken inside Grand Teton National Park is the iconic image of the glorious Grand Tetons behind Moulton Barn, built by original homesteaders, a wink to the western splendor of the Cowboy State.

8. PAINT EN PLEIN AIR

French for "in the open air," this art form is a perfect match for Wyoming's wide-open spaces, mountains, plains, lakes, rivers, and gorgeous light, which are muses for artists. Jackson Hole's National Museum of Wildlife Art even holds an annual Plein Air Fest.

9. TRAVEL BY COVERED WAGON

Experience the American West and the tradition of travel via covered wagon (with a lot more comfort) on a four- or seven-day trek with Teton Wagon Train and Horse Adventure. Dine on Dutch oven meals cooked on the fire, horseback ride, swim, and listen to Old West stories amid Teton and Yellowstone scenery.

10. STOP AT REGISTER CLIFF

West of Fort Laramie, Register Cliff is an important landmark of westward expansion in the mid-1800s. Walk along the soft sandstone cliffs where emigrants carved their names and messages into the rocks as they passed through or camped overnight. Interpretive signs shed light on pioneering tales.

Indian paintbrush

The Painted Hills of John Day
Fossil Beds National Monument
in Oregon (page 525)

Contributors

BLANE BACHELOR covers outdoor adventure, travel, and women doing awesome things for outlets including CNN, *National Geographic, Condé Nast Traveler, Runner's World*, and many others. Her favorite stories to write are those that involve off-the-beaten-path places, colorful characters, and anything spooky. Born and raised in Florida, Blane has lived all over the United States and is now based in Amsterdam. Visit her website at *blane bachelor.com* or follow her on social media @blanebachelor.

KAREN CARMICHAEL is a National Geographic writer, editor, photographer, and expedition leader. Her work has been published in *National Geographic Traveler* and *National Geographic* magazine and more than a dozen National Geographic books, as well as *AFAR, Budget Travel*, and the *Los Angeles Times*. She lives in Washington, D.C., and some of her favorite outdoor places include Natural Bridge in Virginia, Maryland's Chesapeake Bay, and Sleeping Bear Dunes in her native Michigan.

MILES HOWARD is an author and journalist writing about the intersection of outdoor recreation and urban living. Raised in the Boston suburbs—with a brief but impactful stint in Los Angeles—he became obsessed with the question of how to expand public access to the outdoors. His work has appeared in *National Geographic,* the *Boston Globe*, the *New Republic, VICE,* and the *Washington Post.* He writes the hiking newsletter *Mind the Moss,* and his website is *mileshoward.com.* Follow him on Twitter @MilesPerHoward.

ERIKA LIODICE is a digital nomad who spends her free time searching for beauty and meaning in the great outdoors. Her stories have appeared in National Geographic books. She is also the author of the novel *Empty Arms* and the children's book series High Flyers. Explore the world with her at erikaliodice.com and on social media @erikaliodice.

KIMBERLEY LOVATO is a travel writer whose work has appeared in *National Geographic Traveler,* the *New York Times, Condé Nast Traveler, Virtuoso Life, Hemispheres, AARP,* the *Saturday Evening Post,* Ciao Bambino, and the *Best Women's Travel Writing* anthology. She's working on children's picture books inspired by her wanderlust, and always makes time to get outside to sail, hike, bike, snowshoe, and watch the sunset. Read more about her at *kimberleylovato.com* or on Instagram @KimberleyLovato.

RACHEL NG is an award-winning travel and food writer, specializing in adventure, sustainability, history, and culture. She has been published in *National Geographic, AAA,* the *London Times, Outside, Men's Journal, Robb Report, Bon Appétit,* Fodor's, and *Rachael Ray Every Day,* and at TheKitchn.com. Originally from Singapore, Rachel now lives in an old wooden house right outside Hawai'i Volcanoes National Park. Follow her and her ducks on Instagram @rachelloveschicken or read her stories at *rachelng.net.*

STEPHANIE PEARSON is the author of *100 Great American Parks,* published by National Geographic in May 2022. She is also a contributing editor to *Outside* magazine and regularly writes for *Wired* and *National Geographic.* A number of Stephanie's stories have been anthologized in *The Best American Travel Writing.* She lives in Duluth,

Minnesota, and tries to be outside as often as possible.

JILL K. ROBINSON writes about travel and adventure for *National Geographic, AFAR, Condé Nast Traveler, Travel + Leisure, Outside, Sierra,* and more. Her essays have appeared in *The Best Travel Writing* and *The Best Women's Travel Writing*. She has won Lowell Thomas, Society of American Travel Writers, and American Society of Journalists and Authors Awards for her work. Read more about Jill at *dangerjillrobinson.com* or on Instagram @dangerjr.

LINDSAY SMITH is a travel and culture writer whose work has appeared in *National Geographic* magazine, *Metro Parent,* and *Chicago Parent.* She also works with nonprofits, associations, and businesses to craft their editorial content and messaging. Outside the world of words, she can't say no to a waterfall hike, lake jump, or doughnut shop. Find her at *lindsaynicolesmith.com* and @lindsayn_smith.

JOE YOGERST has backpacked the John Muir Trail and Grand Canyon, kayaked the Florida Keys and Alaska's Icy Bay, biked across Hawaiian volcanoes, and canoe camped along the Rio Grande. The author of the best-selling 5,000 Ideas travel series, he has been published in *Outside, Condé Nast Traveler, Islands,* CNN Travel, the *Washington Post,* and numerous National Geographic books, and has earned six Lowell Thomas Awards from the Society of American Travel Writers.

Acknowledgments

Along with the wonderful writers who lent their research and voices to these pages, *Great Outdoors U.S.A.* would not have been possible without the talent and time of the wonderful team at National Geographic Books. In particular, thank you to senior editor Allyson Johnson, design manager Nicole Miller Roberts, photo editors Katie Dance, Matt Propert, and Uliana Bazar, senior production editor Michael O'Connor, production editor Becca Saltzman, senior cartographer Mike McNey, and so many others who helped bring all 1,000 adventures in this book to life.

Maps and Illustrations Credits

Front cover, Ben Herndon/TandemStock; back cover, Anne/Adobe Stock; 2–3, Noppawat Tom Charoensinphon/Getty Images; 4, Bob Norris/Alamy Stock Photo; 6, Rachid Dahnoun/TandemStock; 8–9, Jim Vallee/Shutterstock; 11, Bernard Chen Photography; 12 (UP), Red Mountain Park; 12 (LO), Jeffrey Isaac Greenberg 10+/Alamy Stock Photo; 13, Grandbrothers/Alamy Stock Photo; 14–5, red_pexel/Shutterstock; 16 (UP), lawsonbe/Getty Images; 16 (LO), New Africa/Shutterstock; 17 (UP), sshepard/Getty Images; 17 (LO), JoshuaLee334/Shutterstock; 18–9, Michael Warren/Getty Images; 20, Zachary Frank/Alamy Stock Photo; 21, Scisetti Alfio/Shutterstock; 22–3, Josh Whalen/TandemStock; 26 (UP), DCrane08/Getty Images; 26 (LO), Arturo Polo-Ena; 27 (UP), aperturesound/Shutterstock; 27 (LO), Joerg Clephas/500px/Getty Images; 28–9, NPS/Jacob W. Frank; 30, Jason Jaacks/National Geographic Image Collection; 31 (UP), Simon Evans/Design Pics/Alamy Stock Photo; 31 (LO), frantic00/Shutterstock; 32 (UP), Whit Richardson/Alamy Stock Photo; 32 (LO), V. Belov/Shutterstock; 33, tibu/Getty Images; 34, Amber Johnson/Design Pics/Alamy Stock Photo; 35, Christopher Dodge/Shutterstock; 36–7, Colleen Miniuk-Sperry/Alamy Stock Photo; 39, Louis Arevalo/TandemStock; 40 (UP), Brown W Cannon III/Alamy Stock Photo; 40 (LO), Fsendek/Shutterstock; 41, Pung/Shutterstock; 42–3, Merrill Images/Getty Images; 44 (UP), LHBLLC/Shutterstock; 44 (LO), Alexey Wraith/Shutterstock; 45 (UP), Susan Hodgson/Shutterstock; 45 (LO), Gen Montreuil; 46–7, levifrench.photo/Adobe Stock; 48, Andrew Peacock/TandemStock; 49, Ian Dagnall/Alamy Stock Photo; 50–1, Wesley Hitt/Getty Images; 54 (UP), Dennis Flaherty/Jaynes Gallery/DanitaDelimont/Alamy Stock Photo; 54 (LO), All Stock Photos/Shutterstock; 55 (UP), kerozkeroz/Shutterstock; 55 (LO), Eli Wess/USFWS; 56–7, ODell Outside/Adobe Stock; 58, SnapTPhotography/Alamy Stock Photo; 59 (UP), Barry Hamilton/RGB Ventures/SuperStock/Alamy Stock Photo; 59 (LO), Ruslan Shevchenko/Shutterstock; 60 (UP), Greg Disch; 60 (LO), Rostislav_Sedlacek/Shutterstock; 61, Arkansas Department of Parks, Heritage and Tourism; 62, Walter Bibikow/mauritius images GmbH/Alamy Stock Photo; 63, Madlen/Shutterstock; 64–5, Dennis Silvas/Shutterstock; 67, Chris Moore—Exploring Light Photography/TandemStock; 68 (UP), Ian Shive/Tandem-Stock; 68 (LO), Sandra Foyt/Shutterstock; 69, Brad Scott Visuals; 70–1, Oksana Belikova/Adobe Stock; 72 (UP), Brent Durand/Getty Images; 72 (LO), Sodel Vladyslav/Shutterstock; 73 (UP), Ian Dagnall/Alamy Stock Photo; 73 (LO), Justin Bailie/TandemStock; 74–5, Floris van Breugel/National Geographic Image Collection; 76, Chip Morton/Alamy Stock Photo; 78–9, Matt Dirksen/Getty Images; 82 (UP), Celin Serbo/TandemStock; 82 (LO), Wally Pacholka/AstroPics; 83 (UP), Tetiana Rostopira/Shutterstock; 83 (LO), Faina Gurevich/Alamy Stock Photo; 84–5, wanderluster/Alamy Stock Photo; 86, Randy Langstraat; 87, Jim West/Alamy Stock Photo; 88 (UP), Schrodington/Adobe Stock; 88 (LO), Samuel Acosta/Shutterstock; 89, Steve Krull Leisure and Sports Images/Alamy Stock Photo; 90, Andrew R. Slaton/TandemStock; 91, mountainpix/Shutterstock; 92–3, Allan Wood Photography/Shutterstock; 96 (UP), Michele Ursi/Adobe Stock; 96 (LO), Randy Duchaine/Alamy Stock Photo; 97 (UP), Sofiaworld/Shutterstock; 97 (LO), Michael Whittaker/500px/Getty Images; 98–9, Enrique Shore/Alamy Stock Photo; 100, Stan Tess/Alamy Stock Photo; 101 (UP), The Adventure Parks of Outdoor Ventures; 101 (LO), Richard Griffin/Shutterstock; 102 (UP), Stan Tess/Alamy Stock Photo; 102 (LO), Simon Leigh/Alamy Stock Photo; 103, Stan Tess/Alamy Stock Photo; 104, Shanshan0312/Shutterstock; 106–7, Education Images/Getty Images; 109, Bo Shen/Shutterstock; 110 (UP), Wirestock Creators/Shutterstock; 110 (LO), Elena Milovzorova/Shutterstock; 111, VIKVAD/Shutterstock; 112–3, Abby/Adobe Stock; 114 (UP), Yvonne Navalaney/Shutterstock; 114 (LO), lunamarina/Shutterstock; 115 (UP), Martyshkin Uladzimir/Shutterstock; 115 (LO), Edwin Remsberg/Alamy Stock Photo; 116–7, Darrell Gulin/DanitaDelimont/Alamy Stock Photo; 118, Walter Bibikow/DanitaDelimont/Alamy Stock Photo; 119, Steve Collender/Shutterstock; 120–1, Juan Carlos Munoz/Adobe Stock; 124 (UP), Dawna Moore/Alamy Stock Photo; 124 (LO), Allen Creative/Steve Allen/Alamy Stock Photo; 125 (UP), Jim Polakis/Shutterstock; 125 (LO), Casey Tucker/Florida Department of Environmental Protection; 126–7, Christian Heeb/Prisma by Dukas Presseagentur GmbH/Alamy Stock Photo; 128, blewisphotography/Shutterstock; 129, Steven Widoff/Alamy Stock Photo; 130, Maresa Pryor-Luzier; 131, Ian Dagnall/Alamy Stock Photo;

132, Filippo Bacci/Getty Images; 133, Juanamari Gonzalez/Shutterstock; 134–8 (UP), Sean Pavone/Shutterstock; 138 (LO), Corey Robinson/National Geographic Image Collection; 139, Spring Images/Alamy Stock Photo; 140–1, Gallogly/TandemStock; 142, Joanne Wells/DanitaDelimont/Shutterstock; 143 (UP), Pikoso.kz/Shutterstock; 143 (LO), Kelly vanDellen/Alamy Stock Photo; 144–5, Joanne Dale/Shutterstock; 146, Ian Dagnall/Alamy Stock Photo; 147, Victor Torres/Shutterstock; 148–9, Michael DeFreitas/robertharding/Alamy Stock Photo; 152 (UP), Thomas Kline/Design Pics/Alamy Stock Photo; 152 (LO), Manfred Thürig/Alamy Stock Photo; 153 (UP), duangphorn wiriya/Shutterstock; 153 (LO), Stephanie A Sellers/Shutterstock; 154–5, Chris Abraham/Design Pics/Alamy Stock Photo; 156, John Elk III/Alamy Stock Photo; 157 (UP), Fotosearch RM/age fotostock; 157 (LO), Videowokart/Shutterstock; 158 (UP), Marcel Clemens/Shutterstock; 158 (LO), fotoslaz/Shutterstock; 159, Phil O'nector/Shutterstock; 160, Michael DeFreitas/robertharding/Alamy Stock Photo; 161, Benny Marty/Shutterstock; 162–3, Wirestock Creators/Shutterstock; 165, Krzysztof Wiktor/Adobe Stock; 166 (UP), George Ostertag/Alamy Stock Photo; 166 (LO), Ben Herndon/TandemStock; 167, Pete Zimowsky/Idaho Statesman/Tribune News Service via Getty Images; 168–9, Witold Skrypczak/Alamy Stock Photo; 170 (UP), Steve Bly/Alamy Stock Photo; 170 (LO), CAspinwall/Shutterstock; 171 (UP), wk1003mike/Shutterstock; 171 (LO), Gerhard Zwerger-Schoner/Getty Images; 172–3, Sam Judy/Alamy Stock Photo; 174, Steve Smith/Getty Images; 175, ivandan/Shutterstock; 176–7, SeanPavonePhoto/Adobe Stock; 179, Patrick Gorski/NurPhoto via Getty Images; 180 (UP), Gayle Harper/DanitaDelimont/Getty Images; 180 (LO), Rockford Park District/Jesse Fox; 181, Willard Clay; 182–3, Matthew J. Kirsch/Alamy Stock Photo; 184 (UP), Chestnut Mountain Resort/Joey Wallis; 184 (LO), PixelShot/Shutterstock; 185 (UP), WiP-Studio/Shutterstock; 185 (LO), snikeltrut/Getty; 186–7, D Guest Smith/Alamy Stock Photo; 188, Jon Lovette/Alamy Stock Photo; 189, Michiel de Wit/Shutterstock; 190–1, Tim Fitzharris/Minden Pictures; 193, Bluespring Caverns Park; 194 (UP), Jeff Timmons; 194 (LO), Brent Frazee/Kansas City Star/Tribune News Service via Getty Images; 195, Leah Tribbett/Alamy Stock Photo; 196–7, Rafi Wilkinson; 198 (UP), Brent Waltermire/Alamy Stock Photo; 198 (LO), Bohbeh/Shutterstock; 199, f11photo/Getty Images; 200–1, Anna Miller/DanitaDelimont/Alamy Stock Photo; 202, Everyday Artistry Photography/Alamy Stock Photo; 203, LanKS/Shutterstock; 204–5, Tom Bean/Alamy Stock Photo; 208 (UP),

AP Photo/Telegraph Herald, Jeremy Portje; 208 (LO), AP Photo/Charlie Neibergall; 209 (UP), Ron Buskirk/Alamy Stock Photo; 209 (LO), Wildnerdpix/Shutterstock; 210–1, Stephen Bay/Alamy Stock Photo; 212, Timothy Mulholland/Alamy Stock Photo; 213, Charlie Langton, courtesy Vesterheim Museum; 214 (UP), EJ Rodriquez/Adobe Stock; 214 (LO), Tathoms/Shutterstock; 215, Sean R. Heavey; 216, Peter Blottman/Alamy Stock Photo; 217, Bob Pardue-Midwest/Alamy Stock Photo; 218–9, Lee Rentz/Alamy Stock Photo; 222 (UP), Robin Lorenson; 222 (LO), Ripperger Photography/Adobe Stock; 223 (UP), Susan Hodgson/Adobe Stock; 223 (LO), Amy Coffman/USFWS; 224–5, Jim Richardson/National Geographic Image Collection; 226, Bernard Friel/DanitaDelimont/Alamy Stock Photo; 227 (UP), Laura Rose Clawson/The Nature Conservancy; 227 (LO), specnaz7/Adobe Stock; 228 (UP), Tommy Brison/Shutterstock; 228 (LO), David Herbig/DanitaDelimont/Alamy Stock Photo; 229, Kansas Tourism; 230, pop_gino/Adobe Stock; 231, Urbiik/Shutterstock; 232–3, Jonathan D. Goforth/Getty Images; 236 (UP), Vicki L. Miller/Shutterstock; 236 (LO), Clint Farlinger/Alamy Stock Photo; 237 (UP), Sari ONeal/Shutterstock; 237 (LO), Adam Paris/AP Imagery; 238–9, Patrick Jennings/Shutterstock; 240, Rodrigo Donoso; 241 (UP), Matt McClintock; 241 (LO), FanThomas/Shutterstock; 242 (UP), Alton Strupp; 242 (LO), Valentin Valkov/Shutterstock; 243, FRP LaGrange Quarry; 244, Gary Whitton/Alamy Stock Photo; 246–7, Jaynes Gallery/DanitaDelimont/Alamy Stock Photo; 250 (UP), Carrie Vonderhaar/Ocean Futures Society/National Geographic Image Collection; 250 (LO), Alison Jones/DanitaDelimont/Alamy Stock Photo; 251 (UP), Robyn Mackenzie/Shutterstock; 251 (LO), Jerry Hopman/Getty Images; 252–3, Luke Fater; 254, Carmen K. Sisson/Cloudybright/Alamy Stock Photo; 255 (UP), Dave McNamara; 255 (LO), a_v_d/Shutterstock; 256 (UP), Magnolia Ridge Adventure Park; 256 (LO), Jenny Ellerbe; 257, Tim Mueller Photography; 258, Jamie & Judy Wild/DanitaDelimont/Alamy Stock Photo; 259, Svetlana Foote/Shutterstock; 260–1, Nance Trueworthy/TandemStock; 263, Jerry Monkman/EcoPhotography, LLC; 264 (UP), David McLain/Cavan Images; 264 (LO), Bill Koplitz/Getty Images; 265, Bill Crnkovich/Alamy Stock Photo; 266–7, Cavan Images/Offset; 268 (UP), Washington Imaging/Alamy Stock Photo; 268 (LO), Eric Isselee/Shutterstock; 269 (UP), Erin Paul Donovan/Alamy Stock Photo; 269 (LO), Grispb/Adobe Stock; 270–1, Sean Pavone Photo/Adobe Stock; 272, Mary Liz Austin/Alamy Stock Photo; 273, Charles Brutlag/Shutterstock; 274–5, Michael Rickard/

Getty Images; 278 (UP), Pat & Chuck Blackley/Alamy Stock Photo; 278 (LO), Katherine Frey/The Washington Post via Getty Images; 279 (UP), OSTILL is Franck Camhi/Shutterstock; 279 (LO), Yvonne Navalaney/Adobe Stock; 280–1, Nathaniel Gonzales/Shutterstock; 282, Matt McIntosh/NOAA; 283 (UP), Jon Bilous/Shutterstock; 283 (LO), Quang Ho/Shutterstock; 284 (UP), Philip Scalia/Alamy Stock Photo; 284 (LO), hoangminh1904/Shutterstock; 285, Peter Essick/Getty Images; 286, Pat & Chuck Blackley/Alamy Stock Photo; 287, Eric Isselee/Shutterstock; 288–9, Leong Chee Onn/Dreamstime; 292 (UP), Michael Sean OLeary/Shutterstock; 292 (LO), WaterFrame_eda/Alamy Stock Photo; 293, Susan E. Pease/age fotostock; 294–5, Al Wood Photo/Adobe Stock; 296, Garth Grimmer/Dreamstime; 297, steheap/Adobe Stock; 298 (UP), Lee Snider Photo Images/Shutterstock; 298 (LO), Joe Sohm/Dreamstime; 299, Ed Collier; 300, Paul Mozell/Shutterstock; 301, vvoe/Shutterstock; 302–3, David Hoefler/Getty Images; 305, Jim West/Alamy Stock Photo; 306 (UP), Tane Casserley/NOAA; 306 (LO), Cindy Hopkins/Alamy Stock Photo; 307, Chuck Haney/DanitaDelimont/Alamy Stock Photo; 308–9, Dennis MacDonald/Alamy Stock Photo; 310 (UP), Alex Messenger/TandemStock; 310 (LO), PhotoPaper/Shutterstock; 311 (UP), drohn/Shutterstock; 311 (LO), Michael G Smith/Adobe Stock; 312–3, Brandon Flint/TandemStock; 314, Westend61/Amazing Aerial; 315, styxclick/Adobe Stock; 316–7, Wildnerdpix/Shutterstock; 319, Eitan Simanor/Alamy Stock Photo; 320 (UP), Joe Mamer Photography/Alamy Stock Photo; 320 (LO), Joe Eichele; 321, Clint Farlinger/Alamy Stock Photo; 322–3, Tom Thulen; 324 (UP), Jacob Laducer/Getty Images; 324 (LO), Gilang Prihardono/Shutterstock; 325 (UP), Boris Shevchuk/Shutterstock; 325 (LO), Steve Skjold/Alamy Stock Photo; 326–7, natmac stock/Shutterstock; 328, Jonathan Larsen/Diadem Images/Alamy Stock Photo; 330–1, Jeremy Woodhouse/Getty Images; 333, Lynne Buchanan/Getty Images; 334 (UP), ItsNotLana/Shutterstock; 334 (LO), Longleaf Trace; 335, Michael Ventura/Alamy Stock Photo; 336–7, Robert Zaleski/rzcreative; 338 (UP), terry/Adobe Stock; 338 (LO), Elizabeth Spencer/Shutterstock; 339 (UP), Buddy Mays/Alamy Stock Photo; 339 (LO), Norm/Adobe Stock; 340–1, Daniel Thornberg/Adobe Stock; 342, Tom Sperduto/Cavan Images; 343, Daniel Prudek/Shutterstock; 344–5, Jeremy Mason McGraw/Getty Images; 348 (UP), Eddie Brady/Getty Images; 348 (LO), LanaG/Shutterstock; 349 (UP), ded pixto/Shutterstock; 349 (LO), Robert Charity/500px/Getty Images; 350–1, Westhoff/Getty Images; 352, Rosemarie Mosteller/Shutterstock; 353, Garret Suhrie/Cavan Images; 354 (UP), Courtesy Vail Resorts; 354 (LO), Jennifer White Maxwell/Shutterstock; 355, M.Curtis/Shutterstock; 356, Mark Edward Harris/Getty Images; 357, S Becker/Shutterstock; 358–9, Bill45/Adobe Stock; 362 (UP), Hall Jameson/Shutterstock; 362 (LO), Visit Helena; 363 (UP), George Ostertag/Alamy Stock Photo; 363 (LO), Justin Kauffman, courtesy of Montana's Missouri River Country; 364–5, Douglas Hughmanick/Adobe Stock; 366, NPS Photo/Alamy Stock Photo; 367 (UP), Lee Foster/Alamy Stock Photo; 367 (LO), ppart/Shutterstock; 368 (UP), Zachj6497/Shutterstock; 368 (LO), Joel Sartore/National Geographic Photo Ark, photographed at Milford Nature Center, Junction City, Kansas; 369, Dan Leffel/age fotostock; 370, Jason Hatfield/TandemStock; 371, Marek Mierzejewski/Shutterstock; 372–3, MarekPhotoDesign/Adobe Stock; 376 (UP), Michael Forsberg/National Geographic Image Collection; 376 (LO), dianarobinson/Adobe Stock; 377 (UP), Roblan/Shutterstock; 377 (LO), Chuck Haney/DanitaDelimont/Alamy Stock Photo; 378–9, D. Scott Clark/TandemStock; 380, Visit North Platte; 381, Cheryl-Samantha Owen/NPL/Minden Pictures; 382 (UP), Joel Sartore/National Geographic Image Collection; 382 (LO), Giancarlo Restuccia/Shutterstock; 383, Michael Snell/Alamy Stock Photo; 384, Peter Blottman/Alamy Stock Photo; 385, George Ostertag/Alamy Stock Photo; 386–7, romanslavik/Adobe Stock; 389, Sebastien Fremont/Adobe Stock; 390 (UP), Ellen V Baker/TandemStock; 390 (LO), Rachid Dahnoun/TandemStock; 391–3, Scott Sady/TahoeLight; 394 (UP), Dominic Gentilcore PhD/Shutterstock; 394 (LO), topseller/Shutterstock; 395 (UP), Joseph Navara/Shutterstock; 395 (LO), Scott Smith/Getty Images; 396–7, sixfournorth/Shutterstock; 398, Rachid Dahnoun/Getty Images; 399, Nick Knight/Shutterstock; 400–1, Brent Doscher/Cavan Images; 403, Erin Paul Donovan/Alamy Stock Photo; 404 (UP), Jerry and Marcy Monkman/EcoPhotography/Alamy Stock Photo; 404 (LO), dp Photography/Shutterstock; 405, jmorse2000/Getty Images; 406–7, Pierre Rochon/Alamy Stock Photo; 408 (UP), Jon Bilous/Adobe Stock; 408 (LO), LanKS/Shutterstock; 409, Greg Ryan/Alamy Stock Photo; 410–1, DAVID/Adobe Stock; 412, sphraner/Getty Images; 413, Melinda Fawver/Shutterstock; 414–5, Susan Candelario/Alamy Stock Photo; 417, Henryk Sadura/Shutterstock; 418 (UP), DianaThomas/Stockimo/Alamy Stock Photo; 418 (LO), Marko Subotin/Shutterstock; 419, Yarvin World Journeys/Alamy Stock Photo; 420–1, ARK NEYMAN/Shutterstock; 422, Loralea Dawn Kirby/Getty Images; 423 (UP), Sergey Chips/Shutterstock; 423 (LO), PTZ Pictures/Shutterstock;

716 I GREAT OUTDOORS U.S.A.

Index

Since 1888, the National Geographic Society has funded more than 14,000 research, conservation, education, and storytelling projects around the world. National Geographic Partners distributes a portion of the funds it receives from your purchase to National Geographic Society to support programs including the conservation of animals and their habitats.

Get closer to National Geographic Explorers and photographers, and connect with our global community. Join us today at nationalgeographic.org/joinus

For rights or permissions inquiries, please contact National Geographic Books Subsidiary Rights: bookrights@natgeo.com

Library of Congress Cataloging-in-Publication Data
Names: National Geographic Society (U.S.)
Title: Great outdoors U.S.A : 1,000 adventures across all 50 states.
Other titles: Great outdoors United States of America
Description: Washington, D.C. : National Geographic, [2023] | Includes
    index. | Summary: "This collection offers more than 1,000 escapades
    to experience across the United States"-- Provided by publisher.
Identifiers: LCCN 2022059086 | ISBN 9781426222665 (Paperback)
Subjects: LCSH: Outdoor recreation--United States--Guidebooks. | Tourism--
    United States--Guidebooks.
Classification: LCC GV191.4 .G74 2023 | DDC 796.50973--dc23/eng/20230109
LC record available at https://lccn.loc.gov/2022059086

ISBN: 978-1-4262-2266-5

The information in this book has been carefully checked and to the best of our knowledge is accurate. However, details are subject to change, and the publisher cannot be responsible for such changes, or for errors or omissions. Assessments of sites, hotels, and restaurants are based on the authors' subjective opinions, which do not necessarily reflect the publisher's opinion.

Printed in China
23/PPS/1

SO MANY IDEAS. SO LITTLE TIME.
Travel Planning Made Easy!

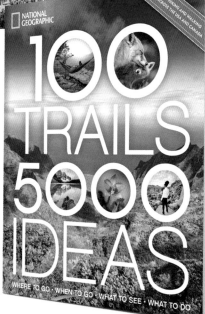

From the waterfalls of Kauai's Nāpali coast to the tests of the Appalachian Trail, *100 Trails, 5,000 Ideas* highlights the preeminent hiking adventures across the United States and Canada. Inside this authoritative travel guide, you'll find National Geographic experts' recommendations for superlative hikes, as well as tips for wildlife spotting, scenic picnic locales, routes with a view, camp sites, and off-trail activities nearby. Plus, you'll discover alternative routes to extend your trek or tackle shorter lengths of some of the country's most iconic journeys. From beginners looking for an easy day hike to advanced trekkers seeking multiweek excursions, this guide is the ultimate keepsake for any hiker.

ALSO AVAILABLE IN THIS SERIES

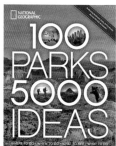

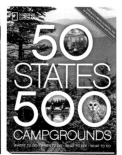

AVAILABLE WHEREVER BOOKS ARE SOLD

 NatGeoBooks   @NatGeoBooks